ETHNOMUSICOLOGY

HISTORY, DEFINITIONS, AND SCOPE

Garland Publishing, Inc.

ETHNOMUSICOLOGY
HISTORY, DEFINITIONS, AND SCOPE

A Core Collection of Scholarly Articles

Edited by Kay Kaufman Shelemay
Wesleyan University

Garland Publishing, Inc.
New York & London
1992

ACKNOWLEDGMENTS

I thank
Philip V. Bohlman, Regula Burckhardt Qureshi, Bruno Nettl,
Adelaida Reyes Schramm, and Ruth Stone
for their advice and assistance.

This volume was originally published in cloth as part of the seven-volume set, the
Garland Library of Readings in Ethnomusicology (1990)

Introduction to the *Garland Library of Readings in Ethnomusicology*
Copyright © 1990 by Kay Kaufman Shelemay

Introduction Copyright © 1992 by Kay Kaufman Shelemay
All Rights Reserved

All articles are reproduced by permission. See Acknowledgments.

Library of Congress Cataloging-in-Publication Data
Ethnomusicology: history, definitions, and scope / a core collection of scholarly articles /
edited by Kay Kaufman Shelemay.
p.   cm. — "Originally published in cloth as part of the seven-volume set, the
Garland library of readings in ethnomusicology (1990)"—T.p. verso.
ISBN 0-8153-0764-0 (alk. paper)
1. Ethnomusicology. I. Shelemay, Kay Kaufman.
ML3799.H58 1992
780'.89—dc20
                                                                91-47978
                                                                CIP

Design: John M-Röblin

Printed on acid-free, 250-year-life paper
Manufactured in the United States of America

INTRODUCTION

This volume brings together articles written between 1909 and 1983 on the history, definitions, and scope of ethnomusicology, providing multiple perspectives of the changing ways in which ethnomusicologists have viewed themselves and others during the first century of ethnomusicological activity. It was originally published in cloth as Volume 1 of the *Garland Library of Readings in Ethnomusicology* (1990).

Ethnomusicologists have long been concerned with their relationship to diverse fields of humanistic and scientific research. The earliest article in this volume, by Gilman (1909), discusses the importance of a then-new technology, the phonograph, and its role as a catalyst in building a new "science of exotic music." The interdisciplinary range of what was to become ethnomusicology is already evident in Gilman's comments, moving from the largely musical issues that occupied scholars of his era to a broader indictment of ethnocentrism and a call for efforts to understand different cognitive systems. Similarly, Charles Seeger's global view of the ethnomusicological endeavor within the framework of systematic musicology, setting forth a "universally valid foundation for the study of music" (1951, 29), resonates in the broad and inclusive agendas later endorsed by Merriam (1975), Nettl (1975), and Simon (1978). The longstanding and symbiotic relationships of ethnomusicology with musicology, anthropology, and dance ethnology are explored and expanded by Herzog (1942), Schaeffner (1961), McLeod (1974), Kurath (1960), McAllester (1963), and Reyes Schramm (1979). Indeed, the very murkiness of these conventional disciplinary boundaries led one scholar to suggest that ethnomusicology had already accomplished its goals and should be abolished (Lieberman 1977).

Given the varied range of activities and divergent agendas of individuals, it is perhaps predictable that many articles are heavily concerned with definitions of the field. Many of these efforts cluster in the quarter century following the founding of the Society for Ethnomusicology and the subsequent incorporation of ethnomusicological studies into American universities. It appears that the growing institutional role of ethnomusicology as a discipline separate from both musicology and anthropology in the United States sparked these publications engaged with self-definition. Included here are an early contribution by Rhodes (1956), and summary statements by Hood (1969), Nettl (1975), Simon (1978), and List (1979). Three seminal contributions by Alan Merriam (1960, 1975, 1977) are also reprinted, including his invaluable compilation of definitions in the final member of that trilogy.

Attempts to synthesize the past and arrive at a mandate for the future have also encouraged a continuing involvement with historical writing. A sample of such efforts is included here. Two early and notable contributions are those by Densmore (1927) and Herzog (1942), each of which recounts the history of the study of Native American musics while touching on broader methodological issues. Several other articles, including Nettl (1958), Schaeffner (1961), and Wiora (1965), are historiographical in their content, emphasizing the importance of ethnomusicological research for the study of music history. The history of specific trends in ethnomusicological thought is further traced in a detailed discussion of paradigm formation by Marshall (1972). All these contributions make clear the manner in which intellectual trends are linked to personal and institutional factors, explicating the ways in which the history of ethnomusicological thought reflects the predilections of its practitioners and their particular situations at specific points in time.

Many of the articles in this volume raise issues that have continued importance in ethnomusicological research. These include Seeger's seminal contribution on the subject of criticism and value (1965), the frequent references to ethical concerns in writings from Densmore (1927) to Nettl (1975), and the recurrent debate over preservation, recast by McLean (1983) from an ethical and political perspective. The concern with new technologies, eloquently addressed by Gilman (1909), echoes in several essays, most notably in Feld's discussion of visual documentation and film (1976).

Given the characterization of ethnomusicology as an "orphan discipline" (Herzog, 1942, 22) and as the "stepchild" (Rhodes, 1956, 33) of both its disciplinary parents, musicology and cultural anthropology, it is perhaps predictable that many have sought to weld the many activities and approaches that have fallen under this rubric into a coherent whole. It is intended that the presentation of these diverse contributions within a single volume gives easy access to a sampling of this lively, and continuing, dialogue.

Kay Kaufman Shelemay

INTRODUCTION TO THE *GARLAND LIBRARY OF READINGS IN ETHNOMUSICOLOGY*

Over a century of ethnomusicological research has given rise to a large if widely scattered scholarly literature. The *Garland Library of Readings in Ethnomusicology* presents a selection of distinguished articles on diverse historical, methodological, and theoretical topics dating from the nineteenth century to the 1980s.

All articles have been photographically reproduced as originally printed, each volume incorporating both older contributions and more recent scholarship, arranged for the most part in chronological order. In this manner, a single volume provides insight into individual approaches to common problems or issues over time, while the series as a whole sets forth an overview of the history and nature of a changing ethnomusicological discourse.

Ethnomusicologists have always published in an international and interdisciplinary array of periodicals and collections of essays, rendering many of the publications difficult of access. For this reason, a special effort was made to incorporate here valuable writings that are difficult to locate or out-of-print. Consideration was given to including important older articles from rare or inaccessible sources while also incorporating more recent contributions crucial to the thorough treatment of a particular theme or issue. Approximately one-fourth of the entries in this series are drawn from *Ethnomusicology*, reflecting its status as a most important venue for ethnomusicological publication during the second half of the twentieth century. The majority of the articles are in English, with a minority of contributions in French, German, and Spanish. Publication of articles in other languages presented issues of translation beyond the scope of this series.

Articles were chosen with primary consideration for their treatment of major issues or problems that have occupied ethnomusicological thought and practice. While many of the selections contain discussion of a particular musical tradition as part of a more general statement or argument, articles were selected with consideration of their contribution to the methodological and issue-oriented focus of the series. No attempt was made to balance geographical coverage or to pi ovide a representative sample of musical traditions that have been the subject of ethnomusicological research. In some cases, copyright difficulties prevented the inclusion of other entries of choice.

In juxtaposing within a seven-volume collection a number of important articles originally conceived independently, the *Garland Library of Readings in Ethnomusicology* brings together individual scholarly efforts in a new context. The rubrics under which the articles have been organized emerged during the process of bibliographic selection. Each volume unites articles that speak in some way to the common theme or problem reflected in its title, although some of the items in the collection could have fit equally well into more than one volume of the series. Volume 7 contains contributions that intersect with and overlap the themes of the other six volumes, each entry representing a new perspective, paradigm, or approach at its respective time of publication.

Ethnomusicologists have since early dates been concerned with both the boundaries and mandates of their discipline. Volume 1 includes articles treating the history, definition, and scope of the field. These range from early summaries of ethnomusicological subject matter and state of research to later, comprehensive discussions spanning the discipline at large, its intellectual history, and future prospects.

Ethnomusicologists have always invoked and applied a wide range of theories and methods in their research. Volume 2 incorporates a diverse collection of articles that either make explicit theoretical or methodological statements, or implicitly set forth approaches that transcend their particular case study. Several contributions define the relationship between ethnomusicology and other fields of inquiry, as well as the impact of the methods and theories of other disciplines on ethnomusicological scholarship.

Attention to the role of music in culture and methods for the study of music in context is the theme linking articles included in Volume 3. All articles in this volume explicitly address the cultural aspects of music making—the role of music in human social life, thought, and action.

Articles discussing the philosophy, methodologies, and technologies of musical transcription are found within Volume 4, while the methods and problems of cross-cultural musical analysis are the subject of Volume 5.

Ethnomusicologists have long been concerned not only with music making, but with music makers and the processes through which musical materials are generated, transmitted, and documented. Volume 6 contains selected articles on musical instruments and musicians, on the processes of composition and performance, and on the technologies and methods through which these materials have been preserved and studied.

Volume 7 presents articles that signalled new trends or subjects of ethnomusicological concern at their time of publication. Their chronological presentation together graphically illustrates the scope and dynamism of ethnomusicological research throughout the first century of its history.

This series is intended to provide a core collection of ethnomusicological articles for libraries that may not own a wide array of periodicals or that may seek to preserve their often fragile originals from heavy use. The volumes can also serve as a convenient resource for teaching and study, a welcome alternative to the dozens of crumpled photocopies that access to these widely dispersed offerings otherwise necessitates. Although no single collection can do justice to the extraordinary diversity of thought that has characterized ethnomusicological inquiry to date, it is hoped that these volumes provide both a partial overview of the past and a useful resource for readers as they draw upon existing research in their search for new intellectual directions.

Kay Kaufman Shelemay

CONTENTS OF THE *GARLAND LIBRARY OF READINGS IN ETHNOMUSICOLOGY*

CONTENTS

ETHNOMUSICOLOGY
HISTORY, DEFINITIONS, AND SCOPE

SPECIAL ARTICLES

THE SCIENCE OF EXOTIC MUSIC[1]

IF architecture is the king of the fine arts, commanding the outward services of others, music is their queen, imposing the inward laws by which all rule themselves. The notions of harmony, pitch, scale, tonality and key, applied in fine art generally, have in music first become clear enough to receive names. The theory of all the arts awaits to this day the exact grasp of these ideas which the investigation of musical structure will some time give.

[1] A. J. Ellis, " On the Musical Scales of Various Nations," *Journal of the Society of Arts*, XXXIII., 1885. J. P. N. Land, " Ueber die Tonkunst der Javanen," *Vierteljahrsschrift für Musikwissenschaft*, 1889, 1. C. Stumpf, " Lieder der Bellakula Indianern," *Vierteljahrsschrift für Musikwissenschaft*, 1886, 4; " Phonographirter Indianermelodien " (review of " Zuñi Melodies "), *Vierteljahrsschrift für Musikwissenschaft*, 1892, 1; " Tonsystem und Musik der Siamesen," *Beiträge zur Akustik und Musikwissenschaft*, 3, 1901; " Das Berliner Phonogrammarchiv," *Int. Wochenschrift für Wissenschaft, Kunst und Technik*, 22 Februar, 1908. Franz Boas, " The Central Esquimo," Bureau of Ethnology, Sixth Anual Report, Washington, 1888; " The Kwakiutl Indians," U. S. National Museum, Report for 1895. B. I. Gilman, " Zuñi Melodies," *Journal of American Archeology and Ethnology*, I., Boston, 1891; " Some Psychological Aspects of the Chinese Musical System," *Philosophical Review*, I., Nos. 1 and 2, New York, 1892; " Hopi Songs," *Journal of American Archeology and Ethnology*, V., Boston, 1908. Miss Alice C. Fletcher, " A Study of Omaha Indian Music: With a Report on the Structure of the Music by John C. Fillmore," Peabody Museum, Cambridge, U. S. A., 1893; " The Hako: A Pawnee

Hitherto the study of music has labored under an essential disadvantage compared with that of painting and sculpture. Passing events can not be scrutinized as permanent objects can. Time is lacking for their close determination; and once experienced they become memories only. Precision and revision —twin essentials of science—are possible in observing a combination of color and form, but not of tone. Hence the study of music as we know it is a study of scores. Connoisseurship, pictorial and plastic, has found its material wherever paintings and sculptures exist: musical criticism only where scores exist; that is to say only in modern Europe. In order to bring accurate method to bear on non-European music some means for reproducing it at will is demanded. If we can choose the moment when data of sense are to present themselves we can prepare for their precise registry; and the power to repeat our impressions gives the power to correct them. Such a means has been furnished within our own time and our own country. Chiefly by the aid of the phonograph inquiries into exotic music have within

Ceremony," Bureau of Ethnology, Twenty-second Report, Part 2, Washington, 1903. O. Abraham and E. M. von Hornbostel, " Studien über das Tonsystem und die Musik der Japaner," *Sammelbänder der Int. Musikgesellschaft*, IV., 2, 1903; " Ueber die Bedeutung des Phonographen für vergleichende Musikwissenschaft " and " Phonographirte türkische Melodien," *Zeitschrift für Ethnologie*, XXXVI., 2, 1904; " Phonographirte indische Melodien," *Sammelbänder der Int. Musikgesellschaft*, V., 3, 1904; " Phonographirte Indianermelodien aus British Columbia," Boas Memorial Volume, New York, 1906. E. M. von Hornbostel, " Phonographirte tunesische Melodien " (1905?); " Notiz über die Musik der Bewohner von Sud Neu Mecklenburg " (1905?); " Ueber der gegenwärtigen Stand der vergleichenden Musikwissenschaft," *Int. Musikgesellschaft*, Basler Kongress, 1906. " Ueber die Musik der Kubu," Städtischer Völkermuseum, Frankfurt, 1908. " Phonographirte melodien aus Madagaskar und Indonesien," Forschungsreise S. M. S. *Planet*, V., 6, Berlin, 1909. Compare also: Charles K. Wead, " Contributions to the History of Musical Scales," U. S. National Museum, Report for 1900. W. C. Sabine, " Melody and the Origin of the Musical Scale," SCIENCE, May 29, 1908.

a generation attained the standing of a branch of science.

The closer study of instrumental forms undertaken in England by the late A. J. Ellis in 1885 and carried on by J. P. N. Land in Holland laid the foundation for the new research. Five years later, in 1890, Dr. J. Walter Fewkes, of the Hemenway Southwestern Expedition, first used the phonograph in the study of aboriginal folk lore, and collected the records of American Indian singing which in the following year formed the basis of the writer's study of Zuñi melodies. The notations of singing in Miss Alice Fletcher's monograph on the " Music of the Omaha Indians," published in 1893 with a report by the late J. C. Fillmore on the structure of the music, although made by ear, were based upon years of experience in the field. In later extended studies of Indian life and art by Miss Fletcher, Dr. Boas and Dr. Dorsey the phonograph has aided. The investigation of exotic music had already occupied Professor Carl Stumpf, now of Berlin and lately rector of the university. Professor Stumpf in 1886 made an accurate study by ear (" gleichsame phonographische Nachbildungen ") of the singing of Bellakula Indians from British Columbia, in 1892 gave an incisive discussion of the Zuñi melodies, and in 1901 published an extended investigation of Siamese music, based on phonographic records and the examination of instruments. Apart from the writer's volume on " Hopi Songs " (1908) all the other contributions to the phonographic study of the non-European art have come from the Psychologisches Institut of Berlin University, of which Professor Stumpf is director, and are the work of his assistants, Dr. E. M. von Hornbostel and Dr. O. Abraham. Meanwhile collections of phonographic records of exotic music have been founded in Berlin, St. Petersburg, Vienna, Paris, Washington, Chicago, Cambridge and elsewhere.

A body of material has thus been gathered and in part investigated, from which already a rich yield of new views of the art of music and its foundations in the mind of its makers either has been reaped or plainly stands ready for the harvest.

First: Anharmonic structure. As far as is known, true harmony does not exist outside of European music. Harmonic feeling has been attributed to the North American Indians; but it does not express itself in part singing and its existence is not yet satisfactorily established. It now seems altogether probable that in spite of the great development of music elsewhere no peoples but the European have ever based an art of tone upon the disturbance and readjustment of consonant combinations of notes.

Second: the isotonic scale. The initial investigations of Asiatic instruments by Ellis and Land pointed to a new formal principle deeply differentiating the music of east and west. There are neither semi-tones nor whole tones in certain scales of Siam and Java. Instead the octave is divided into equal parts, either five $\frac{6}{5}$ tones or seven $\frac{6}{7}$ tones. Professor Stumpf's later phonographic study confirmed these conclusions. A principle of tone-distance supplants the principle of consonance on which the European musical system is based. Music becomes isotonic instead of diatonic as Europeans have hitherto known it. We seem at last out of hearing of Greek tetrachords, as Stevenson, dropping anchor in the harbor of Apia, felt at last beyond the shadow of the Roman law.

Third: heterophony. A Siamese orchestra plays neither in unison nor in parts, for each of the various instruments takes its own liberties with a melody approximately followed by all. To this musical method Professor Stumpf applies the Platonic term " heterophony," and wonders whether the Siamese do not give us a glimpse of what Greek music actually was— which, as Moritz Hauptmann once remarked, " We now know only from the writings of theorists, i. e., do not know at all." Such a structure results sometimes in unisons, sometimes in parallel intervals, but as often in dissonances either transient or unresolved.

Fourth: neo-tonality. As in European music so in many exotic melodies, though not in all, one note is distinguishable as the principal one. But whatever the European feeling of tonality may be, and the point is not yet clear, the regard for a principal note which takes its place among some non-European peoples would appear a widely different thing. In some cases there is no tendency to end on the tonic note. In Kubu scales Dr. von Hornbostel finds absolute pitch an element. There remain the instances like that of Javese music in which no principal note is discoverable at all. New musical factors reaching deep into the heart of the art, seem revealed in these fundamental divergences.

Fifth: rhythmic complication. Hindu and African music is notably distinguished from our own by the greater complication of its rhythms. This often defies notation. Professor Stumpf remarks that a group of African drummers sometimes perform different rhythms simultaneously; as it were a chord of rhythms like the chords of notes to which different performers contribute in harmonic music. For its jejune structure in tone non-European music makes amends by a rhythmic richness beside which that of European music seems in its turn poverty. In Dr. von Hornbostel's words, "The vertical in the score (harmony) is the enemy of the horizontal (rhythm)." It is not impossible that this revelation of elaborate rhythm in non-European music may affect the future development of our own. The east has already profoundly influenced our painting, as it may perhaps, through some view-point hitherto unguessed, yet influence our sculpture.

Sixth: the melody type. For one element in exotic music no recognized counterpart exists in our own, and it is difficult for the European mind to obtain a clear conception of it. This is the Hindu Raga; apparently a type of melody with a delicate and abstract but very definite expressiveness. A certain Raga may, it is said, be attuned only to a certain season or time of day, and may shock the sense at any other time. This is mysterious, but the whole subject of musical expressiveness is wrapped in a mystery which the isolated students who have attacked it inductively are only beginning to enter. How can the choice of a certain step of the scale as tonic determine a "soft Lydian mode" demoralizing to the fancy? Or was modality itself in Greek music a type of melody otherwise determined

and perhaps akin to the Hindu Raga? Why should medieval times have proscribed the major mode as the "*Modus Lascivus*"? In general why should a minor third upward from the tonic sound sad, and downward sound serene? Is the differing imaginative character of different modern keys a fact or a fancy? Do not all consist of the identical scale performed only at a different pitch? That these questions are, in the present state of musical science, unanswerable, evidences the indifferent equipment of Europeans for the study of the Raga. For the present it is another puzzling datum of musical expressiveness which may some day yield an explanation of wide applicability.

Seventh: scale versus song. Still another fundamental difference from European music has been suggested to the writer by the singing of the Pueblo Indians. These musicians do not seem to grasp the notes they utter as steps in any scale at all, but simply as constituents in a familiar sequence of tones, unrolling itself before the memory. This characteristic may prove the differentia of pure song from music as determined by instruments. A scale would then appear the creation of mechanisms giving fixed tones, like the lyre or the panpipes, the voice by itself knowing none. America would appear the continent of song *par excellence*, the one place where instrumental music has never attained a development capable of putting an end to the liberty of the voice. European music, wholly built on instrumental forms, again appears only one among radically distinct varieties of the art of tone.

Hitherto Europeans have believed all this alien music to be rude, primitive and nugatory—an assumption of which the present inquiries amply show the naïveté. The extraordinary exactness of ear and voice revealed in the phonographic records of some Pueblo songs is matched by the achievements of Siamese musicians in tuning their instruments, as tested by Professor Stumpf. They proved able to approximate more closely to their isotonic scale than our piano tuners commonly do to the European octave. The absolute pitch of panpipes from Melanesia proved so closely identical with that of others from Java as to suggest an ethnic or historical affinity between their makers. This close identity between instruments of distant countries, discovered after an interval of years, bears strong testimony at once to native skill and to the accuracy of the methods employed in these studies and to the competence of the students.

To much non-European music the word primitive is wholly inapplicable. An immense development has led up to the isotonic octave. The choice of seven steps is referred by Professor Stumpf to mystic ideas of number; but he also suggests that a diatonic scale, the result of tuning by a chain of fourths, may have preceded the Siamese order. If so, the European scale, which still approximates such a tuning, is the less developed of the two. That of eastern Asia is a modification too radical to have completed itself in less than ages of progress.

Besides its frequent high refinement and artificiality, non-European music has an artistic rank of which it is hard for us to convince ourselves. Rank to its makers, be it added at once; and herein lies the widest lesson of the whole inquiry. This may be described in a phrase as the discovery of how great a part is played by the mind in apprehending a work of art; and how little of the veritable creation can often be grasped by an alien. Professor Stumpf cites a striking example. Since c-e-g on our instruments is a major chord and e-g-b a minor, the two sound to us major and minor, respectively, on a Siamese xylophone, where they are, nevertheless, identical combinations. In like manner a comparison of the tone-material in phonographic records with the same melodies heard currently makes it apparent that Europeans apprehend all music in the diatonic terms familiar to their ears. From the first employment of the instrument doubt began to be thrown on the earlier notations by ear which exhibited exotic music generally as a poor relation of the European family. Psychologically, the value of these results as a notable instance of the dependence of sense on fancy is very great. As a discipline in liberal culture compelling us to seek for the standpoint of other minds, they will be invaluable to all privileged to follow them. It is our own ears that are oftenest at fault when we hear in exotic music only a strident monotony or a dismal uproar to be avoided and forgotten. To most non-Europeans their music is as passionate and sacred as ours to us and among many it is an equally elaborate and all-pervading art.

The influence of European music becomes every day more audible in the singing and playing of non-European peoples. The time seems not far off when the task of dissecting out aboriginal elements will become impossible. As the ornament in Queen Ti's tomb fell to dust at the entry of the explorer, so exotic music is already dying on the ears of its discoverers. The life of the science has inexorable limits, and if it is to yield what it might, the number of those who pursue it and the money at their command must at once be greatly increased. The results of a few years' work by a few students sufficiently show the absorbing interest and the wide-reaching value of the study; and should bring out both material and personal aid in plenty from lovers of music, of ethnology and of the humanities. What men of means or of science will offer their fortunes or themselves for this imperative labor?   Benjamin Ives Gilman

Museum of Fine Arts,
  Boston

THE STUDY OF INDIAN MUSIC IN THE NINETEENTH CENTURY

By FRANCES DENSMORE

THE first specialized study of Indian music was made by a German and published in Germany. Theodor Baker came to America in 1880 and remained among the Seneca Indians of New York during the entire summer; he also visited the Indian school at Carlisle, Pennsylvania. Returning to Germany he wrote a book of eighty-two pages on the music of the American Indians.[1] It is said that he made the research in order to obtain a doctor's degree at the University of Leipzig, but his book does not mention this use of the work. In addition to personal observations among the Iroquois he quotes the best authorities on tribes of the Plains, the Southwest and Mexico. It is to be regretted that so scholarly a work has not been translated into English, for the author makes many statements which have been proven correct by later investigators and other statements which are unique and valuable.

Baker divides the songs into seven classes: Cabalistic (including the individual songs of medicine-men), Religious (including the seasonal ceremonies), Historical, War, Mourning, Love, and Social, the last-named being partly mystical and partly religious in character. Forty-three songs are transcribed in ordinary musical notation, though the author does not claim that the Indians sang the exact tones of the "piano scale." By a system of tabulation he shows the probable keynotes of the melodies and the persistence of the fifth above the keynote. This accords with the observations of later investigators that the Indians prefer tones having simple ratios of vibration. He states that the usual compass of the male voice was two octaves, beginning on F below the bass staff, or on A, on the second space of that staff. Further, he states that the Iroquois women did not take part in the singing, that the musicians did not join in the dancing, and that the

---

[1] Baker, Theodor. Über die Musik der nordamerikanischen Wilden. Leipzig, 1882.

77

Iroquois had neither historical songs nor love songs, though both existed in neighboring tribes.

The following quotations indicate the trend of the book:

The Indians say that the songs connected with religious concepts were of supernatural origin and that the newer songs are only imitations of these songs.

As the Indians live close to Nature they get from Nature the feelings and thoughts which form the largest part of their poetry. These feelings are increased by their superstition.

The metrical dividing of the melodies is a consequence of the rhythmical *feeling* of the natives. This is not accidental but the result of slow development.

The author gives a spirited description of the Harvest Dance of the Iroquois which took place in a room about 30 by 50 feet in size. In the middle of the room were two long, low wooden benches for the musicians, and the warriors danced with short steps around these benches. The leader of the musicians and his principal assistant were at opposite ends of a bench, sitting astride and facing each other. Each held a rattle, the construction of which is not described. The leader struck the bench with his rattle, which was firmly grasped in both hands. His assistant did the same. At first the beats fell slowly and weakly but they gradually increased in rapidity and strength until the proper degree was reached. Then the leader called to the warriors, saying, "Will you begin?" The warriors responded as one man, and the song began to an accompaniment of single beats. The dancers shifted their weight from one foot to the other. Then the accompaniment changed to double beats, given so rapidly that they could scarcely be distinguished from single beats. The dancers lifted their feet. one after another, bringing them down with a violent stamping and gradually working themselves into a fury. The noise was increased by small rattles tied around the knees of the dancers. When the dancing became rapid these small rattles made a noise that was indescribable. The movement of the rattles was varied by what may be termed "false strokes," the leader bringing his rattle downward but not striking it against the bench. These motions alternated with the strokes upon the bench. With the repetitions of the songs he waved his rattle in the air, after the manner of a man conducting a band. No mention is made of a drum at these dances but the author states that the gatherings often were so large that the voices of the singers could not be heard by all the people and that accordingly a stamping of the feet by the dancers "was necessary to keep the music in order." The musical instruments were also described by Baker.

The name of Miss Alice Cunningham Fletcher is forever linked with the music of the American Indian. She went among the Omaha for scientific work in 1883 and early secured the assistance of Mr. Francis La Flesche, a son of the head chief, whose cooperation continued until her death in 1922.   Miss Fletcher was assistant in American Ethnology, Peabody Museum, Cambridge University, and holder of the Thaw Fellowship in that Institution. Her first contribution to the subject of Indian music was entitled *The 'Wawan' or Pipe Dance of the Omahas*[2] and was published in 1884. Ten songs in musical notation were presented in this paper. During the same year she published *The Elk Mystery or Festival*[3] with one song, and four years later an article entitled *Glimpses of child-life among the Omaha tribe of Indians*[4] with three melodies. Her work became more widely known through a later work which will be considered in a subsequent paragraph.

Dr. Carl Stumpf of Vienna published a pamphlet on the songs of the Bellacoola Indians[5] in 1886, thus early presenting material on the Indians of British Columbia. In 1888, Dr. Franz Boas published twenty-three Eskimo songs with analytical notes in his work on "The Central Eskimo."[6] These were transcribed in ordinary musical notation but, in some instances, he indicated the rhythm by accents, omitting the bars. He also published four melodies in his article "On certain songs and dances of the

[2] Fletcher, Alice Cunningham. The "Wawan" or Pipe Dance of the Omahas. Peabody Mus. of Am. Archaeol. and Ethnol. Ann. Rep. 1884, p. 308-333.

[3] *Id*. The Elk mystery or festival, Ogllala Sioux. Peabody Mus. of Am. Archaeol. aud Ethnol. Ann. Rep. 1884, p. 276-288.

[4] *Id*. Glimpses of child-life among the Omaha tribe of Indians. Journal of American Folk-lore, 1888, p. 115-123.

[5] Stumpf, Carl. Lieder der Bellakulla Indianer. Vierfelj. f. Musikwiss., 1886.

[6] Boas, Franz. The Central Eskimo, ln 6th Rep. Bur. Amer. Ethn. 1888.

Kwakiutl of British Columbia"[7] in the same year. Dr. Boas, throughout his writings, has stressed the importance of rhythm in primitive music.

In July 1889, Dr. Jesse Walter Fewkes assumed direction of the Hemenway Southwestern Expedition which had for its object the collection of data regarding the Pueblo Indians. Mrs. Mary Hemenway of Boston was the founder of this Expedition. The following winter Mrs. Hemenway commissioned Dr. Fewkes to visit the Passamaquoddy Indians in Maine, taking with him a phonograph in order to test its practicability for recording the folk-lore of Pueblo tribes. The results were so satisfactory that a phonograph was included in the outfit of the next expedition to Zuñi. Dr. Fewkes wrote an article describing this use of the phonograph[8] and, at the time, could find no printed mention of the recording of Indian songs by means of the phonograph. On his next visit to the Zuñi he made a number of records of their language and of their singing. The study of these cylinder records was entrusted by Mrs. Hemenway to Dr. Benjamin Ives Gilman, who at that time was lecturing at Harvard University on the psychology of music and who later held the position of Curator of the Art Museum in Boston. Dr. Gilman's scholarly treatment of this subject was contained in a paper entitled "Zuñi Melodies."[9] Dr. Fewkes continued his use of the phonograph and published several important articles on the subject.[10]

In 1891, the expedition moved from Zuñi to the Moqui or Hopi villages in Arizona and Dr. Fewkes recorded a number of Hopi songs which were studied intensively by both Dr. Gilman and Dr. Fewkes, the former writing a book of more than 200 pages on

[7] *Id.* On Certain Songs and Dances of the Kwakiutl Indians of British Columbia. Journal of American Folk-lore, Boston, 1888.

[8] Fewkes, Jesse Walter. A Contribution to Passamaquoddy folk-lore, Journ. Am. Folk-Lore, vol. III, no. XI, pp. 257–280. Boston, 1890.

[9] Gilman, Benjamin Ives. Zuñi Melodies, Jour. Am. Archaeology and Ethnology, vol. I, 63–91, 1891.

[10] Fewkes, J. W. On the Use of the Phonograph among the Zuñi Indians. American Naturalist, July 1890, pp. 687–691.

Id., Additional Studies of Zuñi Songs and Rituals with the Phonograph. American Naturalist, Nov. 1890, pp. 1094–1098.

10

the result of this work.[11] Seventeen songs are presented in ordinary musical notation and also in a "phonographic notation" consisting of notes placed on equidistant parallel lines, 11 to 24 in number. The trend of the melodies is also shown by ascending and descending lines on similar parallels.

The position of both Dr. Gilman and Dr. Fewkes, from the beginning of their research, has been radically different from that of Professor John Comfort Fillmore, who wrote on the subject about two years after the publication of *Zuñi Melodies*. Professor Fillmore believed that the Indians have a "subconscious sense of harmony" similar to that which is developed in the music of the white race, while Dr. Gilman denied the existence of even a "sense of scale." Dr. Gilman said:

> What we have in these melodies is the musical growths out of which scales are elaborated, and not compositions undertaken in conformity to norms of interval order already fixed in the consciousness of the singers. In this archaic stage of the art, scales are not formed but forming.[12]

He called the Zuñi songs "examples of music without scale." Concerning the Hopi songs he said:

> The singer's musical consciousness seems restricted to a few intervals of simplest vibration ratio approximately rendered, and to melodic sequences formed by their various analysis and synthesis and rendered with a certain loose fidelity.[13]

After presenting arguments both for and against the existence of "scale" in Indian music the author states that:

> The evidence of the present notations bears strongly against the diatonic theory of this music.

However, he admits that:

> A measure of coincidence with the diatonic scale is implied in a predominant use of approximations to intervals of simplest ratios.[14]

Dr. Gilman states that the intervals of the songs varied greatly in repetitions by the same or another singer. This is not in accordance with the experience of the present writer in recording about 1600 Indian songs and may have been due in part to the lack of

---

[11] Gilman, B. I. Hopi Songs. Boston, 1908.
[12] Zuñi Melodies, *op. cit.*, p. 89.
[13] Hopi Songs, *op. cit.*, p. 5.
[14] Hopi Songs, *op. cit.*, p. 6.

uniform speed in the recording phonograph, a defect which was practically corrected in the phonograph a few years later. The phonograph first taken into the field by Dr. Fewkes was run by a treadle. The machine used in recording the Hopi songs was provided with an electro-motor and a storage battery. Subsequently, the spring motor was found to be a more satisfactory motive power, and the present cylinder type of phonograph became established.

It has already been noted that the study of Zuñi and Hopi music with the phonograph was made possible by Mrs. Mary Hemenway. It is an interesting coincidence that the musical study among the Omaha Indians by Miss Alice C. Fletcher was made possible in its later years by the generosity of Mrs. Mary Copley Thaw. Reference has been made to Miss Fletcher's work on the *Wawan*, published in 1884, which included a consideration of the music. In 1888 she sent an Omaha song to Professor John Comfort Fillmore of Milwaukee, Wisconsin, with a request that he examine it from the standpoint of a musician. This led to an association with Professor Fillmore which continued until his death in 1898. He studied the songs noted down by Miss Fletcher, transcribed her phonograph records and visited the Omaha reservation under the guidance of Mr. Francis La Flesche. This visit enabled him to hear many of the old songs. Miss Fletcher's book entitled *A Study of Omaha Music* was published in 1893 by the Peabody Museum of American Archaeology and Ethnology of Cambridge University and included a "Report on the Structural Peculiarities of the Music" by Professor Fillmore. This book contains 92 Indian melodies, 89 of which were harmonized by Professor Fillmore, somewhat in the manner of hymns or chorals. The remarkable extent of Miss Fletcher's work prior to this time is shown by her statement that during the previous ten years she had "transcribed several hundreds of Omaha songs and . . . . taken down songs of the Dakotas, Otoes and Poncas." Her study had also included the Pawnee and Nez Perce tribes.[15]

---

[15] Fletcher, A. C., aided by La Flesche, F. A Study of Omaha Indian music. With a report on the structural peculiarities of the music by John Comfort Fillmore, A. M., Arch. and Eth. Papers, Peabody Mus., Harvard Univ., vol. 1, no. 5, p. 9. Cambridge, 1893.

12

The following statement by Miss Fletcher concerning the intervals used in Indian songs is interesting and important.

During the earlier years of my studies I was, with other observers, inclined to believe in the theory of a musical scale in which the interval of a tone was divided into many parts; but, for several years now past, having become more familiar with the Indian's mode of thought and feeling concerning music, and as a result of careful investigation of hundreds of songs which I have transcribed, I have been led to account for his peculiar intonations in other ways than in the use of a minutely divided scale.
(From Study of Omaha Music, p. 152)

If Professor Fillmore had limited himself to a statement that the line of least resistance in the songs under analysis appeared to be the upper partials or overtones of a fundamental, he would not have aroused the controversy which befell his work. On the contrary, he claimed that Indians have the same sense of harmonies that is possessed by cultured musicians of the white race, including changes of key, and he made no distinction between the songs as actually sung by the Indians and the same melodies harmonized according to his own ideas with the approval or concurrence of the Indians. The term "Indian music" was applied to both. He spoke and wrote as a musician of the "romanticist" type, and his work was assailed by men who were accustomed to choose their words with care.

The following are among the more conservative of Professor Fillmore's statements concerning the structure of Indian songs:

It seems clear that . . . . the sense of key-relationship and of harmonic relations . . . . is at least subconsciously present in the Indian mind. For when the melodies are given in correct pitch and with natural harmonies the Indians soon come to recognize and enjoy them.

My experience . . . has led me to think . . . . that the harmonic sense is universal. It seems clear to me that the course of these melodies can be accounted for in no other way than on the assumption that the Indian possesses the same sense of a tonic chord and its attendant harmonies that we do; although, of course, it is latent and never comes clearly forward into his consciousness. . . . At first, perhaps, there is merely a feeling for the tonic chord, arising from the complex nature of a single tone with its consonant overtones.[16]

The substitution of the term "major triad" for "tonic chord" would have protected Professor Fillmore from criticism but he *meant* "tonic chord" in the sense of its meaning to a musician.

---

[16] A study of Omaha music, *op. cit.*, pp. 74, 76, 77.

In addition to his work with Miss Fletcher on the music of the Omaha and related tribes Professor Fillmore was associated with Dr. Franz Boas and Mr. H. E. Krehbiel in the study of primitive music at the Columbian Exposition in Chicago, 1893. He prepared a paper treating of the songs of the Navaho, Kwakiutl, Yaqui, Tigua and Omaha, as well as the songs of the Fiji, Dahomey, Arabs and South Sea Islanders, and was on his way to present this paper before the American Association for the Advancement of Science when death ended his labors. One of the last sentences in this paper is,

Folk-melody, so far as now appears, is always and everywhere harmonic melody.[17]

To Professor Fillmore, as well as to Miss Fletcher, the writer desires to acknowledge her indebtedness. It was her privilege to meet Professor Fillmore about the year 1892 and to hear him talk upon Indian music. His enthusiasm was inspiring, and later the gracious kindness of Miss Fletcher encouraged her in the study of Indian music.

Dr. Boas, in his analytical notes on the Eskimo songs published in 1888 stated that "On the whole, the melodies, even to our musical sense, can be traced to a keynote."[18] He divided these songs into two distinct groups, the first containing the tones of what is commonly called the major pentatonic scale, and the second containing the tones of the minor pentatonic scale with the sixth omitted. The seventh is used as a leading tone in the first group. (The scale commonly known as the "major pentatonic" is the "fourth pentatonic" according to Helmholtz and can be played on the black keys of the piano with F sharp as the keynote. The "minor pentatonic" is the "second pentatonic" according to Helmholtz and can be similarly played with D sharp as its keynote.)

An important contribution to the subject of Indian music was made by Dr. Boas in 1896.[19]

---

[17] Fillmore, John Comfort. The Harmonic Structure of Indian Music, American Anthropologist (N.S.), Vol. 1. April, 1899.

[18] Boas, F. The Central Eskimo, *op. cit.*, p. 648.

[19] *Id.*, Songs of the Kwakiutl Indians. Intern. Arch. f. Ethnog., 1896, 9, Suppl., 1–9.

It will be noted that all the writers thus far quoted on the structure of Indian music are agreed on one point, that the songs contain many tones having simple ratios of vibration, these being, of course, the first upper partials or overtones of a fundamental. The divergence among these authorities arises, in part, from the different interpretations placed upon the tones *other* than these, occurring in the melodies. Some regarded these tones as having very great significance, while others held that they had no significance at all. For instance, let us suppose we are considering a melody whose principal tones are C, E, and G, with C in the upper octave and A as an unaccented tone. This suggests the "key" of C, with the simplest overtones of C and with A as a passing tone. Suddenly the tone F sharp is introduced into the song. If we were to follow Professor Fillmore's reasoning we should regard this as an indication of a "change of key," but if we were to follow that of Dr. Gilman we should regard it as "being in itself an argument against the possession of any scale-consciousness by the singers."[20]

A phonograph was used by Dr. Washington Matthews in recording Navaho songs and his book entitled *Navaho Legends*,[21] published in 1897, contained 11 songs which were transcribed by Professor Fillmore. These included "The approach of the war gods," "Song of the war gods," "Daylight song," and a "Night chant." The rhythm of these songs is very simple; they are transcribed in the treble clef, and some are designated as sung in falsetto.

Indian music, as a phase of native life, has always engaged the attention of scientists, and descriptions of musical customs, the words of songs, and some transcriptions of songs in musical notation have been included in their works on the American Indians. It is manifestly impossible to refer to all such data concerning Indian music, and the present paper is limited to Indians living north of Mexico. The following references may, however, indicate the extent to which the subject received attention during the latter part of the nineteenth century.

---

[20] Hopi Songs, *op. cit.*, p. 9.

[21] Matthews, Washington. Navaho Legends, Houghton, Mifflin and Company, New York, 1897.

Twenty songs in musical notation were given by Hoffman in his work on the Midewiwin,[22] and Mooney presented the words of 138 songs with numerous transcriptions in his book on the Ghost Dance,[23] while Dr. Boas published transcriptions of Kwakiutl songs in his work on that tribe.[24] Musical customs were described by Dr. Dorsey[25] and Dr. Fewkes,[26] as well as by other scientists of the United States, and Cringan contributed to the subject in Canada.[27]

Mention should here be made of Carlos Troyer, who went among the Zuñi in 1888 and, during a long residence among these Indians, recorded many of their songs. He was a writer on the subject of Indian music, and also the first musician to arrange Indian songs for concert use, providing words in metric English verse and the conventional form of piano accompaniment.[28]

[22] Hoffman, Walter James, M.D. The Midewiwin or "Grand Medicine Society" of the Ojibwa, in 7th Rep. Bur. Amer. Ethn., Washington, 1891.

[23] Mooney, James. The Ghost Dance Religion, in 14th Rep. Bur. Amer. Ethn. Pt. 2. Washington, 1896.

[24] Boas, Franz. The Social Organization and Secret Societies of the Kwakiutl Indians, in Rep. U. S. Nat. Museum, Washington, 1897.

[25] Dorsey, James Owen. Siouan Sociology, in 15th Rep. Bur. Amer. Ethn., Washington, 1897.

[26] Fewkes, Jesse Walter. Tusayan Katchinas, in 15th Rep. Bur. Amer. Ethn., Washington, 1897.

[27] Cringan, Alexander T. Description of Iroquois Music, in Archaeological Report, App. Rep. Min. Education Ontario, Toronto, 1898; also other Iroquois music.

[28] Miss Densmore's modesty has made her remain silent as to her own contributions. The Editors desire to point out that her studies began as early as 1893, under the stimulation of Miss Fletcher's book, though at first her interest was that of a musician only. From 1895 on she lectured widely on Indian music and availed herself of every opportunity for hearing it. About 1900 she noted by ear melodies sung by Minnesota Indians, and in 1901 made her first field trip to the Ojibwa on the north shore of Lake Superior. Her phonograph studies commenced in 1907, shortly before her connection with the Bureau of American Ethnology. Her subsequent activities in this field are generally known. ED.

RED WING, MINNESOTA.

F. GENERAL

STUDY OF NATIVE MUSIC IN AMERICA

GEORGE HERZOG

Assistant Professor of Anthropology, Columbia University,
New York, New York

The music of the American Indian has an essential unity. That this requires many qualifications hardly needs to be added. In North America much intensive work has been accomplished during the last few decades; yet we are far from having a complete picture of the variety of musical styles and their relationship to each other. In México and Central America much of native music is irrevocably lost, while South American Indian music has not as yet been studied systematically.

In a general description of Indian music various features stand out. The main emphasis is definitely on singing, and there is little instrumental music performed without the voice. Still there is a considerable variety of musical instruments, especially of percussive types, which serve primarily to provide rhythmic accompaniment to singing. This accompaniment is usually of a simple pulsating type which punctuates and emphasizes the rhythmic flow of the singing, rather than to furnish contrasting or independent rhythmic designs as it does so frequently in African music. In North and Central America the typical instruments of accompaniment are drums, while in South America rattles predominate. Independent instrumental music is performed chiefly on wind instruments; these serve either for love making—as so often in North America—or for ceremonial purposes. In addition to strictly musical instruments, there are a great number of sound instruments whose use is non-musical. These are utilized for a number of purposes: in hunting, fishing, for signaling, as toys, and so on.

Many tribes have a predilection for solo singing, which may well be connected with the prominent role the individual plays in dealing with the supernatural through the practices of the shaman or the medicine man. Music is on the whole the man's art in indigenous America; men singers are greatly in the majority, whether within a ceremonial framework or otherwise. Musical instruments which on other continents are often in the hands of women, like the gourd rattle, are played by men here. The man is the musician on this continent just as much as he is, as a rule, the social and political figurehead, the leader of the

203

17

ceremonial, the active participant in drama and dance. More than elsewhere in primitive cultures, music tends to be part of a larger ritualistic, social, or literary setting, it is the favored medium for communicating with the supernatural world, and is indulged in only seldom for the sake of sheer esthetic pleasure, although dances for social entertainment are by no means rare. We seldom find the figure of a singer or musician as a member of a specialized profession, though his skill or good memory may be among the indispensable prerequisites for the office of a priest or a curing doctor.

The more formal aspects of Indian music, too, make for a rather unified general picture. Polyphonic music is almost entirely absent, unless one conceived of the instrumental accompaniment as a voice of its own, furnishing a constantly interrupted drone. However that may be, singing unaccompanied by some rhythmic musical instrument is rare. Not infrequently the melody is split between a solo and a chorus, but this rarely results in the two voices executing at the same time different parts, that is, in true part singing. Some instrumental polyphony has been found in South America.

As in most primitive music, the form is small, built up of a few phrases which are then repeated as often as may be required by some extraneous circumstance: the text, the context of the ceremony, or some other setting. The miniature form tends to assume in Indian music a more clear-cut and architectonic structure, with well-established subdivisions, than is the rule in primitive music. The number of repetitions to which the song-unit is subjected is often fixed—especially in North America—by custom. This, and the connection so often made between the required number of repetitions and the ritual or sacred number, seem characteristic of America. The most complex and intricate musical forms found so far are connected with the masked *kachina* dances of the Pueblo Indians of New Mexico and Arizona. The simplest forms were found on the peripheries of the continent—Tierra del Fuego and the Eskimo—and in pockets where fragments of old population groups must have found a retreat. California is such a pocket on the northern continent; a number of comparable regions where very ancient forms of Indian music must have lingered into the present can be predicted, on the basis of linguistic and ethnological considerations, at various spots in South America.

Beginnings of larger forms, transcending the miniature organization of the song which is so characteristic not only of Indian music or primitive music in general but also of European folksong, can be observed in various Indian styles. There are loosely strung "dance-suites," consisting of an established succession of songs to be sung for the same dance. A development apparently particular to America carries this cumulative principle almost to an extreme; the "song-cycles" or "song-series" which predominate especially in the music of some tribes in the Southwest of the United States of North America. In these forms a large

18

number—even hundreds—of short songs are interwoven in a fixed order. In the music of the Yuman tribes, in western Arizona and southeastern California, these song cycles are built up each from an elementary musical idea so that the entire cycle becomes in some respects comparable to the "Theme with Variations" of Occidental music.

Quite characteristic of Indian music are some specialized features of the technic or manner of singing. A very emphatic mode of manipulating the vocal organs in singing has been observed in the greater part of America north of México, and in some regions of South America. This technic of singing is controlled by strong muscular tension in the vocal apparatus, resulting in glides and glissandos, strong and frequent accents, and pulsations of the voice on longer tones. While this method of singing results in a melodic line that to us at first appears blurred, it is connected with a singular capacity for an expressive molding and manipulation of the single tone. This might be said to compensate for the rarity of dynamic fluctuations of intensity: of crescendos and diminuendos, expressive features not utilized in most of primitive music and folk music. This technic has been recorded also in Eskimo music and in eastern Siberia. Its spread may be connected with the spread of shamanism—and perhaps of the tambourine drum—on this continent. However, it is by no means present in all Indian music as was assumed by Erich M. von Hornbostel, who considered the technic a racially inherited trait of the Indians. Also, Indians who have at an early age lost contact with their tribal culture find it just as difficult to imitate this technic as does the white man.

Other general traits of Indian music may be cited, but these are at the same time common to most if not all primitive music: the strongly descending trend of melody, the avoidance of metrical regularity in rhythm for which our classical music has a predilection, the comparative flexibility of intonation which is connected with the dearth of musical instruments with fixed tones, the absence of music writing, of analytic theory and of an awareness of units of musical construction (tones, intervals, phrases and the like), and the fact that melody is not used for emphasizing or illustrating the dramatic, emotional, or pictorial content of the song text—again a matter of contrast chiefly with our classical and romantic music.

In America north of México both the availability of technical facilities and the existence of a prolific field of anthropology of long standing are reflected in the study of native music We have a fair though far from satisfactory number of monographs on different tribal styles, and a few contributions to the solution or interpretation of anthropological problems through musical evidence. Much of this material serves primarily as raw source material and needs to be re-analyzed in order to free it from the effects of nineteenth century musical thinking. The work of pioneer students like Alice Fletcher and Frederick Burton is chiefly of historical interest today, as against the studies of the late Natalie Curtis-Burlin, of Frances Densmore, Helen H. Roberts, and the author, all in the United States of North America, and of C.-M. Barbeau in Canada.

These studies are almost exclusively based on phonograph records, the profusion of which is not unexpected in the country where the phonograph was invented. Bitter experience has shown that notations of melodies by ear only are almost entirely unsatisfactory in primitive music. There are some fifteen thousands phonograph records of Indian music in this country, cylinders and disks, containing perhaps four times that many songs and pieces.[1] During earlier years, institutions like the Bureau of American Ethnology and the United States National Museum in Washington, D. C., the Departments of Anthropology at the University of California, at the American Museum of Natural History in New York City, and the Field Museum at Chicago, have been particularly instrumental in amassing this material. More recently the Department of Anthropology of Columbia University in New York City has been especially active in the systematic gathering of recordings of Indian music, utilizing modern technical apparatus and methods of musicological analysis. At this institution, in its *Archive of Primitive Music* which is under the author's direction, there are now over 8,000 records of authentic Indian music. Our knowledge of native musical instruments is much less satisfactory. A large number of specimens are preserved in ethnological museums; they have been little studied and are not always annotated or labeled properly. Unfortunately, and unavoidably since they were collected by ethnologists rather than musicologists, data are often lacking to tell about methods of construction, of tuning, if any, and of the exact way of playing.

Almost all the music recordings were made by trained ethnologists, and consequently the connections of music with its cultural setting have been duly considered, although we still lack concrete studies exposing in intimate detail the functioning of music in Indian cultures. The analysis of the relation of music to dance is still a goal for future attainment; the study of native dances itself has hardly begun in this country. More adequate efforts are being made now when it comes to the other important connection of native music, poetry and the linguistic phase. And yet, the greater part of our older music recordings are not supplemented by song texts written down and analyzed by trained linguists, which is a serious drawback. It ought to become standard practice that whenever native music is recorded, the cooperation of qualified linguists be made

---

[1] For a detailed report on the study of native music in this country, with a finding list of the collections, a tribal index, and a selected bibliography, see the author's *The Study of Primitive Music and Folk Music in the United States—A survey,* Bulletin No. 24 of the American Council of Learned Societies, 1936, p. 96, Washington, D. C. (A revised edition is to be issued shortly.)

part of the work of recording and analysis; many basic musical features can be fully appreciated and understood only when they are seen in conjunction with poetic and textual detail.

In México, Central America, and South America work in primitive music has been less systematic, though sometimes excellent. Much has been written from a general and somewhat literary angle, indicating a profound appreciation of the significance of native art for contemporary culture. There is great need, however, for detailed and concrete studies of a monographic type, and for phonograph recordings made with the cooperation of trained linguists. The most important writings are those of the late E. M. von Hornbostel, of the d'Harcourts on Andean music, and studies of Latin American scholars such as González Bravo, Carlos Isamitt, Vicente T. Mendoza, Carlos Vega, and others. The studies of the d'Harcourts are the most extensive, but their value is somewhat impaired by the fact that what is Spanish in style, what is hybrid mixture, and what is pure Indian has not been properly distinguished. Pre-Spanish Inca music has been of especial interest to Latin American writers; the essays of Andrés Sas and Carlos Vega are perhaps among the most important. The study of musical instruments, on the other hand, has progressed in South America much farther than in the North. In addition to the excellent recent monograph on South American Indian musical and sound instruments by Carl G. Izikowitz, we have the detailed discussions especially of E. M. von Hornbostel, E. Nordenskiold, the d'Harcourts, and A. Métraux. There is need for exact tonometric investigations, in order to fit the results more securely into their historical perspective.

In México and Central America too, the investigation of musical instruments has been more active than that of vocal music and musical styles, perhaps because so much of Indian music has disappeared entirely, and because the musical instruments do offer a testimony concerning the pre-Spanish periods of the high Indian civilizations. There are a fair number of brief but instructive essays, beginning with the writings of Eduard Seler, and also a systematic study initiated by the Museo Nacional and the Conservatorio Nacional de Música in Mexico City. It is to be hoped that the first volume of this study, devoted by Daniel Castañeda and Vicente T. Mendoza to percussion instruments, will be followed shortly by others of equal excellence. Indian music has received only cursory treatment in México so far, by folklorists or music historians such as Rubén M. Campos, Gabriel G. Saldivar, and F. Termer. Of Central American native music we know little more than what is contained in a paper by Frances Densmore on the music of the Tule (Cuna) Indians in Panamá, and in a good collection of melodies by Narciso Garay from Panamá.

The study of primitive music is often considered somewhat too technical, since it represents a highly specialized branch both of the study of Man, Anthropology, and of the study of Music, Musicology. It has been rewarding, however, in more than one respect. It has contributed toward our knowledge of the history and prehistory of the American Indian. Musical evidence confirms the migration of Indians from northeast Asia through Behring Strait, and points more and more clearly to southeast Asia. In another direction, intimate trans-Pacific parallels with Pacific and southeast Asiatic forms are indicated by musical instruments in both Americas. Von Hornbostel has pointed to general similarities between the music of the Fuegians and of some Californians, to which may be added eastern Siberians. More specific parallels appear between the music of the Gran Chaco and the North American Great Plains; also, according to the most recent discovery, between the music of Gê tribes in Brazil and the so-called Yuman style which predominates in the melodies of the Yuman tribes of the North American Southwest, but has been located also in California, and again along the Atlantic Seaboard of the United States of North America.

The cultivation of musical study in conjunction with that of the linguistic material in song texts has already led to findings that throw considerable light on processes operative in the rise of poetic forms and meter, and in the growth of musical rhythm. We may well hope that the study of musical instruments, especially if it follows methods of exact tonometrical procedure, for which there has been little opportunity so far, will produce constructive results. Data from this study are apt to be especially reliable for purposes of historical reconstruction; they are of particular interest to the historian of music and the student of acoustics.

The field is in need of material and new data for its share in answering those questions which the anthropologist and the culture historian ask. It needs especially, however, trained workers and exact studies. Collecting by means of modern phonographic devices is essential for scientifically reliable procedure, and for preserving for the future the vanishing records of musical development and experimentation in primitive cultures. Failing intensive collaboration with linguists, much of this work would be doomed at the outset to be inadequate. The combination of the study with that of the associated motor behavior, whether or not it is as highly formalized as in the dance and in work, is very desirable. Intensive work of the type which has been pursued on the northern continent for decades is just beginning in South and Central America. It may be hoped, however, that the experience gained by the trials and errors incurred in the North will be put to good use elsewhere.

As for the proper position of this orphan discipline, it is just as important for the study of primitive music to retain its close connection with the field of Anthropology, as to stimulate the interest of the historical musicologist. The latter has as yet hardly discovered the significance of a comparative perspective reaching beyond the development of European art music; he is just becoming aware of the importance, for the understanding of music, of all music. The varied problems of Psychology, and those on the borderline of Anthropology and Social Psychology, are of paramount interest in the study of native music. It is the potential complexity of this study which should stimulate more interest on the part of all the special fields which contribute to it and to which it in turn makes its contribution. This may be especially true for American native cultures, where so much of the relationship of the individual to his social environment finds expression in songs and music.

Systematic Musicology:
Viewpoints, Orientations, and Methods*

By CHARLES SEEGER

ELSEWHERE,[1] I have called attention to the complementarity and interdependence of historical and systematic orientations in musicology. Theoretically peers, as I see them, equally valid and necessary where comprehensiveness and balance are the aims, they must be expected, as a rule, to serve unequally where precision in matters of detail is required. The student may—indeed, must—choose which of the two he will employ, and the connection and sequence in which he will employ them. Broadly speaking, the aggregate of historical studies presents the history of system; that of systematic studies, the system of history. For system, like history, is ultimately concerned with the relationship of structure and function, event and process, products and the traditions in accordance with which production is achieved. Yet the individual musicological work will inevitably be either a historical or a systematic presentation. It is itself a product in a tradition, a structure, that as soon as publicized takes a place in the stream of that tradition and bears a functional relationship to other products or structures of its kind and, so, to the cultural processes in which all have their being. Thus, it would appear that while the two orientations cannot in fact be totally joined, neither can they for long be held entirely separate. And students will inevitably fall into one or the other of two classifications—of historians or of systematizers—according to the emphasis predominating in their work.

Instances are not rare, of course, in which our knowledge of music is mostly or wholly of one sort. There is history but no music (as in Ancient Mexico) or there is music but no history (as in some primitive cultures at the present day). In such cases, the preliminary work must be entirely of the character of one or the other orientation. But the musicological task cannot be considered much more than begun until, by use of frames of reference, of techniques of comparison, of hypotheses of construction or reconstruction, and of other devices of speech presentation, the purely reportorial phase is followed by that of interpretation, and, finally, by that of integration with the main body of musicological and general thought, at which point the other orientation is inescapable and the theoretical complementarity and interdependence of the two orientations again appear. A balance between them can then be striven for in a speech presentation.

The problem is not, we well know, peculiar to musicology but is encountered to varying extents in other scholarly disciplines. All of them, including musicology, conducted as they are in the art of speech, make use of the power but suffer the limitations of the semantics of that

*This paper was read in Washington on December 29, 1950, at the sixteenth annual meeting of the Society.
[1] *Acta musicologica* XI (1939), pp. 121-128.

240

medium of communication. Musicology, be it said, is in an especially delicate position in this respect. For it has, in addition, its own peculiar problem of semantics (or whatever we call the communicative function of music), study of which, with modern methods of investigation, can hardly be said to have begun.

The considerations of pure theory involved here constitute, then, a perennial challenge to the serious student. And the concrete situation in which we find ourselves is no less compelling. The aim of the present undertaking, therefore, is to propose a sound theoretical basis for systematic musicology in terms of which improved relationships may be established (1) between musical and non- or extra-musical viewpoints, (2) between historical and systematic orientations, and (3) between scientific and critical methods. It is hoped that this apparatus will serve as the base for the description of any music with maximum objectivity. But until it can be tested in many particular cases, claims for its universal validity should not be made. The present proposal, then, is advanced as valid for the Occidental art of music as of the mid-20th century alone— that is, for "music" as the majority of the members of the American Musicological Society living at this time know it.

My first proposition will be that distinction between historical and systematic orientations in musicology may best be made upon the basis of two separate but related concepts of space-time, general and musical: the historical orientation viewing music as occurring in general space-time, the systematic, in music space-time. Although the concept of music space-time is a novel one and has not

yet been given formal statement, it has already been adumbrated in a manner similar to that which led to the formation of its parent, general space-time. Particular experiences of particular persons, observed to be like or unlike, related or unrelated, have been designated by words through group agreement over centuries of time. Ultimately, words of the nature of concepts, that is, symbolizing classes of things talked about, have led to the formation of higher generalizations and abstractions until a formidable structure of speech reference to music has been built, the more deliberately methodical segment of which we call musicology.

The concept of music time (tempo, movement, duration) is highly elaborated and has customarily been correlated easily with the concept of general time. By comparing a clock or a metronome with the beat or pulse of music, musicians and laymen alike easily distinguish roughly wherein music time differs from general time. The conception of musical sound (tone, dynamics, timbre), though even more highly elaborated, has been slow of development into a concept of music space. Derivation and distinction from a concept of general space has been common only recently.

A single concept of space-time is, of course, quite a different thing from two separate concepts of space and of time. It would seem to conform, however, more closely to the facts of direct music experience, in which tonal and temporal factors can be apprehended by us in an intimate fusion or integration that is quite a different thing from the perception of the two as separate objects of attention. A concept of music space-time is therefore advanced here as one quite as necessary to study as the two conventionally accepted separate concepts of space and of time.

It is important at this juncture to point to the relatively opposite situation in which we find ourselves, as students of music, with respect to the instrument of communication we use in our study, namely, the art of speech. We are so attentive to what we say about space and time that there is a constant temptation to forget the fact that what we say occupies itself both space and time. The careful student will keep ever in mind the fact that he is employing one art utilizing a highly selective set of tonal and temporal materials (speech) to deal with another utilizing a somewhat different but no less highly selective set (music). Consideration of the complications of speech alone involved here could easily be so protracted as indefinitely to postpone arriving at a consideration of music. Perhaps it would suffice to suggest that concepts of speech space and speech time—not to mention the possibility of a concept of speech space time—function as a kind of lens through which we observe and report upon music. We cannot pretend to measure the distortion. But neither can we assume there is no distortion.

With this warning (which I beg be taken with utmost seriousness) that the operational idiosyncrasies of our instrument of study, speech, must of necessity color the subject studied, music, in certain predictable ways, I may proceed to more detailed consideration of the nature of music space-time (1) as a phenomenon in general space-time, (2) as a concept derived from objective analysis of musical processes, and (3) as basic in the definition of the

scope, methods, and aims of systematic musicology.[2]

My second proposition is that elaboration of a concept of music space-time rests upon its distinction from a concept of general space-time. I shall review this distinction briefly under seven headings, passing

[2]Concepts of speech space are highly developed and are customarily well integrated with concepts of general space. Such tantalizing parallelisms and apparent contradictions as those between acoustic phenomena and music practice seem not to embarrass the student of linguistics. A concept of speech time, however, is practically non-existent, the only elaboration given to it being in versification. I do not mean to imply that temporal organization is unimportant as a factor in speech technique. Far from it! I might even go so far as to suggest that perhaps some of the many problems posed by the study of the semantics of speech may rest in part upon the lack of a refined concept of speech time and the consequent tardiness in exploration of a concept of speech space-time. Though by implication inescapable in the present undertaking, this last must be considered, for the present, as of the nature of an "imaginary" concept, with a function in the argument analogous to that of the imaginary number in mathematics. Among the predictable distortions of music that may be expected in speech handlings of music might be mentioned: (1) the over-emphasis upon music space in the disciplines of composition (harmony, counterpoint, form, etc.) all of which are heavily implemented by the art of speech; (2) underemphasis upon music time in these same disciplines—both, it would seem, owing to the greater ease with which speech handles spatial concepts as over against temporal; (3) preponderance of analysis as over against synthesis, the event as over against the process, the product as over against the tradition, the structure as over against the function, the static as over against the dynamic, and, consequently, the preference for dealing with spatial and temporal concepts of music separately rather than together.

Perhaps it would not be irrelevant to remark here that concepts of both music and speech space-times should be viewed as specialized examples of the more general class of (human) product space-time. A conception of product space-time refers to the integrated spatial and temporal factors involved in the creation and consumption of products of human ingenuity. Cf. Charles Seeger, "Music as a Factor in Cultural Strategy," Abstract in *Bulletin of the American Musicological Society*, No. 3 (April, 1939; as of June, 1938), p. 18.

from use of the term "music space-time" as a concept to its use as denoting what is conceived.[3]

1. *Occurrence*. General space-time is, to present knowledge, universal. Music space-time occurs within it.

2. *Provenience*. General space-time is, for us, a given thing. Music space-time is man-made.

3. *Identity*. General space-time is unique: whether there is more than one, either in concurrence or in sequence, or whether it is repetitive, duplicative, or runs also backwards (as Gilbert Lewis once suggested) is not known to us. Music space-time, on the contrary, is multiplex: there are as many particular music space-times as there are distinct structures (as, *e.g.*, compositions).[4] It may be repetitive and duplicative in general space-time, occurring in many places at one and the same time, as also at many times in one and the same place. But it is not repetitive or duplicative with respect to itself, *i.e.*, a particular music space-time is not repetitive or duplicative *qua* music space-time. Each structure defines its own music space-time. Any one can be run backwards (*cancrizans*) in time, upside down in space, or both. Two or more can be

combined in one particular instance of general space-time.[5]

4. *Continuity*. General space-time is, as far as musicology is concerned, a completely uniform continuum without known beginning or end. Music space-time is a continuum that varies infinitely among various structures, and has as many beginnings and endings as there are instances of it.

5. *Control*. General space-time is entirely outside our control. Music space-time is entirely within it.

6. *Measurability*. General space-time is measurable by norms of the art of speech, in speech space-time, but is not itself constituted by any known norms of its own. Music space-time, on the other hand, while measurable as a phenomenon in general space-time by these same speech norms (as is speech space-time also), is itself constituted by norms of the art of music known by the carriers of the music tradition or traditions in which any structure is cast.[6] Separate speech norms are conventionally used to designate these music norms as events in music space-time.

7. *Variability*. The norms of speech used in measurement of music space-time viewed as an occurrence in general space-time, *i.e.*, as performance, refer, as far as musicology is concerned, to invariables (cycles, seconds, etc.). Those used with respect to music space-time itself refer to variables (tones, beats, motifs, chords, phrases, forms, etc.). These are variables not only in music space-time but in general space-time as well.

---

[3]"What is conceived" is, in the present instance, an infinite number of particular music space-times, or "area-periods" of music space-time in general. By definition, all exhibit the common characteristics that constitute the class to which the term "concept" is given.

[4]It is comparatively easy to speak of the music space-time (or area-period) occupied or constituted by a composition of which a single authoritative written version exists. The problem arising from the existence of two or more (written) versions, however, is simple in comparison with that arising in the study of the true folk tune, which, by definition, has no one authoritative version, is known only in variants of one or more versions in oral (unwritten) tradition, and is written down only after currency has been effected—not before, as in the case of structures in the fine art.

[5]As, for example, when two tunes, ordinarily recognized as separate, are performed together, thus creating a separate event in music space-time and constituting a new instance of it.

[6]Thus, the tenth measure of the "Eroica" is its tenth second in general space-time, but its tenth measure—a very different thing—in music space-time.

The kind of relationship that obtains among our three space-times should need, perhaps, no further elaboration here. It is plainly that of a fixed system (general) and a variable one (music), both reported in a second variable system (speech). Its recognition, though this be scarcely more than a superficial understanding of the operational details, should at least clarify some of our most vexing problems. Two examples may suffice. The first is the relationship of the invariable system of the harmonic series to the variable one of diatonic harmony. Some parallelism must, it seems, be admitted; but complete causality is questionable. The second is the relationship of a music to the culture in which it flourishes. Some causality, it seems, must be admitted; but complete parallelism is questionable.

Between general and music space-times, then, there should be no postulation of a one-to-one correspondence, least of all when one bears in mind that between neither of them should there be such postulation with respect to the instrumentality of the situation—the art of speech.

My third proposition, and one of an importance to musicology equal to that of the preceding two, is a concept of the music event as occurring in both general and music space-times. In the former, the music event may be regarded as a phenomenon: in the latter, let us say tentatively, as a "normenon."[7] Take, for

example, any musical unit—a primitive ritual chant, a popular dance, a folksong, a symphony, or any part of one of these—for brevity's sake, $a\flat$-g-f-g-$a\natural$ in the tenth to twelfth measures of the first violin part of the "Eroica." Each of the many performances this has been given can be regarded as a separate event in gen-

---

[7] There is, unfortunately, no word to denote, upon the high level of abstraction required here, the class of man-made product that serves primarily a function of communication. The term "art-work," or "work of art," is entirely unacceptable. It is too specialized. And it is clumsy. In coining such a word I have wanted first of all to emphasize the patterns or norms of tradition whose linking together in small and in large units constitutes the essential process of production of the communicative product. At the same time, it has seemed desirable that the word denoting the product as an event in production space-time have a form resembling that denoting it as an event in general space-time, even if the artifice seem a bit more pat than I would like it to be. I am aware that combination of the Latin noun *norma* ("carpenter's square or pattern") with the Greek participle ending results in an etymological mongrel, and had thought of the slightly more proper spelling "nomenon", from νομίζω, future νομιῶ ("use customarily") and related to νόμος ("that which is in continual practice, use or possession"; see Liddell and Scott, *Greek-English Lexicon*, rev. by Jones; Oxford, 1925). But the fact that νόμος was commonly used in a musical sense (meaning "melody") would be confusing to the generalized use of this spelling. On the other hand, I do not wish to become involved with the Greek γνώμων ("carpenter's square," from γνω-.γι γνώσκειν "to know"; see Murray, *New English Dictionary;* Oxford, 1901) for that would suggest an epistomological rather than a semantic function. Furthermore, γνώμενον would suggest a critical function.

Perhaps I should state specifically that the normenon, as here conceived, is not to be confused with the noumenon. If the phenomenon is defined in general space-time and the noumenon (as the class of non-empirical concepts) out of space and time, the normenon will be found in a median position, both a phenomenon and a noumenon, depending upon the viewpoint from which it is regarded. For example, Kant's *Critique of Pure Reason, qua* normenon, has not only its phenomenological aspect (its printed page, the sound of its reading, and its frequent reference to physical reality) but also its noumenological aspect (particularly the non-empirical concepts themselves and the ultimate structure of the content of the work). Bach's *Art of Fugue*, also *qua* normenon, has its phenomenological aspect (its printed page, the sound of its performance, and its aesthetic or other "effect") and as well its communicable content or musical "idea" from which, though we cannot easily circumscribe it in a speech normenon, we cannot reasonably withhold attribution of a homologue of the (speech) noumenon.

eral space-time. But in music space-time, all these performances have been of one single event, one and the same normenon, that is to say, the passage from the "Eroica," unless its identity as such has been conceded to have been lost through excessive variation, in which case the music space-time must be conceded still to have existed in general space-time but occupied, or constituted by, another normenon and peculiar to it, not to the "Eroica."[8]

As long as we confine our interest to the Occidental fine art of music, the plotting of norms of variation may not seem very pressing. Standards of notation and of performance are increasingly uniform and high. But as soon as we extend our view to comprise other musics of the world, we cannot get our study under way for sheer lack of understanding of the nature of these norms and the limits beyond which variation changes identity—limits that vary even in various idioms of our own culture.

Pursuit of this understanding brings us very quickly to the problem of a universally valid foundation for the study of music. It is time we cease analyzing and evaluating other musics, or even other idioms of our

own music, in terms of the Occidental fine art alone. The last attempt to account for the non-European languages in terms of Latin grammar, Leonard Bloomfield tells us, was before 1800.[9]

Organization of such an apparatus is pre-eminently the task of systematic musicology. It would appear to be predicated upon the criterion of the equal importance to study: of both musical (intrinsic) and non- or extra-musical (extrinsic) viewpoints—I and II in the Table (pp. 246-247); of both systematic and historical orientations—A and B in the

[8]The question, "to what extent may performances vary yet still present one and the same normenon?" is an interesting one. The "Eroica" has probably been played with variations of the "standard" A from at least 360 to 600 c.p.s. and still been accepted by competent judges as "the Eroica." Similarly, the tempo of the first movement has probably strayed equally widely from $\downarrow = 60$ with the same result. Which technical factors can be greatly varied without loss of identity and which cannot, and the conditions under which variation can take place almost unnoticed or can effect change of identity should be more thoroughly investigated. Findings would bear upon such diverse critical problems as the artistic validity of the twelve-tone row, the legal claim to copyright, and the definition of what is a version and what a variant in the study of folk music.

[9]Leonard Bloomfield, *Language* (New York, Holt, 1950), p. 8. It might not be out of place here to remark that the progress of linguistic studies, being about a century ahead of those in the field of music, would seem to be worthy of close scrutiny by students of music. For like musicology, linguistics has gone through a period of over-emphasis upon the historical orientation. This was followed by a period of hope that some philosophical or psychological system held the key to the study of speech. Of course, the student of linguistics uses the art of speech to study speech, whereas the student of music uses speech to study another art, whose resemblances to and differences from speech are not easy to trace. The extent to which psychologies, sociologies, and mathematics of music are being produced suggests that we are emerging, in musicology, from the former stage and entering the latter. Remembering that even such an outstanding linguist as Bloomfield had, after disposing of the mantle of the historical method, to work out from under the domination of Wundt's psychology, should cause us to pay special heed to his categorical statement: "In order to describe a language one needs no historical knowledge whatever; in fact, the observer who allows such knowledge to affect his description, is bound to distort his data." This is a thoroughly systematic viewpoint and should be taken as encouragement to equally thorough systematic studies in music. Lest it be taken for a recommendation of artificial contemplation *in vacuo*, let it be said that absence of historical considerations in purely descriptive analysis of primary data does not constitute a vacuum. Rather, it means a clearing away of underbrush and overlying preconceptions. After the ground is accurately mapped and described, there will always be plenty of time for integration with history. The apparatus proposed here is mainly for use in this clearing function.

CONSPECTUS OF THE ORGANIZATION OF MUSICOLOGICAL STUDY UPON A BASIS OF THE SYSTEMATIC ORIENTATION

I. Music Viewpoint (Viewpoint of the knower and valuer primarily of music)

A. Systematic Orientation

⌐―DIRECT EXPERIENCE―⌐

1. *Scientific Method.* Music normena as structures and/or functions of a tradition contemporary with the student and of which he is a direct knower. The science of music in its aspect as what students know *qua* handlers of the forms of music-making in a tradition (or traditions) of which they are carriers.

2. *Critical Method.* Music normena as resources of a tradition contemporary with the student and of which he is a direct valuer. The critique of music in its aspect as what students value *qua* handlers of the values of music-making in traditions of which they are carriers.

Note. Integration of operations I,A,1 and I,A,2 constitutes the systematic study of style as a thing in itself, in time present to the student.

B. Historical Orientation

⌐―INDIRECT EXPERIENCE―⌐

1. *Scientific Method.* Music normena as structures and/or functions of traditions not contemporary with the student and of which he is an indirect knower, *viz.,* through notations. The science of music in its aspect of what students know *qua* students of the forms of music-making in a tradition of which they are not carriers.

2. *Critical Method.* Music normena as resources of a tradition not contemporary with the student and of which he is an indirect valuer. The critique of music in its aspect of what students value *qua* students of the values of music-making in a tradition of which they are not carriers.

Note. Integration of operations I,B,1 and I,B,2 constitutes the historical study of style as a thing in itself in time past to the student. The data and evidence are secondary sources of study (1) because notations are not music but rather blue-prints of it, and (2) because these must be rendered into music by performance using primarily norms of a tradition

⌐―DATA PRIMARY FOR STUDY―⌐

⌐――――――――FOR STUDY―⌐

30

present to the student and of which he is a carrier. Integration of I,A,1 and 2 and I,B,1 and 2 constitutes the comprehensive study of style in a tradition. Comparative studies of style between two closely related traditions, as, for example, between the idioms of fine and folk art in certain Occidental regions, could probably be initiated today. But whether comparative study of style upon a world basis could be initiated in the forseeable future is a question respecting whose answer we can formulate only a few tentative conditions.

II. General Viewpoint (Viewpoint of the knower and valuer primarily of things other than music)

A. Systematic Orientation

  |—DIRECT EXPERIENCE—|

  1. *Scientific Method.* Music phenomena in their aspect as data, present to the student, of physics, physiology, psychology, sociology, etc., viewed in or out of their music context by relatively non-carriers of a music tradition.

  2. *Critical Method.* Music phenomena in their aspect as evidence, present to the student, of other or general values, viewed in or out of their music context by relatively non-carriers of a music tradition.

Note. Integration of operations I,A,1 and 2 and II,A,1 and 2 constitutes the comprehensive study of systematic musicology.

B. Historical Orientation

  |—INDIRECT EXPERIENCE—|

  1. *Scientific Method.* Music phenomena as data for general history—chronology, geography, biography, bibliography, etc., of which the student is an indirect knower, *viz.,* through (speech) writing or other non- or extra-musical media of times past to him.

  2. *Critical Method.* Music phenomena as evidence for general or other history—literary or art criticism, critical philosophy, etc., of which the student is an indirect valuer, *viz.,* through (speech) writing and other non- or extra-musical media of times past to him.

Note. Integration of operations I,B,1 and 2 and II,B,1 and 2 constitutes the comprehensive study of historico-musicology. The term "comprehensive" as used in this and the the three preceding Notes is definitive only. In actual practice, science and criticism, history and system, and, indeed, musical and non-musical viewpoints, can never be wholly separated nor wholly joined.

DATA SECONDARY

DATA TERTIARY FOR STUDY

Table; and of both scientific and critical methods—1 and 2 in the Table.

The Table outlines briefly the function of eight possible operations, each engaging one term of each of these three dichotomies. Competence in handling this apparatus will require, in every one of the eight operations, knowledge and judgment in the handling of the requisite speech norms of both general and music space-times. The four operations under heading I require, in addition, knowledge and judgment in the handling of the requisite music norms. The two operations under I,A refer particularly to traditions of idioms contemporary with the student; the two under I,B, in addition to these, to knowledge and judgment in the handling of one or more notated traditions not contemporary (or not wholly contemporary) with the student. Competence in the four operations under II can be plotted on this pattern, adding or substituting, for the norms of music, the special norms of speech required by one or more of the specialized studies employed.

Attention is called to the fact that the order in which the eight operations are presented here produces an organization of musicological work in which the core is the systematic study of the particular tradition (or traditions) of which the student is a carrier (or has the equivalence in knowledge) around which a succession of layers may be wrapped, each more remote from that tradition until the universe of speech discourse is completely comprehended in its relation to the universe of music discourse.[10]

[10]Or, perhaps we should say in both cases

In conclusion let me say that the apparatus as a whole may hardly be expected to be employed in its full development by any one man. Actually, we each of us carve out, according to our individual interest or competency, a section that we use. It is to be hoped that some day, among the lot of us, all eight operations will be fairly equally deployed.

I hope it is clear that the music event is not to be confused with the verbal report of it. We cannot remind ourselves too often that the sound patterns of speech normena and their meanings cannot represent the sound patterns of music normena and their semantic homologue of speech meaning without distortion. The task is to find a terminology and a method of handling it most suitable to the particular idiom under investigation. Since in this mid-20th century we do not start with a *tabula rasa*, we must, of course, make use of the terms of current acceptance found more nearly universal in application. But we must carefully criticize each one, that it bring not with it preconceptions at variance with the primary data before us. There can be no substitute for the accurate description of a music idiom known first hand by the student, whether or not it has a history, and whether or not it fits into the history of our study. It is only upon such a base that sound comparative studies of separate musics and music idioms can be made and, so, a world view of music envisaged.

Pan American Union

"universe of communication." For the philosopher may justifiably withhold the word "discourse" from use in connection with music, as peculiar to the art of speech alone.

Toward a Definition of Ethnomusicology[1]

WILLARD RHODES
Columbia University

THE increasing interest in music and awareness of its significance as a revealing expression of man and his culture have given a fresh impetus to ethnomusicological research and investigation. Employing the techniques and methods of cultural anthropology and musicology, the discipline has struggled along these past seventy years as a stepchild of both parents, a second class citizen in the society of the social sciences and the humanities. This unenviable position results in part from the cross-relationship of ethnomusicology and the demands which it imposes on the student and scholar, for he must have a working knowledge and facility with the theoretical and empirical aspects of both disciplines if he would deal adequately with his material. The ethnologist with a basic training in musicology is as rare as the musicologist who has worked seriously in anthropology. The progress of ethnomusicology has been limited by the small number of workers who have been able to meet the double qualifications of the discipline.

Why has man's music, so rich and varied and so overtly expressive of his inner life, attracted so few students and scholars? The heavy demands of preparation in two disciplines and the limited opportunities for professional practice of ethnomusicology have conspired to repel all but those persons who, despite lack of support and opportunities, have dedicated themselves to the study of this aspect of culture. But is not the fraternity of ethnomusicologists also responsible for this situation? Have we been as diligent in the promotion and publication of our work as our colleagues in other fields? And have we not been over-zealous in the trusteeship of the discipline and its tradition? A field of investigation already highly specialized has often been made to appear more esoteric and forbidding than was necessary. How many potential workers and patrons have been lost because we failed to communicate with them? Without lowering standards of scholarship we must somehow manage to enlist more workers in ethnomusicology and gain a wider interest and support not only among our colleagues in the related disciplines but among all those who find in man's music an expression of his thoughts and feelings, his inner life.

It may appear pretentious to attempt a definition of ethnomusicology at this late date, but if this paper stimulates thinking and discussion on the subject and contributes in a small way toward a clearer focus on the scope, objectives, problems and methods of our discipline, it will have fulfilled its purpose.

The term musicology, recently adopted from French *musicologie* into English usage to denote the scientific study of music, is the equivalent of the German *Musikwissenschaft*. The German term was first used by F. Chrysander in the preface to his *Jahrbücher für musikalische Wissenschaft* (1863) to emphasize the importance of applying scientific and scholarly standards and methods in musical studies, and since that time scholars of the Western world

457

have been attempting to define the discipline and its province. Guido Adler, in an article *Umfang, Methode und Ziel der Musikwissenschaft* which appeared in the first volume of the *Vierteljahrschrift für Musikwissenschaft* (1885:14), presented a comprehensive system that embraced the entire field of music study and acknowledged the interdisciplinary relationship to the collateral sciences, acoustics, physiology, psychology, logic, grammar, pedagogy and esthetics. Waldo S. Pratt, music historian and American pioneer in musicology, wrote in his article, *On Behalf of Musicology* (1915:3)

> Here genuine scholarship must guard itself against every' species of provincialis n, from the pettiness of the ignorant to the snobbery of professed culture. Its outlook must be determined, as far as may be, not by the impulses of personal preference or prejudice, not by the demands of practical instruction, not even by the problems of library economy and system, but by the essential possibilities of the subject. "Musicology" if it is to rank with other comprehensive sciences, must include every conceivable scientific discussion of musical topics.

This is sound counsel, but Pratt betrays his own provincialism in his discussion of Adler's systematization when he writes, "The application of 'musicology' to comparative ethnological research is surprising, and must be set aside as arbitrary" (1915:2).

Otto Kinkeldey, dean of American musicologists, in his article *Musicology* in the *International Cyclopedia of Music and Musicians* (1939:1218), has broadly defined the subject as "the whole body of systematized knowledge about music, which results from the application of a scientific method of investigation or research, or of philosophical speculation and rational systematization to the facts, the processes and the development of musical art, and to the relation of man in general (or even animals) to that art." Few will take issue with this all-embracing theoretical definition, but an examination of studies and research made under the aegis of musicology reveals the fact that most scholars have been content to work within a much smaller framework.

In the *Harvard Dictionary of Music* (1947:474) Willi Apel presents in a realistic statement the emphasis and orientation of contemporary musicology. He writes, "The important point, however, is that the category of Musical Research (*Musikforschung*) must be given the central position in the plan, with theory, music history, etc., forming the foundation, while aesthetics, acoustics, etc., represent adjunct fields of study."

So much for musicology in its broadest outline. What now of that special field of investigation which we have designated ethnomusicology? Recognized as a division of musicology by Guido Adler in 1885, it has been more or less consistently practiced since that time under the term comparative musicology (*vergleichende Musikwissenschaft*). The comparative viewpoint which prevailed in the early studies of Alexander John Ellis, *Tonometrical Observations on Some Existing Non-Harmonic Scales* (1884:368-385) and *On the Musical Scales of Various Nations* (1885:485–517), is undoubtedly responsible for the qualifying adjective that was introduced to set this field of investigation apart as a distinct branch of musicology. Guido Adler defined its task as "the comparison of the musical works—especially of folksongs—of the various peoples of the earth for ethnographical purposes, and the classification of them according to their various forms" (1885:14).

The inappropriateness of the term has been pointed out on the basis that all scientific investigation employs comparative methods and that "the comparative method is based upon fundamental investigations that are themselves descriptive, analytic, experimental, speculative, and historical" (Haydon 1946:218, 237–238). Jaap Kunst (1950:7) advocated the term ethnomusicology as a more accurate and descriptive designation of the field of research long known as comparative musicology, and this term has received wide acceptance. The linking of ethnology to musicology in the new name emphasizes a phase of the science that has long been recognized but often neglected. With the rechristening of this established discipline it seems timely to survey the achievement of the past, re-examine the boundaries of its field of inquiry and methods of investigation, and project a program of study for the future.

In reviewing the literature of the past one can recognize three types of studies which appear in a time sequence more or less paralleling the evolutionary development of comparative musicology. None of these types are pure, however, nor is the time sequence absolute. The first type includes the earliest studies, many of which were so burdened with the investigation of musicological problems that the material often received scant ethnological treatment (Abraham and von Hornbostel 1909–10:1–25; Stumpf 1901; von Hornbostel 1913:11–23; von Hornbostel and Sachs 1914:553–590). This situation is understandable since the pioneers in comparative musicology had to develop a methodology and techniques for the scientific analysis and classification of their musical data. To these early scholars, Ellis, Stumpf, Abraham, von Hornbostel, and Sachs, the ethnomusicologist of today is indebted for the systematization of the discipline and the establishment of a methodology which with minor variations still serves as the foundation of his science.

The second type may be described as ethnographic, and comprises studies devoted primarily to the analysis and description of the music of an ethnic group in its cultural setting (Densmore 1918; Roberts 1926; Burlin 1907). Although these studies rarely exceed the scope of an ethnographic monograph, they constitute a large and important portion of our literature and working material. Based for the most part on phonographic field recordings, they have preserved for further study musical forms that have since undergone radical change under the impact of an alien culture, or in many instances have died with the last singers and musicians who knew them. In presenting a clear definition of the musical style and practice for an ethnic group, based on sound musical analysis, these monographs have made significant contributions to the work of later scholars whose orientation has been toward ethnological interpretation.

The third type is the ethnomusicological study in which the scholar, after a thorough musicological examination of his material, attempts to see music in its proper relationship to culture and to employ it in "the investigation of theoretical problems that arise out of the analysis of human custom" (Herzog 1935; McAllester 1954; Merriam 1955; Nettl 1955; Rhodes 1952). It is at this point that we so often fail to realize the full resources and possibilities of our discipline. Ethnomusicologists are in constant danger of becoming isolated and insulated in a musical vacuum where they pursue the study of music per se without reference to man and his culture. Herskovits states a fact that bears frequent repetition: "But it is at the core of anthropological thinking that each problem investigated be recognized as only one manifestation of one segment of man's complex culture, and that it be studied with full consciousness of its wide implications" (Herskovits 1948:2).

Each of these three types of study is important to the further development of our discipline and should be continued. The musicological-theoretical problems of transcription and analysis need to be re-examined and discussed. The need for musico-ethnographic monographs is now as great as ever. Despite the great amount of collecting done throughout the world during the past seventy years, there are still cultures whose music remains unrecorded and unstudied. For those ethnic groups that have been adequately recorded and studied, we need contemporary field material in order to measure culture change in music and to gain some insight into socio-psychological processes. Studies in these two categories are preliminary and essential to research in the third category, which represents a fuller realization of the resources and objectives of ethnomusicology.

If the term ethnomusicology were to be interpreted in its broadest sense it would include as its domain the total music of man, without limitations of time or space. This viewpoint was advanced by Charles Seeger and is supported by the semantic implications. It makes historical musicology, which is primarily concerned with the art music of Western Europe during the Christian era, only one division of a universal discipline (Seeger 1933:143–150; 1955). However, both historical musicology and comparative musicology have staked their claims to their respective fields of research, and any attempt to redefine the boundaries at this time appears impractical. Jaap Kunst has defined the study-object of ethnomusicology as "mainly the music and musical instruments of all non-European peoples, including both the so-called primitive peoples and the civilized Eastern nations" (Kunst 1950:7). A survey of the early comparative musicological studies in the first volume of the *Sammelbände für vergleichende Musikwissenschaft* (1922), and the two monographs on folk music, *Das Lied der Deutscher Kolonisten in Russland* (Schünemann 1923) and *Volkmusik der Rumänen von Marmures* (Bartok 1923) which constitute volumes three and four, gives a clear view of the field which the pioneers cultivated and regarded as their rightful province. Here, under the imprint of comparative musicology, are bound together studies of the music of the Near East, the Far East, Indonesia, Africa, the North American Indians, and European folk music. Of those ethnomusicologists whose interests are confined solely to primitive music I ask, "Can we refuse our inheritance?" Let us not be provincial in the pursuit of our discipline. Oriental art music, the folk music of the world, and primitive music, all await our serious study. The historical musicologist has shown scant interest in any of these fields. The fact that they are so vast that no person is able to master them in their entirety should not exclude them or any part of them from ethnomusicology. Within the discipline there are places aplenty for the specialist.

The subject of hybrid music has disturbed some scholars who question whether or not the "impure" music of an acculturated group constitutes material for ethnomusicological study. The question appears rhetorical, but I think there can be no doubt about the right of hybrid music to claim our attention. What anthropologist would disclaim the phenomena of culture change, be it social organization, language, religion, or music, as suitable material for investigation and study? We are derelict in our work if we fail to record and study the contemporary changing music of ethnic groups, few of which are free from the impact of alien cultures. Such music may be less interesting from a strictly musical point of view, but it will undoubtedly cast light on the psychological and sociological processes of the individuals and the groups that produce it.

The invention of the phonograph and its use in the recording of primitive and folk music made possible the amassing of an impressive body of musical material without which ethnomusicology could never have developed to its present scientific status. With the replacement of the wax cylinder by the acetate disc, which in turn was replaced by the magnetic tape, the cost of recording has been steadily reduced, the quality has been improved, and the field worker's problems have been considerably lightened. But we have not yet been able to avail ourselves of electronic equipment for the graphic analysis of our recordings. Charles Seeger has experimented with such an instrument but has not developed it to the point where it can be used widely (Seeger 1951). Development in this direction has been retarded by the tremendous cost of building electronic instruments, and by the little interest that manufacturers and scientists have shown in our particular need for such equipment. Modern electronic instruments for the acoustical analysis of melodies and the measurement of intervals would not only facilitate the ethnomusicologist's work but would give it an objectivity that it can never achieve so long as it depends upon the human ear conditioned by the Western musical system.

Ethnomusicology, twice interrupted by World Wars, has languished from lack of adequate publication and exchange of news and ideas among its workers. Recently the *Ethno-Musicology Newsletter* under the able editorship of Alan P. Merriam has partially filled this gap by re-establishing communication among students and scholars on an international basis. Until the *Newsletter* is firmly established on a sound financial basis and provision is made for the publication of articles, we proceed at a disadvantage. Despite the great amount of collecting that is being done throughout the world, there are still few professional ethnomusicologists qualified to analyze and interpret this material. The lack of trained scholars continues to retard the progress of the discipline. We need to educate a corps of workers, but first we must convince the administrations of our universities and foundations and our colleagues in anthropology and musicology that ethnomusicology has a real contribution to make toward the understanding of man.

In discussing the comparative study of music of people outside the stream of Euro-American culture, Herskovits writes: "For its implications lead us to some of the most fundamental truths about the nature and functioning of culture, and suggest the importance of the contribution that investigations carried on in this special field can make to the study of culture as a whole" (Herskovits 1948:435). Here is our opportunity. The musicologists have developed methods and techniques for analysis of musical material. The anthropologists have provided theories for the interpretation of cultural phenomena. It is the task of the ethnomusicologist to avail himself of the resources of both disciplines in order to give meaning to this significant segment of man's culture. In validating its claim as a scholarly discipline, ethnomusicology can point to a distinct and well defined body of subject matter and field of investigation, and to a methodology unique in its application of anthropological concepts and principles to musicological analysis.

We need to be more imaginative and creative in the interpretation of our material. Such an approach, while calling for a more sensitive insight and understanding, implies no relaxation of rigorous scientific methods. Self-criticism is already arising in our ranks. "Musicology has been mainly absorbed with the mechanics of ethnic music, its collection, classification and analysis from a purely musical-technical point of view. The investigation of music as an emotional expression must go beyond this" (Yurchenko 1955:6). Let us not become narrow in the pursuit of our special field. If ethnomusicology is to achieve its rightful place among the social sciences and humanities it must contribute more generously of its knowledge, insight, and ideas to anthropology and historical musicology.

NOTE

[1] This paper was presented at the fifty-fourth annual meeting of the American Anthropological Association in Boston, November 18, 1955.

REFERENCES CITED

ABRAHAM, OTTO and ERICH M. VON HORNBOSTEL
    1909–10 Vorschlage für die Transkription exotischer Melodien. Sammelbände der internationalen Musikgesellschaft 11: 1–25. Leipzig.

ADLER, GUIDO
    1885 Umfang, Methode und Ziel der Musikwissenschaft. Vierteljahrschrift für Musikwissenschaft 1:5–20. Leipzig.

APEL, WILLI
    1947 Musicology. Harvard Dictionary of Music 473–475. Cambridge, Harvard University Press.

BURLIN, NATALIE CURTIS
    1907 The Indians' Book. New York and London, Harper and Brothers.

DENSMORE, FRANCES
    1918 Teton Sioux Music. Bureau of American Ethnology, Bulletin 61. Washington, D. C.

ELLIS, ALEXANDER JOHN
 1884 Tonometrical Observations on Some Existing Non-Harmonic Scales. Proceedings of the Royal Society of London 37:368–385.
 1885 On the Musical Scales of Various Nations. Journal of the Society of Arts 33:485–517.

HAYDON, GLEN
 1946 Introduction to Musicology. New York, Prentice-Hall.

HERSKOVITS, MELVILLE J.
 1948 Man and His Works. New York, Knopf.

HERZOG, GEORGE
 1935 Plains Ghost Dance and Great Basin Music. American Anthropologist 37:403–419. Menasha.

HORNBOSTEL, ERICH M. VON
 1913 Melodie und Skala. Jahrbuch der Musikbibliothek Peters für 1912: 11–23.

HORNBOSTEL, ERICH M. VON and CURT SACHS
 1914 Systematik der Musikinstrumente. Zeitschrift für Ethnologie 46:553–590.

KINKELDEY, OTTO
 1939 Musicology. International Cyclopedia of Music and Musicians 1218–1221. New York, Dodd, Mead & Company.

KUNST, JAAP
 1950 Musicologica. Koninklijke Vereeniging Indisch Institut, Mededelling No. 90, Afdeling Culturele en Physische Anthropologie No. 35. Amsterdam.

MCALLESTER, DAVID P.
 1954 Enemy Way Music: A Study of Social and Esthetic Values as seen in Navaho Music. Peabody Museum of American Archaeology and Ethnology, Harvard University, Papers 61, No. 3. Cambridge.

MERRIAM, ALAN P.
 1955 The Use of Music in the Study of a Problem of Acculturation. American Anthropologist 57:28–34. Menasha.

NETTL, BRUNO
 1955 Musical Culture of the Arapaho. Musical Quarterly 41:325–331. New York.

PRATT, WALDO S.
 1915 On Behalf of Musicology. Musical Quarterly 1:1–16. New York.

RHODES, WILLARD
 1952 Acculturation in North American Indian Music. Proceedings and Selected Papers 29th International Congress of Americanists, Acculturation in the Americas, Sol Tax, Ed. 127–132. Chicago.

ROBERTS, HELEN H.
 1926 Ancient Hawaiian Music. Bernice P. Bishop Museum Bulletin 29. Honolulu.

SEEGER, CHARLES
 1933 Music and Musicology. Encyclopedia of the Social Sciences 11:244–250. New York.
 1951 An Instantaneous Music Notator. Journal of the International Folk Music Council 3:103–106. Cambridge, England.
 1955 Personal communications.

STUMPF, CARL
 1901 Tonsystem und Musik der Siamesen. Beiträge zur Akustik und Musikwissenschaft 3, reprinted in Sammelbände für vergleichende Musikwissenschaft 1:127–177 (1922). Munich.

YURCHENKO, HENRIETTA
 1905 Communication. Ethno-Musicology Newsletter 65.

Historical Aspects of Ethnomusicology

BRUNO NETTL
University of Kiel

E THNOMUSICOLOGY has traditionally been classified within the systematic branch of musicology rather than the historical, but historical interests and orientations have always played a considerable part in it; indeed, they have at times been the predominant motivating forces in investigation. However, the preference for synchronic and descriptive approaches has evidently caused the historical aspects of ethnomusicology to be left in a methodologically disorganized array. It is the purpose of this paper to work toward a systematization of the various historical aspects; it will utilize approaches followed in the past as well as other theoretical possibilities. Systematizations of this sort have already been attempted in ways which range from early music-historical points of view such as Lach's (1924) through later ones which emerged under the increasing influence of anthropology (Kunst 1955:43–46; Nettl 1955a). The subject matter under consideration has also varied greatly. Beginning with historical speculation in Oriental music (with which we are concerned here only in a secondary sense because of the existence of at least a partially written tradition and a professionalized musical culture) and the role of folk music in the history of European cultivated music, the interests began to follow the trends of anthropological thinking, have occasionally gone their own way, and have sometimes been influenced by other disciplines such as biology and psychology.

In spite of the variety of materials and aims, the historical aspects of ethnomusicology can be grouped into two principal classes, origin and change. Explanation of the origin of various phenomena has been at the root of many developments throughout the field, and has until recently predominated over the study of change. But while the study of origins has in a sense been exhausted or in many cases seems impossible to pursue further, the study of change promises to be of even greater interest when some of the methodological problems have been solved.

The problem of origin can be approached in a number of ways. For example, one may be interested in the manner of origin of a given phenomenon, or in the place of origin. The manner-of-origin approach has been one of the more speculative sides of ethnomusicology, and has provided considerable common ground between that field and general music history. The problem of the origin of music itself falls into this class, although ethnomusicological data can only corroborate or, more frequently, negate. Nevertheless, some theories of the origin of music which indicate the special function of music in primitive culture and its close ties to religion are genuinely based on ethnological information (e.g. Nadel 1930).

The search for the manner of origin of various generalized musical phenom-

518

ena is also involved here. For example, the debate on the origin of polyphony carried through the decades (e.g. Adler 1908; Lachmann 1927; Schneider 1934), the arguments for single versus multiple origins of polyphony, the possibility of various types of polyphony developing separately or together, would all be included in this category. Slightly different is the treatment of specialized and localized musical phenomena. The origin of certain types of scales or meters is relevant here, insofar as the approach does not stress the development of one type from another; the latter would properly be included in the "change" category. An example of this category is the investigation of the origin of the unhemitonic pentatonic scale whether it was derived acoustically through the circle of fifths, through the repetition of a two-tone motif at different pitch levels, or through filling gaps in larger intervals. Another such example is the origin of transposition or melodic sequence, which may be interpreted as variety introduced in a repetitive musical structure, or (since it is most frequently downward movement) as repetition modified by the prevailingly descending melodic contour (Kolinski 1957:3), or in still other ways. It would be difficult to exhaust the examples for the manner-of-origin quest in ethnomusciology, for it may be justly said that it has provided the impetus for a large proportion of the research in this field.

The search for the place of origin of musical phenomena, generalized and specialized, has comprised a number of research problems in ethnomusciology.

Thus, the place of origin of medieval European polyphony (summarized by Reese 1940:249–58), of the styles of some Northwest Coast Indians (Barbeau 1934), of certain musical instruments, and even of individual compositions such as the folk songs in European traditions, to cite only a few examples, have provided a variety of studies and theories. The general problem of place of origin has been approached from the nonmusical side as well; musical materials have been used to ascertain the possibility of cultural contact among widely separated peoples, and it is in this area that the historical orientation of ethnomusicology has made its greatest contribution to cultural anthropology.

The problem of change, although often related to and combined with the problem of origin, requires somewhat different approaches. We are interested in the reasons for change (or lack of change), and in its nature, degree, and rate. This applies to various levels of musical organization. We can study the change in individual compositions or in larger bodies of music. We can try to trace the changes indicated by differences among the variants of a single song, and we can try to identify the reasons for them whether they lie within the structure of the piece or in its cultural context. We can try to measure, for comparative purposes, the amount of change that has taken place and try to determine how rapidly it has occurred. Similar matters can be studied, but with greater difficulty, in entire repertories, whether defined geographically or by their cultural milieu. If more than one composition is involved, certain statistical methods may be drawn upon (as in Merriam 1956). Finally, investigations involving change are frequently associated with those concerning the place of origin of a musical phenomenon, for the obvious reason that if a musical item moves from one place to another it is also subject to change, and it would be impossible to evaluate the change without considering the geographic movement.

It is useless to try within a short space to survey all of the studies in ethnomusicology involving historical perspective. However, the approaches of many of these studies are summarized in the following pages, and we shall attempt to give examples of the general conclusions to which they have led and to formulate some of the general tendencies which seem to prevail.

PROBLEMS OF ORIGIN

The origin of music, as well as of individual musical phenomena, has usually been explained by reference to three possible processes. (The origin theories are summarized in Kunst 1955:46–48 and Nettl 1956:134–36). It may be a coincidence based on the structure of a related phenomenon, it may be motivated by a nonmusical need, or it may be inevitable through some process of evolution in a given direction. Thus, the origin of music in emotional speech (a theory not widely accepted) or in vocal signalling over a long distance (one more widely held) could be based on coincidence. A human need for music, and its resulting invention, are postulated in theories involving rhythmic work and religion as the cradles of music. Music as the human version of mating calls, or as a specialized form which developed from a prelanguage and pre-music generalized type of communication (Nettl 1956:136) are examples of the evolutionary views.

Most origin theories involving smaller-scale phenomena are also based on one of these three approaches. For example, most forms of polyphony are attributed to discovery by coincidence or by faulty rendition of monophonic materials. This point of view does not explain why "faulty" rendition (singing of two variants of the same piece simultaneously, overlap in antiphonal singing, or singing the same melody at different pitch levels) should in some cultures lead to the development of polyphonic style, while in others it is simply written off as error. The origin of some instruments is also attributed to coincidence—for example, the origin of the musical bow from the hunting bow.

It is also possible to postulate the development of musical features in some styles on the basis of esthetic needs. The need for unifying factors in orally transmitted music (explained in Nettl 1957) may bring unity in one element in order to balance the elaboration or heterogeneity in another. It is possible, for example, that a style in which the tonal material is expanded will also introduce melodic sequences in order to offset the diversification. Or a style based largely on repetition of short melodic formulae may introduce and encourage improvisation and variation in order to offset the large degree of unity. This view is supported by the complementary distribution of unifying features in some styles.

The evolutionary view is represented by such hypotheses as that the direction of change remains the same, so pentatonic scales naturally evolve from tetratonic scales if the latter have in turn developed from tritonic scales. The opinion that there are stages through which all (or many) musical cultures pass, discussed below, is also pertinent here.

The problem of single versus multiple origin has occupied ethnomusicologists on many occasions. On the whole, they have adhered to the generally accepted anthropological point of view, using geographic distributions and assuming that the likelihood of multiple origin decreases with the complexity of the phenomenon. They have also used the laws of acoustics (Hornbostel 1910) to explain the presence of the same phenomenon in widely separated areas. The main problem faced here by ethnomusicologists is the measurement of degree of complexity and similarity. This problem is shared with other cultural anthropologists, but is somewhat more specialized here because of the peculiar structure of music. It is possible that musical material, being in its structure relatively independent of other cultural elements and being fairly easy to describe and analyze, is better suited to measuring devices than are many other cultural phenomena (Merriam 1956:465).

PROBLEMS OF CHANGE

Why, how, and under what conditions does music change? Although these questions have not been answered with scientifically predictable results for any type of music, they have considerable significance even for material outside the scope of ethnomusicology, as have the negative versions of the same questions—the identification of stability and stabilizing factors in music.

It is first necessary to define musical change. In non-Western music, change seems to be a phenomenon substantially different from change in a cultivated, Western tradition. While changes through substitution in a repertory occur in both types of cultures, it is only in those which make use of oral tradition that established compositions are altered. Thus, change in a cultivated musical culture tends to be cumulative, new material simply being added to the old; in an oral tradition it may be change in a real sense, old material being eliminated as the new is introduced.

Changes in a repertory, or beyond the simple alteration of individual compositions, occur in various ways. Individual elements of music may undergo change, while others remain the same. New songs may be introduced into a repertory, causing the older material to change by assimilation; or the new material may gradually change to accommodate the style of the old. Changes in a repertory, if not caused by the substitution of new compositions for older ones, are of course determined by the changes wrought in individual compositions. But when change in a repertory is evident, it is often impossible to determine what has happened to individual compositions. Thus the two levels of change must usually be approached in contrastive ways.

There are many reasons for musical change, and the following discussion is limited to those involved in music in oral tradition. However, the same reasons, and perhaps others, may be relevant to cultivated music. We are not in a position to assert under what conditions, how fast, and how much music changes, and which aspects of it are most subject to change. It is possible to divide the scholarly approaches to change into two main classes: those which make use of strictly musical (or esthetic) criteria, concerned with the characteristics of the musical material itself; and those which make use of nonmusical criteria, such as cultural and racial ones. Of course, these approaches are not mutually exclusive; both must be used, and which is finally preferred depends on the individual case.

The first to be generally accepted were racial criteria; these were partially subscribed to by such men as Carl Stumpf, E. M. von Hornbostel, and Marius Schneider (1946). Today they are not generally credited with great validity, although they have been the subject of technical investigation by Metfessel (1928) and Bose (1952). On the whole, racial approaches tend to concentrate more on musical stability than on change. The musical relationships among members of different races are of course entwined with cultural relationships, and to separate the racial factors is a difficult and sometimes impossible task. Nevertheless, statements have been made (e.g. Schneider 1938:290) that the style of music is determined by the culture, but the manner of performance, vocal techniques, and so forth, are determined by the race, and there have been attempts to associate specific traits with certain racially defined groups. Since members of a race have lived in relatively close cultural contact, the existence of common musical traits hardly proves racial or physically inherited traits. Even when the characteristics of a racial group, such as the African Negroes, are brought from one place to another, such as from Africa to the New World, we have no convincing case for racially inherited musical characteristics. The notion that members of a racial group tend to accept musical materials from physically similar groups more readily than from different ones (Schneider 1946) seems too speculative. Moreover, it is negated by such cases as the distribution of individual compositions through the various physical types of Europe, the influence of Arabic music on the African Negroes, and the relatively similar musical styles of Africa and Europe (viewed on a broad scale) as compared to the musical contrast between the African Negroes and the physically similar Melanesians. The accompaniment of cultural influences by racial ones in many cases obscures the problem even more, and we must conclude that the racial approaches to musical change have not contributed much to this field.

Logically related to the racial approaches are those concerned with movements of populations and contact among peoples. It is probable that most documented cases of changing repertories are due to culture contact. Peoples living side-by-side influence each other, and where there is movement of population groups, the greater number of contacts increases the possibility of musical change. One might conclude from this that a tribe which moves about experiences greater or more rapid musical change than does one which remains among the same set of neighbors. The former tribe might have a high rate of elimination of material; or, holding on to old styles as new ones are introduced, it may increase the total number of styles in its repertory. Thus we conclude that a tribe with many outside contacts may have more variety in its music than one with a stable and limited set of contacts. This approach is illustrated by my study (Nettl 1953) of Shawnee music, in which it is shown that Shawnee contacts with other Indian tribes resulted in the introduction of new styles; the Shawnee today have music which can be traced back to their contacts with the Northern Algonquians, the Southeastern United States, and the Plains styles. On the other hand, we find that the Pueblos have a rich and complex but rather unified musical style, perhaps because (at least in recent centuries) their contacts with other tribes have been limited. The generally conservative nature of Pueblo culture may also be involved here.

Another problem involving musical change through cultural contact is the direction of influence. This can generally be answered with some degree of certainty: the more complex style tends to influence the simpler one. This does not necessarily mean that the music of the more complex culture is introduced into the simpler one, for occasionally the simpler culture may have the more complex music. A variety of stylistic combinations may also occur, as indicated below in the discussion of acculturation. In these combinations, however, it seems likely that each culture contributes the elements which it has developed best or to the greatest degree of specialization. For example, the mixture of African and European styles found in Haiti consists of African rhythm, antiphonal singing, and drum accompaniment, but European melodic structure, perhaps because melody is more highly developed in European folk music than in African Negro music.

A musical style may also move from one tribe to another, independently of population movement. It changes the repertories of the tribes through which it passes but it may also undergo change itself, influenced by the tribal styles with which it has made contact. For example, the Peyote style, as defined by McAllester (1949), presumably moved from the Apache and Navaho to the Plains. It retained a feature of Apache music, the use of restricted rhythmic values (only two note-lengths are usually found), but in the Plains it evidently acquired the cascadingly descending, terrace-shaped melodic contour. Possibly the forces described above operated here; the melodic contour of the Plains, a specialized and rather highly developed type, was strong enough to encroach on the Peyote style, but the more generalized rhythmic structure of the Plains was not strong enough to alter the specialized rhythmic organization derived from the Apache. Thus it may be justified to assume (although there are as yet few documented examples) that specialized features in music are less easily changed than generalized ones, and from this to proceed to the hypothesis that generalized features are constantly undergoing change in the direction of becoming specialized. If this were true, a general law of music history could be formulated stating that generalized features change to specialized ones. On the other hand, this process would no doubt be modified by many other forces, and the hypothesis may be applicable only in certain cases rather than generally.

Movement of musical material occurs not only in large bodies of music but also at the level of the individual composition, where the same forces seem to operate. In European folk music it is possible to identify tunes which have moved through large areas. They seem rarely to have influenced the music of these areas to any great extent, but they themselves have changed for reasons which are discussed below in another context. It might be possible to infer that the larger a moving body of music, the greater is its influence on the repertories through which it passes, and the less it is subject to change itself.

Another force toward change may be called assimilation, the tendency of neighboring styles to become similar. While musical material which moves from one place to another influences the styles in its environment, there is also a force of attraction among the styles which are in contact. Thus, an area in which there is little contact among groups is likely to have diverse styles, but one in which the contact is great is likely to have a more unified style. An obstacle to testing this hypothesis is the lack of measuring devices for degree of musical similarity. Yet it is possible to compare an area with much internal communication, such as Europe, with one in which communication is inhibited, such as Oceania, and find the hypothesis substantially borne out. Of course, the presence of other factors must also be considered here.

I doubt whether it is possible to make decisions about musical change, its causes and directions, on the basis of strictly musical information. It is likely that certain directions of change do predominate and that some can in some cases, and with the corroboration of other kinds of information, decide such matters as the relative age of musical styles on the basis of structural features in the music. In most cases, music seems to move from simplicity to greater complexity, so it is assumed by most scholars that the simplest styles are the oldest. As indicated above, there may be movement from generalized to specialized features, if it is possible to classify musical traits in this way. Once a specific direction has been established, there may be a tendency to continue it. For example, if the tones in a scale have been increased from three to four, further increases will follow, or at least a decrease will not ensue. These tendencies are speculative, and beyond the obvious simple-to-complex movement, they have not been used in specific investigations.

Other changes due to musical reasons are related to the basic common feature of folk and primitive music, oral tradition. Because there are mnemonic problems in the oral transmission of music, the material must adhere to certain specifications in order to make retention possible (Nettl 1957). The music must be simple, and there must be some unifying device such as repetition in form, a drone or parallelism in polyphony, isorhythmic structure, repetition of a metric unit, a definitely established tonality, melodic sequence or other transposition, or predominance of a single tone. The necessity for these features tends to inhibit change, and to channel it in specific directions. Thus, perhaps a melody with rigidly isometric structure is free to become heterometric after becoming isorhythmic. A melody with a hierarchical arrangement of tones, in which important and secondary ones are easily distinguished, may lose this arrangement after the introduction of sequences, since there is less need for the unifying function of the tonal structure. Again, these forces have not been studied in many examples; they are presented here as a possibility for future research. They can be observed in some European folk tunes which have undergone change while passing from one ethnic group to another, but whether these changes are due strictly to assimilation is an open question.

Measurement of the rate of change in music, and the amount of change in a given instance, awaits the discovery of proper methods. On the basis of impressionistic observation, particularly in the field of cultivated music, we may assume that change takes place irregularly; it is sometimes rapid, sometimes absent. In European music history there seem to be intervals during which musical style changes rapidly, while between them it changes only slightly over long periods of time. Sachs (1947) believes that this is connected with the length of a person's productive life, and in effect blames it on the turn-over of persons in the population. It is often stated that the music of primitive cultures must be somewhat closer to the beginnings of music than is Western cultivated music, and that primitive music must therefore have changed more slowly. It is also possible that the rate of change is proportional to the complexity of the music. This may be caused by the inherent structural traits; for example, where there are more features (i.e. more tones, more voices, more sections) there is more possibility for change. Or it may be caused by the more generally dynamic nature of complex cultures (open to question because of the large number of exceptions). The fundamental values of the culture are also involved.

There is evidence that in at least some cases, music changes less rapidly than do other aspects of culture. Thus, most primitive cultures which have had close contact with the West have taken on more European material culture, economic organization, and religion than European music. Although reconstruction is difficult, there may be similar examples among primitive cultures which lack Western influence. The Apache and Navaho have possibly retained more of the Northern Athabascan musical heritage than of many other aspects of that culture. The Hungarians have retained some of the musical features shared by other Finno-Ugric peoples such as the Cheremis (Kodaly 1956:23–59), but otherwise their culture has become Westernized. The reasons for this slow rate of change probably vary with the example, and comparison of music with other cultural features is methodologically difficult.

There are two ways of studying individual cases of historical change in folk and primitive music. One can try to reconstruct events of the past, or one can observe the changes occurring at the present time. The latter approach has been used in a number of cases involving acculturation (for example, Merriam 1955); the former has been used less often in cases involving individual repertories or styles (Nettl 1953, 1955b), but more often in general questions such as those involving the relative age of musical features. For example, it has been used to reconstruct the history of European folk songs by comparison of variants. There are definite limitations to both approaches. The reconstruction method is limited by inadequate material and by the fact that definite proof is almost impossible to obtain. The study of change in the present limits the amount of time during which change may take place, and involves specialized situations in which the cultures being studied are usually feeling the influence of Western civilization.

THE ROLE OF THE INDIVIDUAL COMPOSITION

The role of the individual composition must be especially considered in historical research in ethnomusicology. It is a problematic role, for there is no clear-cut definition of what constitutes a composition in folk and primitive music, and this very lack accentuates the importance of historical orientation. Should one consider a group of variants with proved relationship a single unit of musical creation? Most scholars would prefer this to a working definition of a single variant or rendition, but they are then faced with proving the relationship. At the other extreme, one could devise melodic types which may or may not have internal genetic relationship, as has been done by Wiora (1953), and call these individual compositions without considering the question of actual genetic relationship. This would have the advantage of grouping similar materials and simplifying the picture. There are other possibilities, all of which show that isolation of the unit of musical creation is much more difficult in folk and primitive than in Western cultivated music.

The problem of measuring degrees of similarity among different musical items in a style is also unsolved. However, it would appear that in some styles, all or most of the pieces are so similar as to be comparable to related variants of single compositions in other styles. For example, most songs of the Plains Indians appear, by virtue of their specialized melodic contour and form and by use of similar scales, as closely related to each other as the variants of a single English folk song found in several English-speaking countries. Thus the criteria used for one culture do not hold for others. Informants' statements may be of help in some cases, and they have on occasion differed considerably from the writer's own calculations.

Another problem is identification or classification of musical items which, although composed at separate times, are based on each other or on a common model. In many cultures, the priority on originality (however one can define this term) is probably not as great as in Western civilization, and there may be cases in which new songs are created simply by copying an already existing song with only slight changes (Nettl 1954a:83–85). For descriptive purposes in all of these situations it is probably advisable to accept the informant's classification, but for comparative work this is usually not feasible.

The very existence of the problem of identifying individual units of composition points up some of the essential differences in historical change between cultivated and traditional material. In some primitive cultures it seems that entire complexes of musical material are built up from a single composition. This process, described by Roberts (1933) and called by her the "pattern phenomenon," may occur, for example, when a ceremony unites a body of music which then tends to become homogeneous by intensifying the specialized tendencies of its style. In some cultures (Nettl 1954a:89), new material is consciously created from the old, either by elaborating songs already in existence or by combining material from several songs to form new units. The extent to which these products are individual compositions may also be questioned. To be sure, a similar problem occasionally appears in cultivated music, as when the ultimate source of a composition is investigated. In traditional music the problem becomes substantially greater in cultures which encourage improvisation and where music may be performed with considerable change in each rendition. One must also consider the problems of defining a composition if each rendition or stanza is different, and of dealing with entirely improvised material. These examples show why the history of individual pieces has rarely been studied, especially in primitive cultures. (An important exception is Willard Rhodes' investigation, as yet unpublished, of an individual Peyote song.)

SOME METHODS OF INVESTIGATING CHANGE

Among the various approaches to historical problems in ethnomusicology and the interpretation of descriptive data in a diachronic manner, three are selected for brief discussion here: evolutionary, geographic, and statistical. We label an approach evolutionary if it recognizes a generally valid series of stages of musical style, into which the data are fitted. The schemes arranging musical material into a time sequence may apply to generalized concepts or to more specific local ones. For example, it is believed by some that each culture goes through a stage of monophonic music, after which polyphony is developed. Cultures which have a great deal of polyphony, such as many in Negro Africa, are thus assumed to be higher in the musico-evolutionary process than those which have very little polyphony, such as the North American Indians. The difficulty with this view is that the results might be reversed if some other elements of music were considered. It could be postulated, for example, that there is an evolutionary process from short, repetitious forms to longer, strophic ones; in this case the Indians would be ahead of the African Negroes, assuming that typical rather than exceptional examples are used. Such a scheme is used by Lach (1929:17) to classify the music of the Finno-Ugric tribes in Russia. He believes that the simple forms of the Mordvin, which are usually repetitious, place that tribe in a lower evolutionary category than the Chuvash, who have many strophic songs with four different phrases per song. The Cheremis, who have many forms which begin in a typically strophic manner and then go on to repeat one phrase several times, are placed in an intermediate category. The same data could be interpreted differently, and without the use of evolutionary schemes. One of the problems faced by the classifier of tribes according to evolutionary principles is the selection of representative material. There would be different results if one used the average or most common, the simplest, or the most complex material within a repertory as a basis for comparison. Furthermore, the assumption that all cultures ultimately pass through the same set of musical stages is invalid unless one makes only the grossest sort of distinctions. Evolutionary schemes must thus be limited, if they are to serve any useful purpose at all, to restricted areas and phenomena, and the existence of other factors must be admitted.

Universally applicable stages for other elements of music have been postulated. They are usually quite logical and would be accepted as valid for most cases even by opponents of evolutionary approaches. For example, the development of scales from two to three and finally four tones probably took place in many cultures, although a development of tetratonic from ditonic without the intermediate tritonic is also possible. Similarly, most strophic styles probably developed from simple repetitive forms, but this does not necessarily indicate the future development of strophic forms in all styles which consist of a simple repetition of single phrases. There has been particular confusion in the case of rhythm. Some students believe that metric chaos, or absence of metric organization, precedes unification into metric patterns. On the other hand, it might be assumed that metric simplicity, repetition of a simple metric unit, precedes heterometric structure which, to the listener, many appear confusing and unorganized. A given piece may be analyzed as metrically unorganized or complex, and many evolutionary statements in ethnomusicology have been made on the basis of such subjective distinctions.

Evolutionary stages have also been hypothesized for the development of repertories. For example, Bartok (1931:12) postulates three stages in the development of folk music. First the repertory is homogeneous; all songs are in the same style. Then special substyles are developed for certain categories of songs, such as Christmas songs, wedding songs, and music for other ceremonies. In the third stage these ceremonies disappear, and with them the correlation between song functions and musical styles. This scheme seems justified for at least some cases, if we take the music of some primitive cultures as an example of the first stage. It is not known whether Bartok also allows for the appearance of intermediate stages caused by the impoverishment of repertories, whether the third stage is even reached in all cases, or whether the disappearing ceremonies and their peculiar styles are not replaced by other similar categories. Answers to these questions would probably qualify the general validity of this scheme.

Other such schemes have been advanced, largely along lines similar to Bartok's. Characteristically, they divide music history into three stages, a fact which in itself renders them suspect. The general validity of evolutionary schemes has never been established because of the many other factors affecting the material. Their greatest value has perhaps been the arrangement and classification of material.

The geographic approaches to historical questions have been more valuable. They have always been accepted for classificatory purposes, and there are few ethnomusicological studies which do not include some statement of geographic reference. There are perhaps two main uses which ethnomusicologists make of geographic concepts: (1) They plot distributions of musical phenomena, entire styles, individual compositions, but most frequently of individual traits abstracted from their styles, which can be present in various stylistic environments. An example of the latter is a scale type found with various kinds of meter or form, so that its distribution is not affected by the other elements in the same composition. (2) They classify the world in terms of musical areas which exhibit some degree of internal unity and contrast with neighboring areas. The results of these plottings and classifications are then used as the basis for conclusions on origin and change in music.

The plotting of distributions of musical traits is fairly clear-cut, but is limited by several factors: the difficulty of obtaining material which is valid for a given point in time for the entire area to be covered; the reliability of samplings represented by a collection; the necessity for positive statements and the fact that one can rarely vouch for the absence of a certain trait simply because it has not yet been observed; and the identification of similar traits when found in different stylistic milieus. However, these limitations do not pose as great a methodological problem as does identification of musical areas.

The concept of a musical area is difficult to handle because it is necessary first to decide how much homogeneity must be assumed. If based on one main trait, it becomes nothing but a plotted distribution of that trait; but if one expects too great a degree of unity, the musical area will shrink to the provenience of a single tribe, and the original purpose will not be served. It is therefore necessary to guard against overly great concentration on a single trait when making such constructions. Furthermore, there is a temptation merely to describe the music of an established culture area instead of basing the musical area exclusively on musical traits. The very fact that it is possible to identify musical areas at all gives us some insight into the nature of musical change. The areas, rather surprisingly, have fairly distinct borders and sometimes well-marked centers. To be sure, the borders show some influence of neighboring areas, but it is nevertheless remarkable that they set off a geographic unit which has common musical traits but which does not coincide with a language area, a culture area, or a natural area. The evidence thus points to some kind of independent development of the musical area.

Although it is subject to many influences, the musical area may in part be determined by an interaction of stylistic traits which appear because they have complementary functions. The presence of one trait may favor the retention of another one. For example, it is possible that the cascading melodies of the Plains Indians, with their wide range and large intervals, inhibit the development of polyphony and favor retention of a monophonic style. The small intervals and ranges of the Caroline Islands may be responsible for the fact that parallelism is the main type of polyphony rather than, say, imitation; with such a melodic structure, imitation would not be perceived as well as with larger intervals. All of this is highly speculative, but the possibility that musical styles develop on the basis of certain musical forces should be considered, and this can best be done through a study of musical areas. Different sizes of areas, and variety in the accompanying degree of homogeneity, have been noted for

North America in several studies (summarized in Nettl 1954:3), for Africa (Merriam 1953), and for the world divided into three huge areas (Nettl 1956:141).

Most historical conclusions drawn from distributional information are based on several hypotheses. One is a generalized form of the so-called age-area concept—the assumption that the more widely distributed a trait is, the greater its probable age. Thus two-tone scales, found in all parts of the world, are assumed to be older than pentatonic scales, which are less widely distributed; rattle types of instruments are oldest because they are found in more places than other types, and so forth. A complementary hypothesis is the theory of marginal survivals, namely, that traits found only at the geographic limits of an area are older than material found only in the center. This theory has dominated discussions of the origin of European polyphony and its relationship to the folk polyphony of the Caucasus, Eastern Europe, and Iceland (Reese 1940:256–258). Similar conclusions have been drawn for European folk music in the United States, which seems to preserve especially old forms. But isolation may not mean retention of old traits, but rather separate development; this fact precludes the possibility of dogmatic statements regarding age-area and marginal survivals. These theories are less often applicable to individual compositions. For example, the presence of a melody throughout Europe does not mean that it is older than a purely local tune.

Related to these hypotheses are those formulated by the Kulturkreis school, as represented in ethnomusicology by Curt Sachs, Walter Graf, and Werner Danckert, among others. A number of their studies have attempted to reconstruct music history through a study of the distribution of the layers in tribal repertories and in larger areas. This procedure has been subject to many methodological obstacles, but has resulted in some valuable information. Finally, the use of music to establish specific times of contact among cultures has been a contribution to cultural anthropology at large. Common musical traits, particularly if specialized, are usually assumed to be evidence for former contact, if the distribution is not contiguous. The degree of difference among musical styles may indicate the time elapsed since contact. Conversely, if common musical material exists, and the time of contact is known, a minimum age for the material can be established. This is especially applicable to individual compositions, as has been demonstrated by Idelsohn (1921). We may conclude that geographic approaches to historical problems have made greater contributions than have evolutionary points of view.

Statistical approaches have been used only in recent decades, but they seem to be very promising for historical contexts. By statistical we do not mean all approaches which are based on large bodies of music, groups of variants, or other corpora, which attempt to evaluate samplings from a corpus, and which make use of quantitative classification. Statistics in its more technical sense has been used in a recent study by Merriam (1956), which deals with problems not primarily of historical interest. A classical example of a study with historical implications is the description of Suriname music by Kolinski (1936). Here the proportions of African material in music used in the country and in town are compared, and although historical conclusions are not drawn, they are evident. An unpublished study by the present author, comparing variants of British ballads collected in various regions of the Eastern United States, indicates the possibility of using statistics for tracing the history of musical units.

Statistical samplings of the repertories of individual singers and players, and of individual musical elements or traits (considered separately from entire compositions) have yet to be tested. The main problem facing the statistical investigator is again the lack of measuring devices for degrees of similarity, relationship, and importance of musical items, and the necessity of proceeding at present along intuitive lines.

The importance of historical orientations in ethnomusicology can readily be seen. Such orientations can contribute to the knowledge of culture change in general, as well as to a better understanding of the processes of music history.

REFERENCES CITED

ADLER, GUIDO
    1908   Über Heterophonie. Jahrbuch der Musikbibliothek Peters 15:17–27.
BARBEAU, MARIUS
    1934   Songs of the Northwest. Musical Quarterly 20:107–116.
BARTOK, BELA
    1931   Hungarian folk music. London, Oxford University Press.
BOSE, FRITZ
    1952   Messbare Rassenunterschiede in der Musik. Homo 2:4:1–12.
HORNBOSTEL, E. M. VON
    1910   Über einige Panpfeifen aus Nordwest Brasilien. *In* Zwei Jahr unter den Indianern, vol. 2, Theodor Koch-Gruenberg ed. Berlin, Ernst Wasmuth.
IDELSOHN, A. Z.
    1921   Parallelen zwischen gregorianischen und herbräischorientalischen Gesangsweisen. Zeitschrift für Musikwissenschaft 4:515–524.
KODALY, ZOLTAN
    1956   Die ungarische Volksmusik. Budapest, Corvina.
KOLINSKI, M.
    1936   Suriname folk music. *In* Suriname folklore, M. Herskovits ed. New York, American Folklore Society.
    1957   Ethnomusicology, its problems and methods. Ethnomusicology 10:1–7.
KUNST, JAAP
    1955   Ethno-musicology. The Hague, Martinus Nijhoff.
LACH, ROBERT
    1924   Die vergleichende Musikwissenschaft, ihre Methoden und Probleme. Vienna, Academy of Sciences.
    1929   Tscheremissische Gesänge. Vienna. Academy of Sciences.
LACHMANN, ROBERT
    1927   Zur aussereuropäischen Mehrstimmigkeit. Kongressbericht der Beethoven-Zentenarfeier. Vienna, Otto Maass.
McALLESTER, DAVID P.
    1949   Peyote music. New York, Viking Fund.
MERRIAM, ALAN P.
    1953   African music reexamined in the light of new material from the Belgian Congo and Ruanda-Urundi. Zaire 7:245–253.

53

1955   The use of music in the study of a problem of acculturation. American Anthropologist 57:28–34.
1956   Statistical classification in anthropology: an application to ethnomusicology. American Anthropologist 58:464–472.

METFESSEL, MILTON
1928   Phonophotography in folk music. Chapel Hill, University of North Carolina Press.

NADEL, SIEGFRIED
1930   The origins of music. Musical Quarterly 16:531–546.

NETTL, BRUNO
1953   The Shawnee musical style. Southwestern Journal of Anthropology 9:160–168.
1954a   Notes on musical composition in primitive culture. Anthropological Quarterly 27:81–90.
1954b   North American Indian musical styles. Philadelphia, American Folklore Society.
1955a   Change in folk and primitive music: a survey of problems and methods. Journal of the American Musicological Society 8:101–109.
1955b   Musical culture of the Arapaho. Musical Quarterly 41:335–341.
1956   Music in primitive culture. Cambridge, Harvard University Press.
1957   Unifying factors in folk and primitive music. Journal of the American Musicological Society (in press).

REESE, GUSTAVE
1940   Music in the Middle Ages. New York, W. W. Norton.

ROBERTS, HELEN H.
1933   The pattern phenomenon in primitive music. Zeitschrift für vergleichende Musikwissenschaft 1:49–52.

SACHS, CURT
1947   The commonwealth of art. New York, W. W. Norton.

SCHNEIDER, MARIUS
1934   Geschichte der Mehrstimmigkeit vol. 1. Berlin, Julius Bard.
1938   Die musikalischen Bezeihungen zwischen Urkulturen, Altpflanzern und Hirtenvölkern. Zeitschrift für Ethnologie 70:287–302.
1946   El origen musical de los animalos-símbolos. Barcelona, Instituto Español de Musicología.

WIORA, WALTER
1953   Europäischer Volksgesang. Köln, Arno Volk Verlag.

WHITHER ETHNOMUSICOLOGY?

The following is a report assembled from notes on the two panel discussions entitled "The Scope and Aims of Ethnomusicology," held at the meetings of the Society in Boston and Cambridge, Dec. 29 and 30, 1958. The wide range of ideas and opinions expressed at these panels merits their reproduction here. The editor thanks Roxane McCollester for her excellent notes on the first panel and takes full blame for any errors of ommission and inaccuracies of statement or emphasis in this report. The blood is moving vigorously in the veins of our young Society: it is hoped that our readers will be sufficiently stimulated, or even outraged, to respond with opinion, counter-opinion, and new ideas.

PANEL I. Hotel Sheraton Plaza, Boston, Dec. 29, 1958. Chairman: Mantle Hood, Music Dept. Univ. of California, Los Angeles; Panelists: Mieczyslaw Kolinski, New York City; Bruno Nettl, Wayne Univ., Detroit; Nadia Chilkovsky, Philadelphia Dance Academy, Philadelphia; George List, Indiana Univ. Archives of Folk and Primitive Music.

Mr. Kolinski: "The Scope and Aims of Ethnomusicology," There is a dif-

99

ficulty with our name: it suggests that our field is the music of foreign cultures. A Korean student might call the study of Mozart "ethnomusicology." In fact we are committed to both ideo-cultural and allo-cultural studies. There is a close interdependence between historical musicology and ethnomusicology. As Alan Merriam has said, our field is cross-disciplinary between the humanities and the social sciences. "Integral Musicology" should not limit itself to marginal anthropological problems but should use a wide variety of methods including those of acoustics, psychology and still other disciplines. World music as a scholarly study should be approached as one over-all discipline. It may well be time to establish a Center for training and research in the United States which would incorporate the total range of music.

Discussion: It is true that we must use every resource, but we must not lose sight of the social background of music in our research -- All music is really in the oral tradition, no system of notation conveys the actual style of performance -- No disciplines have clearly defined borders -- Can't we define our subject matter not by geographical area or "kinds" of music, but by the social function of music? This is the special emphasis of ethnobotany, ethnohistory and the like. For example, what is the function of rock and roll? No other kind of approach to music is concerned with this -- But ethnomusicology must not be limited to being merely a part of anthropology -- We have to delimit the field, ethnomusicology is a point of view, any scholar from whatever culture must, to be an ethnomusicologist, use that point of view -- What are our basic questions? -- They revolve around the relation between music and culture -- The core of the matter is that we must embrace the subject in its own terms: these may be anthropological, psychological or geographical. They may involve dance, religion and poetry. The difficulty is that we have to use a delimiting label.

Mr. Nettl: "Music Areas." One way to organize this vast body of material and present the information is to do so by geographical area. The "culture area" concept has proved useful in anthropology and so has attracted ethnomusicologists. There are difficulties: unreliable sources, poor transcriptions, varying depths of survey, lack of coherence between different kinds of statistical classification (distribution of instrument types may not coincide with stylistic traits). The basic organic musical unity is hard to define. But to make our work organized and tangible, to be able to integrate new material into some sort of system, especially from the point of view of teaching, a concept like "music area" is useful.

Discussion: (Contra): If it's a real music area, must it not coincide with a culture area? -- Study should derive from the music itself, so area considerations are irrelevant -- It will be decades before we know musics well enough for this sort of work -- Is it good teaching to administer easy "pills of misinformation?" -- acoustics raises problems: acoustically the lute and biwa are the same instrument but they are not related culturally -- It is difficult to determine just what refinement of criteria would work.

(Pro, and other suggestions): Not every trait is identical in all parts of presently accepted culture areas, Madagascar is an example of a region where music and other cultural traits do not match -- Why not start with objective criteria so that expectations of music area do not introduce distortion, and then see if such areas do, indeed, emerge? -- There seem to be some adhesions of stylistic features. We can imagine a kind of musical Grimm's Law. (Are you suggesting a kind of unilinear musical evolutionism?) Not quite, but it might be possible to predict direction of change in music -- It might be possible to find an organic relationship between rhythms, harmonies, and other aspects of music -- These wouldn't have to be universally true to be useful. Everyone here should read Charles Seeger's work on systematic musicology.

Miss Chilkovsky: "Dance and Ethnomusicology," Dance has hardly been asked to participate in scientific discourse as yet. We welcome all kinds of invitations; we have much to offer and much to learn. We are not yet organized as a discipline - we are confined still to the private dance studio, a few conservatories and some colleges. We are very young and in great need of an elevation in prestige. In New Guinea the term "good dancer" means an intelligent man. But here only three conservatories offer a degree in dance. It has been pointed out recently that a full understanding of certain musical forms can only be a-chieved if we know the dance form that accompanies them. Dance belongs in departments of anthropology and music, but is still usually in the physical edu-cation departments of those colleges that offer it. Dance can now offer labano-tation as a functional system of movement notation which could be used in the field by ethnologists and ethnomusicologists. It could be highly useful in the laboratory in the analysis of dance and other movement in ethnographic films.

Discussion: It would be of great value if there were a handbook on dance notation for field workers -- Many of us have been unable to record even very simple dance movement and pattern for lack of any conception of a system of notation -- Most of us have no idea what to look for in analyzing a dance -- The same is true for music for most ethnographers: such a handbook should include instruction for both music and dance -- The Pitt-Rivers Museum in England is preparing a field-workers' handbook and the International Folk Music Council has recently revised theirs -- Could Miss Chilkovsky and others with her train-ing analyze films we now have? -- Shouldn't the Society consider means for mak-ing dance analysis of films possible? -- There are thousands of feet of film al-ready made; we need a center where such material can be stored and studied and from which it can be borrowed -- If this analysis is not too difficult to learn it sould be known by all field workers.

Mr. List: "Problems of Archiving." The Indiana University Folklore Archives and the Archives of Folk and Primitive Music are concerned with the recording and study of all kinds of material in the oral tradition. The original recordings are not available to students but duplicates are. A course in train-ing in techniques of recording, transcription and documentation is offered. Most collections, including too much of the material that comes in to the Archives, are very poorly documented. Reels of tape are often not labeled or numbered, no indication is given as to where one song ends and another begins. There should be an indication as to whether the current running the machine was 50 or 60 cycles. Information should be put on the reel itself, not just on the box. A pitchpipe note on the tape will identify the pitch of the song: if it is known what the pitchpipe note is supposed to be, then correction can be made for various odd speeds of tape. This can be added to the tape after the recording session if necessary. A minimum documentation: the culture (Human Relations Area Files classification is practical) the informant's culture, (you might have a Japanese singing Korean music), location, date, title, if any, the instruments used, if any, texts, if obtainable. The ethnographer should consider himself a heaven-ordained documentor. If at all possible, with songs, full texts and translations should be obtained and information on the function of the song. Photographs should be included. As a last note, the best all round battery re-corder for work away from power sources seems to be the Nagra. (Ed. note: see ETHNOMUSICOLOGY, May 1957, pp. 42-3 for further information on this machine.)

PANEL II, Paine Hall, Harvard University, Cambridge, Dec. 30, Chairman: Leonard Meyer, Dept. of Music, Univ. of Chicago; Panelists: Charles Seeger, Santa Barbara, Calif., Malloy Miller, Dept. of Music, Boston University, David McAllester, Dept. of Psychology, Wesleyan University, and Mr. Meyer. Mr. J. H. Nketia, Univ. College of Ghana, was asked to contribute from the floor.

Mr. Seeger: "Musicology and Ethnomusicology." "Ethnomusicology" has the connotation of "strange" or "foreign." Do we mean only the study of music in a culture and not in itself? Clearly we must study music both in itself and in culture and this is "musicology." All music is in culture so why do we need a term like "ethnomusicology?" The reason is that historians have highjacked the proper term, "musicology." Yet they study a very narrow band of world music and only part of that. They have turned their backs on the only primary source and limit themselves to secondary sources. Compounding the villany, they profess that only through the past can the present be understood. This is

101

57

absolutely false: we can only know the present by knowing it in the present and we only know the past via the present. The past can only enrich and qualify our knowledge of the present; this obsession with the past leads to mere antiquarianism. We had no choice but to use the title we now have, but we have patterned our constitution and organization on that of the American Musicological Society and when semantic sanity returns we must merge the two groups. In the '30's the AMS began as the New York Music Society. It started with the two emphases, systematic and historical both present, but the latter soon dominated.

For the future: 1) we must make our domain world music, including all of Euro-American music, not only folk, popular and tribal music. This includes the fine art - we must look at the monuments too from the ethnologist's viewpoint. There is an ethnology of the Romantic movement, the Gothic, the Renaissance, etc. And it is very much up to us to make this point in a scholarly way.

2) We must persuade historians to engage themselves in the history of other musics. Only the Islamic has the beginnings of a history, we don't have a history of other musics. Let us engage good historians to work with us. The history of our own folk music is very weak. What of the history of our popular music? What are its roots? They seem to be well back in the music of the goliards in the 12th and 13th centuries or even the popular music of the Roman circuses. We must be careful not to get bogged down exclusively in tribal musics, our field is all music. We must define music and music idioms in social depth and keep clear of antiquarian preoccupations with "authenticity" of folk music. We should not oppose change in music. Every music comes from hybridization, but we can document and study the change; let the sentimentalists lament the fate of the Child Ballad in the terrible hands of the Hill Billies and Rock and Roll. Above all, we must strive for bimusicality in our studies of the musics of other cultures. We must learn the critical standards of other peoples and approach their music with their canons, not our own.

Mr. Miller: "Using American Indian Music in Orchestral Composition." I am concerned about what we are collecting as a commodity. As a composer and conductor my interest is both practical and creative. We can use ideas from music outside our culture, but it should not be just for coloring, it must have an integrity of its own. I have attended Pueblo Indian rituals and I have used the music in symphonic composition. One check I rely upon in my use of this material is to take recordings back to the Indians for their criticism. It is not "in the style" unless it is significant for them. Some things we cannot use but there is much that we can, even though our musics differ so greatly. The use of melodic line presents no problems, but what do we do with the rest of the orchestra? Certainly we must avoid melody plus oom-pah-pah bass. Some of the ways in which I try to keep stylistic integrity are: to avoid our triadic harmonies, using neutral harmonies and avoiding parallel fifths and fourths; to keep away from augmented sixths and our strong emphasis on the leading tone; to make strong use of elementary emphatic rhythm; to try to get free from the conductor, which can be done if the primary beat is strong enough; to use strings percussively; to use unison a good deal - this raises the problem of contrast, but this can be achieved with the instrumentation. I do use development, we need it in our listening.

Mr. Nketia: "Musical Synthesis in Ghana." When I was a student I heard for the first time African music played on the harmonium. I remember the tremendous enthusiasm, it was the first time a congregation had heard music that bore some resemblance to our own traditional music. It was close enough so that we all enjoyed it. This new music became very popular; bands of singers, choirs, were formed. I thought it was our native music. My college training included reading African music - this was a new type of literacy in music - from reading African rhythm I went on to write music. Some of the features of this music include considerable use of parallel thirds and a heptatonic scale. We began to see problems such as the conflict of melody with tonal values of

102

58

the words used in songs. Now we are really beginning to use the musical resources of our tribal groups. Our composers are all interested in traditional folk music.

Mr. McAllester: "An Approach to Music." To take my turn at definitions, I will agree that our subject is "musicology," in the sense of world music, but I will put in a special plea for what has already been said for music in relation to its culture because this dimension is not yet enough with us. It is nice to know that a song is a lullaby from Bukabuka - now we can catalogue it - but to satisfy me we have to know what the people of Bukabuka think of this lullaby and about their music in general. I want to know where this song fits into a whole value system. In other words I want to study culture through the avenue of music, to study music as social behavior. Music is essentially a matter of values rather than a matter of notes. With our emphasis on the written word we sometimes confuse speech with writing: it is the same mistake to confuse music with notes. With notes scientific detachment is possible, but not with music as a living part of culture. Then, as Leonard Meyer says, music has "tendency," music has motion, music has emotion, music has, in Miss Chilkovsky's word, "excitement." I believe the approach to living music calls not for curiosity but for love. Only then can we feel the commitment that leads us to a real understanding of the music in its own terms. Only this feeling can interest us enough so that we may have the care and patience enough to approach something like a competency in another musical tradition than our own. I would stress the value of field work - you must experience the music in its setting in order to understand it. The great lesson that our informants teach us in the field is admiration and respect. This depth of appreciation is necessary to induce us to spend the years that are necessary to learn a music. Music is not only a good avenue to the understanding of cultural values, it may well be the best. It is, more than many other aspects of culture, one that we can participate in, however imperfectly at first. The rewards in rapport and insight are very great. Music is not a universal language by any means, but it is a language, and with very hard work it can be learned.

Mr. Meyer: "Music and Values." Ethnologists try to have their cake and eat it too when they claim they are relativists, because at the same time they work from all kinds of absolute assumptions. If you were really a relativist you would not pretend to analyze an tune from another culture. You claim a universal, you can "understand." No linguist would dare take a tape of an unknown language and try to analyze it. The point is, it is not how we analyze it but how they, the native speakers and singers, analyze it, that counts. From their point of view, what is its tendency, how does it want to move? The syntax and grammar of a music must be discovered from the musician's concept of syntax. But there is more than this: there are two elements, 1) the purely cultural, in which sense the vocabulary of music varies from culture to culture, and 2) an overall syntax that may be applied to all music. For some aspects of the latter: there is a natural tendency to make a form complete; skips tend to be filled in; there is a "fifth need:" novelty, the need for information. People in isolation develop hallucinations to satisfy this need. This may be a universal value in music, but the kinds of information vary culturally. We must get out of our chairs and really talk to people to find out how they feel music is articulated. We can experiment with the musician by finding out from him: "can you do this?" This is the only way we can discover meaning. The note that occurs most often does not tell us, necessarily, about the "tonic." Wagner's background of musical thinking is cadential. We have to know this and what the various other backgrounds of musical thinking are in the musics of the world.

Discussion (Panelists were given the first opportunity, then discussion followed from the floor) Seeger: I like what Miller says. This country is far behind in the integration of styles. We have made a few efforts but Brazil and Mexico, for instance, are a full generation ahead of us. In the '90's they realized that stealing tunes did not lead to anything and began to assimilate idioms that produced a music truly Brazilian and Mexican. The German Romanticists

103

59

did the same thing 150 years ago and produced new folk songs from the old. I didn't like Miller's negative approach, though: don't avoid anything! Mc-Allester's view is the real meat of a new musicology. This is uncouth in the European view - it is becoming known as the American view and it is very hard to do. The things Mr. Meyer wants to know are hard to find out. The hazard is communicating about music by speech instead of by music. This leads to "theory," which is nothing but the rules of practice of the immediate ancestors. Music does express values, yes.

Meyer (to Miller) On stylistic integrity, this is not defined by referring back to the Hopis. It is a system of probabilities. You can't have a triad in a twelve tone row because you arouse expectations with no intention of satisfying them. The row has its own logic.

Hood: We must be musicians by trade. We must have basic musicianship whatever culture we plan to work in. It is hard to get them (our informants) to be critical - you must be self-critical to get them to help you. Students in our program at UCLA must be highly qualified Western musicians. When they achieve this literacy they have won the privilege of becoming a beginner all over again in another culture. It is fatal if you go into the field as a V.I.P. or an "expert." You must assure them by actions, not words, that you are a beginner. Then, with reservations, you may begin to see (don't ask) how they regard their music. Many cultures are not theoretical and there you must be careful not to ask questions. If you do you will get answers and fill a notebook and learn very little. Often you cannot get information directly. I once asked "How do you hold a bow?" My informant told me wrong - he didn't know how to tell me. To learn drums (in Indonesian music) you need a new time sense. You need a basic musicianship we don't have. A gamelan is 30 instruments playing like a string quartet. This is hard for us to even imagine.

Barbara Smith: This training in music of another culture can be done long before you are a graduate student. It has been learned naturally by children in some places such as Hawaii. Hood: Yes, in nearly any large town there are other cultures to learn from. Roxane McCollester: How much is it possible to learn in one short year of field work? Hood: Prepare before you go - we have students who, for example, study the koto here before they go to Japan.

Dalia Cohen: I am confused by all the generalizations I have been hearing. On not asking questions, doesn't it all depend on what kind of questions? Many of you sound defensive, critical of the AMS, but you are using subjective terms. "Love" is not objective - any academic discipline requires detachment with participation. I feel a need here for a common language. One scholar can talk with another in the AMS. We must have a common language to be a discipline. I agree with Kolinski that we must have an integrated musicology. Meyer: to deal with a music you must respond to it as they do. This is communication. You take on the attitude of the other, which is love, an absolute must. You can only analyze Beethoven as you respond to it.

: About love being needed for communication, I only know Western and South Indian music, but I had a talk with Nketia and I've learned something about the music of Ghana. I talked with Hood and learned the difference between Javanese and Balinese gamelans. If we are all trained in our own music we can communicate. I am sympathetic to the idea of love, but we must face up to it - we must specialize. To be bimusical is about as far as we can go, but we can still communicate something about other musics. We have to spread the good word. Svatva Jakobson: In the Slavic countries the idea of participation is very much in practice. Folk societies do not meet in Universities but on the top of mountains where the folk are. In Bulgaria all music students must know the folk rhythms. Perhaps the Slavs are still too much their own native informants.

Seeger: Suppose we have 1000 who participate in the music of other cultures like Hood and McAllester - this is the new technique but who is going to digest all the results? It is the Hornbostels who will do so with great and lofty objectivity and together the two techniques will give us the music of mankind.

Richard Waterman: We've said some bad things about the counting of intervals, about statistics. I am an anthropologist. I see great values in analytical work

104

such as careful measurement of acoustical phenomena. There are anthropological problems not related to values. History may be traced through analysis. In seeking to find out things about style the informant may be totally unaware of what you want: such ideas are outside the vocabulary and thought of many peoples. It has been said that the "objective approach" isn't really objective, but there are ways of plotting facts which are objective and convenient. Music is not all the study of values - there are phenomena that can be described in a music even if we hate it. Let's be a little hardboiled.
Meyer: I agree on history, but acoustical phenomena are "sound," not music. If you say "music" you go beyond acoustics. The relationships of tones are psychological in some sense - the only ultimate check is the human ear. And I am not so anti-statistical. Seeger: We must keep our two methodologies: fact-value, statistics-love, equally important or we will be making a cult of one or the other. _____: Perhaps love is for the field work and statistics is for the analysis when you get home. Cohen: Statistics has been singled out for criticism, but means nothing by itself; it is only a tool to help define a style. Kolinski: But remember that one can spend a lifetime counting meaningless things. Perhaps what we mean by love is "enthusiasm." Hood: Yes this is better, and lack of enthusiasm is deadly. To get back to the matter of asking questions, I ask hundreds of questions, but not the direct ones. Cohen: I agree with Kolinski, the word is "enthusiasm." You can have enthusiasm for an idea. Hood: I mean enthusiasm for a subject.
Meyer: On statistics, music has a nature as a probability pattern. Statistics are no guarantee of probability. Waterman: That's probability statistics, I just mean they do help us to figure out a musical pattern. Meyer: One of the big questions is, in what areas are these probabilities intercultural and in what areas are they intracultural? Waterman: Perhaps we can find certain musical patterns that are human, quite independent of cultural patterns. Meyer: Certain things seem to be apparent already, such as the tendency to fill in gaps. Kolinski: There is also a pan-cultural tendency to respond to the pull of octaves, and other similarities, more than we generally think.

* * * * *

Roxane McCollester is in Belgium on a Fulbright fellowship working on the music of the Congo, especially that of the Bushong people, at the Musee de Congo Belge, and at the tape archives of the National Radio Corporation. She reports that the Museum has a tremendous library of material hard to obtain in the U.S., 6,000 instruments which need to be studied by modern ethnomusicological techniques, many hundreds of old wax cylinders and a large tape library which is constantly receiving new additions from the field. Any qualified scholar will find the Museum extremely cooperative and generous with all this wealth of material.

Wanted! Information pertaining to the whereabouts of recordings of St. Francis, Penobscot, Malecite, Abnaki, or Passamaquoddy music or folklore. J. Walter Fewkes made some wax cylinders among the Passamaquoddy in 1889 and an old Passamaquoddy says that he remembers a woman from Boston who made recordings a number of years ago. What has happened to these? Please send any information to Nicholas N. Smith, Seminary Hill Road, Carmel, N.Y.

The ethnographic film The Hunters, taken on the Peabody Museum of Harvard-Smithsonian Institution Kalahari Expeditions, and edited by John Marshall and Robert M. Gardner, is now available for purchase or rental through Contemporary Films, Inc., 267 West 25th St., N.Y. This film won the Flaherty Award for 1958 for its superb presentation of Bushman life in the Kalahari Desert. It is of particular interest to ethnomusicologists for its musical sequences and because of the growing importance of sound film techniques in our field.

105

61

ETHNOMUSICOLOGY
DISCUSSION AND DEFINITION OF THE FIELD

Alan P. Merriam

In a recent article, "The New American Archaeology," Joseph R. Caldwell has pointed out the shift in interests of American archaeology which, he feels, are bringing new kinds of understanding to the field (Caldwell, 1959). Thus he speaks of the earlier archaeology which was preoccupied with "the description of archaeological sites and . . . of prehistoric cultures. . . .The emphasis was on archaeological data as things in themselves rather than on the values offered by different ways of looking at them. Moreover, it was considered, in practice, as important to excavate a site meticulously and to record every scrap of evidence which might conceivably bear on any future problem as it was to have a reason for excavating the site in the first place" (p. 303). However, "the new archaeology in America is tending to be more concerned with culture process and less concerned with the descriptive content of prehistoric cultures. . . .Where formerly we were concerned with the identification of things and of cultures . . . we have added an interest in the identification of culture processes and situations" (p. 304).

It may seem strange that a paper which proposes to discuss and define the field of ethnomusicology should begin with a quotation concerning American archaeology, and yet the analogy between the old and the new archaeology and the old and the new comparative musicology or ethnomusicology presents such striking parallels that it is indeed apropos. More than this, what has happened in archaeology, and is happening in ethnomusicology, is but a reflection of what happens in almost every field of scientific endeavor as the discipline grows, defines its terms more sharply, and begins, eventually, to develop away from the more specific to the broader and more general. What has been quoted for archaeology, then, could almost be re-quoted for ethnomusicology, and this is evident in the increased concern in our field for an understanding of methods, history, and especially what we should study and why.

Our awareness of the history of ethnomusicology as a discipline has shown us a changing emphasis on what is considered to be our "proper" field of study, and, it is clear that like archaeology, we have been moving steadily toward a consideration of broader and broader problems, not so much of definition of music styles as of an understanding of music as a human phenomenon. In this we have perhaps not yet come so far as archaeology, but the movement of our interests is inevitably in this direction. Thus we come to a point at which it seems wise to discuss and attempt to define the field of our concern once again, and in broader terms than has characterized most such discussion in the past.

Without going into the details of the history of ethnomusicology, which has been the subject of study elsewhere (Nettl, 1956: Kunst, 1955), it seems fair to say that earlier studies were marked by an emphasis upon the analysis of melodic and pitch phenomena, including the study of scales, intervals and tonal systems; such investigations dealt also with theories of the origin of music which were thought to be observable in the music of contemporary so-called "primitive" peoples. The emphasis on the study of the structure of music is, of course, perfectly understandable; to bring order out of a mass of data, taxonomy must be established. I should like to add here that this does not imply that early workers in the field ignored problems other

107

63

than structure; a glance at Hornbostel's bibliography, for example, (Anon, 1954), makes clear the wide range of his thinking over many problems of music other than the purely structural. Nor is it suggested that our taxonomies are complete; while we have developed to the point of constructing music areas based on musical characteristics (Nettl, 1954; Merriam, 1959), our knowledge of the specific ways in which the elements of music are put together remains far from complete. But the fact remains that the major emphasis in the work of earlier students of ethnomusicology was oriented toward analysis of the structure of the particular musics they studied.

With the slow emergence of what Nettl has called the American school (Nettl, 1956:28), the emphasis upon music structure as such was joined by a new emphasis upon the relationship of music to culture, and this was pointed up by the quick acceptance of Kunst's recommendation in 1955 (Kunst, 1955: 9) that the old discipline of comparative musicology be rechristened "ethnomusicology," thus stressing the fact that music does not exist by and of itself but is a part of the totality of human behavior.

What has happened in the field of ethnomusicology is an increasing awareness of the fact that there is more to the study of music than the description and analysis of its form, and here again reference may be made to the quotations concerning archaeology which opened this discussion. While this broader view has always been the case to a certain degree, ethnomusicology is today being more and more led by cultural anthropology, or ethnology, a relationship stressed by Hornbostel, among others, as early as 1905 (Hornbostel, 1905:86). What Bascom has said for folklore applies equally to music, and we can substitute one word for the other in reading his remark that "(Music) is studied in anthropology because it is a part of culture. It is a part of man's learned traditions and customs, a part of his social heritage. It can be analyzed in the same way as other customs and traditions, in terms of form and function, or of interrelations with other aspects of culture. It presents the same problems of growth and change, and is subject to the same processes of diffusion, invention, acceptance or rejection, and integration. It can be used, like other aspects of culture, for studies of these processes or those of acculturation, patterning, the relation between culture and the environment, or between culture and personality" (Bascom, 1953:286).

As the earlier formulations of the field stressed units of structural analysis, definitions of its scope tended to define it as geographically and formally descriptive in character, and this point of view has persisted, in varying degree, to the present. Thus Gilman, in 1909, stressed the idea that the study of exotic music comprised primitive and Oriental forms (1909), while Bingham added the music of the Dalmatian peasants (1914). And this point of view has carried through into contemporary definitions which stress the study of all music except that in the Western tradition: thus, the "primary aim [of ethnomusicology is] the comparative study of all the characteristics, normal or otherwise, of non-European [music]" (Schneider, 1957:1); or "the science that deals with the music of peoples outside of Western civilization" (Nettl, 1956:1). But if, indeed, the field of ethnomusicology has developed toward an understanding of the fact that the study of music does not consist solely in analysis of form, then definitions which stress a type of music to be studied can no longer serve the field.

That this has become more and more clearly recognized is indicated by a number of articles in this Journal which stress properly the broader view toward the study of music. Willard Rhodes indicated this, although still tending to speak of the kinds of music which properly fall into the field including that of "the Near East, the Far East, Indonesia, Africa, North

108

64

American Indians and European folk music," as well as "popular music and dance" (Rhodes, 1956:3-4). Later, Kolinski objected to the definition of ethnomusicology as "the science of non-European music," and noted admirably that "it is not so much the difference in the geographical areas under analysis as the difference in the general approach which distinguishes ethnomusicology from ordinary musicology" (Kolinski, 1957:1-2), although he did not go on to define the field. Mantle Hood took his definition from the Journal of the American Musicology Society, with the insertion of the prefix "ethno" in suggesting that "[Ethno] musicology is a field of knowledge, having as its object the investigation of the art of music as a physical, psychological, aesthetic, and cultural phenomenon. The [ethno] musicologist is a research scholar, and he aims primarily at knowledge about music" (Hood, 1957:2). There can be little quarrel with such a definition, save perhaps that it is borrowed from a sister organization as Hood points out. And finally, Chase has indicated that "The present emphasis . . . is on the musical study of contemporary man, to whatever society he may belong, whether primitive or complex, Eastern or Western" (Chase, 1958:7).

It is considerations such as these, then, which lead me to a proposal of a definition of ethnomusicology, not as the study of extra-European music, but as "the study of music in culture." In other words I believe that music can be studied not only from the standpoint of musicians and humanists, but from that of social scientists as well, and that, further, it is at the moment from the field of cultural anthropology that our primary stimulation is coming for the study of music as a universal aspect of man's activities. To define ethnomusicology in this way is in no way to deny its primary connections with the aesthetic and the humanistic, but it is to say that our basic understanding of the music of any people depends upon our understanding of that people's culture, the place music plays in it, and the way in which its role is played. It is through this sort of understanding that we can approach on a firm foundation our further understanding of what structure is and how music achieves whatever aesthetic ends are sought.

This can perhaps be further clarified by attempting to point out the kind of work an ethnomusicologist does, both in the laboratory and in the field situation. It seems to me that any project in ethnomusicology can be conceived to fall into three major parts of which some may be stressed over others: 1) the actual gathering of materials in the field; 2) transcription and analysis; 3) the application of results obtained to relevant problems. I should like to discuss, principally, the first and third of these.

Let us assume for the moment that the extremely important questions of the formulation of the problem to be studied, hypotheses concerning it, theoretical orientation, study of historic material available, and the like, have been solved, and that the researcher is in the field and ready to pursue his study; there are, first, two directions his research can take.

Thus, his study can be either extensive or intensive, depending upon the results desired. In the extensive study, the student is interested in sampling a broad variety of cultures which will lead to generalization about a widely distributed socio-music area; this is primarily a taxonomic approach which leads eventually to the establishment of music areas. On the other hand, in the intensive study, the student restricts himself to a single locale and focuses his attention upon the study in depth of the music he finds there, not only as a musical, but also a social, cultural, psychological, and aesthetic phenomenon. Here fall at least six areas of inquiry to which he will turn his attention.

The first of these concerns the musical material culture, or more specifically phrased, the study of musical instruments and other implements by

109

means of which the music system is carried out. This involves, of course, the various kinds of instruments, ordered in terms of a recognized taxonomy based on division into idiophones, membranophones, aerophones, and chordophones, as well as the study of principles of construction, materials employed, methods and techniques of performance, musical ranges, tones produced, and theoretical scales. In addition there are included here the important questions of the presence or absence of special treatment of musical instruments, problems of ownership, and the economics of instrument construction.

A second category comprises the study of song texts, which may be approached from a number of directions. Obviously, we deal here with text-melody relationships, but the texts themselves can reveal much about the culture of which they are a part. Thus we may study the text itself in terms of literary behavior, linguistic usa‿e, and the presence or absence of permissiveness in regard to language behavior in song. On the other hand, study may be directed toward what the text reflects, that is, the prevailing "ethos" of the culture on the level of a kind of national character generalization, or toward the value systems, in terms both of ideal and real behavior, as expressed in song. Finally, texts reveal history of the group, underlying motivations which are often not otherwise expressed, and deep-seated values and convictions.

The third element of study comprises the categories of music, envisaged by the investigator for convenience, but much more important, by the people themselves as various separable types of songs. It is in this connection, of course, and by this means, that the investigator orders his recording program, arranged to record an adequate sample of all types of music, both in controlled and in actual performance situations.

The role and status of the musician in the society of which he is a part forms the fourth point of interest for the ethnomusicologist. Here he must deal with the problem of professionalism and its ramifications, as well as the problems of the level from which the musician is drawn, the factors which shape his becoming a musician, his attitudes toward the rest of the society and their attitudes toward him, and the ownership of music, whether by the musician or by others. It may be suggested that this is the point at which tests of musical ability enter; it remains to devise such a test which is truly cross-cultural in character, but once established, it should give us a great deal of information about the abilities of musicians and the cultural expectations of his abilities. Are all persons in the society considered to be potentially equal in ability, or are some recognized as superior to others either in latent or manifest abilities, and how does this correlate with a truly cross-cultural test of musical ability?

A fifth area of study concerns the functions of music in relation to other aspects of culture. Here is included the synchronic study of music as a kind of human behavior related to other behaviors including the religious, the dramatic, relationships to dance, social control, enculturation and education, economics, political structure, and other aspects. Thus the investigator is forced to move through the total culture in search of music relationships, and in a very real sense, he finds that music reflects the culture of which it is a part, in much the same way as has been pointed out by Boas in his folklore studies (Boas, 1909-10).

Finally, we study music as a creative cultural activity, including such problems as the sources of musical materials, the standards of excellence in performance, the psychology of music, and the processes of creation. Is music conceived to be an affective activity or is it functional, and what is its relationship to other activities in the fields of graphic and plastic arts,

110

66

oral literature, dance and drama, all of which in our culture we consider to be aesthetic manifestations? Here, too, falls the problem of cultural variation as expressed in individual renditions of songs, which leads to possibilities of understanding internal change; further bearing on this question is obtained from the study of acceptance and rejection of innovations in music in terms of what the culture will allow when presented new elements from outside.

These, then, are some of the kinds of things an ethnomusicologist looks for in the field phase of his study; that there are others is obvious, but in general outline, the intensive investigation leads the student into all aspects of culture in search of the deep-seated attitudes and beliefs about music, as well as its functions and its modus operandi.

The second, or laboratory, phase of ethnomusicological investigation need not concern us here; in this phase the investigator turns to the transcription and structural analysis of the materials he has recorded in the field, and this is, of course, basic in establishing the taxonomy essential to his study.

The third part of his research concerns the application of results obtained to relevant problems, and here a number of questions arise. If we accept the outline of field study given above, then it is clear that ethnomusicology is in no way restricted to the study of particular geographic areas, or supposed kinds of societies, but rather, is applicable to any body of music in any society. If our field can be defined as "the study of music in culture," then it is as applicable to the study of jazz or art music forms in our own society as it is to a non-literate group. It is here that I am in perfect accord with Kolinski when he points out that it is not geographical areas which are important to us, but rather that it is a general approach which we seek; viewed in these terms, ethnomusicology is not a category in which is studied certain kinds of music, but rather a method of study which searches for certain goals in certain ways and which is applicable to any of the varied musical systems of the world.

Let us illustrate this further by using as an example a paper by Herskovits entitled "Freudian Mechanisms in Primitive Negro Psychology" (Herskovits, 1934). In this paper, Herskovits proposes "to indicate certain aspects of the psychology of primitive Negro cultural behavior which may be better understood when some of the broader simpler concepts of psychoanalysis are applied to their interpretation" (p. 76). Taking the concepts of repression and compensation, he points out a number of examples of these mechanisms in Negro cultures, and emphasizes that "there exists both a recognition of the nature of the neuroses as induced by repression, and of the therapeutic value of bringing a repressed thought into the open" (p. 77). His vehicle for the discussion rests partly upon an analysis of song and dance. Thus, he notes:

> In Dahomey, the institution of the avogan, the dance in the market-place, is . . . recognized by the natives as affording release for suppressed emotions. At stated periods the people of each of the quarters of the city of Abomey have in turn their opportunity to stage such a dance. Crowds come to see the display and to watch the dancing, but most of all, to listen to the songs and to laugh at the ridicule to which are held those who have offended members of the quarter giving the dance. Names are ordinarily not mentioned, for then fighting may result. In any event, the African relishes innuendo and circumlocution too well to be satisfied with bald, direct statement. However, everyone who is present already knows to whom reference is being made. Thus the song might be:

111

Woman, thy soul is misshapen.
In haste was it made, in haste.
So fleshless a face speaks, telling
Thy soul was formed without care.
The Ancestral clay for thy making
Was moulded in haste, in haste.
A thing of no beauty art thou,
Thy face unsuited to be a face,
Thy feet unsuited for feet. (p. 77-8)

Such release is also given to co-wives who sing songs against each other.

The lobi singi of the Negroes of the coastal region of Dutch Guiana, especially of Paramaribo, and a very similar phenomenon, is discussed at some length by Herskovits in the same article, as is the institution of fiofio in the same area, and he notes, "What has been shown is that among the . . . Negroes, both in Africa and the New World, patterned types of psychic purges are recognized as valid; what is important for a psychoanalytic approach to the understanding of these social data is the fact that, in every case, the native explanation of the particular type of behaviour, though ordinarily couched in terms of the supernatural, can be restated in terms of the unconscious" (p. 82-3).

How, then, shall we classify this article, of which a brief resume has been given here? Surely, it is psychological in that it deals with Freudian mechanisms; it is anthropological since it is concerned with cultural behavior; but just as surely, it is also ethnomusicological in that it emphasizes the role of music in psychological behavior within cultures. What is important to us is not the fact that it was written by a scholar who would never call himself an ethnomusicologist, but that it represents one facet of the approach to the study of music, used in this case simply as an example, which clearly falls within the scope of that which we would call "ethnomusicological."

We return, then, to the point that ethnomusicology does not deal with geographic areas of research or with certain supposed "types" of people, but that it is clearly a method, an approach, to the study of music in culture. If this be true, however, it is equally clear that method does not operate in a vacuum, and that there must always be a consideration not only of problem, but of the theoretical framework along the lines of which an approach to the problem will be carried out. It has been noted, rightly, that "the relation between research design and theoretical terms of reference in shaping ethnographic studies" is of the utmost importance, and that "techniques are essentially no more than ways of implementing the testing of hypotheses, and that there is no hypothesis which does not arise from a body of theory and concept" (Herskovits, 1954:3,5). It is perhaps at this point that we are least clear in the field of ethnomusicology; our work has proceeded without much clearcut definition of what we are trying to achieve or how we are to achieve it. It is for this reason that I have defined ethnomusicology as the "study of music in culture," and that I believe our objectives are to a considerable extent coincident with those of cultural anthropology. Our interests, I believe, should be directed toward the broader understanding of music, not simply as a structural form, not in terms of particular areas or peoples, and not as an isolate, but as a creative human phenomenon which functions as part of culture. In thus defining the field I have tried to make it as clear as I can that I by no means exclude the purely historic, the purely structural, the purely aesthetic from equal consideration with the ethnological. The point is that the clear understanding of the historic, structural and

112

aesthetic is intimately connected with an understanding of the cultural back-ground in which these aspects operate.

There is one further implication involved in this view, and this con-cerns the problem of whether the ethnomusicologist must, then, spend time in the field gathering his materials at first hand. I believe that this is nec-essary if the studies are to be truly ethnomusicological in their import. The analysis of music for the sake of its structure is a necessary and important step in the processing of ethnomusicological materials gathered in the field, but it is only the beginning. The day of the "armchair ethnomusicologist" who sits in the laboratory and analyzes the music that others have recorded —already passed to a considerable extent in anthropology—is fast passing in our discipline. I do not deny the contribution of such a specialist in the past, nor in the future, but his role is becoming progressively smaller, and rightly so, for method and theory are inseparable in the gathering of data, and the descriptive phase of our study in which we treat simply structural facts is giving way before the broader interpretations. We are beginning to realize that all facts are not equally important, that facts in themselves are primarily understandable in context, and that the formation of the research design must be followed through by a single investigator who gathers his ma-terials in the field, analyzes them himself, and applies the results to the problems he sought to investigate. While the study of music as a structural form and as an historic phenomenon is of high, and basic importance, in my own view it holds this position primarily as it leads to the study of the broader questions of music in culture.

NOTES

I should like to express my appreciation to Mr. J. H. Kwabena Nketia who has read this paper and made pointed suggestion for its improvement; he is, of course, in no way responsible for its final form.

REFERENCES

Anon
    1954   Bibliography: Erich Moritz von Hornbostel. Ethnomusicology Newsletter No. 2:9-15.
Bascom, William R.
    1953   Folklore and anthropology. Journal of American Folklore 66:283-90.
Bingham, W. V.
    1914   Five years of progress in comparative musical science. Psychological Bulletin 11:421-33.
Boas, Franz
    1909-10   Tshimshian mythology. Washington: 31st Annual Report, Bureau of American Ethnology.
Caldwell, Joseph R.
    1959   The new American archaeology. Science 129:303-07.
Chase, Gilbert
    1958   A dialectical approach to music history. Ethnomusicology 2:1-9.
Gilman, Benjamin I.
    1909   The science of exotic music. Science 30:532-35.
Herskovits, Melville J.
    1934   Freudian mechanisms in primitive Negro psychology, in E. E. Evans-Pritchard, Raymond Firth, Bronislaw Malinowski, and Isaac Schapera (Eds). Essays pre-sented to C. G. Seligman. London: Kegan Paul, Trench, Trubner, pp. 75-84.
    1954   Some problems of method in ethnography, in Robert F. Spencer (Ed.). Method and perspective in anthropology. Minneapolis: University of Minnesota Press, pp. 3-24.
Hood, Mantle
    1957   Training and research methods in ethnomusicology. Ethnomusicology Newsletter No. 11:2-8.

113

Hornbostel, Erich M. von
 1905 Die probleme der vergleichende musikwissenschaft. Zeitschrift der Internationale
         musikgesellschaft 7:85-97.
Kolinski, Mieczyslaw
 1957 Ethnomusicology, its problems and methods. Ethnomusicology Newsletter No.
         10:1-7.
Kunst, Jaap
 1955 Ethnomusicology. The Hague: Martinus Nijhoff.
Merriam, Alan P.
 1959 African music, in William R. Bascom and Melville J. Herskovits (Eds). Conti-
         nuity and change in African cultures. Chicago: University of Chicago Press,
         pp. 49-86.
Nettl, Bruno
 1954 North American Indian styles. Philadelphia: Memoires of the American Folklore
         Society, Vol. 45.
 1956 Music in primitive culture. Cambridge: Harvard University Press.
Rhodes, Willard
 1956 On the subject of ethnomusicology. Ethnomusicology Newsletter No. 7:1-9.
Schneider, Marius
 1957 Primitive music, in Egon Wellesz (Ed.). Ancient and Oriental Music. London:
         Oxford University Press, pp. 1-82.

Panorama of

Dance Ethnology

by Gertrude Prokosch Kurath

APPROACH

DANCE as a reaction to life has a long tradition that encircles the globe. Dance ethnology, however, has come into being only within the last few decades. Though studies of dances are to date still individualistic and experimental, the literature as a whole is comprehensive enough so that the time is ripe for a co-ordination of the many different approaches.

COVERAGE AND GAPS

In the course of time, dances from probably every corner of the globe, as well as relevant customs now long vanished, have found their way into literature, for the most part in travelogues or sociological works. The literature of accurate description or analysis falls almost entirely within the last fifty years, and is now also respectable in quantity.

European dance ethnology received impetus from the research of Cecil Sharp in England, early in the twentieth century. Today all European countries can boast large, and sometimes systematic, government-sponsored collections of folk dances, particularly England and the Balkans. The names of the scholars who are most prom-

inent in this work will appear often in the following pages. Wolfram further cites for Austria the work of Ilka Peter, Herbert Lager, and, as the "grand old man," Raimund Zoder; Hans von der Au and Felix Hoerburger, in Germany; Bianca Maria Galanti, in Italy; and Joan Amades and Aurelio Capmany in Catalonia.[1]

While the huge territory of the Union of Soviet Socialist Republics had seemed to be represented only by scattered reports of popular dances in anthologies, the ethnologist, I. I. Potekhin, sent (Dec. 12, 1958) a list of 139 bibliographical items which starts with the year 1848 and reaches to the present time. It includes anonymous surveys dealing with the dances of the U.S.S.R. (*Tantsi Narodov SSSR*), and many items containing choreographies and music of special regions, for instance, Azerbaijan (Almasadze 1950) and Moldavia (Onegina 1938). Accounts of Russian dances have been published in Berlin (Moiseyev 1951), Sophia (Okuneva 1951), Prague (Berdychova 1951), and Yakutsk, Siberia (Zhornitzkaya 1956). Further titles and an appraisal will appear in a 1960 issue of *Ethnomusicology*.

Labanotation, a technique of dance notation described below, under "Second Circuit," is in full swing in Europe. According to Knust, who terms it "Kinetography Laban,"

GERTRUDE PROKOSCH KURATH is Co-ordinator of the Dance Research Center in Ann Arbor, Michigan, U.S.A. She was born in 1903 and educated at Bryn Mawr College (M.A., 1928, History of Art) and at the Yale University School of Drama (1929–30), in the U.S. She also received extensive training in music practice and theory, and in several systems of art dance as well as folk dancing, in Germany and the U.S. From 1923 to 1946, she was active as teacher of Modern Dance, as concert performer, and as producer of pageants and dance dramas. Some of her choreographic compositions were based on research in European dances of the Middle Ages and Renaissance, and in American Indian and jazz dance. Since 1946, KURATH has concentrated on dance ethnology and ethnomusicology. Her research has included field work among the Aztec, Otomí, Tarascan, and Yaqui Indians of Mexico, and the Iroquois, Cherokee, Ottawa, Chippewa, Menomini, Fox, Tewa, and Keresan Indians of North America. Among her many articles and co-authored books, she wrote the dance entries for the *Dictionary of Folklore, Mythology and Legend*, and articles on dance for the *Encyclopedia Americana* and the *Encyclopaedia Britannica*; she is also dance consultant for *Webster's New International Dictionary*.

In June of 1958, KURATH accepted a suggestion from the Editor that she write a survey of dance ethnology for CURRENT ANTHROPOLOGY. To supplement her data on certain parts of the

world, she embarked on eighteen months of correspondence with scholars in various countries. She received answers, information, ideas, manuscripts, reprints, or illustrations from the following correspondents: Renato Almeida, Henry R. Baldrey, Franziska Boas, Donald Brown, Richard L. Castner, Nadia Chilkovsky, Dance Notation Bureau of New York, Edward Dozier, Blanche Evan, William N. Fenton, Josefina Garcia, Erna Gunther, William Holm, Katrine A. Hooper, James H. Howard, Shirley W. Kaplan, Maud Karpeles, Joann Kealiinohomoku, Juana de Laban, Portia Mansfield, Samuel Martí, David P. McAllester, George P. Murdock, I. I. Potekhin, Curt Sachs, Ted Shawn, Estelle Titiev, Frank Turley, K. P. Wachsmann, and Richard Wolfram. Wolfram's contributions were especially substantial.

The first version of this survey, submitted on September 30, 1958, took the form of a symposium among correspondents. By July, 1959, at the suggestion of the Editor, it had taken the present form of an essay, which was then sent for additional CA☆ treatment to eight scholars of whom the following returned comments: Erna Gunther, Fred Eggan, James H. Howard, T.F.S. McFeat, Ted Shawn, and Richard Wolfram. Only contributions of these final commentators are identified by a star. The author and editors wish to express their thanks to the many correspondents and commentators who collaborated on this manuscript.

The exchange of books of Hungarian folk dances containing motifs and whole dances written in Kinetography, against copies of my book and the scores of dances published by my Institute in Essen, is continuing. . . . We have received orders from both Eastern and Western Germany, Yugoslavia, Hungary, Holland, Sweden [for] scores of national and historic dances [1956a].

In Yugoslavia, the Laban system was introduced by Prof. Pino Mlakar . . . the Yugoslav folklore institute has accepted Kinetography as the official method of notation. The first collection of Yugoslav dance scores written in the Laban system has been published.

In Hungary, due to the energetic work of Emma Lugossy and Maria Szentpal . . . the Corpus Musicae Popularis Hungaricae contains a large section in Kinetography, and several folk dance collections containing scores have recently been published. In Poland, Prof. Stanislaw Glowacki advanced the cause of Kinetography in the thirties, and recently a Kinetography group has been formed under the leadership of folklorist Roderyck Lange of Thorn . . . teachers of Kinetography have been trained at the Kinetographisches Institut, Diana Baddeley from Great Britain, Helmut Kluge from West Germany, and Ingeborg Baier from East Germany [1958a].

According to Juana de Laban (letter, Sept. 19, 1958), the Surrey Laban Art of Movement Centre has published national dances of Yugoslavia, Israel, and Austria.[2]

In Asia it is the dances of India which have received most study, especially the art forms, although lately the folk dances have been described as well. In other parts of Asia, save in Bali, theater dances rather than remote folk forms have drawn attention. Dances of Oceania need systematic study, except for the hula. Australian aboriginal dance has been reported only in ethnographic studies; a team of trained dancers produced a ballet and travel book about Australia instead of a much-needed analysis (Dean and Carell 1955).

The spectacular dances of Africa have been studied piecemeal, in connection with research on music. K. P. Wachsmann, a leading musicologist, is optimistic that his new role as Scientific Officer of Anthropology at the Wellcome House, London, will lead to an integration of music and dance study, at any rate in Uganda (letter, Oct. 20, 1958).

In the Americas, most publications use verbal description only. But there are centers of Labanotation in Cuba, Brazil, Argentina, and Chile (Solari 1958), and in New York, Philadelphia, Boston, and other cities of the United States. Andrew Pearse is trying to elevate the prevailing approach toward Caribbean dance from sensational journalism to serious folklore study. In South American countries, folklorists are feverishly collecting and interpreting not only popular dances but also acculturated and indigenous rites expressed in dance. Especially in Venezuela, Brazil, Argentina, and Bolivia, they have been aided both in research and in publication by government agencies. Remote tribes, however, are generally left to ethnologists, missionaries, and adventurers. In Mexico, research has progressed spasmodically, depending on Government attitudes, since a boom in 1922. A recent bibliography of Latin American dances includes a detailed account of research activities and sponsors (Lekis 1958).

The bulk of the dance publications in the United States deal with European folk dances or European derivatives such as squares and longways, and some favorites appear repeatedly. But Latin American dances are now popular in dancing schools, and jazz dance, until recently relegated to collections of ballroom dances, is rising to the status of subject for serious research. Dances of the American Indian have been included in a number of ethnographic accounts, though, unfortunately, choreographers were not engaged by the dance-enthusiast Speck, or by the great teams that studied the Plains Sun Dance and Societies, under Clark Wissler and Robert H. Lowie. Further, Mason (1944) and others initiated a great vogue for distorted Indian dances among countless groups of Boy Scouts and interpretive dancers.

In Canada, the disparate British, French, and Indian traditions have been discussed together in popular lectures by Barbeau. Also, there is a miniature manual of French quadrilles (Lambert n.d.) and a book of children's rounds (Barbeau et al. 1958). Other anthropologists have investigated some of the native tribes in the vast interior expanses of the country. Some repeatedly beat a trail through Six Nations Reserve, and a choreographer followed in their wake (e.g., Speck 1949; Kurath 1951, 1954, MSc, d). On the West Coast, William Holm is justifying Erna Gunther's encouragement in the reconstruction of Kwakiutl dances. Despite picturesque accounts by ethnographers, choreographers have not ventured into the Eskimo's bleak habitat. As the shamanistic ceremonies and mimetic festivals retreat before the white man's ways, chances for comparisons with the also unstudied dances of the Arctic fade, and chances for the analysis of Eskimo square dances improve.

OBJECTIVES OF DANCE ETHNOLOGY

Notwithstanding the energetic collecting of folk dances within the last fifty years, we have but now arrived at a point where we can begin to define for dance ethnology the subject matter, the scope, and the procedures of this emerging discipline. So far, the views of its devotees are characterized by diversity and much disagreement.

The first question that requires discussion is: What is the subject matter of dance ethnology?

Ethnology deals with a great variety of kinetic activities, many of them expressive, rhythmical, and esthetically pleasing. Would choreology, the study of dance, include all types of motor behavior or only restricted categories? If the latter, what identifies "dance," which uses the same physical equipment and follows the same laws of weight, balance, and dynamics as do walking, working, playing, emotional expression, or communication? The border line has not been precisely drawn. Out of ordinary motor activities dance selects, heightens or subdues, juggles gestures and steps to achieve a pattern, and does this with a purpose transcending utility. When walking attains a pattern, it becomes a processional, which is treated as dance by Wolfram (1951: 54–56), ..ennedy (1949: 84–90), and others. A utilitarian activity like rice-planting, rhythmical and often accompanied by song, can easily be stylized into dance (Moerdowo 1957; Shawn 1929: 170). The transformation from occupation to mimetic dance has often been achieved, by processes ranging from imitation to abstraction (Kurath, in Leach [1949–50] 1: 277; Lawson 1953: 11; Wolfram 1954). For example, in the codification of gesture into Plains sign language (Tomkins 1929), gesture remained utilitarian and formally haphazard, while in the choreography of Pueblo Indian Tablita dances (Kurath, in Lange MS; Kurath 1957c), gesture was idealized and integrated into a structure of song, symbolic text, and group movement. In a strict sense, dance ethnology would be confined to patterned phenomena. In a broader sense, it could deal with any characteristic and expressive movement, since everyday motions are the roots of dance. Pursued according to the strict sense, this newest ethnic science would have limited usefulness. Pursued according to the broader sense, its findings would be indispensable to all holistic cultural analyses.

A second, closely related, question is: What is the scope of dance ethnology?

Existent definitions of the science contain varying emphases on ethnic and choreographic content. Franziska Boas calls dance ethnology "a study of culture and social forms as expressed through the medium of dance; or how dance functions within the cultural pattern" (letter, July 30, 1958). Ten years ago Kurath made "ethnochoreography" synonymous with "dance ethnology" and defined it as "the scientific study of ethnic dances in all their cultural significance, religious function or symbolism, or social place" (in Leach [1949–50] 1: 352). (See Gunther [2].☆)

Kurath's definition includes a controversial term, "ethnic dance." In her letter, Franziska Boas identifies ethnic dance with "folk dance." Another dance educator's definition of folk dance would apply equally to ethnic dance: "Folk dance may be defined as the traditional dances of a given country which have evolved naturally and spontaneously in conjunction with everyday activities and experiences of the people who developed them" (Duggan *et al.* 1948: 17). But Wolfram includes folk dance in folklore, "the lore of historical high cultures, to which we have direct access, as we belong to them" (letter, Aug. 22, 1958). A performer, La Meri, restricts the term "folk dance" to "communal dances executed for the pleasure of the executant" (in Chujoy 1949: 177). Chujoy defines folk dance as "dance created by a people without the influence of any one choreographer but built up to express the characteristic feelings of a people" (1949: 191). Thurston defines several categories of folk dances (1954b: 4–5):

(*i*) Dances of folk-lore. The narrowest use. They include religious and magical dances, occupational dances, war dances, and so on.

(*ii*) Dances of the folk. Includes (*i*) and also popular recreational dances, but not skilled step-dances.

(*iii*) Traditional dances. This will differ from (*ii*) in including step-dances.

(*iv*) All non-professional dances. The broadest use.

A class of dances which many people would exclude . . . is the fashionable ballroom dance. . . . But now there is ground for a real difference of opinion.

The American dance-pioneer, Ted Shawn, makes "ethnic dance" subsume "folk dance" as a subspecies, and further distinguishes "ethnologic" or art dance: "I have included pure, authentic and traditional racial, national and folk dance as 'ethnic' and the theatrical

handling of them as 'ethnologic' and the free creative use of these sources as raw material as 'ethnological,' but there is no hard and fast rule, and no clear dividing line" (letter, July 5, 1958). Franziska Boas would "make a distinction between professional dance as distinct from secular folk, much as you might between art and craft" (letter, July 30, 1958). La Meri defines ethnologic dance as "those indigenous dance-arts which have grown from popular or typical dance expressions," excluding folk dance (in Chujoy 1949: 177), but she admits that folk dance "is the dance from which inevitably grows both in technique and spirit the dance-art of a nation" (1948: 33). Thurston (1954b) completely excludes from "folk dance" the commercial dances of the stage and screen, on the ground that the mercenary objectives of commercial dance remove it several notches further from the roots than art dancing.

Ten years ago, Kurath (in Leach [1949–50] 1: 276) inclined to an identification of ethnic and folk dance similar to Thurston's second category above. At present, she would restrict "folk dance" to secular forms, no matter whether of ritual origin; include all types, both secular and ritual, under "ethnic dance"; and agree to the distinction between folk or ethnic dances and art creations.

This still does not settle the question of the scope of dance ethnology, nor have we meant to imply a restriction of scope to ethnic dance. Most students would agree with Boris Romanoff that "the art of ballet cannot be carried into the domain of ethnologic research" (in Chujoy 1949: 92), yet ballet developed from European court dances, just as present-day Japanese Nō drama has its roots in early religious and secular ceremonies (Kurath, in Leach [1949–50] 2: 794). Similarly, while jazz dance originated with the people, it has been adapted to the stage. Nevertheless, jazz, and also modern creative dance, express significant facets of our way of life that are not expressed in square dancing. A culturally complete picture should, as in Miss Boas' definition, include all of these.

This point of view has a champion in an eminent dance historian and musicologist who has considered all forms of dance in his research. Sachs says, "The question whether ethnology includes all forms of the dance must be emphatically answered in the affirmative" (letter, July 7, 1958).

A third question on which there is published disagreement is that of the extent of a need for dance ethnology within the broader field of general ethnology. In part, the answer to this question must await further inquiry into the function of dance in culture, which, in turn, depends on more findings on the relative significance of dance in particular cultures. Scholars have justified their studies on dance, not only by their use to readers in search of information or of material for performance, but also by the functional significance of dance in society.

Thus, Sachs points out that the dance has aided sustenance and well-being (1933: 2). Cherokee dances, like many others, are prophylactic and contain "the principles that insure individual health and social welfare" (Speck and Broom 1951: 19). The Samoan dance aids education and socialization, because it "offsets the rigorous subordination" of children and reduces "the threshold of shyness" (Mead 1949: 82–83). A statement by Mansfield about the Concheros holds for many other peoples as well: "The dance is the most satisfying expression of their religious feeling" (1952). Such motivations of utility or religious feeling are confirmed by many writers, among them Kirstein (1935: 2): "The subject matter of primitive, or source dances are the seasons of man's life, the seasons of vegetation, and the seasons of the tribe's development or mythic history." Two experts on Yugoslav folk dances hold that, "Folk dances . . . composed the dramatic element of various rituals and actions, each of which had for the man of a primitive society significance of a ritual magic action" (Jankovic and Jankovic 1934–51: 48).

In Western culture, religious content is increasingly relegated to art dance, while folk-dance activities are largely recreational (Mayo 1948: 3; Holden *et al.* 1956: v), or they are educational in that they break down ethnic prejudices (Herman 1957: v) and can, thereby, contribute to world unity (Shawn 1929: xii). This shift of purpose from faith to fun spreads inexorably to other parts of the world, as our dances spread; it widely changes public attitudes in the direction of exhibitionism. "First nights" succeed "first fruits" (Singer 1958: 379).

FIRST CIRCUIT

Common Problems of Choreology and Anthropology

Choreology recognizes the cultural setting of dance, including the cultural position of individuals and of the sexes, and patterns of social organization and economic activity. It can identify local styles and styles spread over larger areas. Further, choreologists can design comparative studies to solve problems of prehistory, orthogenesis, diffusion, and internal and acculturation changes.

SOCIAL RELATIONS

Individual and Group: Creativity

The individual dancer's role within the group-dance pattern is a matter of local custom. In relatively few places, he can exercise his creative imagination uninhibited; more often he is submerged within the traditional group pattern, or permitted only some leeway.

In native America, limited freedom is reported by many observers. For example, ". . . every Conchero takes his turn in leading the dance. He can introduce new steps and if the Jefe approves of them they may become favorites" (Mansfield 1952: 151–52). Again, "The Iroquois Eagle Dance illustrates the pattern phenomenon in ritual and it permits the free expression of personality within set forms" (Fenton and Kurath 1953: 75). But contrasting practices between the Woodlands and Plains, and between the Pueblos and the Northwest Coast, are evident. In the Woodlands, "All of these circular and linear formations involve the cooperation of a group, commonly the whole community. . . . Across the

Great Plains and westward, individual exhibitions are at least as popular as group formations" (Kurath 1953: 64). "The joint dances of the Pueblo Indians in which participate a large number of dancers dressed alike and in formation, are quite foreign to the North Pacific coast where the single dance prevails" (Franz Boas 1955: 346).

The role of the individual dancer may vary within a community, according to the function of a dance: ".\ sacred-profane dichotomy is still characteristic of the Pueblos. . . . [In secular dances,] there is no limit to improvisation and to the introduction of novel forms, whereas such innovations are strongly discouraged and controlled in other ceremonies" (Dozier MS: 149).

In modern America, the set patterning of square dances (Mayo 1948) contrasts with the almost chaotic freedom and formlessness of jitterbugging (Kurath and Chilkovsky 1959; Kealiinohomoku 1958).[3] (See Fig. 4.)

Elsewhere over the world, we find similar variety, with freedom generally a male prerogative, however, as in Yugoslavia: "Single folk dancers who are phenomenally gifted introduce into the collective style something of their own individuality. This must remain within the frame of the collective technique" (Jankovic and Jankovic 1934–51: 30). According to Hamza, the Ländler and Schuhplattler dances of Bavaria and Austria permit improvisation only to the male: in former times improvisation was imaginative; today the forms are more stereotyped (1957: 23). (See Fig. 9.) In Samoa, dance is still individualistic, being especially free for the boys: "It is a highly individual activity set in a social framework" (Mead 1949: 78). It is remarkable how male exuberance is similarly expressed in these otherwise contrasting cultures through stamping, leaping, clapping, and slapping of the thighs (Hamza 1957: 24–25; Mead 1949: 80–81).

Male-Female Roles

Let us look now at male-female relationships, first in terms of exclusive societies and the effects of exclusiveness on dance patterns, and then in terms of mingling of the sexes in dancing.

Anthropologists have reported the initiation rites of male dance societies. In addition, a theater expert has made a study of dramatic and choreographic patterns in the masked rituals of Patagonians, Australian Aborigines, and other primitive people (Eberle 1955). These rites, from which women were excluded or by which they were frightened, have now mostly died out. Analogous warrior ceremonies in the North American Plains are also in the throes of extinction or survive only in the War or "Grass" Dance. The reports for these rites are unfortunately too sketchy for reconstruction of their dances (Wissler 1916). In Europe, the traditional ceremonies of surviving male brotherhoods have been carefully described, and sometimes analyzed, for instance, the Calušari of Rumania (Wolfram 1934; Sachs 1933: 227–28), the sword dancers of Austria and England (Wolfram 1951: 66, 82; Kennedy 1949: 60–77), and the puberty rites of Hessen-Nassau; both in Europe and in the Plains, the societies emphasize age-grading (Zoder 1950: 87–90; Wissler 1916).

Women's ritual societies are absent in many cultures. However, in Yugoslavia the rain-bringing Dodole are young girls who dance from house to house (Jankovic and Jankovic 1952*b*: 13). Austrian female societies function at weddings (Zoder 1950: 91–92). The Iroquois have some women's dancing societies (Kurath MS*a*), as do Southern Plains tribes like the Ponca (Howard and Kurath 1959: 5).

Males generally dominate ceremonial activities. Of the ten Kiowa tribal dances, Gamble says that five are exclusively for men, and none are for women alone (1952: 100). Among the Iroquois, on the other hand, the women are more prominent. And in Brazil, Almeida voices surprise at the monopoly of females in the rite, Bumba-meu-Boi, both as chorus and dancers (1958*a*: 12). In Asia, their prominence varies in adjacent countries, and even within a single country. Thus, in the Cambodian dance dramas, girls play both princes and princesses (Shawn 1929: 160), but in Japan and China, female roles are usually played by men (Shawn 1929: 51). In Japan, again, it is priestesses who "perform the type of dancing called Kagura" (Shawn 1929: 37–38).

Customs governing the participation of the sexes recur strikingly throughout the world. To give just one example, for Yugoslavia and the Iroquois, specialists have made identical observations as to separation within a line, alternation, or pairing: "In earlier times men and women danced in separate kolos, but the female kolo was led by a man. . . . Later they danced the same kolo but grouped by sexes" (Jankovic and Jankovic 1934–51: 14). "Each sex fulfills specific ceremonial assignments and enters the dance in a prescribed order. . . . Social dances pair the sexes; most ritual dances segregate them in a line. . . ." (Kurath 1951: 124).

The arrangement of the sexes may provide a clue for relative chronology, for observations from various parts of the world seem to corroborate the statements from Yugoslavia and the Iroquois. Initiation and shamanistic rituals are danced by men alone or women alone (Eberle 1955: 186). Wolfram (1951: 82) considers such rites and their European survivals very ancient. In agricultural ceremonies men and women participate but without contact, as in the Pueblo Corn Dance (Kurath 1957*c*). But in social dances the mingling has become more intimate (Speck and Broom 1951: 66; Gamble 1952: 102).

Though courtship is one of the most fundamental of human activities, couple dances with courting mime appear to be fairly recent. In some couple dances, the man and woman hold hands, perhaps with many intricate arm figures, as in the Austrian Steirischer (Wolfram 1951: 180–83) or the Renaissance Allemande (Horst 1940: 31–40). The embrace dance evolved in Central Europe from the sixteenth-century Weller to the nineteenth-century Waltz (Sachs 1933: 184ff., 257). In American Indian social dances, the man may place his hand on the woman's neck or shoulder (Martí 1959: 143). In modern Pan-Indian couple dances, partners cross arms or lock elbows, but probably as a result of White influence (Kurath 1959: 34).

Organization

Ritual, but not secular, dances are generally organized according to the objectives of the enacting group, be it a small closed ritual society, a hereditary division, an economic group, or some combination of these.

1. *Ritual Societies.* The male societies discussed above have traditional systems of officeholding. Sometimes officers serve for life; sometimes they are elected periodically. The roles of the officials find choreographic expression, and are often identical with leading roles in professional dancing guilds (Wolfram 1934; 1951: 75–85).

In Mexico these organizations tend to be elaborate and often hierarchic, and the reflection of these features in choreographic grouping is evident to both ethnologist and dancer: "The Yaqui have a closely knit organization with three major divisions. The first is the church organization proper, which appears to be allied to the matachin dancers' society. . . . Next is the dancers' society, and thirdly is the fariseo (dancing clown) society" (Beals 1945: 107). "The Yaqui Matachini are led by a monarca and each of the files by a monarca segundo; the rank and file are called soldados" (Kurath 1952: 237).

The hierarchy of the Concheros society has a multiple function: "The organization is military as to discipline and titles, and a religious brotherhood as to purpose and the vows and obligations of members" (Mansfield 1952: 144). The captains also lead the dances (Kurath 1952: 237).

2. *Clan and Moiety Organizations.* Though perhaps modeled on civic organizations, and even linked with them by an overlap in leadership roles, ritual societies remain discrete. However, sometimes ritual organization follows hereditary and antithetical clan or moiety divisions. This phenomenon has survived among North American Indians such as the Creek, Yuchi, and Cherokee in the Southeast, the Iroquois and Musquaki in northern U. S., the Pueblos of the Southwest, and others, and among some of these peoples it finds choreographic expression.

For example, Speck observes of Iroquois dance forms that, "On each 'side' or moiety, there are two groups, the one of males, the other of females" (1949: 39). Similarly, the Seneca Eagle dancers, paired by opposing moieties, "always face their partner" (Fenton and Kurath 1953: 233).

Such relationships affect the spectacles and plaza circuits of the Pueblo Indians as well. In ethnographic terms, "Each Tewa pueblo is comprised of two divisions or moieties," which successively govern the ritual observances appropriate to the summer and winter halves of the ceremonial year (Dutton 1955: 6). In choreographic terms, "The Tewa moiety pattern has a profound effect on the circuits. . . . In San Juan the winter and summer moieties operate in harmony. . . . Santa Clara is split into four parties. All parties follow a set circuit" (Kurath 1958*a*: 24–25).

In other parts of the world, clans and not moieties are the significant hereditary divisions, as in Scotland, and clan totemism produces complex rituals, as in Australia (Eberle 1955: 427–53). However, the relationships between clan divisions and dance patterns have not been clarified, whether because of non-existence, or non-observance by field workers, we do not know.

3. *Economic Groups.* Economic specialization often creates occupationally disparate groups with special

dances, dance organizations, and dance functions. Gorer distinguishes these characteristics in African communities: "The best dancers come from the smaller, hunting tribes. In the larger, agricultural tribes dance diminishes in importance and vitality" (1944: 34). Tax observes that a Guatemalan community "that specializes in maize may pay more attention to the ritual aspects of culture—rain, planting, and harvest ceremonies. . . . Industrial communities should show special characteristics in contrast with agricultural communities. . . . They should be more secular-minded since they are less dependent on the vagaries of nature and more dependent on trade and money" (1952: 63). Agarkar emphasizes the superior dancing of lower castes in the Maharashtra of India, and the difference in dance types among "three main groups that are culturally distinct, namely, the Brahmins and the other advanced classes, the agriculturalists and allied tribes and the hill-tribes" (1950: 3). In Austria, craftsmen and miners retain occupational dances.

Urban-rural and class differences in dance forms exist in the West (Kurath 1952: 237; Lekis 1958: 90), but they are not so sharp as in India with its caste system. Thus in Brazil and Cuba, city has borrowed from country, with mutations (Lekis 1958: 202, 238), and in Europe, the court took from the peasantry (Horst 1940: 99–105), or the two engaged in give-and-take (Kennedy 1949: 102).

CHOREOGRAPHIC AREAS

A survey of dances over the world—or over even a limited area of the world—reveals dazzling variety, as suggested by the following comments on, respectively, Africa, Madagascar, and Greece. "African dancing . . . involves the whole body . . . ; the dance steps are above all acrobatic" (Gorer 1944: 19–20). "The movements . . . are very largely of the hands with rather minute sorts of gestures with the fingers" (Danielli, in Thompson 1953: 41). "The predominant feature of the dances is the variation of rhythm in slow and quick steps" (Crosfield 1948: 23). (See Fig. 5.)

Most students of continental forms have preferred to treat their subject according to political units, e.g., by countries of Europe (Alford 1948–52) or by states of Spain (La Meri 1948). Still other choreologists have delimited studies in terms of linguistic groupings (Lawson 1953) or topographical surroundings (Agarkar 1950: 3). In separate publications, Kurath, Mason, and Mansfield have agreed on the general characteristics of Amerindian dance as distinguished from European-derived dance of the New World; but Mason considers inter-tribal differences inconsequential (1944: 9–10), while Kurath is impressed by the cultural implications of these differences and by the usefulness of area mapping.

Fortún de Ponce (1957) shows Bolivia's regional differences on a map. Dances of native North America may be simpler to map than those of other parts of the world, where castes or racial mixtures complicate the picture, or where surveys are to date still sketchy. However, such mapping is highly desirable and could be carried out in terms of a number of criteria, the most fruitful being that of ecology.

It is certain that environment affects the repertoire, the content, and the form or style of ritual and dance. Common or similar natural resources have produced similar beliefs and dance rituals, for instance, in the Great Lakes region (Kurath 1957a: 1). Primary dependence on a certain commodity, such as maize or buffalo, everywhere inspires dances appropriate to that commodity. Subsequent tribal shift to a new environment enriches the repertoire, witness the Musquaki (Kurath MSd) and the Plains-Ojibwa (Howard MS: 24), both of whom migrated from the Woodlands onto the Plains and took on buffalo ritualism while retaining a residue of Woodland dances.

Such dances may well persevere after the extinction of the object-species, as does the Iroquois Passenger Pigeon Dance at the modern Spring Maple Festival (Fenton 1955: 1–2), or after a new religion has rendered the rites meaningless (Slotkin 1957: 13). On the other hand, the repertoire might change with the loss of aboriginal occupations such as hunting (Gamble 1952; Kurath 1958b). Studies focused on this problem might reveal similar phenomena in parts of the world other than America.

However, an analysis of dance form requires more insight than does an inventory of dance repertoires. Encouragingly, formal and evaluated analyses exist for several ecological zones of the world. Agarkar (1950) has made a noteworthy contribution in relating ecology and dance form in Maharashtra. Lawson has suggested connections between topography and dance movement, such as the traveling movements of steppe dwellers and the leaps of mountain people (1953: 32). Wolfram has made similar observations about Austrian mountaineers and plainsmen (1951: 200). However, Sachs cautions against hasty generalizations about geographical differences, saying "scholarly research into this question is still remote" (1953: 53).

Explanations for these differences are even more hazardous. Ecology certainly is an important factor in determining occupation, ritual, and dance; and it may prove to have an influence on style. Kurath has observed similar dance formations among widely removed agricultural groups (1956a), but doubts the applicability of ecological criteria to finer points of style. In addition, other factors must be weighed. Racial characteristics suggest themselves as a criterion when one compares Gorer's comments on Africa with Courlander's remarks on the "gross, direct movements" of Haitians (1944: 35) and with Dmitri's statement about the "use of the whole body" in Brazilian dances (1958: 9). Such a criterion receives further support from Kealiinohomoku's comparison of African and American Negro styles (1958). Again, Lawson (1953: 202) suggests linguistic affiliation as a reason for choreographic similarities. Several writers have speculated on psychological causes: Holt and Bateson speak of searching for the "cultural temperament" that motivates leaps or shuffles (1944: 52); Sachs has voiced daring theories on the relationship among manner, temperament, and environment (1933: 128–29); and the Jankovics seek the source of style in the "spirit and character of the people" as well as in externals of "social, economic and political conditions, geographical, topographical, and climatic circumstances" (1934–51: 29).

RECURRENT FORMS: ORTHOGENESIS, MONOGENESIS, OR DERIVATION?

As impressive as local variation, and more baffling, is universally recurrent manifestation, e.g., of "Rituals for increasing food supply, augmenting raw materials, controlling the weather, and warding off natural catastrophes" (Titiev 1955: 404–406), and of corresponding dance practices (Kirstein 1935: 1). Three main theories have been advanced to account for this: (1) orthogenesis following parallel invention; (2) common archaic origin, and subsequent migration and local adaptation; (3) derivative diffusion by direct culture contact.

In given cases, definitive explanations are usually wanting, but they can be arrived at by several modes of reasoning. Obvious and simple, or superficial, similarities of form suggest (1), while agreement of many elements and of complex, unusual patterns suggests (2). Further, at times archaeological or historical facts afford helpful evidence. Thus, for the maskers and rounds of Middle America and Central Europe, Kurath suggests independent origin under analogous circumstances (1956a: 296). Again, Spence and Sachs have both historical and formal evidence for direct, ancient connection of the present "Pyrrhic dances of the Balkans, Southern Russia, and even Southern France, which was powerfully affected by Greek culture" (Spence 1947: 3). On the basis of element count, Sachs proposes Rumania as the center of origin for these pyrrhics (1933: 228). On the strength of an equally striking list of common elements, Kurath bases arguments for (3), that is, for the derivation of New World correspondents out of this Old World base. For more recent events, historical documentation can substantiate theories of derivation (Fenton and Kurath 1953; Kurath 1956a: 287, 292). Modern folk dances clearly betray their history of derivation, through name, form, and documentation (e. g., Tolman and Page 1937).

DYNAMIC PROCESSES

Continuity

Thanks to a streak of conservatism, many peoples have retained dances unchanged through centuries, e.g., the Japanese (Matida 1938), the Yugoslavs with their ritual mime (Jankovic and Jankovic 1957: 53–57), and the Pueblo Indians (Dutton 1955: 6–16). All dances have roots in some ancient form, but some cling to the roots with remarkable tenacity. One of the most famous examples of the latter is the European chain-and-song-dance, of which Wolfram says, "A Greek picture from Ruvo (400 B.C.) shows a chain-dance at a funeral. In modern Greece as well as in southern Italy such dance-forms, looking exactly like the old picture, are still current and are called 'Tratta,' for instance, at Megara" (1956: 33–34). These dances have been accurately notated and rhythmically analyzed in Lattimore (1957) and Crosfield (1948: 8). (See Fig. 5.)

Diffusion

One dance has turned up "all over Europe, north, south, east, and west" (Alford and Gallop 1953: 51). "In England it is coupled with the Maypole" (Kennedy 1949: 97). In the district of Parnassus its steps are "the same as on the Faroe Islands" (Wolfram 1951: 90). Wolfram, like others, infers from the steps a relationship between the Faroe rounds, the Yugoslav kolo, the hora of Rumania, and the French branle of today and of the sixteenth century. Yet each of these dances shows peculiarities of local style. (See Fig. 10.)

Some dance phenomena have spread even farther—the hobbyhorse almost around the world during prehistoric times (Spence 1947: 143–44, 167ff.), the modern fox trot under our very eyes. Diffusion can be supported by documentary as well as formal evidence, as in the cases of the Eagle-Calumet complex (Fenton and Kurath 1953) and the Morisca type from the Old World to the New World (Kurath 1949; Lekis 1958). (See Fig. 11.) Examples of postulated diffusion are legion, though not all are equally tenable.

Many diffused dances have entered repertoires alongside forms persevering through continuity. If their origin can be ascertained, the amount of adaptation to local style can serve as a measure of the antiquity of this entrance. The fact that Pueblo Buffalo dances have undergone "Pueblo-ization" implies lengthy presence (Kurath 1958b). The American Pan-Indian dance complex betrays recent origin by its faithful adherence to one style, whether performed in Oklahoma or hundreds of miles away (Howard 1955).

Transculturation

Often borrowings are reciprocal, especially among adjacent groups, to the enrichment of the repertoire of each. One example from the Pueblos will suffice: "Tanoans gave the moiety concept, perhaps animal and hunt societies to Keresans while they received in turn medicine societies, katchina cult, perhaps the clown societies and some notions of the clan. . . . Plains-Pueblo borrowing is a lively process" (Dozier MS: 156). (See also Fig. 12.)

Acculturation

Frequently borrowing is largely one-way, and takes place more or less under compulsion. A potent influence in this process was the expansion of European political control. In the New World, spectacular effects developed as blends with, or adapted borrowings of, European forms. Kurath has discussed such ritual and secular resultants in Mexico (1952); Lekis has identified not only Indian-Spanish but also Indian-Negro-Spanish mixtures in many countries of Latin America (1958). Almeida says of Brazil, "Our popular folk ballets are of three origins: Portuguese, African and Indigenous. . . . The blending was complete and these dramatic dances have been entirely remolded" (1958b: 145). (See Fig. 7.)

Kurath considers it possible to unravel the blends into their components. Mansfield voices some scepticism as to the possibility of identifying native and European steps in, say, the dance of the Concheros (1952: 252).

Enrichment

Change can take place spontaneously, through internal development, or as a result of contact with external forces. Huge and varied repertoires have accumulated through millenia of borrowings, as in Yugoslavia with its many historico-cultural layers (Jankovic and Jankovic 1934–51; Kurath 1956a). The Japanese Nō theater combined many cultural strains (Shawn 1929: 22–37), and, as is usually the case, these borrowings were voluntary. On the other hand, the Mexican Indians accepted, remolded, or created new forms under forceably imposed European influence (Santa Ana 1940: 128), while they abandoned many indigenous ceremonies. In the same way, forced migration, as well as conquest, can develop rich blends, but always with some loss, for instance, the rites of the Haitian Negro (Courlander 1944). The difference between these two processes furnishes a subject for future study in dance adjustments.

Decline

Perhaps all dances are destined ultimately to decline. Currently in all countries, conservatives lament the deterioration of dances under pressures of modern industrial civilization, e. g., Agarkar, Wolfram, Vega. The decline takes various forms: change in overt features, such as paraphernalia (Lange 1957: 72–73); change of function, such as from hunt to weather control (Kurath 1958b: 439); secularization (Gamble 1952: 95); "discrepancy between the ideal and the actual" (Slotkin 1957: 15); deterioration of performance quality (Kurath and Ettawageshik 1955: 3); and simplification (Sturtevant 1954: 64). This pattern, noted among American Indians, is paralleled among the Yugoslavs, according to the observations of the Jankovics (see "Second Circuit," "Hypotheses"), and may well apply over the world.

Resurgence

The phenomenon of resurgence appears in various guises. For instance, renewed enthusiasm for tradition has in Santa Clara and Isleta Pueblos produced "a resurgence of dancing . . . and old dances which have not been performed for years have been revived" (Dozier MS: 148). But in Israel, where immigrants from diverse countries are reviving the ancient Hebrew culture, splendid new folk dances have arisen "from Chassidic and Yemenite traditions, from the energetic Horas of the Balkans, from the Arab 'Debka' . . . a synthesis between Orient and Occident" (Kadman 1956: 166). In Austria, revivals have grown not only out of scholarly, conscious efforts, but also among the folk, for example, the Salzburg "Jakobischützentanz."

Rebound

Rare and entertaining is the rebound of a dance from a land of acculturation to its home soil. Kealiinohomoku, Chilkovsky, and Kurath can corroborate the statement by Herskovits that "the dance itself has in characteristic form carried over into the New World to a greater degree than any other trait of African culture" (1941: 76). Now, reports Jones, the young African neglects his own heritage for a Euro-African song-dance, Makwaya, and for adaptations of modern American ballroom dances (1953: 36–37).

Review

Interpretation of dynamic processes relies on a core of style and structure that is manifested not only in the dance patterns of a culture but also in the human relations, social organization, adaptation to environment, and adjustment to contacts of that culture. The unraveling of dance mixtures depends on separate analysis of both the intruding and the native patterns as well as on analysis of the mixtures. In this way do anthropological and choreographic aims and methods parallel one another.

RELATION TO OTHER FIELDS OF RESEARCH

Psychology

"The anthropologist can find in the study of the dance corroborative materials for his observations, as well as clues which will direct his research toward new aspects" (Holt and Bateson 1944: 52). This applies to normal behavior, to buffoonery (Beals 1945: 102, 129–31), to possession by deities (Sachs 1933: 35, 43; Herskovits 1950: 881–82), and to "holy dancing" of the American Negro (Kealiinohomoku 1958: 105).

From analysis of rhythm and tempo in curative Amerindian rites, it appears that the "effects are the very opposite from the derangement" (Tula 1952: 118–19). Again, symbols have been devised to denote mental states, for example, "extravert" and "intravert," and their corresponding dance postures (Loring and Canna 1956: 7–9). In combination, techniques and findings of this kind have unexplored possibilities for modern psychiatric treatment, as has been pointed out by both a physician and a dancer: "Dance as a therapeutic agency . . . is quite unparalleled in potentialities" (Lawton, in Chujoy 1949: 144); "The possibilities of dance as mental therapy must be explored" (Franziska Boas 1944: 6). Blanche Evan is training her pupils for treatment of neurotic patients and for preventive therapy (brochure, 1959).

Technology

Choreologic findings apply also to technology, especially to the study of work movements. Occupational dances can be magico-mimetic, such as the planting mime of the Portuguese Bugios (Alford and Gallop 1935: 117), or recreational, such as the Philippine Balitao or rice-planting dance (Shawn 1929: 170). They can fall differentially along a scale of stylization, from the realism characteristic of the Balitao to the abstraction that marks the mining symbolism in the Dürnberger Schwerttanz (Wolfram 1954: 1–2). We have already remarked that occupational dances are numerous (Kurath [1949–50]: 277).

Anthropologists have studied traditional movements in work and craft production from a practical point of view (Weltfish 1946), and have evaluated some components of the movements with regard to an economic transition to industrial techniques (Salz 1955: 111, 228). Lately, engineers have clamored for scientific roads to industrial efficiency (Gomberg 1946). Techniques for improving kinetic patterns are available and have had incipient application. Specifically, Laban's system of Effort symbols can be used to notate actions and to expedite efficiency training. The system depends on criteria of "Weight, Space, Time and Control of the Flow of Movement" for well-regulated, less fatiguing actions (Laban and Lawrence 1947: 406).

After all, motions of work and sport have the same dynamic components as those of the dance—"Swing, suspense, sustained resistance, percussive impact, thrust and throw, relaxation" (Prokosch 1938: 294).

Linguistics

There are two promising approaches to the connection between dance and the spoken word. One is the study of the "manifestation of the relation between language and symbolic movements, standardized in each cultural area" (Franz Boas 1955: 346–47). Among the recreational dance-mimes to words, a delightful example is Barbeau's collection of French Canadian children's rounds (1958: 17–18, 98, *passim*). Again, it is often possible to define the connection between the ideology and the patterns of gesture code, as with the Cochiti Tablita-dance gestures (Kurath, in Lange MS).

A second topic for research arises from the question: To what extent are choreographic similarities linked to original linguistic relationships or to later culture contact? Lawson believes that stylistic likenesses between the Finns and Magyars may be due to linguistic affinity, and the differences to separation and different environments (1953: 202–204). Kurath would attribute likenesses between the Iroquois and Cherokee both to linguistic and to cultural connections. She has observed that the long-separated Shoshoneans, the Hopi and Comanche, have different dances, but the unrelated, adjacent, Tewa and Keresan Pueblos share a similar dance culture. Evidently both factors are operative.

Mythology

The spoken word, mythological beliefs, and dance drama are often integrated. In Hawaii, the dancer chants his own accompaniment—"their great dances, the great hulas: they are from the gods" (Campbell 1946; 32)—and with symbolic gestures enacts the words. On the Faroe Islands, dancers enact tales of the Sigurd legend as they sing them. In Malabar and other parts of Asia, a separate chorus sings for the actors of the Ramāyana and Mahabharata (Bowers 1953: 64–87), much as the Greek chorus voiced dramatic words. In America, myths are rarely enacted, but a close relationship between imagery, song, "birdlike dance and the myths" is characteristic of Kwakiutl dances, for instance the *MatEM* (Gunther MS). The Iroquois False-Faces impersonate "the great fellow who lived on the rim of the earth, and secondly, his underlings, the common forest people," by kicking and sparring (Fenton 1941b: 401–402, 420). The more usual situation confronting the dance ethnologist in America is a mere explanation by Indians of a dance's origin, as in the case of the Iroquois *Ohgiwe*, "Death Feast" (see Barbeau 1957, side 2).

Theater Science

In a noteworthy contribution to *Theaterwissenschaft*, Eberle points out that primitive drama mirrors the people's *Weltanschauung*, their beliefs and mythology (1955: 538), and that it does so by a combination of dance enactment, dialogue, music mask, costume, setting, and lighting (pp. 18–19). He shows insight and imagination in his compilation of anthropologists' field materials and in his reinterpretation of them in terms of dramatic structure, though he relies entirely

on verbal descriptions without choreographic symbols or analyses. He confines this work to Australian, Patagonian, and African primitive drama. Others have similarly interpreted the drama of other areas—Spence (1947) largely from literary sources, Alford and Gollop (1935) mostly from observation. While studies of historic medieval dance drama are many, structural analyses of Amerindian forms are few. Speck's study of personally observed Cherokee dance drama (Speck and Broom 1951) suffers from the same omission as Eberle's work—absence of dance and music notation.

Dramatic constituents other than dance and music are often included in choreographic textbooks, e.g., costume and paraphernalia in Alford (1948–52), Evans and Evans (1931), Jankovic and Jankovic (1934–51), Lawson (1953), and Sedillo-B. (1935). The natural setting or native architecture is related to the dances in Bowers (1953), Matida (1938), Dean and Carell (1955), Slotkin (1957), Wilder (1940), and Mansfield (1952). There are also specialized studies: many on masks (Fenton 1941b; see Bibliography to Kurath [1949–50] 2: 687); some on costuming (see notes in Kurath 1958b: 44); and one a penetrating analysis of Melanesian settings (Schmitz 1955). Gunther [3]☆ comments on these aspects; see also Figure 1 for integration of several aspects. Instruments, often described, are sometimes also related to the dance (Wilder 1940).

Archaeology and Art History

Students of early historic or prehistoric dance drama have consulted sculpture, painting, or architectural remains from those periods. Schmitz lists a respectable number of archaeological sources for his study of the development of ritual settings (1955). Hickman has reinforced his inferences from ancient Egyptian bas-reliefs by observing the contemporary dances of the same region (1957). Nellie and Gloria Campobello have found confirmation on Maya antiquities in the modern Maya movement style (1940: 13–27). Sachs, as reinforcement for his text, reproduces art works of prehistory (1933: Pl. 1), antiquity (Pls. 8–11), and the Middle Ages (Pls. 17–24). Europeanists have a secure basis for historic reconstruction of the Middle Ages and Renaissance in a combination of pictures, verbal descriptions, codes and notation schemes dating from those centuries, as well as modern survivals. Among those who have availed themselves of this rich heritage are Sachs, Wolfram, Gallop, Kennedy, Walter Wiora, and Maurice Louis.

Kurath believes in conferring with the archaeologists themselves, and approached Homer Thomas for chronology in connection with Eurasian ritual drama ([1949–50] 2: 946–47), Joffre Coe for Tutelo mortuary customs (1954: 161), and Bertha Dutton for leads on Pueblo dance prehistory (1958b: 447). Such co-operation could have two-way benefits if choreographers aided archaeologists to reconstruct ground plans and movement styles.

Musicology

While integration of choreology with most of the above-mentioned disciplines lags, the close association of dance and music are fully realized. Although there are dance studies without reference to music, and musicological analyses of dance music without kinetic references, a huge literature combines these arts. Textbooks for prospective dancers combine the steps with musical measures and counts, by means of various notation techniques discussed below under "Second Circuit." (See Fig. 8). Scholarly analyses go still further than such juxtapositions, particularly in the Balkans where prevalent rhythmic complexities have inspired mathematically exact concordances (Jankovic and Jankovic 1955). Kurath attempted a possibly too detailed analysis of the two arts and their synthesis in the Iroquois Eagle Dance (Fenton and Kurath 1953). Mansfield has demonstrated how "the Concheros steps fit the music so precisely that the playing of the concha becomes an integral part of the dance" (1952: 183).

Yet a vast field remains to be worked. For instance, no one has correlated the intricacies of jazz rhythms with motor responses. Also, no one has gone beyond mathematical counts in the attempt to base musical rhythms on the force and nature of the motor impulses guiding the dances, though Sachs envisions the following process: "Organized in regular patterns, motor impulses pass from the moving limbs to the accompanying music, only to revert from voices, clappers, and drums as a stronger stimulus to the legs and torsos of those who dance" (1953: 38). A very few authors have suggested relationships between emotions, expanse of movement, and melodic lines (Kurath 1954: 160; Lawson 1953: 52; Sachs 1953: 128ff.). In a noted musicologist's opinion, "In dance is found the overt physical expression in visual form of the physical and spiritual aspects of music" (Rhodes 1956: 4). This merges into esthetics.

Symbolics

Dance patterns, gestures, and paraphernalia transcend an ornamental purpose. Indeed, investigators have asked whether ideas symbolized in dance are also expressed by all other arts within a culture. Sachs and Wolfram have speculated on such a connection between arts and culture symbols. Sachs, with caution, suggests an inherent connection (1933: 116–17). Wolfram points out interlaced motifs in crafts and dance (1951: 34–35).

In a discussion of ground plans, Sachs recognizes a widespread, perhaps universal, symbolism in certain circuits, serpentines, and interweavings (1933: 99–119). Today a symbolic significance is attached to the formations of many ritual dances, even in Europe and America, but it has faded from recreational repertoires. How many participants in American square dances realize the original vernal meaning of their "Grand Right and Left" (Kurath [1949–50] 1: 290)? Experts in the *mūdras* of India can communicate, yet foreigners and even Indian government members fail to grasp this gesture code (Singer 1958: 369, 375). The ancient combat symbolism of Moriscas is not apparent to all spectators, and not even to all performers.

Such facts cast doubt on the "universal language" of dance. Yet choreologic methodology rests on the assumption of some universality, and must proceed on the basis of this assumption.

SECOND CIRCUIT: CHOREOGRAPHIC PROCEDURES

Certain procedures used in choreographic analysis, such as observation, interviewing, consultation of secondary sources, and re-study, are shared with ethnologists. However, the analysis of dance requires additional, specialized devices. Dance constituents are only partially revealed by general verbal description. For comparative purposes, symbols are required. Such symbols have been systematized by dance specialists trained in kinesiology and art dance, but these symbol systems, with their respective types of analysis, apply equally well to ethnic dance and art dance, and also to utilitarian activities.

ANALYTIC RECORDING

The recording, and analysis, of dance movements entails breaking them down into their space and time components.

GROUND PLANS

Track drawings, with solid or dotted lines, are commonly employed to depict solo or group movement along the ground, though other schemes serve related but special purposes (e.g., Jankovic and Jankovic 1952a: 58; Hutchinson 1954: 84–87). For complex progressions by large groups, it is customary to draw a series of ground plans. For the identification of males and females, officials, dramatis personae, and the directions they face, choreographers have used diverse symbols, identified by a key (Duggan *et al.* 1948; Mason 1944; Vega 1952; Laban 1928; Hutchinson 1954; Kurath 1951, 1958a, b). Figure 1 shows an attempt to depict in one diagram the ground plan, setting, and dramatis personae of the Iroquois Eagle Dance (Fenton and Kurath 1953: Fig. 4 by Kurath). The dotted lines indicate the path of the Eagle Dancers. Labels *A*, *B*, *A'*, and *B'* refer to the structure of the music and dance as related to the path of movement. The positions of the other actors are identified by numbers. Furnishings are spelled out. Ethnologists have often attempted similar diagrams for placement of participants or path of locomotion. Beals has successfully shown both placement and path (1945: 177–79).

Ground plans can be juxtaposed for comparison. Figure 2 illustrates a clockwise circle and a counterclockwise ellipse. In both cases the singer (*S*) is in the center. Such diagrams are instructive for area studies, e. g., for contrasting the paths of Great Plains and Woodland Indians' dances (Kurath 1953: 61–62). More complex diagrams can also be juxtaposed, but there is a limit to the amount of material that can be integrated on one page.

BODY MOTION

The graphic representation of three-dimensional body movement on a two-dimensional written or printed page poses problems. Textbooks for schools and the general public have usually bypassed this problem, and depended on technical terms in verbal descriptions, tabulating the verbal phrases with counts and beats. Their authors have often employed stick figures (Mason

1944; Evans and Evans 1931), full-figure drawings (Herman 1947; Mayo 1948), or photographs (Blanchard 1943; Agarkar 1950; And 1959), by way of graphic aids. Raphael Mova has drawn expressive stick figures for Campobello and Campobello (1940), and John Bancroft has given stick figures locomotor value in Lawson (1953). A device for showing footwork is a set of footprint outlines in numbered positions (Shomer 1943: 8, 11–15, 17; Vega 1952: 364–65, 369).

The inadequacy of these devices has for many years led to experiments with symbols. The most complete symbol system, and the one in widest use, is that of Rudolf Laban, termed "Labanotation" in the United States. It is not, however, the simplest one. Other ingenious systems have found useful application in field work and for special dance styles. None of these systems can here be explained in full, but the principles of Labanotation will be illustrated as applied to selected stylistic problems and comparisons. A few examples of other systems, which can combine dance notation with musical rhythms and structure, will also be given.

The Laban System of Notation and Stylistic Analysis

"In 1928, Rudolf Laban published a new system of notation in which he introduced the vertical, symmetrical staff, read from the bottom up and clearly picturing, for the reader facing the score, right and left, front and back. The other invention is . . . using the length of the symbol on the staff to indicate duration of movement" (Hutchinson 1954: 3; see Shawn [5]✩). The level of movement—upward, downward or horizontal—is indicated by the shading of the symbol (Hutchinson 1954: 14; Knust *et al.* [1958] 2: 9–12). The Dance Notation Bureau of New York worked out some officially approved modifications and sponsored the publication of Labanotation for trained dancers (Hutchinson 1954) and for beginners (Chilkovsky 1955–56). Folklorists and anthropologists can find introductions to the system in Pollenz (1949) and in Juana de Laban (1954).

The Laban system records the motion of every part of the body. It can distinguish between a natural walk and various kinds of stylized walk. In Figure 3, (a) represents an ordinary, normal forward walk; (b) represents a shuffling walk, as in American square dancing and in some American Indian stomp or round dances; and (c) represents an elastic, syncopated progression, as in the Pueblo Tablita dances (Kurath 1957c). The system can also show creative or local variants. In Figure 4, individual, creative variation is illustrated by two versions of the Lindy jazz dance, from the notes of Nadia Chilkovsky. In Figure 5, local variation is illustrated by the Greek Syrtos and Kalamatianos, from the notes of Alice Lattimore. Variants of the notations in Figures 4 and 5, as well as symbols in Figures 3 and 7, were approved by the New York Dance Notation Bureau for publication in the *Dance Notation Record* ([1957] 8, No. 2: 6; [1960] 11, No. 1).

Style, or quality, can be shown more precisely by "diacritical" symbols for flexion or extension, accent, dynamics (strength), and effort. These useful symbols can be written separately as style indices (Fig. 6) or attached to a notation staff (Fig. 7). In Figure 6, the most basic style symbols (a) are compared with three other, more abbreviated, devices for showing posture variants.

Thus (a) exemplifies stick figures from Campobello-and Campobello (1940: 21 [Maya], 89 [Tarascan], 158 [Yaqui]), the left one indicating erect posture, the middle one indicating stooped posture, and the right one indicating greatly flexed posture. While the other symbols vertically aligned with these in each of the three cases indicates the same posture as the stick figures in the top row, (b) are symbols used in goniometry (cf. Kurath 1954: 160); (c) are symbols equated with extravert or intravert mental stages (Loring and Canna 1956: 9, key 1); and (d) are Labanotation extension and flexion symbols (Hutchinson 1954: 184, 264–65; Knust *et al.* 1958, 2: 5–6, 72–73, 78–79).

Figure 7 illustrates the compactness of the Laban system when applied to an acculturation problem in choreology. The illustration tabulates symbols for dance steps (co-ordinated with their rhythm), and for four aspects of style—posture in torso tilt and flexion, dynamics (degree of tension or relaxation), and effort (strong or weak impact). The problem is the discernment of native and Spanish elements in several hybrid Mexican Indian dances. Example (a) shows a typical step of the native base line in the Yaqui Indian masked Pascola dance (Kurath, field notes; Beals 1945: 120); (b) shows a step from the importation, the Spanish zapateado (Tsoukalas 1956: 19). The native qualities are forward tilt and slight flexion of the torso, relaxation, and fast, direct, strong effort; the alien qualities are erect and extended torso, tension, and fast, direct, light effort. The blends (b), a step of the Yaqui unmasked Pascola, and (c), a step of the Concheros, use the zapateado step, but maintain slight variants of the native qualities. The Concheros step receives a verbal description, with counts, in Mansfield (1952)—upbeat, slight lift on left foot, extended right foot; count 1, step on left foot to left side; count 2 brush right heel forward; count 3, step on right foot, closing to left foot. The efficiency in the use of symbols should be apparent.

Other Systems and Their Application to Musical Problems

All systems have attempted some combination of music with dance steps. The Laban system is convenient in this regard, for the dance symbols can be lined up alongside the musical notation. Several other systems have, however, achieved the graphic integration equally well, for example, those of Stephan Toth in Bratislava, Boris Zaneff in Sofia, Raina Katsarova-Kukudova in Sofia, Rudolf Benesch in London, and Eugene Loring in Los Angeles. The combination of dance notation and rhythm, specifically of long and short impulses, is shown in Figure 8, where (a) depicts a typical Pueblo Indian step (music fragment from Yellow Corn Dance of San Juan in *Midwest Folklore* [1958] 8, No. 3: 157), according to the Kurath system (see Kurath 1953, 1954; Thompson 1953: 35–38); (b) depicts the Mexican Jarabe Tapatio in the Sedillo system (1935: 14) and (c) depicts it in the Mooney system (1957: 28 [Fl means flat; b, ball; S, stamp]); (d) depicts the Bowarian "Zwiefacher"—the Ländler, with changing meter—according to Hoerburger (1956: 101 [D means "Dreher," or two-count turning step; W, waltz in three-counts]); and (e) depicts the

81

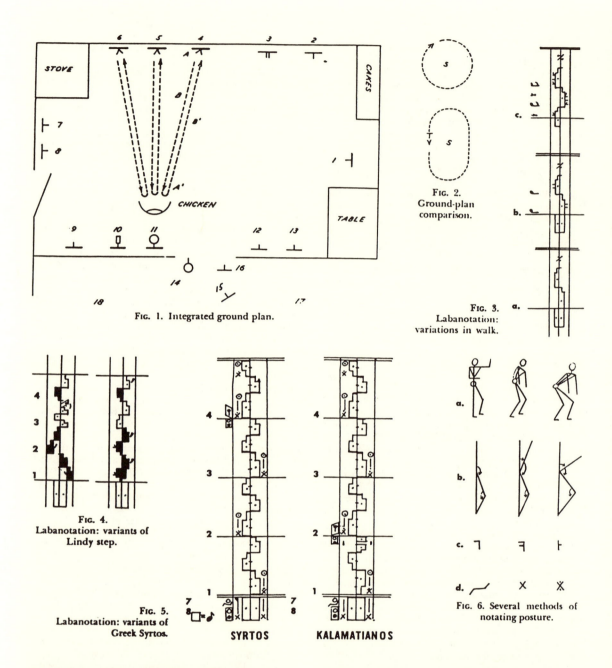

Fig. 1. Integrated ground plan.

Fig. 2.
Ground-plan
comparison.

Fig. 3.
Labanotation:
variations in walk.

Fig. 4.
Labanotation: variants of
Lindy step.

Fig. 5.
Labanotation: variants of
Greek Syrtos.

SYRTOS

KALAMATIANOS

Fig. 6. Several methods of
notating posture.

Yugoslav Invertita, in the Proca system (taken from Balaci and Bucsan 1956: 224 [for principles, see Proca 1956, 1957]).

Several systems include devices for showing rhythmic stamps or hand claps. Ilka Peter and Herbert Lager devised one such method, for recording the stamps and leaps of the Perchten of Pinzgau, Austria. Figure 9 illustrates two methods for depicting hand strikes, on various parts of the legs or feet, in two male dances—the Austrian Schuhplattler (a) and the Rumanian Calušar (b). In Figure 9, (a) shows the "Sechserschlag" step in the Schuhplattler dance, according to the Horak system

(1948: 155), which places the dance rhythm on a musical staff (on counts 1 and 3, right hand strikes right thigh; on counts 2, 4, and 6, left hand strikes left thigh; on count 5, right hand strikes sole of left foot, while hopping on right foot). Directly underneath these symbols are the corresponding symbols (Greek letters, delta and sigma, for right and left) for these hand strikes, in the Proca system (1957: 87–92). These constitute (b).

The juxtaposition of dance notation with musical rhythm and/or melody can show the nature of phrasing. It can show, for instance, whether the dance and music phrases or meters coincide or overlap. Such relation-

244

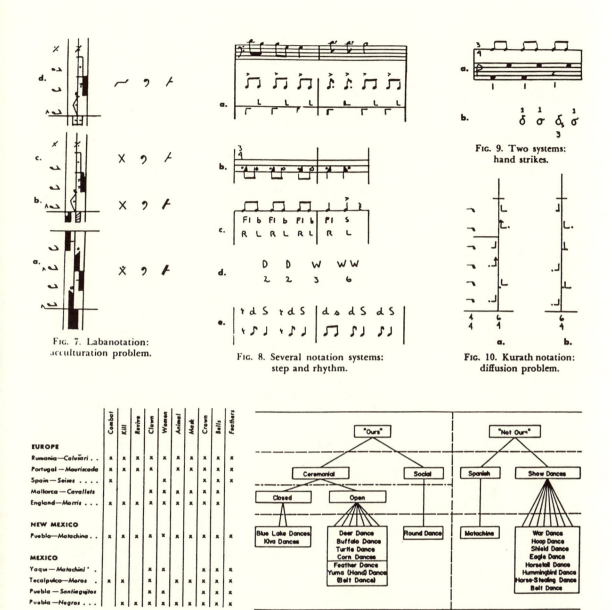

Fig. 7. Labanotation: acculturation problem.

Fig. 8. Several notation systems: step and rhythm.

Fig. 9. Two systems: hand strikes.

Fig. 10. Kurath notation: diffusion problem.

Fig. 11. Tabulation: symbolic elements in acculturation problem.

Fig. 12. Classification of Taos dances (1958).

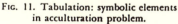

ships are often important indices of local or national style, e.g., in German and Scandinavian dances, the meters usually coincide, while in the Balkans, Rumania, and Palestine, they often overlap. Once a local or national style is determined, by this criterion of phrasing, problems in diffusion can be investigated through comparison of the diagrams which reveal the nature of phrasing. Figure 10, for example, indicates diffusion of the Hora step to the Branle and Faroe step: (a) shows the phrasing of the Hora of Rumania or Palestine (step with left foot; step with right foot; hop on left foot; hop on right foot), while (b) shows the phrasing of the Faroe

step and the French Branle to be essentially the same as that of the Hora, though a toe-touch replaces the hop.

The larger structure of a dance also can be analyzed in relation to the accompanying music, and with the aid of musical precepts, since, as a rule, the structure of the dance matches the music structure. Again, analysis of a folk dance can lean on methods for analysis and composition of art dance, since similar forms recur in both types of dance—the "binary" form of two themes (A B), the "ternary" (A B A), the "rondo" (A B A C A), and so on. After the basic form of the dance has been established, the dance score can be further labeled for its significant parts, such as phrases and larger sections. Art dancers have published explanations of these structural units, and their works can be consulted for details (e.g., Hayes 1955: 74–87). In dance ethnology, such structural analysis constitutes an interesting study for its own sake, and it can also illuminate problems of local style or of derivation and mixture of styles (Kurath 1954, 1956b, 1959; Kurath, in Lange MS).

ORGANIZATION OF MATERIALS

Distribution maps of stylistic features of dance rarely contain notation symbols, despite the potentialities of symbols for this purpose. Thus, Kurath used other devices to tentatively map choreographic areas (1953: 69) and diffusion paths (Fenton and Kurath 1953: Fig. 30) in North America. Kennedy published a map of England's Ceremonial Dances (1949: 72–73). Several authors have provided pictorial maps of regional dances in Europe (La Meri 1948; Duggan *et al.* 1948: Alford and Gallop 1948–52; Wolfram MS; Zoder 1938: 174–75).

Tabulation has served as a clarifying device in many studies, though, like maps, without benefit of notation. Sachs made frequent use of tabulations for summarizing element distributions (e.g., 1933: 111). La Meri used tabulation in assigning Spanish dances to their various regions and origins (1948: 171–80), and Lekis in charting Latin American dances (1958). In an acculturation study of Mexican Moriscas, Kurath tabulated symbolic elements found in dances of Mexico, New Mexico, and Europe (see Fig. 11, condensed from Kurath 1949: 105–106). Kurath has also tabulated dance concepts and patterns ([1949–50] 1: 280–83, 288–93; 2: 748).

Classification of dances has been carried out according to a number of categories: region (Jankovic and Jankovic 1952b; La Meri 1948; Lawson 1953; Lekis 1958); period (Czarnowski 1950; Kealiinohomoku 1958); social class (Agarkar 1950); origin (Tolman and Page 1937; La Meri 1948; Lekis 1958); function (Kurath 1949; Speck and Broom 1951; Wolfram 1951; Brown 1959); form (Sachs 1933; Vega 1952; Holden *et al.* 1956); and ground plan (Howard and Kurath 1959: 8–11). Kurath's classification of Iroquois dances (MSa) follows Fenton's classification "into three groups according to their function of bringing man into rapport with particular spirit-forces" (1941a: 144). Brown (1959) has based his classification of Taos dances on native opinions (Fig. 12). Taos Indians have accepted Plains show dances, but have attitudinally kept them separate from their own religious dances. Within each category Brown distinguishes subdivisions, by sacredness or origin.

Evaluation of dance depends on both cultural and choreographic criteria, which vary from place to place. It hinges primarily on stylistic definition, but also an appraisal of factors such as creativity, precision, acrobatic skill, and dramatic ability. Slotkin (1955) devised a ruse for eliciting native standards with respect to a Menomini Contest Dance. Agarkar describes the dances of Maharashtra and publishes the dance-songs in Devangari music script "with a view to evaluating their social significance and to show the place occupied and purpose served by them in the complex social fabric" (1950: 12). Hein (1958) combines cultural and artistic criteria in evaluating the Rām Līlā of North India. None of these evaluations has relied on notation, either during investigation or for publication of findings.

HYPOTHESES

Reliable workers have generally hypothesized only in connection with specific problems; often the hypotheses have received subsequent confirmation. Thus Cecil Sharp's theories of the origin and function of the Morris dance have been confirmed and amplified by Alford, Gallop, Kennedy, Sachs, and Wolfram. At times, experts have evolved theories from regional observations which may have universal application. For example, the following findings of the Jankovics on change in ritual dances seem to pertain in parts of the world other than Yugoslavia: (1) change of dance rites, while choreographic elements are preserved; (2) change of choreographic and other elements, while ritualistic purposes are preserved; (3) change of ritual paraphernalia; (4) change of specified age and sex of the participants; (5) disconnection and dissipation of component parts of dance rites, which join and amalgamate with other parts and with folk dances (1957: 58).

Sachs has courageously speculated on symbolism of forms, on paths of diffusion, and other phenomena, prying into prehistory and history to correlate dance patterns with cultural layers, from earliest times up through the periods of Neolithic nobility and peasantry (1933: 148). Frances Wright has been working on a tabulation integrating dance, music, and religious forms through the ages.

Theories must rest on exact and manageable information. Solutions to questions posed above in the "First Circuit" regarding ecology, universality and diversity, psychology, artistic patterns, and practical application await systematic compilation of reliable data.

THIRD CIRCUIT: PRACTICAL CONSIDERATIONS

Past and future accomplishments depend, in part at least, on practical considerations such as the availability, cost, and differential usefulness of recording machinery; the training of workers in the field; and relationships between scholars and laymen.

TECHNOLOGICAL AIDS

FILMS

Dance films cannot replace dance notation, any more than recordings can replace music notation. Even where finances permit photography, no film can supply the data for complete choreographies. Professional films usually cut both dance and music into fragments and obscure them with an educational drone; sometimes they are not authentic. Films by ethnographers often contain short dance excerpts which can serve as a reliable basis for some stylistic notation, but they are, after all, only excerpts. Films by choreographers, though perhaps technically inferior, are more likely to contain essential data because the choreographer tries to phrase the shots by dance sections and to co-ordinate them with notes taken on location. Although, in cases of unposed performances, they may miss some phrases during re-winds. Kaplan, Kurath, Kealiinohomoku, and Mansfield have made good use of such films for notations.

Techniques are being developed for viewing films at different speeds, repeatedly and backwards, and for halting at particular frames when necessary. Splicer viewers provide a simple tool for the scrutiny of single frames. Connecticut College School of Dance has a three-year Rockefeller grant to work out such techniques with a special projector (Rogers 1958: 5). The English Folk Dance and Song Society is experimenting with the use of films in stylistic analysis (Williams 1958: 111).

Problems relating to film techniques were discussed by the International Folk Music Council at its meeting in 1950, and by the Folklore Conference of 1950. Fragments of a conversation from the latter follow (Thompson 1953: 39–40):

THOMPSON: I was very much interested in Brazil to find that they were beginning a rather systematic collecting of dances . . . of the State of São Paolo. And they were sending out sound trucks with movies. They were able at that time to make a record with sound and also with pictures of these dances, but they had not worked out the technique of co-ordinating these.
KURATH: I regret that we do not have more of these motion pictures and photographs of dances. There is a great technical difficulty in getting all around the dance to see from all points of view. There are two techniques. . . . In the old one you set up a camera and then take the dance from one angle. . . . I think that is the best method for ethnologists. But nowadays there has been developed the artistic method of moving the camera around and getting shots from above and below . . . we are mixed up with tabu. . . . You are not permitted to take movies of any of the ceremonies.
SEAN O'SUILLEABHAIN: We have done some recordings of certain types of folk dances in Ireland. We have the mummers . . . we sent out our gramophone to record them and also sent a camera two years ago where we made an hour-long film recording one of these dances. And we also took a record of the people speaking their parts. We had no difficulty whatsoever, and there is no tabu on recording the dance.

Still photography, monochrome or color, can have some value for the analysis of posture, costume and so on, especially if the pictures are taken in series. Such pictures are also more practicable for publication than are frames from films, and have been used to excellent effect in many books, for example, the beautiful set of Ainu dances in a book by Kawano (1956). They cannot convey the kinetic element, however, and thus can only supplement notes and films.

RECORDINGS

Field recordings on disc or tape have the same value for dance study as for music study, because they can supply the basis for the music notation that is vital to the dance score. Recordings are complete and can be used to fill structural gaps left in the films, though the reeling off of the film and the tape can co-ordinate only by chance. Kurath found that a simultaneous use of a recording and a film was very helpful in the analysis of Pueblo and Menomini dances.

Publication of interrelated records and books on dance has unfulfilled possibilities. Popular combinations for folk-dance groups have been sponsored by the Folk Dance House of New York and the Jewish Education Committee of New York, and great quantities of Folkcraft records have been produced to accompany a *Syllabus* by Herman and a pamphlet by Lapson (1954). The Folk Dance Federation of California has issued sets of interrelated discs and volumes of European and American folk dances. Ethnic Folkways records often are accompanied by dance descriptions. The Folk Dance House of Manchester, England, and other European centers have similar projects.

TRAINING OF DANCE ETHNOLOGISTS

"We should send trained dancers in company with mechanical technicians into all the countries where the native dancing is still true and untouched."

This vision of Ted Shawn's (1929: xiii) has not been realized for several reasons. First, suitably trained dancers do not grow on every bush, as do mechanical technicians. In fact, an adequate course of training—which should include courses not only in anthropology but also in kinesiology or "modern" dance (not ballet), folk dancing, dance notation, and music, preferably by the Dalcroze system of kinetic rhythmic analysis—does not exist. The usual graduate-study requirements in anthropology leave no room for three-year courses in choreography. Moreover, few schools offer the needed artistic combination. Those which do, include the Juilliard School of Music in New York and Rosalie Chladek's School in Vienna. Some have taught ethnic dance routines, such as Shawn's University of the Dance and La Meri's former Ethnologic Dance Institute. All colleges in the United States include modern dance in their physical education curriculum; many, such as Berea, include folk dance; some, for instance Swarthmore and Women's College of the University of North Carolina, have added courses in Labanotation. An increasing number confer higher degrees in dance. Some have accepted Ph. D. projects on ethnic dance, among them Texas Woman's University in Denton (Garcia 1958) and New York University (Mansfield 1952), where Sachs formerly gave a course in dance history. Nevertheless, colleges do not offer rounded courses or degrees in the combined disciplines. As a unique instance, John Mann offers a course on Ethnic Dance in the Social Science Department at Northern Illinois University. The course includes practical and theoretical training in history, forms, techniques, relation to music, and in Labanotation, with emphasis on dances of Polynesia and of the European Renaissance and Baroque periods, and with a more general survey of other styles.

Research that is sound must be done by dancers who have achieved the insight and point of view of the ethnologist, or by musicians and ethnologists with dance training. It is difficult for an anthropology graduate without previous dance training to learn dance theory and notation in a few spare hours. Even the simple Kurath shorthand cannot be learned in a hurry. Prospective field workers whose schedule cannot include choreography may resort to a check-list on dance in the *Guide for the Human Relations Area Files* (Murdock *et al.* 1954); to two questionnaires prepared by Kurath (*Midwest Folklore* [1952] 2: 53–55 and *American An-*

thropologist [1956] 58: 177–79); and to an amplified list being prepared by Kealiinohomoku.

SCHOLAR AND SCHOLAR

TEAMWORK

It would be a big order for one person to go to the field as choreographer, musician, photographer, technician, ethnologist, folklorist, linguist, and psychologist, and to continue as historian and archaeologist, not to speak of geographer and botanist. Consequently, teamwork is essential. Each member of a team may well master two of the above specialties, and they need not all enter the field at the same time, though this is preferable (see Gunther [4]☆ and Shawn [2]☆).

EXCHANGE OF IDEAS

Conferences

Mailed exchange is possible at a distance, but it is not conducive to alert repartee. Publication often lags years behind discovery, and may, even then, not become known or available to all who are interested. Personal meetings are preferable. The International Folk Music Council gives dance an equal place with music at its annual conferences in various countries. In the United States, the Society for Ethnomusicology and the regional and national folklore societies welcome dance topics. But American dancers rarely attend the former conferences because of the expense, and few belong to the societies. European scholars have profited from frequent meetings. Wolfram, together with forty other experts from Germany, Austria, and Switzerland, was active in the founding of a "Studienkreis Volkstanz" in 1957 in Stuttgart. Under its auspices folk-dance leaders and groups from eight countries met for ten days in August, 1957, at Diest. Again, an international notation congress, held in Dresden during October 1–4, 1957, brought together scholars from many European countries. It was initiated by Wilhelm Fraenger, the Co-Director of the Institut für Deutsche Volkskunde an der Deutschen Akademie der Wissenschaft zu Berlin, and was organized by the Institut für Volkskunstforschung beim Zentralhaus für Volkskunst zu Leipzig. The frequent European folk-dance festivals also provide opportunities for discussion and seminars. In the United States, the National Folk Festival, managed by Sarah Gertrude Knott, has added small conferences occasionally. But, in the main, outside of Europe, dance scholars have had inadequate opportunities for interchange of knowledge. They have had even less opportunity for consultation with experts in the various anthropological sciences.

Centers

Another requirement for sharing knowledge is a clearinghouse for information. As in the case of ethnology, field materials on dance are strewn about in many archives and private collections, and manuscripts remain in private files unless some publisher has the courage to print them. Films, recordings, and even publications fail to reach interested students, though many items are available in the libraries of centers listed under "Selected Source Materials," below. To an extent,

published items appear in various current bibliographies, in *Ethnomusicology,* and in the *Journal of American Folklore.* For the ethnological aspects of dance, the research scholar can refer to the Human Relations Area Files (headquarters: 421 Humphrey Street, New Haven, Conn., U.S.A.), which are available at several universities in the United States: full quotations on the dance are assembled mainly under Number 535, but also under related topics such as Gestures, Posture, Recreation, Theater, Therapy, Funerals, and Ceremonies. In 1959, a dozen American dance scholars formed the Dance Research Center, with headquarters in Ann Arbor, Michigan. The associates provide and receive information on research activities, publications, and films, and are planning several co-operative projects.

However, Latin American dance folklorists have received government support (see list of sponsors in Lekis 1958) covering both field work and publication. Some groups, such as the African Music Society, successfully turn to UNESCO. In the United States, individual scholars have some small chance at foundation sponsorship for research, but none for processing and publication. Yet the expense of the latter is high. For instance, the preparation of the score for a solo dance, in Labanotation, costs U.S. $40.00 and, for a group dance, U.S. $75.00, not to speak of clerical and other costs. But the Dance Notation Bureau is in a position—if financed—to aid individual field and publication enterprises, as Chilkovsky suggests (1958: 1):

We believe that the best assurance will come through a publications program broad enough to include . . . national and folk dance material, and composition studies. Cooperative interchange of ideas by the leading practicioners of movement notation will then result in a widely representative publishing outlook so that all notation needs on all levels and in all centers may be consulted. European countries have already released a wealth of notated national and folk dances. Why not publish books on American Indian dances, jazz steps, West Indian dances, Hawaiian dances?

In the interest of extending notation activity on a world scale, we should like to suggest that the Bureau or Music Publishers Holding Corp., or both, assume leadership in organizing an advisory council composed of notators in all centers, who can act as a clearinghouse for publishable materials. Such a council might be empowered to make recommendations to publishers on the basis of a broad overall perspective.

SCHOLAR AND PUBLIC

Another sponsor of publication must not be overlooked. That is the dancing public, which has determined the policy of many a publishing house and has prompted publication of works by Czarnowski, Herman, and other folk-dance specialists. The dancing public, which receives the information, may at times also provide recruits for research. Educators around the globe have found stimulus in lay demands.

The dance descriptions with their music, songs and social setting . . . are published at this time because of the great demand for this material during the three years of the California Centennial celebration, as well as to satisfy the eager desire on the part of California dancers to learn more about the pioneer dances of their state [Czarnowski 1950: 8].

It is due to this revival [in schools] that an attempt has been made in this book to put into written form some of the dance-lore, traditional steps and music of South India [Spreen 1949: vii].

Those of us who are engaged in making folklore available to the public are performing a fascinating, interesting and very valuable task, but one that has a good many difficulties. The greatest of these, I think, is that in many cases we are trying to take over a tradition that has developed unconsciously and graft it onto a conscious culture. . . .

Now, as you know, the revival of folk music in England is mainly due to Cecil Sharp. He was not the first person to collect folk songs or perhaps even dances—but he was the first, or one of the first, to see the implications . . . as a form of artistic expression to a modern generation. . . . In 1911 the English Folk Dance Society was formed and from that seed grew our present organization. The methods adopted were classes, country parties, festivals, demonstrations [Maud Karpeles, in Thompson 1953: 199ff.].

The majority of its members come to its dances, classes and festivals for recreation and enjoyment, and . . . a small and serious body of people look to it as a focus for research [Williams 1958: 110–11].

As a result of these activities in England, a society was formed in the United States. At first it was a branch of the English Folk Dance Society, but later it became the autonomous Country Dance Society of America.

Similar societies have mushroomed throughout Europe, at first under scholarly guidance, but recently also without it. For instance, in Scandinavia "thousands and thousands have joined in the dance societies so that just now in Helsinki this summer we have a dancing festival with 1500 dancers from all of the northern parts of the country" (Otto Anderson, in Thompson 1953: 242–43).

That Switzerland has a wealth of old dances became known only slowly after 1930. Volumes of dances were published after that date [by Louise Witzig and others]. . . . Now Switzerland is industrialized, but since 1935 various dance-groups have been formed. . . . The groups also make tours abroad. Thus the groups' repertoires contain both Swiss and foreign dances, though the latter cannot really be transplanted [Klenk 1954: 13].

The Catalan folklorist, Señor Capmany . . . has worked to introduce Catalan dances and folk songs into schools, and has encouraged *Esbarts*, or societies for folk dance. . . . His solid work in *Folklore y Costumbres de España, El Baile y la Danza* . . . was done in 1931, when traditional dances were left to the people of the soil which bred them, and had not suffered the dangerous invasion by hundreds of youth-groups with diverse foundations unconnected with either soil or dance [Alford 1949: 54–55].

American-born folk-dance groups, as well as immigrants to the United States, show their fondness for European forms. Lately they have become captivated by the sophisticated Balkan and Israeli rounds. These groups greatly surpass the "Amerindian" imitators in desire for accuracy, desire for expert advice, and an increasing demand for background knowledge. All depend for this knowledge largely on books and records, and provide a market for good publications. Some, such as the Philadelphia Folk Dance Center, co-operate with dance notators. (See Lattimore project.)

SCHOLAR AND SHOWMAN

The relative excellence of productions of traditional dances by non-native dancers depends on the integrity of the leaders, as well as on the quality of the members, of the dance group. At times the work of such groups leads to scholarly research by its members. Thus, after two decades as concert performer of Plains Indian dances, Reginald Laubin in 1959 undertook a research project on the history and cultural place of American Indian dances. Again, Bill Holm's interest in Kwakiutl dances has developed as follows (letter, Oct. 10, 1958):

Boas' *Social Organization and Secret Societies* is and has been our "Bible," supplemented by the material in *BAE* 35th Annual Report. It wasn't until about seven years ago that the opportunity came to see real Kwakiutl dancing, and from that time to the present we have been getting firsthand information at an ever increasing rate. Four years ago a group of us began building a Kwakiutl-style house. Two years ago we developed a really rewarding relationship with Mungo Martin and his family.

I always try to stick to the traditional form of the dance as I know it, subject to the limitations imposed by space, number of performers available, and the million other things that can make it difficult to reproduce a dance. .

From performances given at his Jacob's Pillow University of the Dance, Shawn notes: "It is interesting to me to see that Shrimathi Gina [an American] gives a meticulously correct rendition of the various schools of Hindu dance, whereas Ram Gopal, a real Hindu, is more theatrical and free in his dances than Gina" (letter, July 5, 1958).

Josefina Garcia states frankly: "My work has been mostly ethnological instead of ethnic" (letter, July 28, 1958).

On the other hand, Paul Virsky, Director of the Ukrainian State Cossack Company, is quoted in Purdon (1958: 162) as saying that, "The future blending of folk dance and classic dancing . . . is not, therefore, to present untouched folk dances of Ukraine, but to express by their means choreographic ideas in a theatrical form."

Again, Franziska Boas says that when she uses "any ethnographic material in my choreography, I use it from the present creative dance point of view and weave it into the choreography" (letter, July 30, 1958).

The scholar may function as performer, though more often he will counsel backstage. Thus Kurath and Ettawageshik, in the course of an acculturation study, assisted the Ottawa in a production of a "Sun Ceremony." Ethnologists are evaluating the Pan-Indian powwow (Howard 1955; Schusky 1957).

By their stage performances, native and non-native professionals have performed a valuable public service (see Shawn [4]✩). Such artists adapt, and often change, the materials for theatrical purposes, hence face problems different from those of the choreologist, who emphasizes accurate recording.

PROSPECT

This completes the circle back to the question of definition and scope of dance ethnology, to the distinction between dance of the people and of the artist. Shall we accept Thurston's broad category of "folk dance" and admit the latest jazz steps, which, in Shomer's words, are "as timely as to-day's headlines in the newspapers, as interesting as the pulse of America" (1943: 5)? Shall we accept Sach's all-inclusive concept of dance ethnology? Franziska Boas proposes: "It would be interesting to trace relations between folk, ritual and twentieth century modern movement, particularly into the ritualistic aspects of the 'Modern Dance' of the twenties, and what has become of it now" (letter, July 30, 1958).

Any dichotomy between ethnic dance and art dance dissolves if one regards dance ethnology, not as a description or reproduction of a particular kind of dance, but as an approach toward, and a method of, eliciting the place of dance in human life—in a word, as a branch of anthropology.

To establish dance ethnology as a subdiscipline, ethnologists must accept choreology as a science, and choreologists must accept the scholarly responsibilities of being ethnologists. Let us hear the point of view of an ethnologist, James H. Howard (letter, Oct. 16, 1958; see also Shawn [1]☆):

The study of the dance, or choreology, is not only a legitimate but a very necessary part of the ethnological study. It is sometimes difficult for persons in our own culture, where the dance has been relegated to (1) performances of a spectacular nature by a few professional artists and to (2) a rather mechanical means by which members of one sex meet the other half of the population, to understand the importance of dance, as dance, to members of other cultures. Perhaps because of the relative unimportance of dance in Western European culture, most ethnographers ignore the dance completely, as something beneath their consideration, or content themselves with descriptions of the dance costume plus a few striking features (i. e. the "torture" feature of the Sun dance, the "shooting" dance of the Midewiwin). It is necessary, however, if we are attempting to describe a culture, to at least accord the dance the same importance as it is given by members of that culture. Lines of direction, characteristic steps and movements are culture traits and as such are capable of, and deserve, the same sort of treatment as other cultural elements. It would be well for each ethnographer, as part of his training, to learn some form of dance notation in order that he might record the dances of the group he is studying with the same accuracy he employs in recording kinship data, basket weaves, or irrigation techniques.

Again, William N. Fenton states in a letter (Oct. 29, 1959):

There is now evidence to demonstrate that music and the dance of primitive peoples can be analyzed and published and that these materials make very good tools for cultural and historical analysis and reconstruction. To linguistics is now added a second and third dimension of motor behavior that expresses the covert culture. These externalize the behavior systems that are manifest in language, the dance, and music and they used to baffle the field ethnologist who knew them as the most real expression of the culture but they frustrated him because they eluded his net. Now there are devices for recording these cultural expressions with some hope that they can be analyzed.

Teamwork is the best solution to problems of effecting comprehensive coverage and accurate analysis, given the increasing scope and specialized demands of dance research. This means teamwork between choreographers for standardization of analytic methods and for exchange of data, teamwork between choreographers and ethnographers for constructive application of these methods, and even teamwork between scientists and laymen, the public, the therapist, and the industrialist.

Only teamwork can cope with the widening scope and rapidly changing subject matter of dance ethnology. By the time that choreology is an established subdiscipline, the aborigine will have vanished, and we will have to assess the place of dance not only in mestizo culture but in our own materialistic, hybrid culture.

Notes

1. Space does not permit a historical survey of research activities. However, my brief comments have been augmented by some valuable information on Europe by Wolfram. See Wolfram☆, the English of which is a free translation from his German.

2. Wolfram☆ mentioned a number of publications which are not readily available in the United States. They have been incorporated into the Bibliography below, identified by a star. Wolfram considers Müllenhoff (1871) to be a notable pioneer effort, and considers that Böhme (1886), though not based on personal observations, is a valuable compilation of early source materials.

3. McFeat☆ comments, "I disagree with the statement . . . regarding 'the formlessness of jitterbugging.' My impression, especially when attending student dances, is that jitterbugging, which has been in form for at least twenty years, is a very conservative term for what is now called 'rock and roll.'" But I would answer that "rock 'n roll" is derived from jitterbugging and is equally lacking in formations.

Comments

By ERNA GUNTHER☆

[1] This is an overwhelming paper in its scope and may stimulate further work or frighten anyone inclined to timidity. I would prefer a separation between the true ethnological field and the folk dance of the European and American cultures. ꞌ can see the relationship theoretically, but the students in these two fields have such totally different background and orientation that it is difficult to include all their needs and attitudes in a single study.

[2] The definitions of dance ethnology which are quoted need closer scrutiny. I prefer the one of Franziska Boas, which would appeal most to the anthropologist. Kurath's definition of ethnochoreography says really the same as Boas, but it should be a definition of dance ethnology rather than "choreography," since the latter is limited in general usage to the dance pattern and its execution rather than the cultural relations of the dance.

[3] In the great mass of categories for study, there is one absent which I consider of interest, namely, the relation between the dance, costumes, and the place of performance. For instance, a dance executed by firelight before a large group is often seen in silhouette and demands large dramatic gestures, whereas one done for an intimate group in good light can use facial expressions and minute hand movements. If the dancer must handle any part of his cos-

tume, it restricts his arm movements. The relationship of costume to movement in the choreography of a modern dance is very apparent, and leads one to realize that in ethnic dances two lines of development often meet in traditional clothing, on the one hand, and dance gestures and stance, on the other. How are they reconciled?

[4] I hope this study will be the impetus to more accurate field work by teams, as suggested, as well as a detailed appraisal and review of what is actually hidden in many ethnographic sources, that deal with the dance only casually.

By TED SHAWN☆

[1] It seems to me that Kurath has done the most complete assembling of facts, and from all possible angles, on her subject. This is an extremely valuable survey, for it places in one article everything that anyone could ask about what knowledge has been accumulated, where it can be found, and evaluations of work done, and it sets out all of the fields of further and necessary research.

I am delighted that anthropologists are finally waking up to the importance of dance. And I feel that dissemination of Kurath's article will promote recognition of the absolute necessity of including study of ethnic dance in any complete dance curriculum.

[2] I am completely in accord with Kurath's ideas on the necessity of teamwork by the dancer-choreographer, trained anthropologist, photographer, sound recorder, and dance notator. Wanting to have my own eyes and ears undistracted during the five days of the Corroboree given in my honor in Australia in 1947, I had a writer for the *Australian National Geographic Magazine* take the motion and still pictures, unsupervised. He shot only on climaxes —the fastest and most violent movements—whereas many of the slower passages were of equal significance.

[3] Kurath probably does not know of the amount of ethnic film I have in my possession: besides that on the Australian Aborigines, I have films taken during my tour (1925–26) in India, Java, Ceylon, Darjeeling (Tibetan lamas), Japan, and many other parts of Asia. I also have films of dancing in Bali, a "Bee Dance" by Moros in the Philippines, of some Oklahoma Indians taken by a surgeon who had access to dances not seen by any other White man, etc. etc. All these are catalogued, and a copy of this list is available to Mrs. Kurath or to anyone else who wants it (write: Ted Shawn, Jacob's Pillow Dance Festival, Inc., Box 87, Lee, Mass., U.S.A.). These films will eventually be added to the Denishawn Collection in the Dance Archives of the New York Public Library.

[4] Also, she does not give full credit to some of the people who have done a lifetime of research on dance—Roger and Gloria Ernesti, who have specialized on the Indians of the Pacific Northwest, and Mme. La Meri (Russell Merriweather Hughes), whose Ethnologic Dance Institute was the finest clearinghouse for knowledge and information on ethnic dance that ever existed, but had to be closed for lack of funds.

[5] Ann Hutchinson, President of the Dance Notation Bureau of America and author of a textbook on Labanotation, agrees with me that the training of notators for the special purpose of working on a dance ethnology team is an admirable project and one which she will endeavor to promote. The most important fact to be faced is that a system of notation to give the greatest service must be *universally accepted*. Exchange of information freely between anthropologists and dance ethnologists can come about only if everyone, everywhere, accepts and uses one system, and Labanotation is the most complete and scientific system ever evolved. Even if a "shorthand" system is used in the field, the shorthand notes should be transcribed into Labanotation at the earliest possible moment, while memory is still fresh.

By RICHARD WOLFRAM☆

Folk-dance revival in Europe received its earliest impetus from Sweden and South Germany. In Sweden a student organization, "Philochorus," was founded in 1880. The founder, Philochorus, drawing inspiration from a Swedish ballet master who arranged folklike dances for the Royal Opera, made field trips and presented dance arrangements on the stage. Besides these staged "national" dances, true folk dances persevered in Sweden and engaged the attention of the Folkdansens Vänner (1893) and other organizations. This movement stimulated research in Denmark and the founding in 1900 of the Danish Foreningen for Folkedansens Fremme. This organization, in turn, stimulated Cecil Sharp, who had already collected dances and songs in England and who then founded the English Folk Dance Society in 1911. Swedish developments also influenced North Germany and its Wandervogel and Jugendbewegung. On the other hand, the Trachtenvereine of South Germany arose independently in 1884, and soon extended their interest from costumes to dances, though always for show purposes.

Serious research scholars had to counteract the emphasis on the stage. Like Cecil Sharp, with his accurate field work, Raimund Zoder in Austria accumulated accurate notes from 1903 on, then Ernst Hamza in 1914, and then others. The scholarly preoccupation spread to Germany, which has produced many exact descriptions and analyses since 1920. France has produced some clean-cut work, such as Monique Decitre's "Dansez la France." Among Romance nations, the Spanish, Bretons, and Catalans have best preserved their traditions. The Basques have also. Italy and France tend to arrange their dances for show purposes. In Russia, Yugoslavia, and Rumania, the government tries to preserve traditions and to encourage research, as well as large ensembles for displays.

National Folk Festivals began in the 1920's in Scandinavia and England. The first all-European folk-dance festival took place in 1934, in Vienna. Out of this came the important festivals and congresses which took place in London in 1935, and in Stockholm in 1939. And out of these grew up the International Folk Music Council and subsequent conferences in Switzerland, Italy, U.S.A., Yugoslavia, England, France, Brazil, Norway, Germany, Denmark, Rumania, and Austria.

Selected Source Materials

Of the published items annotated below as containing useful bibliographies, see especially Lekis (1958) and Horak (1959). For an almost complete list of journals containing articles on dance, see W. Edson Richmond's *Annual Bibliography of Folklore (Journal of American Folklore Supplement* [April, 1959] Pt. 2: 19–22).

A compilation of theses and dissertations based on dance research is for sale by the National Section on Dance, American Association for Health, Physical Education and Recreation, 1201 Sixteenth St. N.W., Washington 16, D.C.

Films, recordings, notes, manuscripts, and rare books from various countries are on file in the libraries of the Dance Notation Bureaus of New York City (47 West 63 St.) and Philadelphia, Pennsylvania (271 South Van Pelt St.); the Jacob's Pillow University of the Dance (Lee, Massachusetts), The English Folk Dance and Song Society (Cecil Sharp House, 2 Regent's Park Road, London, N.W. 1), The Laban Art of Movement Centre (Addlestone, Surrey, England), the Manchester Folk Dance House (505

Wilbraham Road, Manchester, England), the Folkwangschule der Stadt Essen (22 A Essen-Werden, Germany), the Tanzarchiv of the Musikwissenschaftliches Institut in Regensburg, Germany, and other centers.

The addresses of persons holding private collections of any kind of material relevant to dance ethnology are available from the continually growing files of the Dance Research Center, 1125 Spring Street, Ann Arbor, Michigan, U.S.A.

Bibliography

AGARKAR, A. J. 1950. *Folk-dance of Maharashtra.* Bombay: Joshi.

AKIMOTO FUMI. 1953. Japanese dance. Unpublished M.A. thesis, Juilliard School of Music, New York. (Labanotation.)

ALFORD, VIOLET (Ed.). 1948–52. *Handbooks of European national dances.* London: Parrish; New York: Crown Publishers.

———. 1949. Don Aurelio Capmany. *Journal of the International Folk Music Council* 1:54–55.

ALFORD, VIOLET, and RODNEY GALLOP. 1935. *The traditional dance.* London: Methuen.

ALMASADZE, G. 1950. *Ansambly Azerbaijanskovo Narodnovo Tantsy.* Baku, Azerbaijan: Azerbaijan State Philharmonic Society.

ALMEIDA, RENATO. 1958a. O Bumba-Meu-Boi de Camassari. *Modulo* 2, No. 9:7–13. Rio de Janeiro.

———. 1958b. Brazilian folk ballets. *Folklorist* 4:145–48. Manchester, England.

AND, METIN. 1959. Dances of Anatolian Turkey. *Dance Perspectives* 1, No. 3.

ARNHEIM, RUDOLPH. MS. "Movement and the psychology of expression," in The Function of Dance in Human Society (Second Seminar) (ed. FRANZISKA BOAS), New York, 1946.

BALACI, EMANUELA, and ANDREI BUCSAN. 1956. Folclorul coreografic din Sibiel. *Revista de Folclor* 1:213–47. Bucharest.

BARBEAU, MARIUS. 1957. *My life in recording Canadian Indian lore.* Ethnic Folkways Record FG 3502.

BARBEAU, MARIUS, et al. 1958. *Dansons à la ronde (roundelays).* Ottawa: National Museum of Canada.

BEALS, RALPH L. 1945. *The contemporary culture of the Cahita Indians.* Bureau of American Ethnology Bulletin 142.

BERDYCHOVA, JANA. 1951. *Tance Sovetskych Narodu.* Popis s obrazky a hudebnim doprovodem. Prague.

BLANCHARD, ROGER. 1943. *Les danses du Limousin.* Paris: Maisonneuve.

BOAS, FRANZ. 1944. "Dance and music in the life of the Northwest Coast Indians of North America (Kwakiutl)," in *The Function of Dance in Human Society (First Seminar)* (ed. FRANZISKA BOAS), pp. 7–18. New York: Author.

———. 1955. *Primitive art.* 1st ed., 1927. New York: Dover.

BOAS, FRANZISKA (Ed.). 1944. *The function of dance in human society (first seminar).* New York: Author.

———. MS. The function of dance in human society (second seminar), New York, 1946. (Typed copy provided by JOANN KEALIINOHOMOKU.)

BÖHME, FRANZ M. 1886. *Geschichte des Tanzes in Deutschland.* 2 vols. 339 pp. text, 221 pp. music. Leipzig.☆

BOWERS, FAUBION. 1953. *The dance in India.* New York: Columbia University

Press.

BROWN, DONALD N. 1959. The dance of Taos Pueblo. Senior Honors Thesis, Harvard University, Cambridge, Mass.

CAMPBELL, JOSEPH. 1946. The ancient Hawaiian hula. *Dance Observer* 13, No. 3:32–33.

CAMPOBELLO, NELLIE, and GLORIA CAMPOBELLO. 1940. *Ritmos indigenas de México.* México, D.F.: Oficina Editora Popular.

CAVALLO-BOSSO, J. R. MS. Kumanche of the Zuni Indians of New Mexico. Thesis submitted at Wesleyan University for B.A., with distinction in Ethnomusicology, 1956.

CHILKOVSKY, NADIA. 1955–56. *Three R's for dancing.* (Series.) New York: Witmark.

———. 1958. Editorial. *Dance Notation Record* 9, No. 2:1.

———. 1959. *American bandstand dances in labanotation.* New York: Witmark.

CHUJOY, ANATOLE (Ed.). 1949. *Dance encyclopedia.* New York: A. S. Barnes.

COURLANDER, HAROLD. 1944. "Dance and dance-drama in Haiti," in *The Function of Dance in Human Society (First Seminar)* (ed. FRANZISKA BOAS), pp. 35–45. New York: Author.

CROSFIELD, DOMINI. 1948. *Dances of Greece.* (Handbook series.) London: Parrish.

CZARNOWSKI, LUCILLE. 1950. *Dances of early California days.* Palo Alto, Calif.: Pacific Books.

DEAN, BETH, and VICTOR CARELL. 1955. *Dust for the dancers.* New York: Philosophical Library.

DEMPSEY, HUGH A. 1956. Social dances of the Blood Indians of Alberta, Canada. *Journal of American Folklore* 69, No. 271:47–52.

DMITRI. 1958. Characteristics of Brazilian dance. *Dance Notation Record* 9, No. 2: 9–11.

DOZIER, EDWARD P. MS. The Rio Grande Pueblos (including analyses of dance types and organization), in seminar on Differential Culture Change, University of New Mexico, 1956.

DUGGAN, ANNA S., et al. 1948. *Folk dances of the United States and Mexico.* (From "Folk Dance Library" Series.) New York: A. S. Barnes. (Useful bibliography.)

DUTTON, BERTHA P. 1955. *New Mexico Indians and their Arizona neighbors.* Santa Fe: New Mexico Association on Indian Affairs.

EBERLE, OSKAR. 1955. *Cenalora: Leben, Glaube, Tanz und Theater der Urvölker.* Switzerland: Walter Verlag. (Large bibliography.)

EVANS, BESSIE, and MAY G. EVANS. 1931. *American Indian dance steps.* New York: A. S. Barnes.

FENTON, WILLIAM N. 1941a. Tonawanda longhouse ceremonies ninety years after Lewis Morgan. Bureau of American Ethnology Bulletin 128:140–66.

———. 1941b. Masked medicine societies of the Iroquois. *Smithsonian Report for 1940,* pp. 397–430.

———. 1955. The maple and the passenger pigeon in Iroquois life. Albany: University of the State of New York.

FENTON, WILLIAM N., and G. P. KURATH. 1953. *The Iroquois eagle dance, an offshoot of the Calumet dance.* Bureau of American Ethnology Bulletin 156. (Large bibliography.)

FORTÚN DE PONCE, JULIA ELENA. 1957. *La navidad en Bolivia.* La Paz: Ministerio de Educación. (Good bibliography.)

GAMBLE, JOHN I. 1952. "Changing patterns in Kiowa Indian dances," in *Acculturation in the Americas: Proceedings of the Twenty-Ninth International Congress of Americanists* (ed. SOL TAX), Vol. 2, pp. 94–104. Chicago: University of Chicago Press.

GARCIA, JOSEFINA. 1958. Latin-American dances. Unpublished Ph.D. dissertation, Texas Women's University, Denton, Tex.

GILLESPIE, JOHN D. MSa. Notes on the Shawnee bread dance.

———. MSb. Some Eastern Cherokee dances and songs.

GONYEY, SANDOR, and LASZLÓ LAJTHA. 1937. *Tánc.* Magyarság Szellemi Néprajza IV. Budapest.☆

GÖTLIND, J., and H. GRÜNER NIELSEN (Eds.). 1933. *Idrott och lek, Dans.* Nordisk Kultur XXIV. 198 pp. Stockholm, Oslo, Copenhagen. (Dance in Denmark, Norway, Faroes.)☆

GOMBERG, WILLIAM. MS. "Time and motion studies in modern industry," in The Function of Dance in Human Society (Second Seminar) (ed. FRANZISKA BOAS), New York, 1946.

GORER, GEOFFREY. 1944. "Function of dance forms in primitive African communities," in *The Function of Dance in Human Society (First Seminar)* (ed. FRANZISKA BOAS), pp. 19–34. New York: Author.

GUNTHER, ERNA. MS. A preliminary analysis of Kwakiutl dance.

HAMZA, ERNST. 1957. *Der Ländler.* Forschungen zur Landeskunde von Niederosterreich, Bd. 9. Vienna.

HARASYMCZUK, ROMAN W. 1939. *Tance Huculskie.* 304 pp. text, 56 pp. music. Lwów, U.S.S.R.☆

HAYES, ELIZABETH R. 1955. *Dance composition and production.* New York.

HEIKEL, YNGVAR. 1939. *Folkdans.* Finlands Svenska Folkdiktning 6. 496 pp. Helsingfors: Svenska Litteratursällskapet i Finland.☆

HEIN, NORVIN. 1958. The Rām Lilā. *Journal of American Folklore* 71, No. 281:279–304.

HERMAN, MICHAEL. 1947. *Folk dances for all.* New York: Barnes and Noble.

HERSKOVITS, MELVILLE J. 1941. *The myth of the Negro past.* New York: Harpers.

———. 1949–50. "Possession," in *Dictionary of Folklore, Mythology and Legend* (ed. MARIA LEACH), Vol. 2, pp. 881–82. 2 vols. New York: Funk and Wagnalls.

HICKMANN, HANS. 1957. Danses de l'Égypte pharaonique et moderne. *Folklorist* 4:14–17.

HOERBURGER, FELIX. 1956. *Die Zwiefachen.* Berlin: Akademie Verlag.

HOLDEN, RICKEY, et al. 1956. *The contra dance book.* Newark, N. J.: American Square Dances.

HOLT, CLAIRE, and GREGORY BATESON. 1944. "Form and function of the dance in Bali," in *The Function of Dance in Human Society (First Seminar)* (ed. FRANZISKA BOAS), pp. 46–52. New York: Author.

HORAK, KARL. 1948. *Schuhplattlerschlüssel: Beiträge zur Volkskunde Tirols.* Festschrift zu Ehren Hermann Wopfners. Schlern-Schriften, Bd. 53. Innsbruck.

———. 1959. *Bibliographie des Volkstanzes in Österreich.* Innsbruck: Author.

HORST, LOUIS. 1940. *Pre-classic dance forms.* New York: Dance Observer.

HOWARD, JAMES H. 1955. Pan-Indian culture of Oklahoma. *Scientific Monthly* 81, No. 5:215–20.

———. MS. The Turtle Mountain Plains-Ojibway. (Sections on dance organizations and forms, and partly transcribed song tape, by G. KURATH.)

HOWARD, JAMES H., and G. KURATH. 1959. Ponca dances, ceremonies and music. *Ethnomusicology* 3, No. 1:1–14.

HUTCHINSON, ANN. 1954. *Labanotation.* New York: New Directions.

JANKOVIC, LJUBICA S., and DANICA S. JANKOVIC. 1934–51. *Folk dances 1–6, a summary*

of Narodne Igre. Belgrad: Council of Science and Culture.
———. 1952a. *Narodne Igre,* Vol. 7. Belgrad.
———. 1952b. *Dances of Yugoslavia.* (Handbook series.) London: Parrish.
———. 1955. Provilno u Nepravilnome (Le Regulier dans l'Irregulier), Zvuk. *Jugoslavenska Muzicka Revija* 2–3:65–79.
———. 1957. *A contribution to the study of the survival of ritual dances.* Serbian Academy of Sciences Monographs, Vol. 271. Belgrad.
JONES, A. M. 1953. Folk music in Africa. *Journal of the International Folk Music Council* 5:36–39.
KADMAN, GURIT. 1956. The folk dance of Israel. *Folk Dancer* 3, No. 1:165–67. Manchester, England.
KAPLAN, SHIRLEY. MS. Notes on folk-dances of India. (Film and tape.)
KAWANO HIROMICHI. 1956. *Ainu Odori.* Tokyo: Nirei Shobo.
KEALIINOHOMOKU, JOANN. 1958. A comparative study of dance as a constellation of motor behaviors among African and United States Negroes. Unpublished M.A. thesis, Northwestern University, Evanston Ill. (Analysis of Africa from films, of America from observation; dance notation.)
KENNEDY, DOUGLAS. 1949. *England's dances.* London: Bell.
KIRSTEIN, LINCOLN. 1935. *Dance: A short history of classic theatrical dancing.* New York: Putnam.
KLEIN, ERNST. 1937. Om Polskedanser. *Svenska Kulturbilder,* n.f., Bd. 5, Div. IX. X. Stockholm.☆
KLENK, KARL. 1954. Der Volkstanz in der Schweiz. *Folk Dancer* 1, No. 5:9–13.
KNUST, ALBRECHT. 1956a. Letter to the editor. *Dance Notation Record* 6, No. 5–6:13.
———. 1956b. *Abriss der Kinetographie Laban.* Hamburg: Das Tanzarchiv.
———. 1958. Letter to the editor. *Dance Notation Record* 9, No. 1:3–4.
KNUST, ALBRECHT, with the assistance of DIANA BADDFLEY and VALERIE PRESTON. 1958. *Handbook of kinetography Laban.* (English version of 1956b.) 2 vols. Hamburg: Das Tanzarchiv.
KONYVKIADO, MUVELT. 1954. *Hungarian dances.* (Series Neptancosok.) Budapest.
KURATH, GERTRUDE P. 1949. Mexican Moriscas: A problem in dance acculturation. *Journal of American Folklore* 62, No. 245:67–106.
———. 1949–50. "Dance, folk and primitive" and other entries, in *Dictionary of Folklore, Mythology and Legend* (ed. MARIA LEACH), pp. 276–96, *passim.* 2 vols. New York: Funk and Wagnalls.
———. 1951. Local diversity in Iroquois dance and music. Bureau of American Ethnology Bulletin 149, Pt. 6:109–37.
———. 1952. "Dance acculturation," in *Heritage of Conquest* (ed. SOL TAX), pp. 233–42. Glencoe, Ill.: Free Press.
———. 1953. Native choreographic areas of North America. *American Anthropologist,* n.s., 55:153–62.
———. 1954. The Tutelo harvest rite. *Scientific Monthly* 76, No. 3:87–105.
———. 1956a. Dance relatives of mid-Europe and middle America. *Journal of American Folklore* 69, No. 273:286–92.
———. 1956b. Antiphonal songs of Eastern Woodland Indians. *Musical Quarterly* 42:520–26.
———. 1957a. *Algonquian ceremonialism and natural resources of the Great Lakes.* Reprint 22. Bangalore: Indian Institute of Culture.
———. 1957b. Basic techniques of Amerindian dance. *Dance Notation Record* 8, No. 4:2–8.
———. 1957c. Notation of a Pueblo Indian

corn dance. *Dance Notation Record* 8, No. 4:9–11.
———. 1958a. Plaza circuits of Tewa Indian dancers. *El Palacio* 65, No. 1–2:11–26.
———. 1958b. Game animal dances of the Rio Grande. *Southwestern Journal of Anthropology* 14:438–48.
———. 1959. Menomini Indian dance songs in a changing culture. *Midwest Folklore* 9, No. 1:31–38.
———. MSa. Seneca song and dance style. 1951. American Philosophical Society Library. (Dance notation.)
———. MSb. Onondaga ritualism. 1952. New York State Museum Educational Library. (Dance notation.)
———. MSc. Tutelo dances and songs. 1953. (Dance notation.)
———. MSd. Animal rites, dances and songs of Eastern Woodland Indians. 1955. (Dance notation.)
———. MSe. Tewa Indian dance and music. 1957–58. (Dance notation; film and tape.)
KURATH, GERTRUDE P., and NADIA CHILKOVSKY. 1960. Jazz choreology. *Proceedings of the Fifth International Congress of Anthropological and Ethnological Sciences* (ed. ANTHONY WALLACE). Philadelphia: University of Pennsylvania Press.
KURATH, GERTRUDE P. and JANE W. ETTAWAGESHIK. MS. Religious customs of modern Michigan Algonquians. 1955. American Philosophical Society Library. (Dance notation.)
LABAN, JUANA DE. 1954. Movement notation: its significance to the folklorist. *Journal of American Folklore* 67, No. 265:291–95.
———. MS. Notes on Hungarian dances. (Labanotation).
LABAN, RUDOLF. 1928. *Kinetographie.* 2 vols. Vienna.
LABAN, RUDOLF, and F. C. LAWRENCE. 1947. *Effort.* London: MacDonald and Evans.
LAMBERT, OMER. n.d. *Danses Canadiennes.* Quebec: Imprimerie Nacionale.
LA MERI. 1948. *Spanish dancing.* New York: A. S. Barnes.
LANGE, CHARLES H. 1953. Economics in Cochiti culture change. *American Anthropologist* 55:174–94.
———. 1957. The Tablita, or corn dance of the Rio Grande Pueblo Indians. *Texas Journal of Science* 9, No. 1:59–74.
———. MS. The Pueblo of Cochiti, New Mexico: past and present. Austin: University of Texas Press. In press. (Chapters on ceremonialism, with dance and music analysis by G. KURATH.)
LAPSON, DVORA. 1954. *Dances of the Jewish people.* New York: Jewish Education Committee of New York.
LATTIMORE, ALICE. 1957. Kalamatianos. *Dance Notation Record* 8, No. 1:8.
LAWSON, JOAN. 1953. *European folk dances.* Toronto and London: Pitman.
LAWTON, SHAILER U. MS. Physiological determinants in movement, in The Function of Dance in Human Society (Second Seminar) (ed. FRANZISKA BOAS). New York, 1946.
LEKIS, LISA. 1956. Origin and development of ethnic Caribbean dance and music. Unpublished Ph.D. dissertation, University of Florida, Gainesville, Fla.
———. 1958. *Folk dances of Latin America.* New York: Scarecrow Press.
———. MS. Notes on Peruvian and Ecuadorian dances.
LORING, EUGENE, and A. J. CANNA. 1956. *Kinetography.* Los Angeles: Author.
LUGOSSY, EMMA, and SANDOR GONYEY. 1947. *Magyar Nepi Tancok.* Budapest.

MANN, JOHN. MS. Teaching and research in ethnic dance. *Ethnomusicology.* In press.
MANSFIELD, PORTIA. 1952. The Conchero dancers of Mexico. Unpublished Ph.D. dissertation, New York University, New York, N.Y. (Music by RAOUL GUERRERO.)
MARIÁN, RETHEI PRIKKEL. 1924. A Magyasag Tancai. 311 pp. Budapest.☆
MARTI, SAMUEL. 1959. *Danza precortesiana.* Sobretiro de Cuadernos Americanos, No. 5 de 1959.
———. MS. *Canto, música y danza precortesiana.* México; D.F.: Fondo de Cultura Económico and Instituto Nacional de Antropología e Historia. In press.
MASON, BERNARD S. 1944. *Dances and stories of the American Indian.* New York: A. S. Barnes.
MAYO, MARGOT. 1948. *The American square dance.* New York: Sentinel Books.
MATIDA KASYO. 1938. *Odori (Japanese dance).* Tokyo: Board of Tourist Industry, Japanese Government Railways.
McALLESTER, DAVID P. MS. Comanche sign language. Paper in Ethnomusicology, at Columbia University, 1941.
MEAD, MARGARET. 1949. *Coming of age in Samoa.* New York: Mentor Books. First published in 1928.
———. MS. "Dance as an expression of culture patterns," in The Function of Dance in Human Society (Second Seminar) (ed. FRANZISKA BOAS), New York, 1946.
MOERDOWO, R. 1957. Dances in Indonesia. *Folklorist* 4:63–66.
MOISEYEV, IGOR. 1951. *Tänze der Völker der Sowietunion.* Berlin.
———. 1952. *Orosz Heptsancszvit.* Budapest.
MOONEY, GERTRUDE X. 1957. *Mexican folk dances for American schools.* Coral Gables, Fla.: University of Miami Press.
MÜLLENHOFF, K. 1871 (and later supplements). *Über den Schwerttanz.* Berlin.☆
MURDOCK, GEORGE P., et. al. 1954. *Guia para la clasificación de los datos culturales.* New Haven and Washington, D.C.: Pan-American Union.
NIELSEN, H. G. 1917. *Vore äldste Folkedanse.* 71 pp. text, 24 pp. music.☆
———. 1920. *Folkelig Vals.* 83 pp. text, 47 pp. music. Kopenhagen.☆
OKUNEVA, B. B. 1951. *Russkie Narodnye Chora i Tantsy.* Sophia.
ONEGINA, T. D. 1958. *Moldavsky Tanets.* Moscow.
POLLENZ, PHILIPPA. 1946. Some problems in the notation of Seneca dances. Unpublished M.A. thesis, Columbia University, New York. (Labanotation.)
———. 1949. Methods for the comparative study of the dance. *American Anthropologist,* n.s., 56:428–35.
PROCA, VERA. 1956. Despre notarea dansului popular rominesc. *Revista de Folclor* 2, No. 1–2:135–71. Bucharest.
———. 1957. Despre notarea dansului popular rominesc. *Revista de Folclor* 2, No. 1–2:65–92.
PROKOSCH, GERTRUDE. 1938. Rhythms of work and play. *Journal of Health and Physical Education* 9:294–97.
PURDON, M. E. 1958. Ukrainian Cossack Company. *Folklorist* 4, No. 6:158–62.
RHODES, WILLARD. 1956. On the subject of musicology. *Ethnomusicology Newsletter* 7:1–9.
ROGERS, HELEN P. 1958. A complete record for the dance. *Dance Notation Record* 9, No. 1:5–6.
SACHS, CURT. 1933. *Eine Weltgeschichte des*

Tanzes. Berlin: Reimer. (Huge bibliography.)

——. 1953. ·*Rhythm and tempo*. New York: Norton.

SALZ, BEATE. 1955. *The human element in industrialization*. Memoir, American Anthropological Association, No. 85.

SANTA ANA, HIGINIO VASQUEZ. 1940. *Fiestas y costumbres Méxicanas*. México, D.F.: Ediciones Botas.

SCHMITZ, CARL A. 1955. *Balam: Der Tanz- und Kultplatz in Melanesien*. Emsdetten, Westphalia: Lechte Verlag.

SCHUSKY, ERNEST. 1957. Pan-Indianism in the eastern United States. *Anthropology Tomorrow* 6:116–23. Chicago: University of Chicago Anthropology Club.

SEDILLO-B., MELA. 1935. *Mexican and New Mexican folk dances*. Albuquerque: University of New Mexico Press.

SHAWN, TED. 1929. *Gods who dance*. New York: Dutton. (Valuable bibliography.)

SHOMER, LOUIS. 1943. *Swing steps*. New York: Padell Book Co.

SINGER, MILTON B. 1958. The great tradition in a metropolitan center: Madras. *Journal of American Folklore* 71, No. 281:347–88.

SLOTKIN, J. S. 1955. An intertribal dancing contest. *Journal of American Folklore* 78, No. 268:224–28.

——. 1957. *The Menomini powwow*. Milwaukee Public Museum Publications in Anthropology No. 4.

SOLARI, MARIA LUISA. 1958. Notación de la danza. *Revista Musical Chilena* 12, No. 58:42–58.

SPECK, FRANK' G. 1949. *Midwinter rites of the Cayuga longhouse*. Philadelphia: University of Pennsylvania Press.

SPECK, FRANK G. and LEONARD BROOM. 1951. *Cherokee dance and drama*. Berkeley and Los Angeles: University of California Press.

SPENCE, LEWIS. 1947. *Myth and ritual in dance, game and rhyme*. London: Watts.

SPREEN, HILDEGARD L. 1949. *Folk-dances of South India*. New York: Oxford University Press.

STURTEVANT, WILLIAM C. 1954. The medicine bundle and busks of the Florida Seminole. *Florida Anthropologist* 7, No. 2:31–70. (Bibliography.)

Tantsi Narodov SSSR. ("Folk Dances of the USSR.") 1955. Moscow: Iskusstvo.

TAX, SOL. 1952. "Economy and technology," in *Heritage of Conquest* (ed. SOL TAX), pp. 43–75. Glencoe, Ill.: Free Press.

THOMPSON, STITH (Ed.). 1953. *Four symposia on folklore*. Bloomington: Indiana University Press.

THUREN, HJALMAR. 1908. *Folkesangen paa Färöerne*. Folklore Fellows Publications, Northern Series 2. 337 pp. Kopenhagen. (Over 100 songs.)☆

THURSTON, HUGH A. 1954a. *Scotland's dances*. London: G. Bell.

——. 1954b. What is a folk dance? *Folk Dancer* 1, No. 1:4–6.

TITIEV, MISCHA. 1955. *The science of man*. New York.

TOLMAN, BETH, and RALPH PAGE. 1937. *The country dance book*. New York: A. S. Barnes.

TOMKINS, WILLIAM. 1929. *Universal Indian sign language*. San Diego, Calif.: Author.

TSOUKALAS, NICHOLAS. 1956. *Spanish dancing: zapateado movements*. Detroit: Author.

TULA. 1952. Therapeutic dance rhythms. *Dance Observer* 19, No. 10:117–18.

TURLEY, FRANK. MS. The present-day Oklahoma fancy war dance. 1959.

VEGA, CARLOS. 1952. *Las danzas populares argentinas, Vol. 1*. Buenos Aires: Ministerio de Educación de la Nación. (Comprehensive bibliography.)

VENABLE, LUCY, and FRED BERK. 1959. *Ten folk dances in labanotation*. New York: Witmark.

VISKI, KÁROLY. 1937. *Hungarian dances*. 193 pp. text, 34 pls. London and Budapest.☆

VYCPALEK, JOSEF. MS. *Ceske Tance*. Czechoslovakia. In press.☆

WELTFISH, GENE. MS. "Patterns of work in primitive industry," in The Function of Dance in Human Society (Second Seminar) (ed. FRANZISKA BOAS), New York, 1946.

WILDER, STAFFORD. 1940. The Yaqui deer dance. Unpublished M.A. thesis, University of Arizona, Tucson, Ariz. (Diagrams.)

WILLIAMS, RALPH VAUGHAN. 1958. The English folk dance and song society. *Ethnomusicology* 2, No. 3:108–12.

WISSLER, CLARK. 1916. General discussion of shamanistic and dancing societies. *Anthropological Papers of the American Museum of Natural History*, Vol. 2, Pt. 12.

WOLFRAM, RICHARD. 1931. Volkstanz—nur gesunkenes Kulturgut? *Zeitschrift für Volkskunde*. Berlin.☆

——. 1933. Die Frühform des Ländlers. *Zeitschrift für Volkskunde*. Berlin.☆

——. 1934. Altersklassen und Männerbünde in Rumanien. *Mitteilungen der Anthropologische Gesellschaft in Wien* 64:112–28.

——. 1937. Deutsche Volkstänze. *Bilder der deutschen Volkskunde* (ed. A. SPAMER), Vol. 5. 49 pp. text, 44 pls. Leipzig, Germany.☆

——. 1951. *Die Volkstänze in Österreich und verwandte Tänze in Europa*. Salzburg: Müller. (Large bibliography.)

——. 1954. *Der Schwerttanz. Helleiner Heimatbuch*. (Series Heimat Osterreich.) Graz, Drechsler.

——. 1956. European song-dance forms. *Journal of the International Folk Music Council* 8:32–35.

——. MS. Schwerttanze Europas. 800 pp. Three fascicles appeared Bärenreiterverlag, Kassel. (Diagrams of 30 dances.)

ZHORNITZKAYA, M. YA. 1956. *Yakutskie Tantsy*. Yakutsk, Siberia.

ZODER, RAIMUND. 1938. Der Deutsche Volkstanz. *Deutsches Volkstum* 3:137–84. Berlin.

——. 1950. *Volkslied, volkstanz und volksbrauch in Osterreich*. Wien: Doblinger.

Projects

CASTNER, RICHARD L. A history of traditional American country dancing, to 1800.

CHILKOVSKY, NADIA. Observation and notation of national traits in effort behavior. (Laban Effort symbols.)

CHILKOVSKY, NADIA, and Students of Philadelphia Musical Academy and Philadelphia Dance Academy. Notes on regional jazz dances. (Labanotation.)

DELZA, SOPHIA. Notes on Chinese dances. (Labanotation.)

GARCIA, JOSEFINA. Labanotation of Latin American dances.

HOERBURGER, FELIX. Bibliography and critical inventory of folk dance publications in Europe.

HOLM, WILLIAM. Reconstruction of Kwakiutl dances.

KURATH, GERTRUDE P., and Dance Research Center Associates. Ritual Drama of the American Indian. (For *Dance Perspectives*.)

LATTIMORE, ALICE. Notes on mudras of India, on Balkan, Slavic, Greek and other folk dances. (Labanotation.)

LAUBIN, REGINALD, and GLADYS LAUBIN.

A historical study of American Indian dances.

MARTI, SAMUEL, and G. KURATH. Manual of dance analysis. (For SAMUEL MARTI MS.)

THURSTON, HUGH A. Dictionary of folk dance terms.

WEST, LA MONT. American Indian sign language. Indiana University thesis.

Non-Commercial Films

BOAS, FRANZ. Kwakiutl dances. University of Washington.

CHILKOVSKY, NADIA and LEAH DILLON. Complete vocabulary of Hindu mudras. Philadelphia Dance Academy.

DEAN, GETH, and VICTOR CARELL. Australian dances.

DEHN, MURA. History of Jazz Dance.

ENGLISH FOLK DANCE AND SONG SOCIETY. English dances. Cecil Sharp House.

FIRST, GEORGIA. Dances of Fox Indians. (Also slides.)

GERSON-KIWI, EDITH. Wedding ceremonies and dances of Kurdistan Jews.

IRISH FOLKLORE COMMISSION. Mummers and other Irish dances.

KAPLAN, SHIRLEY WIMMER. Folk dances of India.

(a) Twenty-one dances during Republic Day Celebration, New Delhi, Jan. 1957. Partial notation of nine dances, from Assam, Himachal Pradesh, Kashmir, Kerala, Orissa, Uttar Pradesh. (600 ft. color; taped music expected from Sangeet Natak Akadami.)

(b) Kandyan dance in Ceylon. (300 ft.; tape of drum and voice.)

(c) Girls' dance from Ellora. (100 ft.; no tape.)

KURATH, GERTRUDE P. Edited tapes and slide series at Dance Research Center, *inter alia*:

(a) Michigan Indian dances. (150 ft.: tapes.)

(b) Menomini dances. (100 ft.; tape.)

(c) Santa Clara plaza dances. (150 ft.; tape.) Copy at Wenner-Gren Foundation.

(d) Jazz dances of White and Negro teenagers of Ann Arbor. (100 ft.)

MANSFIELD, PORTIA. Edited films. Copies, Perry-Mansfield School of Theater.

(a) The Conchero dancers of Mexico. Sound, music arr. by RAOUL GUERRERO. (Two reels: Background [10 min.], Ceremonies [18 min.])

(b) Cowboy squares. (12 min.)

(c) Southwest Indian dances (Tewa Pueblos, Acoma, Cochiti, Taos). (12 min.)

(d) Nepalese dances. (Not edited.)

MERRIAM, ALAN P. Ekonda, Africa. (Edited.)

NICHOLLS, THAD. Yaqui Easter fiesta, Pascua, Arizona. (Edited.)

PETER, ILKA, and HERBERT LAGER. Austrian "Trestern."

PINKERSON, FRANCES. Ceremonial dances of Mexico (Volador, Moros y Cristianos, Apaches, Pastorcitas, etc.). (400 ft.; edited.)

POSPISIL, F. German Sword Dances.

RAYE, ZELIA. Hawaiian dances. 40 King's Road, London.

SHAWN, TED [3]☆ Dances of India, Java, Ceylon, Darjeeling, Tibet, Japan (1925–26), Australian Corroboree (1947), Bali. Philippine Moros, Oklahoma Indians, and others. List, Jacob's Pillow University of the Dance, Lee, Mass.

STREHLOW, THEODOR G. H. Aranda and Loritja totemistic ceremonies, Australia.

TURNER, ALONSO. West African journey.

WOLFRAM, R. Norwegian "Springar" (1939).

92

The Contribution of Ethnomusicology to Historical Musicology
Der Beitrag der musikalischen Volks= und Völkerkunde zur historischen Musikforschung
Contribution de l'ethnomusicologie à l'histoire de la musique

Chairman: Paul Collaer, Brussels
1st Paper: André Schaeffner, Paris

IL SERAIT vain de vouloir réveiller d'anciennes querelles. Mais peut-on vraiment parler d'une «contribution» de l'ethnomusicologie à l'histoire de la musique? On rappellera d'abord que le terme d'ethnomusicologie est récent et n'a fait que se substituer à celui de musicologie comparée (vergleichende Musikwissenschaft) désignant, dans les pays de langue germanique, une discipline vieille d'au moins un demi-siècle et qui a produit de nombreux travaux. D'aucun les historiens ne paraissent avoir tiré profit.

Pour ne citer qu'un exemple, la communication d'Erich von Hornbostel sur la polyphonie extra-européenne date de 1909; elle fut lue au cours d'un congrès international de musicologie qui passa d'autant moins inaperçu qu'il se tint à Vienne lors des fêtes célébrant le centenaire de la mort de Haydn. Depuis, des publications se sont multipliées, des disques même ont été édités, attestant un emploi délibéré de la polyphonie chez un grand nombre de peuples, à des niveaux différents de culture. N'utilisant que les phonogrammes conservés à la phonothèque de Berlin, M. Marius Schneider présentait en 1934, dans le premier volume de sa Geschichte der Mehrstimmigkeit, près de 200 notations offrant des exemples indiscutables de polyphonie vocale à 2 ou 3 voix, en Océanie comme en Afrique noire. On n'en a pas moins continué de nier l'existence d'une véritable polyphonie soit hors de l'Europe soit, en Europe, avant le Moyen âge ou en dehors de la musique dite savante. Les arguments sont demeurés les mêmes: en l'absence de toute écriture une polyphonie ne peut être que le produit du hasard ou, mettrait-on celui-ci hors de cause, ne mérite de toutes façons le nom de polyphonie. A vouloir ainsi réserver ce terme à des procédés contrapunctiques très spéciaux, ne voit-on pas que même en Occident ils ont été employés par un nombre relativement restreint de compositeurs? Autant considérer comme exceptionnel l'usage de la polyphonie dans notre propre musique, et accorder à Verdi ou à Offenbach une place qui serait refusée à Debussy. Ce dernier, il est vrai, s'était condamné lui-même en prétendant qu'une musique de tradition orale comme le gamelan javanais «observe un contrepoint auprès duquel celui de Palestrina n'est qu'un jeu d'enfant». En fait de jeu, Debussy savait qu'il jouait ici sur les mots — mais pas plus que les historiens sur celui de polyphonie.

Qu'attendre de l'histoire si ceux mêmes qui la pratiquent ne se libèrent d'une conception de la musique qu'ils tiennent de leur éducation première? C'est elle qui cause le plus d'erreurs de jugement, et il ne semble pas qu'un domaine ou qu'une méthode de recherche plus que d'autres en garantissent l'historien. Outre qu'elle raccourcit l'horizon, elle prédispose à ériger en règles générales ce qui n'a jamais été que conventions du moment ou appuis passagers. Tant de libertés prises à toute époque montrent que rien n'est absolument fixe en notre propre musique, sous quel angle que nous l'envisagions. Déjà sa notation, qui lui semble pourtant essentielle, est remise sans cesse en question, la précision qu'elle apporte étant relative. La part de tradition orale dans l'exécution de nos œuvres, même modernes, reste considérable. Ce qu'on entend d'ordinaire par «fidélité» d'interprétation ne résiste pas à l'examen. Rien que ce fait devrait vaincre certaines préventions contre des musiques sans écriture, et qui ne sont pas pour autant improvisées.

Au moins en matière de *tempo*, la plupart de ces musiques observent une rigueur dont nos exécutions sont fort éloignées. Des raisons purement rituelles peuvent toujours s'opposer à une variation quelconque des formules rythmiques ou mélodiques, encore plus si ces formules sont calquées sur le langage parlé ou répondent à un mode de communication, à une séméiographie sonore. Les ornements, s'il s'en trouve, sont stéréotypés et ont généralement leur place déterminée. De toutes façons le matériel ou vocabulaire dont on dispose est peu étendu; la marge de variation est nécessairement limitée. Enfin, il faut considérer la situation du musicien dans des civilisations différentes de la nôtre. L'assujétissement à des règles est d'autant plus grand que le lien entre le musicien et la société est plus étroit et que cette société même est plus intéressée au parfait accomplissement des rites — autant dire: qu'elle vit en économie plus fermée. Toutes raisons techniques, psychologiques ou sociologiques pour que se produise ou se tolère un minimum d'écarts.

Qu'on ait trouvé trace de notations musicales, ou prétendues telles, dans de hautes civilisations de l'Antiquité ou de l'Orient, a plutôt contribué à égarer les esprits. A l'exception de l'écriture tibétaine (la seule qui n'ait pas été étudiée, alors que son existence en une région aussi reculée et son tracé lié et curviligne posent maints problèmes), les fragments de notation découverts jusqu'ici font douter qu'elle ait servi effectivement à la pratique musicale. Autant prendre des pierres tombales ou des ex-voto pour un cabinet de lecture. Si l'emploi d'une chironomie paraît certain, au moins en ancienne Egypte et quelle que soit la nature de ses indications, on peut s'étonner que les artistes de l'Antiquité, qui ont reproduit avec tant de minutie des scènes de musique ou de danse, aient figuré rarement, et de façon si peu évidente, des musiciens lisant un texte. Trouverait-on d'ailleurs des pièces plus probantes qu'on devrait quand même se demander à quel usage une notation était réservée et quelle classe d'individus était capable de la déchiffrer (au sens propre du terme). Ici intervient la notion de « musique savante ».

La rareté des notations, leur imprécision ou leur déchiffrement difficile, leur apparition toujours tardive, sinon leur absence dans de grandes civilisations à écriture, eussent dû faire réfléchir les historiens et les amener à voir en elles soit un instrument inventé pour les besoins de la théorie et de la spéculation (ce qui est probablement le cas dans l'ancienne Grèce), soit un code ou aide-mémoire qu'un accroissement du répertoire liturgique et une profusion non moins croissante de variantes avaient rendu nécessaire, mais que pouvait utiliser seulement un petit nombre d'initiés. Qu'elle soit destinée à l'usage philosophique ou culturel, toute notation se ressent de la nature de son objet. On ne doit espérer en déduire les caractères d'une musique qui, ni savante ni religieuse, au moins autant instrumentale que vocale, était la plus répandue dans une société où philosophes, théoriciens et chantres constituaient une minorité et qui avait ses métiers, ses réjouissances profanes, ses célébrations civiques.

Une remarque du même ordre peut être faite à propos des musicographes anciens dont les écrits, loin de renseigner sur une pratique musicale connue alors de chacun, s'attachaient plutôt à des cas singuliers, curieux et même imaginaires. Les spéculations sur les intervalles et les échelles proviennent moins d'un milieu de musiciens praticiens que d'un cercle d'esprits géomètres et quelque peu sophistes. Il ne s'agit nullement de rejeter les écrits des théoriciens grecs, mais de les consulter avec prudence, sachant leur objet, leur rapport lointain avec une réalité musicale qui, de ce fait, nous échappe presque entièrement. Comme nous échappe une musique du Moyen âge dont la notation est particulièrement tardive, marquée par le caractère spécial du répertoire auquel elle fut adaptée, et de toutes façons lacunaire.

Tant d'incertitudes et d'obscurités devraient inciter à moins de méfiance à l'égard de musiques de tradition entièrement orale, mais dont la variabilité a des limites et qui offrent l'inestimable qualité d'être vivantes. Qu'on puisse les enregistrer et en même temps interroger les hommes qui les exécutent, observer le comportement de sociétés entières vis-à-vis de celles-ci, constitue un avantage inappréciable. Il n'y a pas lieu d'insister sur ce point.

On marquera plutôt que le travail de l'ethnologue n'est pas tellement différent de celui de l'historien. Une société n'est jamais sans passé, pas plus qu'elle ne se présente devant l'observateur comme une masse uniforme. Sans parler d'instruments de musique dont l'usage s'est à peu près perdu mais dont on retrouve des exemplaires sur le lieu même, ni de chants anciens dont de vieux témoins nous parlent et se rappellent les paroles à défaut de la mélodie, il se rencontre des individus que leur âge ou leur dignité ont fait les spécialistes d'un certain répertoire, moins appelé à s'altérer, des sectes aussi ou des rituels à plus ou moins longue périodicité, ayant leur musique propre, vraisemblablement ancienne ou d'origine étrangère. Des différences de style apparaissent et dont on peut, grâce aux témoignages des indigènes ou par comparaison avec des musiques avoisinantes, découvrir la cause. Toute enquête sur le terrain ne saurait d'ailleurs être exclusivement musicologique : elle implique une connaissance profonde des institutions locales. Ce sont elles qui déterminent, mieux que les caractères intrinsèques de la musique, la stratification de celle-ci.

D'autre part, voici plus d'un demi-siècle qu'on se livre à des enregistrements. Dans le nombre des phonogrammes conservés peuvent se trouver des pièces se rapportant à des régions où l'on est revenu depuis, sinon aux confins desquelles l'on a enquêté de façon plus exhaustive. Ainsi en est-il pour plusieurs tribus de Pygmées au centre de l'Afrique, dont les chants ont été enregistrés à plusieurs reprises au cours des cinquante dernières années. Ainsi en est-il encore pour le théâtre chinois, javanais ou balinais, et vraisemblablement pour divers chants de l'Inde.

A défaut de remonter plus haut dans le passé, l'ethnomusicologue a devant lui un espace largement ouvert. Encore qu'il reste bien des points du globe où aucun enregistrement n'a été effectué, le champ des connaissances s'est considérablement accru. Les découvertes se sont multipliées. De deux sortes : existence de procédés (surtout vocaux) encore inouïs ; traits communs à des musiques dont il paraît impossible que les possesseurs soient jamais entrés en contact, vu la distance qui les sépare. A vrai dire la distance n'est pas un argument absolu, pas plus qu'inversement la proximité n'en constitue un autre. Le musicologue a trop d'occasions de constater que des populations voisines tantôt se font des emprunts tantôt s'y refusent totalement : ici c'est l'ethnologue ou le sociologue qui donne la raison d'un comportement si différent. En matière de distance l'historien des civilisations ou le comparatiste sont seuls juges. Dans des cas de convergence le psychologue aura le dernier mot. De toutes façons la solution échappe au musicologue.

Il n'en reste pas moins que tant de façons si peu naturelles de chanter (ou qui nous paraissent telles), tant de timbres étranges produits par les instruments caractérisent la musique primitive. Quelle que soit leur imagination, les hommes durent souvent recourir aux mêmes procédés. Ni l'organe vocal ni les matériaux avec lesquels le primitif fabrique ses instruments ne permettent de dépasser certaines limites, que sans doute aujourd'hui nous sommes prêts de connaître. Un inventaire de tous ces procédés reste à faire, une terminologie à établir. Peut-être marquera-t-on des distinctions qu'on n'avait pas encore envisagées. Alors seulement décidera-t-on si la multiplication d'un même phénomène relève de la diffusion ou de la convergence.

L'organologie primitive peut apporter beaucoup à l'histoire et à l'acoustique de nos instruments. Leurs formes si complexes, baroques, que les physiciens expliquent rarement et qui ont subsisté malgré l'évolution du goût musical, ont une origine lointaine. La facture même moderne ne s'est jamais entièrement dégagée des formes qu'avaient imposées les premiers matériaux utilisés (coques de fruits, etc.), un désir de représentation plastique si vif chez le primitif et qui s'accorde avec ses conceptions religieuses, enfin la recherche d'un timbre artificiel et très surprenant. On peut se demander jusqu'à quel degré notre art vocal lui-même n'a pas pendant longtemps, au moins jusqu'à la Renaissance, été tributaire des modes étrangers d'émission qui sont encore courants si près de l'Europe, et même dans certaines de nos campagnes. Point que toute écriture musicale est incapable de révéler.

D'autres questions controversées auraient trouvé une solution si les purs historiens avaient eu également recours à la méthode comparative. Par exemple, les *hauts* et *bas* instruments. Chaque société, même primitive, a ses « hauts » et ses « bas » instruments, répartis entre des individus de classes, de castes et même de sexes différents, ou se faisant entendre dans des répertoires entièrement distincts (service du culte, exercice du pouvoir, musique profane, publique ou privée). Mais sont venues des explications *a posteriori*. Il est normal que des règles se perpétuent alors qu'on ne sait plus pourquoi elles avaient été instituées. A partir d'une certaine époque, en quelques régions de l'Europe occidentale, on a pensé que hauts et bas instruments se distinguaient selon la force ou la douceur de leurs sonorités; or le partage avait été établi au préalable d'après d'autres critères, uniquement d'ordre sociologique, et que l'on retrouve à peu près partout, dans des civilisations supérieures comme inférieures.

C'est pourtant en un pareil domaine touchant à la sociologie qu'historiens et ethnologues pouvaient s'entendre; encore eussent-ils dû confronter les résultats de leurs recherches particulières. Les uns et les autres ont étudié d'assez près:

la situation sociale du musicien (qu'il soit créateur ou interprète);

les circonstances et les conditions matérielles de l'exécution musicale;

le genre de public auquel celle-ci s'adresse;

enfin, les moyens par lesquels une musique se répand hors de son lieu d'origine.

En ces matières les observations ont abondé de part et d'autre. On connaît mieux qu'auparavant le statut du musicien dans différentes civilisations ou à diverses époques, la répartition des instruments entre les classes d'une même société, la composition variable des orchestres (à la cour, à l'église, dans les fêtes). Enfin les exemples se sont multipliés d'échanges de musiques, soit grâce aux migrations ou au tournées de musiciens, soit par la voie, aujourd'hui, de l'imprimé, de la radio, du disque.

Mais le principal apport de l'ethnomusicologie est de mettre en doute que l'évolution de notre propre musique se soit réellement faite comme l'historien le décrit sur la foi des théoriciens ou à l'appui uniquement des documents notés. Outre que l'écart entre des principes énoncés et la pratique peut toujours être considérable (c'est ce que constate l'ethnologue sur le terrain), bien des phénomènes n'ont pas été mentionnés, soit parce qu'ils apparaissaient dans l'usage seulement populaire soit, au contraire, qu'ils étaient tellement courants qu'on ne les apercevait plus. Ainsi en est-il d'une polyphonie qui se pratiquait d'instinct et dont on ne trouve trace que lorsqu'elle est passée dans la musique religieuse. Ainsi en est-il des échelles musicales qui n'ont jamais réalisé la somme totale des sons produits; tout au plus peuvent-elles indiquer que certains d'entre eux sont privilégiés et sont relativement stables, tandis que la hauteur des autres est sujette à variations. Encore faudrait-il comparer la fréquence des premiers à celle des seconds.

ETHNOMUSICOLOGY, THE FIELD AND THE SOCIETY[1]

David P. McAllester

The roots of the Society for Ethnomusicology in the work of Stumpf, Ellis, Hornbostel and others and in the Zeitschrift für Vergleichende Musikwissenschaft have been delineated ably and in detail in earlier issues of ETHNOMUSICOLOGY and elsewhere (Seeger 1956; Rhodes 1956; Kolinski 1957; Nettl 1956: 26-44).

My pleasant task is to recount the developments that have taken place in our Society, and in the field of ethnomusicology in the United States, since 1953. The description of events at such close range cannot be termed history but should be considered as an interpretation, or what one person thinks has been happening. I hope the thoughts set down here will elicit from other interested persons the corrections and amplifications that will help round out the picture.

This particular decade has been more eventful for ethnomusicology than has all the history of our field before the founding of the Society in 1953. The formation of the Society was only one indication of the ground swell of a very large international movement with many manifestations indeed. Musically this ten-year era is very much akin to the Age of Discovery with Prince Henrys suddenly appearing on the horizons of a dozen new continents at once.

If any gauge is needed for the strength of the work it can be seen with sociological perspective in the rise of institutions. Where once was an archive in Berlin and two or three beginnings in the United States, are now innumerable sophisticated collections both special and general. Where once was a single perishing publication are now at least a dozen journals of all sorts, national and international, including one devoted to archiving. Most of them represent organizations or societies and this means regular meetings of scholars. Very importantly, where once were wax cylinders is now magnatic tape, affording a convenience and fidelity undreamed of a few years ago. In addition to all this there is the popular enthusiasm for folk music which is beginning to extend to world music. In ways perhaps too subtle to assess this awakening of general interest means support for the scholar.

A recent survey lists thirty educational institutions in the United States offering anywhere from one course, in or related to ethnomusicology, to as many as fourteen (Winkelman 1963). In addition there are institutions and have been special meetings that are hard to classify, such as the Institute for Ethnomusicology at UCLA and the Symposium on Ethnomusicological Field Method at the University of Washington held in March 1963. Large scale projects involving a number of researchers focussed on a single problem are another new manifestation in the field.

I shall discuss certain of these indications of the impressive vitality of ethnomusicology in my effort to describe what I think are major trends in our field and in our Society. Since the borderline between suggesting trends and coming right out and making predictions is a fine one, I shall not hesitate to assume a prophetic mien.

182

The emphasis in our work alternates between studying music to find out more about culture and vice versa. Which it is, of course, is simply a function of the interest and background of the particular investigator. The marriage between music and the social sciences is celebrated anew with each issue of our journal. It is a sometimes uneasy union but it is evident that since each partner has so much to learn from the other, neither can afford a divorce.

Most of the Jobs Are in Music

It is interesting that at the beginning of our decade the academic jobs in ethnomusicology seemed to be in a few anthropology departments and that now they are much more plentiful and seem to be largely in music departments. It is in the latter that ethnomusicology majors are beginning to appear. The plain fact is that music departments are beginning to shake themselves awake to the fact that music, real music, is a world phenomenon. There are more and larger music departments than there are anthropology and sociology departments in American universities. It is to be expected therefore that greater academic muscle will be brought into play by musicians than by social scientists. More degrees in ethnomusicology will go to Calliope than to Caliban.

This may be seen at UCLA where the largest graduate program in the field is to be found (Hood 1957). The extent of the training offered at Los Angeles does not appear in the Winkelman survey. This is especially true with regard to the many "study groups" in the theory and performance of different musics such as Mexican mariachi, Javanese gamelan, African drumming, and Chinese orchestra. The excellent argument is made that the actual performance of an exotic music is essential to the full understanding of its structure and purpose. A strong aspect of the UCLA program is the presence of native musicians from the many cultures represented. Equally important is the practice of sending the advanced student to the country whose music he is studying for one or two years of research and apprenticeship. When he returns such a student is likely to be in a position to write the first definitive book in English on the music of his area of study (Malm 1959) and typically carries the study group idea with him as he begins his teaching career: Robert E. Brown, South India, Wesleyan University; Robert Garfias, Japan, University of Washington; William P. Malm, Japan, University of Michigan.

The anthropology in the UCLA program is "home grown." The students who undergo a musical apprenticeship overseas in India, Africa, etc. develop what anthropological perspective they may from the necessities of first hand experience. This method has its disadvantages but at present the program at Los Angeles is moving towards intensive musical analysis in terms of computer theory and melograph techniques rather than a deepening exploration of the insights of the social sciences.

More Money in Connection with Anthropology

To look at the other side of our equation, the group research projects are finding their impetus in anthropology. For better or worse, the sciences at present are receiving greater support from national foundations than are the arts. Two current programs rising out of anthropology may be cited to illustrate this trend. Alan Lomax is investigating a system of musical

analysis which involves linguistic, psychological, physiological and social
factors as well as musical ones. The National Institute of Mental Health is
supporting this two year study which involves Victor Grauer and Conrad
Arensberg and has benefited from the advice of Margaret Mead, Edith Trager
and others. The publications of the project have appeared in anthropological
journals (Lomax 1959, 1962). It is significant that the scope of the project
permits secretarial help—a commonplace in the sciences but an unheard-of
luxury in ethnomusicological research. Wesleyan University has received a
grant from the National Science Foundation for a three-year study of Navaho
ceremonialism. Here again the emphasis is to be on the interrelatedness of
various aspects of culture. The study is linguistic and sociological as well
as musicological. Charlotte Johnson, Kätchen Coley, and Gerry Johnson, all
graduate students, are assisting in the project and here again secretarial
help is available.

     Due to the availability of large funds "task force" projects are on the
increase in anthropology. The Columbia University project in culture and
linguistics under George Herzog included the study of Comanche music
(McAllester 1949) and the Harvard University studies in comparative values
included ethnomusicology as an avenue to the understanding of deep-seated
attitudes (McAllester 1954). Nicholas England's studies of Bushman music in
the Kalahari Desert have been in cooperation with an extensive joint project,
the Marshall-Peabody Museum Expeditions, involving many people, mostly
anthropologists.

More Success in Interrelating the Two Disciplines

     How well music and social science may be blended in a single institu-
tion is more likely to be a matter of atmosphere and personalities than of
disciplinary ideologies. The University of Hawaii may be cited for the happy
interrelation between the music department and anthropology, as represented
by the Department of Anthropology at the University and the Bernice P.
Bishop Museum of Honolulu. The East-West Center at the University of
Hawaii profits by this cooperation and its combination of students from Asia,
Oceania, and the United States. Hawaii also demonstrated its aloha spirit
last year by its invitation to an anthropologist to be a visiting professor of
music. Indiana University shows excellent promise of cooperation between
music and the social sciences with Walter Kaufmann in music, Alan Merriam newly appointed in anthropology, and the superb Archive of Folk and
Primitive Music under the direction of George List. The recent appointment
of Nicholas England to the Music Department at Columbia and the purchase
of the Laura Boulton Collection gives this department unusual strength. Willard Rhodes's extensive training in anthropology and England's anthropological research in connection with his Bushman studies gives this team an impressive breadth of perspective. Richard Waterman and Bruno Nettl teach in
the anthropology and music departments, respectively, of Wayne State University. The projected Theater-Art-Music Center at Wesleyan University
will include ethnomusicology under its aegis. This reflects a mutuality of
interest in these departments that suggests an interesting variation on the
music-anthropology axis. A similar trend can be discerned at the University of Washington where music and the Center for Asian Arts (including
theater) are in active cooperation. It was the Center, at Washington, that
sponsored an unusual and imaginative symposium on ethnological field method this spring. A glance at the many offerings at the University of Hawaii

shows a similar awareness of the mutual dependency of the arts, particularly dance and music.

The examples given here were chosen to exemplify the trends that have developed in our decade. Their effects on the Society as such are represented in various ways in the Journal. The intimate relationship of music to dance has been acknowledged from the first by the inclusion of dance articles, bibliography, and news, and a dance editor on the staff of the Journal. One can feel sure that a similar hospitality will be extended to the graphic arts and literature as research finds the way to significant relationships between them and music. What will become then of our already difficult name is hard to imagine: "Ethno-Arts"? "Ethnohumanities"? In any case interrelatedness is clearly a permanent part of the ethos of the Society.

The Journal, the principal enterprise of the Society, is finding increasing support in the scholarly world at large. More subsidies of various kinds from universities, foundations, and other institutions, a steady growth in size as finances permit, are all indications of good health and gratifying recognition.

The Society serves as a clearing house for information in ethnomusicology and related fields. Inquiries of many kinds come to the officers and editors and the existence of the Society enables them to find the right person to answer these inquiries. As this function develops it seems entirely likely that the Society as such will come to act as referee in a variety of scholarly contexts. Hopefully it may find itself in a financial position to offer grants-in-aid for research. Here the possibility would arise of a Board sponsored by the Society which could use our resources to suggest fruitful or crucial areas of research and introduce an element of planning into the activity of the field as a whole.

Our initial purpose when the Newsletter was begun, ten years ago, was to encourage communication between ethnomusicologists and foster scholarship in the field. The pages of our Journal and the forum of our meetings have contributed considerably toward these goals. It is plain that there are still other ways, dreamed of and as yet undreamed of.

Wesleyan University
Middletown, Connecticut

FOOTNOTE

1. This paper is based, in part, on remarks made by the author at the 1962 annual meeting of the Society for Ethnomusicology in Bloomington, Indiana.

REFERENCES ⁻ITED

Hood, Mantle
    1957   "Training and research methods in ethnomusicology," Ethnomusicology
            Newsletter no. 11, 2-8.
Kolinski, Mieczyslaw
    1957   "Ethnomusicology, its problems and methods," Ethnomusicology Newsletter no. 10, 1-7.
Lomax, Alan
    1959   "Folk song style," American Anthropologist 61:927-54.
    1962   "Song structure and social structure," Ethnology 1:425-51.
McAllester, David P.
    1954   Enemy Way music. Cambridge, Mass.: Peabody Museum Publications in
            Anthropology 61, no. 3.

McAllester, David P.
    1949   Peyote music. New York: Viking Fund Publications in Anthropology no. 13.
Malm, William P.
    1959   Japanese music and musical instruments. Rutland and Tokyo: Tuttle.
Nettl, Bruno
    1956   Music in primitive culture. Cambridge: Harvard University Press.
Rhodes, Willard
    1956   "On the subject of ethnomusicology," Ethnomusicology Newsletter no. 7,
            1-9.
Seeger, Charles
    1956   "Past organization," Ethnomusicology Newsletter no. 6, 1-3.
Winkelman, Donald M.
    1963   "Ethnomusicology at American universities: a curricular survey," ETHNO-
            MUSICOLOGY 7:113-23.

PREFACE TO THE CRITIQUE OF MUSIC

by CHARLES SEEGER

It is our misfortune today that both the predominantly historical study of the professional, elegant or fine art of European music that we know as "musicology" and the predominantly systematic study of the total music of the world that we know, perforce, as "ethnomusicology" have both been developed mainly as descriptive sciences. Neither has had a comparably organized critique. Neither has taken any cognizance of general value theory. Yet both have been bound by assumptive value judgments which, though quite different, are the more dominating for lack of explicit statement. These judgments hold apart the two branches of what eventually must be a single study and provide an almost impassable barrier to the integration of either with the rest of the humanities.

Historicomusicology has assumed that the single idiom with which it deals is the only one worth its serious attention. Other musics - and the folk and popular idioms of the European tradition - have been regarded variously as irrelevant, inferior, "bad," barbarous, or not music at all. To ethnomusicologists, from Stumpf, Abraham, von Hornbostel, with the possible exception of Sachs, down to the present day, this ethnocentric and class-conscious bias has been anathema. Yet a uniform approach to their field embodying another highly restrictive value judgment, discarded long ago by historicomusicologists, has been adopted uncritically by most ethnomusicologists, and has been a prime conditioning factor in what has and what has not been collected, studied and published qua ethnomusicology. Another single value - purity or authenticity - has taken the place of the "good music" of the historicomusicologists. Between two items, one of which showed changing features, the apparently unchanging has almost always been considered the proper ethnomusicological datum. Only too often the former has not even been considered worth recording. Sometimes its very existence has been deplored. This is ethnocentrism in reverse - broader, it is true, and not biased in favor of "own" music, but still ethnocentrism in the sense that change seems usually to be induced by outside influences, among them acculturation, and is therefore "bad." Thus, ethnomusicology has tended to be for the most part archaistic rather than realistic in its approach to its field. Stability has been weighted against change. To the student of a music not his own, changed or changing traditions in it have seemed the lesser value. Certainly, they are more difficult to study. But to the carriers of them change must, usually, constitute a reaching for higher values even though this may later prove to have been mistaken or overdone, and result in attempted revival of the values that have been forsaken. Survival, continuity, stability, variation, change, diversification, consolidation, revival, decay and other such concepts must be employed with care to avoid bias toward one or another. They refer to aspects of the equally valid holistic concept of the propensity for music-making - the musicality - of man, a universal behavioral continuum that the student himself personifies, emergent in him from prehistory and persistent through his day into the unforeseeable future.

I am not depreciating the achievements of this century of historicomusicology and half-century of ethnomusicological work. Even as for the former, so for the latter, salvage, preservation and study of survivals is a task of prime importance. If we do not know the relatively stable, how shall we measure change? If we do not have a single concept "music", how shall we decide what are and what are not musics? Without a concept of value, how shall we order, among the musics of the world, the multiplicity of value-systems which they are? What is value, anyway, and a value-system? Shall we regard criticism as the valuing of fact or the fact of valuing? And what is the relation of music-value to other values and to value in general?

Such questions and many like them can be dealt with properly only by a critique with a method as comprehensive and as carefully thought out as that of science. Although both methods were well-launched by the ancient Greeks, Christianity put a stop to cultivation of that of

2

science and developed its own over-mastering value-theory and supporting dialectic in whose terms were settled, supposedly for good, all the questions raised by the Greek philosophers, both scientific and critical. Scientists, from Galileo on, had to fight a bitter, three-century war for independence from ecclesiastical value-theory. The last notable challenge may have been the Scopes trial in Tennessee, in 1925. But although on the whole the churches lost the war with science, they seem to have held criticism to something like a draw. Unlike the scientists, the critics never fought a unified war of independence. Some remained in the church and maintained the essentials of the religious value-theory intact. Some declared and won doctrinal independence, but maintained the value-theory in modified forms. Criticism in the arts seems to have been, on the one hand, exploited, and, on the other, to have "bored from within", with the result that the early puritanism of Christian religious organizations gradually gave way to increased use of the arts as supports and vehicles for religious activity. Criticism of the arts, at first entirely subordinate to ecclesiastic value-theory, gradually emphasized artistic value until it became a separate, independent literary genre. By the time of Galileo, public art-criticism, as in the Artusi-Monteverdi controversy, was possible because it seemed to have nothing to do with ecclesiastic value-theory. Ecclesiastic value-theory was not value-theory. It was the Word of God, or at least of church doctrine. Thus, by the early 18th century, when letters, art, and music became recognized as appanages of the prosperous middle-classes instead of a small number of princes and nobles, critical activity was firmly split into two domains, an ecclesiastic and a secular, whose separation some tried to reason away, bridge or unify to no avail. For the split, like a geological fault, produced innumerable ancillary splits - - separate literary, art and music criticisms - - among which there has been no substantial connection.

What the founders of Christianity seem to have realized is that the art of speech--at least in the languages of the Western World--depends for its operation, wherever there is even a modicum of rationality, upon a recurring alternation of analysis-synthesis, synthesis--analysis, in which analysis, a splitting technique, and synthesis, a technique of joining the split parts, effect an appearance of one-to-one correspondence between the verbal symbols of speech and the apprehensions of our senses and the promptings of our feelings. The utter fragmentation of this apparent correspondence in Greco-Roman sophistry and the cynicism of Roman imperialism, presented in crisis form a need and a demand to control what amounted to run-away verbal inflation. Assumption of the single, unequivocal supremacy of the Word--an unanalyzable, unsynthesizable, eternal oneness of primitive and ultimate value, knowable only by faith but backed by sufficient physical power, personal, social and political--met both need and demand and endured intact for well over a thousand years and still carries enormous weight throughout the world.

It is neither necessary nor appropriate for the present undertaking to trace in detail the nearly 2000 years history of this split in the value-theory of the Western World. Suffice it to say that music has always been valued in both ecclesiastic and secular terms, i.e., in terms extrinsic, contextual, to music, as incidental or exemplary in studies other than of music. Very much to the point, however, are the principal ways in which general value-theories have laid bases upon which music has been valued in accord with them in these terms. I list eight of these, to which I shall add separately, at a later point, a ninth.

Valuation of Music in Extrinsic Terms

I.   Denial of the reality both of the problem of fact vs. value and of its constituents in the practice of a discipline designed to transcend belief in them. Fact and value, and, so, any relationship between them, are illusions. There is a problem in man's enslavement to illusions. It can be solved by discipline. The Rigveda seems to have been the fountainhead of this adjustment. The discipline of yoga taught escape from illusion by experiential union, physiological, affective and intellectual, with the Brahman or ineffable. There was one fact and one value be-

3

105

coming nothing. Music seems to have been ignored in the basic texts, but was employed in enticement and entertainment of the god. Krishna, an avatar of Vishnu, played the flute. Taoism and Buddhism adopted this solution of the problem, made much mention of music and gave it an honored place.

II.   Denial of the reality of the problem but not of its constituents; and postulation of a reasoned integration of them in "correct" or "wise" conduct. This adjustment would appear to be made in the name of "common sense." Confucius was the outstanding exponent of this middle of the road approach. One finds oneself in a situation in which the fact of a social and political authority is so unquestionable that a practical value-adjustment to it seems inevitable. Successful adjustment is possible and can be achieved as the supreme value. Music has an honored place.

III.   Postulation of a reasoned primacy of value. Idealist philosophy from Plato on has relied upon this adjustment of the dilemma. Reason is employed to establish and give order to value--especially the highest value or values--with fact in a secondary place or even shunned, as by Plato, because the attempt to attach ideas to the infinite multitude of facts would be an endless and frustrating task. Socrates took refuge in ideas of the just, the beautiful and the good and let the rest go. Music was honored but subject to stringent control by verbal formulas.

IV.   Assertion of an unreasoned primacy of value. The Judaic-Hellenic-Christian epos seems to have been a syncretion of the Judaic passionate mysticism, Greek intellectualism and the Roman genius for social-political organization. Of course, there were other ingredients, notably Orphic and Mithraic traditions. Reason, though not employed to establish the primacy of value, was employed to support that primacy and to order the facts of life in accord with the policies of the institutions set up to control private, social, political and economic affairs. The relative dependence upon unquestioned assertion of value and upon a reasoned support of it, varied enormously. In Islam, in the words of such Saints as Juan de la Cruz and Santa Theresa, and in the writings of F. W. Nietzsche, the role of reason is more subordinate than in, for example, St. Augustine and the long line of Christian apologists, philosophers and reformers of an idealist cast since his time. In the presence of suppression by doctrinal law, music throve to whatever extent that the right hand knew not or ignored what the left hand did.

V.   Postulation of a reasoned primacy of fact. This adjustment was stated clearly in Francis Bacon's First Aphorism:

> "Man, being the servant and interpreter of nature, can do and understand so much and so much only as he has observed in fact or in thought of the course of nature: beyond this he neither knows anything or can do anything."

Other early scientists adhered to this view. Music was interesting especially for the number relations it exhibits but variously for its form and content. Merz[1] classed music as unmethodical thought.

VI.   Assertion of an unreasoned primacy of fact. As Western science became more diversified and specialization, in many minds, took the place of the comprehensive synoptic view, the primacy of fact was often taken for granted or as self-evident. Value became subordinated to, and used and defined in, terms of special fields--moral, aesthetic, economic, psychologic, etc. Often as not, it was retained only in a technical sense, as, for example; in economics as the measure of use and exchange; in the visual-arts as the name for a characteristic of color; and in music, for the relative length of notes. The tendency, outside of art-criticism, was to denigrate music, especially in England and America.

---

1 J. T. Merz. *A History of European Thought in the Nineteenth Century.* Edinburgh and London, 1896-1914.

4

VII. <u>Search for a bridge between the poles of the problem</u>. This adjustment was pre-eminently the achievement of Immanuel Kant, who may be regarded as the founder in his <u>Kritik der Urteilskraft</u>, of "modern" critical method. The aim was to reason away the dualism and substitute a monism. The argument, as it deals with music, runs: music is one of the proper objects of aesthetic contemplation because, (a) it is "free" beauty (a flower is another example), i.e., without intellectual content (meaning, presumably, speech-intellectual content), and because (b) it is only in free beauty that man can see a unity in fact and value.[2]

VIII. <u>Acceptance of the problem as insoluble</u>. A few writers tried to see both sides of the problem, without trying to reconcile them. In his <u>Mission of Music</u>, Thomas Mann wrote eloquently:

> "Music is a great mystery . . . by virtue of its sensual-spiritual nature and the amazing union it achieves between strict rule and dream, good form and magic, reason and emotion, day and night, it is without a doubt the most profound, most fascinating, and, in the eyes of the philosopher, most disquieting phenomenon . . . Music is a theology of number, an austere, godlike art, but an art in which all demons are interested and which, of all the arts, is most susceptible to the de-moniac. For it is both moral code and seduction, sobriety and drunkenness, a summons to the highest alertness and a lure to the sweetest sleep of enchantment, reason and anti-reason--in short, a mystery with all the initiation and educative rites which ever since Pythagoras have been part and parcel of every mystery; and the priests and masters of music are the initiates, the preceptors of that dual being, the divine-demoniac totality of the world, life, mankind and culture."

Any survey of the enormous number of complex arguments bearing upon value in general (i.e., extrinsic, to music) must disclose such extremes as blanket condemnation or prohibition of music by the Apostle Paul, early Islam and some later Protestant sects, and the opposite, unexceptionable approval, in the Kantian position, of all music without words and the extreme permissiveness of contemporary American life. Discrimination has varied from the severe reasoning of Plato and the vehement affective bias of Nietzsche to the statistics of the psychological laboratory and the public polls of musical taste by public relations companies. The contradictions among them and the manifest invalidity for musicology of some of the assumptions upon which they are based (such as the Kantian, that music is without intellectual content, with "no perfection of any kind, no purposiveness"[3]) together with the persuasiveness of their presentation, make confusing reading for students of music, excepting, possibly, the last two, the second of which effectively denies the problem and poses a dilemma in its place. But before either can be recommended for musicological consideration they will need essential qualification. (See, later, a ninth way of handling the situation.)

Now, one would think, would one not, with this incessant concern with value, that both general and critical philosophy--not to speak of the galaxy of special studies--would have organized a general critical method comparable in comprehensiveness and precision, and acceptable to a consensus such as that with which the scientific method has been accepted. Kant had, however, injected the problem of value into 19th-century thought in such emphatic terms that it became an increasingly absorbing concern of every branch of learning. Pietistic handlings were made by theologians, from Albrecht Ritschl to Rudolph Otto; materialistic, by economists, from Carl Menger to Thorstein Veblen. But it was not until nearly the end of the 19th century that the concept of a unified value theory was adumbrated. Perhaps, it was in part Nietzsche's "transvaluation of all values" that shocked students in every field to an awareness of the chaos in a situation in which they were all equally involved.

---

2 Immanuel Kant. Critique of Judgment, J. H. Bernard trans. New York, 1951, section 16.
3 *Loc. cit.*

5

Around 1900, a philosophy of value, since known as the "Austrian," came into being through the work of Franz Brentano, Alexius von Meinong[4] and Christian von Ehrenfels.[5] Under the names "general value theory" or "general theory of value," the predominant emphasis was psychological. The members of the Austrian group were primarily psychologists. But nearly every facet of philosophic and humanistic thought became involved--epistemology, metaphysics, ethics, aesthetics, logic, scientific methods, etc. George Santayana,[6] W. M. Urban,[7] Hugo Münsterberg,[8] John Dewey[9] and R. B. Perry[10] were among the first in the United States to carry on the work of the Austrians. In the Postscript of his first substantial volume, the last named sums up his view, of which the following quotations give a fair notion:

"There are three accepted classifications of values. . . the trinity of canonized values, known as the "True, the Beautiful and the Good"; or the tetrad in which to these three there is added the higher unity of God. This classification employs two principles: a triadic psychology, which divides mind into thought, feeling and will; and an absolutist philosophy, which affirms that these three acts define a convergent goal of aspiration. The absolute or God, when thought is Truth, when felt is Beauty, and when willed is Goodness. . .

"A second mode of classification is that which, assuming values to be functions of interest, divides them in accordance with the several modalities of interest or the different relations which objects may sustain thereto. Such a classification has been virtually provided in the present work. . .

"The third mode of classification is that which adopts the divisions already made among the several moral or social sciences. . ."

Perry finds the first "is objectionable on several grounds;" the second, because it "tends to be excessively detailed and schematic" is "easy to make and likely to prove barren when made." His last words commit him to the third alternative in his second volume:

"A fruitful theory of value will accept those stable and well-marked unities in which the values of life are already grouped. The great foci of interest are science, conscience, art, industry, state and church. Perhaps there is no absolute reason why this should be so, but there is no denying the fact that it is so. . ."

A crisis seems to have been reached in the attempt to set up value-theory as a semi-independent division of philosophy on a par with epistemology, ethics, metaphysics, aesthetics. H. O. Eaton[11] hazarded the opinion that ". . . a value which is neither economic, ethic, aesthetic, nor any other of the specific types of value seems unthinkable." About the same time, H. Osborne[12] wrote of "The deplorable imbroglio in which philosophy of value is entangled. . ." J. W. Smith[13] surmised ". . . perhaps we had better abandon the value program altogether."

---

4 Alexius von Meinong. *Ueber Annahmen*. Leipzig, 1902.
5 Christian von Ehrenfels. *System der Werttheorie*. Leipzig, 1897.
6 George Santayana. *The Sense of Beauty*. New York, 1896 and 1936.
7 W. M. Urban. *Valuation: Its Nature and Laws*. London and New York, 1909.
————————. "Value, Theory of ." *Encyclopaedia Brittanica*, Chicago, 1946.
8 Hugo Münsterberg. *The Eternal Values*. New York, 1909.
9 John Dewey. "Theory of Valuation," *International Encyclopedia of Unified Science*, II, Part 4. Chicago, 1939.
10 R. B. Perry. *General Theory of Value*. Cambridge, 1926.
————————. *Realms of Value*. Cambridge, 1954.
11 H. O. Eaton. *The Austrian Philosophy of Values*. Norman (Okla.), 1930.
12 H. Osborne. *Foundations of the Philosophy of Value*. London and Cambridge, 1933. p. 1.
13 J. W. Smith. "Should General Theory of Value Be Abandoned?," *International Journal of Ethics*, LVII, 4 (July 1947), Part I, pp. 274-88.

6

The historic procedure, of course, has been to include consideration of value in the body of the comprehensive philosophical enquiry. This has also characterized the main body of later 20th-century concern with value by many writers, among whom we may mention C. I. Lewis,[14] M. R. Konwitz,[15] D. J. McCracken,[16] P.W. Taylor[17] and S. C. Pepper.[18] The last-named states[19] plainly that "The Basis of Criticism in the Arts must ultimately lie in a complete philosophy" and it would be hard to disagree with him. He presents an analysis of the valuing process[20] showing

> ". . . the need of considering the thing we call a work of art as a nest of objects. . . that. . . consists. . . of three closely interrelated objects: First, the physical vehicle; second, the object of perceptual immediacy. . . third. . . the object of criticism. . ."

this last being made possible

> "by the process of funding, through which earlier perceptions fuse their contents with later ones making possible an intuitive sense of a perceptual whole spreading over a wide period of discrete stimulation."

A physical vehicle would be the acoustic sound of speech or music. An object of perceptual immediacy would be the sound as apprehended and perceived by a listener. This would vary extensively; but a norm of amateur or of professional competency could be conceived. An "object of criticism" would include, in the case of music, an assemblage of discrete apprehensions and perceptions of the object of perceptual immediacy, funded in a frame of contextual relevance in which many factors bearing different weights have become fused in a single unified understanding of the nest in its relation to the valuer and to the situation in which the valuer values it.

The student of music cannot but be impressed with the enormous advance made in the study of value both as a semi-independent general theory and as an essential part of philosophy during the first half of the 20th century. Its bearing upon musicology should be obvious. But the extent of the literature, its complexity, the increasingly unfamiliar terminologies and, above all, the vast extension of its viewpoint beyond that of the musicologist seem to have discouraged his interest in it. It seems virtually unknown to American musicologists, or, in cases where it is, must be regarded as irrelevant; for it remains unused by them. At a three-day Symposium on Music and Criticism[21] held at Harvard University in 1947, there was not a mention of general theory of value in spite of the fact that Perry, who had taught at Harvard for most of his life, lived only a few blocks away. His name was not mentioned nor was his substantial first volume, which had been in use for twenty years as a prime reference in uncounted university and college courses throughout the country. Yet the prime concern of criticism, whether of music or anything else, is value. And just as in science there must be many particular scientific methods there must be at the same time one over-all theory within which they may be distinguished and related, so in criticism we must accept the probability that there will be many specialized critical methods but eventually, we may hope, one over-all general theory within which these particular methods will be distinguished and related.

The early 20th-century burst of enthusiasm for "a" general theory of value may simply

14 C. I. Lewis. *An Analysis of Knowledge and Valuation.* La Salle (Ill.), 1946.
15 M. R. Konvitz. *On the Nature of Value: Philosophy of Samuel Alexander.* New York, 1946.
16 D. J. McCracken. *Thinking and Valuing.* London, 1950.
17 P. W. Taylor. *Normative Discourse.* Englewood Cliffs (N. J.), 1961.
18 S. C. Pepper. *The Work of Art.* Bloomington (Ind.), 1955.
19 ————————. "Some Comments on Professor Kahn's Paper," *Journal of Aesthetics,* IX, 1 (Sept., 1950), p. 51.
20 ————————. *The Work of Art,* p. 30 ff.
21 R. F. French, ed. *Music and Criticism: A Symposium,* Cambridge, 1948.

have been premature. Until the specialized theories of the arts can catch up with those of economics, theology, sociology, philosophy and the others, it may not be feasible. However, this may be, in any other than a superficial approach to a critique of music it must be obvious that the history of the first effort to formulate a general theory of value must be required reading for musicologists. Some of the salient features may be summarized as follows.

1. Clear distinction must be made between value and values, between valuation as a past, present and future act, and validation of past, present and future valuation.

2. In most discussion of value and valuation such as the present and the sources cited in it, there is a tendency, because of the type of speech-usage adopted, to regard value and values as existent because they can be referred to as either manifest in an external, physical universe or in the universe of (speech-) discourse. Both references are generic. Valuation, however, is for the valuer, always a particular act in a particular situation. Indeed, it can be looked at as the particular answer to the particular question, explicit or implied: "What shall I do?"

3. What is done may, indeed, result in part from consideration of such generic reference; but in how many cases can we say that action results entirely from such generic reference? Candor must compel us to admit that we can never know and weigh exactly all the consciously and unconsciously relevant factors.

4. Furthermore, the particular act is always in a particular situation that is unique. For example, let us suppose that one is walking up the street and meets face to face another pedestrian walking in the opposite direction whose path one cannot predict. One may wait for him to act with respect to which side he will pass one on, or one may oneself make the decision. Whichever one of the two makes the decision or if, by chance, they both act at once, successfully or unsuccessfully, so as not to collide, the decision in either case is a value judgment. Whether either or both do or do not want to collide is beside the point.

5. In the absence of a judgment based upon the complete analysis of all the known and unknown factors leading to the passage to the right or left of the other, either the one who has taken the situation in hand and decided it has, or the both of them have, tried to control it and performed, insofar as there was a value in avoidance of collision, a creative, valuative act. This act was directed toward an end. It was purposive and its effect was predicted upon an estimate of the other person's behavior. Knowable factors certainly may have been operative in it; but equally certainly, there were unknowable factors.

6. Barring its simplicity and the relatively low coefficient of value created, this example seems to be typical of the act of valuation throughout the parameter of speech-usage of the terms "value" and "valuation," from the most trivial to the most exalted.

7. Disposition of the terms value, values, valuation and validation in relation to existence, reality, will and other basic concepts must be one of the main concerns of a critique. Trivial and basic, primitive and ultimate values are necessary assumptions, or, as Urban [22] translates von Meinong's Voraussetzungen, presuppositions of all use of speech. They are more often felt than reasoned. Only too often it is forgotten that every science and critique rests upon a judgment that its cultivation is "worth while."

8. It would be a grievous mistake, however, for musicology to attempt to make such dispositions upon the basis of values extrinsic to music alone. For just as every act of the non-musician is valual as well as factual, so is every act of the musician. But in addition, the musician's act is musically valual and musically factual.

---

22 Urban. *Valuation: . . .*, p. 38.

8

Valuation of Music in Intrinsic Terms

Coming, then, to the question whether intrinsic or textual value can be distinguished in music through expression in literary form, it must be admitted that no such survey as I have hazarded of the literary expression of extrinsic values can be made. Agreement seems general that "musical criticism", as at present known, has tried to do this. In earlier days it was closely associated with literary criticism itself. To paraphrase Saintsbury,[23] it has been an exercise of "that function of the judgment which busies itself with the goodness and badness, success and ill-success of (musical) literature (and its public performance) from a purely (music-) literary point of view"; which is to say it is "pretty much the same thing as the reasoned exercise of (musical) taste" expressed in words rather than music, by musicians and musical amateurs engaged in the concert-life of the well-to-do bourgeosie of the Western World. It has been wholly "particular and actual. " (parentheses mine - CS)

While we still await a history of this musical Fachkritik comparable to Saintsbury's compendious work, useful handbooks by Armand Machabey[24] and Max Graf[25] are readily available, as are articles on the subject in the standard dictionaries and encyclopaedias of music.[26]

The problem that musical critics have faced has been: how to express in terms of the art of speech what, as musicians or musical amateurs, they know, feel and imagine is music-value. From Mattheson to Hanslick most of the earlier appraising and praised critics were professional musicians. They were able to sit down with other musicians and perform in ensembles with that unity of musical knowledge, feeling and imagination that only trained musicians can have sufficiently in common to make the result successful. But after the music has been played, the talking and writing has begun. And then, the greatest variety of opinions, judgments, and even statements of fact may have been held by the very same persons who, while making music, showed such remarkable agreement that they almost seemed like one person in separate bodies. The content of music, what music "means", what it "does", "what it communicates" is either held to be exactly or substantially the same as speech; or, the two are mutually exclusive; or have something in common.[27] The longer one listens to the talk or reads the written criticisms, the more it appears that whatever musical knowledge, feeling, and imagination musicians and critics have, becomes expressed in non-musical terms, i.e., in terms extrinsic to music, e.g., of Affektenlehre, of enlightened reason, of personal genius, of evolutionary progress, of historical periods, of technical mastery, of newness, of contemporaneity, of experiment, or other. The critical process is sometimes taken to be a mere translation, as from one mode of thinking to another. But often as not, it is, rather, a re-creation that alters, distorts, and in many cases completely misrepresents. The result has been a widening of a gap between critic and composer that some critics claim is unbridgeable.[28] Composers are likely to agree, in spite of the fact that they themselves, when they talk or write about music, usually do so like critics.

There seem to be two main reasons for this unfortunate situation. First, music-critics write mainly for newspapers and periodicals for general readers. General readers are mostly city people who are listeners rather than producers of music. The critics tend, therefore, to

---

23 George Saintsbury. *A History of Criticism.* Edinburgh and London, 1948, Vol. I, pp. 3-4.
24 Armand Machabey. *Traité de la critique musicale.* Paris, 1947.
25 Max Graf. *Composer and Critic.* New York, 1946.
26 H. H. Stuckenschmidt. "Musikkritik," *Musik in Geschichte und Gegenwart,* 9, Kassel, 1961.
Winton Dean. "Criticism," *Grove's Dictionary of Music and Musicians,* Fifth Edition, New York, II, 1955.
27 Charles Seeger. "On the Moods of a Music Logic,"*Journal of the American Musicological Society,* XIII (1960), pp. 225-6.
28 E. M. Forster. "The Raison d'Etre of Criticism in the Arts," in French, *op. cit.,* p. 30, *passim.*

9

write as listeners. This is so much the fashion that even composers, when they branch off into criticism as they commonly do, speak of music as something to be listened to.

Second, it would seem to stand to reason that if there is intrinsic value in music, it would be the producer of it who would know what it is. To the extent he can use technical terms that the critic must either eschew because his public would not like them or because he does not understand them, he may make some headway. But - whether or not, owing to the listening attitude or a lack of skill in using reasoned speech - all one has to do to start a knock-down drag-out battle among composers or critics alike is to ask what is meant by some common music-technical term such as melody, rhythm, meter, form, or such. The argument about music becomes unnoticeably one about speech. There seems to be nearly as much difficulty in settling the question of intrinsic fact in music as in dealing with the question of intrinsic value.

Suffice it to say: the current conception of "musical criticism", whether by professional critics or professional musicians, is no base or surrogate for a critique of music. Newspaper criticism serves a definite journalistic function, but stands no higher, if as high, as newspaper science. Niels Bohr, Enrico Fermi and Albert Einstein did not base their mathematical physics upon, or direct their professional careers in terms of, newspaper science; nor did Meinong, Dewey, or Pepper, their critical thinking and scholarly careers upon a base of newspaper criticism. As a branch of daily journalism, musical criticism is largely a public-relations service for composers, performers, concert-managers and that amorphous cross-section of the urban population known as "music lovers." It furnishes prime data for study of a single stratum of the musicality of the social continuum (i. e., of the idiom of the elegant or fine art of the Western World), but is neither a base nor an aid for the criticism of any other idiom or music or for the formation of a critique that may adequately serve either historico-musicology or ethnomusicology.

How, then, shall we go about building a critique for musicology that will comprehend all substantial aspects of the association of the concepts of music and value, textual as well as contextual? That it has never been more than adumbrated is, perhaps, testimony for its difficulty. That every musicologist, musician, and music critic acts as if one existed (for, otherwise, how would any of us ever get down to work?), and that at least he had a correct understanding of it attests to its need of formal statement. I venture to propose here, therefore, one way in which I believe a comprehensive and adequate critique can be set up. I am well aware of the fact that there may be others and of the probability that before a critique of music can be considered to be as maturely thought out as was the method of science, let us say, in the early 19th century, many students will have contributed. But it is time a start were made. As in all pioneer ventures, a degree of freshness and independence is to be expected. It needs no apology. Indeed, that both qualities may be advantageous seems, in the light of history in other fields, to be possible.

With respect to the difficulty of the venture, two considerations should be remarked. Whether or not with Pepper's dictum in mind, the first is general: in the critique of any field the specialist finds himself face to face with all the problems of philosophy. Shall he take time off and settle them all to his satisfaction so as to be able to found his musicology on solid rock? Should he try, he will never reach musicology, nor, surely, even the end of philosophy. Throughout history, philosophers have spent whole lives in the attempt. And while they seem to know a lot more about them today than yesterday, there is still as much disagreement as - perhaps, even more than - there ever was. Yet the crux of the matter is precisely this: without supposed or hypothesized "solutions" of these problems there can be no musicology. Candidly, from a strictly musicological viewpoint, the so-called solutions cannot be solutions because the problems are not problems. Without pretending here to tell the philosopher about his own business, we can say that as far as musicology is concerned, in the use of the art of speech we are in a predicament. If the philosopher answers that, nevertheless, we are trespassing upon his domain, we can reply that throughout history non-musical writers generally, including philosophers, have felt free to say whatever they chose about music, and that at last the worm is turning and we are going to say something about the use of speech in connection with music. And that is: in talking about music we are in a predicament and it is a speech-predicament. We can name it, if we like, "the linguo-centric predicament." And we can hold that its problems are dilemmas met by us in the use of the art of speech. If the philosopher must draw more general conclusions from this particular field, that is his concern. We are in a linguo-centric predicament in the sense that there is no avoidance of it except (1) not to enter it or (2) if one has entered it, to withdraw oneself and what one has said or written. If one remains in the predicament, one has to make tentative, or hypothetical, adjustments of the horns of the dilemmas that will enable one to begin and to proceed. The situation might be compared to building a path upon swampy ground. One can throw down planks. But to keep one's balance is essential. For it is as easy to fall off one side as the other. The swamp is the same - the swamp of controversy. The musicologist will be wise, therefore, not to rely too much upon either horn of a basic dilemma. If he must lean far to one side, let him correct his course by leaning equally far to the other. If, by his peculiar nature, he lean toward the Cartesian "I think therefore I am", let him compensate to the best of his ability by "allowing equal time" to the existentialist "I am therefore I think", or vice versa. What is a basic dilemma has been virtually decided for us in most cases by the history and present state of philosophy. The musicological juncture presents us with a novel one. What is compensation for excessive leaning upon one rather than another horn of a dilemma is partly a matter of logic, partly a matter of judgment. For some, a middle ground can be found, as, for example: between right and wrong, justice; between knowledge and ignorance, wisdom; good and evil, charity; reason and ecstasy, common-sense (in a non-pejorative sense). For others it is more difficult: fact vs. value, appearance vs. reality; being vs. non-being; subjectivity vs. objectivity; general vs. particular; concrete vs. abstract; particular vs. general; absolute vs. relative; part vs. whole. The horns of the basic dilemmas are the lode-stars of all writing, the points of the compass by which we plot and direct its course, the terms in which it is cast. But as musicologists we must take care not to think that they must, therefore, be either our goals or the stuff about which we wish to communicate. Let us question with special care, then, all musical theory based upon one horn of a basic dilemma to the exclusion of the other, as, for example, intellect vs. emotion, practical vs. theoretical, old vs. new.

The second consideration to be kept in mind is that use of the art of speech to deal with the art of music is in one respect unique: it deals with another means of communication among men, a means that employs the same medium - sound. This at once facilitates the dealing in some ways, but limits it in others. The predicament can be shown as follows: operation of both arts, in their simplest forms, requires (1) a producer or maker of a sound-signal, (2) a receiver or listener. If both producer and receiver carry the same tradition or closely related traditions of communication, the sound-signal may be intended to be received as a message and may be received as such by the receiver. Under optimum or normal conditions, the receiver will "understand" the message. If, however, the receiver carries a more distantly related tradition, he may recognize the signal as a message but not understand it. If he carries a totally different tradition, he may not even recognize the sound as a message - perhaps he might think that a tone-language were music or music, speech. What is understood in the first case and is imperfectly or not understood in the second and third, is what may be referred to in both speech and in music as the "content" of the message. If this content is sufficiently not understood, it is quite possible that the receiver may not perceive the signal is a message, or, perhaps, even a speech- or music-signal. In such a speech-operation no substantial value will have been communicated. Is this also the case with the music-operation?

There seems to be a profound difference between speech- and music-communication in the locus and nature of the content - and hence of valuation - in the two processes. The difference in locus can be observed in the facts that (a) the speech-signal can be completely altered, as by translation from one language to another, while the content remains practically the same, as in ordinary and scholarly prose, or recognizably related, as in a poem, whereas (b) if the music-signal is completely altered, as by playing a Beethoven symphony by the orchestra of the Japanese gagaku, or a Javanese _gending_ by a Western string quartet, the content will be completely, probably unrecognizably, altered. The conclusion must be that the content of - and hence valuation in - music-comunication lies also in the music-signal, or, more precisely, in the sensation and perception as well as in the conception and understanding of the message and, therefore, that the signal is part of the content. Thus, the concept of "content" although it facilitates to some extent the dealing with music by speech, is in turn broadened by it. The questions present themselves: is the sensed and perceived part of the content of music conceivable and understandable _qua_ music only by receivers who carry the same or a closely related tradition of music and not at all by receivers who do not? Or are there two kinds of music value: the sensed and perceived, and the conceived and understood?

In all Western languages, understanding of content in a related tradition would probably not extend much beyond, if as far as, the difference of high and low German or Southern USA and Brooklynese dialects. But ethnomusicological experience has shown that the specimens of musics as unrelated as are Javanese or Japanese to the Western elegant or fine art have been instantly, upon first hearing, conceived and understood by carriers of only one tradition or the other as music in the sense that subsequent training and practice has confirmed rather than altered the original reception. Among ethnomusicologists who have had this experience with even more than one music not their own, the probability is taken very seriously that the contents of all musics may be closely related in terms of the first two phases of the signal-message-content syndrome - sensation of the sound-signal and its perception as a message - and, though less closely in terms of the second two phases - conception of content and its understanding - are far more closely related than in many languages. The old cliché "music is a universal language" might have some validity if re-stated "music is a more uniform means of communication than language." Bimusicality and multimusicality seem to be at least as easily demonstratable as the analogous abilities in language.

This train of thought would seem, however, to leave us still with the question: are there two kinds of music content, one sensed and perceived, another conceived and understood; or is the content one homogeneous Gestalt?

Here, the matter of performance style must be considered. And to do so means returning once more to the signal-message-content process. Whorf [29] and others have shown the importance of the signal to the understanding of the speech-message. Its content may be largely modified by the inflection of the signal, its "performance-style." The tone of voice, the stress, the speed, loudness, and nuances of delivery of the signal may support but may also question, distort, even contradict, the literal content; but only when the literal content is understood. If this is not understood, the performance-style, not having anything to support or modify, would function independently, as it so often does in communication between persons who do not carry each other's traditions of speech.

Because performance-style can serve somewhat similar ends in music (barring, of course, contradiction, because it cannot be attributed to music except in terms of highly subjective writing), a case is customarily made for a duality of music-content, as, for example, aesthetic and intellectual. Surely this is a convenient distinction in (speech-) literary dealing with music. But doubt may be entertained that it is musically valid. Most musicians would, I believe, regard performance style as so inextricably a part of compositional style that performance in a style other than of the tradition to which it belongs, i. e., in which it originated and has been cultivated, is a violation of the integrity of the content. Indeed, composition is _for_ a performance style and improvisation is _in_ one. But even granting that optimum performance in any music tradition requires the performance style peculiar to the tradition, we must admit that increasing numbers of situations are coming to our notice in which traditions and, so, performance styles are becoming mixed, as by inter-traditional borrowing

29 B. L. Whorf. _Language, Thought and Reality_. Boston and New York, 1956.

and by acculturation. Aesthetics, of course, will be primarily interested in such optimum performance as can result only from an undifferentiated signal-message-content process and sensation-perception-conception-understanding syndrome fused in one holistic Gestalt. But although also concerned with the exceptional, musicology cannot afford such limitations. It is concerned as much with the quantitative as with the qualitative functions of the world-wide musicality of man, and with changing as well as with comparatively stable traditions. Moreover, in this wider field the exceptional and optimum is rare. For the axiology as well as for the phenomenology, therefore, of paramount importance are the norms of traditions, how they are established and what they are. The exceeding of them is not more important than the meeting of them or the falling short of them. Its concerns are equally the individualities and the universals among them. The factual aspects of the situation are no more important than the valual. For both the phenomenology and the axiology of a mature musicology, nothing is more imperatively required than to know not only how the distinction of the one from the other can be made, but also when it cannot be made.

So much regarding the locus of the content of music must suffice for this present undertaking. Regarding the nature of this content there must be much more to say, for in comparison to the voluminous literature upon music in non-musical terms very little has been in musical terms--if, indeed, this is possible. What are and what are not musical terms is not any too easy to say. Are they musically factual, valual, both at once or mere linguistic projections of linguistic terms peculiar to the formative or informative techniques of reference in a language or language family?

Surely, we may accept the (speech-made) proposition that the musician knows, musically, what he is doing when he writes, sings or plays a note, measure, phrase, period, section or what-not that we may call "X" and follows it with a note, measure, phrase, period, section or what-not that we may name "Y." Whether nor not he has the Gestalt Z in mind or builds it from X'es and Y'es is, perhaps, irrelevant for the moment. Does any musicologist believe that the musician is necessarily thinking in words: "Now I'll put this note down on paper (or sing or play it) and it is a fact in the physical universe; I think I'll give it such-and-such value"? Or vice versa? If we are to make any sense at all in talking about music, it seems that we must admit, upon the basis of our own experience in composing, performing and listening to music, that we may do this or we may not, depending upon the work-habits of the individual person, the occasion and other factors. One need not--and one receives the impression from other musicians that they need not--think separately of the facts and the values of what they are doing when they make music. The factor of speech is, simply, absent. And when it intrudes is more than likely to stop efficient progress of musical action. That this must be in every respect completely describable or even conceivable in terms of speech seems, however, unreasonable.

I propose, therefore, a ninth way in which the dilemma of fact vs. value may be adjusted for musicology.

IX. <u>Acceptance of the problem of fact vs. value as a dilemma of the linguo-centric predicament inescapable in speech-communication, but denial of it as a necessary factor in music-communication.</u>

Must we conclude, then, that in terms of the speech-description of music-fact and music-value further investigation of value by musicology is a fruitless task? I believe not. We must admit the limitations of speech and stay within them. And we may often arrive at results whose truth or untruth it may be difficult or impossible to prove (in terms of speech). May it not be, simply, that the typical or normal act of producing music is at once both factual and valual? Surely, in all optimal cases the note Y is the "best" choice a composer or improviser can make in a situation. His best is not produced in a vacuum but in two related contexts: one, the tradition of music in which he operates, some of whose norms he has

13

represented, others he has re-presented; the other, the bundle of traditions or culture of which the music-tradition is one. If a consensus comes into being among the effective judges of intrinsic value to the effect that this best has exceeded the norms of the tradition, and has enriched its repertory and extended its capabilities, a work may take its place as a master-work. If it merely meets the norms but does not seem to aid the growth, of the tradition, it may still be valued as nourishing its vigor and serving its continuity. If it falls short of these requirements it may be forgotten or kept in storage as a datum for statistical studies, doctoral dissertations or research for the maintenance of academic status.

But note: in all these cases, as well as in the many that fall between them, the producer himself has functioned as a judge of music-value. Every act of composition, performance and improvisation is a critical act. The prime critic of music is the producing musician. For him the music-critical act can be entirely free of the speech-dilemma fact vs. value. But to the extent that he talks about music or allows speech-thinking to intrude in or influence his music-thinking, to that extent he is in thrall to the verbal dilemma intrinsic vs. extrinsic and must accept the predicament in which he has placed himself.

A similar view may be taken of the second context in which the producing musician acts: the society and culture in which he lives. Here, judgment of others passes upon whether the product is socially or culturally valuable above, equal or below the requirements of non-musical norms. These may or may not coincide with the musical. At different times, the coincidence may vary.

It would seem, therefore, that we should understand the nature of the linguo-centric predicament as thoroughly as possible. Such understanding is both a musical and a linguistic job, in short, it is the task of musicology.

Here, everything hinges upon where and how we begin. "The most difficult part of any inquiry," writes Northrop,[30] voicing a very general belief, "is its initiation. One may have the most rigorous methods during the later stages of investigations, but if a false or superficial beginning has been made, rigor later on will never retrieve the situation."

Although the tap-roots of any musicological enquiry may be traced into nearly every domain of scholarly endeavour and into an uncountable number of daily experiences, we cannot, I believe, find any pre-existent ground, concrete or conceptual, firmer than what I have referred to as the "musicological juncture." The beginning of every particular instance of talking or writing about music takes place in, and is a product of, this juncture. Its facts precede and underlie citation of all further facts. Its values precede and underlie citation of all further values. The relation between these facts and values are set up in the juncture, whether or not we are aware of such setting up. If we adopt the present fashion of the "problem approach," this is the problematic situation, as Dewey labelled it. Our known and unknown assumptions, preconceptions and prejudgments are evidenced by our behavior in the juncture. For though we can generalize it as the situation in whose terms the foundations of the discipline must be stated, each one of us behaves in a different manner when we enter it, i.e., concretely, when we talk or write about music. The situation, or "juncture", as I prefer to name it, cannot, I believe, be reduced to any more fundamental terms; nor is there any posibility that such may be found elsewhere, for even the search for them must take its start from the juncture and be carried on it and in its terms.

Elsewhere,[31] I have dealt with the phenomenology of the juncture--music as fact. The

---

30 F. S. C. Northrop. *The Logic of the Sciences and the Humanities.* New York, 1959, p. 1.
31 Charles Seeger. "Preface to the Description of a Music," *Kongress—Bericht. Internationale Gesellschaft für Musikwissenschaft, Utrecht 1952,* p. 363.

14

axiology--music as value--follows, I believe, the same six-fold pattern. For present purposes, I re-state it here as comprising:

I. the student himself, with the particular value-inclinations his since birth and cultivated by him through training and experience;

II. the value-inclinations, individual and collective, of persons with whom he has close contact as teachers and colleagues, and of those to whom he addresses his talking and/or writing about music;

III., IV., V. the valual capabilities of two traditions and one sub-tradition of communication that he has inherited, cultivates and transmits, respectively, a speech, a music and a musicology;

VI. the general value-structure and value-functions of the music-cultural continuum that he enters, lives in and departs from.

Upon entering the musicological juncture, the musicologist faces, then, either knowingly or unknowingly, the following considerations.

1. Speech is the tool of musicology; music, the material worked upon with the tool by the musicologist. This is possible because of the high development of the principal features of the tool: informational reference (naming) and formational reference (connecting of names) in the languages of the Western World.

2. Music is only one of the many referents (items named) and dealt with (worked upon) by the art of speech. The musicologist uses, therefore, a tool of many uses for one particular use. ("Referent" may be pronounced "référent".)

3. As a tool, the art of speech is in part a mirror, in part a light upon, what it deals with. As a mirror, it takes on to some extent the likeness of its informational referents; as a light, it imposes upon its reference to these referents, to some extent, the idiosyncrasies of its formational reference. Philosophers have contended endlessly upon this dual role.

4. The present character of the art of speech, as manifest in the principal languages of the Western World, has been formed more in connection with its dealing with non-musical than with musical referents. We may, therefore, suspect the possibility of a non-musical linguistic bias in musicology--a tendency to cast its reference to music into the likeness of other foci of speech-interest and usage.

5. Music is also a tool of musicology; but not, customarily, one with which the musicologist deals with speech. Music also makes use of reference. The extent to which this resembles what is known in speech as "naming" has long been a matter of controversy. Formational reference (relationship among sounds in time accepted qua music in a culture) is characteristic of highly developed musics and perhaps of all musics. Music is admittedly weak in reference to the referents of speech-reference. Are we, then, to infer that it makes no informational reference? Surely, few musicians would defend such a notion. The conclusion must be that we should make allowance for a substantial difference between speech-reference to what is not speech and music-reference to what is not music. For though these may overlap in some areas (about which there is endless controversy) they certainly do not, in others. The vast area of what is neither speech nor music may be dealt with variously by both, but with two very different techniques of reference.

6. There is no direct check in terms of music upon the mirroring and illuminating of music in terms of speech. In the absence of such check, non-musicians - and sometimes

15

117

musicians - philosophers, religious leaders, politicians, moralists, and others have dealt freely with music, influencing and not seldom controlling its cultivation. Though often forced into subservience to speech-formulae, even by musicians themselves, ways of modifying or circumventing verbal restraints have often been found.

7. <u>There is no way in which the domination of music by speech has been more common or more effective than in terms of value.</u> An indirect check upon the mirroring and illuminating of music in terms of speech would seem to be possible through the use of speech-concepts of music-fact and music-value that are referent to factors in the art of music that resemble factors in the art of speech in some ways but differ from them in others. If there are such factors in the art of music and if we can describe or circumscribe them in speech, negatively if not positively, the musicologist should be able to identify them because he is a competent musician and be able to report upon them because he is a competent speaker or writer.

It will be observed that the musicological juncture has been presented here in its valual aspect as a complex of facts. The naive reader might, at this point, become impatient for some definitions. In the kind of speech-usage accepted by musicologists in the 20th century, definition of fact is not difficult. This usage, to which I habitually refer as "deliberately methodical" or "rational," favors a definition of the term "fact" in musicology that might read as: "musical fact is that which is or might be accepted by a consensus of musicologists as existent." Definition of the term "value" in musicology is, however, prejudiced by this usage. It tends, as just noted, to factualize it; to cast it in the form "is that which" entertains, pleases, interests us, or "is what" we prize, want, will, ought, must, etc. I would prefer, therefore, to eschew definitions at this point and to proceed, rather, to a circumscription of the way the words "fact" and "value" are used. For in the various sciences and critiques, most of which treat of music in the non-musical terms proper to each, both terms vary enormously in meaning. This circumscription will begin with a consideration of the senses in which the two terms and their relationship to each other may be most advantageously understood as prime speech-concepts in musicological theory.

Fact and Value as Speech-concepts

Let us suppose that the total possibilities of speech-usage, i.e., the universe of discourse, is a variable whose parameter, or field of variance, is represented by the line LM, when L stands for logic and M for mysticism, after Russell,[32] or myth, after Cassirer.[33]

Figure 1.

At the L limit, a particular speech-product (instance of talking or writing) uses words, or symbols for words, that may have no reference outside the universe of discourse. Meaning is entirely endosemantic, word to word, symbol to symbol, i.e., intrinsic to speech. Thus, some tell us, in pure mathematics and logics, constructions can be true in themselves regardless whether they are true in the objective or physical universe of which our senses give us

32 Bertrand Russell. *Mysticism and Logic and Other Essays.* London, 1917.
33 Ernst Cassirer. *Language and Myth,* S. K. Langer, trans. New York, 1946.

evidence or in the subjective human experience of affections.[34] Such reference is purely formational.[35] It follows strict rules of inference from a minimal roster of stated postulates. A content can be infinitely comprehensive and absolutely precise, and can, if we are to believe the great mathematicians and logicians, be proved without exception to be true--in terms of this usage.

At the M limit, a particular speech-product uses words that may have no reference to the universe of discourse but only to items outside it. Meaning is entirely ectosemantic, word to sensed, perceived or imagined referent, i.e., extrinsic to speech. Such reference is purely informational. Words may derive their meaning purely by belief or from subjective experience, sometimes so exceptional that the terms "inspiration" and "revelation" have been accepted by many as the only suitable explanation, if such it is. A content may be infinitely comprehensive and absolutely precise, and can, if we are to believe the great mystics and religious teachers, be proved to be without exception true--in terms of insight, intuition, inspiration, faith, God-consciousness or other. Kyrie eleison, la ilaha illa allah, glossolalia, speaking in tongues, OM.

Between these extremes or, as they are sometimes called, "poles" of the parameter of speech-usage, there are many varieties of traditional speech-usage combining the characteristics of both. These combinations are formational in that mathematical and/or logical usage is "applied" or "extended" in the grammar and syntax of traditional speech as, in languages of the Western World, words refer to other words in sentences as subjects, verbs, predicates, adjectives, adverbs, etc. They are informational in that dictionary meanings, when not formational, refer to sensory, perceptive or subjective referents.

In these traditional combinations of usage, the concepts employed tend to gravitate toward one or the other limit or pole of the parameter; or, to reverse the metaphor, the formational usage tends to divide the available vocabulary into pairs of opposites. Thus, along with logic and mathematics, we find, near the L limit of the line in Figure 1., such concepts as those of reason, described fact, appearance, law, objectivity, manyness, causality, intellect, generality, determinism, etc. Along with myth and mysticism are customarily ranged intuition, felt value, reality, subjectivity, oneness, will, purpose, teleology, desire, affection (emotion, feeling) faith, free will, etc. Northrop[36] places apprehended fact in the latter category and I concur. Similarly, I would place statements and behavioral evidence of value judgement in the former.

Criticism as a scholarly discipline--as a critique, equally a reasoning of valuing and a valuing of reasoning--would seem to range over an area midway between the extremes of L and M. As a less circumscribed activity, the term "criticism" is commonly given to value-judgment in areas a and b in Figure 2. The nature of these will be dealt with presently.

---

34 Bertrand Russell. *Principia Mathematica.* New York, 1950, p. viii: "In practice, a great deal of mathematics is possible without assuming the existence of anything." Rudolph Carnap. *Meaning and Necessity.* Chicago, 1947, p. 1: "It is seen from the definition of L(ogical)-truth that it holds for a sentence if its truth follows from the semantical rules alone without reference to (extra-linguistic) facts." (First parentheses mine—CS).

35 In a paper "Music as a tradition of Communication, Discipline and Play" (*Ethnomusicology*, VI, 3 (Sept. 1962), p. 156), I used the word "operational" in this sense. Perhaps it would be better to reserve the word to designate the combination of informational and formational reference, which characterizes most speech-usage.

36 *Op. cit.,* p. 40.

17

Figure 2

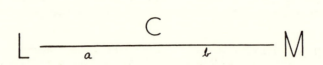

The natural sciences--physics, astronomy and geological sciences, biology, physiology and some psychology--would range over the area a; anthropology, the rest of behavioral sciences, sociology, aesthetics, over the middle area; ethics and metaphysics might barge into area a. Philosophy, of course, would range over the whole parameter.

As one of the humanities, musicology would be centered in area C. But all the sciences bear, either practically or theoretically, upon music. Thus, acoustics, the physiology and psychology of music would stem from area a; criticism, from area b. For any particular instance of speech-communication must, of necessity assume some one point in the parameter as that of its beginning.

Figure 3

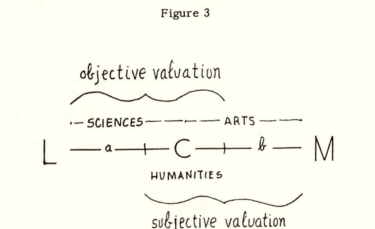

Every beginning must take many things for granted: on the one hand, the vocabulary, grammar, syntax, rhetoric, etc., of the language used and, on the other, the data and dicta that delimit the field envisaged. Since these initial assumptions determine to a large extent the substance of the communication, including its conclusions, the farther they are from L, the less the substance will be found to partake of the character of L; and the farther they are from M, the less the substance will be found to partake of the character of M. Let us indicate the tendencies of these subordinate parameters as plus (+) and minus (-), noting that the subordinate parameters l→m and m→l do not begin and end at L or M, but stop a little short of them. For it is quite impossible, so far as we know, to deal to any effect with beauty, love, virtue, God or Brahma, in terms of pure mathematics or logic, or with these latter in terms of poetry or ecstatic rhapsody. Our single line of variance in speech-usage LM, in Figures 1 and 2, turns out to be, therefore, a dual highway upon which one can travel in either direction from any point of beginning, remain in that vicinity, explore its width, the air above it and the ground below.

18

Figure 4

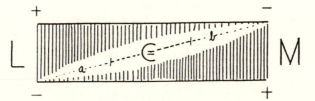

Of the many possibilities, only two will be singled out for mention here. Both have been explored by literary and art criticism as well as by musical criticism. The names customarily given to them are not very satisfactory; on the one hand, the scientific, rational or objective; on the other, the impressionist, affective or subjective. Both have available to them one and the same aggregate of sources or body of evidence. It comprises: (1) past judgments of value and valual trends contemporary with the critic and (2) potentialities of the arts of speech and music and of the culture of which they are parts. For convenience and economy, I shall first list this aggregate or body of evidence under eight main headings and second show how the same materials can be made to appear in two opposite lights as a result of their handling by the two opposite critical procedures.

Sources of the Evidence of Value-judgment

Figure 5

1. INDIVIDUAL TASTE

2. COLLECTIVE TASTE
(General)
Religion, Ethics,
Mores, Folklore,
etc.

3. COLLECTIVE TASTE
(Musical)
Arbiters, Critics,
Box Office, Sales,
etc.

4. HISTORY
(General)

5. HISTORY
(Musical)

6. SCIENCES
(Non-Musical)
Physics, Physiology,
Psychology, Aesthetics,
Anthropology, etc.

7. SCIENCES
(Musical)
"Theory" of Melody,
Counterpoint, Form,
Style, etc.

8. LAW

19

Under source 1., Individual Taste, I mean to include not only each individual's deep-set preferences and prejudices, which are prone to spontaneous expression in action or words, but also the modifications and extensions of them that have become built into the personality under influence of additional evidence of judgment by other persons and of training, maturing thought and experience involving, variously, the other seven sources, that may have been knit into habit. Thus, the referent is intended to comprehend manifestation and operation of both known and unknown--even unknowable--affections, feelings of pleasure and pain, inclinations of esteem, favor, approval, interest and their opposites--in short, what we do and do not want, prize, will, ought and must, whether or not we have conscious knowledge of it.

Under source 2., Collective Taste (General), I mean to include here groupings of tastes that operate in a community in such a way as to appear to transcend individuality and, so, present to any individual valuer a weight of authority sanctioned to the extent of the status of the persons represented in the grouping by custom and mores. Such taste, made evident by organized religious, social and civic groups through the music they employ, bears strongly upon the position and role of a music-tradition in a society and hence is a source of a large number of criteria in whose terms music-value judgments are made. The terms of such criteria are likely to be contextual, i.e., extrinsic, to music.

Source 3., Collective Taste (Musical), designates a similar grouping of taste and is more likely to be expressed in terms intrinsic to music, as by composers in their music, and in language by appointed or self-appointed arbiters of taste, whose word carries widely among amateurs and professionals alike. Such taste, also made evident by the same agencies as those mentioned in connection with general collective taste, finds specific expression in the sale of tickets at the box office, the cost of instrumental and vocal instruction, the financing of orchestras, opera houses, in concert management, etc.

The three sources (1., 2., and 3.) are to be regarded as contemporary by anyone adducing criteria from them.

Sources 4., History (General), and 5., History (Musical), comprise record and review of such criteria and judgment made in accord with the collective taste of former times. It will be observed that all of these criteria were, originally, based upon subjective, largely non-rational and predominantly mystical experience.

Source 6., Sciences (General), comprises values as expressed in terms of non-musical sciences, ranging from the natural (physics, physiology), near the L limit, to the humanities (anthropology, aesthetics, communications theory and philosophy) nearer the center of the parameter of speech semantics. These sciences can regard objectively the subjective judgments of sources 1. to 3. to the extent that these have been verbally expressed or can be inferred from the acts of those that hold them. For verbal expression, although a dictum for the producer of the expression, constitutes a datum for an observer. If he chooses, even the producer of a dictum can regard it, after it has been produced, as a datum.

Source 7., Science (Musical), comprises strictly musical value-judgments that are counterparts of those comprised by Source 6. The procedures outlined in conventional books on melodic, harmonic, contrapuntal and formal composition and in writings upon the more theoretic aspects of music and music-making can be regarded as constituting this source.

Evidence drawn from former writings of the classes of sources 6. and 7. can be comprised in sources 4. and 5., as were those of the classes 2. and 3.

Source 8., Law, comprises a class of criteria not now valid for the majority of populations in the Western World. In the early centuries of Christian Churches, criteria classifiable as "canon law" were operative. Even today, among some small religious sects, no music or only certain kinds of music are permitted. The Soviet Union has attempted to codify music-value upon a large scale. It may not be possible to attempt evaluation of this venture for some time to come. The effectiveness of either religious or political law for music has never been studied upon a broad or comprehensive scale. To best of present knowledge, verbal expression of law refers, or is supposed to refer, to strictly objective values -- that is to say: manifest in some kind of behavior. But it is a matter of common knowledge that obedience no less than enforcement varies widely according to strictly subjective values that are not necessarily expressed in verbal form. Musicians, like other people, have sometimes obeyed, sometimes evaded, sometimes flouted it.

Criteria

Criteria, or standards of value judgment, may be a posteriori generalizations of evidence or a priori assumptions of principles. (Ultimate or highest values, drawn from source 1., may be themselves criteria.) They may, therefore, be classified under the eight sources already given for evidence. The aggregate criteria and evidence funded in the memory, habits, outlook and will--the Gestalt--of any one of us must be random and highly miscellaneous, part consciously and part unconsciously held, now rational, now non-rational, and defying complete analysis. It forms the bulk of the subjectivity that science flees but is the basis of our beliefs, faith and hopes. Other persons can regard ours but not their own, objectively, as we can theirs. Each one of us must accept our own funded aggregate as our own individual value system, our "taste." The other sources of criteria and evidence may be variously represented in the source 1. that is our individual taste. Experience shows, I am sure we agree, that just as we differ in stature, physiognomy, perception, action and other definitive qualities of personality, so we differ in our valuative capacities and tastes. Surely, the serious student strives toward the balanced judgment by due consideration of evidence and criteria from all of the eight sources I have listed, but will never achieve the perfect balance. Indeed, as a denizen of an "unbalanced world," one of his chief aims in living in it must be to compensate for its unbalance to the extent to which he may be able and to take arms against a sea of troubles and by opposing not end but bring more into balance their oppositions as far as his individual need may require or desire it and his ability may achieve it. Thus, the problem of the subjective judgment in its relation to the objective situation has come to be dealt with, traditionally, by the formation of two distinct types of speech-usage. Both are known as well in the field of music as in speech-literature, drama, the visual arts and in philosophy.[37]

The scientific, objective or rational criticism regards the gamut of evidence and criteria in terms, typically, of what can be known of the valuative activity of others. Its typical exponent must suppress his own valuative activity, as well as he can, as bias invalidating his results. The dicta tend to be concerned with the relation between a datum and a perceiver so that value becomes a relative matter. There may be a hierarchy of values with a sharp distinction between one and another. It is the fact, the physical sound of the music that is real. The question whether value exists, subsists or has any reality apart from man is irrelevant Value is, thus, a function of fact, i.e., music must be perceived as fact before value may be attributed to it. Beauty is not in the symphony but is an attribution to it. In such attribution, a person acts in his capacity of membership in a community by which he has inherited, cultivates and transmits a tradition of valuing. Carriage of such a tradition implies training in and exercise of not only skill but taste. The scientific criticism is interested in the norms of the tradition, in individual variation among the users of it, and in what, if anything, in it can be found in other musics and what in all musics, i.e., what is universal in it. A posteriori reasoning and appeal to authority are characteristic of this procedure. Prediction is ventured only in terms of hypothesis. Evidence must be susceptible to verification by one or another scientific method and can be both quantified and qualified. Emphasis is not upon a few supreme values but upon as many as there are criteria from which they can logically be drawn. The attitude of the valuer is observant--ethically responsible [37] -- rather than emotional or worshipful. The aim is a balanced judgment.

37 Cf. Max Weber's *Verantwortungsethik* and *Gesinnungsethik*, quoted in Morris Ginsberg, "Facts and Values," *Advancement of Science*, XIX, 81 (Jan. 1963), p. 108.

21

The impressionistic, subjective or affective criticism regards the gamut of evidence and criteria in terms, typically, of direct expression of the individual valuer's intuition and taste. The typical exponent is likely to disregard the taste of others unless they agree with him or he wishes to denounce them. The dicta tend to be concerned with the exceptional, rather than with the norm, and to "either-or" or "all-or nothing" types of valuation, without gradation. Exceptional value tends to be regarded as value itself--unchanging, absolute, eternal, subsistent in the universe, as if it were the only reality and, as such, outside of general space and time and of mankind. Thus, fact tends to be a function of value. The stimulus, its apprehension, perception, conception and understanding tend to be merged. Beauty is one of the words for the oneness of things. Or the "one-manyness." It takes the exceptional person not only to create and perform the exceptional work, but also to achieve the empathy with it, its creator and performer in which alone the full experience of it can be realized. The exceptional is rare. The exceptional person can be sure of this. Hoi polloi must take his word for it. They can be ignored, just as lesser values, if they intrude, can be ignored. Norms are unimportant. A priori reasoning and assertion of authority are characteristic of this procedure. Prediction is easy, for it does not have to be based upon anything but a wish to predict. Neither evidence nor criteria are necessary. Certainly, they can be neither quantified or qualified. Whether regarded as a trinity of beauty, goodness and love or as the unity of God, the Brahman or the ineffable, the very nature of value is to be beyond rationalization and, therefore, mystical. The attitude of the impressionistic critic is emotional and worshipful--"true to himself"[38]--rather than observant. The balanced judgment is irrelevant.

Although clearly discernible as types of procedure, formal reliance upon either one of the two to complete exclusion of the other is not often met with in musicology. Alternation or mixing of them seems to be more common. But no critical undertaking can, I aver, escape classification as, on the whole, belonging to one or the other of these two types. The very nature of the technique of speech-communication, of the assumptions that must be made before the undertaking can get under way and can never be entirely divested of their origin in either logical postulates or mystical assertions, and, above all, the inescapable postulate that music must be able to communicate value in its own way that is not entirely commensurable with the value that language can communicate - all these hazards of the musicological juncture inevitably throw any critical undertaking into one or the other of the two categories. Of course, this is expressed, here, in terms of the so-called "scientific or objective" approach. The impressionistic or affective critic can answer: "You can't prove the supremacy of reason by reason." To which the scientific critic may reply, "Well, you can't prove the supremacy of intuition just by shouting louder."

Absurd though the confrontation may appear, it seems to have been even more clear and far-reaching (though expressed in more refined verbiage) in the actual course of philosophy during the last 150 years, in which logical positivism[39] has tried to establish a reality of fact free of, basic to or above value, and existentialism,[40] a reality of value free of, basic to or above fact. Contrary to this dependence upon one or the other of the horns of the dilemma that makes the confrontation seemingly inevitable and irreconcilable, the proposal here is that the dilemma--the confrontation itself--is the very crux of the matter. The two types of speech-usage must be admitted to be equally indispensable and each, without the other, equally futile.[41] Whether or not this adjustment of the dilemma is acceptable outside of musicology, I hold that we must accept it within musicology. The task of this "Preface" is merely to call attention to the situation as inherent in the musicological juncture. The details of the adjustment are the concern of the critique proper.

38 loc. cit.
39 Bertrand Russell. *Religion and Science*. New York 1933. Chap. IX.
40 John Wild. *The Challenge of Existentialism*. Bloomington (Ind.). 1959. pp. 1-26.
41 Risieri Frondizi. *What is Value?* Solomon Lipp, trans. Lasalle (Ill.). 1963. Chap. 5.

22

The Modalities of the Critique

As a deliberately methodical dealing with music and value in the art of speech, the critique will, then, be cast in the manner of the scientific criticism as far as the nature of its speech-usage is concerned. This will automatically tend to give it the backward-looking, fact-describing bias of the scientific or objective criticism which is one of the two terms of a dichotomy he is attempting to mediate and, so, will seem effectively to preclude achievement of the balanced judgment it seeks. Compensation is, to some extent, possible. It seems unlikely that full compensation can be found for such bias in any one piece of critical writing. A nearly balanced theory is probably more possible of attainment than a balanced style-criticism; and a balanced style-criticism more easily attainable than a balanced judgment of a particular contemporary composition. We should distinguish, therefore, a least three modalities of the critique of music--three distinct levels upon which it may operate most conveniently and economically in musicology:

1. the critique proper--the purely theoretical adjustment of the dilemmas met with in the musicological juncture;

2. style criticism--the application of pure theory to a particular tradition of music;

3. what is commonly known as "musical criticism" or Fachkritik--the application of the applied theory to particular items of composition, performance, personalities and the organizational activities in connection with them.

The speech-usage appropriate to the critique proper will be the deliberately methodical, objective or rational criticism; to style-criticism, an artistic (we may hope) blending or alternating of this and the impressionistic, subjective or affective; to music-journalism, the latter.

As to content, it is to be hoped that all three would bear in mind that like a circus-rider with each foot upon a different horse, the writer's task is to guide his speech-knowledge and taste in the same direction as his music-knowledge and taste. Reference to the second in terms of the first will be in words; but that of the second to the first must be for the most part not in words but by some alchemy of the imagination wherein the musically concrete, though ineffable, is credited with being linguistically concrete.

It is to be hoped also that although the value-judgments of others and even one's own, once stated, can be regarded objectively, everyone will bear in mind that the moment of making a judgment is a valual act, a continuing function, one extending from the valuer's past through his present into his future. It is essentially creative, forward-looking, teleological. The more importance given to it, the more nearly it is rooted in pure belief, the inclination of faith and of destiny--and so much the less rational. There is nothing more futile than for the rational criticism to "prove" by reason its superiority to the affective--or, for that matter, the reverse operation. The task of the critique is precisely to employ one kind of speech-usage to deal with its opposite in a single, coordinated content. Lest this be dismissed as mere paradox, let me assure the reader that at least for the present and the foreseeable future I see no likelihood that the critique of music will express mystical vision in terms of mathematics or symbolic logic, or mathematical truth by speaking in tongues. But let us not forget that from a mystical viewpoint paradox may be nearer the truth than is consistency. Imagination can--and perhaps should--take off where reason falters and where mystical insight becomes encased in dogma. Indeed, looking once more at our initial diagram (Figure 1.) of the parameter of speech usage, we might come nearer the truth--or, at least, clarity (although it would hopelessly confuse redrafting of Figures 2-4)--if we would represent it as a curve rather than as a straight line. For both our extremes, L and M, transcend both common sense and the "uncommon sense" of the humanities. And it is not seldom that we encounter suggestions that mathematical and mystical symbolisms are not as far apart as

23

the straight line makes them seem to be. Both seem to move in equally rarified and, perhaps, not entirely foreign territories. Either mystic or mathematician might accept a spiral, L + M, as at _a_ in Figure 6. But surely the "perfect" mystic would insist upon a circle, L equal M, as at _b_.

Figure 6

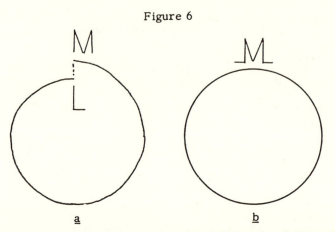

a   b

In closing, it may be worth remarking that the middle area of the parameter of speech-usage to which I have assigned the critique and the normative disciplines is one in which neither logic nor mysticism is at full strength. But do not underrate criticism on that account. Rarely do men act upon either pure reason or ecstatic contemplation. The facts as well as the values of life must, usually, first be funneled through the sieve of criticism before any substantial action is taken, whether in international politics, the little amenities of human intercourse or in scholarly talking or writing.

It is to be hoped that this exceedingly simplified exposition of one possible adjustment of the predicament that the musicologist finds himself in whenever he enters the musicological juncture is not, as Whitehead is said to have once remarked of a student's paper, "clearer than the truth." Although the critique lacks both the methodological power of incontestable logic and the passionate conviction of absolute belief, its strength is the rarity of either of these ultimates in the day-to-day life of the musicologist and the possibility when they do manifest themselves that either one may be used as a check against the other.

EDITORIAL NOTE

This monograph complements the author's "Preface to the Description of a Music" (Société Internationale de Musicologie,Cinquième Congrès, Utrecht, 3-7 Juillet 1953: Compte Rendu: Amsterdam, Vereniging voor Nederlandse Muziekgeschiedenis, 1953).One half was read at the First Inter-American Conference on Ethnomusicology held at Cartagena de Indias, Colombia, February 24-28, 1963; the other, at the First Inter-American Conference on Musicology held at Washington, D.C., U.S.A., April 29 - May 2, 1963. The combined text (Primera Conferencia Interamericana de Etnomusicología, Trabajos Presentados: Washington, D.C., Pan American Union, 1965) has been slightly revised. The author was Chief of the Music Division of the Pan American Union from 1942 to 1953 and is at present Research Musicologist in the Institute of Ethnomusicology of the University of California at Los Angeles.

PAN AMERICAN UNION
Washington 6, D.C., U.S.A.

PENALTY FOR PRIVATE USE, $300
EXENTO DE FRANQUEO POSTAL
ISENTO DE FRANQUIA POSTAL

OFFICIAL BUSINESS

Ethnomusicology and the History of Music

W. WIORA

Saarbrücken

1. Integration or Isolation

That ethnomusicology and the history of music depend on each other and should be closely connected has been suggested frequently, from Guido Adler and Carl Stumpf to the present day. In 1919, Georg Schünemann's inaugural speech at the University of Berlin dealt with "the relations between comparative musicology and music history". Several scholars have devoted their life's work to this task, for instance, Curt Sachs and Marius Schneider. As to the present time, I would point to the Hungarian school of musicology. The relations between ethnomusicology and the history of music have been chosen as a principal subject at several congresses, especially in 1953 at Bamberg, in 1961 in New York, and in 1964 in Budapest.

But in spite of all the efforts towards integration, these two sections of musicology remain rather isolated from each other, or their separation has even increased. Most historians of music take into account neither primitive nor oriental nor folk music, even in fields where it is necessary to do so, such as plainsong and hymnody research. Conversely, historical viewpoints and methods are scarcely applied in the majority of folklore and ethnological studies.

To justify their self-sufficiency, several historians of music maintain that ethnomusicology has not yet reached the rank of a scientific discipline with agreed principles and convincing results. They claim that the history of Western art music is and has to be the centre of musicology, because this highly cultivated art is more *historic* and more *historical* than all the other musics in the world. It seems to be more historic on account of its great composers and works of art and of its memorable evolution. On the other hand, it seems to be more historical than the music of any other culture because only Western civilization since the Middle Ages has had a fully developed musical life with a script culture and because only notated music, like written poetry, *i.e.* literature, can

St. Musicologica VII. (1965)

be investigated by really historical methods. Those historians are sceptical about the historical approach to ethnomusicology because it lacks a large number of written documents and is on the whole restricted to oral traditions so that many tasks of historical investigation, such as absolute chronology, are not practicable here. They assume that ethnomusicologists can give only single data, not the picture of a whole development. Moreover, folk-song and primitive music seem to be unchanging with time in several essential features, so that historical problems are at least subordinate in these fields.

Such arguments may be effective, but they are not true. The critics leave out of account the contribution of ethnomusicology to the *prehistory of music* and on the other hand to its *contemporary history*, *e.g.* the research into acculturation in all continents and other changes towards global industrial civilization. They have no regard for the very great importance of oriental music in the investigation of classical antiquity. They underestimate the results and possibilities of ethnomusicological contributions to the history of Western art music since the Middle Ages, *e.g.* the rhythm of medieval monody or the relationship of folk music to art music.

Let me, however, omit discussion of all these aspects and let me restrict myself to the problem as to whether Western art music alone, and its investigation, are historical in any adequate sense of the word.

2. History of Non-literate Cultures

It is true that the music of non-literate cultures has no historical existence in the same full sense of the word as western art music. It is lacking in elements such as a proper theory, an elaborated notation and higher forms of consistent evolution from stage to stage, like the evolution of opera or symphony. It lacks consciousness of evolution and with it "historia" in the sense of "res scriptae". But no people is so lifeless that it has no history at all. At least it lives in *elementary categories of history*, such as origin, change, influence, acculturation, suppression, decline.

Moreover, entirely non-literate cultures and the fully developed script cultures are at opposite poles. Between them there are different kinds and degrees of historical existence and they call for correspondingly different kinds of historical investigation. Have not the high civilizations of the orient, beside their predominantly oral methods of communication,

St. Musicologica VII. (1965)

written systems of music theory and philosophy, several kinds of notation, and records of memorable musicians?

As to European folk music, written sources are much more numerous
than has hitherto been supposed. Many melodies are hidden in plainchant,
in contrafacta, in the refrains of Troubadours and Trouvères. Moreover,
political events provide data for a chronology of folk music, for instance,
the immigration of the Magyars about 900. As in general ethnology, early
references to and descriptions of folk music are an important source for
absolute chronology; we have to study such sources methodically, following the American concept of *Ethnohistory*.

According to a general principle of scientific research, sources and
literature should be used in their entirety. All written testimonies of
the past have to be confronted with the oral traditions, and all criteria
for a chronology have to be combined, such as geographical dissemination and the superposition of different strata. The application of these
methods and their convincing results can be seen in historical linguistics
and other disciplines of comparative research. In view of their results
it is nonsense to deny the possibility and necessity of comparative
investigation of oriental and primitive cultures, wherever the constellation of sources is favourable.

3. An Approach to a Historical Outline:
German Folk-Song from its Beginnings to the Present Day

One of the fields with a favourable constellation of sources is folk-
song in the German-speaking countries. Moreover, historical research
on German folk-song is especially well developed. Based on this research,
not only can single results be collected, but a comprehensive outline may
also be attempted, at least as a framework for the main trends and
periods. Let me briefly point out this framework, emphasizing those
features which are to be found in several other countries also.

In the history of German folk-song three ages can be distinguished,
corresponding to the three historical periods: Germanic and German
Antiquity, the Middle Ages and Modern Times.

The stage of Antiquity in many areas extends into the Middle
Ages as is testified by clerical interdictions of pagan traditions; it survives as long as and insofar as christianization and the superposition
of cultural strata are not yet fully realized. Combined with archaic
oral traditions in remote regions, records and reports from TACITUS'

St. Musicologica VII. (1965)

Germania to several documents about 900 and 1000 — for instance some charms and the dance song at Kölbigk — bear witness to various structures and functions: epic songs with a free change in the number of syllables in each line and of lines in each stanza, pagan formulas, used not only as single incantations, but also as burdens, and so on. By comparison with Magyar and Czeremiss melodies, archaic types of strophic tunes, with a descending octave, prove to be older or even much older than 900. Comparison with other old European traditions discloses various stylistic elements, for instance types of pentatonism, jubilation and polyphony.

The Middle Ages of German folk-song, which reach into the Reformation epoch, may be divided into two stages, beginning about 900 and in the fourteenth century respectively. Compared with the first age, the social situation has changed through the superposition of feudal, clerical and learned music in which folk music now becomes the basic stratum. Its history from now on consists to a great extent in its relation to the other strata. Pagan traditions were suppressed or transformed, for instance types of ritual song in Christian festival songs. Besides spiritual songs stemming from the people, others were created by clerics. Under the influence of plainsong and art music the heptatonic modes became widespread and superseded older systems. Stichic forms were supplanted by strophic structures, alliteration by rhyme, and free rhythm by regular metre.

The second stage of the Middle Ages is determined primarily by the rise of urban culture; most of the folk-songs from written sources were sung in towns and in their vicinities. Moreover, in the late Middle Ages folk melodies began to be notated, especially in *contrafacta* and other spiritual songs. Besides improvised polyphony, the contrapuntual setting of folk-song developed and soon led to the golden age of this genre. Urban culture, notation and art music influenced the style of folk music, at first in the towns alone, whereas in the country and especially in remote regions old traditions lived on.

The Modern Period of German folk-song can be divided into three stages: from the time of the Reformation to the time of Enlightenment, from Herder to the Youth movement, and finally the present stage of technical and industrial civilization with its new forms of folklore.

During the first of these three stages, the changes which have led to the present critical situation of folk-song are already apparent. Songs were now partly spread in print by people making a trade of selling broad-sheets and teaching their melodies to the crowd. The authorities continued to suppress and pour scorn upon customs and songs. Alongside the people's dispossession of their indigenous traditions, the styles of folk-song became simpler and narrower. Instead of the former variety of tonal systems, rhythms and structures, the stereotyped model of major melodies, simple rhythmic formulas and symmetrical strophic forms became almost exclusive. Genres formerly accompanying customs and work now changed to selfconscious representation of professions and other groups. Besides the genuine folk-song, other kinds of popular song developed: the congregational song which supplanted the spiritual folk-song in protestant regions, the "Neue Zeitung" and the "Bänkelsang" which were folk-songs only in part, and further the popular art song and songs offered to the people by the philanthropic "enlightenment".

The stage from Herder to the Youth movement is characterized by two opposite processes: the decline of the genuine folk traditions and the renewal of the ancient folk-song which, however, was only a partial revival. Collection and investigation began to produce their lasting effects on musical life. The "Gesangverein" devoted itself to the concert performance of old songs in new arrangements. The *"Deutscher Liederhort"* of ERK and BÖHME became the depository of practical song-books such as the "Zupfgeigenhansl" and the "Kaiserliederbuch". In publication and performance, melodies were modified towards sentimentality and romanticism. Still more than before spontaneous folk-song was supplanted by "Kunstlieder im Volksmunde", by popular singing in church and school, by patriotic songs and "Heimatlieder", by "Gassenhauer" and operatic tunes. On the other hand, its melodiousness survives in the popular art song and other kinds of art music from the Viennese classics to Gustav Mahler and Paul Hindemith.

In the present industrial civilization, the situation of folk-song is being radically changed by the urbanization of the country folk, by mass media, by the submersion of the whole population in popular and art music, and by the growth of tourism and the fully developed entertainment industry. The genuine traditions and the spontaneous variation vanish almost completely, even in remote regions. On the other hand, the very same factors help to develop the secondary existence of folk music as a classical heritage and as mass entertainment. Folklore study and pseudofolklore have become main features of an epoch. Thus the new period brings to an end old trends which have pervaded the history of German folk-song since the Middle Ages.

St. Musicologica VII. (1965)

4. Need for Historical Ethnomusicology

We cannot understand the present changes if we follow the view of a simple revival after a period of decline, or if we maintain the present situation as being provoked by no previous trends other than the technical revolution. In view of its crisis, we are urged to study the history of folk-song as well as of other musical traditions of mankind, more intensively than ever.

The general view of the historical development will have to be supported by the detailed investigation of both written and oral sources. We have recently founded a musicological study group which will list the sources of ancient German folk-song in a comprehensive repertory. Corresponding projects could be inaugurated within the wider frame of the International Folk Music Council. Three of these tasks may be named: first, a repertory and edition of the written sources of European folk melodies from Antiquity to the end of the Middle Ages or, at least for some countries, to the eighteenth century; second, a collection of reports on folk music in the same period since Antiquity; third, extension of the systematic catalogue of melody types outlined in my collection *Europäischer Volksgesang*.

Historical research is not an addition to but a main task of ethnomusicology. It has to consist of *historical* as opposed to *semi-historical* studies such as the mere enumeration of sources. It includes critical interpretation, investigation of absolute chronology and causality, wherever this is possible, and finally a conception of historical development.

On the other hand, the fragmentary state of the sources does not permit of a complete and detailed picture of musical development in every country. The constellation is favourable only for some areas; but at least an approach to historical ethnomusicology and the working out of historical outlines seems to be practicable everywhere. For the general history of World music the contribution of historical ethnomusicology is no less necessary than the contribution of music history in the conventional sense of the word. This contribution is indispensable. Let us aspire and hope that it will become important and essential too.

More Recent Literature

Concerning the General Problem :

Der volks- und völkerkundliche Beitrag zur Musikgeschichte "Congress Report", Bamberg 1953, pp. 157—215, Kassel 1954.

The Contribution of Ethnomusicology to Historical Musicology "Congress Report", New York 1961, I: pp. 376—385; II, pp. 153—157, Kassel 1961 & 1962.

St. Musicologica VII. (1965)

Origins of Western Polyphony, ibid., I, pp. 161—183; II pp. 107—111.

BRAILOIU, C.: *Musicologie et Ethnomusicologie aujourd'hui*, "Congress Report", Köln 1958, pp. 17—29, Kassel 1959.

COLLAER, P.: *Polyphonies de tradition populaire en Europe méditerranéenne*, "Acta Musicologica", 32, 1960, pp. 51—66.

FENTON, W., N.: *The Training of Historical Ethnologists in America*, "American Anthropologist", 54/3, 1952, pp. 328—339.

HAEKEL, J.: *Zum heutigen Forschungsstand der historischen Ethnologie* in "Die Wiener Schule der Völkerkunde", Wien 1956, pp. 17—90.

HARRISON, F. LL.—HOOD, M.—PALISCA, C. V.: *Musicology*, Princeton University, New Jersey 1963.

MOSER, H.: *Gedanken zur heutigen Volkskunde*, "Bayrisches Jahrbuch für Volkskunde" 1954, pp. 208—234.

NETTL, B.: *Theory and Method in Ethnomusicology*, The Free Press of Glencoe 1964.

WIORA, W.: *The Concept and Method of "Comparative" Musicology*, "Congress Report", Salzburg 1964 I, pp. 3—10.

id., *Musikwissenschaft und Universalgeschichte*, "Acta Musicologica" 33, 1961, pp. 84—104.

id., *Musikgeschichte und Urgeschichte*, "Studier tillägnade Carl-Allan Moberg" 1961 = Svensk Tidskrift för Musikforskning 43, 1961, pp. 375—396.

id., *Die vergleichende Frühgeschichte der europäischen Musik als methodische Forschung*, "Congress Report", Basel 1949, pp. 212—221, Basel 1949.

id., *Die vier Weltalter der Musik*, Stuttgart 1961; English edition, *The Four Ages of Music*, New York 1964.

id.—ALBRECHT, H.: *Musikwissenschaft*, "Die Musik in Geschichte und Gegenwart".

Concerning the history of German folk-song:

Deutsche Volkslieder mit ihren Melodien, Herausgegeben vom Deutschen Volksliedarchiv, Vol. I ff., 1935 ff., Berlin/Leipzig.

"Jahrbuch für Volksliedforschung", I—VIII, 1928—1951; IX ff. 1964 ff., Berlin.

"Musik in Geschichte und Gegenwart", ed. F. BLUME, art. *Deutschland*.

HEILFURHT, G.: *Das Bergmannslied*, Kassel 1954.

MEIER, J.: *Abriss der Geschichte des deutschen Volksliedes*, in "Deutsche Literatur in Entwicklungsreihen, herausgegeben von Heinz Kindermann"; Reihe: 'Das Deutsche Volkslied', Vol. I, Leipzig 1935.

MÜLLER-BLATTAU, J.: *Deutsche Volkslieder*, Königstein/Taunus 1959.

SALMEN, W.: *Das Erbe des ostdeutschen Volksgesanges*, Würzburg 1956.

id., *Der fahrende Musiker im europäischen Mittelalter*, Kassel 1960.

SEEMANN, E.—WIORA, W.: *"Volkslied"* in "Deutsche Philologie im Aufriss", 2nd edition, herausgegeben von *Wolfgang Stammler*, Berlin|Bielefeld|München 1957.

WIORA, W.: *The Origins of German Spiritual Folk Song : Comparative Methods in a Historical Study*, "Ethnomusicology" VII/1, 1964, pp. 1—13.

id., *Zur Lage der deutschen Volksliedforschung*, "Zeitschrift für deutsche Philologie", Vol. 73, 1954, 197 ff.

Das Volkslied heute, "Musikalische Zeitfragen", herausgegeben von W. WIORA, Vol. VII, Kassel 1959.

BAUSINGER, H.: *Volkskultur in der technischen Welt*, Stuttgart 1961.

MOSER, H.: *Vom Folklorismus in unserer Zeit*, "Zeitschrift für Volkskunde", Vol. 58, 1962, pp. 177—209.

Ethnomusicology. A term coined by J. Kunst to replace "comparative musicology" (G. *verglei-chende Musikwissenschaft*) on the ground that the comparative method is employed in every scientific discipline. Ethnomusicology is an approach to the study of *any* music, not only in terms of itself but also in relation to its cultural context. Currently the term has two broad applications: (1) the study of all music outside the European art tradition, including survivals of earlier forms of that tradition in Europe and elsewhere; (2) the study of all varieties of music found in one locale or region, e.g., the "ethnomusicology" of Tokyo or Los Angeles or Santiago would comprise the study in that locality of all types of European art music, the music of ethnic enclaves, folk, popular and commercial music, musical hybrids, etc.; in other words, all music being used by the people of a given area.

In the 18th and 19th centuries an interest in what was then termed "exotic music" led to studies in Chinese music (J. B. du Halde, 1735; J. M. Amiot, 1779) and Arab music (Andres, 1787; R. G. Kiesewetter, 1842). As early as 1768, the *Dictionnaire de musique* of Jean-Jacques Rousseau contained examples of Chinese, Canadian Indian, Swiss, and Persian music. It was not until the end of the 19th century, however, that a few writers began to realize that the musical cultures of the non-Western world merited the same serious scholarship that was being focused on the European art tradition (e.g., C. R. Day, *The Music and Musical Instruments of Southern India and The Deccan*, 1891, with an Introduction by A. J. Hipkins; F. T. Piggott, *The Music and Musical Instruments of Japan*, 1893; F. Bose in *AMW* xxiii, 239ff).

About the same time, two developments provided essential tools for the ethnomusicologist: the Ellis cent system and the phonograph. In 1884–85 the British mathematician and philologist, Alexander John Ellis, aided by A. J. Hipkins, demonstrated that there are a great variety of tuning systems and scales built on different principles from those known in western Europe. He showed that these are accepted by accustomed ears as normal and logical. His method in these studies was based on the arbitrary division of the tempered octave into 1,200 parts or

298

134

"cents" [see Cents]. The first phonographic field recordings were made in America by J. W. Fewkes in 1890 and transcribed by B. I. Gilman in 1891 ["Zuni Melodies," in *Journal of American Archaeology and Ethnology* i, 68]. In 1900 C. Stumpf and O. Abraham made the first German recordings of this kind when a court orchestra from Thailand and musicians from South Africa visited Berlin. Today innumerable collections have been amassed by universities, state-supported institutions, and centers for research all over the world, with the tape recorder having largely replaced the phonograph.

In Germany the term *vergleichende Musikwissenschaft* became associated with the systematic studies inspired by Stumpf and Abraham and subsequently led by E. M. von Hornbostel. The interest of German scholars was concentrated on acoustics, psychology, and physiology in an effort to understand principles of tuning systems, scales, and organology, leading to a number of speculative theories founded on the *Kulturkreislehre*. In the United States studies in comparative musicology, pioneered by Fewkes and Gilman and carried on by Frances Densmore and others, showed the influence of anthropological interest in the American Indian. The methods developed under Hornbostel's brilliant leadership were introduced in the United States in 1928 by one of his pupils, G. Herzog ("The Yuman Musical Style," *Journal of American Folklore* xli, 183–231). Both German and American scholars emphasized cross-cultural comparisons.

An early concern with comparative method, before the subjects under comparison could be understood, led to some imaginative theories but provided very little accurate information. Nonmusical standards relating to economic status, technology, and relative social isolation were responsible for the general use of such terms as "primitive music" and "exotic music." It was not until 1928 that M. E. Metfessel documented the need for a device that could register musical sounds objectively, independent of the aural prejudice of the transcriber, showing subtleties of pitch, duration, attack, release, and other details of performance style that resist transcription in Western music notation (*Phonophotography in Folk Music,* 1928). Various approaches to this problem have been undertaken in Japan, Norway, Israel, and the United States.

In 1941 C. Seeger wrote that actual performance of music of another culture must carry far more weight than mere listening to it ["Music and Culture," MTNA, *Proceedings,* 35th series, pp. 112–22], an observation made a few years earlier by P. R. Kirby [Preface, *The Musical Instruments of the Native Races of South Africa,* 1934; repr. Johannesburg, 1953]. Foreshadowed by Seeger and Kirby, a new kind of program that has had a profound effect on training and research elsewhere in the United States and abroad was begun in 1954 at the University of California, Los Angeles. The program includes training in basic musicianship of non-Western musical cultures in order to provide a firm foundation in the performance skills of specific African, Oriental, and other types of music. Also, as Manfred Bukofzer indicated in 1956 ["Observations on the Study of Non-Western Music," *Les Colloques de Wégimont,* Brussels, Elsevier, 1956, p. 35] and as practical studies in performance have borne out, the research methods of Western historical musicology are inadequate for non-Western studies. As a result, new field and laboratory methods are rapidly being developed. The basic elements of music—rhythm, melody, harmony, tone color—have developed differently and with varying degrees of emphasis in different cultures. In the Middle East, Africa, South and Southeast Asia, and the Far East, rhythm and melody are expressed in subtle, rich, and complex forms. Among the gong-chime cultures of Southeast Asia orchestras composed of bronze instruments have developed a rich harmonic texture founded on the principle of orchestration known as stratification. In Western music, the primary emphasis on harmonic development represents an entirely different utilization of the basic elements of music. A comparison of the rhythm and melody of India with those elements in European art music (or American jazz, for that matter) serving as models is no more enlightening than a comparison of Tamil with Latin and Greek.

Recent studies not only document Ellis' assertion regarding the "musical scale" but also indicate that the musical practices, cultural contexts, and value systems of cultures throughout the world are highly individual, varying often in principle and always in detail from region to region and locale to locale (e g., see under Bali, Java, Thailand, Vietnam, etc.). A vast number of musical cultures of the non-Western world are yet to be studied systematically and the music of the European art tradition re-examined in the light of newly emerging concepts before comparative methods can "give musicology a truly world-wide perspective."

299

135

Lit.: For bibl. through 1958, see J. Kunst, *Ethnomusicology*, 3rd ed. (1959) and Suppl. (1960). Also see E. M. Hornbostel, *Opera Omnia*, ed. K. Wachsmann (in preparation, 1966); C. Sachs, *The Wellsprings of Music*, ed. J. Kunst (1962); A. P. Merriam, *The Anthropology of Music* (1964); B. Nettl, *Theory and Method in Ethnomusicology* [1964]; *id.*, *Reference Materials in Ethnomusicology* [1961]; G. Herzog, *Research in Primitive and Folk Music in the United States, a Survey* (1936); C. Seeger, "Systematic Musicology: Viewpoints, Orientations and Methods" (*Journal of the American Musicological Society* iv, 240–48); *id.*, "Semantic, Logical and Political Considerations Bearing Upon Research in Ethnomusicology" (*Ethnomusicology* v, 77–80); *id.*, "Music as a Tradition of Communication Discipline and Play" (*Ethnomusicology* vi, 156–63); M. Hood, "Music, the Unknown," in *Musicology* (1963).   M.H.

TWO PARADIGMS FOR MUSIC:
A SHORT HISTORY OF IDEAS IN ETHNOMUSICOLOGY[1]

Christopher Marshall
Department of Anthropology
Cornell University

ABSTRACT

Ethnomusicology presents an interesting case for scientific
historians. A paradigm, or body of shared assumptions,
existed even before the field did; a second paradigm
emerged without a scientific revolution; and the two
coexist without either giving way. The reasons for these
features are to be found in the history of the field and
the influence of humanism and social science on it; the
first paradigm is derived from old humanistic assumptions,
the second from newer anthropological ones. Anthropological contributions to ethnomusicology have not been as
great as they could be, owing to certain preconceptions
about the field, but it can be shown that it is a valid
and necessary occupation for anthropologists.

Thomas Kuhn, in his The Structure of Scientific Revolutions (1962),
outlines a pattern of development which he feels may be deduced from the
history of scientific theory. Science is not a gradual accumulation of
knowledge or an incremental discovery of truth through time; rather, its
history is characterized by a movement from one world view to another
according to a characteristic cycle of change. In its normal course, a
science has its own body of theory, methodology, and research design which
serves to define its domain of study and makes possible communication and
consensus among its members: Kuhn refers to this body as a paradigm. Men
who share a paradigm work within it on the problems it poses, seeking to
elaborate the paradigm, until it happens that an instrument fails to behave
as expected or an experiment reveals inexplicable anomalies. When major
anomalies are perceived the paradigm is threatened by its inability to account
for them; some scientists will try to explain away the anomalies so as to
defend their paradigm, others will reject the old paradigm and propose new
ones. When consensus over the paradigm breaks down a scientific revolution
occurs -- a period of turmoil followed by the rise of a new, more satisfactory
paradigm inconsistent with the old one. We must also mention preparadigmatic
science, when no standard set of methods or phenomena has yet been agreed on
and schools and subschools proliferate; this type of science occurs only in
the earliest days of the field, and some fields have always had paradigms.

---

1. I should like to express my debt to Alan P. Merriam of Indiana University
   for many of the ideas expressed in this paper. Naturally this does not
   mean that he is in agreement with all the ideas presented.

75

With reference to Kuhn's theories, the history of ethnomusicological theory is sufficiently interesting to merit some study. The field came into being all at once, without a preparadigmatic period and with a tremendous degree of consensus about the basic paradigms right from the start; later a new paradigm emerged to challenge it, but not as a result of perceived anomalies; and now the two paradigms seem to be coexisting, with no sign of one giving way to the other. This paper will attempt to outline the general history of the theory of ethnomusicology, showing how its seemingly unusual features came into being /for histories of ethnomusicology, see also Nettl (1957) and Kenst (1959)/. In a field as small as this one, institutional and social history have done much to mold the history of theory, and these influences will also be discussed. Finally, some suggestions will be made about the role of anthropologists in ethnomusicology and the possibilities inherent in the field for them.

The field of ethnomusicology came into being about the 1890' , as the result of two important forces. One force was the invention of the gramophone, which for the first time made it possible to examine non-written music in detail by creating concrete, replayable documents. Previously what work had been done on non-notated music had depended on hand notation in the field, a laborious process requiring the incessant resinging of a piece of music until the scholar had it all written; and such notation was so difficult and limited in the amount of data it recorded that it was hardly practiced at all. Now it was possible to preserve a large number of items easily for study by any number of scholars, none of whom even had to enter the field. The second force was the great interest in and investigations of nonwestern peoples, especially colonial peoples, during that century. This was the era of several large-scale ethnographic expeditions, such as the Torres Straits Expedition, going out of Europe to the colonies. Their goal was to record as many aspects of native life as possible, so it was natural that they brought along the newly invented gramophone to record copies of native song as well.

There was no field of ethnomusicology in those days. Various men from various disciplines converged independently on the study of nonwestern music within their own fields of study. Ethnologists, physicists, psychologists, and acousticians were all involved in this study. A number of archives were founded in Europe for the preservation and study of phonograms, wax cylinders, and other recordings, usually in connection with psychological institutes; the archives made sure that every expedition went into the field with a gramophone, and formed the nuclei around which the students of "exotic music" gathered.

Though they did not think of themselves as sharing a common field, these men were nevertheless working with the same set of assumptions about music, sharing the same paradigm of music, of culture, and of their interrelations. These assumptions were held by all, in fact were scarcely questioned, a fact which might seem odd in view of Kuhn's ideas about how a science begins. Why were these years not marked by a conflict of pre-paradigms, since the phenomenon of nonwestern music, brought back in recorded form, was so new to Western ears? The fact is that, although the serious study of exotic music had not begun until this time, there were already pre-existing paradigms about the nature of music in general and its relations to culture. These paradigms were the common heritage of Western culture and held by practically all without question. When the phonograms began to make it clear that there were many kinds of musics, the general Western paradigm of what music was was simply extended to cover them as well. This would explain the remarkable degree of consensus in the new study of "exotic music" -- the paradigm was already agreed upon even before the science came into being. What was this paradigm? Music was seen as a <u>self-contained, bounded system of sound capable of being fully understood in its own terms</u>.

The search for the origins of this theory of music takes us in many directions, but we can be aided to some extent by a comparison with the current theory of language, which we find very similar; in fact, the same paradigm, as stated above, could hold for almost all linguistic research at the time. Let us first examine why music, like language, was seen as "self-contained" and "bounded". This implies a detachment from other human creations, a separateness and freedom from ties to other phenomena. In large part this attitude can be traced to an anthropomorphic concept of culture, according to which culture consisted of many discrete institutions like organs, each playing a unique role in keeping the social body alive, yet each somehow functionally independent of the others. All cultures apparently had the same institutions, whether more or less developed; and like the comparative anatomist, the student of culture could compare the same institutions in different cultures. Language was one such institution or organ of culture; music was another. As such, every culture had them, but every culture had them differently, and because they were discrete subunits of culture one could compare them cross-culturally without any problem.

What was meant by "system" in the paradigm of music? Language was seen to be systematic in the sense that it operated according to a finite number of statable laws (a grammar) and consisted of an unambiguous hierarchy of units (sounds, words, sentences). In observing language, one went to texts and abstracted these rules and units, finally presenting them in the form of grammars and dictionaries. The system of language was to be separated from the humans who spoke it; only the product of speaking, as it were, was of interest. Music was also seen to be systematic; it was believed that there were rules to all music and that it consisted of clear units -- notes, scales, songs, meters. To understand music, one went to recorded and written texts and abstracted rules and units, with the hope of making statements about the internal regularities of a culture's music. Lastly, music could very well be studied by people who had never seen the field; the whole of a piece of music was contained on a wax cylinder, without any ties to the people who sang it; only the product counted.

Just as language consisted of words which could be gathered to form a dictionary, music was seen to consist of songs: discrete, unchanging, beginning and ending things which could be collected. Music was thus made up of a theoretically countable number of <u>things</u>, brick-like items which went together to build the whole structure. Songs were taken out of their living context as wax cylinders -- things, with beginning and end -- songs could be replayed many times on cylinders without changing -- things, unchanging -- and songs could be investigated to reveal the rules of music -- things, structured according to a sort of grammar.

We have already seen, I think, some of the reasons why music was to be studied "in its own terms", without reference to other elements of culture. But there was another reason for this, a more subtle one perhaps. Music was defined as an <u>art</u>. Now, in the West art is seen to be different from ordinary life and cannot be judged by the same standards; it is defined as being aesthetic (that is, we have to look at it differently), as being non-useful, and as understandable only in its own terms and in terms of inexpressable feelings. If music is art, then it must be judged with relation to itself and not to other, prosaic aspects of life. The emphasis on the "artisticness" of music had another effect, to reinforce the idea of music as thing. What we in the West appreciate about art is the product of the artist, the "work of art", not the process of making it; this is evidenced by our naming of works of art and the institution of copyright, among other things. Thus, if music be defined as art and art as product, then we study the product of the musician only, not the way he makes it or why he makes it.

As we have seen, the paradigm for music stemmed from all sorts of pre-existing ideas about music and culture. When the students of "exotic music" began their studies, their paradigm permitted them to ask certain kinds of questions and use certain types of methods. Evolutionary theories of music became possible -- since music was structured, was there a pattern of growth from a simple structure to a complex one? Diffusionist theories were even more popular -- since music consisted of discrete items (songs, scales, and so on), might not these items be borrowed successively outwards from certain areas? Music could be separated from culture, and items of music could ne separated still further from others; thus it became possible to use the comparative method, abstracting isolated features from various bodies of music. Just as philologists were attempting to collect units of language for their dictionaries and grammars, music scholars were interested in collecting units of music (rather than observing their social context or talking to the musicians). The origins of music were traced, not to present culture processes, but to the distant human past.

At the same time that psychologists, ethnologists, and other such folk were becoming interested in "exotic music," Western musicians were developing the field of musicology. Founded on essentially the same paradigm of music we have been discussing, the musicologists too sought to get at the rules of music, this time only Western music. Contact between the musicologists and the students of exotic music increased steadily, and because the only real difference between the two was an areal bias, they finally came to be thought of as merely different aspects of the same field. The contact with the more respectable musicologists had two effects on the students of exotic music: first, it strengthened their paradigm, and second, it gave them an institutional base out of which most are still operating -- departments of music.

The conjunction of the two fields took place gradually, and coincided with a drift within the paradigm. The old paradigm of music was not changed in any of its fundamentals; what gradually changed were secondary features. To be more exact, scholars began to realize that music was not as simple a structure as they had thought. At first, no one had regarded musical structure as being particularly complex. Songs had been seen as stable through time; one song could be taken to represent an entire body of music, since a culture's music was homogeneous; and so on. These assumptions made the comparative method and evolutionary-diffusionist theories possible. But it began to appear, as scholars turned their attention to music in more detail, that a song is not unitary through time and space; that a body of music is not homogeneous; in short, that the structure of music was not as simple and clear-cut as had been supposed, and that the free-wheeling theories would have to be shelved for awhile until music was better understood. Formal description, then, became an end in itself; it was repeated faithfully that comparison and generalization cross-culturally were the utlimate goals of the science of exotic music, but less and less of either came to be done. People began to write incredibly detailed "musical ethnographies." All this work remained faithful to the old paradigm of music, but with a shift in emphasis. Music was still seen as a self-contained, bounded system of sound understandable in its own terms; but the system, it appeared, was less homogeneous and more complex than it had first appeared. Few doubted that the proper study-object of the field was music sound.

This drift toward description rather than generalization, and the increased technicalization of music study (aided in large part by the musicologists) had a number of effects on the field. First of all, the anthropologists became less and less interested in the field (which by this time was actually called comparative musicology) partly because of the technical skills which were becoming necessary. Anthropologists continued to be active in the collection of music, it is true, but they were rarely able to do anything with the music itself. But the failure of anthropologists to take hold in the arts, I think, was also due to another factor; they never seriously questioned the paradigm of music. Art, they must have felt, is not part of ordinary life; you cannot elicit the same sort of information about music as you can about kinship; it is hard to fit it into a functionalist model of culture; and its study requires too much technical training. Most of all, though, anthropologists never saw the need to look at music as something other than sound -- as behavior, as concepts -- because they unquestioningly accepted the prevailing definition of music.

Since there was little social-scientific interest in music, the field was taken over completely by humanists, a process which was already taking place anyway as a result of contact with the musicologists. Anthropology has always been characterized, at least to some degree, by a search for generalizable principles, by the construction and testing of hypotheses, and by cross-cultural comparison. Under the humanist domination of comparative musicology all these languished. The humanities are not characterized by a devotion to a search for the general; the social sciences are. As a result, comparative musicology became the study of musics rather than of music; a strong Boas-like reluctance to compare went hand in hand with a fascination with the particular. And throughout this whole period no one ever questioned the basic paradigm of music, because no one was really thinking theoretically.

One wonders whether "scientific revolutions" occur in the humanities at all. It would seem likely that something comparable to Kuhn's description of revolution in the "hard" sciences does take place in the very "soft" humanities -- new styles of literary criticism rise on the ashes of old ones, for example. But whether or not this constitutes revolution, it would seem that humanists are not given to the conscious stating and elaborating of a paradigm, let alone the questioning of an old one. Humanistic scholars of music have found nothing wrong with their paradigm yet; one of their safety valves has been to state that there is a component in music that cannot be stated in words (for instance Seeger, 1965), and this may sometimes be used to justify their failure to try. But whatever the case, the humanistic study of music is still going strong today and shows no sign of a scientific revolution within its ranks.

World War II was a watershed for the study of music, just as it was for the study of everything else. For one thing, the war did much to weaken American comparative musicology (which had had strong ties to the old German and Austrian scholars), financially and institutionally; the field was hit hard by the Depression and almost finished off by the War. But a whole new current of students began to enter the field. Some were music students interested in broadening their field; but many were ex-G.I.'s, men who had fought in distant parts of the world and had had experience with nonwestern peoples. These new students had dual training -- almost all had one of their degrees in music but another in anthropology. They were familiar with comparative musicology, since they had studied with the old masters, but were also aware of the principles of anthropology, particularly the emphasis on generalization and theory, the elaboration and definition of models, and most of all the idea of culture as an integrated whole. By the application of their anthropological ideas to music they evolved what may be seen as a new paradigm. Music was culture, rather than being in culture. Not only was it a system of sound; it was also a way of behaving, a pattern of action necessary to create or appreciate sound properly; and it was a system of concepts about what behavior and sound was correct. Music was no longer defined solely as sound in cultural context, as the old paradigm had had it -- music was now sound, behavior, and concept all together, and any separation, though analytically useful, would be essentially distorting (Merriam, 1964).

This whole new movement (which began to take form around 1948) was connected with the appearance of a new term for the discipline, significantly enough. "Ethnomusicology" appeared about this time, and "comparative musicology" was gradually phased out. Clearly, something was happening within the field, something that required redefinitions; even the old-line comparative musicologists felt that some sort of redefinition was necessary. What was happening, of course, was a confrontation of paradigms; music in culture was being confronted by music as culture, and the definitions of "music" and "culture" were very different.

This confrontation is still going on today, and there is no sign of it letting up. Supposedly, according to Kuhn, one paradigm should be giving way to the other, more effective one, but there is no sign of this either. The reason is that neither group can understand the fact that the other is operating according to a different set of definitions of "music" and "culture", and therefore there is no dialogue. In the opinion of the proponents of the older paradigm, the new people are not studying music but the context of music; according to the followers of the new paradigm, the old ones are analyzing only one isolated segment of music and neglecting a great deal of the subject. The talking at cross-purposes that has resulted has not benefited from some humanists' unwillingness to define their terms, a tendency resulting from their non-generalizing, nontheoretical approach; they have been particularly loose in the way they use the term "culture", commonly used but never to my knowledge defined in the writings of a first-paradigm scholar.

There have been many attempts to bridge the ever more apparent gap between the two groups, but none to my knowledge have viewed it as resulting from differences in the basic paradigms of music and culture. The anthropological, second-generation ethnomusicologists, however, have come closest to it; Merriam, for example, has noted the humanities-social sciences split in method, technique, and general outlook between the two (1969). Kolinski (1967), Hood (1963), and other proponents of the older paradigm have been no less concerned with the problem, but in my opinion have not examined it in enough theoretical depth to get at the real nature of the problem. Such scholars have tried to define the field in broad enough terms to encompass both camps by saying that it is to study both music and its cultural context, or music in itself and music in the world. This produces rather strange results if one goes to define ethnomusicology from it; for, in their view, ethnomusicology is concerned basically with music (that is, sound), while at the same time it is to be <u>equally</u> concerned with things that are <u>not</u> music (the "cultural context"). This position is theoretically untenable if one believes that a discipline is defined mainly by what it studies, for here we have ethnomusicology apparently giving equal weight to the context of what it studies as well. But the paradox is only a seeming one; although the proponents of the first paradigm have been more than generous in their stated definitions of the field, in fact they continue to act as if music (music sound) were the most important study-object of the field. It would appear that they are not aware of the paradox, largely because they have little inclination to examine their presuppositions theoretically. Given this humanistic tendency to be uncritical of one's paradigms and definitions, there is little hope of serious contact between the two camps within the field. (I do not mean to slight the humanistic approach, a very valuable one in the case of music. But I am writing from the perspective of anthropology, a social science /at least compared to musicology/, and am trying to stress the ways in which the difference between "their" approaches and "ours" has led to misunderstandings in the field of ethnomusicology.)
Kuhn does not mention the possibility of such situations in his discussion, perhaps because it is much less important in the hard sciences; yet it is a frequent occurrence that conflicting paradigms can exist side by side without one overpowering the other, due to a failure to communicate. In anthropology the Americans and the Dutch have had very little contact with each other, and there is no chance of either one's paradigm being swallowed up by the other; here distance and language work against communication. Closer to home, sociologists and anthropologists have very different paradigms for society, and the differences are sustained by the (rather arbitrary) system of separate departments. At any rate, there seems to be little meaningful dialogue at present between the adherents of the older, humanistic, music-<u>in</u>-culture paradigm and the proponents of the newer, anthropological, music-<u>as</u>-culture paradigm; and the signs for change do not seem to be there.

The number of scholars interested in the new music-as-culture paradigm is very small; we might mention Alan Merriam, Alan Lomax, John Blacking, and William Kay Archer as examples. All of these men have had anthropological experience, a great many are anthropologists now. In comparison to the large number of musicological ethnomusicologists they are a small number indeed. Why have so few proponents of the second paradigm emerged? Clearly, the paradigm of music as culture depends on modern anthropological concepts of culture, and thus proponents of the second paradigm should come from anthropology. Let us rephrase the question: why then, are there so few anthropologists in ethnomusicology?

The reasons are probably the same ones that led anthropologists to drop out of the field in the early decades of this century. Anthropologists still have the feeling that music is an art, and the arts are still regarded as non-useful, as being of a different order of reality than that which the anthropologist is accustomed to dealing with, as somehow not rooted in clear Malinowskian biosocial needs. This whole idea of art is questionable, for one thing; Merriam (1964) has shown that the concept of art is by no means a cross-cultural one, especially with relation to music. But anthropologists are unwilling to question their deep-seated Western beliefs about the specialness of art. Another problem, and this one the most commonly voiced, concerns the need for specialized training in music if one is to study ethnomusicology. While there is unquestionably a tremendous advantage in knowing something about the technicalities of music sound, there is much that anthropologists can do concerning people's philosophies of music, their musical behavior and values, and other studies which do not require such specialized training. Perhaps the greatest problem of all is the fact that anthropologists have tended not to question the common Western conception of music. Music has been seen as technically organized sound, not as sound produced by human behavior and organized by concepts, and as such has been relegated to the specialists since it does not be definition have anything to do with people's behavior and values. In fact, as we have seen, music may be viewed as much more than an isolated system of sound, for sound is produced by social behavior according to cultural concepts, and therefore seems to demand study by the anthropologist.

Many studies which have been carried out by anthropologists have been quite successful. Alan Lomax has shown that correlations exist between musical style and social structure (1968); Alan Merriam has compared the ways in which music is viewed cross-culturally to show that our concept of art is not universal (and such projects involve practically no knowledge of the technicalities of music sound, be it noted) (1964); and others could easily be cited. There is no question, then, that anthropologists working with a new paradigm of music, without necessarily any formal training in music sound, can achieve significant results; and there is no question that the new paradigm is a viable one, one which can solve many of the problems of both fields. Up till now anthropologists have treated ethnomusicology as a curious, obscure little field straddling the bounds of anthropology. Let us hope that they come to question their own values about music and the arts in general, for it seems evident that ethnomusicology is obscure only for lack of attention, and lies squarely within the boundaries of anthropology.

REFERENCES

Hood, Mantle. 1963. "The Quest for Norms in Ethnomusicology." Inter-American Music Bulletin 35.

Kolinski, Mieczyslaw. 1967. "Recent Trends in Ethnomusicology." Ethnomusicology 11:1.

Kuhn, Thomas. 1962. The Structure of Scientific Revolutions. Chicago: University of Chicago Press.

Kunst, Jaap. 1959. Ethnomusicology. The Hague: Nijhoff.

Lomax, Alan. 1968. Folk Song Style and Culture. American Association for the Advancement of Science Publication #88. Washington, D.C.

Merriam, Alan. 1964. The Anthropology of Music. Northwestern University Press.

Merriam, Alan. 1969. "Ethnomusicology Revisited." Ethnomusicology 13:2.

Nettl, Bruno. 1956. Music in Primitive Culture. Cambridge: Harvard University Press.

Seeger, Charles. 1965. "Preface to the Critique of Music." Inter-American Music Bulletin 49.

ETHNOMUSICOLOGICAL RESEARCH AND ANTHROPOLOGY

§ 9537

Norma McLeod
Program of Comparative Studies, University of Texas, Austin, Texas 78712

INTRODUCTION

As of the present writing, ethnomusicology has developed in several directions, some of which are of only marginal interest to anthropologists because of the specialized nature of the researches. Among these developments are the computerization of pitch measurement data, the discussion of tuning patterns in the absence of information concerning form, the development of notational techniques in the Far East, and other subjects of similar interest to musicologists. For the purpose of this paper, information not of central interest to the discipline of anthropology will be deliberately excluded in order to concentrate upon the relationship between music and culture.

Music as a variety of human behavior can be classed as one of the most highly patterned cultural activities. In fact, patterning is so heavy that as a sound phenomenon, music can be estimated at approximately 90% redundancy, as compared to an estimated 50% redundancy for language (50). While language is describable as a phenomenon with a small repertoire of phonological constituents organized into an immense number of lexemes, music has a small number of phonological constituents organized into a small number of phrases or motifs, each of which is frequently repeated. On a larger order of form, language may represent an infinite number of possible combinations of sentences into paragraphs and other larger units, no one of which may ever be repeated, while music is organized into a small number of large forms, each of which is usually repeated. Thus music is a setpiece phenomenon, and its level of redundancy is very high.

The very prominence of pattern in music has led to a vast amount of work on the particulars of pattern; in fact, so much has been done that Merriam (36) made this complaint:

99

> In the history of ethnomusicology we have given undue importance and stress to musical sounds as things in themselves. That is, we have taken the sounds produced by any particular group of people as a phenomenon made up of interrelated parts which behave according to certain principles and regularities inherent in themselves. We have looked at musical sound as a structural system, i. e. in static synchronous terms, and we have tended to make our analyses without reference to the human behavior out of which the sound system arises (36, pp. 211-12).

The trend Merriam suggests is indeed a part of the history of ethnomusicological research; however, I would disagree that any structural studies, in present terminology, were done until quite recently. Rather, music seems to have been used as a particularly apt arena for the demonstration of intellectual theories in vogue at any given time. To my knowledge, no study of music as a phenomenon of interrelated parts was attempted before 1954 (Nettl 40), and even then not all of music was viewed as a single structure.

More pertinent to Merriam's comments is the fact that early work on music did concentrate almost exclusively on the music itself, with subsequent neglect of the cultural factors which are inherently significant to the creation of any art. So much is this the case, that Kolinski was able to maintain as late as 1957 that music was so similar from culture to culture at least in respect to pitch that it could be explained by . . . "basic similarities in the psycho-physical constitution of man" (26, p. 5), i.e. that psychic unity is a rational explanation of music and that cultural variation is not pertinent.

This point of view results from two factors: a lack of concrete studies by musicologists of contextual features of music before that time, and a lack of knowledge on Kolinski's part of the work that had been done previously by anthropologists on the relation of music to culture.

Since this is the first review of ethnomusicology to be presented in the *Annual Review of Anthropology*, it seems necessary to give a short review of the history of the studies on non-Western music in order to provide the reader with a better understanding of the later trends.

HISTORICAL OVERVIEW

Before 1882, mention of music of non-Western cultures is found for the most part in the works of travelers, explorers, priests, and missionaries. Robert Stevenson (53, 54) summarizes what is known of the music of North American Indians. In other parts of the world, attention was directed mainly to the high art of civilizations, and little or no emphasis was placed on either folk music outside of Europe (indeed, the folk music of India is little known even today) or on the music of nonliterate peoples. Such information as is available on music is usually embedded in works on other subjects, and it is grossly misleading because of the problems of transcribing music of non-Western cultures into the European notational system.

The practical aspects of field work began with Theodore Bäker, who studied the

Seneca Indians of New York State (1882), giving both musical and cultural information. He used the terminology of Western music for the former and general description for the latter. Nettl has characterized the work of German scholars who followed him as the German school of comparative musicology (41, p. 28), and maintains that they were guided by two principals—exact sound measurements of pitch and some cultural description. The main work was influenced by German psychologists, primarily Carl Stumpf, who studied the Bella Coola Indians and founded the Berlin archives, and his pupil, E. M. von Hornbostel. The intellectual impetus was the desire to understand "the place of music in the framework of the human mind" (41, p. 28), and they worked with non-Western music because of its divergencies in type. Special emphasis was placed on pitch and melody, which were expected to reveal mental trends. The purpose was comparative; the tool, the highly structured nature of pitch systems; the aim, threefold.

At first scholars adopted the framework of unilinear evolution. Attempts were made to show that one style of music was older than another within a given culture; Bäker concluded for the Seneca, for instance, that the rhythmic dance was older than the recitative style (Densmore 14, p. 77). From this first aim came the work of Curt Sachs and his pupils, primarily Rose Brandel, who have attempted to organize all musical phenomena in evolutionary sequences from least to most complex. Sachs was extremely prolific, and his approach has deeply influenced musicologists interested in non-Western music. Although anthropologists have abandoned unilinear evolution, Brandel was attempting to prove Pygmy music was older than Nilotic as late as 1961. It is to be deeply regretted that naive comparisons couched in evolutionary terms should have survived until so recently. As with others it can only be assumed that anthropological theory was not widely known among many persons interested in music.

The second aim stressed the *Kulturkreis* theory of Schmidt and Graebner, particularly in the worldwide distribution of instruments but also in connection with music. Pitches were used by von Hornbostel in a number of studies designed to show that the primary center of distribution for world music was somewhere in Southeast Asia. The best known of these theories is that of the cycle of blown fifths, designed to show that African xylophones are derived from Indonesia. Although the theory has been ably exploded by several musicologists (e.g. 24, 41), A. M. Jones is still maintaining its validity.

Once American diffusionist theory came into vogue, the same materials were used to demonstrate music areas, beginning with von Hornbostel's study on Africa (1928) and continuing with work by Herzog, Roberts, and Nettl. Of these scholars, the contributions of Helen H. Roberts are the most meticulously done, and her study of the musical relationships between the Luiseño, Gabrielño, and Catalineño Indians of California stands out as a fine example of trait and complex listing and manipulation (45). Other works, however, such as Roberts' and Nettl's attempts at music areas in North America and Merriam's classification of African music were looser and less satisfactory. The latest attempt at defining music areas is that of Lomax (30a), which outlines music areas for the entire world. Again the criteria chosen are too loose and the trait list involves too few items to be convincing to any scholar familiar with the works of Spier or Kroeber.

The trends begun by the German scholars have two factors in common: bits of music are lifted out of the totality and used to prove whatever theory is wished; and the theories are globalistic in nature. The lack of understanding of the influence of context upon content is a familiar one. What is surprising is that this should have been done with a behavioral syndrome of so systematic a character.

In late nineteenth century America, interest in music was also developing, as displayed by the works of Alice Cunningham Fletcher, who worked with the Sioux and Omaha and who described her interest as "the consideration of the relations existing between the Indian's music and his life, social and individual" (17, p. 237). While her work is far from good by today's standards, it represents the beginning of a trend that was immensely aided by Franz Boas.

Boas is of primary importance in the present trends of the study of music. While he had no relevant theory and did not do supremely good work on music himself, his constant emphasis on the arts as a source of information on culture deeply influenced his students. This, combined with the sense of urgency to collect information before it faded away before the onslaught of Western culture, led many of Boas' students not only to take a kind view of music, but to actively collect it whether they knew how to handle it or not. The end result is a magnificent set of collections of recordings, along with data which in many cases are sufficiently meticulous to allow a modern scholar to work successfully with them. It is a source of wonder to me to read the early works of Speck and to find in them all the wealth of detail a modern ethnomusicologist could desire (along with some aspects we have since forgotten to consider!).

Boas' lack of global theory, his distaste for theorizing in the absence of data, and his insights into small detail have left all anthropologists, including ethnomusicologists, with a rich heritage to explore and understand without the constraints of a priori assumptions about the nature of reality to skew our thinking. Boas supported no particular theory that is evident in his works. As Spier (51) has put it, "he regarded all the arts as aspects of the interplay of imagination and convention" (p. 150). While this might be regarded as a truism today, it is for the most part an unexplored truism; Boas' comments on the relationship between esthetics and technical control in the arts have been worked out for some graphic art styles, but remain to be studied in music. Although it is clear that, depending upon the construction of an instrument, some melodies will be easier to play than others for technical reasons, no study of the relationship between a technical Gestalt and an esthetic Gestalt has been done.

It would not be possible in a short review to mention all that Boas and his students did; a mass of recordings, transcriptions, and descriptions of ceremonial and musical activities remain to be plumbed. The main line of continuity to the present, however, is Melville J. Herskovits, who believed that music might be a clue to the understanding of New World Negro culture, and who urged William Bascom, Richard Waterman, and Alan P. Merriam to investigate the relationship between African music and New World Negro music on some stable basis. The best description of the final system is to be found in Freeman & Merriam (18).

Briefly defined, the system involves the counting of intervals and the presentation of interval percentages in chart form; the expression of melodic range by a mathematical formula; a formula for melodic direction based on beginning, ending, highest and lowest tones; the discussion of prominent interval patterns; and a description of modal structure—especially anhemitonic pentatonic modes (modes of five tones without half steps). All descriptions are presented numerically; two musical systems so described are compared to one another, and probability statistics are applied to determine their possible relationship. Through time it has been discovered that certain of the above aspects of music are better indicators of relationship than others. While the final statement of the method is yet to be written, it is now clear that New World Negro music has retained its African character remarkably well. In some cases the retention is uncanny. Herskovits asked a modern Yoruba speaker to listen to some Brazilian candomblé music in 1956 in London. The origin of the songs was Ketu, a group in Togo speaking a Yoruba dialect. Although the Yoruba gentleman was unable to understand the modern words, he was able to reconstruct the texts by listening to the pitches of the melodies, which had remained completely stable (Herskovits, personal communication). In another experiment, Darius Thieme asked a Yoruba speaker to attempt to extract linguistic terms from New World Yoruba drumming. The result was a long series of praise names of the gods being drummed for. Once again the system had remained stable in spite of long separation (Darius Thieme, personal communication).

These comparisons led to an understanding of the conservatism of music, a factor which has puzzled ethnomusicologists for some time. While the number of cases is too large to explore here, one example perhaps will indicate just how conservative music is. In a recent article, Charlotte Frisbie (19) has pointed out that the similarities between Pygmy and Bushman music are so many and so consistent as to preclude the possibility even of diffusion. Rather, their musics are clearly derivable from a single style. When we consider the amount of time that must have passed since these peoples were even in contact, music can be seen as a highly retentive behavioral syndrome.

This latter trend is but one of the influences on modern studies which have derived from Boas. The most prominent example of a variety of approaches of strictly anthropological interest is to be found in Merriam's *The Anthropology of Music* (37), which, in spite of all the criticisms directed at it, is the best statement of possibilities for the study of music in print today. This work is clearly in the Boasian tradition; Merriam discusses a wide series of possible approaches, without emphasizing any one at the expense of the others. While the work lacks a central viewpoint, it offers the student of music a series of choices for study which do not depend upon a knowledge of music, and thus it allows scholars without musical background to envisage an investigation into the nature of music as culture rather than as form or style. Merriam has thus repeated Boas' *tour de force* for the arts in general, and has materially broadened the study of anthropology without the imposition of restricting a priori theory. The results of his endeavor have only begun to be felt; such a work as Boissevain's *Saints and Fireworks* (9), with its inclusion of information on Maltese music, would have been unthinkable to British social anthropologists some years ago. Today, however, such scholars as Maurice Bloch are investigating the use of music in ritual and inviting the help of ethnomusicologists in the completion of the work in much the same way that Helen H. Roberts and other American scholars of music were asked for similar aid three decades ago.

Several attempts have been made to create a typology for music, particularly for folksong. The Finnish attempt, begun by Ilmari Krohn (27), led to an index based on the first few notes of a melodic line. A highly specific index was created by Bartok and Kodaly for Hungarian music, and attempts have been made to apply it to other Slavic musics, with varying degrees of success. Samuel P. Bayard ordered the British traditional material by an extremely complex system, claiming that his index of 55 categories "will account for by far the greater part of all the musical settings of our traditional songs in English" (3, p. 15). His criteria were mainly melodic; three years later he added rhythmic similarities and order of phrases (4).

In the same year, Sirvart Poladian (44) attempted to set up criteria for variance in indexing. After due consideration of those factors which might influence variance, such as syllabic distribution in the text, dance motions, and other culturally determined factors, she was left with two factors which might be culture free: the superimposition of variants on one another in such a manner that the accented tones were aligned, and the principle of melodic contour. The second factor, she warned, does not always define the same level of generalization about music; among the Pima, it defines a musical substyle, among the Yuma a musical area, and in Armenia it is diagnostic for the culture.

This work clearly demonstrated the difference in aims between a comparative system and a cultural description. The items Poladian extracted from her index were all context-sensitive, and in comparative studies they are the first to be thrown out. Again, no attempt is made to treat music as a system nor to place it in context; rather, bits of music are discarded until nothing is left but series of variant phrases. The end is pure classification, but without the refinements of typological analysis with which archeologists are cognizant.

Poladian's work had consequences in folklore. In 1944, Bronson (12) suggested that the limitation of the study to the music alone might be a mistake; perhaps text and tune should be studied together. Two years later he added modes (the pitches used in given set-pieces) to the classification. By 1948 the ramifications of simple typology were becoming unwieldy; Bayard, reporting on a committee effort to solve the problem, pointed out two factors which made the work difficult. First, text variants and musical variants do not coincide. Second, the bulk of British-American material was so great that the time for its study was prohibitive.

Bayard was losing heart before the complexity of the problem. He quotes Phillips Barrys' opinion that

The study of even a single traditional ballad was ceasing to be a one-man job; that it required instead the joint efforts of a folklorist, a musicologist, an anthropologist, a psychologist, and a literary scholar. He might well, perhaps, have added a linguist, among others, to this list; but his statement in itself is an accurate expression of the feeling we folk song students share as we contemplate the ever-increasing magnitude of our tasks (5, p. 298).

Bronson finally turned the problem over to computer analysis, in the hope that mechanical sorting would cut down the time involved (13).

A feeling of helplessness now spread to every corner of the study. In the succeeding years, simple descriptions continued, utilizing the four main principles discussed above: unilinear evolution, Kulturkreis theory, culture-area concepts, and classification. But it was now recognized that music would not yield easily to simplistic listings. The phenomenon was too complex; no writing system had developed which was valid for all styles; formal analyses differed from scholar to scholar; and context sensitivity was regarded as a problem rather than an area for investigation. Nettl went so far as to state that formal analysis could not be done (41).

The earlier period was also characterized by massive efforts at collection of the world's music, purely aside from anthropological collecting. Prominent among those fired with the need to collect the music of the world before it disappeared were Hugh Tracey, Laura Bolton, Kurt Reinhardt, Charles Duvelle, Wolfgang Laade, Bela Bartok, and John and Alan Lomax. Major archives were begun in Germany by E. M. von Hornbostel, and in America by George Herzog. Unfortunately, the vast majority of the early collections were done without stable reference to cultural facts; as a result, many recordings are today useless for other than strictly analytical purposes.

MODERN TRENDS

Beginning about 1954, the scholars interested in ethnomusicology began to realize that their task was immense, and specialists began to appear, each of whom concentrated either upon a particular tradition or a particular set of problems. In one sense this was unfortunate, since it meant that for at least a decade few works of a general nature would be done. On the other hand, the intensity of concentration upon particular types of problems has led to resources for future scholars who wish to investigate cross-cultural or universal problems.

One may characterize the developments in the past two decades in two major areas: the relationship of music to culture, and the development of models for musical analysis, the latter mainly taken from linguistics. Of the two, the use of linguistic models and variants from them has been a prominent feature of this period and will be discussed first.

Linguistic Models for Music

The interest of Jakobsen and his followers in poetic meter produced speculation on the relationship between music and its text. The first statement, dating from

1942, was that of John Lotz (31), whose ideas were taken up later by Jakobsen. Basically Lotz proposed that both music and poetry should be amenable to structural analysis because both were closed systems with formal-restrictive character; i.e. both were heavily constrained varieties of sound. Constraints on the free flow of sound can be viewed as norms, and once such norms are established, it becomes possible to consider variance from norms.

Jakobson (25) and Sebeok (49) assumed that for poetry and regularly recurring variants from norms, such as features characteristically found at the beginnings and ends of lines or phrases but nowhere else, might prove to be significant and therefore formal constraints. This opinion was broadened by the work of Springer (52), who set the tone for later investigation. He suggested that formal relationships between features in music are the more significant because of the vast amount of variation upon a general format that is characteristic of music.

The first papers to explore this idea restricted themselves to the relationship between music and its accompanying text. Coincidence of structure was demonstrated by Bartok & Lord (2), Robins & McLeod (46), and Nettl (43) for text phrase and musical phrase. Other interrelationships of a more intimate kind also appear in some traditions. Bright (10, 11) showed that syllabic length was tied to the duration of pitches in South India; McLeod (33) found a similar relationship between diphthongs and a congeries of musical features in Vaninankaratra music. Durbin's (15) demonstration of deep structure difference between prose, poetry, and song texts in Gujerati tends to indicate that language shifts in the context of both poetics and music.

The problems that arise from such studies are amply demonstrated by Nettl (39), when he attempts to show the relationships between music and text in Arapaho. He chose as his coordinates linguistic tone, vowel length, and stress (a feature of high tone in Arapaho), and compared these to duration length and stress in music. In assessing musical "stress," however, Nettl chose any tone coming at the beginning of a measure: "A stressed tone is one in a potentially stressed condition . . . the first tone of a measure is potentially stressed (39, p. 196).

The correlation, naturally, was negative; the musical information was not based on actual features but potential ones. Nettl's assumption is based upon an older European concept of the nature of rhythmic subdivisions in music, and is characteristic of the lack of empirical analytical procedures in music study.

In contrast, List (28) attempted to show the relationship between linguistic tone and musical pitch in Thai songs, and concluded that while in traditional music pitch does indeed follow tone, in artistic classical songs nonsense syllables and continuants were used to allow melody to supersede linguistic tone. List also studied forms intermediate between speech and song (29).

Many strictly musical studies tend to take their models from structural linguistics. Nettl (42) and Bright (11) tried a phonemic approach to music without success. Ruwet (47), McLeod (34), and Arom (1) have tried to create a formal definition for larger units such as phrases and motifs on the basis of either a behavioralist or a structuralist model. Boilès (8) began a trend toward the use of transformational and other generative models which continues until the present.

Sapir (48) has attempted an etic-emic study by using native song terminology and a transformational approach.[1] Perhaps the most interesting is the attempt of Blacking (6, 7) to align the concepts of competence, performance, deep structure, and surface structure.

While the terminology of linguistics is clearly present in this period, very frequently the papers lack the presentation of basic materials and explanation of testing procedures so normal to linguistics. As a result, these first attempts at structural analysis in music tend on the whole to be unconvincing. In spite of this, the trend to use the analogy of linguistics has brought a serious problem into the foreground for all scholars: is music a separate or indeed a separable entity? If not, what conceptual frameworks can be viewed as rational for its proper description?

It is a commonplace to view music as an entity, separable and somehow different from other types of human behavior. Once it is labeled an "art," music comes to be viewed as esthetic, and thus to be in that category of human behavior which is called "creative," that is, an expression of human ideals at their highest. This ethnocentric viewpoint underlies many of the assumptions made not only by ethnomusicologists but also by anthropologists about music. Yet there are musical traditions, such as the Hopi, to which no new pieces of music are presently being added. While fine art musics do indeed exist in civilizations, the position of music in nonliterate societies belies the assumption that music is created by the few and the gifted for the appreciation of the elite and the sophisticated. On the contrary, music is to be found as one feature among many on public occasions throughout life, often performed by a personnel which includes most of those present. In many communities, all interested persons make music; in others, music-making is restricted to social pariahs.

Music is judged; set-pieces stay in or drop out of currency on the basis of that judgement. There is close association between music and ritual, and one just as close between music and recreation. It may be a legal mechanism, as among the Eskimo, or an expression of sexual hostility, as in Tikopia. It may be the only vehicle for abstract poetry, as among the Betsileo, or a magical act, as among the Bara. In short, music performs such variant functions from society to society that the assumption that it is the prerogative of the few, and an extractable entity or even an esthetic activity must be seen as an ethnocentrism. Like language, music is a commonplace in culture.

More bewildering yet, it is almost impossible to define music as an entity apart from other structured sound phenomena. The Maori *haka* is spoken, yet is considered music; the Koran is sung, yet is not music. The line between highly ordered ritual speech and "song" is so thin that in Black Southern Baptist churches the sermon progresses from the one to the other without a break. In view of this, it would be difficult to assume a comparative approach for music alone, since comparative techniques involve the creation of a priori hypotheses which do not take the particulars of cognitive categories into account. Unfortunately, the only method of defining what music is in a particular society is to use native categories.

[1] My thanks to Stephen Feld for bringing this work to my attention.

This view of music could have arisen only through the failure of previous attempts to understand it, and thus it represents a point of significance for anthropology. At last a human behavioral syndrome has been found which defies categorization by any means yet employed. For ethnomusicologists, the discovery has been a galvanizing force, driving them to attempt a better understanding of the nature of particular musics in the hope of revealing a partial hypothesis of a universal nature. We are so confused that we are thinking.

The Study of Music in Culture

Only three principles appear relevant. First, whatever a particular society calls music is very highly ordered. Second, wherever else it may appear, music is always connected with ritual. And third, music is always context-sensitive.

The first principle is often helpful in defining the difference between similar types of sound activity in the same society. For instance, while the Koran is "performed" with pitch, there is no larger formal order to the pattern of its performance. Even though the *haka* is not pitched, its formality is of a higher order than that of poetry. Few comparative studies of prose, poetry, and music text in the same society have been done; however, Durbin's study of Gujerati shows that while song texts retain the same grammatical form as poetry, continuants and extra syllables occur in the text, indicating that the act of singing imposes yet another set of constraints upon the linguistic text. Thus for Gujerati speakers a song is a combined form having the constraints of poetics plus the added constraints of rhythm, the formality of a larger order, and the arbitrary display of pitch in a patterned way. The articulation of these sets of constraints may, of course, differ from society to society. Among the Yurok there is an absolute collocation between the meaning of a textual line and a musical phrase, such that where a variant of a meaning is expressed in the text, a variant of its accompanying musical phrase occurs in the music. In Italian opera, on the other hand, there is no tight congruence between a phrase of text and a phrase of music.

In view of its highly patterned nature, it is not surprising that music should be associated with ritual. When speech comes into the context of ritual, it frequently becomes ritualized, and added constraints appear. The extremely high level of redundancy in music, plus the repetitiveness of set-pieces, is a natural accompaniment to highly redundant behavior of other kinds. This, of course, leads to the question of the reason for such a high level of redundancy. Is music a behavioral syndrome, derived from ritual, which has spilled over into less complex areas of human life? Or does its patterning result from something else? Perhaps the most pertinent study was done by Fogelson and Herndon (16, 21) in connection with the Cherokee Ball Game. These paired papers were done by two scholars studying the same phenomenon, using some of the same informants, within a 10 year time span. It is natural that their conclusions should be similar; what of their study is pertinent to this question is the fact that the music in use at particular moments in the Ball Game ceremonial cycle reflects the magic numbers of the Cherokee. Major sectioning is either in fours or sevens; the arrangement of pitches suggests an attempt at a four-part concept. Thus a major detail of musical patterning among the Cherokee is a reflection of the system of magic numbers in force. In a less dramatic way, the music of Malta tends to reflect a dichotomous world view, as suggested by Boissevain. In musical terms, while there are three guitarists, there are only two names for guitarists. The major song types are conducted by two or four singers. Meter is divided into two; guitar improvisations stress the repetition of units (cf Herndon 22).

Thus it is clear that there is an interpenetration of values and meanings, world view and concepts, into music. The most prominent view of this is expressed by Lomax, who maintains that the redundancy of music is an expression of purely cultural patterns, and who has attempted to correlate all musical features with all known cultural patterns for the world. While this work clearly heralds a new understanding of music for anthropologists and musicologists alike, it is unfortunately based on several concepts of music which considerably reduce its validity. First, Lomax has assumed that a subjective analysis of music will suffice. The types of small detail mentioned above for the studies of Durbin and Herndon would not be revealed by his analytical techniques. Second, and perhaps most significant, each culture is viewed as having only one musical style, and a master format for the culture is prepared. It is this point of view which has not allowed Lomax to perceive anything but the Cushite nature of Bara music and the East African nature of Sakalava music. There are some substyles within both cultures which are neither Cushite nor East African. Malta has influences from North Africa and Europe; Kutenai music has characteristics of the Basin, Plateau, Plains, Northwest Coast, and others yet unknown. The same is probably true of other musics as well.

Thus we are presented with a dilemma: if Lomax can produce a map of music areas from his data, and if music is frequently borrowed, how can it be specific to particular cultural patterns? If the form of music is culturally determined, as Herndon's study indicates, then a borrowed form would not necessarily be context-sensitive. The crucial data for this dilemma come from the Pygmy-Bushman case. These musics show striking similarity, yet the cultural patterns underlying them are highly divergent. How then can music be context-sensitive?

Lomax explains this case by the assumption that both systems exhibit hocketting, a musical technique in which the melodic line is not sung by a single person or group but rather is cut up into bits. A single individual or a group of persons will sing a particular bit and then drop out. Another group will then sing another bit, and so on to the end of the performance. In the strictest type of hocket, each performer would have only one tone and would insert his or her tone into the total fabric whenever required. Thus the final product in hocketting is a group effort. Since both Pygmy and Bushman groups are presently acephalous, Lomax concludes that group singing is an expression of the lack of leaders in these societies.

This explanation appears satisfactory on the surface. Unfortunately, the assumption cannot be reversed. While Pygmy and Bushman groups do indeed hocket, other acephalous groups do not. Furthermore, there are groups who hocket who are not acephalous. Hocketting occurs in the kingdom of the Central Sakalava of Madagascar, for instance. Not all Sakalava music has this feature, but it is present. More striking is the example of hocket in 13th and 14th century Europe and in the 20th century works of Webern. At neither of these points in history can European society be said to be acephalous.

The dilemma therefore remains. Music may indeed be context-sensitive, but borrowing and cultural conservatism in music do not appear to be in keeping with the idea. This problem may be the most significant one for musical study at present. It is clear that music is responding to culture at the same time that it is borrowed freely from group to group. It is also clear that many musics are highly conservative. The solution to the problem lies in concentrated study upon single areas where close investigation of musical and cultural concepts together may indicate a rational solution.

Several modern studies hint at a solution. Gourlay's article (20) on cueing behavior is a case in point. Among the Karimojoŋ, each type of music performed has embedded within it a set of signals that indicate which substyle is about to be sung. In addition, just prior to beginning the musical performance one or more linguistic cues are given which are also specific to particular substyles. Thus, as with folktales and other linguistic forms, music has *marking behavior*. Native categories are signalled both linguistically and musically. This being the case, the solution to context sensitivity may lie at the level of substyle and not at the level of culture. My own study of the Kutenai Blanket Rite (35) confirms this and also aids in understanding the use of borrowed materials. In the Blanket Rite, all the *nupika* (*manitou*) are called to the ceremony by the presentation of their specific songs. Each spirit has only one song, which has variants related to different ceremonies. Thus there is a song for calling Coyote or Grandfather Bear into the Blanket Rite, and a variant of that song for calling Coyote or Grandfather Bear to the Sweathouse ceremony. Further, all spirits are believed to come in groups of three or seven. There are, for instance, three Bears: Grandfather Bear, Mother Bear, and Child Bear. Similarly there are three Canines: Dog, Fox, and Coyote. The songs for groups of spirits show a high level of similarity. Each song signals not only its specific spirit but also indicates the group into which it fits. The songs for the groups mentioned here are borrowed. As could be expected, the Canine songs are characteristic of Plains music and probably came to the Kutenai with the adoption of the Crazy Dog Society. The Bears, on the other hand, are clearly Basin in origin and represent the borrowing of the Bear cult. Both have been fitted into the larger cosmology of the Kutenai, and in the process of identification between song and spirit, some borrowed songs have changed markedly from their original pattern in order to make them distinctive enough to represent a particular spirit.

The process of borrowing has been so profound among the Kutenai that it is no longer possible to describe a musical style for the culture. In this case at least music is context-specific but not culture-specific. This case then represents the reverse of the Pygmy-Bushman, and indicates once again that there is no simple answer to the relationship between music as patterned structure and culture.

Variation of another kind may help solve the problem of the relationship between music and various types of human activity. Because of the vast number of constraints inherent to it, one may assume that music is like ritual speech. It is clearly the most redundant form of human behavior. It is thus not surprising to find music associated with ritual where other forms of human behavior become similarly redundant. However, music is also associated with recreation, which is theoretically less organized than ritual. If the redundancy of music is a ritualization of behavior, then music should not appear in recreational contexts. This implies that redundancy is not operating here in the same manner as is ritual speech, which seems somewhat illogical.

A comparison of activities within a single culture helps to explain this problem, although it does not solve it. In Tikopia, music is created by stringing short phrases or motifs together into a larger form. Each native category of music differs from every other by the way the motifs are put together and also by which specific motifs are used. In the *matavaka* (canoe-bow dance), for instance, there is a relatively large repertoire of motifs from which composers may choose when producing a new song. In *fuatanga* (funeral dirges), there are relatively few motifs to choose from, and a given song may repeat a motif several times. Dirge music can thus be said to be more redundant than dance music. For Tikopia, therefore, relative redundancy rises as activity becomes more ritualized, in the same manner as speech. It is to be hoped that similar types of study in other societies might reveal the same tendency.

This, of course, does not solve the problem of why music is found in association with recreation. It merely indicates that music is less redundant in recreational situations. However, even there music is still highly redundant. Lomax explains this redundancy as a group-organizing function that displays the "behavioral norms which are crucial to a culture" (30a, p. 15). Thus in his terms music has two simultaneous functions: to organize groups of people into activity; and to demonstrate, within that activity, certain core-concepts which represent a skeletal statement of the major values of a society. Lomax further describes music as a form of communication in that it signals cultural patterns in specific, symbolic ways.

The view of music to be derived from Lomax is thus of a phenomenon which can only occur when a group is present, since it is a group-organizing activity. Once the group is acting out (or performing), music then symbolizes basic cultural qualities; as Lomax puts it, "Behavioral norms crucial to culture are then set forth and reinforced in such terms that the whole community can accept them and join in their restatement" (30a). Music should thus be a group activity which tends to support cultural norms, display them in symbolic form, and by forcing their performance in a public arena through the agency of activity on the part of the culture-bearers, insure the acceptance (and thus reinforcement) of a basic ethos.

Unfortunately, once again, music does not do what Lomax suggests. It can be sung by an individual alone. There are numerous cases of entire substyles which are never sung in public and which have no audience. Among the Bara of Madagascar, persons troubled with a problem go off into the desert and sing a song which specifies their personal problem. They may stay away from others for as long as three days, singing the same phrase over and over. They go alone; no group is organized; and the ideas expressed in this music are highly personal. Further, music does not always support the social order. So common is this that it is a truism among ethnomusicologists that song texts allow persons to sing what they cannot say. Lomax (30), in discussing blues, quotes an informant as saying "The blues is just *revenge*. Like you'll be mad at the boss and you can't say anything. . . . That's the way with the blues; you sing those things in a song when you can't speak out" (pp. 7–8).

It is more difficult to ascertain the reasons for the inclusion of music in recreational situations than in ritual situations because there is as yet a dearth of information concerning recreation. Perhaps the best account is that of Whitten (55). In his discussion of the lowerclass Negro of the Pacific littoral of Columbia and Ecuador, he describes two recreational occasions, the *currulao* or marimba dance, and the saloon or dance hall. In the marimba dance, men and women do not touch each other while dancing, but rather advance and retreat. Whitten maintains the dance symbolizes men's prerogative to change wives, as well as women's attempts to hold men. The saloon, on the other hand, is an occasion for the symbolic exchange of tokens (dances and drinks) which establish networks for future cooperation in the economic sphere, plus the opportunity for men and women to seek new partners.

The marimba dance emphasizes the fragility of dyadic relationships. In contrast, the saloon offers the opportunity to establish new sexual relationships and to develop, for future economic exploitation, personal networks which are necessary in a region of intense economic fluctuation. Reading this into the situation then, it appears that the recreational occasions in question tend to emphasize those areas in the culture which are the most uncertain and least controllable by the culture bearers.

This assumption is partially substantiated in Tikopia. Recreational occasions are centered around basic structural divisions where antagonism is potential, such as sexual, district, and clan rivalry. In most cases, the occasions both express and mitigate rivalry by presenting it in a controlled environment where exchanges of food, personnel, and bark-cloth temporarily damp down feelings of antagonism (McLeod 32). The assumption is most clear for Malta, where recreational music is heavily weighted toward song duels between individual men. Malta is characterized by factionalism and by vendetta. Public argument is extremely dangerous, and must be sublimated by social institutions which remove the individual from the central position. In recreational singing, however, two individuals perform mock fights, called 'fighting with words,' for the benefit of large audiences of admirers, each of whom chooses one or more 'champion' and follows him from bar to bar to hear him publicly insult others (22, 23). Fear of the consequences of vendetta prevents public quarreling outside of the musical context; such feuds might go on for generations. Yet it is this potentially disruptive social factor which is played out by recreational music.

Thus it would appear that music is sensitive to contexts of social instability rather than stability. Rather than being a focus for the restatement of cultural norms, it may be the focus for the restatement of uncertainty. This point of view would accord well with the assumption that ritual behavior is a response to anxiety; the constant association of music with the supernatural or social instability is more reasonable than the assumption that music is a group-organizing activity.

Such a view helps to explain Needham's insight into percussion (38). While the view is more limited than I like, it does point out some aspects of music in a rational manner. Restated in a broader context, percussion becomes part of a series of *constraints upon sound*, viz:

1. Rhythm, in percussion or music, is a constraint upon noise.
2. Pitch is a constraint upon noise.[2]
3. Mode is a constraint upon pitch.
4. Melody is a constraint upon mode.
5. Form is a set of constraints upon rhythm and melody.

Thus music is a set of constraints upon sound. If a linguistic text is added to music, it is usually altered so as to fit the musical constraints already set up. The totality then becomes a highly redundant sound bundle.

Needham goes on to point out the connection between percussion and transition, both in terms of rites of passage and the change of state necessary in dealing with the supernatural. I would add to that the additional change of state implied by the public presentation of social uncertainty. In all cases, what music symbolizes is an altered state of consciousness, be it a transition from one status to another, the adoption of a ritual attitude, or the acting out of personal or social impotence in the face of tensions implicit in the social structure. In all cases, music is directed at areas regarded as uncertain.

Like accusations of witchcraft then, music tends to occur at points of conflict, uncertainty, or stress within the social fabric. Its function may also be viewed as cyclical; it tends to damp down anxiety and irritation, but does not permanently alter the situation. This helps to explain the potential conservatism in music, but does not imply its use in connection with the reinforcement of norms unless those norms involve an element of uncertainty. Thus music would not support a basic ethos—unless one assumes that an ethos is constructed as a barrier against the unknown.

Music then can be viewed in the same category as, but a less extreme form than, such phenomena as psychotic humming, the *lala* of Southeast Asia, and conversion hysteria. Its common association with trance and shamanism helps define it as a more generalized mechanism for dealing with anxiety, whatever its cause. It helps to explain the use of music as a background to other things: the music professor who listens to Mozart to stay sane; less dramatically, the anthropologist who listens to classical music while writing to "order his mind"; or the dentist who uses Muzak through headphones to soothe his patients.

This places music in a state accessible to anthropologists, whether they have musical training or not. It can be viewed as a phenomenon which signals social

---

[2] Acoustically, pitch is a selection of some frequencies occurring in noise.

stress. The potential for the study of music in culture is presently very great; however, there are a limited number of ethnomusicologists trained in anthropology. They cannot conceivably advance the study rapidly by themselves. Unless anthropologists take an interest in this area, the development of meaningful statements will be slow.

Literature Cited

1. Arom, S. 1970. Essai d'une notation des monodies à des fins d'analyse. *Rev. Musicol.* 55(2):172-216
2. Bartok, B., Lord, A. 1951. *Serbo-Croatian Folksong.* New York: Columbia Univ. Press
3. Bayard, S. P. 1939. Aspects of melodic kinship and variation in British-American folk tunes. *Int. Congr. Musicol.* NY 9:11-16
4. Bayard, S. P. 1942. Ballad tunes and the Hustvedt indexing method. *J. Am. Folklore* 55:248-52
5. Ibid 1948. Report of the folk song committee of the comparative literature II section of the Modern Language Association, 1947. 61:298-304
6. Blacking, J. 1971. Deep and surface structures in Venda music. *Yearb. Int. Folk Music Counc.* 3:69-98
7. Blacking, J. 1971. Towards a theory of musical competence. In *Man: Anthropological Essays Presented to O. F. Raum,* ed. E. J. DeJager, 19-34. Cape Town: C. Struik
8. Boilès, C. 1967. Tepehua thought-song: a case of semantic signalling. *Ethnomusicology* 11(3):267-92
9. Boissevain, J. F. 1965. Saints and fireworks: religion and politics in rural Malta. *London Sch. Econ. Monogr. Soc. Anthropol.* 30. London: Athlone
10. Bright, W. 1957. Singing in Lushai. *Indian Ling.* 17:24-28
11. Bright, W. 1963. Language and music: areas for cooperation. *Ethnomusicology* 7(1):23-32
12. Bronson, B. H. 1944. The interdependence of ballad tunes and texts. *Cal. Folk. Quart.* 3:185-207
13. Bronson, B. H. 1949. Mechanical help in the study of folksong. *J. Am. Folklore* 62:81-90
14. Densmore, F. 1927. The study of Indian music in the nineteenth century. *Am. Anthropol.* 29(1):77-86
15. Durbin, M. A. 1971. Transformational models applied to musical analysis: theoretical possibilities. *Ethnomusicology* 15(3):353-62
16. Fogelson, R. 1971. The Cherokee ballgame cycle: an ethnographer's view. *Ethnomusicology* 15(3):327-38
17. Fletcher, A. C., LaFlesche, F. 1893. A study of Omaha Indian music. *Archaeol. Ethnol. Pap. Peabody Mus.* 1(5):251-382
18. Freeman, L. C., Merriam, A. P. 1956. Statistical classification in anthropology: an application to ethnomusicology. *Am. Anthropol.* 58(3):464-72
19. Frisbie, C. J. 1971. Anthropological and ethnomusicological implications of a comparative analysis of Bushmen and African Pygmy music. *Ethnology* 10(3):265-90
20. Gourlay, K. 1972. The practice of cueing among the Karimojon of Northeast Uganda. *Ethnomusicology* 16(2):240-46
21. Herndon, M. 1971. The Cherokee ballgame cycle: an ethnomusicologist's view. *Ethnomusicology* 15(3):339-52
22. Herndon, M. 1971. *Singing and politics: Maltese folk music and musicians.* PhD thesis. Tulane Univ., New Orleans, La.
23. Herndon, M., McLeod, N. 1972. The use of nicknames as evaluators of personal competence in Malta. *Texas Work. Pap. Socioling.* 14
24. Hood, M. 1966. Javanese music. *Harvard Dictionary of Music,* ed. W. Apel. Cambridge: Harvard Univ. Press
25. Jakobson, R. 1952. Studies in comparative Slavonic metrics. *Oxford Slav. Pap.* 3:21-66
26. Kolinski, M. 1957. Ethnomusicology, its problems and methods. *Ethnomusicol. Newslett.* 10:1-7
27. Krohn, I. 1903. Welches ist die beste Methode, um Volks- und Volkmässige

Lieder nach ihrer melodischen (nicht textlichen) Beschaffenheit lexikalisch zu ordnen? *Sammelbande Int. Musikgesellschaft* 4(4):643–60

28. List, G. 1961. Speech melody and song melody in central Thailand. *Ethnomusicology* 5(1):16–32

29. Ibid 1963. The boundaries of speech and song. 7(1):1–16

30. Lomax, A. 1959. *The Rainbow Sign.* New York: Duell, Sloan & Pearce

30a. Lomax, A. 1968. Folk song style and culture. *Am. Assoc. Advan. Sci.* 88

31. Lotz, J. 1942. Notes on structural analysis in metrics. *Helicon* 4:119–46

32. McLeod, N. 1957. *The social context of music in a Polynesian community.* MA thesis. London Sch. Econ.

33. McLeod, N. 1966. *Some techniques of analysis for non-Western music.* PhD thesis. Northwestern Univ.

34. McLeod, N. 1968. *The definition of the phrase.* Presented at Ann. Meet. Soc. Ethnomusicol.

35. McLeod, N. 1971. The semantic parameter in music: the blanket rite of the Lower Kutenai. *Yearb. Inter-Am. Musical Res.* 7:83–101

36. Merriam, A. P. 1963. The purposes of ethnomusicology, an anthropological view. *Ethnomusicology* 7(3):206–13

37. Merriam, A. P. 1964. *The Anthropology of Music.* Evanston: Northwestern Univ. Press

38. Needham, R. 1972. Percussion and transition. In *Reader in Comparative Religion*, ed. W. A. Lessa, E. Z. Vogt, 391–98. New York: Harper & Row

39. Nettl, B. 1954. Text-music relationships in Arapaho songs. *Southwest. J. Anthropol.* 10:192–99

40. Nettl, B. 1954. La musica folklorica. *Folklore Americas* 14 (Dec.):15–34

41. Nettl, B. 1956. *Music in Primitive Culture.* Cambridge: Harvard Univ. Press

42. Nettl, B. 1958. Some linguistic approaches to musical analysis. *J. Int.*

Folk Music Counc. 10:37–41

43. Nettl, B. 1964. *Theory and Method in Ethnomusicology.* New York: Free Press

44. Poladian, S. 1942. The problem of melodic variation in folk-song. *J. Am. Folklore* 55:204–11

45. Roberts, H. H. 1933. *Form in Primitive Music.* New York: Norton

46. Robins, R. H., McLeod, N. 1956. Five Yurok songs: a musical and textual analysis. *Bull. Sch. Orient. Afr. Stud.* xviii/3:592–609

47. Ruwet, N. 1966. Methodes d'analyse en musicologie. *Belge Rev. Musicol.* 20:65–90

48. Sapir, J. D. 1969. Diola-Fogny funeral songs and the native critic. *Afr. Lang. Rev.* 8:176–91

49. Sebeok, T. A. 1956. Sound and meaning in a Cheremis folksong text. In *For Roman Jakobson*, ed. M. Halle, 430–39. The Hague: Mouton

50. Shannon, C. E., Weaver, W. 1949. *The Mathematical Theory of Communication.* Urbana: Univ. Illinois Press

51. Spier, L. 1959. Some central elements in the legacy. In *The Anthropology of Franz Boas*, ed. W. Goldschmidt. *Anthropol.* 61(5):146–55

52. Springer, G. P. 1956. Language and music: parallels and divergencies. In *For Roman Jakobson*, ed. M. Halle, 504–13. The Hague: Mouton

53. Stevenson, R. 1973. Written sources for Indian music until 1882. *Ethnomusicology* 17(1):1–40

54. Ibid. English sources for Indian music until 1882. 17(3):339–442

55. Whitten, N. E. Jr. 1970. Personal networks and musical contexts in the Pacific lowlands of Colombia and Ecuador. In *Afro-American Anthropology: Contemporary Perspective*, ed. N. E. Whitten Jr., J. F. Szwed, 203–17. New York: Free Press

163

articles

ETHNOMUSICOLOGY TODAY[1]

Alan P. Merriam

I confess at the outset that I am hesitant lest what I say be taken as anything but the set of suggestions it represents: ethnomusicology is currently in a startling state of flux, and quite probably no one either does, or can, grasp all its complexities. Six years ago, when I undertook the discussion "Ethnomusicology Revisited"[2] it all seemed reasonably simple and clearcut; while I still support—and might well elaborate—the thrust of those remarks, they represent today only one part of what ethnomusicology involves. While we could speak then of ethnomusicology as a field in terms of a set of dichotomies between musicological and anthropological approaches, it is now evident that the intervening period has witnessed the emergence of a host of other specialists who call themselves ethnomusicologists, or who at least use the word in conjunction with their activities. Whether they are, in fact, ethnomusicologists, and whether what they do is ethnomusicology may be debatable, but the fact remains that they exist, they act, and they are part of some kind of entity which involves in some way the word "ethnomusicology."

We have sometimes in the past defined ethnomusicology as "what ethnomusicologists do," a tautology by no means confined to practitioners of our field. Such a definition is unsatisfactory, of course, because it demands that we have prior knowledge of what an ethnomusicologist is, and thus we could just as well reverse the words and define an ethnomusicologist as "someone who does ethnomusicology." It *is* a tautology, and never-ending in its circularity. But looking at what persons who call themselves ethnomusicologists, or who use the word in association with their activities, do, does have a certain utility, and what it shows us is that things have changed in the past few years. Who, then, are the people who today speak of themselves as having something, at least, to do with ethnomusicology?

One such group consists of the players of ethnic music,[3] who today are legion. Some of them play well and some badly, some for fun and others for profit, but what they show us, among many other things, is that bimusicality is rapidly becoming a fact of musical life in our Western world, as it has been for some time in other worlds, such as that of the North American Indian for example.[4] Some players of ethnic music are self-taught, but most of them, I believe, are either first or second generation students of ethnomusicology programs which have laid heavy emphasis

50

upon performance, such as U.C.L.A., Wesleyan, Michigan, and Washington. Indeed, it is my impression that a number of academic institutions in the United States teach some ethnic music performance without pretending to offer any sort of ethnomusicology program per se.

Many fascinating offshoots have emerged from the rapid proliferation of performance of ethnic music: for example, the now well-known House of Musical Traditions, which began in New York City, and is now located in Takoma Park, Maryland. I do not, of course, presume to comment upon its financial success, about which I know nothing, but evidence of its continuity and growth is seen both in its extensive displays at the annual meetings of the Society for Ethnomusicology, and in the expansion of the list of instruments it offers for sale. In its advertisement in the September 1973 issue of *Ethnomusicology*, for example, it advertises not only the instruments of India, which formerly constituted almost its entire stock, but also the "dulcimer, dumbek, oud, zils, koto, lute, classical guitar, kalimba, khene, musettes, shakahachi, cheng, recorders, and strings," to say nothing of instruction books to assist the neophyte performer in mastering these instruments. That the business exists, and to outward appearances, at least, thrives, is testimony to the importance of performance and the values for which it stands.

The players of ethnic music may or may not call themselves ethnomusicologists, but clearly what they are doing is broadly viewed as a part of ethnomusicology and, particularly for those who study in various universities, *as* ethnomusicology.

A second large, and rapidly growing, group is comprised of music educators, and I am thinking here in the main of primary and secondary school teachers. The chief aim of activity in this area is to teach the appreciation of ethnic music, and within the rubric of music education rather than of ethnomusicology as such. A high point in this development was reached with the publication of the October 1972 issue of the *Music Educators Journal*, a special issue titled "Music in World Cultures." This publication was primarily the work of professional ethnomusicologists: Barbara Smith was its special editor; the Music Education Committee of the Society for Ethnomusicology was responsible for compiling bibliography and discography; Elizabeth May put together a filmography; and the list of ethnomusicologist, and other, contributors included Yamaguchi, Susilo, Menon, Slobin, Goines, Grame, McAllester, Kennedy, Gillett, Reeder, Tait, Trimillos, Malm, Wolz, and Klotman. In addition, reviews were published by Rhodes, Lieberman, Nettl, Wade, and Thieme, and I am sure that many others contributed in other ways.

It is my impression that the issue was a landmark in music education, and that it has led to an increasingly higher level of interest in teaching ethnic music in our schools. As this interest is a spin-off from ethnomusicology, so it has produced spin-off of its own, which appears in a

51

variety of forms, such as books designed specifically for teachers in primary school,[5] source books for teachers in secondary school,[6] and developed course materials for college teachers.[7] It also appears in filmstrips accompanied by teaching manuals, such as "The Music of Primitive Man," issued in 1973.[8] The September 1974 issue of *Ethnomusicology*, carries an advertisement for an elaborate 4-LP or cassette package prepared by Louis W. Ballard on "The Words, the Sounds, the Cultural Story of the American Indian," including, according to the copy, a special feature: "Dr. Ballard teaches the songs & culture of 22 tribes in 27 songs." The May 1974 issue of *Ethnomusicology* carries an advertisement for 16 mm. color films on various ethnomusicological subjects, distributed by Flower Films. The list is long, the variety of materials substantial and growing, and the main thrust directed toward music teachers.

This group is probably the fastest growing of those with some sort of ethnomusicological interest, and the evidence of its importance lies not only in that which I have noted above, but in the fact that the influence has reached so deeply into the education field that the publisher of *down beat*, long the bible of the jazz field, began his regular column not long ago by writing, "Consider this a first call for a Constituent Assembly to consider the promulgation of a Music Bill of Rights," and he listed a number of items, including the following:

> Requirements for a music teacher's certificate shall include demonstrated ability in the following areas: instrumental and vocal world music (Western, Eastern, African, American); various large and small ensembles; individual creativity (improvisation, composition, etc.); therapy (not necessarily as a specialty); contemporary materials literature; and technology.[9]

I am sure that many similar statements are being made in many other journals.

A third group of persons having something to do with ethnomusicology involves all those who see ethnic music in the context of a global view of music, vis à vis, particularly, the study of Western "classical" music. Thus Lipiczky can write, for example, that at Wesleyan University, and presumably elsewhere as well, "there is a thrust toward dealing with Western European art music as just one of the many expressions of culture in the musics of the world . . ."[10] and Palmer refers repeatedly to non-Western music forms in relationship to their contribution to an "American music."[11]

Further, composers are well aware of the potentials involved; Reich points out that for today's Western composer, the solution is not to be an ethnomusicologist per se (and he employs the term), or to "give up composing and devote himself to trying to become a performer in some

52

non-Western music," but rather, to ". . . continue composing, but with the knowledge of non-Western music one has studied . . ." The mechanism he has chosen is to

> . . . create a music with one's own sound that is constructed in the light of one's knowledge of non-Western *structures*. . . . Instead of imitation, the influence of non-Western musical structures on the thinking of a Western composer is likely to produce something genuinely new.[12]

Similarly, Jean Schwarz speaks of "une meilleure connaissance des musiques du monde"[13] in connection with his own electronic music compositions, and others could be cited.

I am not suggesting that these persons necessarily call themselves ethnomusicologists, or that they see their work as ethnomusicology, but they are clearly cognizant of the field, some of them - *are* ethnomusicologists, and they are all keenly aware of the use of ethnic music in Western art music composition. It is, of course, reminiscent of Arthur Farwell and his Wa-Wan Press, which published the North American Indian music-influenced compositions of Charles Wakefield Cadman, Horace Alden Miller, himself, and others, at the turn of the century.

A fourth group is a heterogeneous one made up of persons with a variety of interests, all of which are in some sense "applied." Included here are those professional ethnomusicologists who feel it important to make their knowledge available to teachers for dissemination to school children, a move toward application of materials learned and theory accumulated. Included also is a person such as Chenoweth who, if I understand her work correctly,[14] wishes to analyze music so well that "a description of it enables a foreign musician to understand its theory sufficiently to compose intelligently in the system,"[15] and that the composition itself will be useful in Christian mission endeavors. Although not called ethnomusicology, similar applications of music knowledge have long been made in many parts of the world.[16]

Still another possible entry in this group are music therapists, who may or may not be turning to ethnomusicology for assistance. Some of the problems faced have recently been considered important enough to have been discussed in Robertson-DeCarbo's 1974 article in *Ethnomusicology*.[17] Finally, and on admittedly shaky grounds, I have recently received a newspaper clipping from Hawaii which indicates that the East-West Center Culture Learning Institute is in the midst of a program designed specifically to foster interethnic group understanding through ethnomusicology.[18] Some of these activities are more nascent than actual at this point in time, but it seems probable that they will develop further, and that other applied roles will be found for ethnomusicology.

53

The two final groups of persons calling themselves ethnomusicologists are the same two on which so much attention has been focussed in the past, i.e., the musicologists and the anthropologists, and I will return to them later.

What does all this add up to? What does the proliferation of ethno-musicological activities imply? The answer is that within the past five to ten years ethnomusicology has become "popular," and this, in turn, involves several further ramifications. We have, for example, the simple fact that a rapidly increasing number of people is interested in the field, and this is apparent in such a substantial number of ways that documentation is hardly required—let me only cite, therefore, the steady growth in the membership of the Society for Ethnomusicology, as well as in the number of performers of ethnic music.

This increase in numbers means, in turn, a greater variety of inputs into the field and out-takes from it; one result is that while we do not necessarily have more definitions of the word representing the field, we most certainly have more meanings of it to different groups of people. The term "ethnomusicology," then, has acquired a popular meaning which standardizes as it disseminates. Further, the word has become "valuable" for purposes which are not necessarily academic, and I wish to illustrate this with three examples.

Many of us have recently received an advertisement from Banjar Records in Minneapolis, which informs us of the issuance of a record of Norwegian-American folk music. What is important for the present discussion is that its player-producer is specifically identified as an ethnomusicologist; although the word is used in this sole connection in the advertisement, it is apparently important and valuable enough to *be* used. In other words, the term, "ethnomusicology," has selling power. As a second example, for the first time to my knowledge a trade book on ethnomusicology is planned for publication, in 1976 by Scribners, New York. Up to the present, books in ethnomusicology have been textbooks, learned expositions, theoretical works, monographs—in short, thoroughly academically oriented writing; the new work will be directed toward the general public. Third, Air India has recently advertised a "23-day musical odyssey through India and Nepal," under the title "Musical India." The brochure announces that "on this tour you will visit both traditional and modern cultural centers throughout the country and watch and hear some of India's greatest artists perform. You can also take part in discussions and seminars where leading Indian musicians and dancers will explain to you the subtleties of their art." Although the word "ethnomusicology" is not featured in the brochure, the two leaders of the tour are both identified with "World Music," and one of them is spoken of as a teacher of "World Ethnomusicology." Again, the word has economic power, as well as "popularity," in the general sense of that term. And perhaps the

54

clearest evidence of the latter is that at the last two annual meetings of the Society for Ethnomusicology, persons who can only be described as "ethnomusicological groupies" have been in full evidence for the first time.

I am suggesting, then, that ethnomusicology has become popular in the sense that it is a known term in the general lexicon as it has never been before; that it is a "valuable" term; and that because it has become popular, it has acquired new meanings. The next question, of course, is what these new meanings are, and thus what the term "ethnomusicology" is, as understood by most of the people who use it. In these terms, and constructing the definition on the basis of "ethnomusicology is what ethnomusicologists do," then "ethnomusicology is the practice and dissemination of ethnic music."

I am not saying that this is my definition or your definition, but rather, that it is probably the definition of ethnomusicology used by most people who have some casual acquaintance with the word and the field. I am also saying that, on another level, it accurately represents the use to which the work of the academic ethnomusicologist is being put. And, of course, it is of our own doing, and of our own conscious doing, with which we associate a positive affect.

From the mid-1950's on, for example, Mantle Hood has consistently espoused performance practice, and has set the example for others through his gamelan (and other) performance groups at U.C.L.A. Indeed, ethnomusicology owes a not insubstantial portion of its growth in that period and through the succeeding ten to fifteen years, to his espousal of the idea that people can be bimusical, and his demonstration of it. His work in this direction led both his own students and others to follow up his success, so that now, Wesleyan University, for example, devotes a substantial amount of energy to ethnic music practice and performance as a fundamental part of its music curriculum.[19] Further, our own general teaching has expanded enormously in recent years, and for the first time, it can be said that we have reached, and are reaching, truly substantial numbers of people. It is a rather extraordinary experience to compare the first course survey undertaken in this country with the most recent one. In the *Etho-Musicology Newsletter #3*, Bruno Nettl was able to list eleven universities and their course offerings, as well as eight other institutions less centrally concerned, on two 8½" x 11" typewritten pages.[20] Almost exactly 20 years later, three compilers required an entire issue of the *S.E.M. Newsletter* to list 75 institutions and their courses on 42 8½" x 11" pages, and in much smaller type.[21] The number of persons being reached through formal teaching of ethnomusicology has expanded almost unbelievably, and this says nothing of extra-institutional teaching of various sorts.

Another influence which has widened the knowledge of ethnomusicology has been the Music Education Committee of the Society for Ethno-

55

musicology, which has been in operation since 1968. Considerable support for its projects, most of which have involved the teaching, practice, and dissemination of ethnic music, has been evidenced by the Board of Directors of the Society, by its Council, and by its individual members. Further, the establishment of a resource such as Robert Brown's Center for World Music and Related Arts has the same kind of influence, since its teaching is highly professional and since its mission is viewed precisely as a "cause."[22] Indeed, the devotion of many professional ethnomusicologists to the preservation and dissemination of ethnic music has become almost messianic.[23]

All these movements toward "popularizing" the field of ethnomusicology must be viewed against the background of at least three other currents of the times which have meshed perfectly with the changes in our field. One of these is the extraordinary change wrought in the past thirty years, and perhaps particularly in the past ten to fifteen, in world communications systems, which has brought about greatly increased public awareness of the world itself and, as a part of the world, music. Concomitant, and surely partly as a result of the changes in world communication, has been the upswing in the booking of concerts by non-Western musicians. It sometimes seems that Ravi Shankar has always been with us, but it was not too long ago that the *Ballet Africaine* wowed the United States public with the question of whether the ladies would or would not wear brassieres. At the time of this writing, Duro Ladipo has brought his folk opera company from Nigeria to the United States for a tour under a professional booking agency. Equally interesting is the fact that organizations considered to be at least partly professionally ethnomusicological arrange bookings as well. Thus the January 1975 issue of *Ethnomusicology* carries an advertisement for "The Performing Arts Program of the Asia Society," which offers booking dates for a Bengali and a Pakistani dance-music troupe. Once again, note that the popular definition of ethnomusicology turns out to be valuable, else professional agencies would not continue to book ethnic music groups. Finally, the third contributing influence has been the development of what we know now as the counter culture and its taking seriously and to itself the performance of local folk musics and then the music of other societies—the perfect way to be different.

All this is in no sense intended to be a gloomy or critical description; rather, it is simply the situation that has developed around us. In sum, the concept "ethnomusicology" has come to be known, and to be popular, for a rapidly increasing number of people. The result is that the term itself has become valuable for them, but in an increasing variety of ways. The most visible way in which ethnomusicology as a field is viewed is as "the performance and dissemination of ethnic music." The question now

56

is what effect and meaning this has for those who regard themselves, rightly or wrongly, as the core professionals in the field.

Some it affects enormously, particularly those who have staked much on performance, which is certainly a firmly established part of our field. But performance cannot very well be transferred to the printed page, and this means that those who espouse it reach a different kind of audience than those whose inclinations lead them to express themselves in writing rather than in music sound (some do both, of course). Therefore, both the Society for Ethnomusicology, and its journal, remain rather firmly in the hands of one portion of the membership.

Four broad groups seem, then, to be active today:

1) A large, essentially non-academic group whose members use ethnic music for a variety of purposes: for the pleasure of performance, as a part of the teaching curriculum, to make money, and for a number of other purposes.

2) A small group of professional ethnomusicologists who are more or less in the middle, acting as it were as culture brokers between the "popularizers" and the other professionals. Their role in this connection (and they have others) is to translate back and forth between the two groups, disseminating the knowledge of the professionals to the performers, and always urging the former to make their knowledge more widespread, especially through school teaching.

3) A group which in size lies somewhere between the first two, whose members can still be called "musicologists," i.e., those who see the focus of their study as music sound, with their basic definition often taken from Mantle Hood: "Ethnomusicology is an approach to the study of *any* music, not only in terms of itself but also in relation to its cultural context."[24]

4) A small group (quite probably the smallest, but among the noisiest) whose members can still be called "anthropologists," i.e., those who see the focus of their study as human beings and work out from there saying that "music *is* culture" and "what musicians do *is* society."

The situation seems novel to me, although it may characterize many fields. The first two groups are facing outward to the general public, stressing "the performance and dissemination of ethnic music"; while the second two are facing inward and away from the general public, stressing intellectual problems, and acting as the central group in the Society for Ethnomusicology and the management of its journal. The first two groups can also be combined on the broader level; those involved tend to turn away from formal definitions, to turn toward performance as the central focus in ethnomusicology, to view academic study and the speech .node[25] of music as less valuable and viable than the music mode, and to value the feeling and experience of music sound. The second two groups also

57

171

form a single, larger group, whose members tend to see performance as one mode of reaching a broad understanding of music and not as an end in itself, to view academic study and the speech mode of music as being as valuable as they ever were, but probably in the end being forced in upon themselves while watching their numbers decreasing *proportionately* to all those who call themselves ethnomusicologists or who regard themselves as being involved with ethnomusicology in some way.

It is my conviction that we cannot define ethnomusicology as "what ethnomusicologists do," or as "the performance and dissemination of ethnic music," and I doubt that many, if any, professional ethnomusicologists would use these definitions seriously either. If I am correct in this as a general supposition, then it appears to me that we find ourselves today back in an old situation but in a somewhat different way. The "old situation" is that the "professionals" are also the "academicians," and the academicians, of course, are the musicologists and the anthropologists. The "different way" is that while these two groups once saw themselves as having antithetical interests, they now find themselves, by chance of fate over which they have little real control, allied together "against" a rapidly growing body of persons who identify themselves in some way or another either as ethnomusicologists or as doing ethnomusicology, but whom they regard as neither, except possibly tangentially. In saying this I do not in any way mean to indicate that all the groups cannot get together, or that yawning gulfs separate us all, but that rather, by intellectual interest and inclination, new alignments have appeared with the emergence of new perspectives which mark the popularity of ethnomusicology. "Revisiting ethnomusicology" is by no means as easy as it once was, simply because the threads are now so much more complex than they formerly were.

One of these complexities, from my perspective, is that I am much less sure now than I once was as to what musicology is, since it appears to have fragmented in the past few years as much as any other field. Historical musicology still seems fairly sharply delimited; systematic musicology is apparently defined in a number of different ways now; some musicologists simply refer to themselves as ethnomusicologists; others refer to themselves as musicologists but say they regard what they are doing as ethnomusicology, and so forth. Still, if one were to make his judgment on the basis of the journal *Ethnomusicology*, he would be forced to say that the musicologists and the anthropologists have not really come much closer together than they were six years ago. Each seem to be doing much the same things as then: in the past year, in *Ethnomusicology*, the musicologists have written about the history of Korean music, or Samoan musical instruments, and the anthropologists have written about linguistics and ethnomusicology, or music as therapy. While we certainly

58

have much more awareness of each others' points of view, we have not done a great deal about it.

I would like to say as clearly and as emphatically as I can that I am not interested in finding out whose "fault" this is, or in placing "blame" at one point or another; I do not think of the problem in these terms, and in fact, never have. Rather, while I do not claim to be an historian of science, it is from that perspective that the situations in which ethnomusicology finds itself fascinate me. I have always believed that good and compelling, if involuntary, reasons existed for the two approaches so manifest in the field, and in the end, I think it is healthy that we have multiple approaches. I do regret, however, that we do not seem to have been able ever to create a true discipline of ethnomusicology, as opposed to a musicology of music and an anthropology of music living rather uneasily together under an artificial rubric.

Be this as it may, I wish to turn now to a brief summary of what I think anthropologists interested in music (ethnomusicologists of a sort) are doing today. In undertaking to do so, I must enter two caveats: the first is that I am speaking primarily, of course, from my own experience and that of graduate students with whom I work at Indiana University, and I do not know how typical this experience is. Second, I believe, however, that the general threads of interest I will indicate are similar to those in anthropology all over the United States, at least, but that their specific application to ethnomusicology may perhaps be more intense at Indiana than elsewhere. I wish also to point out that graduate students in ethnomusicology at Indiana are artificially separated by academic boundary into those who will earn doctorates in anthropology and those who will earn them in folklore (with a smattering of graduate student interest in the School of Music), but the two groups function to a considerable extent as one, for students are free to take courses and to have advisors across the boundaries, and they are constantly thrown together in a variety of ethnomusicological events.

I think that those looking at music from the point of view of social science today feel even more isolated from the mainstream of ethnomusicology than they did six years ago, and they are thus placing less and less emphasis on the sounds of music, and more and more on other aspects of the music phenomenon. One hears more talk today about organizing ethnomusicological panels within the framework of the American Anthropological Association's annual meetings, as an increasingly attractive and natural forum for discussion. The reason is that music is being viewed in quite different ways from what it was six or seven years ago: the revolution that has recently struck anthropology has had similar impact on ethnomusicologists in anthropology.

These changes must be projected against the background of the general

59

173

climate of anthropology and intellectualism in our society, and here I wish to note two streams which are having enormous impact. The first is that the speed of change in anthropological theory has become almost unbelievable in recent years. This is partly because some general intellectual revolutions have occurred, and partly bcause as more and more persons enter the field, it becomes increasingly important for each to stake out his own individual piece of intellectual turf, so to speak. One of the many results is that anthropology shows a widening gap between theory and evidence, simply because theory is generated faster than it can be verified through research. For example, when *The Anthropology of Music* was published some eleven years ago,[26] it represented a new paradigm, but while aspects of that paradigm have come to be accepted theoretically, very few of the suggestions made therein have been tested empirically in field research. Or again, the structuralism of Lévi-Strauss, so important and so "hot" such a short time ago, is already coming under severe criticism. Anthropology is flashing through ideas at this point in its history; it is a very exciting time, but it is also a very frustrating one, and the discipline is presently becoming a less data-oriented and more theoretical discipline.

The second background stream is the intellectual era in which we find ourselves living today; one of its characteristics is the science-antiscience debate, and this is deeply affecting anthropology, and by extension, ethnomusicology. Nicholas Wade for example, has summarized the views of Theodore Roszak, one of the foremost critics of science, as follows:

> ... the objectivity of scientific inquiry is not merely a convenient tool for arriving at agreed results, but rather an ingrained, philosophical attitude, cold, depersonalized, and spirit-sapping, which dehumanizes science and indeed aridifies Western civilization itself, since the scientific view of reality has succeeded in ousting all others. ... the trouble with science is that it provides only information about the world, without the meaning. Real knowledge . . . avoids the Cartesian apartheid which science has imposed on itself and seeks the 'meaningfulness of things which science has been unable to find as an objective feature of nature.'[27]

This debate leads, in turn, to the argument about the merits of positivism, structuralism, and transcendentalism (though, I believe, often leaving out humanism as such[28]), and in the first two the discussion focuses on what we now call surface structure versus deep structure. Anthropology today is asking itself all the questions being asked in the other scientific disciplines: What is science? What is it supposed to do? How do we verify results and data without scientific methodology? Do intuition and empathy really substitute for science's supposed objectivity? This is not the

60

forum to argue about these, and the myriad of similar questions, but all are of high importance.

It is difficult to relate this directly and methodically to an anthropological view of music, but perhaps the matter can be approximated in this way: students today are often finding their prime interest to be the meaning of human interactions in the artistic performance event. This problem set has developed from the cultural anthropological approach commonly labeled cognitive anthropology, the core of which is expressed by Stephen A. Tyler in the following manner:

> . . . cognitive anthropology . . . focuses on *discovering* how different peoples organize and use their cultures. This is not so much a search for some generalized unit of behavioral analysis as it is an attempt to understand the *organizing principles underlying* behavior. It is assumed that each people has a unique system for perceiving and organizing material phenomena—things, events, behavior, and emotions . . . The object of study is not these material phenomena themselves, but the way they are organized in the minds of men. Cultures then are not material phenomena; they are cognitive organizations of material phenomena.[29]

Interest in cognitive anthropology has led to, and interacted with, other ideas in anthropology, which have been applied, then, to ethnomusicology. For example, the importance of the psychobiological background of cognition is receiving strong recognition; its interaction with music and the resulting altered states of consciousness form the basis for the studies of some persons. The problem of split-brain research and its implications, not only for music but for the other arts as well, is particularly fascinating, as are more specific inquiries such as the correlation between the speed of drumming and the frequencies of brain waves, to say nothing of the effects of circadian and other rhythms.

Communications theory has had a strong impact, beginning with the simple ideas of a sender, a message, noise, a receiver, and feedback, and moving on to more complex models. Involved heavily with linguistic theories and models, a number of students have returned to the problems of meaning: what is the message being sent, and what are the means through which it is sent? But this is a rather different view of meaning than that discussed by ethnomusicologists in the past, and understanding of it is to be reached by rather different means.

Cultural concepts are to be understood as consisting of those ideas, feelings, expectations, beliefs, values, ethics, assumptions, and metaphysical constructs present in a given culture. These do not necessarily find expression in language, since the penchant for verbalization of

61

ideas is cross-culturally variable. They do not necessarily find behavioral expression in particular non-linguistic expressive genres of a culture, since cultural 'oughts' are often not equivalent to cultural 'ises.' Often their existence can only be ascertained through the observation of their effect in a number of seemingly unrelated and subtle behavioral manifestations, for example, through the gradual understanding of the symbolic meaning of kinesic and paralinguistic data. Thus, the elucidation of some cultural concepts cannot be arrived at through the use of quantitative methods, although such methods may be used to reify hypotheses about their existence; qualitative methods, such as those used by phenomenologists, symbolic anthropologists, and symbolic interactionists, are often the only ones amenable to the collection of such materials . . .[30]

It is this view which has led to the proliferating ethnomusicological-anthropological studies of symbolism, phenomenology, and symbolic interactionism, and since such studies are viewed as essentially novel, they also require novel techniques of study, such as componential analysis, "an approach to finding significant differences in meaning among a set of terms . . .";[31] ethnoscience or ethnosemantics, a method in which distinct domains of meaning are isolated in the language of another society in order to understand meanings;[32] the importance of emic, as opposed to etic, data, as used by Harris;[33] the probings of the ethnomethodological approach;[34] and many others.

At the moment, much of this has focussed upon the performance event itself as the unit of analysis, since it sharply delimits the problems and allows the researcher to probe deeply into structure,[35] and the various linguistic, kinesic, gestural, and proxemic codes, often with the use of videotaping equipment as an addition to standard ethnographic techniques. This leads, one hopes, to an understanding of the multiple aspects of the messages being sent between and among persons in the interacting network, the multivocality of those messages, and an ultimate focus on the meaning of what is going on to the people who are doing it.

What has been said here is the briefest of resumés which only touches swiftly upon a few of the aspects of current anthropology-ethnomusicology. In order to make the point clearer, I should like to quote briefly from three research proposals which have recently been formulated and submitted at Indiana University: all three have been funded.

The proposed research will focus upon the interaction and communication processes in musical performance events among the (X people) of (Y country) in order to explain how participants dynamically create, maintain, and change musical meaning and structure. It will investigate the interpretive process in which participants evaluate relevances and expected responses as they construct their per-

62

formance. More specifically, it will study the 'ambiguity' resulting from partially shared interpretations as exemplified in the differences between intent on the part of the actor and inference on the part of the audience. These musical cognitive processes will also be compared with other cognitive processes in (X people's) interactional situations, such as face-to-face conversations and court hearings. . . . The conceptual framework for this study will derive from the assumptions of symbolic interactionism about the centrality of meaning for actors and audience in the processual construction of performance. . . . It will also draw upon the semiotic-cybernetic aspect of communication theory by utilizing the specific concepts of channel, feedback, redundancy, and noise. . . . The research will begin with the event. . . . Videotape recording equipment will be employed. . . . The act of studying the event will also be considered a social process . . .

* * * * *

The purpose of this research is to investigate the socio-cultural meaning of musical symbols among the (X people) of (Y country) as they are revealed by interaction and behavior before, during and after musical events. The (X people) . . . are particularly suited for this research because they are articulate critics, both verbally and behaviorally, of their music making activities. It is these points of criticism that will reveal important data about the meaning of musical symbols among the (X people). It is my contention that research among the (X people) will provide an example of the general principle that meanings associated with music in any culture can be isolated and illuminated through an analysis of interactions surrounding musical behavior.

This writer discusses the hypotheses which underlie his research, including the ideas that "musical behavior . . . is a symbolic system, communicating meaning," that "musical expectations may be grouped for purposes of analysis in terms of general cultural expectations for any musical performance," and that "these expectations may be expressed either verbally or through culturally acceptable gestures and movements in terms of universal human emotions or feelings, or in terms of culturally specific ideas related to form, structure, sound and movement," and that "musical symbols may be related to other cultural symbolic systems such as religion, myth and values."

* * * * *

The purpose of my research is to make an ethnolinguistic inquiry into musical conceptualization in the dialect of (X people). . . . This project is aimed towards making linguistic, ethnomusicological, and ethnographic contributions to the study of (X) culture.

63

Rather than focusing on the extrinsic study of musical sounds . . . or on the social-behavioral study of musicians, music-making, and the functions of musical events, my research will pose what I see as a more basic human question: What is the cognitive basis for humanly organized sound in this particular culture? The aim of this orientation is to understand an *ethno*-logic; to explore a domain of culture *in its own terms* and thus to seek out its own internal organizing principles.

In order to work at this level of abstraction, I will be using theories and methods refined in the subfield of ethnolinguistics that has been dealing with formal cultural semantics.

These three examples, literally chosen at random, exemplify the directions in which research is moving today, but this general approach is not without its difficulties, of which I wish to note three in passing. The first is that the kind of research proposed here is essentially microethnography, and the problem is how to relate it to macroethnography. Second, as we dig ever deeper, through the use of more sophisticated concepts and methodological tools, the data become increasingly complex. All ethnographers-ethnomusicologists are thus forced to take more and more material on faith, since the data are less and less subject to verification without the minutest reexamination of the same subject. Third, anthropology, and in this case ethnomusicology by extension, has always claimed to be a generalizing science based on the comparison of data. But it is becoming more difficult to compare data simply because of their increasing complexity, and furthermore, part of the overall scene is a clear disinclination to probe comparative problems. But one cannot help asking whether it will pay to understand more about less if it does result in less comparison, and thus generalization. Or are we on the way to becoming a theoretical, and descriptively-analytic discipline, instead of a theoretical, comparative, and generalizing one? These questions, of course, return us to the problems of positivism-structuralism-transcendentalism-humanism, and to those of surface versus deep structure.

My remarks have been drawn in avowedly broad strokes, and much detail has been omitted. What I have attempted is to give you an idea of what I think ethnomusicology is doing today, and from that, an overview of what is going on among some ethnomusicologists who view themselves as anthropologists. In my association with ethnomusicology through some twenty-five years now, it seems to me I can see a progression (though not in a teleological sense) from a focus on music sound structure, through a concern with music as a socio-cultural phenomenon, and on now to a preoccupation with musical emotion, feeling, and meaning. It is my contention, however, that we have not provided an adequate data base for any one of these three broad views; while I always find it useful to at-

64

tempt to generalize on the basis of the data at hand, it would be reassuring to have more data.

The development of these differing views in ethnomusicology (whatever that elusive word may mean) is, of course, fascinating to watch. I cannot help but recall a spirited but amicable argument in which Charles Seeger and I engaged some years ago within the confines of the Council of the Society for Ethnomusicology. We jokingly evolved the problem in terms of what would happen to the Society were 1000 drummers suddenly to become members: it was Charles' contention that this would be an upsetting experience of potential dire consequence; I remember it seemed to me at the time, and still does, that it would only mean we would become the Society of Drummers.

NOTES

1 This paper was originally delivered from notes at a meeting of Professor Dieter Christensen's ethnomusicology seminar at Columbia University in March, 1975. In putting together a written version, I have attempted to keep the informality of the occasion intact, save that I have added some citations for those who may wish to look further into some of the points made. I wish to emphasize that the talk was a general one, meant to indicate overall trends in ethnomusicology as I saw them at that point in time. Both Frank Gillis and Valerie Christian have read the manuscript and made friendly and wise suggestions toward its improvement.

2 *Ethnomusicology* 13 (1969) pp. 213-229.

3 I am not particularly pleased with the phrase "ethnic music," but use it here because it is common parlance. For me, it has only relative meaning, and its connotations are faintly pejorative.

4 Alan P. Merriam, *Ethnomusicology of the Flathead Indians* (Chicago: Aldine, 1967).

5 Elizabeth Crook, Bennett Reimer, and David S. Walker, *Silver Burdett Music* (Morristown, N.J.: General Learning Corporation, 1974).

6 James A. Standifer and Barbara Reeder, *Source Book of African and Afro-American Materials for Music Educators* (Washington, D.C.: Contemporary Music Project, 1972).

7 Vada E. Butcher, *Development of Materials for a One Year Course in African Music for the General Undergraduate Student* (Washington, D.C.: U.S. Department of Health, Education, and Welfare. Office of Education: Bureau of Research, 1970).

8 Stamford, Conn.: Educational Dimensions Corporation, 1973.

9 Charles Suber, "The First Chorus," *down beat* 41 (1974) no. 3, p. 6.

10 Thom Lipiczky, "Report from Wesleyan University: The Wesleyan World Music Program," *Current Musicology* 15 (1973) p. 21.

11 Bob Palmer, "What is American Music?" *down beat* 42 (1975) no. 4, p. 11.

12 Steve Reich, "A Composer Looks East," *The New York Times*, 2 September 1973, section 2, p. 9.

13 Jean Schwarz, *Programme-Bulletin: Groupe de Recherches Musicales* 7 (Paris: Service de la Recherche de l'O.R.T.F., 1974) p. 20.

14 Vida Chenoweth, *Melodic Perception and Analysis: A Manual on Ethnic Melody* (Ukarumpa, E.H.D., Papua New Guinea: Summer Institute of Linguistics, 1972); V. Chenoweth and Darlene Bee, "Comparative-Generative Models of a New Guinea Melodic Structure," *American Anthropologist* 73 (1971) pp. 773-782.

15 Chenoweth, "Melodic Perception," p. 10.

65

[16] John F. Carrington, "African Music in Christian Worship," *International Review of Missions* 37 (1948) pp. 198-205.

[17] Carol E. Robertson-DeCarbo, "Music as Therapy: A Bio-Cultural Problem," *Ethnomusicology* 18 (1974) pp. 31-42.

[18] George Furakawa, "Course Preserves 'Cultcha!'" *Ka Leo O Hawaii*, 3 March 1975, p. 6.

[19] David P. McAllester, "Cerebration or Celebration," *Current Musicology* 15 (1973) pp. 95-97.

[20] Bruno Nettl, "A Survey of Courses in Ethno-Musicology and Related Subjects," *Ethno-Musicology Newsletter* 3 (1954) pp. 5-6.

[21] R. A. Black, C. J. Frisbie, and E. Zonis, "Ethnomusicology Curricula Survey," *S.E.M. Newsletter* 8 (1974) no. 3.

[22] Robert E. Brown, *The American Society for Eastern Arts: Center for World Music and Related Arts* (Berkeley: The Center for World Music and Related Arts, 1974).

[23] See Alan P. Merriam, "Purposes of Ethnomusicology: An Anthropological View," *Ethnomusicology* 7 (1963) pp. 206-213, and McAllester, "Cerebration or Celebration."

[24] Mantle Hood, "Ethnomusicology," *Harvard Dictionary of Music*, ed. Willi Apel (2nd ed., Cambridge, Mass.: The Belknap Press of Harvard University Press, 1969) p. 298.

[25] Charles Seeger, "Preface to the Description of a Music," *International Society for Musical Research, Fifth Congress, Ultrecht 1952: Report* (The Hague: N.V. Drukkerij Trio, 1953) pp. 360-370.

[26] Alan P. Merriam, *The Anthropology of Music* (Evanston, Ill.: Northwestern University Press, 1964).

[27] Nicholas Wade, "Science and Its Critics: Must Rationality be Rationed?" *Science* 185 (1974) pp. 925, 927.

[28] Mina Rees, "The Scientist in Society: Inspiration and Obligation," *The American Scientist* 63 (1975) pp. 144-149; Gunther S. Stent, "Limits to the Scientific Understanding of Man," *Science* 187 (1975) pp. 1052-1057.

[29] Stephen A. Tyler (ed.), *Cognitive Anthropology* (New York: Holt, Rinehart, and Winston, 1969) p. 3.

[30] Nahoma Sachs, "Music and Meaning: Musical Symbolism in a Macedonian Village" (Ph.D. diss.: Indiana University, 1975) p. xiii.

[31] James P. Spradley, *You Owe Yourself a Drunk: An Ethnography of Urban Nomads* (Boston: Little, Brown and Company, 1970) p. 76.

[32] Charles R. Adams, "Ethnography of Basotho Evaluative Expression in the Cognitive Domain *Lipapali* (Games)" (Ph.D. diss.: Indiana University, 1974).

[33] Marvin Harris, *The Rise of Anthropological Theory* (New York: Thomas Y. Crowell, 1968) pp. 568-604.

[34] Harold Garfinkel, *Studies in Ethnomethodology* (Englewood Cliffs, N.J.: Prentice-Hall, 1967).

[35] Fremont E. Besmer, *Kídàn Dárán Sállà: Music for the Eve of the Muslim Festivals of 'Id Al-Fitr and 'Id Al-Kabir in Kano, Nigeria* (Bloomington, Indiana: African Studies Program, Indiana University, 1974).

66

THE STATE OF RESEARCH IN ETHNOMUSICOLOGY, AND RECENT DEVELOPMENTS[1]

Bruno Nettl

This article attempts to assess the general state of research in the field of ethnomusicology. It pretends to be nothing more than a personal statement of opinion, and I find myself making it with considerable anxiety, for our field has become so large, in terms of its scholarly, human, and musical populations, that it is impossible for one person to control the data of the entire field in a way which makes feasible a good evaluation of recent developments and current affairs. I often look back to my student days, in the late 1940s and early 1950s, when a candidate coming into the doctoral examination might be expected to know nearly all of the significant publications in the field. Now, students of mine grow despondent when confronted with the need to know the whole field. I therefore approach my task humbly, for I certainly cannot claim to know, with any sort of even emphasis, the entire recent literature, and you will no doubt sense that I am best acquainted with what has been published in North America. I therefore intend my remarks to be suggestive, the basis for discussion, rather than in any way definitive. And the reader may find my remarks rather more pessimistic than he might expect; but salvation does not lie in self-congratulation.

Instead of proceeding by continent or country, by culture type or musical stratum, by school of ethnomusicology or approach, I have organized my remarks into a series of numbered statements, each briefly amplified. These statements outline what has been going on in the last ten or fifteen years, what is going on now, and what may perhaps transpire in the immediate future. Some of the statements are simply descriptive. They attempt to give the facts of the situation. More, however, are analytical or synthetic, indicating how I think we as a profession have performed the tasks we set ourselves decades ago, and also how we have encountered problems that we have not been able to solve. Thorough footnoting of a presentation such as this is not practicable. I therefore restrict myself to the occasional mention, in passing, of a scholar or a significant work, and apologize to all whose publications should also have been included.

* * *

1. We are having trouble defining our field of study. In the United States, debates on the definition and the essence of ethnomusicology have been going on for years. This uncertainty is perhaps due to the fact that

67

ethnomusicology in my view is not a discipline, though surely it claims occasionally to be one, but that it is a *field* which draws members from other areas, particularly from the disciplines of musicology, anthropology, and folklore. I am not sure whether the question of defining ethnomusicology is an issue elsewhere in the world. I would surmise that perhaps it is not, that elsewhere scholars have more often taken a practical approach, setting themselves certain specific tasks and carrying them out within a practical framework decided in advance. But we do frequently read statements that ethnomusicology is simply the study of non-Western musics, which may sound ridiculous to many non-Western scholars; we do deal with the question of ethnomusicology as a study of music that exists in oral tradition, though we realize that the contact between oral and written traditions in many cultures, particularly those of Europe, has always been very close. We grapple with the notion of ethnomusicology as the study of music in culture, of the role which it occupies in human society and societies, and of music as not only sound and associated behavior but a complex which includes, on equal terms, sound and behavior; then we are faced also with a substantial school of musicologists who say that this indeed is the stuff of musicology itself. (Actually, I count myself among them.) We have definitions of ethnomusicology as a field dealing with musical cultures synchronically, rather than diachronically, which is the task of the music historian. But again we look at ethnomusicological literature and find that it is full of history in the sense of "history is what happened," not in the sense of "history is processes," the credo of many social scientists. We are faced with a definition of ethnomusicology as the comparative study of musical systems and cultures, but we are also told that comparison is premature, and that indeed cultures are not really comparable. And if we finally hear that this definition—the one I could subscribe to most readily—narrows the field too greatly, and that in Jaap Kunst's words, there is no more comparison in ethnomusicology than in other disciplines, we can see that we really have not arrived at a definition which is shared by all people who feel that they are somehow subscribers to and workers in this field. Fortunately, students do not worry about this quite as much as their professors, though I have run into some students who have almost despaired because of the difficulty which they had in deciding whether what they were doing was indeed ethnomusicology or not. Sessions of the Society of Ethnomusicology have been devoted to this problem, and publications by Hood, Merriam, Reinhard, Daniélou and others speak to it.

Let me comment just a bit on one of the widely used definitions of ethnomusicology, that it is the study of music in oral traditions. One thing that has become clear to me is that it is difficult to identify this music, in contrast to other kinds. Sure enough, the polarity between the

68

music of an isolated tribal group and the most academic music of Europe is not difficult to handle, and it has served as a model for much scholarly thought. But perhaps most of the music of the world lies along a continuum between the written and the oral; yet we have assumed that it is easy to place all music in one camp or the other. I believe the dichotomy is erroneous. The aural component in the learning of music of all sorts is enormous—if we discount only some of the most avant-garde music of recent times. Even the current performance practice of Mozart and Beethoven has significant components that are transmitted in oral tradition. Moreover, much of the music which we regard as definitively folk music, around the world, has close relationships to written traditions, especially if we consider the words as well as the music. I feel therefore that I should not devote myself simply to what we call orally transmitted music, or what we were once permitted to call folk music, but instead to the study of all music from the point of view of its oral tradition; and this, for me, is one of a number of acceptable definitions of the field of ethnomusicology. At the same time, let us try not to delude ourselves. The cultures we are studying have changed more than have we, in recent times. And within this context, to which the mass media have contributed mightily, we ought to clarify the entire question of the oral and the aural, and to take a realistic look at its relationship to the written and the recorded.

Nonetheless, we do not have much difficulty deciding what music actually constitutes the core of our field. It is the outskirts, the borders, that are difficult to define. But they are, of course, crucial because it is at these borders that we would expect new kinds of work (by "new" I mean the study of "popular" music, the development of a cognitive ethnomusicology, or the notion of an "applied ethnomusicology"). There are new approaches, there are new ideas, but have these had the thrust of innovation that one might expect? In other words, it is curious that, despite new technology and greater accessibility of field research, we are still rather close, in our kinds of activity, to those carried out by the grand old men and women who founded our field: Erich von Hornbostel, Belá Bartók, Carl Stumpf, Frances Densmore, and the others. Is this perhaps in part because the borders of the discipline are not very well defined and the scholar who wishes to investigate at these borders is in a certain sense discouraged? The point that I must reluctantly make is that recent developments are, in my view, not dramatic in their impact on our scholarly consciousness *because* we have had trouble defining our efforts. But let me move on to a second, related statement.

2. We are having trouble communicating. One reason for this is of course the size of the field. If we have not progressed in dramatic impact, we have certainly increased in numbers and in a recognition of the com-

69

plexity of the network of world musical cultures. A specialist in the folk music of one Eastern European nation has his hands full controlling the data, the multitudinous song types, styles, dances, instruments, culture types, text-music relationships in different languages, and with the large multi-lingual literature of that field. One can hardly expect him also to know a good deal about the music of Korea, Java and South America. Yet the student of the music of Java or Korea or South America may be doing precisely the kinds of things that our Balkan specialist also wishes to do. And he needs to be aware of them.

When ethnomusicologists meet, they have a small amount of common knowledge, and even this seems to me to be decreasing. There is very little subject matter which one can expect all ethnomusicologists to hold in common. Moreover, scholars with a number of differing approaches have difficulty communicating with each other, in dialogue or in publication. There are scholars who regard themselves primarily as performers and propagators of non-Western and folk music. There are schools in which social science-style model building is the most important activity, and there need be almost no direct contact with musical material or indeed even with the facts of human musical behavior. There are the comparativists. And then there are, of course, the scholars who have emerged from the world's new nations, from what we still call the Third World, and these scholars sometimes have difficulty being persuaded that others—Europeans, North Americans—will ever really understand the musics which they are studying, to say nothing of the artists and intellectuals coming from these cultures. It is difficult to refute this argument; within the system, musical and social, of the music of a West African nation, or of Iran or Thailand, the Western ethnomusicologist plays a distinctively minor role, that of contributing what insights an outsider, *because* he is one, can provide, adding them to what we must regard as the primary view, that of the music by its own culture. But it is not surprising that ethnomusicologists coming from such diverse backgrounds, with so many different approaches and motivations, do not always communicate well. This lack of communication, curiously, is a development we must take into account.

3. The grand old men really had the answers. We are filling gaps in the field, but there are times when the field of ethnomusicology seems to give us substantially no new ideas of what the world of music is like. Have we discovered all musics? I do receive many new ideas of how to work, ideas on methodology and theory, but the substantive descriptions of musical style and musical culture seem to me to have changed relatively little. After carrying out some studies in Persian and Arabic improvisation, I again looked into Robert Lachmann's little book, *Musik des Orients*, and realized that either explicity or by implication he already, almost 40 years ago, had stated in a few sentences what I had stated in a

70

series of articles. Among the most significant developments is the republication of classics and of earlier writings, going back to the 16th century. What emerges from this rather critical catalog is the idea that we are indeed filling gaps in our understanding of the musical ethnography and the musical style map of the world, but we have found few surprises. The area in which we are making progress and in which we must seek for excitement is the area of theory and methodology.

4. We are becoming comparative again. If we are discovering or rediscovering our own past, perhaps we are going back to earlier precepts, and this trend runs counter to our having trouble communicating. The reprinting of the work of such scholars as Hornbostel and Brailoiu is a stimulus for those who feel that it is possible for someone to comprehend a number of musical systems sufficiently well to compare them. Really formidable obstacles stand in the way of comparison, obstacles that extend from the difficulty of controlling a sufficient quantity of data, to the epistemological problems of comparability. We are again returning to the idea that musics can be compared, that they lend themselves, at some level of study, to quantified comparison and that one is perhaps unable to absorb information about a new musical culture except by making implicit comparisons to something already known. This has educational as well as scholarly implications. To me the most exciting work of a comparative nature in recent years has been the work in the cantometrics project, headed by Alan Lomax. I must say that while I feel critical of its techniques and methods of approach, I feel also very sympathetic to its basic assumptions—that musics *can* be compared, that one *can* find an appropriate sampling for each of the world's musics (treating this concept now like languages) and that in some way a music *must* reflect the cultural and social system that produces it.

5. The question of transcription seems to have receded. Transcribing music in order to analyze and preserve it in that most important artifact of Western tradition, the book, was once regarded as a major activity of the ethnomusicologist. In the 1950s and 1960s, technological progress reached even into our field, and a number of highly sophisticated approaches to transcription were developed, including—as Mantle Hood summarizes them—an approach involving the traditional notation systems as they exist in non-European cultures, another one making very precise phonetic notations with the use of electrical and electronic machinery, and a third proposing the inclusion, in a transcription, of all aspects of musical and associated behavior. If one now looks through publications from the last few years one finds, indeed, that there are still scholars who regard transcription as a very important preserving force and as a way of presenting material for analysis and description of musical features and musical style. More often, however, we find that transcription lately has not been treated as an absolute and monolithic concept, but one

71

which is flexible and thus more of a tool for arriving at particular kinds of information than for a complete presentation of the music in visual form. Exceptions to this seem to me to be found primarily in European folk music, an area which for obvious reasons has all along probably lent itself better to the notation of transcription in Western notation. But what surprises me is the relatively small number of publications that have actually made use of new methods of transcription. (I must mention a recent special issue of the UCLA *Selected Reports* as an exception.) I suppose that we are simply interested in other matters, and that we have finally begun to use recordings in a way that will make visual presentation of music gradually less and less important and desirable. At any rate, it is interesting to see that the old whipping boy of the enthusiasts of transcription, Western notation, is still very much in use, with the symbols and types of symbols developed for it by the ethnomusicologists of the early 20th century. Again, perhaps we are rediscovering our past and recognizing that these early scholars had many of the answers.

6. Interesting developments are occurring in the area of analysis and description. I believe that transcription and analysis are, to a substantial extent, part of the same process. While straight transcription itself seems not at the moment to be highly productive, the activities resulting from transcription are. Perhaps the most important of these involves the introduction, by such scholars as Nattiez, of the concept of semiotics into music, a concept which has almost acquired the force of a bandwagon movement. The use of linguistic models, first from the structural linguistics of Jakobson and later from transformational grammar, has become popular, although it has been criticized. The idea that any form of communication has certain elements which are significant and other elements which, because they are predictable or devoid of specific symbolism, are less significant, is easily accepted. The notion that a musical system can be described by a rather small number of basic rules and operations in the manner of transformational grammar is also very attractive, but does not seem to me to have been stated with sufficiently convincing force.

Some of the studies which attempt to show that music can be understood in the same terms as language seem almost to be contributions more to linguistics than to musicology or ethnomusicology, for they demonstrate the elegance of linguistic analysis but, as David Feld has recently indicated, do not necessarily tell us anything about the music that we do not already know intuitively from hearing it.

The main issues in the area of analysis seem to me to be two. First there is an infinity of statements we can make about a piece of music, and even a semiological analysis seems to me to be large and perhaps cumbersome. Therefore we may have difficulty saying anything about an entire body of music. Indeed, this kind of analysis may give us trivial in-

72

formation. Second, there is inevitably a collision between the scholar who believes that one can discover the essence of *a* music by an analysis of its structure and the scholar who believes that only the person who understands the culture by having internalized it, either as a native or as an intensive participant-observer, can have the proper insight. This conflict seems to me to be symptomatic of the stress between the outsider and the insider as the scholar of greatest consequence. I cannot say that I have resolved it in my own mind.

But the significant point is that, on the one hand, we find scholars attempting to create universal systems for analysis and others urging us to use the cognitive framework of a culture for analysis of its own music. And on the other hand, the analytical sophistication of many recent publications comes from a willingness to limit analytical methods and techniques to what is needed for the task at hand, the questions being asked in a particular research project. (I should refer you, by the way, to a recent article by Marcia Herndon, treating this subject in detail.) So, I would venture to say that the success of recent work in analysis is due to its particularism, to the concept of analysis not as something one does to all music, automatically and always following a single rigorous procedure, but as a tool for answering a multitude of questions with a large repertory of approaches.

7. We are more interested in how musical *repertories* came to be as they are, and we are looking at them with a new perspective. Formerly, we tended to take for granted that the concept of music everywhere was that of the "piece" as it is in Western music, that pieces consist of notes, which we regard as the smallest units of Western musical thought, and so on. We are now beginning to be interested also in such strictly musical matters as processes: composition, improvisation, models, and types of tradition. In other words we are interested in looking at the motivating forces behind the creation of music. Of three examples, let me mention first the study of music in culture, or music as culture, to which we have always paid lip service, but which, until recently, has been treated rather by the publication of simple ethnographic statements—an overt use of a song, the overt uses of music in a tribal group, and the like. Lately, the interaction of music with other elements of culture has been treated with more sophistication (by scholars such as Merriam and Blacking), the way in which culture types are related to musical styles has begun to be restudied, and generalized models have been constructed to explain the role of music vis-à-vis other elements in human culture (by such scholars as William Archer, Klaus Wachsmann, and Charles Seeger). A second area generally neglected in the past is that which we may (reluctantly) call performance practice, including such matters as singing style, which has been subjected to melographic and sonographic examination and to quantification by scholars such as Ruth Katz, Födermayr, and

73

Lomax. Third, we would like to find out what is the structure of the processes by which music comes about, be it improvisation on a model such as a maqam or a dastgah, or the development of a tune family, or indeed the establishment of a system of stylistic boundaries to which composers adhere and beyond which they are permitted to go only in exceptional cases. It is particularly interesting to see the large number of recent studies on improvisation and it is gratifying to see that this whole concept is undergoing substantial examination and revision, by scholars from Germany, North America, South and West Asia, and even historians of Western music such as Leo Treitler. Sophistication has increased in the area of tune classification, particularly in Eastern Europe, and I would venture today that an understanding of the genesis of orally transmitted repertories is the basic reason for this trend as well. At any rate, I think it would be fascinating to examine the earlier and recent changes in our field, in such basic concepts as "the piece," "composition," "the musician," and "music."

8. We have moved from history to synchronic study and now back again to history with a new slant. Ethnomusicology has always been oriented toward history. In its beginnings, the reconstruction of man's early music was a major stimulus. Then, for a time, the field was dominated by descriptive, preservative, and functionalist studies. In the last decade we have become more interested in the processes by which music and musical cultures change and in the *kinds* of change, rather than the specific individual changes. Following as usual in the footsteps of anthropology, we have become interested particularly in the kinds of change that are engendered by the rapid modernization and Westernization of the world. We are therefore changing our conception of authenticity; in the early days of the International Folk Music Council, authenticity, as I remember it from the conference at Indiana University in 1950, was one of the hotly debated key issues. This authenticity was essentially defined as synonymous with the old, the unchanging, music untouched by the modern world. We have had to abandon this essentially romantic view.

Today many significant studies in ethnomusicology involve recent change of the sort that occurred because of the enormous impact of the West upon the musical life of the world, and because of the coming of the mass media. In the past, ethnomusicologists regarded urban music as something exceptional, as an unusual kind of rural music which required adjustments in the standard model for the field. We have moved away from that unrealistic stance. Rather than maintaining the substance of the field as rural, we now accept urban venues of music and musical culture and we even accept popular music, because its tradition is essentially oral. Most of the interest in what is new and recent comes not from the desire to study what is now socially or politically relevant, but rather because it demands an approach to the processes of history in which the

74

source materials change before our eyes. There is no doubt in my mind that certain new areas, such as urban ethnomusicology and studies of modernization and Westernization and culture change as reflected in music, will be far more significant contributions to an understanding of the history of music, than will the once widespread reconstruction of the musical pre-history of man. A more realistic view of the nature of 20th century culture, already heralded by Walter Wiora and now perhaps fully accepted, seems to me to be a significant "recent development."

9. Our attitude toward field work has changed. We are more interested in participating rather than just observing—although I am aware of important exceptions. We have, in recent years, come to expect of a field worker much more intensive contact with his object culture than was the case 20 or 30 years ago. It is more common now for a scholar to make a career of repeated visits to one culture. On the other hand, the "field" comes to us, as cultures throughout the world begin to broadcast and to issue records for their own use, records that we can buy, analyze, and use in some ways more confidently than elicited field tapes.

Moreover, the concept of field work has also changed. In earlier days most scholars were expected to do more or less the same thing in the field. There was even a time when the IFMC attempted to establish guidelines to standardize field research. But now the assumption is that each scholar must develop field methods and techniques of his own, in order to solve his own special problems. The notion that one goes into the field in order to comprehend the whole musical culture and to make a truly representative sampling of recordings has had to go by the wayside, as we begin to recognize the enormous complexity of musical cultures everywhere, including even the simplest, and as we begin to accept the fact that cultures are constantly changing and have always been changing.

Field methods are becoming more problem-oriented. Field techniques have also changed as technology advances. Recording devices of enormously high fidelity and, of course, sound film are the most recent significant developments. These we accept with pleasure. At the same time we are faced with yet another aspect of modernization which impinges on our field work, the role that the field worker has in the lives of the people whose music and musical culture he is studying.

I am speaking, of course, about the question of ethics in field research and the whole problem of the field worker's obligation to the people who are helping him. Is he to present himself as a buyer or as a student? Should he help people to preserve their music, whether they wish to have this done or not? Should he share with them some of the fruits of his work? We do face ethical and moral issues. To be sure, most of us do not make much money from the issuing of recordings or books about the music of folk and tribal and Oriental cultures. Nevertheless, most of us

75

are building careers which result from the willingness of our so-called informants to help us understand their music. Do we have the right to study the music of a tribal group if this tribal group will soon itself produce ethnomusicologists who may do an altogether different but in some ways much better job? Do we have the right to record music and information which the majority of people in a culture do not want recorded, even though the musician who is working with us is quite willing, for a price, to divulge the material? These kinds of questions have always been with us but they have only been recognized in recent times. No doubt, suspicion of the West and of modern ideas by members of many cultures throughout the world affects ethnomusicological field research. All of this has helped to raise questions in the minds of many scholars, questions whose answers will have far-reaching effects on the future of our field. Certainly this is one area in which the social and political changes in the world have had an enormous impact, and the changing relationship between field worker and informant is a significant "recent trend." A final word on this topic: the emergence of many scholars from non-European societies, whose main aim is the study of their own musical cultures, inevitably puts the concept of "the field" into a completely different perspective.

10. Ethnomusicology is being greatly influenced by other disciplines. That ethnomusicologists were influenced by the leading natural scientists, from geology and biology to psychology, of the late 19th and early 20th centuries, has been eloquently stated by Walter Graf in a paper to be published in our *Yearbook*, Volume 6. In the 1960s, ethnomusicology, at least in North America, was substantially under the influence of historical musicology, and particularly of that branch which maintained an interest in the performance by the musicologist of unusual and old musics, and in the study of performance practice. And this no doubt is in part responsible for the wide popularity of the participant-observer approach in field work and the performance approach in teaching. Today, we are again being influenced substantially again by anthropology with its interests in model building, by linguistics and particularly the wide net linguists have thrown over a number of disciplines, and by the field of dance research, which is beginning to emerge as a major force in the Academy of the Humanities. The association of music and dance has never really been denied, but only in recent years has it come to be recognized for its full significance.

11. We are redefining our categories. At one time ethnomusicology was regarded as the study of folk music. Indeed all music that was not the art music of the Western world was classified as folk music by some individuals. We were rather vague about the role of what we at one time called primitive music in this whole scheme, making it at one point coeval with folk, at other points the non-Western equivalent to the whole

76

complex of folk-popular-art musics found in modern industrialized societies. I suppose some of us have always been troubled by these rather facile distinctions, by the notion that one can readily distinguish art music from folk music in any culture, including our own. We have now turned away from this kind of classification to some extent, and are more willing to approach the music of a culture as a total unit. Hand in hand with this tendency goes the recognition that each culture is likely to have its own kind of musical stratification. Such diagnostic traits of art music as professionalism among musicians, a training system, and theory may all in varying ways be present in the cultures which have heretofore been thought to have no art music at all: the kinds of distinction between the "art" and the "folk" that we have come to expect in Western culture must actually almost be reversed to understand certain cultures. We are, therefore, beginning to realize that our classification does not work everywhere, and that what we once thought was simple, tribal, homogenous has its own complex systems of social and musical stratification, perhaps analogous, conceptually, if not in detail, to the distinction made in the highly complex Western culture which has served as a model for our classifications. In essence, we are finding that each musical culture has its own distinct musical and social stratification, and its own way of classifying its music.

12. We have developed very little theory. Perhaps this is characteristic of a humanistic field. The humanities do not, as a whole, develop bodies of theory which holistically explain the major facts of the data with which they deal. But in its association with the social sciences, in its interest in comparison, in processes, and in the role of music in human life, one would expect ethnomusicology to generate theories. I mean theories that tell us how to proceed and theories that explain our findings. We have very few of these. Not long ago I taught a seminar involving recent change in musical cultures of the world, and I found myself hard-pressed to provide students with any body of theory specific to music around which we could work. Indeed, I found that practically the only kind of theory that has been developed to account for musical change is the well-known and already much criticized concept of syncretism developed by Herskovits, Waterman, and Merriam. It is important to realize that in earlier days, scholars such as Sachs, Hornbostel, and Lach made approaches to this question. But their theories are not really taken very seriously by the scholars active today, and these younger scholars have not developed materials to take their place, perhaps because they are enveloped in a kind of particularism that, I must admit, goes contrary to my earlier statements about the comparative nature of the field.

I hope I will be forgiven for turning what was originally intended to be a discussion of recent developments into a critical, exhortative, and in some ways negative and pessimistic, though perhaps in other ways en-

77

thusiastic, appraisal of the state of our art. I am also sorry that it has not been possible to discuss certain areas, such as the study of attitudes and of aesthetics, tune classification, computer applications, the attention paid to minority cultures, and other trends, which surely form an important component of recent developments. I have not discussed the enormous recent changes in world musical cultures, and of the impact of these changes on the musical awareness of the world's Western or Westernized public—perhaps because they have not been all that influential on our work as yet. I have consciously avoided discussion of many specific studies because they are too numerous, because some of my points are taken from between the lines, and because I feel that it would be offensive to single out a few significant works. But since this paper is to lay the groundwork for discussion I believe that some generalizations about our current place in the history of ideas are useful for assessing just where we seem to be headed.

NOTE

1 This article was originally prepared as a lecture for presentation at the 23rd Conference of the International Folk Music Council, Regensburg, in August 1975, and entitled "The State of Research in Orally Transmitted Music." It was also given as a lecture in a seminar at the Columbia University Center for Studies in Ethnomusicology in February 1975. I should like to apologize for its informality, and to explain that it was indeed intended for oral presentation. And I should like to express my gratitude to Professor Dieter Christensen for suggesting that I write it in the first place, and for inviting me to present it at Columbia, where I found the reactions of the student and faculty audience most stimulating.

78

ETHNOMUSICOLOGY AND VISUAL COMMUNICATION[1]

Steve Feld

> "Home movies are the closest thing to life itself."
> Advertisement

> "If I went over there, I'd see a bunch of grass and a bunch of trees. You can tell about as much about a country as you can by looking at moving pictures."
> Governor George Wallace

> "Hey, . . . what ya see ain't what ya get!"
> Teenage filmmaker

> "Every photographic image is a sign, above all, of someone's investment in the sending of a message."
> Allan Sekula

The use of film as a medium of presentation and research in ethnomusicology[2] is an area marked by considerable recent interest, though hardly without some confusion. The interest seems due to the explosive fascination with audio-visual media in both the humanities and the social sciences. The confusion, it seems, is due to several forms of inability to disentangle the manner in which one deals with audio-visual media in a humanistic or social scientific context from the popular roles these media play in our larger cultural milieu.

Our media awareness derives from two daily cultural contexts of involvement. One is "entertainment"—Hollywood feature films, network television, and social moviegoing. The other is "documentation"—news reports, photojournalism, home movies and photographs, educational and instructional media. The interest in media is in part a testimony to their pervasiveness in shaping our communicational settings. On the other hand, failure to examine with some care what judgments and values derive from these variously overlapping contexts (e.g., ideas about film *qua* truth, reality, illusion, fantasy, reporting, showing vs. telling, education, mechanical reproduction, symbolic communication) can easily create a trivializing and unscholarly effect on the use, discussion, and evaluation of film in ethnomusicology.

Given this perception of our state of affairs, the purpose of this paper is to enhance the interest and reduce the confusion. I hope to demonstrate that there are innovative and exciting potentials for film in ethnomusicological work, but that reaching these potentials requires attaining a kind of conceptual clarity that does not, at the moment, totally prevail.

My format will be largely synthetic but also suggestive, and my emphasis

293

will be conceptual rather than technological.[3] In the first portion of the paper
I discuss the situation, trends, problems, and scholarly status of film work in
ethnomusicology.[4] In the next part I present a discussion largely drawn from
recent work in the anthropology of visual communication. Here I pose some
problems and approaches to the social organization surrounding the scholarly
uses of film, and argue for the necessity of a certain kind of social
organization that is most relevant to studying and sharing ideas and information about human musicality and music making.

I

There are several ways to document the development of ethnomusicological interest in film. A quick look at the publication history of the journal
ETHNOMUSICOLOGY provides one starting point. Although the journal had
a regular "techniques and devices" column beginning in 1959, its first mention
of films appeared in the form of "special bibliographies" of dance films in
1963 (Kurath 1963a, 1963b) continued in 1964 and 1965 (Braun 1964a,
1964b, 1965). These bibliographies (more properly "filmographies") covered
the areas of Africa, Afro-America, Asia, and Australia. Also in 1965, the
journal carried its first review of visual materials, namely a film for teaching
Hawaiian hula, and a filmstrip of Hawaiian musical instruments (Kealiinohomoku 1965). Publication of filmography materials continued with a list of
"folk music & folk dance" films (Archive of Folk Song, Library of Congress
1967), a list of "documentary films on ethnomusicological subjects" (Institut
für den Wissenschaftlichen Film 1968), and Polynesian Dance films (Miller
1970). Film reviews have been sporadic; after the initial 1965 effort, one
appeared in 1968 (Snyder 1968), then not another until January 1973
(Montgomery 1973). Beginning with the May 1973 issue of the journal,
William Ferris became the Film Review Editor; from that point through the
September 1975 issue, five reviews have appeared (Vignos 1973, Dwyer-Shick
1974, Gillis 1975, Feld 1975a, 1975b).

Looking at other ethnomusicology journals, it is only recently that
articles have been published, for instance Kubik's papers (1965, 1972) in
African Music, and Dauer's (1969) in *The Yearbook of the International Folk
Music Council.* Others have appeared, also recently, in anthropology journals
(Rouget 1965, 1971) and film journals (Dauer 1966, Lomax, Bartenieff and
Paulay 1969, Lomax 1971). Similarly, reviewing the major book length
statements on the field and its methodology (Kunst 1959, Nettl 1956, 1964,
Merriam 1964, Hood 1971, Lomax 1968) we find an abrupt shift from no
statements on film at all, to full blown discussion of film production (Hood
1971, chapter 5) as a *basic* skill, and film analysis (Lomax 1968: chapters 10
and 12, especially pp. 263-264) as a *basic* means for data retrieval. Hood and

Lomax treat the making and analysis of film as a principled and central ethnomusicological concern, like the writing of research monographs or preparation of transcriptions.

The last ten years have also seen a growing concern for adequate cataloging of films. Major filmographies have been prepared for Africa (CIFES 1967), the Pacific (CIFES 1970), and North America (Williams and Bird 1973). In addition to specific catalogues of ethnographic films published by distributors (e.g., Audio-Visual Services, Pennsylvania State University 1972 and 1975-1976 supplement), the Comité du Film Ethnographique in Paris published two general catalogues of ethnographic films (CdFE 1955, 1956), and Karl Heider's *Films for Anthropological Teaching*, sponsored by the American Anthropological Association (first through its Program in Ethnographic Film, and now through its expanded Society for the Anthropology of Visual Communication) has gone through several editions (5th Edition 1972; 6th Edition in preparation; to appear in Fall 1976). This too has been influential. A joint project of the International Folk Music Council and UNESCO produced the first international catalogue of films on "traditional music & dance" (Kennedy 1970); my own filmography of African humanities (1972) covered films on African music.

In addition to articles and bibliographic publications, there are other good indications toward deeper involvement with film. Formal and informal film screenings at the annual meetings of the Society for Ethnomusicology have expanded, and the audiences have become larger and more aware of various kinds of films made and used for different purposes. In 1973, at the Urbana meetings, I led a study session on film and film analysis that was well attended by a lively and enthusiastic group; several people have since written to me to suggest that a non-hardware film workshop be a regular activity at the annual meetings.

Recently, the advertisement pages of the Journal have carried notes from film distributors, and the Newsletter has begun to publish notices of film activity, training opportunities, and the like.

This, of course, is only a small part of the story. Many ethnomusicologists have collaborated with filmmakers or made films for a variety of purposes. To mention just some of the better known and more widely distributed 16mm films: Nicholas England has worked with ethnographic filmmaker John Marshall on some of his many films of the Kalahari Bushmen; *Bitter Melons* and *Num Tchai* are the most widely known by ethnomusicologists. England and Marshall have collaborated more recently in Ghana. Johanna Spector has worked in film for several years in the Middle East, recently directing *The Samaritains: The People of the Sacred Mountain*. John Blacking participated in the production of Derek Lamport's *Murudruni*, a film about circumcision rites and cultural transmission among the Pedi in

South Africa. Robert Garfias is the editor of the University of Washington Press' Ethnic Music and Dance Series, and has himself made several films in the series. Mantle Hood has made *Atumpan,* dealing with talking drums of the Ashanti of Ghana, and promoted the making and distribution of musical performance films at the former Institute of Ethnomusicology at UCLA. William Ferris has made several films in the Mississippi Delta in collaboration with the Center for Southern Folklore. Gei Zantzinger has collaborated with Andrew Tracey and the International Library of African Music to film dances of South Africa, and most recently, Chopi Mgodo performances. And after several years of work in cantometrics and choreometrics, Alan Lomax and his collaborators have assembled *Dance and Human History.* This work has blossomed in the last ten years.

In France, the work of major ethnomusicologists has been represented in several films published by the Centre National de la Recherche Scientifique, in conjunction with the Comité du Film Ethnographique of the Musée de l'Homme. Gilbert Rouget has had a keen interest in film since his involvement in the 1946 Ogooué-Congo expedition to Equatorial Africa. On this expedition ethnographers and filmmakers collaborated to produce the first films made in Africa with original soundtracks of musical and ethnographic sophistication (see Rouch 1975:53-54). The best known of the three films made during this mission is *Au Pays des Pygmées.* In the past fifteen years, Rouget has made three important films, each with the participation of Jean Rouch; these are *Sortie de Novices de Sakpata* made in Dahomey, *Batteries Dogon,* made in Mali, and *Danses des Reines à Porto-Novo,* also in Dahomey. During his research in the Solomon Islands on 'Are'Are panpipe music, Hugo Zemp made *Bambous Frappés,* and then in nearby Ontong Java, *Danses Polynésiennes Traditionelles.* Zemp also collaborated with Daniel and Christa deCoppet on *'Are'Are Massina,* and filmed again during his recently completed fieldwork among the Are'Are. In the Central African Republic, Simha Arom made *L'arc musical Ngbaka,* and then, with Geneviève Dournon-Taurelle, among the Gbaya, *Les Enfants de la Danse.* Among the Zarma-Songhay in Niger, Bernard Surugue has made two films, *Godié,* on the construction and playing of the one-stringed bowed lute, and *Goudel,* on possession dances; more recently he has made *Le Balafon,* concerning the construction and performance of the Bambara xylophone. At a meeting of the Département d'ethnomusicologie at the Musée de l'Homme in the Spring of 1974, I had a chance to see the workprint of films in progress by Bernard Lortat-Jacob, one concerning instrument construction, made during fieldwork with the Berbers of North Africa, another, made with Jean-Dominique Lajoux of the Musée des Arts et Traditions Populaires, on traditional vocal and accordion music in a region near the Franco-Italian border. All of this work (with the exception of Rouget's first two films) dates since 1968.

In Germany, the Institut für den Wissenschaftlichen Film in Göttingen established the Encyclopaedia Cinematographica in 1952; this collection is comprised of research films in three areas: Biology, Ethnology, and Technical Sciences. The Institute has published their catalog in English (Wolf 1972, 1974-1975); in 1968 they prepared a special list of their films relating to ethnomusicology (Institut für den Wissenschaftlichen Film 1968). An overview of the Institute's aims and methods specifically related to music and dance study is found in Dauer (1969). The Institute is also responsible for the publication of the journal *Research Film/Le Film de Recherche/Forschungs-film*.

Although I have learned that film is being used by ethnomusicologists in Denmark, Romania, Russia, and several other European countries, I am unfortunately ignorant of these activities.

This too, is merely the surface. Photographic and film equipment have become a basic part of the toolkit taken to the field by ethnomusicologists. Many have used visual products to create illustrative material for lectures, books, and records. If we were to conduct a survey of fieldworkers in ethnomusicology, it would most probably show that in the last ten years virtually miles of silent super 8mm and 16mm film have been exposed, and countless slide and print images made. Like many anthropologists, ethnomusicologists have used this material to advantage not in the mass distribution situation, but in their own classrooms (see Goodman 1975), as a valuable resource when contextualized by verbal accounts.

Aside from ethnomusicologists *per se*, ethnographic, documentary, and educational filmmakers have conventionally filmed music and musicians. Music making has been prominent in many of Jean Rouch's films, like *Yenendi de Gangel, Tourov et Bitti,* and the *Sigui* series, to mention but a few of the most recent. Among documentary filmmakers of the American cinéma-vérité ("uncontrolled" documentary) school, one need only think of D. A. Penne-baker's film about Bob Dylan, *Don't Look Back,* and the whole wave of concert films (made in 16 mm and blown up to 35 mm or 70 mm commercial screen format). Mixtures of portrait and performance are also found in the blues films of Les Blank. And as ethnomusicology becomes a larger part of the classroom material of music education, this too is reflected in trends in educational films. The twenty film *Discovering Music* series of BFA Educational Media thus includes titles on African, Amerindian, Japanese, Indian, Middle Eastern, Latin American, and American Folk musics, in addition to standard subjects (such as music of the middle ages, renaissance, baroque period) and contemporary ones (such as jazz and electronic music).

In the last few years as well, we are beginning to see films by filmmakers from cultures that have previously only been the object of study; and music and music making are among their concerns. N. Moise Zé's film, *Le*

Mvet (see Feld 1975b) is the first African music film by a professional African filmmaker; Francis Bebey, also of Cameroun, and well known for his guitar music and poetry, as well as his books on African radio (Bebey 1963) and music (Bebey 1969), is also now making films. In North America, American Indian filmmakers Larry Bird and George Burdeau have produced a series of films for KSPS-TV in Spokane, Washington, and National Educational Television; the musical sequences in these films, and overall use of music on the soundtrack, demonstrates an orientation to sound unlike that of documentary filmmakers working in the tradtion of European and American film conventions.

Thus, the proliferation of interest in ethnomusicology film is readily documented by increased activities in the last ten years. The interest substantiated, I would like to turn to the nature of the products themselves, and to my second claim, namely that the interest goes hand in hand with a certain confusion about what makes film interesting to begin with. I will thus turn back to discussing some of the literature and films just mentioned, not for purposes of assessing their individual merit or aesthetic qualities, but to focus the discussion conceptually.

Consider the ways that films have been discussed in the journal. Generally there occur three kinds of comments. One is content description, translation of visuals to words. Another concerns the technology of the film. Another is how the film may be used in classrooms.

When we observe the verbal descriptions of visually selected, encoded, and structured images we see an interesting tendency. The images are described as if they were real. But there is a difference between a man playing a drum and pictures of a man playing a drum. The former is a natural event, the latter a mediated symbolic event. The former is once observed and experienced. The latter is a structured selection for the purposes of communicating something of that observed experience (see Worth and Gross 1974). Reviewers seem to not make the difference. We may be told that the film depicts a man playing a drum but we are rarely told what particular kind of selection (spatially, temporally, framing, etc.) we are being shown and how this is purposive. I believe this is a consequence of not approaching film from the point of view of symbolic communication, not being aware of our own cultural categories of spatial and temporal selecting for the purposes of breaking down aspects of real events to make communications about the entirety. When we read a review of a book we are frequently told the point of view, biases, and aims of the writer, and how these are manifest in the particular selection and arrangement of information that the writer has chosen. When we read reviews of films this is not the case. It is what is "in the images" that is stressed, not how the images have been selected, put together, and ordered so that the filmmaker communicates a point of view and aim. The implicit claim is that the pictures are intrinsically meaningful, that the camera passively records what is real and then the filmmaker simply presents this. That the filmmaker systematically makes selections in every stage of the planning, shooting, and editing, and that these choices constitute the way interpretive communication with the film medium works, seems to be outside of the conscious awareness of many.

There is also a fascination with the technology of film, and it tends to be substituted for discussion of how specific technology articulates with particular aims and selecting by the filmmaker. A recent review tells us what kind of camera the filmmaker used. Why? Does this explain why the images look the way they do? Stressing the technology implicitly stresses tools over and above the articulation of ideas, concepts, and concerns by using the technology in a particular way. As Paul Byers has written, just as pencils and typewriters don't write books, "cameras don't take pictures" (Byers 1966). People take pictures; using a variety of instruments and a variety of imaging conventions and strategies, they attempt to communicate feelings, concerns, stories, and experiences. Without a tie to some relevant dimension of the structure and intent of a particular communication—the way it is shaped— commentary on the type of hardware preferred by a filmmaker is trivial. How a mode and manner of structuring articulates with a problem, idea, or story is not trivial.

Reviews also like to tell us what kind of classroom a film is suited for. This is a carry-over from the audio-visual aids approach to film, a favorite ideology of academic film people, one that is perhaps more suited to the military than to education. It strikes me as peculiar that this is isolated; we are not told what verbal information is required to profitably use a film in an educational setting. Nor are we told to what relevant ethnomusicological issue, to what problem or concern area a discussion or study of the film might be illuminating. It is the content area of the film that is stressed, and how it corresponds to some content area in the curriculum.

I believe that this approach is also trivializing. It is underlied by two of our particularly strong cultural myths—that film is entertainment, and that film is a show and tell item that bears some intrinsic meaning. Throughout my entire experience in schools, films were sho..n when teachers were sick, out of town at meetings, or used on the last day of classes, or as a "treat" for the class right after an examination. I do not think that my experience is unique; what is more, it was as predictable in graduate school as it was in grade school. Furthermore, I do not ever remember a discussion of a film that dealt with any more than the content, assuming it to be real, nor can I recall ever being asked to read or otherwise prepare for seeing a film.

I think these tendencies are indicative of the confused unscholarly manner we unconsciously choose and use for dealing with film. I have rarely read a review of an academic film that scrutinizes it the way reviews are expected to scrutinize academic books. This derives, I believe, from the expectation that film is and can be no more than an adjunct, a form of entertainment, that is, in scholarly terms, frivolous, or simply the product of technology that "objectively records" natural events and truths rather than of a complex symbolic communication system.

This level of confusion and ambivalence is also apparent in how we relate film to verbal and print accounts of what the film is about and how it is made. An interesting folkloric theme in our culture is that "a picture is worth a thousand words." Frequently this bit of folklore leads filmmakers and their naive academic counterparts to statements that the film is "total"; that "there is nothing else to say," especially in print. When films are made, and used in an academic context for humanistic or scientific purposes, these folk myths and their manifestations amount to a certain form of stubborn anti-intellectualism which vitiates many purposes of film for communication.

It seems clear that depending upon what one knows, what one wants to know, and how one attempts to use film in this process, a thousand words can not only equal but greatly surpass the information level of the still or moving image.[5] In the context of documentary presentation and study, it seems hardly contestable that there are uses for the printed word. Different kinds of information are handled best in different types of media. To those who argue that accompanying film with print materials destroys the fabric of the film medium, I would reply that it is the use of the soundtrack of the film to make a lecture, thereby cramming an exasperating amount of verbal information onto the film format itself, that virtually ruins the filmic quality more than any printed text ever could.

There are some happy situations where the publication of a monograph fills in and contextualizes the details of an existing film. Surugue, for example, recently (1972) published his monograph on possession music of the Zarma-Songhay. This monograph gives precise ethnographic, acoustical, and organological information on the *gòjé*, thus perfectly complementing his film *Godié*, which documents the techniques of construction, consecration, and performance of this instrument.

The Encyclopaedia Cinematographica has endeavored to provide short descriptive brochures to accompany their distributed films. I have found that the quality of these booklets varies considerably; some are sparse, others thick, some quite superficial, others very informative. These booklets are mailed in the film can, and not published separately. Hence, when ordering a film not used previously there is no precise way to determine what type and quality of information about the film one is to have.

In the field of ethnographic films, Karl Heider has championed the need for and utility of ethnographic companion modules, designed to contextualize and enhance the value of films for teaching (Heider 1974:3-4). Modules by Heider (1972b) for the film *Dead Birds*, and by Rundstrom, Rundstrom, and Bergum (1973) for the film *The Path*, have appeared, and several others are in preparation. The first ethnomusicological films to be provided with such a modular companion are *1973 Mgodo wa Mbanguzi* and *1974 Mgodo wa Mkandeni*. These represent the important collaborative work of Gei Zantzinger and Andrew Tracey. This module (Zantzinger and Tracey 1976) provides basic ethnographic and musical information (including valuable material on the texts) as well as discussion on the manner in which the films were conceptualized and made. Combined with Hugh Tracey's landmark *Chopi Musicians* (1948) and the International Library of African Music's over twenty recordings of Chopi music, these materials make available a greatly valuable teaching and research resource of tremendous depth.

Most of the publication in ethnomusicology concerning film is in the area of film for research; this is hardly surprising inasmuch as one would not expect those who have used film for illustrative purposes to do much writing about it. Dauer stresses the advantages of using film for making "an uninterrupted synchronous recording of a complete process" (1969:226) such as song, instrumental music, or instrument making. In doing so, the Institute's purpose "is to produce informational content, not beautiful pictures" (ibid: 227) so that the films can be used for comparative research or frame-by-frame analysis.

Kubik's paper (1972) elaborating his work with research film points out that the kind of material necessary to answer preconceived research questions is film of musical events in their entirety, but with a highly selected frame. Kubik used 8mm silent film to record East African xylophone performances; simultaneously the music was recorded on audio tape, and precise measurements of the instrument's tuning were also made on the tape. For transcription, however, only the silent film was used. The transcription was first made in graphic notation, like tablature. The film was viewed frame by frame, and whenever a key was struck a mark was made on the graph. Then a basic pulse unit was determined by calculating the shortest visible point between two entries, and the graphic notation rewritten according to this rhythmic division, with the values for the notes given in Hz. Finally the speed of the music was calculated. As a result of having made many such transcriptions since 1962, Kubik also realizes the problems inherent in doing analysis from film—the possibility that certain levels of description might be an artifact of the technology.[6] He thus cautions:

> The danger exists, in interpreting transcriptions from film, of over or under-estimating the importance of small deviations. By comparing them with the size of the basic pulses and other structural characteristics of the music transcribed we must find out in every case what are *intentional* and what are *accidental* (tolerated) deviations from rhythmic regularity" (Kubik 1972:33).

Thus, Kubik has demonstrated that with inexpensive equipment, a set of research questions (like his own concerning "inherent rhythms" in African music, and the motor organization of four hand xylophone playing), and an analysis method, one can retrieve vitally important levels of data from film. His method is also open to test and verification by independent analysis, as well as to cross-checking through traditional methods of transcription from audio tape recordings.

In France, Gilbert Rouget has taken the use of film for research in another direction by combining the use of cinema to recover basic data with its capacity for presentation of research information. Rouget has written two short informative papers concerning his two recent films (on *Batteries Dogon* see Rouget 1965; on *Danses des Reines à Porto Novo* see Rouget 1971). Each of these papers, and the films, bring out three factors: an ethnomusicological problem, an appropriate technological approach for recovering the data, and a statement on the relation of film to the nature of the problem, the data, and its presentation.

In *Batteries Dogon* the problem involved the organization of motor behaviors in polyrhythmic drumming and percussion (idiophone) music. The technological approach was to use wireless synchronous sound recording methods for sampling sets of ensembles. The method was to film in two ways—first to separate the players and rhythms, then to film the ensemble. Filming was done in the Bandiagara cliffs, the traditional home of the Dogon, where the rhythms were first demonstrated by the striking of stones against larger surfaces of the cliff; latter sequences involve playing slit logs, and drums with hook sticks. A final sequence has the same rhythmic structure successively played on rock, then log drum, and finally on the skin-headed drum. Another sequence presents sections of footage from a funeral which allows us to see drumming in context (ensembles of 5 to 10 drums, and dancers). The film thus presents materials both for analysis and synthesis, by juxtaposing preconceived controlled sequences with naturally occurring ones.

In *Danses des Reines à Porto Novo,* the problem was the synchrony of music and movement. The extremely innovative technological approach was to devise a system for recording and presenting synchronous sound footage where the images were in slow motion and the sound was stretched and kept at pitch, in sync with the picture. This research technique is combined with traditional documentary devices (still photographs, narration) as well as with real time footage of the palace context. There are five dance sequences. The fourth dance is shown twice, the second time using the sequences in synchronous slow motion (at one half their normal speed).

These films are very important both for their subject matter and innovative techniques, and perhaps more because they do not fall into the trap of artificially dichotomizing "research" film and "presentation" film.

Both show that when edited together with purposive interpretive images, analytic footage is interesting to watch and is no less filmic than any other kind of image. Rather than have the analytic materials kept away in an archive for use only by specialists, Rouget has shown us the kind of research data we are capable of obtaining and in addition, how the data fit into a larger picture. While the materials exist for analysis and can be recovered and printed from the entire footage, audiences can also have access to seeing and hearing the fascinating decomposition and synthesis of Dogon polyrhythms, and the delicate and complex synchrony of the Porto Novo court dances.

Although none of the work in cantometrics specifically utilized film, it seems important here to mention the use Alan Lomax and his collaborators in the choreometrics project have made of film for extracting data on world dance movement styles (see particularly Lomax, Bartenieff, and Paulay 1969, and Lomax 1975). Drawing upon the methodologies of students of body motion communication (Birdwhistell 1970, Scheflen 1973, Condon and Ogston 1966) and culture and communication more generally (Bateson and Mead 1942, Hall 1959), Lomax and his colleagues began macro and micro analysis of dance and work movement pattern from a film sample of cultures of the world, developed a coding and rating system, established world style areas, and generated and tested (computationally) hypotheses about the correlation of dance style and other cultural elements. As a byproduct of this work, Lomax has travelled the world tracking down ethnographic films with valuable dance footage, has urged the propriety of extensive ethnographic filming (1973), and has even written some guidelines for filmmakers (1971) aimed at helping to make larger amounts of commercial film footage usable for analytic purposes.

In the major statement to date on the use of film documentation as a field methodology, Hood (1971:269-283) outlines some aspects of motion picture technology for ethnomusicologists. While he stresses that ethnomusicologists should aspire to a professional level of competence in recording and still photography, he notes that due to expense and lack of qualified personnel, film's role in ethnomusicological work is not yet clear. Hood provides his own suggestions based on field experience (making *Atumpan*); these relate to technological alternatives, different styles of ethnomusicological film (narrative, documentary, documentary-narrative), editing, and crews.

Among Hood's most interesting comments to filmmakers and ethnomusicologists are a list of nine "violations" (Hood 1971:208-209) in film which he feels minimize their usefulness to ethnomusicology. I am ambivalent about those "violations." I too have seen and choked over countless insensitive, out-of-context, artificial, insulting films, films ruined by unaware filmmakers, slickness, monotonous lecture style narrations, staged and gimmicked action, theatrical license, unplanned and uninspiring visuals, and arbitrary usage of musical materials. Yet Hood's chastizing of these is incongruous with his own film and his suggestions for making film. Hood's suggestions for documentary and narrative approaches derive completely from the same pretty picture tradition that has made so many of these awful films. The scripted and directed story telling documentary tradition, with its Hollywood heritage, is precisely the tradition that so many documentary and nontheatrical film-makers rebelled against in the early 1960's with the development of cinéma-vérité filming in America; the ideological split between observational and scripted documentary cinema helped clarify why the theatrical documentary film was as arbitrary and manipulative as the slick fictional feature films.

On the one hand Hood puts down the "cyclops" approach (fixed cameras) as boring and unvisual; on the other hand he puts down filmmakers for all of the things they have done in their own hostile reaction to "objective" or static means of filmmaking. But *Atumpan* and many other films I have mentioned use both of these poles in filming and then rely on a professional editor to salvage the result. When this happens, the film must fall back on the use of narration to help the bad cuts pass; frequently too it is exactly this type of situation which forces editors to use all of their slick film techniques in order to create the illusion of narrative and causal linear continuity in the film, as the flow of the images does not accomplish this by itself. I think it is the case that many of the procedures and styles that Hood advocates are the very causes of the aspects of film that he finds so appalling.

In sum then, several factors have been singled out. First, there are some exciting thinking and achievement in the area of research film in ethnomusicology and some overall tendencies of note. However, recent examples of suggestions for making documentary illustration film, and recent canons of film criticism in this Journal fall short in coming up to a similar level of sophistication and explicitness. While Hood and others have taken the important step toward deeper and more meaningful ethnomusicological involvement with film, there is a confusion, an element of unawareness of our own cultural predispositions towards film, that is still unresolved.

II

I will now provide a larger context into which we can fit the levels of interest and confusion that have been characterized in ethnomusicological work with film. This is a perspective that has evolved in the areas of "ethnographic film" and "visual anthropology" and now forms part of the "anthropology of visual communication" (see Worth 1974 on the switching of labels). The factors I have noted *qua* ethnomusicology have had a long and persistent history in anthropology, dating to the time of the camera's invention. The concern is a common one—use of visual methods and means for discovering, exploring, and presenting facets of human being. Hence in using film for ethnomusicological research we need not reinvent the wheel. The anthropology of visual communication has struggled with these ideas scientifically and humanistically, and has provided some conceptual clarity which emerged as a product of critical perspectives on how people of one culture tend to image people of other cultures for research, study, and sharing.

From the time of its inception the camera was used for scholarly concerns. At the same time that academic ethnomusicology was being born (the 1880's) Felix Regnault was using film to study body movement and posture cross-culturally. In the field the camera was used as early as 1898, when Alfred Cort Haddon, zoologist turned anthropologist, filmed during the Cambridge expedition to the Torres Straits. For Regnault the camera was a research tool, capable of creating basic data for analysis; for Haddon, and many anthropologists after him, it was a supplement, an instrument of salvage, a peripheral aid that could be used at random, without the rigor that one need devote to verbal and written collection procedures (for accounts of the history of ethnographic film, see De Brigard 1975, i.p.; on the history of research film, see Michaelis 1955). The tension between the development of research methodology rationales for the use of film, and its use for commercial, educational, and other illustrative purposes, has been upon us ever since.

In the late 1930's, when Gregory Bateson and Margaret Mead were using still photographs and 16mm film for personality and child development studies in Bali and New Guinea (Bateson and Mead 1942, and the *Character Formation* films), other famous ethnographers of the day, like Marcel Griaule in France, and Melville Herskovits in the United States, were using film as an adjunct, for either commercial purposes or for the sake of record and posterity. Today when we read *Balinese Character* and watch *Trance and Dance in Bali, Bathing Babies, Childhood Rivalry in Bali and New Guinea, First Days in the Life of a New Guinea Baby, Karba's First Years*, or *A Balinese Family*, we see an extraordinarily provocative and rich demonstration of the lasting value of film when used in an explicit program of research. The questions Bateson and Mead were asking continue to be central to the anthropological study of personality and ethos. The data they gathered with their 22,000 feet of 16mm cine film and 25,000 still photographs, the ways they hypothesized about and interpreted them, and the ways they presented and published them so that others could share and scrutinize the data as well as the mode of analysis, remain a model for the use of still photography and cinema for research about human behavior.

On the other hand, what do we have today when we return to Griaule's

Au Pays Dogon, and *Sous les Masques Noirs*? We have commercial movies, at times embarrassing to watch, and more painful to listen to as we are subjected to their "insensitive editing, Oriental music, and [a] newsreel style commentary more befitting of a sportscast" (Rouch 1974:39). When we compare this to the legacy of Griaule's elegant *Masques Dogon* (1938) or *Dieu d'Eau* (1948) we see that the films give us little more than some picture postcards of the Dogon as they appeared in the 1930's, framed and edited according to the conventions of European commercial cinema at the time. The empathy and affection so clear in Griaule's writings in no way surfaces in the films; the ethnographic temperament and spirit of the author was lost in the translation forever.

The situation is similar with Herskovits. Recently some of his footage was salvaged, transferred to safety film, and viewed publicly. What one sees is virtually incomprehensible. With Herskovits gone, and no notes for us to decipher the contexts of what we are seeing and how we are to look at it, the value of the footage is quite reduced. Again, when we compare this to the enormously rich products of Herskovits' skill at descriptive historical ethnography (such as the volumes on *Dahomey,* 1938) we are left all the more with the realization that sporadic, illustrative, commercial, and other adjunct uses of the camera are not unquestionably important and do not produce unquestionably meaningful documents for present and future generations of viewers (with scholarly or other concerns).

I do not mean to demean Griaule or Herskovits; both were superb anthropologists. While many had used film and thought about its utility before their time, film was looked upon with utter disdain by many academics. Like us all, Griaule and Herskovits suffered from the cultural constraints and cultural notions about such media. Many of their contemporaries damned the camera as the toy of magicians, and damned those whom they found silly enough to use it.

Anthropology was and is a discipline steeped in print. As Margaret Mead has said, visual anthropology has always existed in a discipline of words (Mead 1975). The pity of the footage of many anthropologists of the past years is that in thinking of film as an "other" activity, they were looking at the importance of the medium the way Hollywood filmmakers look upon amateur home movies—something that need not be considered with the seriousness that they gave to the written word. For them, its truth value as realist imagery clearly transcended the need to be explicit—they conceptualized film as intrinsically explicit.

The tendencies apparent at the turn of the century and pre-World War II which I have noted are still partially with us today. Yet there are some differences. Now there is a literature, now there are some sophisticated practitioners, now there is a Society for the Anthropology of Visual Communication (which evolved from the Program in Ethnographic Film of the American Anthropological Association). PIEF had a newsletter, the Society has a journal, *Studies in the Anthropology of Visual Communication* which began in the fall of 1974.

Besides scholarly development there are two other important changes. One is in the caring. There is now a National Anthropological Film Center at the Smithsonian Institution charged with the responsibility to develop methodological guidelines for research filming, to encourage the making of a world ethnographic research film sample, to serve as an active collection facility where scholars can deposit and retrieve film information, and most importantly, film information that is annotated and grounded in full ethnographic materials (Sorenson 1975b discusses these facilities; Sorenson 1974 discusses some of the factors that make such a collection so important). Combined with the important work of the Comité International des Films de l'Homme (formerly the Comité International du Film Ethnographique et Sociologique) in Paris and the Institut für den Wissenschaftlichen Film in Göttingen, we are now seeing the beginning of efforts to develop international measures to more adequately film, preserve, and disseminate film materials on the human family. In 1973, at the International Congress of Anthropological and Ethnological Sciences, held in Chicago, a special conference on visual anthropology adopted a resolution on the urgency of adequately filming the existing varieties of cultural diversity and adaptation on the planet, and, for gathering and preserving existing footage for the benefits of researchers, future generations, and indigenes alike. This resolution was passed by this world congress as but only second in seriousness to the resolution on world population (see Hockings 1975:483-484).

A second change is in the technology itself and in its implementation. Miniaturization in professional quality 16mm rugged noiseless synchronous sound equipment has taken incredible steps since World War II (for a good overall summary of the technological changes as they effect field filming see Rouch 1974). Today we have portable battery driven cameras that weigh 15 pounds and can run noiselessly for 12 full minutes in perfect synchronization with a portable battery operated tape recorder that weighs even less; with quartz crystal controls and radio transmission systems, there need not even be a connection between them and the camera can start and stop the recorder with its own on/off switch. Synchronous sound has also reached the super 8mm format, with the camera and recorder together weighing less than 15 pounds. Film stocks have improved, last longer and have greater latitudes for encoding light, shadow, and color. Portable generator and powering supplies have miniaturized, and solar power generators are developing rapidly. In short, the days of the ritual of theatrical cinema in the field are over. The other part of the equation is that there are now sophisticated and experienced people teaching the skills needed to do the work. No longer is it the case that social scientists and humanists need turn to theatrical film technicians who have no conception that there are ways other than the Hollywood way, that there are aims and purposes for film other than those of mass commercial entertainment. Now there are places where experts in film who are also serious students of the human sciences do research, teach, consult, and aid people in the technical and methodological skills needed to independently make film for their own research and presentation goals. With this situation, these instruments can be put in the hands of the trained fieldworker, no longer being novel toys but creative and forceful ways to study and share information about the spectrum of human behaviors, whether in dance, music, drama, social organization, religion, personality development, or anything else.

In short, now there are no more excuses for trivializing the doing of anthropology with film. Where trivializing exists, where there is insistence on treating film as a novel, frivolous, or anti-intellectual endeavor, it can no longer be blamed on lack of resources, but is more of an indication of our own cultural dogmatism, our Hollywood Tarzan heritage, shining through at its very worst.

Countless fieldworkers take still and cine cameras, and videotape apparatus to the field. The now customary few pages on photography in standard field methods books in anthropology (e.g., Pelto 1970:142-145, Williams 1967:34-37, Royal Anthropological Institute 1951:353-361) legitimize making pictures as something important "to do." But when we turn to the "whys" of making pictures or films, the legitimizing remarks turn soft. Take still photos for instance; Williams writes:

> The most important function of large numbers of photographs is to allow the observer to check the distortion of his observations because of his own cultural experience. If a large number of photographic sequences of interpersonal behavior are made immediately after entering the field, it is often possible after formulating hypotheses to return to photos made before the hypotheses were articulated. In returning to the pictorial detail of the situation that may have given rise to an insight, the observer can check his inclination to distort cultural data in the direction of his own cultural learning. (1967:35)

What this comment indicates is Williams' own cultural mythology of photographic realism, namely that a photograph is a reality substitute, true, and intrinsically meaningful (see Sekula 1975). What he does not mention is that the *way* the photograph is made—its own structuring and selection—is deeply indicative of the anthropologist's own "cultural experience"; this may also be another order of "distortion of data" due to the anthropologist's own cultural learnings and visual categories. Moreover, this approach dismisses the fact that photographic meaning, interpretation and knowledge are contextually bound; photographs change meaning as knowledge of a situation changes, and, photographic interpretation strategies change as ethnographic interpretation competence deepens (for discussion see Feld and Ohrn 1975).

Recent work by Ohrn (1975), Ruby (1973), and Scherer (1975), building on the foundations set by Bateson and Mead (1942), Byers (1966), and Collier (1967), adds important clarity to research making, use, and interpretation of still photographs.

Developing a retrieval system and cataloguing scheme for an African Studies slide library consisting of photographs taken by tourists and field workers, Ohrn realized the problems inherent in reducing slides that were imaged and conceptualized in a personal home photograph style to "data" and "reality substitutes." In the transformation between "home-mode" and "data-mode," Ohrn found that the cataloguing and classifying procedures could obscure the real utility of photographs by eliminating the verbal contextual materials, eliminating information about intention, and fragmenting images taken in series. In this case, assumptions about the objective, context-free, intrinsic truth of the photograph was the basis for setting up a system where interpretation of photographs based on the intention and context of the maker was impossible. Ohrn makes valuable suggestions for the development of less reductive data-mode uses of photographs that were made in a home-mode context.

In studying the photographs and photographic interpretation strategies of ethnographers, Ruby attempted to determine just how it might be that these photographs are in fact anthropological at all. He found that anthropologists pretty much take pictures of the same subjects that attract tourists' attention, and that they structure and image these subjects in the same patterned ways. Ruby concluded that these photographs are thus more indicative of the imaging predispositions of our culture than they are of any particular organizing framework derived from anthropological theories, principles, or problems. His work is an important step in the direction of developing interpretive photography based on imaging codes that derive from concerns other than those of "pretty pictures"; it is also valuable for helping photographers see their own cultural biases of imaging.

Researching historical still photographs of American Indians, Scherer found that interpretation and ethnographic research use was limited without documentation about "limitations of early photographic equipment, [a] comprehension of the photographer's biases and goals, and [a] knowledge of the inclinations of the subject being photographed" (1975:67). Scherer found that early photographers used a variety of tricks to get commercial results; these included printing techniques, dressing Indians in out-of-context costumes, posing them in garments that they didn't even own, or in combinations of garments from many tribes. So famous an anthropologist as Major John Wesley Powell was actually involved in such conscious distortions for monetary gain. And Scherer (1975:77) concludes:

> The value of these North American Indian photographs then is primarily that they reveal how American photographers, even anthropologists, distorted the view of Indians for commercial, aesthetic, and other purposes. These distorted photographs obviously cannot in themselves be used indiscriminately by anthropologists in a study of the ethnology of American Indian tribes.

This research is important in documenting the culturally circumscribed nature of photographic communication; photographers, photography, and photographic imaging conventions are the products of cultural milieux; without an understanding of a specific milieu, image interpretation is impeded.

This work is complemented by recent studies in the area of ethnographic film. Jay Ruby's concern with still photography carries over equally to ethnographic film (Ruby 1975b). In asking "Is an ethnographic film a filmic ethnography?" he echoes an important point made by Sol Worth (1972, 1974), that all films about people—whether by Federico Fellini or the social scientist—can be ethnographic, depending on the modes of their use and contextualization, and how they are communicated about and with. Thus, for example, anthropologists interested in Eskimos can use Nicholas Ray's *Savage Innocents* just as anthropologically as they can use Robert Flaherty's classic *Nanook of the North*, or Asen Balikci's fascinating reconstruction films of the Netsilik (see Balikci 1975). Writing historically, Worth notes:

> It becomes clear that merely attaching the term "ethnographic" did not help us to distinguish between films, or between what was or was not ethnographic. However, knowing what anthropologists did with films, how they used them, made them, and analyzed them, did help us to understand not only films, but anthropology, culture, and communication." (1974:1)

Ruby's conclusions about film are much the same as those drawn for photography; he argues from this point that to reach another level of sophistication there need be a switch from making "film about anthropology" to "anthropological film." Ruby draws this distinction by analogy to the ideas of the French Marxist filmmaker Jean-Luc Godard, who (see Henderson 1970-71) distinguishes "film about revolution" from "revolutionary film." The step in each case is one toward deeper interpretation and away from descriptive recording. For Ruby, a filmic ethnography is a film communication deliberately structured in such a way as to convey ethnographic research ideas; he contrasts this with the use of conventional film techniques for describing (theatrically, academically, fictionally) people and their life situations. Like Rouch (1974), Ruby is arguing for a more "authored" approach where ethnographers take intellectual and personal responsibility for making their intentions, biases, and interpretations explicit through the use of film structuring systems that communicate their concepts and feelings.

Recent work in research filming bears out several of these remarks. The rules of the Institut für den Wissenschaftlichen Film (IWF 1959) were strenuously rejected by De Heusch (1962:21), who argues that these theories add up to a kind of "blindness." By this he means that the concern with neutrality and objectivity has caused them to retreat to a brute empiricism that ignores the basic phenomenological fact of photography: that cameras do not reproduce reality. De Heusch, in the tradition of Flaherty and Rouch, develops a strong position in favor of the "participating" camera approach (also see Rouch 1974), arguing that inasmuch as film objectivity and truth are illusory, the best ethnographic approach is one taking the most advantage of the sophisticated subjectivity of the filmmaker-ethnographer.

Recent work by myself and Carroll Williams at the Anthropology Film Center (Feld and Williams 1975) has also led to critical evaluation of fixed and hidden camera "objective" approaches that supposedly record "total" raw data. We stress the impossibility of "total" raw data; all data are recoded memories, descriptions or transcriptions of what was once experienced, they are thus never total or raw. Since lenses and microphones perform reduced optical and electronic-acoustical imitations of a small portion of human seeing and hearing, the notion that total data is recorded when a subject is entirely within the image and sound is incorrect. We thus argue that the filmer is always collecting samples, and that a more researchable approach to making film is one that starts with maximizing the possibilities of getting more sophisticated samples from the experience of the observer. We also critically discuss how such an approach is impossible when one works in the framework of theatrical conventional film. Our work here goes hand in hand with that of Lajoux (1974), who has discussed the entire problem of temporal condensation in ethnographic films. We end up arguing for a position that stresses film as a qualitative methodology; this means structuring film not on the basis of *a priori* conventions but as a record of the experiential response and intuition of the informed observer in filming naturally occurring phenomena. We thus see (similar to Ruby) a cinema praxis motivated and justified by an anthropological rationale, namely making a communication about the shape of ethnographic observation in a sampling context. We suggest a methodology for bringing film closer to the experience of ethnographic observation. Other work along these lines is represented in the methodology statement by Sorenson and Jablonko (1975), who discuss the interplay of opportunistic, programmed, and digressive sampling strategies in the filming of naturally occurring events. The importance of their approach is that it clarifies the relation between filming by predetermined research plan and filming according to opportunity and intuition exploration.

Tying the making of film back into its uses for analysis in the field, Stephanie Krebs (1975) has worked on the methodology of using film to elicit conceptual categories of culture. Working with Thai dance, she used film to question dancers and audiences about movements, aesthetics, and structural

organization. The relations between still photography and elicitation procedures have been discussed by Collier (1967). In both cases, the materials can
be the basis of presentation as well. This methodology was employed by the
Rundstroms for *The Path*. They first made still photographs of the Japanese
tea ceremony, used the photographs for aesthetic elicitation, and then made a
film structured according to the elicitations, utilizing the categories of the
respondents rather than the categories of the filmmaker's own culture (see
Ruby 1975a). Needless to say, this approach has numerous ramifications for
ethnomusicology.

A final note here concerns the ethics and politics of this work. Recently
many have been concerned with the responsibilities of visual anthropology
vis-a-vis the peoples and cultures who are filmed. Alan Lomax has stressed the
need for cultural feedback and renewal.

> The filmmaker, working with feedback, can defend the age old rights of people
> to the earthly and spiritual terrain they occupy. His function, his reason for
> filming, is to raise morale. His films will be works of art and history around
> which nonindustrial cultures can regroup and rally. In this way, ethno-
> graphic filmmaking can play a part in social and cultural therapy, by giving
> not only voice and image, but heart, to flagging cultures. (1973:480)

Lomax cites the comments of several anthropologists and filmmakers on the
positive responses they have received when playing back footage and film in
the field.

It seems however, that positive responses from native viewers who were
previously filmed is not synonymous with the idea that films will stimulate
and promote traditional culture. Among the Biami in Papua New Guinea,
Edmund Carpenter found that when people confronted their own visual image
for the first time, the result could be terrifying and destructive; the
photograph and moving image did "steal their souls." Moreover, a situation
arose where after a film was made of an initiation, the elders considered
abandoning the rite in favor of erecting a sacred enclosure where the film of it
could be endlessly shown (1975:457, from material originally in Carpenter
1973). Carpenter (1973:190) also reports that when the much acclaimed film
Dead Birds (about warfare among the West Irian Dani) was shown at a college
in Papua New Guinea, "one student angrily turned off the projector: 'what
right does anyone have to record what we choose to forget.' His statement
was applauded." Thus Sorenson writes:

> A quick way to unpopularity in New Guinea would be to suggest that these
> people keep their stone axes or high infant mortality rates and the kind of
> cultural organization that go with them. The argument that we should make
> movies for their cultural renewal would be laughable to them and should be
> to us, for we are not likely to be receptive to the suggestion that we renew
> ourselves by going back to the conditions of the early industrial revolution,
> the sixty hour work week, or an agrarian horse-and-buggy way of life. . . .
> Such cultural renewal is reminiscent of the cultural zoo philosophy. At its

worst it encourages people to remain in the backwash of history; at its best
it gives moments of nostalgia to the old folks. (1975a:465-466)

While Sorenson supports the idea that films may be valuable in teaching
people about their heritages, he finds it dubious that their making and
playback will lead to reestablishing that heritage.

The issue here is particularly pertinent in the matter of ethnomusicological film. We know that the tape recorder can and has had a role in
cultural preservation and teaching, and at times in renewal. What role will the
playback of musical performances on film have for the peoples of the world?
Will film feedback encourage and/or promulgate traditional music? If we look
to the situation with records we see several, sometimes contradictory tendencies. Among North American Indians in the Southwest, for example, recordings of traditional music on labels specifically aimed at an Indian market (as
opposed say to a scholarly one) sell substantially. I know that Indian singers
use these records to learn songs from other tribal groups and that there is a
concern with well recorded traditional music. In Africa, on the other hand, I
am told that recordings of traditional music sell nowhere near as well as those
of modern popular music, and that there is little indication that recordings of
traditional music are forces of cultural-musical continuity. And to take one
example from films, Senegalese director Ousmane Sembène, the most widely
acclaimed African filmmaker in the world, has recently made quite a bitter
filmic statement about the "folklore" of the African nations. In *Xala* he
shows African elites engaged in the wholesale peddling of the exotic image of
barebreasted dancing to wild drum music and uses this vehicle to express how
their African consciousness has been warped to colonialism's patronizing of
these forms of "authentic African culture." It is clear that this topic is crucial
to an ethnomusicological politics of media. The questions of sharing the
airwaves, symbolic domination, and media imperialism have been with us,
though less explicitly, in the past; now for the first time, it is impossible to
conceive of filming without considering them.

III

What things then do we do in ethnomusicology that we might enhance,
do more completely, or communicate more effectively about through the use
of film? In the more musicological realm, it seems that film will be of much
importance to developments in the theory and method of transcription. In the
transcription of African dance drumming for instance, recent work by
Serwadda, Ladzekpo, and Pantaleoni has demonstrated a tablature system that
encodes the importance of playing techniques as they relate not only to
rhythmic organization but to timbre as well (Serwadda and Pantaleoni 1968,

Ladzekpo and Pantaleoni 1970, Pantaleoni 1972a, 1972b, 1972c). Pantaleoni (1972a:3) has mentioned the problems of transcribing in such depth from videotape; it does not have adequate resolution, nor can it be played in slow motion without very expensive equipment. As we move toward less reductive and ethnocentric forms of transcription (i.e., away from Western notation, which has always been so problematic to Africanists because of its implication of stressed beats) we move closer to describing the relations between motor behavior, sound production, and sound itself; this can now profitably be done with the use of Kubik's silent film method as well as with double system synchronous sound, or Rouget's method of slow motion synchronous sound. With these possibilities, as well as Arom's (1973) ingenious audio playback method-for transcription of polyrhythmic and polyphonic music, we could be on the frontier of tremendous advances in transcription method and theory.

In the ethnographic and organological study of musical instruments, film is of clear importance in documentation of the entire process of construction and tuning. One can readily look through Merriam's informative field notes on Bala Basongye drum-making (1969) visualizing a film. The work of Zemp, Surugue, Lortat-Jacob, Hood, and filmmakers with the Institut für den Wissenschaftlichen Film provide films in this area upon which further thinking and refinement can be based.

In the broad area of the ethnography of music making there seem to be so many possibilities in the use of film that one does not know where to start mentioning them. In the study of musical performance, film could enhance research enormously in several areas such as music and motion synchrony, the relationships between performers and audiences, the study of musical cueing, and relations between performing, rehearsing, and musical instruction. Turning to the role of music in community life film can enhance our documentation of the social organization surrounding musical occasions, the study of musicians in society, the process of musical socialization, and the place of music in culture change. In conjunction with specific research problems, film can be used in all of these areas to gather basic data for elicitation research and analysis and can be used to communicate more completely the findings and interpretation of such research.

When we read through a musical ethnography, such as Zemp's excellent *Musique Dan* (1971) we can see that nearly every subject heading lends itself to visual research and documentation: instruments and their uses, status, role, functions, beliefs and practices of musicians, and the place of music in the life cycle and in the community cycle. Moreover, through the interpretive uses of verbal materials, animation, and visuals, it would also be possible to use film to present nondirectly observable behaviors such as Zemp's material on the role of music in the non-human world, or myths about the origin of instruments, or ethnoaesthetic musical evaluation.

In sum, doing ethnomusicology with film is part and parcel of doing better ethnomusicology. By using film in planned programs of research we can avail ourselves of better data modes, better methodologies of elicitation, and testable modes of analysis. By publishing films and writing about them, we can share aspects of field experience—both its data and interpretation—at a new level of communication. There are then scholarly and genuine motivations for doing ethnomusicology with film—not just that film turns the students on, increases enrollments and popularity, is something the departmental secretary can schedule when one is sick or out of town, can be pretty and entertaining, or the right thing for "light" moments such as before vacations and after examinations.

IV

At the very opening of *La Maison de Rendez-vous*, Alain Robbe-Grillet (1966) offers the following author's note:

> This novel, cannot, in any way, be considered as a document about life in the British Territory of Hong Kong. Any resemblance to the latter in setting or situations is merely the effect of chance, objective or not.

There the note stops, but it continues on the following page:

> Should any reader familiar with Oriental ports suppose that the places described below are not congruent with reality, the author, who has spent most of his life there, suggests that he return for another, closer look; things change fast in such climes.

This bit of masterfully felicitous insincerity sets the reader up for a book where vividly realistic descriptions and objective reporting suddenly turn to dreams, lies, and fantasies, and vice versa. I think this juxtaposition exactly provokes our ambivalence about film. On the one hand it is clearly not objective or real, but symbolic, the product of authorship. It was once the tool of magicians and today pervades our mass symbolic environment as the tool of the Hollywood shamans, masters of American fantasy (see Powdermaker 1950). It is the soap selling medium the celluloid dream world, utterly manipulable and manipulating. On the other hand, when compared to other modes of memory, description, and recoding, its objective fascimile and illusion of iconic realism is incredibly strong. In the hands of the documentary and observational shamans it has brought us several magnificent slices of the state of human being, transporting us through thousands of miles, through separate realities, sometimes with brilliant authenticity, sincerity, and understanding. In the hands of researchers it has brought us, at times elegantly and at times dryly, the potential and the actualization of increased knowledge and comprehension of many varieties of human activity.

We are now at a point where a resolution is at hand. Transcending naive claims to hyperobjectivity, truth, reality and unquestionable intrinsic meaningfulness, transcending the collect-it-before-it-dies dinosaur bone approach, and other forms of the objective realist folk myth, we are at a point where the human conceptual equation—that of authored mediated communication—can take over from the "cameras take pictures" technological muddle. Similarly, transcending the pretty picture mentality, the culturally arbitrary story telling conventions, the avoidance of personal and political responsibility through sole allegiance to the high god of ART, the imaging of third world peoples as exotic freak acts for the artistic delights of civilized voyeurs, and other forms of the personal expression and art folk myth, we are at the point where the cinema's subjectivity can be turned into a sensitive, concerned, and intellectually sophisticated means for better mediated communication, to the benefit of all those who care about the potential of visual sharing and visual knowing.

And where is ethnomusicology in all of this? Perhaps it is at the best possible point, because it has the opportunity to tap directly into the foundation being built in the anthropology of visual communication. This requires a non-dogmatic and professional attitude by ethnomusicologists toward film—an openness to deal with film not just as a classroom gimmick, but as a viable scholarly means for the study and sharing of information about human musicality and music making.

NOTES

1. This paper was written while a Research Fellow at the Anthropology Film Center in Santa Fe, New Mexico. My warm thanks go to Carroll and Joan Williams, the Center's co-directors for numerous hours of stimulating talk on topics discussed herein as well as for providing me with a working space for studying ethnomusicology and anthropology of visual communication without compromising either. Thanks too to Diane Bacon for doing the filmography and for feedback. I am also grateful to Gilbert Rouget, Hugo Zemp, Simha Arom, Jean Rouch and particularly to Marielle Delorme for discussion, locating materials, and making films available to me during the semester I spent at the Musée de l'Homme in 1974. Finally, a caveat before beginning: the reader will find that the bulk of my citations are to Africanist materials; I have tried not to exclude other important work but confess far less competence in most other geographical areas.

2. Although it is obviously impossible to neatly separate ethnomusicology film from dance ethnography film, I must exclude discussion of the latter for reasons of both space and competence. It will become apparent, however, that the approach I outline is applicable to both, and I will touch upon the overlaps in the review of some recent work (specifically that of Rouget and of the Choreometrics project).

For those wishing to dive into the large literature of dance and film, I suggest starting with Allegra Fuller Snyder's (1965) discussion of three types of dance film. She distinguishes (1) documentary filming of important dancers/dances for the sake of history of performance/performers, (2) filming records of dance for transcribing, learning, and reconstructing specific dances, and (3) ciné-dance, a combined art form multiplying the visual aspects of movement by the interpretive abilities of the cinema. Other interesting readings are: Dance/Film issues of *Dance Perspectives* (1967), and *Filmmakers' Newsletter*

(1970), Snyder's thesis (1967), Jablonko's dissertation and accompanying film (1968), and articles by Kurath (1963c), Snyder (1969), Bouchard (1951), and Hungerford (1951).

3. As I do not discuss hardware here, the following books are suggested for those wishing a crash course in the nuts and bolts aspects of film and sound: Churchill (1972), Lipton (1972), Malkiewicz (1974), Pincus (1969), and Runstein (1975). These books deal principally with 16mm and 8mm film and ¼" audio. Despite portability, the marginal visual and audio quality of videotape makes it of reduced value for most ethnomusicological research work; the major exception, of course, is the important use of video for instant playback and elicitation in the field. Video primers are: Video Freex (1973), Marsh (1974), and Murray (1975). The tradeoff between portability and dubious quality is truest of the audio cassette format. Labov (1972:110, footnote 6), discussing linguistic methodology, notes that the frequency response of cassette recorders is not even adequate for the study of everyday speech. This of course is much worse with music. In addition, motor instability common to inexpensive cassette recorders inevitably causes variable speed errors, thus distorting both pitch and tempo in music. The Nagra SNN is the only reliable professional quality miniature recorder that uses cassette size tape (though not on cassettes) and operates at 1-7/8 ips.

4. By "film work in ethnomusicology" I will limit the discussion to the uses of the film medium for ethnomusicological research and presentation. For the present then I am placing aside the other important relation between ethnomusicology and film, namely the cultural/musical study of sound tracks, film scores, and television sound. There are obviously several interesting dimensions to this latter area; one need only think about the ways music has been used in exotic movies, adventure films, and travelogues to realize the wealth of data here. Studying the sound symbolism of films of the *Mondo Cane* genre seems as worthy an ethnomusicological topic as any.

I can think of little relevant work in this area to date. Jean Rouch, calling music "the opium of the cinema" (1974:42) has made several interesting observations on the politics of the uses of music in ethnographic film soundtracks. Nazir Jairazbhoy (1973) presented a very interesting paper on Indian film music at the 1973 SEM meeting. One of my own current projects is a study of the music of the Mickey Mouse Club television show (Feld, ms.). A frequent song on this show was titled "Fun with Music"; the song proclaims that "music is a language we all understand" (Walt Disney's contribution to the semiotics of music!). Each successive chorus is laced with hackneyed stereotypes of various European, Asian, and other musics; I try to show why this sort of sound symbolism constitutes an interesting problem in the ethnography of sound communication.

For perspectives on the cultural analysis of visual and sound media, see Carpenter (1974), Schwartz (1973), and Weakland (1975).

5. For those wishing a demonstration I suggest the marvellously visual verbal *Snapshots* of Alain Robbe-Grillet (1968).

6. On questions of using film for frame-by-frame microanalysis, see the writings of Birdwhistell (1970), Condon and Ogston (1966).

REFERENCES CITED

Archive of Folk Song, Library of Congress
    1967   A Brief List of 16mm Sound Motion Picture Films on Folk Music and Folk Dance, with Rental Distributors. ETHNOMUSICOLOGY 11:375-385.

Arom, Simha
    1973   Une méthode pour la transcription de polyphonies et polyrythmies de tradition orale. Revue de Musicologie 59(2):165-190.

Balikci, Asen
    1975   Reconstructing Cultures on Film, *in* Paul Hockings, Ed., Principles of Visual Anthropology. The Hague: Mouton, pp. 191-200.

Bateson, Gregory and Margaret Mead
    1942   Balinese Character. New York: New York Academy of Sciences.

Bebey, Francis
    1963   La Radiodiffusion en Afrique Noire. Seine: Éditions Saint-Paul.
    1969   Musique de l'Afrique. Paris: Horizons de France.

Birdwhistell, Ray
    1970   Kinesics and Context. Philadelphia: Univeristy of Pennsylvania Press.

Bouchard, Thomas
    1951   The Preservation of the Dance Score Through Filming the Dance, *in* Walter
            Sorrell, Ed., The Dance Has Many Faces. New York: World pp. 46-61.

Braun, Susan
    1964a   Films of Dance, Part 3; Australian Aboriginal Dance Films. (Editor) ETHNO-
            MUSICOLOGY 8:170-171.
    1964b   Films of Dance, Part 4; Selected Asian Dance Films. (Editor) ETHNOMUSI-
            COLOGY 8:295-296.
    1965   Films of Dance, Part 5; Films of Australian Aboriginal Dance. (Editor)
            ETHNOMUSICOLOGY 9:153-154.

Byers, Paul
    1966   Cameras Don't Take Pictures. Columbia University Forum 9(1):28-32.

Carpenter, Edmund
    1973   Oh, What a Blow That Phantom Gave Me! New York: Holt, Rinehart, and
            Winston
    1975   The Tribal Terror of Self-awareness, *in* Paul Hockings, Ed., Principles of Visual
            Anthropology. The Hague: Mouton pp. 451-461.

Churchill, Hugh
    1972   Film Editing Handbook; Technique of 16mm Film Cutting. Belmont, Ca.: Wads-
            worth.

(CdF-E) =
Comité du Film Ethnographique
    1955   Catalogue des Films Ethnographiques Français. UNESCO Reports and Papers
            on Mass Communication, n. 15. Paris: UNESCO.
    1956   Catalogue des Films Ethnographiques Étrangers. Paris: Comité du Film
            Ethnographique, Musée de l'Homme.

(CIFES) =
Comité International du Film Ethnographique et Sociologique
    1967   Films ethnographiques sur l'Afrique Noire. Paris: UNESCO.
    1970   Films ethnographiques sur la region du Pacifique. Paris: UNESCO.

Collier, John
    1967   Visual Anthropology: Photography as a Research Method. New York: Holt,
            Rinehart, and Winston.

Condon, William and W. D. Ogston
    1966   Sound Film Analysis of Normal and Pathological Behavior Patterns. Journal of
            Nervous and Mental Disease 143:338-347.

Dance Perspectives
    1967   Issue on Dance/Film. Number 30.

Dauer, A. M.
    1966   Afrikanische musik und volkerkundlicher tonfilm; ein beitrag zur methodik
            der transkription. Research Film/Le Film de Recherche/Forschungsfilm 5(5):
            439-456.
    1969   Research Films in Ethnomusicology: Aims and Achievements. Yearbook of
            the International Folk Music Council 1:226-231, and 2 pp. graphs.

De Brigard, Emilie
    1975   The History of Ethnographic Film, *in* Paul Hockings, Ed., Principles of Visual
            Anthropology. The Hague: Mouton pp. 13-44.
    i.p.   Anthropological Cinema. New York: The Museum of Modern Art.

218

De Heusch, Luc
  1962   The Cinema and Social Science. Paris: UNESCO.

Dwyer-Shick, Susan
  1974   Film Review: *The Loon's Necklace, Anansi the Spider,* and *Eskimo Artist—Kenojuak.* ETHNOMUSICOLOGY 18:487-490.

Feld, Steve
  ms.   Hey There Mouseketeers, It's Time for Fun with Music! Notes towards a cultural analysis of a Mickey Mouse Club song.
  1972   Filmography of the African Humanities. Bloomington, Indiana: African Studies Program, Indiana University.
  1975a Film Review: *Discovering the Music of Africa,* and *Discovering American Indian Music.* ETHNOMUSICOLOGY 19:341-343.
  1975b Film Review: *Le Mvet.* ETHNOMUSICOLOGY 19:513-514.

Feld, Steve and Carroll Williams
  1975   Toward a Researchable Film Language. Studies in the Anthropology of Visual Communication 2(1):25-32.

Feld, Steve and Steven Ohrn
  1975   I Guess You Could Say This is About Why You Can't Make Chicken Liver Out of Chicken Shit. Folklore Forum, Bibliographic and Special Series, Number 13. pp. 94-103.

Filmmaker's Newsletter
  1970   Issue on Film/Dance. Volume 4, Number 1.

Gillis, Verna
  1975   Film Review: *Dry Wood,* and *Hot Pepper.* ETHNOMUSICOLOGY 19:339-341.

Goodman, Felicitas D.
  1975   Films for the Classroom: The Home-Mode on Super 8. Folklore Forum, Bibliographic and Special Series, Number 13. pp. 59-62.

Griaule, Marcel
  1938   Masques Dogons. Paris: Institut d'Ethnologie (Travaux et mémoires, no. 33)
  1948   Dieu d'Eau: entretiens avec Ogotemmêli. Paris: Éditions du Chêne (English translation, 1965, as Conversations with Ogotemmêli: An Introduction to Dogon Religious Ideas. Oxford University Press).

Hall, Edward T.
  1959   The Silent Language. Garden City: Doubleday.

Heider, Karl
  1972a Films for Anthropological Teaching. Fifth Revised Edition. Washington, D.C.: American Anthropological Association.
  1972b The Dani of West Irian: An Ethnographic Companion to the film *Dead Birds.* New York: MSS Information Corporation.
  1974   Ethnographic Films. Lifelong Learning, Two-74:1-5 (Volume 44, Number 21). Berkeley: University of California Extension Media Center.

Henderson, Brian
  1970- Towards a Non-Bourgeois Camera Style. Film Quarterly 24(2):2-14.
  1971

Herskovits, Melville
  1938   Dahomey: An Ancient West African Kingdom. New York: Augustin, 2 Volumes.

Hockings, Paul, Editor
  1975   Principles of Visual Anthropology. The Hague: Mouton.

Hood, Mantle
1971 The Ethnomusicologist. New York: McGraw-Hill.

Hungerford, Mary Jane
1951 Technological Progress and the Dance: The Dance in Movies, *in* Walter Sorell, Ed., The Dance Has Many Faces. New York: World pp. 97-110.

Institut für den Wissenschaftlichen Film
1959 Rules for Documentation in Ethnology and Folklore Through the Film. Research Film/Le Film de Recherche/Forschungsfilm 3:238-240.
1968 A List of Documentary Films on Ethnomusicological Subjects. ETHNOMUSICOLOGY 12:397-409.

Jablonko, Allison
1968 Dance and Daily Activities Among the Maring People of New Guinea: A Cinematographic Analysis of Body Movement Style. Unpublished doctoral dissertation, Dept. of Anthropology, Columbia University.

Jairazbhoy, Nazir A.
1973 How "Indian" is Indian Film Music? Paper presented at the 1973 SEM meeting, Urbana, Illinois.

Kealiinohomoku, Joann
1965 Film Review: '*Ula Nōweo*; a film for the teaching of the Hawaiian Hula, and Filmstrip of Hawaiian Musical Instruments. ETHNOMUSICOLOGY 9:207-208.

Kennedy, Peter, Ed.
1970 Films on Traditional Music and Dance: A First International Catalogue. New York and Paris: UNESCO.

Krebs, Stephanie
1975 The Film Elicitation Technique, *in* Paul Hockings, Ed., Principles of Visual Anthropology. The Hague: Mouton pp. 283-302.

Kubik, Gerhard
1965 Transcription of Mangwilo Xylophone Music from Film Strips. African Music 3(4):35-51.
1972 Transcription of African Music from Silent Film. African Music 5(2):28-39.

Kunst, Jaap
1959 Ethnomusicology. The Hague: Martinus Nijhoff.

Kurath, Gertrude P.
1963a Special Bibliography: Films of Dance, Part 1. ETHNOMUSICOLOGY 7:46.
1963b Special Bibliography: Films of Dance, Part 2. ETHNOMUSICOLOGY 7:125-126.
1963c Photography for Dance Recording. Folklore and Folkmusic Archivist 5(4):1,4.

Labov, William
1972 Some Principles of Linguistic Methodology. Language in Society 1(1):97-120.

Ladzekpo, Seth Kobla and Hewitt Pantaleoni
1970 *Takada* Drumming. African Music 4(4):6-31.

Lajoux, Jean-Dominique
1974 La durée des films ethnographiques. Research Film/Le Film de Recherche/Forschungsfilm 8(3):233-245.

Lipton, Lenny
1972 Independent Filmmaking. San Francisco: Straight Arrow.

Lomax, Alan
1968 Folk Song Style and Culture. Washington, D.C.: American Association for the Advancement of Science.

1971   Choreometrics and Ethnographic Filmmaking. Filmmaker's Newsletter
        4(4):22-30.
1973   Cinema, Science, and Culture Renewal. Current Anthropology 14(4):474-480.
1975   Audio-Visual Tools for the Analysis of Culture Style, in Paul Hockings, Ed.,
        Principles of Visual Anthropology. The Hague: Mouton pp. 303-322.

Lomax, Alan, Irmgard Bartenieff, and Forrestine Paulay
    1969   Choreometrics: A Method for the Study of Cross-Cultural Pattern in Film.
            Research Film/Le Film de Recherche/Forschungsfilm 6(6):505-517.

Malkiewicz, J. Kris
    1973   Cinematography. New York: Van Nostrand Reinhold.

Marsh, Ken
    1974   Independent Video. San Francisco: Straight Arrow.

Mead, Margaret
    1975   Visual Anthropology in a Discipline of Words, in Paul Hockings, Ed.,
            Principles of Visual Anthropology. The Hague: Mouton pp. 3-10.

Merriam, Alan P.
    1964   The Anthropology of Music. Evanston, Ill.: Northwestern University Press.
    1969   The Ethnographic Experience: Drum-making Among the Bala Basongye.
            ETHNOMUSICOLOGY 13:74-100.

Michaelis, Anthony R.
    1955   Research Films in Biology, Anthropology, Psychology, and Medicine. New
            York: Academic Press.

Miller, Hugh
    1970   Polynesian Dance Films in Color with Sound. ETHNOMUSICOLOGY
            14:315-320.

Montgomery, Lou Estes
    1973   Film Review: *The Holy Ghost People.* ETHNOMUSICOLOGY 17:158-159.

Murray, Michael
    1975   The Videotape Book. New York: Bantam.

Nettl, Bruno
    1956   Music in Primitive Culture. Cambridge: Harvard University Press.
    1964   Theory and Method in Ethnomusicology. Glencoe: The Free Press.

Ohrn, Steven
    1975   I've Been Duped: Reducing the Home-mode to Data. Folklore Forum,
            Bibliographic and Special Series, Number 13, pp. 37-44.

Pantaleoni, Hewitt
    1972a   Toward Understanding the Play of *Sogo* in *Atsia.* ETHNOMUSICOLOGY
            16:1-37.
    1972b   Toward Understanding the Play of *Atsimevu* in *Atsia.* African Music
            5(2):64-84.
    1972c   Three Principles of Timing in *Anlo* Dance Drumming. African Music
            5(2):50-63.

Pelto, Pertti J.
    1970   Anthropological Research: The Structure of Inquiry. New York: Harper and
            Row.

Pennsylvania State University, Audio-Visual Services
    1972   Films: The Visualization of Anthropology. University Park, Penna.: Audio-
            Visual Services, Pennsylvania State Univeristy.
    1975   Supplement to: Films: The Visualization of Anthropology. University Park,
            Penna.: Audio-Visual Services, Pennsylvania State University.

Pincus, Ed
  1969   Guide to Filmmaking. New York: Signet.

Powdermaker, Hortense
  1950   Hollywood, The Dream Factory. Boston: Little, Brown and Company.

Robbe-Grillet, Alain
  1966   La Maison de Rendez-vous. New York: Grove Press.
  1968   Snapshots. New York: Grove Press.

Rouch, Jean
  1974   The Camera and Man. Studies in the Anthropology of Visual Communication
         1(1):37-44.
  1975   The Situation and Tendencies of the Cinema in Africa (Part I). Studies in the
         Anthropology of Visual Communication 2(1):51-58.

Rouget, Gilbert
  1965   Un Film Expérimental: Batteries Dogon: Éléments pour une étude des
         rythmes. L'Homme 5(2):126-132.
  1971   Une expérience de cinéma synchrone au ralenti. L'Homme 11(2):113-117.

Royal Anthropological Institute
  1951   Notes and Queries on Anthropology. Sixth Edition. London: Routledge.

Ruby, Jay
  1973   Up the Zambesi with Notebook and Camera, or, Being an Anthropologist
         Without Doing Anthropology ... with Pictures. SAVICOM Newsletter
         4(3):12-15.
  1975a Film Review: The Path. American Anthropologist 77(2):464-466.
  1975b Is an Ethnographic Film a Filmic Ethnography? Studies in the Anthropology
         of Visual Communication 2(2):104-111.

Rundstrom, Donald, Ronald Rundstrom, and Clinton Bergum
  1973   Japanese Tea: The ritual, the aesthetics, the way: an ethnographic companion
         to the film The Path. New York: MSS Information Corporation.

Runstein, Robert E.
  1975   Modern Recording Techniques. Indianapolis: Bobbs-Merrill.

Scheflen, Albert E.
  1973   How Behavior Means. New York: Gordon and Breach.

Scherer, Joanna Cohan
  1975   You Can't Believe Your Eyes: Inaccuracies in Photographs of North American
         Indians. Studies in the Anthropology of Visual Communication 2(2):67-79.

Schwartz, Tony
  1973   The Responsive Chord. New York: Anchor/Doubleday.

Sekula, Allan
  1975   On the Invention of Photographic Meaning. Art Forum 13(5):37-45.

Serwadda, Moses and Hewitt Pantaleoni
  1968   A Possible Notation for African Dance Drumming. African Music 4(2):47-52.

Snyder, Allegra Fuller
  1965   Three Kinds of Dance Film. Dance Magazine 39(9):34-39.
  1967   A Filmic Approach to Dance. Unpublished M.A. thesis, Dept. of Theatre Arts,
         University of California, Los Angeles.
  1968   Film Review: Kashia Men's Dances: Southwestern Pomo Indians, and, Dream
         Dances of the Kashia Pomo. ETHNOMUSICOLOGY 11:428-430.
  1969   Films—Who Can Make Them? How Can We Use Them? Dance Magazine
         43(4):38-41.

Sorenson, E. Richard
  1974   Anthropological Film: A Scientific and Humanistic Resource. Science
         186:1079-1085.
  1975a Visual Records, Human Knowledge, and the Future, *in* Paul Hockings, Ed.,
         Principles of Visual Anthropology. The Hague: Mouton pp. 463-476.
  1975b To Further Phenomenological Inquiry: The National Anthropological Film
         Center. Current Anthropology 16(2):267-269.

Sorenson, E. Richard and Allison Jablonko
  1975   Research Filming of Naturally Occurring Phenomena: Basic Strategies, *in* Paul
         Hockings, Ed., Principles of Visual Anthropology. The Hague: Mouton pp.
         151-163.

Surugue, Bernard
  1972   Contribution a l'étude de la musique sacrée Zarma-Songhay. Études
         Nigériennes, no. 30. Niamey, Niger: Centre Nigérien de Recherches en Sciences
         Humaines.

Tracey, Hugh
  1970   (1948) Chopi Musicians. London: Oxford University Press.

Video Freex
  1973   The Spaghetti City Video Manual. New York: Praeger.

Vignos, Paul
  1973   Film Review: *Bitter Melons, Berimbau,* and *Gravel Springs Fife and Drum.*
         ETHNOMUSICOLOGY 17:597-601.

Weakland, John
  1975   Feature Films as Cultural Documents, *in* Paul Hockings, Ed., Principles of
         Visual Anthropology. The Hague: Mouton pp. 231-251.

Williams, Carroll and Gloria Bird
  1973   A Filmography for American Indian Education. Santa Fe, New Mexico: Zia
         Ciné

Williams, Thomas R.
  1967   Field Methods in the Study of Culture. New York: Holt, Rinehart, and
         Winston.

Wolf, Gotthard, Ed.
  1972   Encyclopaedia Cinematographica (U.S. Edition). University Park, Pa.: The
         Pennsylvania State University.
  1975   Encyclopaedia Cinematographica–Supplement 1972-1975. (U.S. Edition). Uni-
         versity Park, Pa.: The Pennsylvania State University.

Worth, Sol
  1973   Toward the Development of a Semiotic of Ethnographic Film. PIEF News-
         letter 3(3):8-12.
  1974   Editor's Introduction. Studies in the Anthropology of Visual Communication
         1(1):1-2.

Worth, Sol and Larry Gross
  1974   Symbolic Strategies. Journal of Communication 24(4):27-39.

Zantzinger, Gei and Andrew Tracey
  1976   A film companion to *1973 Mgodo wa Mbanguzi* and *1973 Mgodo wa Mkandeni.*
         Roodeport, South Africa: Occasional Papers of the International Library of
         African Music.

Zemp, Hugo
  1971   Musique Dan. Paris: Mouton.

FILMS CITED

Note: Where films have been enlarged or reduced, the first format denotes the original. The films distributed by the Comité du Film Ethnographique are not yet available in the United States and cannot be mailed here.

L'arc musical Ngbaka. Simha Arom. 1970, 16mm, black and white, 10 minutes; Comité du Film Ethnographique.

'Are'Are Massina. Daniel and Christa de Coppet and Hugo Zemp. 1970, 16mm, color, 33 minutes; Comité du Film Ethnographique.

Atumpan. Mantle Hood. 1963, 16mm, color, 40 minutes; Institute of Ethnomusicology, UCLA.

Au Pays des Pygmées. Jacques Dupont. 1947, 35/16mm, black and white, 25 minutes; Comité du Film Ethnographique.

Au Pays Dogon. Marcel Griaule. 1938, 35/16mm, black and white, 15 minutes; Comité du Film Ethnographique.

Le Balafon. Bernard Surugue. 1969, 16mm, color, 20 minutes; Comité du Film Ethnographique.

Bambous Frappés. Hugo Zemp. 1970, 16mm, color, 10 minutes; Comité du Film Ethnographique.

Batteries Dogon. Gilbert Rouget, Jean Rouch, and Germaine Dieterlen. 1964, 16mm, color, 26 minutes; Comité du Film Ethnographique.

Bitter Melons. John Marshall. 1971, 16mm, color, 30 minutes; Documentary Educational Resources.

Character Formation Films. Gregory Bateson and Margaret Mead. 1952, 16mm, black and white, New York University.
 (1) *Trance and Dance in Bali*; 20 minutes.
 (2) *Bathing Babies*; 9 minutes.
 (3) *Childhood Rivalry in Bali and New Guinea*; 20 minutes.
 (4) *First Days in the Life of a New Guinea Baby*; 19 minutes.
 (5) *Karba's First Years*; 20 minutes.
 (6) *A Balinese Family*; 17 minutes.

Dance and Human History. Alan Lomax. 1976, 16 mm, color/black and white, 40 minutes; Extension Media Center, UCB.

Danses des Reines à Porto Novo. Gilbert Rouget. 1971, 16mm, color, 30 minutes; Comité du Film Ethnographique.

Danses Polynésiennes Traditionelles. Hugo Zemp. 1969, 16mm, color, 11 minutes; Comité du Film Ethnographique.

Dead Birds. Robert Gardner. 1963, 16mm, color, 83 minutes; Contemporary/McGraw Hill.

Don't Look Back. D. A. Pennebaker. 1966, 16/35mm, black and white, 95 minutes; Leacock-Pennebaker Inc.

Godié. Bernard Surugue. 1968, 16mm, color, 14 minutes; Comité du Film Ethnographique.

Goudel. Bernard Surugue. 1967. 16mm, black and white, 30 minutes; Comité du Film Ethnographique.

Maring in Motion. Allison Jablonko. 1968, 16mm, color, 18 minutes; Center for Mass Communication, Columbia University.

1973 Mgodo wa Mbanguzi. Gei Zantzinger and Andrew Tracey. 1974. 16mm, color, 53 minutes; Pennsylvania State University, Audio-Visual Services.

1973 Mgodo wa Mkandeni. Gei Zantzinger and Andrew Tracey. 1974, 16mm, color, 48 minutes; Pennsylvania State University, Audio-Visual Services.

Murudruni. Derek Lamport. 1962, 16mm, color, 60 minutes; Extension Media Center, UCB.

Le Mvet. N. Moise Zé. 1972, 16mm, color/black and white, 15 minutes; Mozes Films.

Nanook of the North. Robert Flaherty. 1922, 35/16mm, black and white, 55 minutes; New York University.

Num Tchai. John Marshall. 1969, 16mm, black and white, 20 minutes; Documentary Educational Resources.

The Path. Donald Rundstrom, Ronald Rundstrom, and Clinton Bergum. 1973, 16mm, color, 34 minutes; Extension Media Center, UCB.

The Samaritans: People of the Sacred Mountain. Johanna Spector. 1974, 16mm, color, 30 minutes; inquire of author.

The Savage Innocents. Nicolas Ray. 1959, 35/16mm, color, 90 minutes; Films Inc.

Sigui (series of seven films). Jean Rouch and Germaine Dieterlen. 1968-1974, 16mm, color; Comité du Film Ethnographique.

Sortie de Novices de Sakpata. Gilbert Rouget and Jean Rouch. 1959, 16mm, color, 25 minutes; Comité du Film Ethnographique.

Sous les Masques Noirs. Marcel Griaule. 1938, 35/16mm, black and white, 15 minutes; Comité du Film Ethnographique.

Tourou et Bitti. Jean Rouch. 1972, 16mm, color, 10 minutes; Comité du Film Ethnographique.

Xala. Ousmane Sembène. 1974, 35/16mm, color, 123 minutes; New Yorker Films.

Yenendi de Gangel. Jean Rouch. 1973, 16mm, color, 40 minutes; Comité du Film Ethnographique.

Should Ethnomusicology be Abolished?

Position Papers for the Ethnomusicology Interest Group at the 19th Annual Meeting of the College Music Society, Washington D.C., November 1976

FREDRIC LIEBERMAN
University of Washington

O NE OF THE WORLD'S NATURAL WONDERS is the consistent way in which social organizations imitate biological ones. Once in existence they grow, reproduce, and hang on to life. How frequently do committees or commissions dissolve themselves when their original purposes are fulfilled?

My thesis is that ethnomusicology—specifically academic ethnomusicology as represented by the Society and its Journal—gives no evidence of having become an independent scholarly discipline, and has, therefore, no logical reason for continued existence other than the purely social needs of its members. Furthermore, the continued existence of the pseudo-discipline of ethnomusicology might well hinder rather than promote the avowed goals of its practitioners.

Since its inception, ethnomusicology has been searching for a definition of itself. There is still very little agreement as to its goals, boundaries, methods, requisite skills, or curriculum. As Alan Merriam points out in his recent article "Ethnomusicology Today" (1975),[1] ethnomusicology has made little or no progress in developing a theory.

All sorts of people are identified, or identify themselves, as ethnomusicologists nowadays: anthropologists specializing in music; performers interested in learning to play music of other cultures (some years ago the term "ethnomusician" was proposed); musical tourists of the "Have Nagra, Will Travel" variety; music educators of multi-ethnic persuasion; media mongers

[1]Alan P. Merriam, "Ethnomusicology Today" in *Current Musicology* 20:50-66.

interested in cross-cultural communication; and musicologists who do not limit themselves to the study of Western art music.

On the other hand, some people have reacted against inclusion in the ethnomusicological grab-bag. Ravi Shankar has expressed in print the dismay of Indian musicians and musicologists at being considered part of ethnomusicology rather than musicology. They consider "ethno-" synonymous with "primitive," hence derogatory. More and more of our subjects of study are beginning to feel this way. Despite all high-minded definitions of ethnomusicology as an all-inclusive science of music as human behaviour, those we study see it simply as a form of demeaning neo-colonialism.

More than a few Western specialists in Oriental art musics feel that their work demands total attention to one culture, even one period, exactly as in historical musicology, and feel neither a need nor inclination for comparative or ethnographic studies. Several years ago a Chinese graduate student in ethnomusicology asked me why she was required to take so many courses in anthropology, linguistics, and musics of Africa, Indonesia, et cetera, particularly when this prevented her from taking the courses in literary Chinese, sinological method, Japanese language, and other ones she would need in order to do advanced research in Chinese music. When I explained the premises of the curriculum, aimed at producing ethnomusicologists who could bridge the gap between music and anthropology and help advance our knowledge of human music-making around the world, she replied that that was all very well, but that she was in the program because it was the only way she could major in Chinese music.

What sort of training is appropriate, for example, for a Korean vocalist, with basic training in Western music theory, who wishes to do graduate work abroad and then return home to teach and practice Korean music? (I shall avoid, here, the question of such foreign students who prefer to remain abroad as permanent exiles.) A typical musicology program would excessively involve Western music history and literature; an ethnomusicology program would require excessive work in peripheral areas. Yet there is much that such a student could learn that would assist in his or her life-work: general methods of scholarship, mechanics of reference and bibliography, text-criticism, recording, filming, and archiving techniques, laboratory techniques such as pitch and tempo measurement, and so forth. Publications by Asians who have been exposed to the scholarly apparatus of Western musicology can be significant contributions to knowledge. Without such trained personnel, however, such publications are frequently unreliable—not due to insufficient ability of their editors, but to their lack of understanding of the kinds and quality of evidence and proof required by the international scholarly community.

The Society for Ethnomusicology was formed because musical anthropologists and musicians interested in non-Western musics felt that they had much to share and could talk to each other better than to their colleagues in anthropology and musicology. The two groups soon became armed camps, however, skirmishing regularly even today. Each pays lip-service to the other's expressed values, but neither group comes near to merging the two points-of-view into a synthesis.

When the Society for Ethnomusicology was organized in the early 1950s the musicological establishment was perceived as unreceptive or even hostile to studies of non-Western music, and anthropology was still busily compiling ethnographies of moribund tribelets. Charles Seeger felt that there was no real distinction between musicology and ethnomusicology, but that since historical musicologists had pre-empted the former name, ethnomusicology was a necessary, though ideally temporary, expedient.

From all outward indications, however, things have changed. Within ethnomusicology there has been a continuing broadening of horizons until most of my colleagues would accept Seeger's contention that no music (including Western art or popular music) should be rightly excluded from ethnomusicology. A similar broadening has been evident in musicology.

In 1963 Frank Harrison said " . . . it is the function of all musicology to be in fact ethnomusicology, that is, to take its range of research to include material that is termed sociological."[2] And in the same volume Claude Palisca considered the dilemma of the student of Asian art music, realizing that "neither *comparative* nor *ethnomusicology* is a fitting label. . . . Such a scholar is a musicologist in the same sense as a historian of Western music is, except that he specializes in a foreign musical culture. . . . The inevitable conclusion is that there is only one musicology and its branches are primitive music, folk music, European, Asiatic, Oceanic, African, North and South American music, and their subgroups."[3]

A more recent statement of this exemplary ecumenism is anonymously published on the prospectus of the Twelfth Congress of the International Musicological Society to be held in August 1977:

> Musicology today embraces the music of the entire world as the subject of its research. Scholars in every corner of the globe are studying their own music or that of others. And more than ever they are reaching outside their own discipline for tools and methods for analysis and research. The Twelfth Congress aims to reflect the global and interdisciplinary nature of contemporary musicology.

Let us not be afflicted with that ubiquitous disease of aging academics,

[2]Frank Ll. Harrison, Mantle Hood, Claude V. Palisca, *Musicology* (Englewood Cliffs, N.J., 1963), p. 80.
[3]Ibid., pp. 107-108.

hardening of the categories; and let us not allow false pride to prevent a re-union. Ethnomusicology has served its purpose, run its course. The study of music is not one of the highest of our national priorities today, and there is much to be gained both academically and strategically from putting arbitrary and obsolete divisions behind us and forming a united front to advance knowledge of music and, through music, of man.

RESPONSE BY E. EUGENE HELM
University of Maryland, College Park

The background of these remarks is my conviction that we seem to have forgotten about *quality*. I do not advise my graduate students in historical musicology to resurrect inferior composers of the past, and by the same token I am not ready to treat all non-Western musics as equally worthy of study. All art is not the same. I agree with R. F. Goldman (in his article in *Symposium*, Vol. 16) that a Gothic cathedral is, pure and simple, superior to an igloo.

Yes, strictly speaking, ethnomusicology remains undefined, though we now often say that it is part of musicology, or that there is ideally no difference between the two. So back we go to trying to define musicology. Faced with many systematic outlines of the discipline, we disagree as to whose array of pigeonholes is most attractive. Nevertheless, in the past century our *actions* have at least broadly defined the field: musicology is what we do musically when we put our instruments down, when we stop singing, when we stop composing. Everywhere in the world, musicology is everything musical except performance and composition.

That definition is enough for anybody who is going to live forever. In real life, of course, we cut the definition down to size by declaring some of it to be peripheral, or by simply ignoring part of it. Thus we are willing to give up acoustics if only we can spend more time with a Mozart concerto or a Javanese *Wayang*. We care little if some of Adler's or Pratt's pigeonholes have remained virtually empty all these years. In limiting our actions and our interests, we follow, in the long run, the criterion of *quality*. In the long run we decide, perhaps unconsciously, that all music is not equal. Scholarly manifestoes notwithstanding, we turn out to be unwilling to devote as much time to the songs of Stephen Foster as we do to the songs of Brahms. What's wrong with that? Nothing. That's musicology self-defined; that's life. But it is only *ethnomusicology* if one belongs to the musicological rather than the ethnological side of the fence. If one belongs to the ethnological side, then musicology and ethnomusicology will never be equated.

Professor Lieberman reports that the natives are getting restless at the idea of being placed in glass cases for inspection by Americans. Indeed, this seems inevitable. In the future the *natives* are going to be the ones who most intelligently represent their musics to the world. When this happens, then at some point Professor Lieberman's future students of Chinese music, realizing, as he says, that such a subject by itself is worthy of a lifetime of study, will go to China for *all* of their training, and his students of other musics (if their ambitions are similarly concentrated) will do the same in the appropriate parts of the world, and he will be out of business unless he is able to offer, and justify the existence of, a musicological smorgasbord. I don't think finished scholars from other countries will be coming to America or to any other "musicological" country merely to learn how to write about their own music.

Can ethnomusicology be defined at present? Yes, if it rides on the coattails of musicology. No, if it rides on the coattails of anthropology. Should ethnomusicology be abolished? Yes, if it is part of musicology. No, if, according to the ethnological view, all music is equally worthy of study.

RESPONSE BY CLAUDE PALISCA
Yale University

There are, of course, two sides to this question, but there are also two aspects. One concerns the definition of the field—is the term *ethnomusicology* necessary to define a particular field; does such an independent and discrete field exist? The other side is the association and organization of the practitioners of what is called ethnomusicology—should there be societies, departments, professorships of ethnomusicology as distinguished from musicology? These questions are more than a matter of terminology; how one defines and organizes a field affects very much how one operates within it.

There is no agreement among practitioners concerning what musicology is. The study of music, of all the arts, is the most difficult to circumscribe as a discipline. As soon as you probe its problems with any depth, it spills into neighboring fields—the social and physical sciences, literature, philosophy, and history. It is easier to identify musicologists than to define musicology.

Fluidity of boundaries is inherent in the nature of the subject. Of human sensations, sound is one of the least concrete or measurable; it therefore presents almost insurmountable problems to the psychologist and aesthetician, and the critic who seeks an objective appraisal of music must be a little of both. Music is a purely subjective experience, having no tangible physical existence save as a fleeting pattern of energy in a medium.

No wonder it is the object of so many subspecialists. Its complex raw material requires a student competent in physical acoustics. To study the sensation itself requires a psychologist. Music is made with instruments built by craftsmen and technologists, and to understand them one must be one or the other. It is also made with the voice, which involves physiology. To bring music to listeners often requires highly articulated social organizations; so some musicologists must be sociologists. Music is also associated with rituals and ceremonies, both sacred and secular, and the forms these take demand both theological and anthropological sophistication. Music as an art-product is studied to reveal its structure, its values, and its meanings. The various forms music has taken over the ages have to be subjected to the methodology of the historian. Music expresses the values, forms of thought, and human relationships of a people or ethnic group, and as such is susceptible to the methodology of the geographer and ethnographer.

By necessity, then, there are many subspecialties within musicology. You can, if you wish, give them all names—ethnomusicology, anthropomusicology, physicomusicology, historicomusicology, psychomusicology, theoreticomusicology. One of the sessions in this meeting was entitled: "Women's Studies in Music"; so we now also have gynomusicology. Nor can we omit its correlate, andromusicology—what the gynomusicologists would say we have been pursuing exclusively all along.

"Ethnomusicology" is perhaps the least offensive of these sesquipedalians. There should be no stigma attached to "ethnic." We all belong to some ethnic group; it does not suggest to me, as to our Indian colleague mentioned by Professor Lieberman, something primitive. Besides, few of us subscribe any longer to such categories as "primitive." Cultures foreign to ours may seem primitive until we try to imitate their behavior, when we discover they are very complex. The prefix *ethno* suggests an approach to the study of music that recognizes its being imbedded in a particular culture. Not all music has an ethnic orientation—certainly much contemporary music is in an international style that does not lend itself to an ethnomusicological approach.

To me, then, ethnomusicology is a subdivision of musicology, just as historical musicology is. I once put forward a definition of musicology, and although it was published fourteen years ago, I would still stand by it:

> The musicologist is concerned with music that exists, whether as an oral or a written tradition, and with everything that can shed light on its human context.[1]

This definition does not exclude anything the ethomusicologist does, but it does put the focus on *music*. It places the art of music, the works created, performed, and contemplated by men at the center. The musical work is the principal object, on which structural analysis, historical explanation, ethnic characterization, and critical evaluation converge.

[1]Ibid., p. 116.

Music-centered musicology has not been universally endorsed, even by historians of music. Jacques Handschin urged scholars to turn their lenses not so much on music as on musical man.

> What, then, is the true object of musicology? It is nothing but man, who, standing in a certain location in space and time, impresses his artistic striving in an appropriate music; thus man in his musical activity, man artistically forming something that he leaves behind to posterity.[5]

François Lesure has reinforced this thought:

> The final goal ought, evidently, to be to discover what the music tells us about man that is different from what language, religion, law teaches us about him.[6]

Lesure cautioned scholars to beware of isolating works of art from their context and the conditions which brought them into being, and particularly from the social, political, and economic functions in which musical life is embedded.[7]

A cleavage between those who place the emphasis on music and those who center studies in man and society is even more characteristic of the field of ethnomusicology. Here the older German tradition of comparative musical studies clashes with the more recent orientation toward field work. Even among field workers there is a split between those who as detached observers study musical behavior and those who undergo rigorous apprenticeships with native musicians in order to know a musical practice from the inside. While the anthropologist-musicologist tends to concentrate on the behavior of musicians and the function of their music, the musician-ethnologist tends to study the character of musical art as a living component of a culture.[8]

Both historical and ethnic musicologists, then, are divided in their opinions as to whether to place music or man at the center of their studies. If the ethnic scholars were clearly man-centered and the historical clearly music-centered, we would have a distinction. But, in fact, not the least of what we have in common is this division of opinion.

The other side of the question is whether there ought to be separate societies for historical and ethnic musicology. This is more a practical than an ideological issue.

[5]Jacques Handschin, "Der Arbeitersbereich der Musikwissenschaft," *Gedenkschrift J. Handschin* (Bern and Stuttgart, 1957), p. 24, my translation.
[6]François Lesure, "Musicologie" in *Encyclopédie de la musique* (Paris, 1961), III, 268f., my translation.
[7]François Lesure, "Pour une sociologie historique des faits musicaux" in *Report of the Eighth* [IMS] *Congress, New York 1961*, ed. Jan LaRue, I (Kassel, 1961), 333ff.
[8]I deal more extensively with these trends in my section on music in Chapter V, "Aesthetics and the Science of Art" in *Main Trends of Research in the Social and Human Sciences*, Part II, ed. Mikel Dufrenne, scheduled to be published by the UNESCO Press, Paris, in 1977.

The ethnologists broke off from the American Musicological Society in 1953 to found the Society for Ethnomusicology. The Western musicologists have made attempts to win the ethnologists back, and both national and international musicological meetings have striven to include ethnic material on their programs. The most integrated program that has ever been attempted is that of the Twelfth Congress of the International Musicological Society of 1977 in Berkeley. A high proportion of the panels wed the two points of view or are strongly ethnographic in their focus and personnel. In my opinion the Society for Ethnomusicology should stop trying to be an international organization; it should admit to its North American bias with respect to meetings and membership, continue to cultivate foreign members as do most national organizations, but work with the IMS to make that truly representative of all musicology in its membership and interests.

On the national level the SEM has demonstrated the practical advantage of organizing scholars around a subspecialty that shares a methodology and combination of interdisciplinary relationships. Independence has been all the more necessary to ethnomusicology because it had to break away from two traditional fields, anthropology—a social science—and traditional musicology—a branch of the humanities—to assert its identity as a field that is neither social science, history, linguistics, psychology, nor acoustics, to mention some of the principal components. The anthropological component no longer seems a dominant one, and I would question the proposition that a curriculum should aim to produce people who "bridge the gap between musicology and anthropology."[9] The gap we should be bridging is that between cultures.

Ethnomusicologists have thrived since they declared their independence, because they have met together and strengthened each other's sense of identity and compared methodologies and findings. The number of university chairs is multiplying; as are the number of dissertations, books, articles, grants, prizes, and, too, the number of hangers-on—perhaps the best measure of success. I should not want to see this movement stopped. A vigorous association of ethnomusicologists can do more to promote the field than an infusion or diffusion of ethnomusicologists within the AMS or CMS. Occasional joint national meetings such as we have had from time to time, and particularly international meetings such as that of 1977, are excellent means of bringing the Western and non-Western oriented scholars together.

Even more beneficial, in my opinion, would be joint regional meetings. A number of the AMS chapters are languishing, and there are not always enough SEM members to form a viable chapter. Local meetings are an ideal medium for establishing relationships among those interested in Western and art music on the one hand and those interested in non-Western,

'See Fredric Lieberman's contribution to this panel, above.

popular, and folk music on the other. Regional inter-university cooperation can also reap benefits, as has been experienced by Yale and Wesleyan. In the spring of 1977 Mantle Hood occupied a joint visiting professorship sponsored by the two institutions. In the fall of 1976 David McAllester of Wesleyan taught a course on American Indian music at Yale, bringing Wesleyan students with him for each meeting. Previously Craig Wright of Yale taught a course in Renaissance music at Wesleyan while Gen'Ichi Tsuge taught Japanese music at Yale, and in spring 1977 Craig Monson of Yale taught a seminar in Elizabethan music and culture in Middletown.

We hope to continue this collaboration in the future, taking advantage of each other's strengths to plug some of our own curricular holes and to bridge a cultural gap that is bigger than the stretch of Interstate 91 that separates us. Well might we say: *"Vive la difference!"*

DEFINITIONS OF "COMPARATIVE MUSICOLOGY" AND "ETHNOMUSICOLOGY": AN HISTORICAL-THEORETICAL PERSPECTIVE[1]

Alan P. Merriam

Readers of this, and other, journals hardly need be reminded of my persistent interest over the years in definitions of what ethnomusicology is and what it ought to be (e.g., Merriam 1960; 1969; 1975). It is now more than 25 years since, according to common belief, Jaap Kunst first put "ethno-musicology" into print (Kunst 1950), and we thus ought to be able now to look back with some objectivity at what has since happened to that word, and what happened to its predecessor—"comparative musicology"— before it. In other words, the points are now historic, though the end result is far from settled, and it is in this spirit that I wish to treat the materials to be discussed herein. While I have not gone through the literature with a fine-toothed comb in an attempt to find *all* definitions, I have located a substantial number of them, enough, I trust, to indicate fairly the overall trends and changes. Neither have I gone outside the United States for the most part, though some such definitions are included where they seemed especially pertinent. My major purpose, then, is to discuss what happened over time to these two terms in the United States, and what consequences occurred because of the changes that took place.

Problems of definition can, of course, be extremely sticky. When we define a concept, are we attempting to deal with what it is or with what it ought to be? The former, of course, is based upon the premise that a definition—in this case of ethnomusicology—can be based upon what it is that ethnomusicologists do; in other words, it is essentially descriptive and is drawn from observation of normative activity. The difficulty with this approach is that it is essentially uninformative, both because it is only descriptive, and because it is circular. That is, in order to know what ethnomusicology is, we must be able to identify the ethnomusicologist, but the latter is only definable in terms of the former.

On the other hand, if we are concerned with a definition which tells us what ethnomusicology ought to be, we enter into the debatable realm of advocacy. My own bias, however, is toward the latter type of definition since it attempts to set the standard for the field.

Another difficulty centers on the problem of whether the item to be defined is, in fact, definable. The answer of the strict positivist, of course, is

189

that it is, and that any phenomenon is susceptible of definition "by means of symbolic logic in empirical terms" (Ladd 1973:418). The answer of the Ordinary Language philosopher is different, however, in that his approach "gives full recognition to the fact that there are some valid, rational concepts that are not strictly definable in scientific terms . . . ," these being "inexact, fuzzy concepts that are quite different from scientific concepts. . . ." Thus, for example:

> Aesthetic and ethical concepts are distinct from purely descriptive, empirical concepts in that they a) are open-textured, b) are multi-functional, c) involve criteria, d) are essentially contestable, and e) employ persuasive definitions. (*loc. cit.*)

While examination of some definitions of ethnomusicology might well persuade the reader that they meet these criteria, and that, indeed, the term is not definable, I do not believe this to be true. By the very nature of the word itself, ethnomusicology is linked to science: "logy" as a root is a combining form which names sciences or bodies of knowledge. If our definitions frequently seem primarily persuasive, it is not the fault of the word form, but that of the definers!

We can also, in definition, find ourselves struggling with the very words we use. Thus, for example, Hood, in the Introduction to *The Ethnomusicologist*, writes that "One point is clear: The *subject* of study in the field of ethnomusicology is music" (1971:3). While surely almost all of us would agree that this is so, we have only to stop to wonder how to define "music" to discover ourselves in difficulty again. That is, if ethnomusicology is cross-cultural in its approach, which it certainly is, the problem of identifying the phenomenon "music" becomes crucial. Ethnomusicologists need hardly be told that people in some societies simply have no concept "music," and that others who do, view it in a sharply different light from what is implied in Hood's statement. The point here is not that the statement is incorrect, in the conventional sense of the word, but rather, that it is not cross-cultural, and that the difficulties inherent in making it cross-cultural are almost overwhelming in their magnitude. Perhaps in this case, we *are* dealing with a concept which does not lend itself to definition in the scientific sense, but this, in turn, leads us still further afield and is not of central concern to the present discussion.

Despite these, and other, problems, ethnomusicologists have defined their field of study over and over again, and rightly so, since definition is of primary importance, and for a number of reasons. In the first place, because we are professionals in a field of study, we wish to understand all we can about ethnomusicology; this is at the root both of intellectual curiosity and professional responsibility. Second, the most cursory examination of the content of our publications reveals an extraordinarily mixed bag of interests, and this becomes a puzzle in itself, for what kind of field is it that can encompass such variety, and how can it possibly be defined?

More important are two further reasons for seeking definition of the field. The first is that theory, method, and data are inextricably intertwined: one simply does not exist without the others, and all three constantly interact in any intellectual enterprise. Without theory we can hardly have significant method, not only in the sense that no method *can* be theory-free, but also that no method *should* be theory-free. And without method, no significant gathering of data can occur, for the results will inevitably be random. Finally, both in inductive and deductive procedures, theory is based upon data. The point is not only that the three are interrelated, but that if one cannot define his field of study, he can have no theory in respect to it, for he is dealing with it as an amorphous area of concern which he can only treat in the most general terms.

Thus definition is of vital concern because we can face no other questions until this one has been faced; and once it has been faced, then we arrive at the absolutely necessary position of having to face all questions. In short, all disciplines must question all assumptions; all assumptions derive in one way or another from what its practitioners claim their field, or discipline, to be. Definition is crucial because it forces us to face the bases of our intellectual activities; lacking such honest confrontation, we can have little hope of changing ethnomusicology from the status of a variegated field of study to that of a real discipline. Such status in no way implies uniformity of view, study, or approach, but it does imply commonality of purposes and goals.

I

The earliest definition of "comparative musicology" *per se* was that proposed by Guido Adler in 1885 (see Appendix for definitional quotations), and his emphasis was laid upon "folksongs . . . of the various people of the earth," both for "ethnographical" and classificatory purposes. Hornbostel seems never to have put forward a definition as such, and perhaps the earlier days of the field were less marked by definitional concerns than the later, as, for example, those of Lachmann in 1935, and Roberts a year later. However, the summary definition of comparative musicology in the United States was made by Glen Haydon in 1941 in his *Introduction to Musicology*. Thus:

> Non-European musical systems and folk music constitute the chief subjects of study; the songs of birds and phylogenetic-ontogenetic parallels are subordinate topics. (p. 218)
> If *comparative musicology* means the study of extra-European musical systems, it is natural that the study of Chinese, Indian, Arabian, and other musical systems should fall to the lot of comparative musicology. (p. 235)

Comparative musicology has its characteristic subject matter chiefly in extra-European and folk music.... (p. 237)

Most, if not all, of the music studied in comparative musicology is transmitted by oral tradition.... (p. 219)

These statements carry two important messages, the first of which is advanced more forcefully than the second. They are that comparative musicology is the study of "extra-European and folk music," and that comparative musicology studies music which is "transmitted by oral tradition." Both themes had been foreshadowed, of course, and both were repeated over and over by subsequ.nt authors, but it was the "non-European" aspect of the definition that received the greatest play; it is echoed by Sachs (1943), Apel (1946), Herzog (1946), Koole (1955: "exotic" is the term used), Bukofzer (1956), Nettl (1956), Rhodes (1956), Schaeffner (1956: but note the disclaimer as to whether comparative musicology should study these musics), Schneider (1957), Kunst (1959), and Seeger (1961), among many others.

By 1961, the use of "comparative musicology" as a label had disappeared except in historic references; while it reappeared later (Kolinski 1967), it was no longer applied to the field in general but rather, to a portion of it. Indeed, both Kunst and Seeger, in the citations immediately above, were already using the term historically, and from Nettl, in 1956, forward, the two terms "comparative musicology," and "ethnomusicology" were used together as synonyms. This period of overlap occurred roughly during the latter half of the decade of the 1950's.

Three major points can be made concerning these definitions. First, they are virtually identical and unanimous in what they stress. Second, they define comparative musicology unanimously in terms of certain musics to be studied, namely, either "non-Western" (or an equivalent term such as "exotic"), or "orally transmitted" musics. Third, they do not deal with what is meant by "comparative method" or what the aim of comparison is; indeed, they seldom stress anything comparative at all.

It was the question of the "comparative" in comparative musicology, however, which led ultimately to the abandonment of the term. While it has sometimes been suggested that the question of comparativism arose at the same time as, and as a consequence of, the introduction of the new term, "ethnomusicology," the evidence does not support the case. Two main arguments have been advanced for the inadequacy of the term.

The first can be expressed roughly in the statement: "Because we don't compare any more than anyone else does," and this kind of objection appeared almost as soon as the term itself (Hornbostel 1905). Haydon again provides us with a clear statement:

The term [comparative musicology] is not entirely satisfactory, however, for the comparative method is frequently used in the other fields of musicology, and studies in this field are often not directly comparative. (p. 216)

This point of view was expressed over and over again in essentially the same form, by, for example, Sachs (1943:29), Herzog (1946:11), Kunst (1950:7), Koole (1955:228), Rhodes (1956:459), List (1962:20), and others. The unanimity of the argument is notable in the following passage by Sachs, written twenty years after Haydon's statement:

> But today 'comparative musicology' has lost its usefulness. For at the bottom every branch of knowledge is comparative; all our descriptions, in the humanities no less than in the sciences, state similarities and divergences. . . . Walter Wiora is certainly right when he emphasizes that comparison can denote only a method, not a branch of learning. (1961:15)

The second objection came at a much later time, and was probably an outgrowth of factors other than those which motivated the scholars noted above. This is the view that comparison itself is not central to ethnomusicology's concern, and it has been expressed in two ways. The first is that comparison in ethnomusicology has been undertaken prematurely, and this has been emphasized by Hood, for example, who wrote in 1963:

> . . . it seems a bit foolish in retrospection that the pioneers of our field became engrossed in the comparison of different musics before any real understanding of the musics being compared had been achieved. (p. 233).

Hood later expressed the point of view somewhat more strongly when he wrote in 1969:

> An early concern with comparative method, before the subjects under comparison could be understood, led to some imaginative theories but provided very little accurate information. . . . A vast number of musical cultures . . . are yet to be studied systematically . . . before comparative methods can 'give musicology a truly world-wide perspective.' (p. 299)

The second anti-comparative view was expressed earlier in time; it hinges on the idea that since meanings may differ from one culture to another, comparison of musics may be comparison of unlike things. One of the early statements of this objection is Meyer's opinion written in 1960.

> Appearances are often deceptive. For instance, two cultures may appear to employ the same scale structure, but this structure might be interpreted differently by the members of each culture. Conversely, the music of two cultures may employ very different materials, but the underlying mechanism governing the organization of these materials might be the same for both. (pp. 49-50)

John Blacking was expressing the same point of view when he wrote:

> Statistical analyses of intervals, . . . are all very well, provided that we know that the same intervals have the same meanings in all the cultures whose music we are comparing. If this is not certain, we may be comparing incomparable phenomena. In other words, if we accept the view that patterns of music sound in any culture are the product of concepts and behaviours peculiar to that culture, we cannot compare them with similar

patterns in another culture unless we know that the latter are derived from similar concepts and behaviour. Conversely, statistical analyses may show that the music of 2 cultures is very different, but an analysis of the cultural 'origins' of the sound patterns may reveal that they have essentially the same meaning, which has been translated into the different 'languages' of the 2 cultures. (1966:218)

Other objections to comparison have been made, but they are not central to the present discussion. What is important is that the reaction against the term, "comparative musicology," was first expressed, in print, at least, in terms of the suppositions that its practitioners did not compare any more than anyone else, and that comparison was both premature and dangerous.

II

These objections bracket in time one of the most significant periods of development in the history of our field of study. This period occurred in the first half of the decade of the 1950's, and it was marked by the appearance for the first time in the United States of a small group of specially trained students who were disciples of older men in the field: I am thinking here of such persons as Mantle Hood, David McAllester, Bruno Nettl, myself, and others. It was also marked by the organization of a successor to the American Society for Comparative Musicology which had existed briefly in the 1930's. This effort was begun in 1953, and the formal organization of the Society for Ethnomusicology took place in 1955. And finally, the increase in activity in the field was marked by the introduction of the new term, "ethnomusicology."

It is unanimously agreed, so far as I know, that the first use of the term in print occurred in Jaap Kunst's little booklet, *Musicologica* (1950); it is interesting to note that Kunst was reacting against "comparative musicology" on precisely the grounds cited previously herein. He wrote: "The name of our science is, in fact, not quite characteristic; it does not 'compare' any more than any other science. A better name, therefore, is that appearing on the title page of this book: *ethno-musicology*" (p. 7). I do not know whether, in fact, this *was* the first printed appearance of the word, and it is quite possible that an industrious search would reveal an earlier citation, for certainly the word was in currency before 1950. Regardless of this possibility, the Kunst usage is the significant emotional one for students of the field, and will quite possibly always remain so.

Two important points must be made concerning the introduction of this new term. The first is that it was accepted virtually immediately, and undoubtedly the establishment of the Society for Ethnomusicology (without the hyphen) had a very substantial impact upon the new public convention.

By the second half of the decade of the 1950's the two terms were being used simultaneously as synonyms, and by the end of the same decade, "comparative musicology" had been reduced almost exclusively to the status of an historic term which only referred to something in the past. Thus within five years a significant change had occurred, and within ten, the earlier term had been almost completely replaced as a working symbol.

The second point is that the very speed of acceptance must have indicated a significant desire for change, and the assumption is strengthened when we recall that the first objections to the prior term had been raised at least as early as 1905! This in itself has certain implications:

1) something must have been lacking in the old term, i.e., it did not adequately express what the practitioners of comparative musicology felt they were doing, or ought to be doing;

2) something fresh must have been visualized in the new term, which better expressed the sense of the field and the ideas or ideals of its practitioners;

3) something must have changed in the minds of the persons involved in the field that required a change in its appellation.

The fact that these assumptions did not, for the most part, turn out to be true, does not affect them as reasonable hypotheses. A change of name of an entire field of study, coupled with its eager and virtually immediate acceptance, is not an event to be dismissed lightly.

A considerable amount of similarity was noted in the definitions of "comparative musicology"—in fact, they tended to be as alike as peas in a pod. The definitions of "ethnomusicology," however, do not follow quite the same pattern. Two major types can be distinguished in the twenty-odd years after Kunst's publication, of which the first can be subdivided into three related, but slightly different, approaches.

The first type consists of definitions which closely parallel, or are identical to, those which had been used for comparative musicology, and the first subtype includes those based upon the named kind of music being studied. Thus in 1950, Kunst included as the object of study, "mainly the music and the musical instruments of all non-European peoples, including both the so-called primitive peoples and the civilized Eastern nations" (1950:7), and in Third Edition of the same work, he spoke of "*traditional* music and musical instruments of all cultural strata of mankind," but specifically named "tribal and folk music," and "every kind of non-Western art music," while specifically excluding "Western art- and popular (entertainment-)" music (1959:1). This lead was followed by others, such as Nettl, who wrote "Ethnomusicology . . . [is] . . . the study of non-Western music and, to an extent, ... folk music ..." (1961:2) and others, including, for example, Greenway (1962), Hood (1963), and Nettl again (1965).

The second subtype takes the second stressed aspect of the old comparative musicology definitions and makes it the central focus of the new definition; this concerns music as oral tradition, which Lachmann had emphasized as early as 1935, and which had been a part of Haydon's (1941) and Kunst's (1959) discussions. Characteristic here is List's statement that "ethnomusicology is to a great extent concerned with music transmitted by unwritten tradition" (1962), a position he has reiterated since (1963; 1969), and one which has also been suggested by others (Gillis 1969). More recently, Nettl has discussed the same matter, but from a rather different standpoint, noting that *all* music traditions employ a strong oral component. He writes:

> I feel therefore that I should not devote myself simply to what we call orally transmitted music, or what we were once permitted to call folk music, but instead to the study of all music from the point of view of its oral tradition; and this, for me, is one of a number of acceptable definitions of the field of ethnomusicology. (1975:69)

The third subtype defines the field as showing primary concern with music "outside one's own society." Statements of this type are less frequent than the others, but they have been made by Nettl (1964:11; 1965), and perhaps most specifically in print by Wachsmann, who wrote: "... ethnomusicology is concerned with the music of other peoples" (1969).

These definitions of ethnomusicology are all of one essential type, for they approach the problem from the standpoint of what the supposed sphere of interest is, conceptualized in terms of things. Of the three subtypes, the first two represent essentially different emphases on the same point, and both are used today, though with decreasing frequency. The third has dropped almost completely out of the picture, under the criticism of Kolinski (1957) and Seeger (1961), among others, both of whom pointed out that such a statement is basically ethnocentric and that by its tenet, the definition of what ethnomusicology is depends at any given point on who is studying what.

In sum, the definitions discussed to this point parallel the prior definitions of "comparative musicology," for they are statements of what particular kinds of music should be studied. Further, they represent by far the largest proportion of definitions suggested for the new term, and, contrary to expectations, they do not represent a change in position or in thought. Instead, these majority definitions seem to indicate that for their proponents, ethnomusicology represented no significant break with comparative musicology.

The second kind of definition does indicate the beginnings of a sharp rupture with the past, for in this case, process is stressed over form: the kind of music to be studied is no longer central, and instead, the focus of attention is placed upon the way it is to be studied. While these definitions are relatively rare, they become more common through time; and while the early examples are groping, and perhaps even accidental, they do represent a new feeling about the field of study.

Early in the field was McAllester's report of the organizational meeting of the Society for Ethnomusicology, in which he spoke of the "general concensus" as favoring the idea that ethnomusicology "is by no means limited to so-called 'primitive music,' and is defined more by the orientation of the student than by any rigid boundaries of discourse" (1956). A year later, Hood borrowed a definition of ethnomusicology from musicology which mentioned no types of music to be studied, but instead emphasized "the investigation of the art of music. . ." (1957). In 1960, I suggested a flatly processual definition of ethnomusicology as ". . . the study of music in culture" (1960), and two years later Nketia wrote that "the study of music as a universal aspect of human behavior is becoming increasingly recognized as the focus of ethnomusicology" (1962). Hood's well-known definition in the *Harvard Dictionary* spoke of ethnomusicology as "an approach" (1969), and others have followed with variations on the same general theme, including Seeger (1970), List (1971), Chase (1972), and Merriam (ca. 1973).

These definitions represent a qualitative difference from others in that they stress process rather than form. By defining ethnomusicology in terms of "things," the scholar is constantly forced into making taxonomies, into cutting and splitting, drawing boundaries, differentiating between one thing and another: the conclusion must always be that a significant difference exists, as Hood (1969) and others (Seeger 1961, for example) insist, between music sound and the context of music sound, and that both for practical and analytic purposes, never the twain shall meet.

On the other hand, definitions which stress process force the investigator to focus on a totality rather than a set of component parts, to view description as a beginning in the course of study, and to conceptualize music sound not as separate from, but as a part of the totality of society and culture. The debate between the two views is a continuing, and healthy one which represents a hoary division of intellectual domains in Western thought: it is sharply reflected in the definitions put forward for the word, "ethnomusicology."

III

In the 1970's, definitions of the field have declined in number, presumably either because ethnomusicologists tired of the subject or because they felt that definitional problems had been solved and that they could operate comfortably with one or another of the formulations previously suggested. Further, most of the more recent definitions have been very broad and general, almost as if whatever battles had been fought were no longer appropriate, or as if the problem did not require further sharp and precise thinking. Thus Chenoweth says only that "ethnomusicology is the study of the musical practices of a particular people" (1972), and Blacking writes that "Ethnomusicology is a comparatively new word which is widely used to refer to the study of the different musical systems of the world" (1973; see also Blacking 1974). Nettl has recently suggested a broadly encompassing working definition which he regards as descriptive of most study currently being done in the field.

> Ethnomusicology is the comparative study of musical cultures, particularly as total systems including sound and behavior with the use of field research. (1974)

At the same time, a few definitions have recently appeared which represent either idiosyncratic ideas of what ethnomusicology is, or new directions in which it may be going. Thus it has been suggested that the primary task of ethnomusicology may be to seek correlations between music sound structure, on the one hand, and society and culture, on the other. I have recently commented that if we do "define" ethnomusicology in terms of "what ethnomusicologists do," and given the significant expansion of "world music performance groups," ethnomusicology might well be forced into such a definition as "the performance and dissemination of ethnic music" (1975:56). This suggestion goes against my own strong conviction that no field of study can be defined on such a basis. Most recently, the growing concern manifested by students and professors around the world with the problems of logical positivism and the scientific method, have been reflected in yet another definition, one which stresses, perhaps, things to come: "Ethnomusicology is the hermeneutic science of human musical behavior" (Elizabeth Helser 1976).

The definitions of comparative musicology and ethnomusicology cited here reflect their eras and the thinking of their proponents, as is to be expected. But by looking at them in historic perspective, we learn something not only of the history of our field of study *per se*, but of its intellectual development as well. I have no doubt that new definitions of ethnomusicology will continue to be proposed and that they, too, will reflect the growing maturity of the field and its practitioners.

NOTE

[1] I wish to express my deep appreciation to Frank Gillis, Elizabeth Helser, and Bruno Nettl, each of whom has given me permission to quote his or her unpublished definition of ethnomusicology. I trust I have not distorted any of these friends' views in so doing.

REFERENCES NOT CITED IN APPENDIX

Blacking, John
    1966   Review of The Anthropology of Music. Current Anthropology 7:218.

Hood, Mantle
    1971   The ethnomusicologist. New York: McGraw-Hill.

Hornbostel, Erich M von
    1905   Die Probleme der vergleichenden Musikwissenschaft. Zeitschrift der Internationalen Musikgeselschaft 7:85-97.

Kolinski, Mieczyslaw
    1957   Ethnomusicology, its problems and methods. Ethnomusicology Newsletter No. 11:2-8.

Ladd, John
    1973   Conceptual problems relating to the comparative study of art. *In* Warren L. d'Azevedo (Ed). The traditional artist in African societies. Bloomington: Indiana University Press, pp. 417-24.

Merriam, Alan P.
    1969   Ethnomusicology revisited. ETHNOMUSICOLOGY 13:213-29.
    1975   Ethnomusicology today. Current Musicology No. 20:50-66.

Meyer, Leonard B.
    1960   Universalism and relativism in the study of ethnic music. ETHNOMUSICOLOGY 4:49-54.

Sachs, Curt (Edited by Jaap Kunst)
    1962   The wellsprings of music. The Hague: Martinus Nijhoff.

APPENDIX

References are cited in chronological, rather than alphabetical, order.

Adler, Guido
    1885   Umfang, Methode und Zeil der Musikwissenschaft. Vierteljahrsschrift für Musikwissenschaft 1:5-20.
           p. 14: "... die vergleichende Musikwissenschaft, die sich zur Aufgabe macht, die Tonproducte, insbesondere die Volksgesänge verschidiner Völker, Länder und Territorien behufs ethnographischer Zwecke zu vergleichen und nach der Verschiedenheit ihrer Beschaffenheit zu gruppiren und sondern." ("... comparative musicology has as its task the comparison of the musical works—especially the folksongs—of the various peoples of the earth for ethnographical purposes, and the classification of them according to their various forms.")

Lachmann, Robert
    1935   Musiksysteme und Musikauffassung. Zeitschrift für Vergleichende Musikwissenschaft 3:1-23.
           p. 1: By implication "non-European music," as in the following: "Aussereuropäische Musik wird ohne das Mittel der Schrift überliefert; ihre Untersuchung erfordert daher andere Methoden als die der abendländischen Kunstmusik." ("Non-European music is handed down without the means of writing; its investigation demands, therefore, other methods than those for Western art music.")

Roberts, Helen H.
    1937   The viewpoint of comparative musicology. Proceedings of the Music Teachers National Association for 1936, pp. 233-38.

p. 233: "... the kind of studies that are now coming to be classified under the term 'comparative musicology' deal with exotic musics as compared with one another and with that classical European system under which most of us were brought up."

Haydon, Glen
    1941   Introduction to musicology. New York: Prentice-Hall.
        p. 218: "Non-European musical systems and folk music constitute the chief subjects of study; the songs of birds and phylogenetic-ontogenetic parallels are subordinate topics."
        p. 235: "If *comparative musicology* means the study of extra-European musical systems, it is natural that the study of Chinese, Indian, Arabian, and other musical systems should fall to the lot of comparative musicology."
        p. 237: "Comparative musicology has its characteristic subject matter chiefly in extra-European and folk music. ..."
        p. 219: "Most, if not all, of the music studied in comparative musicology is transmitted by oral tradition. ..."

Sachs, Curt
    1943   The rise of music in the ancient world east and west. New York: W. W. Norton.
        p. 29: "comparative Musicology ... [is] ... the primitive and Oriental branch of music history."

Apel, Willi
    1946   Harvard dictionary of music. Cambridge: Harvard University Press.
        p. 167: "Comparative musicology ... [is] ... the study of exotic music."
        p. 250: "Exotic music ... [is comprised of] ... the musical cultures outside the European tradition."

Herzog, George
    1946   Comparative musicology. The Music Journal 4 (Nov.-Dec.): 11 et seq.
        p. 11: "There are many other musical languages, employed by Oriental and primitive—preliterate—peoples. The study of these bodies of music is Comparative Musicology, which aims to discover all the variety of musical expression and construction that is to be found within the wide array of types of cultural development all over the world. Comparative Musicology embraces also folk music. ..."

Kunst, Jaap
    1950   Musicologica. Amsterdam: Koninklijke Vereeniging Indisch Institut.
        p. 7: "To the question: what is the study-object of comparative musicology, the answer must be: mainly the music and the musical instruments of all non-European peoples, including both the so-called primitive peoples and the civilized Eastern nations. Although this science naturally makes repeated excursions into the field of European music, the latter is, in itself, only an indirect object of its study."

Koole, A. J. C.
    1955   The history, study, aims and problems of comparative musicology. South African Journal of Science 51:227-30.
        p. 227: "The Englishman Alexander John Ellis ... is rightly considered to be the founder of this branch of science [comparative musicology], for although a few studies of exotic music had been published. ..."

Bukofzer, Manfred F.
    1956   Observations on the study of non-Western music. *In* Paul Collaer (Ed). Les colloques de Wégimont. Bruxelles: Elsevier, pp. 33-36.
        p. 33: "From the beginning [musicology] has included also the study of oriental and primitive music or what can best be summarized as non-western

music. This special branch is known by the somewhat clumsy name 'comparative musicology' or 'ethnomusicology.'.... The study is supposed to include
also the musical folklore of western nations." (See remarks in opposition by
Constantin Brailoiu, pp. 35-36.)

[McAllester, David P.]
    1956 The organizational meeting in Boston: Ethno-musicology Newsletter No.
          6:3-5.
          p. 5: "The proper subject matter for the society was discussed at length. The
          general consensus favored the view that 'ethno-musicology' is by no means
          limited to so-called 'primitive music,' and is defined more by the orientation
          of the student than by any rigid boundaries of discourse.... It was further
          felt that the term, 'ethno-musicology' is more accurate and descriptive of this
          discipline and its field of investigation than the older term, 'comparative
          musicology.'"

Nettl, Bruno
    1956 Music in primitive culture. Cambridge: Harvard University Press.
          p. 1: "The study of primitive music falls within the scope of comparative
          musicology, or, as it is often termed, ethnomusicology, the science that deals
          with the music of peoples outside of Western civilization."

Rhodes, Willard
    1956 Toward a definition of ethnomusicology. American Anthropologist 58:457-63.
          p. 460-61: "Here, under the imprint of comparative musicology, are bound
          together studies of the music of the Near East, the Far East, Indonesia,
          Africa, the North American Indians, and European folk music. Of those
          ethnomusicologists whose interests are confined solely to primitive music I
          ask, 'Can we refuse our inheritance?' Let us not be provincial in the pursuit of
          our discipline. Oriental art music, the folk music of the world, and primitive
          music, all await our serious study."

Schaeffner, André
    1956 Ethnologie musicale ou musicologie comparée? In Paul Collaer (Ed). Les
          colloques de Wégimont. Bruxelles: Elsevier, pp. 18-32.
          p. 24: "J'ai dit... que rien dans son nom ne spécifiait que la musicologie
          comparée étudierait plutôt les musiques non-européennes. Or elle s'est
          intéressée essentiellement à celles-ci." ("I said that nothing in its name
          specified that comparative musicology must study non-European musics. But
          it is interested essentially in these.")

Hood, Mantle
    1957 Training and research methods in ethnomusicology. Ethnomusicology News-
          letter No. 11:2-8.
          p. 2: "[Ethno]musicology is a field of knowledge, having as its object the
          investigation of the art of music as a physical, psychological, aesthetic, and
          cultural phenomenon. The [ethno]musicologist is a research scholar, and he
          aims primarily at knowledge about music."

Schneider, Marius
    1957 Primitive music. In Egon Wellesz (Ed). Ancient and Oriental music. London:
          Oxford University Press, pp. 1-82.
          p. 1: "This new discipline was called 'comparative musicology', its primary
          aim being the comparative study of all the characteristics, normal or other-
          wise, of non-European art."

Kunst, Jaap
    1959 Ethnomusicology. The Hague: Martinus Nijhoff, Third Edition.
          p. 1: "The study-object of ethnomusicology, or, as it originally was called:
          comparative musicology, is the *traditional* music and musical instruments of

all cultural strata of mankind, from the so-called primitive peoples to the civilized nations. Our science, therefore, investigates all tribal and folk music and every kind of non-Western art music. Besides, it studies as well the sociological aspects of music, as the phenomena of musical acculturation, i.e., the hybridizing influence of alien musical elements. Western art- and popular (entertainment-) music does not belong to its field."

Merriam, Alan P.
1960   Ethnomusicology: discussion and definition of the field. ETHNOMUSICOL-OGY 4:107-14.
p. 109: "... the study of music in culture."

Nettl, Bruno
1961   Reference materials in ethnomusicology. Detroit: Information Service, Inc., Detroit Studies in Music Bibliography Number 1.
p. 2: "Ethnomusicology ... [is] ... the study of non-Western music and, to an extent, ... folk music. ..."

Seeger, Charles
1961   Semantic, logical and political considerations bearing upon research in ethno-musicology. ETHNOMUSICOLOGY 5:77-80.
p. 79: "The study of non-European musics was launched in 1900 ... and was eventually given the name 'comparative musicology.'"

Greenway, John
1962   Primitive music. Boulder: University of Colorado.
p. 1: "... the systematic study of music as it is manifested among the more primitive and unfamiliar peoples of the world...."

List, George
1962   Ethnomusicology in higher education. Music Journal 20:20 et seq.
p. 24: "Ethnomusicology is to a great extent concerned with music trans-mitted by unwritten tradition."

Nketia, J. H. Kwabena
1962   The problem of meaning in African music. ETHNOMUSICOLOGY 6:1-7.
p. 1: "The study of music as a universal aspect of human behavior is becoming increasingly recognized as the focus of Ethnomusicology."

Hood, Mantle
1963   Music, the unknown. In Frank Ll. Harrison, Mantle Hood, and Claude V. Palisca. Musicology. Englewood Cliffs: Prentice-Hall, pp. 215-326.
p. 217: "The discipline is directed toward an understanding of music studied in terms of itself and also toward the comprehension of music within the context of its society. Ethnomusicology is concerned with the music of all non-European peoples ... and includes within its purview the tribal, folk, and popular music of the Western world, as well as hybridizations of these forms. It frequently crosses into the field of European art music, although such material is only an indirect object of concern. In other words, ethnomusi-cology embraces all kinds of music not included by studies in historical musicology, i.e., the study of cultivated music in the western European tradition."

List, George
1963   Ethnomusicology and the phonograph. In Kurt Reinhard and George List. The demonstration collection of E. M. von Hornbostel and the Berlin Phono-gramm-Archiv. New York: Ethnic Folkways Library, album notes for FE 4175, pp. 2-5.
p. 2: by implication: "[Ethnomusicology is] the study of aurally transmitted music. ..."

Nettl, Bruno
1964   Theory and method in ethnomusicology. Glencoe: Free Press.

p. 1: "...ethnomusicologists in the past have been students of the music outside Western civilization and, to a smaller extent, of European folk music." p. 11: "We can summarize the consensus in stating that ethnomusicology is, in fact as well as theory, the field which pursues knowledge of the world's music, with emphasis on that music outside the researcher's own culture, from a descriptive and comparative viewpoint."

Nettl, Bruno
   1965   Folk and traditional music of the western continents. Englewood Cliffs: Prentice-Hall.
          p. 26: "The field that provides research in ... [folk and non-Western music] ... is now known as ethnomusicology. Before about 1950 it was commonly called comparative musicology, and it is a sort of borderline area between musicology (the study of all aspects of music in a scholarly fashion) and anthropology (the study of man, his culture, and especially the cultures outside the investigator's own background)."

Kolinski, Mieczyslaw
   1967   Recent trends in ethnomusicology. ETHNOMUSICOLOGY 11:1-24.
          p. 5: "One of the most ambitious objectives of musicological research is the comparative analysis of the known musical styles of the world's peoples designed to establish their distinguishing features and, ultimately, to search for universals providing a common basis for the immense variety of musical creations. The most appropriate term for this field of study appears to be *comparative musicology.*"

Gillis, Frank
   1969   Personal communication.
          "[Ethnomusicology is] the study of those world musics which are aurally tramsmitted."

Hood, Mantle
   1969   Ethnomusicology. *In* Willi Apel (Ed). Harvard dictionary of music. Cambridge: Harvard University Press, Second Edition, pp. 298-300.
          p. 298: "Ethnomusicology is an approach to the study of *any* music, not only in terms of itself but also in relation to its cultural context."

Wachsmann, K. P.
   1969   Music. Journal of the Folklore Institute 6:164-91.
          p. 165: "....ethnomusicology is concerned with the music of other peoples.... The prefix 'ethno' draws attention to the fact that this musicology operates essentially across cultural boundaries of one sort or another, and that, generally, the observer does not share directly the musical tradition that he studies.... Thus it cannot surprise us that in the early stages the emphasis was on comparison, and the field was known as comparative musicology until, in the 1960's, it was renamed."

List, George
   1969   Discussion of K. P. Wachsmann's paper. Journal of the Folklore Institute 6:192-99.
          p. 195: "A third definition (and one to which I subscribe) defines ethnomusicology in the broadest sense as the study of traditional music. What does the term 'traditional music' mean? It refers to music which has two specific characteristics: it is transmitted and diffused by memory rather than through the use of writing, and it is music which is always in flux, in which a second performance of the same item differs from the first."

Seeger, Charles
   1970   Toward a unitary field theory for musicology. Selected Reports 1(3):172-210.
          In reading the following, one should recall that Seeger holds "ethnomusicology" to be the proper term for what is now called "musicology."
          p. 179: "....musicology is (1) *a speech study,* systematic as well as

historical, critical as well as scientific or scientistic; whose field is (2) *the total music* of man, both in itself and in its relationships to what is not itself; whose cultivation is (3) *by individual students* who can view its field as musicians as well as in the terms devised by nonmusical specialists of whose fields some aspects of music are data; whose aim is to contribute to *the understanding of man*, in terms both (4) of human *culture* and (5) of his relationships with the *physical universe.*"

List, George
    1971   Inter-American program in ethnomusicology. Bloomington: Indiana University Publications.
            n.p.: "Ethnomusicology is conceived as an interdisciplinary study in which approaches derived from many disciplines can be usefully applied."

Chenoweth, Vida
    1972   Melodic perception and analysis. Ukarumpa, Papua New Guinea: Summer Institute of Linguistics.
            p. 9: "Ethnomusicology is the study of the musical practices of a particular people."
            Repeated in Second Edition, 1974.

Chase, Gilbert
    1972   American musicology and the social sciences. *In* Barry S. Brook, Edward O. D. Downes, and Sherman Van Solkema (Eds). Perspectives in Musicology. New York: W. W. Norton, pp. 202-26.
            p. 220: "I favor the *idea* of an 'ethnomusicology' . . . but I do not favor the terminology. . . . What we need is a term of larger scope. . . . For this I propose the term 'cultural musicology' [the task of which is] 'to study the similarities and differences in musical behavior among human groups, to depict the character of the various musical cultures of the world and the processes of stability, change, and development that are characteristic to them.'"

Blacking, John
    1973   How musical is man? Seattle: University of Washington Press.
            p. 3: "Ethnomusicology is a comparatively new word which is widely used to refer to the study of the different musical systems of the world."

Merriam, Alan P.
    ca 1973   Unpublished thoughts.
            "Ethnomusicology is the study of music as culture."

Blacking, John
    1974   In memoriam António Jorge Dias. Lisboa, Vol. III, pp. 71-93.
            p. 74: "The discipline is concerned chiefly with 'ethnic' or 'folk' music and thus tends to be an area study. The methods used are generally anthropological and sociological, or musicological: thus scholars are concerned with either the rules of a particular society or culture, of which music-making is a feature, or the rules of a particular society's musical system."

Nettl, Bruno
    1974   Personal communication.
            "Ethnomusicology is the comparative study of musical cultures, particularly as total systems including sound and behavior with the use of field research."

Nettl, Bruno
    1975   The state of research in ethnomusicology, and recent developments. Current Musicology No. 20:67-78.
            p. 69: "[Ethnomusicology is] the study of all music from the point of view of its oral tradition; . . ."

Helser, Elizabeth
    1976   Personal communication.
            "Ethnomusicology is the hermeneutic science of human musical behavior."

PROBLEME, METHODEN UND ZIELE DER ETHNOMUSIKOLOGIE

von
ARTUR SIMON (Berlin)

1. Wissenschaftsgeschichtliche Aspekte

1.1. „Vergleichende Musikwissenschaft" und „Musikethnologie"

Seit den Anfängen einer neuzeitlichen Musikwissenschaft hat ein – wenn auch anfangs nur kleiner – Teil von Musikwissenschaftlern die Betrachtungsweise nicht nur auf die Produkte der europäischen Musik und deren Produzenten beschränkt, sondern die Musik aller Menschen, ja den *musikalischen Menschen* per se und die musikalischen Kulturen der ganzen Menschheit zum Ziel wissenschaftlicher Erforschung erklärt. Es steht heute außer Frage, daß dieses ohne Vorurteile und Eurozentrik geschehen muß, will man dem Anspruch der Wissenschaftlichkeit gerecht werden.

Aus verschiedenen Gründen, die vor allem im methodischen Bereich, aber auch dem der praktischen Durchführbarkeit lagen, hatte sich schon bald eine Teildisziplin der Musikwissenschaft etabliert, die sich als „Vergleichende Musikwissenschaft" bezeichnete und die es sich nach Guido Adler zur Aufgabe gemacht hat,

> die Tonproducte, insbesondere die Volksgesänge verschiedener Völker, Länder und Territorien behufs ethnographischer Zwecke zu vergleichen und nach der Verschiedenheit ihrer Beschaffenheit zu gruppieren und zu sondern. (Adler 1885: 14)

Obwohl dieser Terminus sich bis heute hier und da erhalten hat, ist er nach dem zweiten Weltkrieg von den meisten Fachvertretern zugunsten des Begriffs *Ethnomusikologie* (engl.: *ethnomusicology*, franz.: *ethnomusicologie*, deutsch: *Musikethnologie*) aufgegeben worden, ohne zunächst auch eine inhaltliche Wandlung mitzuvollziehen. In dieser Begriffsbildung ist die Vereinigung von *Ethnologie* und *Musikologie* vollzogen, die sich schon vorher angekündigt hatte. Ohne auf ihre unterschiedlichen Inhalte und Aspekte eingehen zu wollen, seien einige Arbeiten genannt, die in ihrem Titel eine gewisse Adhäsion beider Bereiche erkennen lassen, wie z. B. Simmel: Psychologische und ethnologische Studien über Musik (1882), Wallaschek: Musikalische Ergebnisse des Studiums der Ethnologie (1895), Myers: The ethnological study of music (1907), Tiersot: Notes d'ethnographie musicale (1909), Hornbostel/Stumpf: Über die Bedeutung ethnologischer Untersuchungen für die Psychologie und Ästhetik der Tonkunst (1911), Lenoir: La musique comme institution sociale (1933), Schneider: Ethnologische Musikforschung (1937) und Howes: Anthropology and Music (1945) (vgl. auch Howes 1948). Bereits 1949 verwendet Fritz Bose den Begriff *Musikethnologie* – ohne ihn besonders hervorzuheben – mit einer Selbstverständlichkeit, die darauf hindeutet, daß diese Bezeichnung schon vorher bekannt gewesen sein muß:

> Bisher war die deutsche Vergleichende Musikwissenschaft ... vorwiegend Musikethnologie, eine musikalische Völkerkunde, die kulturhistorisch orientiert war. (Bose 1949: 255)

8

Kurz darauf erscheint, programmatisch und exponiert, der neue Begriff *ethno-musicology* in Jaap Kunsts „Musicologica", um den der *Vergleichenden Musikwissen-schaft* abzulösen:

> The name of our science [comparative musicology] is, in fact, not quite characte-ristic; it does not "compare" any more than any other science. A better name, therefore, is that appearing on the title page of this book: ethno-musicology. (Kunst 1950: 7)

In der englisch-sprachigen wissenschaftlichen Welt hatte sich der neue Terminus bis zum Ende der 50er Jahre durchgesetzt, was sich auch im Namen der neuen ameri-kanischen „Society for Ethnomusicology" manifestierte. (Merriam 1977: 194 f.). Un-ter dem Namen *Musikethnologie* wurde die neue Bezeichnung in der deutsch-spra-chigen Wissenschaft eingeführt, ohne jedoch den bereits institutionalisierten Terminus der *Vergleichenden Musikwissenschaft* ganz zu verdrängen. Seitdem herrscht hier eine gewisse Unsicherheit des Gebrauchs, weil man annahm, eine Bezeichnung der Disziplin beinhalte gleichzeitig deren Definition und darüber hinaus deren Zielsetzung, ein Gesichtspunkt, der durch die zusätzliche Einführung des Namens *Ethnomusikologie* eine weitere Nuance erhielt. Es hat nun aber –, wie wir noch im einzelnen sehen werden –, zumindest in Deutschland und anfänglich auch in den USA de facto keinen substantiellen Unterschied – weder in der Definition noch in der Zielsetzung – zwi-schen der *Vergleichenden Musikwissenschaft* und der *Musikethnologie* gegeben, so daß beide im Grunde genommen die gleiche Teildisziplin der Musikwissenschaft bezeich-neten. Auch die Musikethnologie ist immer eine Musikwissenschaft geblieben, so daß, zunächst gesehen, für die in den letzten Jahren ebenso verwendete artifiziellere Na-mensvariante *Ethnomusikologie* eigentlich keine Notwendigkeit besteht. Wir werden jedoch noch an anderer Stelle erörtern, daß Gründe, die sich aus einer neuen inhalt-lichen Definition heraus ergeben, für die Übernahme dieses Begriffes sprechen.

Die Reflexion über ein wissenschaftliches Fachgebiet, die sich aus den verschiedenen Fachbezeichnungen und deren Pro- und Contra-Diskussion herauslesen läßt, ist an sich kein wissenschaftliches Dilemma. Eine Wissenschaft, die ihren Standort und ihre In-halte nicht ständig überdenkt und modifiziert, gerät in ein Stadium der Verkrustung, in dem neue Impulse und Ideen nicht mehr Entfaltung finden können. Die Musik-ethnologie hat nach dem zweiten Weltkrieg gewaltige Fortschritte erzielt, die sie gerade ihrer Fähigkeit verdankt, transdisziplinär zu arbeiten und neue Methoden von anderen Disziplinen zu übernehmen, um sich so aus der kulturhistorischen und evo-lutionistischen Zwangsjacke zu befreien und der historischen die anthropologische Dimension entgegenzusetzen.

1.2. Vom Evolutionismus zum Kulturalismus
      Tendenzen der ethnomusikologischen Forschung

Es ist hier nicht beabsichtigt, die Geschichte der Musikethnologie respektive der Vergleichenden Musikwissenschaft darzustellen, zumal das schon wiederholt geschehen ist (z. B. bei Bose 1953; Nettl 1956; Kunst 1959; Reinhard 1968; McLeod 1974; Graf 1974). Das soll nicht heißen, daß ein erneuter wissenschaftlicher Abriß heute nicht erforderlich wäre, denn jede historische Darstellung spiegelt auch den augen-

9

blicklichen Erkenntnisstand und die vom Zeitgeist bedingte Sicht ihres Verfassers wider. Da es hier um eine Standortbestimmung der Ethnomusikologie geht, mag es genügen, nur die wichtigsten Tendenzen vergangener Zielsetzung zu umreißen, damit die im nächsten Abschnitt dargestellten Definitionen des Forschungsbereichs verständlicher werden.

Die Entwicklung der vergangenen 100 Jahre läßt sich vielleicht am anschaulichsten in den folgenden Begriffspaaren darstellen, wie:

vom Evolutionismus zum Kulturalismus,
von der historischen zur kulturanthropologischen Forschung,
vom Diachronen zum Synchronen,
von den „Vorformen" der europäischen Musik zu den Kulturformen der gesamten Menschheit,
von der musikalischen Urgeschichtsforschung zur musikalischen Gegenwartsforschung,
von den „Anfängen" der Musik zu den biologischen Universalien,
vom Primitivismus zum relativierten Kreativismus,
vom Eurozentrismus zum Ethno-Konzeptionalismus,
vom Formalismus zur sozio-kulturellen Kontextforschung,
von der Auffassung vom Statischen zu der vom Dynamischen,
von der Analyse des Musikprodukts zu der des Musikprozesses,
von der musikalischen Strukturanalyse des Klangdokuments zur Strukturanalyse der musikalischen Verhaltensweisen,
von der Zufallsdokumentation zur gezielten Feldforschung,
von der mono- zur bi-kulturalen Musikalität,
vom naiven Vergleich zur objektivierten Differenzierung,
von der Spekulation zur Empirik,
von den globalen Ideen zur Detailforschung.

Skalen, Tonsysteme, Stimmungen und die Analyse von Melodien, die man von Walzenaufnahmen transkribiert hatte, standen in der ersten Phase im Mittelpunkt des wissenschaftlichen Interesses. Einige Arbeitstechniken (Abraham/Hornbostel 1909) waren am Ende dieser ersten Phase zu einer erstaunlichen Perfektion verfeinert, wie zum Beispiel in den Transkriptionen Béla Bartóks, die nach dem zweiten Weltkrieg durch physikalische Meßtechniken noch übertroffen werden sollten (Pegelschreiber, Sonagraph, Melograph, Frequenzanalysator etc.). Man betrachtete die Musik formalistisch als Material, mit dem man arbeitete, und versuchte dieses in entwicklungsgeschichtlicher Denkweise als „Vorformen" der europäischen Musikwerke einzuordnen. In dieser Art der Material- oder Werkbetrachtung unterschieden sich die vergleichenden Musikwissenschaftler nicht von den Musikhistorikern, mit dem einen Unterschied, daß erstere sich nach allgemeiner zeitgeistiger Auffassung mit den „niederen" und letztere mit den „höheren" Formen der Musik beschäftigten. Damit man im exklusiven Kreise der hehren Kunstwissenschaftler überhaupt geduldet wurde, suchte man nach einer Legitimation des eigenen Tuns und fand sie im evolutionistischen Gedankengut, das im Terminus der *primitiven Musik* seinen deutlichen Ausdruck fand. Curt Sachs, das muß heute bei aller Würdigung seiner wissenschaftlichen Leistung (v. a. „Reallexikon der Musikinstrumente", Berlin 1913) gesagt werden, hat mit seinen theoretischen Äußerungen zur Vergleichenden Musikwissenschaft der Musik-

10

ethnologie einen denkbar schlechten Dienst erwiesen, weil man sich zum Teil noch heute auf seine unhaltbaren Denkansätze beruft. Er betrachtete die Erforschung der *primitiven* und *orientalischen* Musik als einen Zweig der Musikgeschichte (Sachs 1943: 29). Auf die von ihm selbst erhobene Frage nach der Legitimation der Disziplin antwortete er noch 1959 folgendermaßen:

> Denn was uns die Wissenschaft von der Musik fremder Kulturen zeichnet, ist das Schicksal, das *uns* geführt hat und führen wird, und den Weg, den *wir* gegangen sind. Die tausendfältigen Äußerungen menschlichen Lebens, die wie ein buntfarbiger Teppich über alle Erdteile gebreitet sind, sie bilden nur Rückstände einer Entwicklung, die unsere eigenen Vorfahren durchgemacht haben. (Sachs 1959: 5)

Es sei hier die an gleicher Stelle publizierte *historische Definition* wiedergegeben, deren prominentester Vertreter Sachs ja war:

> Die Wissenschaft von der Musik fremder Kulturen handelt von den musikalischen Äußerungen der nichteuropäischen Völker gleichviel welcher Kulturstufe. Europäischen Boden betritt sie nur an denjenigen Stellen, wo sich, weitab von den eigentlichen abendländischen Formen des Musiklebens, Reste altertümlicher Musikübung erhalten haben, die den nichteuropäischen gleichen. Ihr alter Name „Vergleichende Musikwissenschaft" führt irre und ist allgemein aufgegeben worden. Sie „vergleicht" nicht weniger und nicht mehr als jede andre Wissenschaft: sie beginnt geschichtlich zu scheiden und die Hauptzüge einer Entwicklung bloßzulegen, die von rohen Anfängen bis zu der Ebene steigt, auf der sich das Hochgebirge der modernen europäischen Tonkunst aufbaut. (Sachs 1959: 5)

Wesentlich differenzierter äußert sich demgegenüber Schünemann (1919), dem es mehr um Analogien ähnlicher musikalischer Phänomene aus verschiedenen Kulturen geht, womit er sich auf dem gleichen Boden vergleichender Forschung befindet, wie später Wiora (1975):

> Alle diese Analogien müssen besonders behandelt werden, da die Voraussetzungen gleicher Erscheinungen oft der verschiedensten Natur sein werden. Überhaupt führt von diesen Beziehungen und Übereinstimmungen der Weg weiter zu allgemeinen und speziellen psychologischen und ethnologischen Grundfragen. Aber die hier gegebenen Grundlinien der Vergleichung werden wenigstens die Tragweite und Fruchtbarkeit dieser Studien gezeigt haben. Sie wollen die Ergebnisse der Vergleichenden Musikwissenschaft auch der Musikgeschichte dienstbar machen, sie wollen Beobachtungen und Erfahrungen aus dem Studium außereuropäischer Musikübung zur Lösung alter Probleme der Musikgeschichte ausnutzen und damit ein neues Feld für die Beurteilung und Erklärung früher Kunstformen und Ausdrucksmittel erschließen. Diese Vergleichung der Musik außereuropäischer und einfach gebliebener Völker mit der abendländischen Kunst wird alten Fragen neue Lösungen geben. Sie führt weiter zu allgemein geltenden Naturgesetzen und durchdringt eine nur in Handschriften und Traktaten stehende Musik mit einer ähnlich geformten und gleich wirkenden lebendigen Kunst. (Schünemann 1919: 194)

Neben den Vorformen und Analogien zur europäischen Musik war man auch an der Frage nach dem Ursprung der musikalischen Äußerungen interessiert, allerdings kam diese Problemstellung weniger aus dem Bereich der historischen, sondern aus dem

11

255

der psychologischen Forschung. Stumpfs „Anfänge der Musik" (1911) ist das prominenteste Werk dieser Richtung.

Die kulturhistorische Ausrichtung Sachsscher Prägung läßt es nur als allzu verständlich erscheinen, daß die vergleichenden Musikwissenschaftler mit Begeisterung eine ethnologische Richtung übernahmen, die als *Kulturkreislehre* Epoche machen sollte. (Vgl. A. Schneider 1976). Sie hat bis in die 50er Jahre hinein die europäische Musikethnologie wesentlich bestimmt.

Globale Aussagen und Vergleiche wurden auf einer äußerst schwachen Quellenbasis getroffen, die sich aus mehr oder weniger zufällig zustande gekommenen Klangdokumenten zusammensetzte, die nur einen höchst unvollkommenen Eindruck der jeweiligen Musikkultur vermitteln konnten. Wir wissen heute, wie differenziert die musikalischen Erscheinungen bereits innerhalb einer einzigen Kultur oder ethnischen Gruppe sein können. Ich möchte daher diese Epoche als *Phase des naiven Vergleichens* bezeichnen und Arbeiten wie „Asiatische Parallelen zur Berbermusik" (Hornbostel/ Lachmann 1933) (mit den daraus folgenden Arbeiten) und „Die musikalischen Beziehungen zwischen Urkulturen, Altpflanzern und Hirtenvölkern" (Schneider 1939) als ihre typischen Ergebnisse ansehen. Diese Arbeiten standen im Zeichen des extremen Universalismus, der im absurden Gegensatz zur Quellenbasis stand, die in den meisten Fällen keiner Quellenkritik unterzogen worden war. Außerdem war der sozio-kulturelle Kontext der Musik ausgeklammert, obwohl Hornbostel diesen bereits 1905 als betrachtenswert angedeutet hatte:

> Eine vergleichende Betrachtung verdienen ferner nicht nur die speziellen Gebrauchszwecke einzelner Musikinstrumente, sondern die Gelegenheiten, bei denen musiziert wird. (Hornbostel 1905)

Auch der Engländer Charles S. Myers nennt programmatisch einige Punkte, die erst viel später Bedeutung erlangen sollten:

> Music is a recognized means of intercommunication, and must hence be regarded as a language. (Myers 1907: 236)
> The position of music within a community is no doubt largely responsible for the number of coexisting styles of music, and for the degree of conservatism obtaining. (Myers 1907: 240)

Bereits gegen Ende der dreißiger Jahre zeichnet sich eine bevorstehende Abkehr von der ersten Phase des Sammelns und Vergleichens ab, was Schneider (1938) folgendermaßen umreißt:

> Die Zeit der ersten Überraschungen und der naiven Sammelfreude ist vorbei. Es hat den Anschein, als ob die wesentlichen musikalischen Formen heute bekannt seien. Es geht jetzt darum, tiefer in die Ideologie des Phänomens einzudringen, die Zusammenhänge zwischen Musik und Sprache zu erforschen, Melodiebildung, Vortragsweise und Stimmansatz zu relativieren, nicht nur irgendwelche Lieder eines Stammes aufzunehmen, sondern möglichst das gesamte Repertoire in seinen richtigen Proportionen und inneren Zusammenhängen zu erfassen und seine jeweiligen Beziehungen zu der wirtschaftlichen, sozialen und geistigen Kultur aufzudecken. Wir müssen versuchen, die psychologischen Grundlagen zu erfassen (wozu

12

insbesondere die Erfassung des musikalischen Wortschatzes neben der direkten Befragung der Sänger sehr dienlich ist), und insbesondere das Bewegungsphänomen und den Stimmklang, den Zusammenhang zwischen körperlichen und musikalischen Bewegungsformen mit der melodischen und dichterischen Gestaltgebung näher ins Auge zu fassen. (Schneider 1938: 42)

Nach dem zweiten Weltkrieg erfuhr die musikethnologische Forschung einen gewaltigen Aufschwung. Die Fortschritte in der Aufnahmetechnik ermöglichten eine umfassendere Dokumentation und intensivere Feldforschung. So wuchs zum Beispiel der Bestand an Tonbandaufnahmen des Berliner Phonogramm-Archivs (heute Musikethnologische Abteilung des Museums für Völkerkunde) von 1961 ca. 7000 Aufnahmen bis 1973 um gut 340 % (1973: ca. 24 000). Man begann die verschiedenen Musikkulturen der Welt zu studieren, mehr in ihrer gegenwärtigen kulturalen Dimension und weniger in ihrer historischen. Es ist dies die Zeit, in der der ethnologische Aspekt der Forschung den vergleichend-historischen (vgl. Lach 1924: 7) ablöste, was auch in der Namensänderung der Disziplin zum Ausdruck kam. Der Erkenntnisstand, den die musikethnologische Detailforschung in den vergangenen dreißig Jahren erreicht hat, ist gewaltig, gemessen an der relativ kleinen Zahl von Spezialisten (und Idealisten), die daran beteiligt waren.

Man begann, sich von der Vorstellung zu lösen, die Musik nur als reines Klangmaterial anzusehen, das es zu analysieren galt, und interessierte sich mehr und mehr auch für die Musikpraxis und Gestaltungsprozesse. Man wollte sich auch das Wesen der Musik als Teil ihrer Gesamtkultur erschließen.

Einen möglichen Weg hierzu sah man in der sogenannten *bi-musicality* (Hood 1960) oder *bi-kulturalen Musikalität*. Noch unter Jaap Kunst begannen in Amsterdam Studenten, javanisches Gamelanspiel zu erlernen. Mantle Hood war einer der eifrigsten Verfechter dieses Weges in den USA. An einer Reihe amerikanischer Universitäten wird heute praktischer Unterricht in der traditionellen Musik aus Japan, China, Korea, Indonesien, Indien, Iran sowie arabischen, afrikanischen und anderen Ländern erteilt – ein Weg zur bi-kulturalen Musikalität, den jene Länder in umgekehrter Richtung durch Aufnahme der europäischen Musik auch gegangen sind.

Eine andere Methode, welche die Musik von „innen heraus" zu erschließen versucht, indem der Wissenschaftler sich als teilnehmender Beobachter in die jeweilige Musikpraxis innerhalb des authentischen kulturellen Umfelds integriert, hat bereits zu beachtlichen Ergebnissen geführt (z. B. Kubik 1970), die man als moderne musikalische Strukturanalysen bezeichnen kann.

Mit zunehmender Feldforschungstätigkeit fand die Frage nach dem sozio-kulturellen Kontext stärkere Beachtung. Die Frage, *warum* die Musik so beschaffen ist – und nicht allein *wie* – führte zwangsläufig zur ethnologisch und kulturanthropologisch orientierten Untersuchung der Musik, des Musiklebens, der Musikgestaltung als Teil der Kultur (Merriam 1960).

Die wesentlichen Impulse hierzu empfing die Musikethnologie von der amerikanischen ethnologischen Schule um Franz Boas (1858–1942). Vor allem von der kultur-relativistischen respektive kultur-pluralistischen Richtung von Melville J. Herskovits führt ein direkter Weg zu Richard Waterman und Alan P. Merriam:

13

257

The principle of cultural relativism, briefly stated, is a follows: Judgements are based on experience, and experience is interpreted by each individual in terms of his own enculturation. (Herskovits 1955: 15)

... important as it is to discern and study the parallelisms in human civilizations, it is no less important to discern and study the different ways man has devised to fulfill his needs. (Herskovits 1955: 33).

Danach ist Musik eine hochgradig schematisierte menschliche Verhaltensweise, die kulturspezifisch bedingt und geprägt ist und ein großes Beharrungsvermögen besitzt. In diesem Sinne spricht Herskovits zum Beispiel von „patterns of Negro music" (Herskovits 1941). Musikstilistische und typologische Unterschiede innerhalb einer Kultur ergeben sich aus der speziellen Kontextabhängigkeit. Die übergeordneten kultur- und untergeordneten kontextspezifischen musikalischen Verhaltensweisen müssen hierbei unterschieden werden, was besonders bei fremdkulturellen Überlagerungsprozessen wichtig ist (vgl. McLeod 1974: 110).

Die zentrale Figur, die auf die Bedeutung kulturanthropologischer Betrachtungsweisen und Methoden für die Ethnomusikologie überzeugend hingewiesen hat, ist zweifellos Alan P. Merriam (v. a. 1960, 1963, 1964, 1969, 1975, 1977). Sein Buch: The Anthropology of Music (1964) gehört heute zu den Standardwerken der Ethnomusikologie. Merriam selbst bringt seine – eigentlich selbstverständliche, bis dahin allerdings nur unzureichend beachtete und dargestellte – Konzeption auf folgenden Nenner:

It involves study on three analytical levels –
conceptualization about music,
behavior in relation to music,
and music sound itself. (Merriam 1964: 32)

Ethnomusicology, then, makes its unique contribution in welding together aspects of the social sciences and aspects of the humanities in such a way that each complements the other and leads to a fuller understanding of both. Neither should be considered as an end in itself; the two must be joined into a wider understanding.

All this is implicit in the definition of ethnomusicology as the *study of music in culture*. There is no denial of the basic aim, which is to understand music; but neither is there an acceptance of a point of view which has long taken ascendancy in ethnomusicology, that the ultimate aim of our discipline is the understanding of music sound alone.

As in any other field of study, the work of the ethnomusicologist is divided roughly into three stages ... The first of these lies in the collection of data, ... Second, ..., the ethnomusicologist normally subjects them to two kinds of analysis. The first is the collation of ethnographic and ethnologic materials into a coherent body of knowledge about music practice, behavior, and concepts in the society being studied, as these are relevant to the hypotheses and design of the research problem. The second is the technical laboratory analysis of the music sound materials collected, and this requires special techniques and sometimes special equipment for the transcription and structural analysis of music. Third, the data analyzed and the results obtained are applied to relevant problems ... (Merriam 1964: 7 f.)

14

Merriams Konzept geht bereits weit über das bloße Beschreiben sozialer Bezüge und Brauchtumsbindungen, wie es bis derzeit üblich war, hinaus und begreift Musik als sozialpsychologischen musikalischen Prozeß, eingebettet in die sozio-kulturellen Werte und Normen: beim Erlernen, bei der Gestaltung, der Perzeption, der Transmission und der Innovation. Neu ist auch die Betonung des Funktionalen („uses and functions") und des individuell Kreativen („The process of composition"). Es ist der lange Erkenntnisweg von der Mystifizierung des Magischen (z. B. bei Marius Schneider), vom Glauben an die stampfende und stammelnde Urhorde („Musik der Primitiven") zum Menschen als *Creator Musicus*, von einer „ethnomusicologica speculativa" zu einer Anthropologie der Musik.

2. Forschungsbereich und Abgrenzung in der Retrospektive

Es hat bisher eine Vielzahl von Definitionen gegeben – Merriam (1977) hat unlängst über 40 von ihnen zusammengetragen –, die alle irgendwie den geistigen Prozeß reflektieren, den das Fach seit den Anfängen bis heute erlebt hat, die sich auf der anderen Seite jedoch durch eine überraschende Einmütigkeit ihrer Verfasser auszeichnen. Sie zeigen jedenfalls, daß über den Forschungsbereich eine große Übereinstimmung besteht, auch wenn dieser sich im Laufe der Jahrzehnte von der Untersuchung der bloßen „Tonprodukte" (wie bei Adler) – eine Sicht, die ganz vom europäischen Musikleben des 19. Jahrhunderts geprägt war – zu einem Studium der Musik als spezifische Verhaltensweise des Menschen im sozio-kulturellen Kontext erweitert hat.

Auf die musikalischen Folklore-Definitionen wird hier nicht näher eingegangen, weil sie in der Mehrzahl nur einen Teilaspekt der Ethnomusikologie behandeln oder sich mit den hier aufgeführten Aussagen ohnehin überschneiden. Ihre Bedeutung als Beitrag für die heutige Theoriediskussion bleibt damit unbestritten. In jüngster Zeit sind zwei umfassende Darstellungen zur Musikfolklore veröffentlicht worden, die von Elbourne (1975) und Baumann (1976), auf die hier verwiesen wird.

2.1. Die regionale Abgrenzung

Die Mehrzahl der Definitionen grenzt den Forschungsbereich regional auf die außereuropäische Musik ein: z. B. Adler (1885), Lachmann (1929, 1935), Sachs (1943 und 1959), Herzog (1946), Bose (1949, 1953), Schneider (1957). Sachs (1943) unterteilt – gefolgt von Herzog (1946) – die außereuropäische Musik in primitive und orientalische Musik und betrachtet deren Erforschung als einen Zweig der Musikgeschichte. Sachs (1959) führte auch den Begriff der Fremdkulturen ein, der sich jedoch nicht durchsetzen konnte. Auch der Begriff der *exotischen Musik* taucht vereinzelt auf: z. B. bei Gilman (1909), Lach (1924), Roberts (1937) und Apel (1946). Viele Forscher beziehen auch die europäische Volksmusik – oft als *folk music* bezeichnet – mit ein: z. B. Bingham (1914), Haydon (1941), Bukofzer (1956), Schaeffner (1956), Rhodes (1956), Nettl (1956, 1961, 1964, 1965, 1975) und Kunst (1959). Auch das Gegensatzpaar *non-Western* und *Western music*, z. B. seit Bukofzer (1956), wird verwendet. Als Beispiel für die regionale Definition mag hier die von Jaap Kunst (1959) stehen:

15

The study-object of ethnomusicology, or, as it originally was called: comparative musicology, is the *traditional* music and musical instruments of all cultural strata of mankind, from the so-called primitive peoples to the civilized nations. Our science, therefore, investigates all tribal and folk music and every kind of non-Western art music. Besides, it studies as well the sociological aspect of music, as the phenomena of musical acculturation, i. e. the hybridizing influence of alien musical elements. Western Art – and popular (entertainment) – music do not belong to its field. (Kunst 1959: 1)

In den neuesten Definitionen – wie noch aufgezeigt wird – hat die regionale Abgrenzung eine andere Dimension erhalten, in der die Gegensatzpaare Europa – Außereuropa (Western – non-Western) keine theoretische, sondern allenfalls eine wissenschafts-praktische Relevanz behalten haben.

2.2. Die Primitivismus-Definition

Der Begriff der *primitiven Musik* wurde seit den Anfängen der Vergleichenden Musikwissenschaft verwendet, ohne daß jemals begründet wurde, warum (z. B. Wallaschek [1893], Heinitz [1931], Herzog [1932], Roberts [1933], Reinhard [1951], Nettl [1956], Schneider [1957]). Später sprach man von der „sogenannten primitiven Musik" („so-called primitive" s. o. bei Kunst). Doch auch ohne Beifügung hat sich der Begriff bis in die jüngste Zeit hartnäckig gehalten (z. B. bei Bose 1975; Schneider 1975), was auf einen Mangel an Reflektion über den heutigen semantischen Wert des Begriffs hindeutet; wissen wir doch aus zahlreichen musikethnologischen Analysen wie wenig primitiv die „sogenannte" primitive Musik bei richtiger Betrachtung eigentlich ist. Tatsächlich geht der Gebrauch des Begriffs nicht nur auf falsche evolutionistische und entwicklungspsychologische Vorstellungen zurück, sondern in erheblichem Maße auf die zu geringe Qualität und Quantität der zunächst vorhandenen Informationen, das heißt auf den zu kleinen Bekanntheitsgrad.

Wir bemerken früh bei den Menschen der höher entwickelten Zivilisationen eine Neigung zum Regreß ins Archaische, welcher unter Anknüpfung an die Nachrichten von Randvölkern dann leicht zur Konstruktion von *Naturzuständen, Natürlichkeitsideen* führt, und die in der abendländischen Geistesgeschichte als eine komplexe Einstellung unter dem Titel des *Primitivismus* beschrieben werden kann (Lovejoy und Boas 1935). Und wenn auch schon bei Herodot sich eine gegensätzliche Stilisierung der Einfachheit der Barbaren zur Kompliziertheit der hellenischen Kultur angedeutet findet, so liegt hierin bereits ein Vorklang jener kulturkritischen Haltung, die *Natur* und *Kultur* einander entgegensetzt und die Rückkehr von dieser zu jener propagiert. (Mühlmann 1968: 26)

In diesem Sinne und in Anlehnung an den ethnologischen Gebrauch sprach man nicht nur von der *Musik der Primitiven*, sondern auch von der *Musik der Naturvölker* (z. B. Bose 1949; Schneider 1958 und 1975; Oesch 1972) und bezeichnete damit die Musik von Stammesgesellschaften.

Eine primitivistische Komponente erhielt dieser Terminus vor allem durch die Bildung der Gegensatzpaare: *Natur-Kulturvölker* (respektive orientalische Kulturvölker), *Naturvölker* – (orientalische) *Hochkulturen* sowie *primitive* und *orientalische*

16

Musik. Von der „Musik der Natur- und orientalischen Kulturvölker" spricht Lach (1924). Bei Lachmann (1929) heißt es „Die Musik der außereuropäischen Natur- und Kulturvölker". Gilman (The science of exotic music, 1909), Sachs (1943), Herzog (1946) und Bukofzer (1956) unterscheiden *primitive and Oriental music*, wobei letzterer auch das Paar *non-Western* und *folk music* erwähnt. Man ist mit den Bezeichnungen unzufrieden und beginnt zu differenzieren:

> Here, under the imprint of comparative musicology, are bound together studies of the music of the Near East, the Far East, Indonesia, Africa, the North American Indians, and the European folk music. Of those ethnomusicologists whose interests are confined solely to primitive music I ask, "Can we refuse our inheritance?" Let us not be provincial in the pursuit of our discipline. Oriental art music, the folk music of the world, and primitive music, all await our serious study. (Rhodes 1956: 460 f.)

Reinhard (1968) unterscheidet *Naturvölker, Mittelkulturen, Volksmusik der Hochkulturen* und *Kunstmusik der Hochkulturen*. Nettl (1956) kennt *Oriental, folk and primitive music* und umschreibt diese, wahrscheinlich beeinflußt von der Definition der „peasant society" und „folk society" bei Redfield (1956; 1947), folgendermaßen:

> *Oriental:* high cultures of Asia, from China, Japan, and Indonesia to India, Persia, and the Arabic countries. It is not elementary but is cultivated by professional musicians and is in many ways, although not stylistically, comparable to Western European music. *Folk music,* on the other hand, is the music of social groups which are part of higher cultures but are not themselves musically literate. It is common knowledge that folk songs are often composed anonymously and passed from singer to singer by oral tradition. In this way folk music resembles *primitive;* the main difference is that the former is always found in a culture that also has cultivated music, which usually influences its style, while the later belongs to simple cultures that have no writing and are not directly associated with any high cultures. (Nettl 1956: 1)

Nettl definiert die *primitive Musik* für folgende Bereiche (Nettl 1956: 7 f.): 1. Religion, 2. Tanz, 3. Liebeswerbung, 4. gesungene Geschichten, Erzählungen, 5. Kriegsgesang und -tanz, 6. Unterhaltung und 7. Signalgebung.

> It is difficult to find any essential difference between the role of music in primitive societies and the role of music in high cultures. . . .
> . . . The chief distinction in role is quantitative: among primitive people, functional music is far more frequent in proportion to the total amount of music performed. (Nettl 1956: 10)

Diese Aussage steht in einem gewissen Widerspruch zur folgenden, in der dem „Primitiven" die Möglichkeit, Musik auch zu seiner Freude oder Unterhaltung zu machen, abgesprochen wird:

> [entertainment music] occurs only in areas where both culture and musical style are relatively complex. (Nettl 1956: 8)

Fast 20 Jahre später – und hier läßt sich beispielhaft die Entwicklung der Musikethnologie demonstrieren – will Nettl dieses nicht mehr gelten lassen:

17

A third issue is a recognition of the sophistication of all musical cultures of the world, and the difficulty which we have placed in our own way by distinguishing sharply among the folk, the so-called primitive or tribal, and the high cultures. To be sure, different degrees of development in various respects, technical, intellectual, artistic, can be recognized. But by now we must understand that even the world's simplest musical cultures are in themselves sophisticated and complex organisms, and that a certain kind of stratification, a recognition of music excellence, and a certain kind of specialization of musical activity exists in all of them. In other words, the concept of folk and primitive music is really no longer viable. (Nettl 1975: 14)

2.3. Die schriftlose Existenz, orale und aurale Transmission, Variabilität

Die sich auf fremdes und neues wissenschaftliches Terrain vorwagenden vergleichenden Musikwissenschaftler, die alle der europäischen Kultur entstammten und damit Musik nur als in Notenschrift fixierte musikalische Kompositionen kannten, wurden mit dem Dilemma konfrontiert, daß ihr Forschungsgegenstand nicht schriftlich niedergelegt war, sondern ein akustisches Ereignis mit einem zeitlichen Anfang und Ende, das festzuhalten erst mit Hilfe des Edison-Phonographen gelang. Die schriftlose Existenz und mündliche Überlieferung ist in der Tat ein so gravierender Unterschied zur speziellen Entwicklung der europäischen Musik der Kirche, Höfe und Bürgerhäuser, daß er sich in der Definition zur Vergleichenden Musikwissenschaft und Ethnomusikologie niederschlagen mußte (Haydon [1941], List [1962, 1963, 1969], Nettl [1975] u. a.). Als Beispiel sei hier George List zitiert, der am stärksten auf diesen Punkt hinwies:

> A third definition (and one to which I subscribe) defines ethnomusicology in the broadest sense as the study of traditional music. What does the term "traditional music" mean? It refers to music which has two specific characteristics: it is transmitted and diffused by memory rather than through the use of writing, and it is music which is always in flux, in which a second performance of the same item differs from the first. (List 1969: 195)

Wir stellen hier zunächst fest, daß auch die Variabilität des Musikereignisses von allergrößter Bedeutung für die ethnomusikologische Forschung ist, was nicht ausschließt, daß auch starre Vortragsformen (z. B. im Repertoire des japanischen Hoforchesters, bei magischem Ritualgesang u. a.) und Notationen vorkommen.

Auch Bruno Nettl mißt in seiner jüngsten Definition der Frage der mündlichen Überlieferung große Bedeutung bei, schränkt diese jedoch gegenüber anderen Äußerungen etwas ein:

> (Ethnomusicology) is the study of musics in oral tradition. It is true that such study requires different methods and techniques than does the study of written musical documents such as scores, but we have come to realize that the oral component in even those musics which are written is of enormous importance, and that musical notation systems as well as the writings of words in the "oral" cultures is a significant factor which must be taken into account, and thus that there is perhaps no sharp line dividing the oral and the written traditions. (Nettl 1975: 12)

18

Wir werden noch sehen, daß Nettls kritische Einwände zum Gegensatzpaar münd-
lich-schriftlich gerechtfertigt sind, und es zusätzlicher Kriterien zu einer Definition
des ethnomusikologischen Forschungsbereichs bedarf.

Von seiten der europäischen Musikgeschichte hat es den Einwand gegeben, es gäbe
in orientalischer Musik, z. B. in der chinesischen, auch Notationen, das heißt schriftlich
fixierte Musikstücke, und aus diesem Grunde gehörten diese Musikkulturen nicht in
den Bereich des Musikethnologen, sondern in den des Musikhistorikers. Das kann
zum einen – wir werden die Abgrenzung zur europäischen Musikgeschichte im Abschnitt 3.2 ausführlicher darstellen – damit beantwortet werden, daß trotz sporadi-
scher Fixierung (eine durchgehende schriftliche Tradition existiert ohnehin nicht) die
Musik im Unterricht nach dem Gehör und dem Gedächtnis überliefert wird. Wir können jene Charakterisierung, die der Folklore-Forscher Alan Dundes von der Folklore
im allgemeinen gibt, ohne Einschränkung auf die Musik übertragen, mit der sich
der Musikethnologe beschäftigt:

> In actual practice, a professional folklorist does not go so far as to say that
> a folktale or a ballad is not a folklore simply because it has at some time in its
> life history been transmitted by writing or print. But he would argue that if a
> folktale or ballad had *never* been in oral tradition, it is not folklore. (Dundes
> 1965: 1)

2.4. Die kulturanthropologische Abgrenzung

So wichtig die bisher erwähnten Abgrenzungen des ethnomusikologischen Forschungsbereichs, wie die regionale und jene der oralen Transmission für eine Standortbestimmung waren, so haben doch erst die kulturanthropologischen Definitionen den
Weg zu einer heute akzeptablen und zufriedenstellenden Standortbestimmung dieser
Musikwissenschaft gewiesen. Wir haben gesehen, daß die Ethnomusikologie seit Be-
ginn dieses Jahrhunderts unter dem Einfluß ethnologischer Forschungsrichtungen
stand (Abschnitt 1.2.). Die hier gemeinte kulturanthropologische Abgrenzung verläßt
nun die kulturhistorische Interpretation und begreift die Musik als Teil der Gesamtkultur und eingebettet in diese. Die Kulturrelativisten, aber auch die Funktionalisten
hatten diesen Weg ethnologisch bereits vorgezeichnet, so daß die Ethnomusikologen
ihn nur noch auf ihre spezielle objektbedingte Problematik zu modifizieren brauch-
ten. Vielleicht nicht mit den Worten des heutigen kulturanthropologischen Sprach-
gebrauchs, jedoch sinngemäß hatte bereits 1953 Fritz Bose darauf hingewiesen:

> Eine solche Darstellung muß auch von der Musikgeschichte unabhängiger sein,
> als die „Vergleichende Musikwissenschaft". Sie muß ebensosehr der Ethnologie und
> Anthropologie wie der Musikwissenschaft verpflichtet sein. Musik als der körper-
> hafte Ausdruck seelischer und gedanklicher Inhalte erfordert eine ganzheitliche
> Betrachtung im Sinne der Leib-Seele-Einheit, sowohl von der Seite der Psycholo-
> gie wie der Physiologie her. Eine Darstellung der Musik des Erdballs muß daher
> notwendig auch ganzheitlich auf das Stoffliche wie Geistige des Erscheinungsbildes
> gerichtet sein. Um diese größere Unabhängigkeit von der historischen Musikwis-
> senschaft und die engere Zugehörigkeit zu einer auf den ganzen Menschen gerich-
> teten psychosomatischen Ethnologie und Anthropologie auszudrücken, nennen wir
> sie „Musikalische Völkerkunde". (Bose 1953: 27)

19

Als einer der Hauptvertreter der kulturanthropologischen Richtung in der Ethnomusikologie muß Alan P. Merriam angesehen werden (ich deutete bereits im Abschnitt 1.2. darauf hin). Von ihm gingen und gehen wesentliche Impulse aus. Ethnomusikologie als „study of music *in* culture" wurde von ihm zum ersten Mal 1960 definiert:

> It is considerations such as these, then, which lead me to a proposal of a definition of ethnomusicology, not as the study of extra-European music, but as "the study of music in culture". In other words I believe that music can be studied not only from the standpoint of musicians and humanists, but from that of social scientists as well, and that, further, it is at the moment from the field of cultural anthropology that our primary stimulation is coming for the study of music as *a universal aspect of man's activities.* To define ethnomusicology in this way is in no way to deny its primary connection with the aesthetic and the humanistic, but it is to say that our basic understanding of the music of any people depends upon our understanding of that people's culture, the place music plays in it, and the way in which its role is played. It is through this sort of understanding that we can approach on a firm foundation our further understanding of what structure is and how music achieves whatever aesthetic ends are sought. (Merriam 1960: 109)

Musik sollte nach Merriam nicht losgelöst vom sozio-kulturellen Kontext oder von ihren kulturellen Bedingungen und Voraussetzungen untersucht werden. Musik wird hier ganzheitlich, das heißt in allen kulturellen Aspekten betrachtet. Nicht nur das musikalische Phänomen an sich, wie man es zum Beispiel mit dem Tonbandgerät – quasi als Momentaufnahme – festgehalten hat, steht im Mittelpunkt des Interesses, sondern auch die musikalische Gestaltung, der musikalische Prozeß und die musikalischen Verhaltensweisen mit ihren sozialen und psychischen Faktoren sowie die Position, die die Musik innerhalb der Gesamtkultur einnimmt. Diese Betrachtungsweise mußte bei konsequenter Weiterführung zwangsläufig zur Aufgabe der regionalen Abgrenzung und zum Ganzheitsanspruch der Ethnomusikologie führen. In demselben Aufsatz schreibt daher Merriam an anderer Stelle:

> If we accept the outline of field study given above, then it is clear that ethnomusicology is in no way restricted to the study of particular geographic areas, or supposed kinds of societies, but rather, is applicable to any body of music in any society. (Merriam 1960: 111)

Bereits 1957 hatte Mantle Hood das gleiche angedeutet:

> (Ethno)musicology is a field of knowledge, having as its object the investigation of the art of music as a physical, psychological, aesthetic, and cultural phenomenon. (Hood 1957: 2).

1963 kommt Hood wieder auf die regionale Abgrenzung zurück, betont jedoch auch die Kontextbezogenheit der Musik:

> The discipline is directed toward an understanding of music studied in terms of itself and also toward the comprehension of music within the context of its society. ...

20

264

> Ethnomusicology embraces all kinds of music not included by studies in historical musicology, i. e. the study of cultivated music in the western European tradition. (Hood 1963: 217)

Neu ist an dieser Definition, daß hier zum ersten Mal der Gesichtspunkt der *Ethnotheorie (ethnoscience)* berücksichtigt ist ("understanding of music in terms of itself"), der heute eine eminente Rolle spielt. Die regionale Abgrenzung gibt Hood dann später wieder zugunsten des universalen Anspruchs auf, unter Betonung der Kontextbezogenheit:

> Ethnomusicology is an approach to the study of any music, not only in terms of itself but also in relation to its cultural context. (Hood 1969: 298)

Der Ganzheitsanspruch ethnomusikologischer Betrachtungsweise kann auch umgekehrt, von der europäischen Musikgeschichte her kommend vertreten werden, wie zum Beispiel bei Frank Harrison:

> The traditional enterprises of musicology can no longer be pursued in *vacuo*. For their ultimate meaning and value rest on their contribution to restoring silent music to the state of being once more a medium of human communication. Recreation in any full sense cannot be divorced from the original function of the music, any more than a musical work from another society can be fully understood apart from its social context.
>
> Looked at in this way, it is the function of all musicology to be in fact ethnomusicology, that is, to take its range of research to include material that is termed "sociological". This view would still assume the basic importance of analytical and stylistical studies, but look further than has been customary in investigating the various aspects of music as an expression of an individual in his social context. (Harrison 1963: 79 f.)

In Harrisons Definition wird der Teil "ethno" im Begriff *Ethnomusikologie* soziologisch verstanden: "*ethno*" steht für die Betrachtung von "Musik im sozialen Kontext" und "Musik als Ausdruck eines Individuums in seinem sozialen Kontext". Wir werden noch sehen, daß diese Eingrenzung des Ethnischen für eine ethnomusikologische Definition nicht ausreicht, so neu und anregend sie seinerzeit gewesen ist. *Ethnomusikologie* ließe sich in diesem Sinne auch durch "Musiksoziologie" ersetzen, oder der "Ethno"-Teil könnte ganz wegfallen, wenn man davon ausgeht, daß die Einbeziehung einer Sozialgeschichte der Musik in den Rahmen der Musikgeschichte eigentlich eine Selbstverständlichkeit sein sollte.

Dem universalen und kosmopolitischen Anspruch musikethnologischer Forschung gibt auch die semantische Definition von Charles Seeger Ausdruck, für den Musikologie eigentlich Ethnomusikologie ist:

> musicology is
> (1) a *speech study*, systematic as well historical, critical as well as scientific or scientistic;
> whose field is
> (2) the *total music* of man, both in itself and in its relationships to what is not itself;

21

265

whose cultivation is

(3) by *individual students* who can view its field as musicians as well as in the terms devised by nonmusical specialists of whose fields some aspects of music are data;

whose aim is to contribute to the *understanding of man,* in terms both

(4) of human *culture* and

(5) of his relationships with the *physical universe.*

(Seeger 1970: 179)

Einen anderen kulturanthropologischen Aspekt, der hier noch erwähnt werden muß, betont Chase, der für eine *kulturelle Musikologie (cultural musicology)* eintritt:

I favor the *idea* of an "ethnomusicology" ... but I do not favor the terminology. – What we need is a term of larger scope. – For this I propose the term "cultural musicology" ... to study the similarities and differences in musical behavior among human groups, to depict the character of the various musical cultures of the world and the processes of stability, change, and development that are characteristic to them. (Chase 1972: 220)

Dieser Terminus der *cultural musicology* hat sich bis heute nicht gegenüber der *ethnomusicology* durchsetzen können, vermutlich zum einen, weil er zu diffus ist und zum anderen, weil der Ethnos-Begriff mit seiner modernen Definition (siehe Kapitel 3.1.) zu einer genaueren Bestimmung des Forschungsbereichs beiträgt.

Die kulturanthropologische Abgrenzung bedeutet, daß die Ethnomusikologie sowohl von anderen musikwissenschaftlichen Disziplinen als auch von der Kulturanthropologie und Ethnologie im allgemeinen ihre Betrachtungsweise und Methoden bezieht. Gerade der Durchbruch hierzu hat uns die interessantesten Ergebnisse gebracht. Man kann daher sagen: *Die duale Natur der Ethnomusikologie ist nicht ihre Schwäche, sondern ihre Stärke.*

The dual nature of ethnomusicology is clearly a fact of the discipline. The major question, however, is not whether the anthropological or the musicological aspect should gain ascendancy, but whether there is any way in which the two can be merged, for such a fusion is clearly the objective of ethnomusicology and the keystone upon which the validity of its contribution lies. (Merriam 1964: 17)

2.5. Die methodische Abgrenzung

But today "comparative musicology" has lost its usefulness. For at the bottom every branch of knowledge is comparative; all our descriptions, in the humanities no less than in the sciences, state similarities and divergences ... Walter Wiora is certainly right when he emphasizes that comparison can denote only a method, not a branch of learning. (Sachs 1962: 15)

Umreißt man den Objektbereich der Vergleichenden Musikwissenschaft nicht regional, so bleibt die Frage nach dem Wesen vergleichender Untersuchungen. Hierbei haben sich zwei extreme Standpunkte herausgebildet: der historische von Walter Wiora und der naturwissenschaftliche, von Robert Lach vertretene. Wiora unterscheidet

22

266

zwischen ethnologischer und vergleichender Musikforschung (Wiora 1975: 7) und „erhebt den Vergleich zu ihrer konstitutiven Aufgabe" (S. 1).

> Vergleichende ist verbindende Forschung ... Sie wirkt zumal dem kontakt-armen Nebeneinander von nur-europäischer Musikgeschichte und primär außer-europäischer Musikethnologie entgegen. Sie kann zur notwendigen Integration der Musikwissenschaft beitragen. Systematische Musikwissenschaft handelt von Grund-phänomenen, wie Tonalität oder Gefühlsausdruck, und vergleichende Forschung untersucht deren Geltungsbereiche: wo in der Welt sie verbreitet sind und wie sie abgewandelt werden. (Wiora 1975: 13)

Vom natur-evolutionistischen Ansatz abgesehen, steht bei Lach (1924) die Frage nach den erbbiologischen Universalien und psychologischen, physiologischen und an-thropologischen Entwicklungsfaktoren im Mittelpunkt, was später durch Walter Graf in Wien weiterverfolgt wurde (vgl. Graf 1968). Nach Lach (1924: 11) betrachten vergleichende und systematische Musikwissenschaft die Musik vom naturwissenschaft-lichen Standpunkt aus:

> Im Gegensatz zur Musikgeschichte fragt also die vergleichende Musikwissen-schaft nach den biologischen Quellen der musikalischen und musikhistorischen Phänomene ... Der Musikhistoriker fragt nach dem Was? und Wie?, der verglei-chende Musikforscher dagegen nach dem Warum? Woher? Wohin? Wozu?, der Musikhistoriker danach, was und wie ein Tongebilde (historisch) geworden ist, der vergleichende Musikwissenschaftler danach: warum es so werden mußte .../
> ... der vergleichende Musikwissenschaftler dagegen fragt nach den psychologi-schen, physiologischen, anthropologischen Wurzeln . . . Daher wird er Anthropo-logie (speziell Ethnographie und Ethnologie) wie Psychologie (speziell Völker-, Tier- und Kinderpsychologie sowie Psychopathologie), Physiologie (speziell Pho-nations- und Sprachorgane sowie -phänomene, also vor allem Phonetik) wie Bio-logie (speziell der Vögel und Säugetiere), Sprachwissenschaft (speziell verglei-chende Sprachwissenschaft) wie allgemeine Kunstwissenschaft, -psychologie und Ästhetik in den Kreis seiner Betrachtung hereinziehen. (Lach 1924: 11 f.)

In ganz anderer Weise definiert Merriam (1960) im Sinne seiner Forderung „study of music in culture" die Musikethnologie als Methode, womit ein universaler An-spruch erreicht ist, der sich an das unter 2.4. Dargestellte anschließt:

> Ethnomusicology is not a category in which is studied certain kinds of music, but rather a method of study which searches for certain goals in certain ways and which is applicable to any of the varied musical systems of the world. (Merriam 1960: 111)

> Our objectives are to a considerable extent coincident with those of cultural an-thropology. Our interests, I believe, should be directed toward the broader under-standing of music, not simply as a structural form, not in terms of particular areas or peoples, and not as an isolate, but as a creative human phenomenon which functions as part of culture. In thus defining the field I have tried to make it as clear as I can that I by no means exclude the purely historic, the purely struc-tural, the purely aesthetic from equal consideration with the ethnological. The point ist that the clear understanding of the historic, structural and aesthetic is intimately connected with an understanding of the cultural background in which these aspects operate. (Merriam 1960: 112 f.)

23

3. Ethnomusikologie heute

Ethnomusikologie ist selbstbewußter geworden, vielleicht unter dem Eindruck, daß Musik aus Indien, Indonesien und anderen Ländern in Europa und Nordamerika heute bekannter ist als deren Musik der Gegenwart, und das ist keine augenblickliche Modeerscheinung mehr. Für den Ethnomusikologen ist die euro-spezifische Entwicklung der abendländischen Opusmusik nur eine der vielen ethno-kulturalen Möglichkeiten. In diesem Sinne beginnt John Blacking sein in mehrfacher Hinsicht aktuelles Buch „How musical is man?" (1973) mit einer Definition, die sich dem bereits erwähnten (2.4.) universalen Anspruch der Ethnomusikologie zugesellt:

> Ethnomusicology is a comparatively new word which is widely used to refer to the study of the different musical systems of the world. Its seven syllables do not give it any aesthetic advantage over the pentasyllabic "musicology", but at least they may remind us that the people of many so-called "primitive" cultures used seven-tone scales and harmony long before they heard the music of Western Europe. Perhaps we need a cumbersome word to restore the balance to a world of music that threatens to fly up into clouds of elitism. We need to remember that in most conservatoires they teach only one particular kind of ethnic music, and that musicology is really an ethnic musicology. (Blacking 1973: 3)

Die in dieser Aussage steckende Problematik wird etwas deutlicher, wenn wir uns den folgenden Fragen gegenübergestellt sehen: 1. Ist der afrikanische Musikwissenschaftler, der die traditionelle Musik der Kultur untersucht, in der er aufgewachsen ist, ein Ethnomusikologe? 2. Ist der japanische Musikwissenschaftler, der sich mit Beethoven beschäftigt, ein Ethnomusikologe? 3. Ist für einen Inder die Musik Beethovens in erster Linie „ethnische Musik", weil er jene zuallererst mit der deutschen Kultur verbinden würde?

Die Antworten, die der Ethnomusikologe hierauf zu geben vermag, lauten heute: Entscheidend ist nicht, *wer, wo, was* untersucht, sondern, *wie* was untersucht wird, das heißt mit welcher Problemstellung und mit welchen Methoden. Es geht hier nicht so sehr um das „Insider-outsider"-Problem oder das des „Fremdverstehens" (vgl. Brandl 1977), sondern um die Benennung der Objektbereiche der Musikwissenschaft und die Methoden ihrer Untersuchung. Wir werden sehen, daß sich bereits aus der Problemstellung eine Abgrenzung ergibt, wie sie auch in den neuesten Definitionen enthalten ist.

Für Merriam besteht heute das wichtigste Ziel der Ethnomusikologie darin, „to seek correlations between music sound structure, on the one hand, and society and culture, on the other". (Merriam 1977: 198).

Bruno Nettl (1975) faßt alle hinreichend bekannten Aussagen, deren Einzelaspekte bereits dargestellt wurden (s. Abschnitt 2.), noch einmal zusammen. Hierzu muß einschränkend gesagt werden, daß es sich um Aspekte handelt, die für den Ethnomusikologen überwiegend Gültigkeit besitzen, wobei die Betonung auf *überwiegend* liegt. Das gilt auch für alle Abgrenzungen gegenüber anderen Gebieten der Musikwissenschaft. Nach Nettl ist Ethnomusikologie in den Aussagen der Mehrzahl ihrer Vertreter:

24

1. ... tne study of non-Western and folk musics,
2. ... the study of music outside one's own culture. This is perhaps more acceptable [als Punkt 1.], but there is no doubt that there are many ethnomusicologists throughout the world who study their own culture ...
   ... thus this definition relegates to ethnomusicology a marginal kind of
   value ...,
3. ... the study of musics in oral tradition ...,
4. ... the study of music in culture or as culture ...,
5. ... the study of contemporary musical cultures ...,
6. ... the comparative study of musical cultures, a definition once widely accepted and then discarded because it was thought that ethnomusicologists do
   not in fact spend any more time comparing than do members of other humanistic disciplines. I must say that I tend towards the sixth of these definitions,
   for it is the notion *that musics can be compared which distinguishes* the ethnomusicologist from other scholars involved in music. We do not all spend our
   time comparing, but we feel that insights can be gained from comparison
   and we prepare our data in such a way that they lend themselves to comparison. (Nettl 1975: 11–13)

Wir werden noch sehen, daß die heutige vergleichende Forschung kein Sprung
zurück in die frühere naive Phase ist, sondern sie sich bewußt ist, daß die Darstellung
universaler Elemente, Faktoren, Funktionen und Strukturen erst möglich ist, wenn
die strukturellen Einzelanalysen vieler unterschiedlicher Systeme vorliegen und die
kritischen Dimensionen des interstrukturellen Vergleichs bekannt sind.

Eine umfassende Standortbestimmung der heutigen Ethnomusikologie hat Max
Baumann (1976) vorgenommen. Da die dort abgehandelten Begriffs- und Methoden-
erklärungen in ihrer Mehrzahl nicht im Widerspruch zu unserer Darstellung stehen,
sondern diese grundlegend ergänzen, sei ausdrücklich darauf verwiesen. Baumann
stellt folgende Definition an den Anfang seiner Ausführungen:

Unter Ethnomusikologie verstehen wir hier ganz allgemein jene Wissenschaft,
die die musikkulturalen Werte ethnischer Gruppen außerhalb oder in Bezug zur
Kunstmusik untersucht, Erwerb und Vermittlung dieser Werte in Objektivationen
und Subjektivationen beschreibt und analysiert und ihre verursachenden Verhältnisse und begleitenden Prozesse erklärt. Mit „ethnisch" bezeichnen wir keine
statisch biologischen Determinationen – sie gehörten in den Bereich der biologischen Anthropologie –, sondern jene spezifischen Eigenschaften einzelner Gruppen, die sich von einer größeren Gesellschaft durch physische, kulturelle, nationale,
sprachliche, religiöse, politische, ökonomische oder ideologische Interessen und Be-
sonderheiten abheben und deren Mitglieder sich durch ein gemeinsames Band von
Brauchtumsgewohnheiten, Handlungsabsichten, Verhaltensweisen, Intentionen usw.
miteinander verbunden fühlen. Wo solche ethnischen Gruppen in Wechselbezie-
hung zu musikalischen Phänomenen und Praktiken stehen, die ihrerseits als gruppenspezifisch erscheinen oder als gruppenspezifisch empfunden werden, sprechen
wir von *musikethnischen Gruppen.* Musikethnische Gruppierungen sind (in ihrem
Sachverhalt) gegenüber ähnlichen Gruppenbildungen in der „Kunstmusik" durch
die besondere Art und Weise des Tradierens von musikalischen Inhalten und Wer-
ten abgegrenzt. Die primär mündliche Weitergabe des Musikgutes in der „Volksmusik" findet ihr Gegenbild in der primär schriftlichen Überlieferung der Kunstmusik oder jener Musik, die auf Kunstmusik bezogen ist. (Baumann 1976: 17)

25

Diese zunächst überzeugende Definition hat eine schwache Stelle: den Begriff der *Kunstmusik*, der dann auch bezeichnenderweise im vorletzten Satz mit Anführungszeichen erscheint. Auch die dort (S. 17) getroffene Unterscheidung von usueller und artifizieller Musik muß vom Standpunkt des Ethnomusikologen kritisiert werden. Das von Baumann ausführlich dargestellte abgrenzende Kriterium der spezifischen „Theorielosigkeit (pragmatisches Musikverständnis)" (S. 48 ff.) kann nur dann eine gewisse Gültigkeit besitzen, wenn es 1. nicht mit den Vorstellungen Lévy-Brühlscher Prägung vom „Prälogischen Denken" (vgl. Mühlmann 1968: 175 ff.) sympathisiert und 2. mit den Erkenntnissen der Ethnotheorie (Ethnoscience) übereinstimmt, was noch zu verifizieren wäre. Wir sehen hieraus, daß wir noch mitten in der ethnomusikologischen Basis-Diskussion stehen. Die Abgrenzung zur sogenannten Kunstmusik des Abendlandes ist insofern wissenschaftspragmatisch sinnvoll, sofern diese Opusmusik mit historischen Methoden und mit einem eurozentrischen Geschichtsbewußtsein untersucht wird, wie das weitgehend bei der Musikgeschichtsforschung auch der Fall ist. Wenn nun zum Beispiel die mit einer relativ hohen Theoriebezogenheit behaftete Hindustani- und karnatische Musik vom Ethnomusikologen untersucht wird und nicht von der Musikgeschichte, so hat das andere Gründe als den der Theoriebezogenheit, wie wir noch sehen werden. Es ist allerdings dem Musikhistoriker unbenommen, auch diese Musik zu untersuchen, sofern er methodisch dazu in der Lage sein sollte.

Die hier angeschnittenen Fragen machen es erforderlich, den Begriff des *Ethnischen* oder besser gesagt den der *Ethnizität* näher zu umreißen, der meiner Meinung nach ein Grundpfeiler jeder Definition der Musikethnologie respektive Ethnomusikologie ist. Auch das Problem einer Abgrenzung der Musikethnologie zur abendländischen Musikgeschichte bedarf der Erörterung.

3.1.   Der Begriff der Ethnizität

Die Ethnomusikologie untersucht im allgemeinen Sinne alle musikalischen Verhaltensweisen, Phänomene und alle mit diesen zusammenhängende Ursachen und Wirkungen, die sich ethnisch definieren lassen.

Dabei wird auf die folgenden Begriffe zum *Ethnos* und zur *Ethnizität* Bezug genommen.

Mühlmann definiert *Ethnos* oder *Ethnie* als

> die größte feststellbare souveräne Einheit, die von den betreffenden Menschen selbst gewußt und gewollt wird. Eine Ethnie kann daher auch eine Horde, ein Klan, ein Stamm, sogar eine Kaste sein; was sie *de facto* ist, kann nur empirisch festgestellt werden, indem man versucht, in die kollektive Intentionalität einzudringen. (Mühlmann 1964: 57)

Die Frage der „kollektiven Intentionalität" führt uns zu den Begriffen der *Ethnizität* und *Gruppenidentität*, wie sie in der (vor allem amerikanischen) Anthropologie und Soziologie in den letzten Jahren erörtert worden sind (vgl. Glazer/Moynihan [ed.] 1975; Despres [ed.] 1975). Im *American Heritage Dictionary of the English Language* (1973) wird *Ethnicity* zum Beispiel definiert als:

26

1. The condition of belonging to a particular ethnic group;
2. Ethnic pride. (nach Glazer/Moynihan [ed.] 1975: 1)

Es hat demnach eine objektive und eine subjektive Komponente, die es gilt, von Fall zu Fall empirisch zu ermitteln:

> Ethnicity is both an objective and a subjective phenomenon, the interrelation between these two aspects being, once again, an empirical question. Any conception of ethnicity which reduces either the objective or the subjective side of it to an insignificant role distorts reality. ... Ethnic groups are defined by the objective cultural modalities of their behavior (including most importantly their linguistic behavior) and by their subjective views of themselves and each other. (Van den Berghe nach Despres [ed.]1975: 72).

Der Ethnizitätsbegriff, wie er – nicht ohne Kontroverse, das sei einschränkend gesagt – in der oben genannten Literatur beschrieben wird, hat gerade seinen besonderen Reiz für die Verhältnisse in pluralen Gesellschaften und gewinnt für die Ethnomusikologie an Bedeutung, wenn es darum geht, umstrittene Begriffe wie den der „Volksmusik", durch den der *ethnischen Musik pluraler Gesellschaften* abzulösen, der auch die Musik weiterer *musikethnischer Gruppen* (vgl. Baumann 1976: 68 ff.) umfaßt als bisher üblich. Im übrigen sei hier auf die von Baumann (1976) gegebene Darstellung hingewiesen. Nettl hatte das Prinzip der musikethnischen Gruppe bereits angedeutet, als er schrieb:

> For some people folk music must sound a certain way, it must be composed in a particular style and any music which conforms to this style is folk music. If one follows the other approach, one accepts as folk music all music produced by a particular group in society, which one calls and defines as the "folk". (Nettl 1960: 1)

3.2. Ethnomusikologie und Musikhistorik

> Die Ethnologie interessiert sich auch für Völker, die die Schrift kennen: das alte Mexiko, die arabische Welt, den Fernen Osten; und man hat sogar die Geschichte von Völkern geschrieben, die nie eine gekannt haben, wie zum Beispiel die der Zulus. Auch hier handelt es sich noch um einen Unterschied der Orientierung nicht des Objekts, und um zwei Arten, Begebenheiten zu organisieren, die weniger heterogen sind, als es scheint. Der Ethnologe interessiert sich besonders für das, was nicht geschrieben ist, nicht so sehr, weil die von ihm untersuchten Völker nicht schreiben können, sondern weil das, wofür er sich interessiert, sich von allem unterscheidet, was die Menschen gewöhnlich auf Stein oder auf Papier zu fixieren lieben. (Lévi-Strauss 1967: 40)

Diese Feststellung von Lévi-Strauss besitzt auch für die Ethnomusikologie weitgehend Gültigkeit. Wenn hier die Ethnomusikologie von der Musikgeschichte abgegrenzt wird, die sich hauptsächlich mit der abendländischen Musik beschäftigt, dann geschieht das in der Weise, daß jeweils die Aspekte aufgeführt werden, die primär oder überwiegend für das eine oder andere Gebiet Gültigkeit besitzen. Es wird immer Ausnahmen und damit Überschneidungen geben, die es schwierig erscheinen lassen, eine bis ins Detail zufriedenstellende Abgrenzung und Gegenüberstellung aufzustel-

27

len, was auch gar nicht notwendig ist. Es ist auch nicht beabsichtigt, irgendeine Wertung zu implizieren oder künstlich Gegensätze zwischen zwei musikwissenschaftlichen Disziplinen aufzubauen, die sich durch wechselseitige Beeinflussung eher befruchten sollten.

1. Der Musikethnologe oder Ethnomusikologe untersucht primär Musik der Gegenwart, der Musikhistoriker jene der Vergangenheit. Der Musikethnologe hat dabei die Möglichkeit, die lebendige Musikpraxis, die musikalischen Verhaltensweisen – und bei optimaler Feldforschung durch teilnehmende Beobachtung – zu studieren. Für den Historiker ist es unmöglich, in der Kulturepoche, aus der die von ihm zu untersuchende Musik stammt, direkte Beobachtungen anzustellen, es sei denn, er beschränkt sich auf die zeitgenössische Musik.

> Die musikethnologischen Methoden schließen ... auch Befragungen und Beobachtungen und darüber hinaus sogar die Möglichkeit des Erlernens der betreffenden Musik in ihrer eigenen kulturellen Umgebung ein. Die Musikgeschichtsforschung konsultiert nur Schrift- und Bildquellen; Beobachtung und Befragung sind ausgeschlossen. (Laade 1976: 25)

Auch Gilbert Chase betont den Gegenwartsaspekt:

> The present emphasis (of ethnomusicology) is on the musical study of contemporary man, to whatever society he may belong, whether primitive or complex, Eastern or Western. (Chase 1958: 7).

Das soll nicht ausschließen, daß der Musikethnologe in bestimmten Fällen auch historische Problemstellungen behandeln kann (vgl. z. B. Nettl 1958). Er wird es immer dort tun, wo das der umfassenden Fragestellung nützt, die jedoch nie *ausschließlich* historisch sein wird.

2. Der Ethnomusikologe untersucht in erster Linie ein Musikereignis, einen Musikprozeß. Jede Tonaufnahme ist für ihn nur eine Momentaufnahme, ein Ausschnitt. Die Musikabläufe, die er registriert, können mehr oder weniger variabel sein; es kann Abläufe geben, die niemals exakt wiederholt werden. Bei jeder Transkription einer Tonaufnahme muß sich der Ethnomusikologe dieser Problematik bewußt sein. Die Tonaufnahme impliziert die Gefahr der Fixierung und Betrachtung der Musik als feststehendes Ereignis. Demgegenüber studiert der Musikhistoriker Artefakte, fixierte, notierte und meistens in sich abgeschlossene Musikwerke. Zwar beschäftigt er sich auch mit der Aufführungspraxis dieser Artefakte, beachtet dabei jedoch peinlich die Werktreue. Sein Ideal ist das invariable Musikereignis. Dem Phänomen der Improvisation gegenüber, das es immerhin bis ins 19. Jahrhundert hinein gab, befinden sich Historiker wie Interpreten in einem erheblichen Dilemma, da schriftliche Quellen meistens fehlen. Der Musikhistoriker untersucht Notationen, die als Basis für die Aufführung durch Interpreten dienen. Die Notationen haben präskriptiven Charakter. Der Ethnomusikologe fertigt Transkriptionen an, die als Hilfsmittel der Analyse und Beschreibung dienen, sie haben deskriptiven Charakter. Auch die wenigen Notationen, die uns aus außereuropäischen Kulturen überliefert sind, dienten nicht unbedingt präskriptiven, also aufführungspraktischen Zwecken.

28

3. Für den Ethnomusikologen stehen Interpret oder Interpreten und die Perzipienten im Mittelpunkt des Interesses, sofern darin überhaupt ein Unterschied besteht; denn nicht selten sind alle Personen aktiv am Musikereignis beteiligt. Für den Historiker der abendländischen Musik besitzen die Komponisten, deren Werke und deren historische Einordnung das zentrale Interesse. Fragt der Ethnomusikologe zuerst nach dem soziokulturellen Kontext, so der Historiker zuerst nach der historischen Stellung eines Musikereignisses.

4. In allen vom Ethnomusikologen studierten Musikkulturen wird die Musik nach dem Gehör tradiert und erlernt. In der europäischen Tradition hingegen basiert der Musikunterricht in der Regel auf notierter Musik.

5. Wer behauptet, analog zur Bildung von Indologie, Sinologie, Japanologie, Arabistik, Iranistik etc. habe sich auch das Musikstudium dieser Kulturen zu verselbständigen und von der Ethnomusikologie zu trennen, der vergißt sowohl die quantitativen wie auch qualitativen Unterschiede zwischen den schriftlichen Quellen zur Sprache und denen zur Musik dieser Kulturen. Es kann nur immer wiederholt werden, daß die Erforschung dieser Musik grundlegend andere Methoden erfordert als die der Musikgeschichte. Die „Geschichte der arabischen Musik" von Farmer zum Beispiel ist eine Geschichte des höfischen arabischen Musiklebens und nicht der arabischen Musik. Der Grund für die methodischen Unterschiede liegt jedoch tiefer. Was die Musikgestaltung in vielen Kulturen von der abendländischen unterscheidet, ist ein grundlegend anderes *Zeitgefühl!* Dieses ist ein elementarer Faktor in der Struktur aller musikalischen Verhaltensweisen. Die Konzeptionen der musikalischen Gestaltung werden bis ins Detail von diesem in jeder Kultur wieder differenzierten Zeitgefühl bestimmt. Das ist der Grund dafür, warum wir Ethnomusikologen bis heute an der Analyse, Erklärung und Wesenserfassung von Phänomenen wie Alāp, Rāg, Taqsīm, Mawāl, Maqām arbeiten. Indische und arabische Wissenschaftler stehen hier vor den gleichen wissenschaftlichen Problemen wie ihre europäischen und amerikanischen Kollegen. In diesem Zusammenhang sind auch das unterschiedliche, tonräumliche Empfinden in der melodischen Gestaltung, die anders beschaffenen Hörgewohnheiten, ja die gesamte Struktur einer alles regulierenden *sonischen Ordnung* (vgl. Blacking 1973: 11) zu nennen. Dieses *„Musik in Zeit und Raum"-Problem* hat für den Ethnomusikologen vorrangige Bedeutung und nicht das historische Ordnen und Auslegen theoretischer Dokumente und schriftlich fixierter Musikwerke.

> Die Geschichte ordnet ihre Gegebenheiten in bezug auf die bewußten Äußerungen, die Ethnologie in bezug auf die unbewußten Bedingungen des sozialen Lebens. (Lévi-Strauss 1967: 32)

3.3. Ziele und Methoden der Ethnomusikologie

Es gibt in vielen, wenn nicht sogar in der Mehrzahl aller Kulturen und Sprachen kein eigenständiges Wort für „Musik", sondern differenziertere Begriffe, wie „Singen", „Tanzen", „ein Instrument spielen, schlagen, blasen" und viele andere. Die arabische Sprache besitzt nicht den Terminus „Pferd", wohl aber den für „Stute", „Fohlen", „Hengst" und noch eine Reihe mehr. An abstrakten Farbbegriffen kennen manche Sprachen weniger als andere, obwohl die gleichen Farbvorstellungen existie-

29

ren; sie werden nur anders umschrieben. Es dürfte auch keiner ernsthaft leugnen wollen, daß das Phänomen, das wir mit dem Begriff „Musik" bezeichnen, ein universales ist. Nur hat es bei den einzelnen ethnischen Systemen und Kulturen eine spezifisch differenziertere Bedeutung, so daß wir besser von den musikalischen Verhaltensweisen und Aktivitäten sprechen. Musikalische Aktivitäten – seien sie produktiv oder rezeptiv – können in den unterschiedlichen Kulturen unterschiedliche Sinngehalte besitzen und dann jeweils anders bezeichnet werden. Diese Sinngehalte sind Bestandteil dessen, was wir in Anlehnung an Blackings Begriff der „sonic order" (1973: 11) als *sonische Ordnung* bezeichnen. Hierunter verstehen wir:

> die Struktur musikalischer Verhaltensweisen als die Totalität musikalischer Aktivitäten in ihren – zum Teil wechselseitigen – Abhängigkeiten und Beziehungen zu den von verschiedenen Ebenen her wirkenden Faktoren wie den biologischen, sozialen und ökologischen Bedingungen, den Funktionen und der beabsichtigten Wirkung dieser Aktivitäten. (Simon 1977)

Ziel der heutigen Ethnomusikologie ist die Erforschung der sonischen Ordnung aller ethnischen Systeme, der interkulturelle Vergleich ihrer Elemente und deren wechselseitige Beeinflussungen in den interethnischen Beziehungen. Die Vergleichende Musikwissenschaft schließlich beschäftigt sich mit den Fragen nach den *biologischen*, den ererbten Determinanten, den *Universalien* und den kulturbedingten *Varianten* der musikalischen Verhaltensweisen.

Die sonische Ordnung ist ein feinstrukturiertes, feinnerviges komplexes Gebilde, das mit seismographischer Empfindlichkeit auf Veränderungen seiner Elemente reagiert. Die Kenntnis der sonischen Ordnung ist von grundlegender Bedeutung für das Studium der Innovation und des Wandels von Musik, weil diese auf eine Änderung in der sonischen Ordnung zurückgehen. Eines der Ziele der Ethnomusikologie ist auch die Erforschung musikalischer Wandlungs- und Erneuerungsprozesse im kulturdynamischen Sinn.

Die Ethnomusikologie kennt eine Reihe von verschiedenen Methoden, die hier nur summarisch aufgeführt und nur in einigen wichtigen Aspekten erläutert werden sollen, die bisher nur unzureichend behandelt worden sind. Dabei wird, wo es möglich ist, auf einige beispielhafte Arbeiten verwiesen, in denen diese Methoden mit guten Ergebnissen Anwendung fanden. Die Methoden sind nicht isoliert zu sehen, sondern greifen in der Regel ineinander, was sich nach der jeweiligen Problemstellung richtet. Eine wertende Rangfolge ist mit dieser Aufzählung nicht beabsichtigt. Die Anwendung einiger dieser Methoden ist ohne Feldforschung nicht möglich. Sie ist die *conditio sine qua non* für das Studium der Musik als Teil der Gesamtkultur, für die Erforschung des sozio-kulturellen Kontexts und der Relevanz der Musik für Mensch und Gesellschaft.

1. Die *Dokumentation* der musikalischen Aktivitäten. Sie umfaßt deren Aufzeichnung auf Tonband, Film, Video, Photo, Zeichnungen und in Protokollen. Ebenso gehören hierzu die Niederschrift der Gesangstexte und die organologische Bestimmung der Musikinstrumente (vgl. Hood 1971: 143 ff., 247 ff.). Zur Problematik der dokumentarischen Arbeit in der Feldforschung sei auf die Ausführungen Brandls (1973) hingewiesen.

30

2. Die *Klassifikation*. Im Grenzbereich von Dokumentation und Strukturanalyse liegen, je nach Gewichtung und Wertung der Problemstellung, die Klassifikationen musikalischen Materials. Wenn bisher überwiegend Melodien nach verschiedenen Gesichtspunkten hin klassifiziert wurden (vgl. Elschekova 1966), so ist es durchaus denkbar, daß auch andere Parameter eines Musikereignisses berücksichtigt werden. Grundlegende Arbeiten zur Klassifikation sind die von Alica Elschekova (1966) und Bielawski (1973). Probleme der musikalischen Stratigraphie und der historischen typologischen wie stilistischen Entwicklung stehen, abgesehen von einer allgemeinen Notwendigkeit des Systematisierens, wie sie sich großen Archiven stellt, im Mittelpunkt klassifikatorischer Methoden in der Ethnomusikologie.

3. Die *musikalische Strukturanalyse*. Sie kennt zwei methodische Ansätze, die hier als a) *externe Analyse* und b) als *interne Analyse* bezeichnet werden sollen. Beide kennen die Transkription eines Musikereignisses als deskriptives Hilfsmittel. In der externen Analyse wird ein auf Tonband (früher auch Wachswalze und Schallplatte) gespeichertes Musikereignis transkribiert und dann musikalisch analysiert. Die Arbeiten Hornbostels können als beispielhaft für diese Methode gelten, obwohl die Technik der Transkription seit den „Vorschläge(n) für die Transkription exotischer Melodien" (Abraham/v. Hornbostel 1909) bis in die Gegenwart mit Hilfe von Tonhöhenschreibern, wie zum Beispiel dem Melographen (vgl. Reinhard 1975) und Frequenzanalyseverfahren (vgl. Simon 1972: II, 30 f. und I, 148 ff.) immer mehr verfeinert worden ist. Der Einsatz des „Sonagraphen", ein nach der Suchtonmethode arbeitendes Gerät (vgl. Graf 1969: 23 ff.), eröffnete neue Wege der Klangforschung und bereicherte die musikalische Strukturanalyse um die Dimension der Klangfarbe (vgl. z. B. Rouget 1970). Die externe, von außen kommende, am Material arbeitende Analyse mit der ihr zugrunde liegenden Transkription vom Tonband ist nicht ohne Problematik (vgl. D. Stockmann 1966; Symposium on Transcription and Analysis 1964; Reinecke 1970 u. a.). Reinecke faßt das folgendermaßen zusammen:

> 1. In die Analyse gehen nur diejenigen Elemente und Beziehungen ein, die vom Transkribenten bemerkt und auch nur in der Form, in der sie von ihm eingeschätzt wurden. Dabei besteht nicht nur die Gefahr, daß Einzelheiten überhört werden, sondern vor allem auch diejenige, daß musikalische Zusammenhänge unter dem vom Transkribenten vorgefaßten Erwartungsschema in einer Weise notiert und kodiert werden, die den musikalischen Prämissen des Objektes nicht voll entspricht.

> 2. Die geläufigen Transkriptionen erfolgen aus Gründen der unmittelbaren *Lesbarkeit* in einem unserem klassischen Notierungssystem ähnlichen Verfahren. Es werden Zeichen und Symbole benützt, die einem ganz bestimmten Bereich abendländischer Musik entspringen; sie gelten dem europäischen Musiker als *evident*, werden hier aber mit Korrekturzeichen versehen und für musikalische Strukturen angewendet, bei denen die Gültigkeit unserer musikalischen Grundannahmen zumindest in Frage zu stellen ist. Dieses Verfahren ist also mit Schwierigkeiten belastet, die allein schon daraus entstehen, daß durch den Kodierungsmodus der Primat des europäischen Denkens impliziert wird. Und gerade die Prämissen europäischer musikalischer Kategorien des 20. Jahrhunderts sind dort am gefährlichsten, wo sie nicht mehr als solche ins reflektierende Bewußtsein dringen.

31

Die Frage, die aus diesen wie aus mancherlei anderen Gründen immer wieder diskutiert wird, heißt daher: Wie kann man von der Transkription weg zu *objektiven* Verfahren gelangen, um brauchbare Strukturanalysen zu gewinnen? (Reinecke 1970: 154)

Auch sogenannte *objektive* Verfahren lösen jedoch nicht die hier angeschnittenen Probleme, da sie die Klangvorstellungen und Hörerwartungen der jeweiligen Kulturträger, von denen das so analysierte Stück stammt, nicht berücksichtigen. Das „objektive" akustische Bild kann Parameter enthalten, die für die musikalische Gestaltung und Perzeption völlig irrelevant sein können. Letztlich ist es auch hier wiederum der – meistens – kulturexterne Wissenschaftler, der die aus *objektiven* Verfahren gewonnenen Ergebnisse interpretiert. Wir sind damit wieder am Ausgangspunkt unserer Problemstellung angelangt und können feststellen, daß die bisher in der Ethnomusikologie gebräuchlichen Transkriptionsverfahren – bei allen zu Recht kritisierten Unvollkommenheiten – nach wie vor ein im allgemeinen unerläßliches Hilfsmittel für die musikalische Strukturanalyse sind.

Dieser Unzulänglichkeiten wegen die Transkription als Methode und als Ergebnis abzulehnen, wäre ungerecht und unklug. Dem Leser einer Abschrift sollte es aber möglich sein, sich gegen die angeführten Nachteile zu schützen. Dazu kann ihm bei schon mehr oder weniger erschlossenen Musikkulturen die eigene Sachkenntnis helfen; ferner eine Vorstellung von der Verfahrensweise und den Neigungen des Transkriptors. Vordringlich ist bei all dem, daß der Leser das klingende Musikstück zur Hand hat, dessen Transkription e in einer Publikation vorfindet. Anhand der Klanggestalt kann er die Abschrift überprüfen und die Besprechung des Stücks genauer verfolgen. Erst im Zusammenwirken mit Klangfassung und Analyse des Stücks erfüllt die Transkription im vollen Umfang ihren Zweck. Letztlich besteht er darin, das Ohr des nicht-einheimischen Zuhörers mit Hilfe des Auges zu schärfen. (Kuckertz 1977)

Aus dem oben geschilderten Dilemma der externen Analyse vermag die sogenannte *interne Analyse* hinauszuführen. Diese setzt beim inneren Prozeß eines Musikereignisses an, zum Beispiel bei den Bewegungsabläufen oder der Spielweise eines Instruments. Im Gegensatz zur externen Analyse, bei der zunächst das auf Tonband gespeicherte musikalische Gesamtergebnis übertragen und erst im zweiten Gang nach der Strukturierung der einzelnen Teile gefragt wird, beginnt die interne Analyse bei den einzelnen Elementen eines Musikereignisses und setzt diese dann zum Gesamtbild zusammen. Die interne Analyse kann mit der Film- oder Videoaufzeichnung arbeiten (vgl. Dauer 1966) oder aber durch aktive teilnehmende Beobachtung und das Erlernen der Spielweise eines Instruments erreicht werden.

In gewisser Hinsicht ist die Bild-Ton-Aufzeichnung der teilnehmenden Beobachtung sogar überlegen. Dauer (1966) weist in seiner methodisch beispielhaften Analyse einer afrikanischen Tanzmusik aus dem Süd-Wadai darauf hin:

Es läßt sich heute jedoch zeigen, daß der synchrone Tonfilm bei entsprechender Aufnahme nicht nur die Forderung des Dabeiseins weitgehend erfüllen kann, sondern noch viel mehr. Er kann dem einzelnen Musiker wie der ganzen Gruppe, ohne sie zu stören, so nahe auf den Leib rücken wie kein noch so geschickter Beobachter, er kann zum Zwecke genauester Beobachtung die Bewegung verlangsamen oder beschleunigen, er kann sogar anhalten, ohne daß die geringste Gefahr einer Verfälschung entsteht oder Musiker und Gruppe dadurch aus dem Konzept gebracht werden.

Schließlich hat der Tonfilm, genau wie das Tonband, den Vorzug der unbeschränkten Wiederholbarkeit. Aber auch hier gehen seine Möglichkeiten über das Tonband und andere ähnliche Verfahren hinaus, weil gleichzeitig mit dem akustischen Geschehen auch die Bewegungsvorgänge wiederholt werden. Das ließ sich bisher nur mit dem tatsächlichen Versuchsgegenstand, also der Person oder Gruppe an Ort und Stelle durchführen, wobei jedermann weiß, daß diese Methode regelmäßig eine baldige Erschöpfungsgrenze zu erreichen pflegt. (Dauer 1966: 441)

Ebenso wie das von Dauer vorgelegte Ergebnis sind die von Kubik erarbeiteten Strukturanalysen afrikanischer Instrumentalmusik, zum Beispiel der Amadinda-Xylophonmusik aus Uganda, ohne interne Analyse nicht denkbar (Kubik 1969, 1970). Kubik geht von der teilnehmenden Beobachtung der Spielweise des Instruments aus sowie von der genauen Aufzeichnung der einzelnen Partien, die die am Instrument sitzenden Musiker ausführen. Außerdem arbeitete er mit der oben erwähnten Filmanalysetechnik (Kubik 1965). Kubiks Ergebnisse belegen anschaulich, daß die interne Analyse am ehesten geeignet ist, von der hier nicht optimalen Transkription in europäischer Notation zu neuen Notationsmöglichkeiten zu führen, wobei die deskriptive Aufzeichnung zu einer präskriptiven werden kann:

Es gibt derzeit mehrere Möglichkeiten, *Kiganda*-Xylophonmusik aufzuschreiben: a) Mit der europäischen Notenschrift. Sie hat die Vorteile der Vertrautheit und der großen Übersichtlichkeit. b) Mit der graphischen Notationsmethode, die ich seinerzeit beim Transkribieren von 8-mm-Filmen mit Xylophonmusik aus Moçambique entwickelte. c) Mit Buchstaben oder Ziffern, die Xylophonplatten repräsentieren.

Die letztgenannte Methode ist sehr einfach. Sie ist auch leicht erlernbar und mit ihr läßt sich zumindest Xylophonmusik absolut genau notieren. Schon 1962 versuchte ich mit Evaristo Muyinda ein leichtfaßliches System zu entwickeln, das ihm und seinen Schülern ermöglichen sollte, ihre Musik selber zu transkribieren. Wir schrieben zuerst die Basisthemen mit den Buchstaben C D E G A (entsprechend den pentatonischen Noten) auf, später nur noch mit den Ziffern 1, 2, 3, 4, 5. Diese Notation hat den Vorteil, keinerlei Assoziationen zum europäischen Tonsystem zu erwecken. Mit der Ziffernschrift lassen sich auch lange Stücke auf kleinstem Raum zusammenpressen. (Kubik 1970: 113 f.)

Basiert die interne Analyse in erster Linie auf der teilnehmenden Beobachtung, so kann damit bereits der enge Rahmen der ausschließlich musikalischen Strukturanalyse überschritten und um die Frage nach den idiokulturalen Konzeptionen, die sich die ethnotheoretische Analyse stellt (vgl. 5.) wie der nach dem sozio-kulturellen Kontext (vgl. 4.) erweitert werden. Vor allem in den Arbeiten Kubiks läßt sich diese Entwicklung deutlich erkennen (vgl. v. a. Kubik 1977).

4. Die *Ethnographie der musikalischen Verhaltensweisen*. Diese erfaßt, beschreibt und analysiert alle musikalischen Aktivitäten und Verhaltensweisen, deren Anlässe und Zweckbestimmungen innerhalb der ethnischen Gruppe, ihre sozialen Bezüge,

33

277

ihre Relevanz als Audruck sozialer und kulturaler Wertvorstellungen und die soziale Stellung der Musikausübenden.

Man unterscheidet hierbei die Ethnographie
a) der musikalischen Produktion und Kreation,
b) der Aufführung und Ausführung (ethnography of performance, Blacking 1977) und
c) der Kommunikation und Rezeption im sozialen Sinne.

Es handelt sich im Grunde genommen um eine semantische Analyse der musikalischen Aktivitäten. Sie ergänzt sich zu der unter 7. genannten Funktionsanalyse und überschneidet sich mit der ethnotheoretischen Methode (5.).

Eine grundlegende Arbeit in dieser Richtung ist die von Michael G. Smith (1957): *The Social Functions and Meaning of Hausa Praise Singing.*

> Semantic analysis – the determination of meanings – refers to the values or conceptual aspects of particular forms as more or less consistent ideational systems, the correspondence and relations of which to other parts of the social structure remain to be investigated. (Smith 1957: 40)

Die Methode einer *Ethnography of musical performance* hat in jüngster Zeit auf dem 12. Kongreß der Internationalen Gesellschaft für Musikwissenschaft (Berkeley 1977) neue Impulse erhalten. Blacking (1977) faßt die wesentlichen Punkte hierzu folgendermaßen zusammen:

> 1) Who performs, and who listens? What are their group allegiances? And what ideas about music and society do they bring into the performance situation?
> 2) How does the performance situation affect the structures of the music either directly, through improvization, variation and audience response, or indirectly, through composition for a particular occasion?
> 3) What is peculiarly *musical* about the performance and performance response, as distinct from being social, political etc? And how are musical features inescapably tied up with other features, such as dance?
> 4) How do the musical aspects of the performance affect individual participants and so influence decision-making in non-musical spheres? (Blacking 1977: 8)

Methodische Ansätze zu einer Ethnographie der musikalischen Verhaltensweisen findet man zum Beispiel in folgenden Arbeiten: Ames (1973), Brandl (1975; 1977a), Henry (1976) und Kaden (1976, 1977). Hatte Smith (1957) die Relevanz musikalischer Aktivitäten der Hausa als Ausdruck sozialer und kulturaler Wertvorstellungen sowie den Preisgesang als soziales Regulativ gedeutet, so bringt Ames (1973) einen sozio-kulturellen Überblick über diese Aktivitäten, über die Rolle und den Status der verschiedenen Hausa-Musiker innerhalb der Gesellschaft.

Brandl (1975) gibt mit seiner Ethnographie musikalischer Aktivitäten auf der griechischen Insel Karpathos einen protokollarischen Abriß über die volkskundliche Rolle der Musik, der Bedeutung der Musik für die Angehörigen der betreffenden ethnischen Gruppe und der Biographien von Musikern und Informanten. In einer weiteren Arbeit behandelt Brandl „musiksoziologische Aspekte der Volksmusikinstrumente auf Karpathos" (1977a).

34

Henry (1976) weist aufgrund eigener Feldforschungen auf die Mannigfaltigkeit musikalischer Aktivitäten und Ausdrucksformen innerhalb eines nordindischen Dorfes hin und widerlegt die von Lomax (1962 und 1968) aufgestellten Hypothesen einer direkten Verbindung von musikalischer und sozialer Struktur (vgl. 7.).

Kadens Arbeiten (1976, 1977) enthalten Beiträge zur Methodik der Ethnographie musikalischer Verhaltensweisen und Interaktionen, die ein Höchstmaß an Objektivierung zulassen, vorausgesetzt, die in den mathematischen Prozeß eingegebenen Daten stimmen. Zu den Aufgaben künftiger ethnomusikologischer Forschung dürfte es gehören, die bisher in den genannten methodischen Ansätzen aufgezeigten Richtungen weiter zu verfolgen.

> We may attempt to define the concept of music by reference to "how the African *thinks* about his music", to the "musical mind" of the African – an approach often stressed by Jones in his writings on African rhythm (see, e. g., Jones, 1959), or we may approach the problem by considering what the African *does* when he makes music, what resources he uses, how and when he uses them, and from these deduce – in the light of our knowledge and experience of this music in its cultural context – what can be stated to constitute music and what the concept of music involves. (Nketia 1973: 582; zuerst 1961)

5. Die ethnotheoretische Analyse

> Ein Verständnis außereuropäischer Musikformen ist dem Betrachter oft nur möglich, wenn versucht wird, in jene musikalischen Denkvorgänge einzudringen, die diese Musikformen mitbestimmend gestalten. Die Frage, was geht in der Vorstellung afrikanischer Musiker eigentlich vor, wenn sie ihre komplexen rhythmisch-melodischen Formeln und Themen komponieren oder spielen, ist zu einem zentralen Anliegen der musikethnologischen Feldforschung in Afrika geworden. (Kubik 1970: 109)

Die hier geforderte Erweiterung des analytischen Umkreises soll als ethnotheoretische Analyse bezeichnet werden. Sie besteht in der Erforschung idiokulturaler Konzeptionen auf der bereits in Anthropologie und Linguistik erprobten Basis der Ethnotheorie (Ethnoscience) und Ethnographie der Kommunikation (vgl. Sturtevant 1964; Hymes 1964).

> Much progress has been made in the analysis of music, and in the establishment of the use of native taxonomies and approaches to music as a basis for description, and of systems (some of them based on linguistic models) which might lend themselves to universal and comparable descriptions of the musics of the world. (Nettl 1975: 13)

Um nur einige Punkte herauszugreifen: Es genügt heute nicht mehr herauszufinden, in welcher Weise ein Musikereignis variabel ist, sondern die Frage ist, welche Relevanz diese Variabilität für den Kulturträger, die jeweiligen Interpreten und Perzipienten selber hat (vgl. auch Brandl 1977). Es genügt nicht die Feststellung, daß eine Musik in einer bestimmten Weise mehrstimmig ist, sondern warum sie so ist und wie Interpret und Hörer der jeweiligen Kultur zu diesem Phänomen stehen. Bittet man einen ägyptischen Musiker, zum Beispiel einen Rebāba- oder Arġūl-Spieler,

35

einem eine Tonleiter vorzuspielen, so wird man auf Unverständnis stoßen oder irgendein melodisches Gebilde vorgespielt bekommen, das vielleicht entfernt an die europäische Vorstellung von Tonleitern erinnert. Den Schluß, den wir daraus zu ziehen haben ist nicht der, daß der Musiker nicht in der Lage ist, eine Tonleiter zu spielen – er ist es sehr wohl, nachdem man ihm erklärt hat, was man darunter versteht –, sondern daß die sonische Ordnung eine andere ist und die Konzeptionen des melodischen Gestaltens von anderen Voraussetzungen ausgehen als vom europäischen Tonleiter-Denken (vgl. auch Nketia 1962: 1 f.). Auch Leonard B. Meyer hat in seinem Aufsatz zu einigen grundlegenden Fragen der heutigen Ethnomusikologie bereits 1960 auf diese Probleme hingewiesen:

> Appearances are often deceptive. For instance, two cultures may appear to employ the same scale structure, but this structure might be interpreted differently by the members of each culture. Conversely, the music of two cultures may employ very different materials, but the underlying mechanism governing the organization of these materials might be the same for both. The possibility of such discrepancy calls attention to the importance of methodology and definition. (Meyer 1960: 49 f.)

Von hier führt ein direkter Weg zur ethnotheoretischen Analyse, in der die Konzeptionen, Klassifikationen, Benennungen und Vorstellungen der Angehörigen der zu untersuchenden ethnischen Gruppe hinsichtlich der Relevanz zur Musik und allen mit ihr verbundenen Fragen berücksichtigt werden.

Von dem Linguisten Pike stammt die Unterscheidung einer *emischen* und *etischen* Betrachtungsweise, abgeleitet aus dem Begriffspaar phonemisch und phonetisch.

> The study of phonemics involves the examination of the sounds used in a particular language, while phonetics attempt to generalize from phonemic studies in individual languages to a universal science covering all languages. By analogy, *emics* apply in only a particular society, while etics are culture-free or universal aspects of the world (or if not entirely universal operate in more than one society). (Berry/Dasen 1974: 16)

Pike charakterisiert emisch-etisch so:

Emic approach	*Etic approach*
studies behaviour from within the system	studies behaviour from a position outside the system
examines only one culture	examines many cultures, comparing them
structure discovered by the analyst	structure created by the analyst
criteria are relative to internal characteristics	criteria are considered absolute or universal

Die „emische Analyse" ermöglicht es uns, musikalische Phänomene und Verhaltensweisen hinsichtlich ihrer idiokulturalen Wertung und Konzeptionalisierung zu sehen. Man könnte diese auch als *Ethnohermeneutik* bezeichnen. Techniken hierzu sind die teilnehmende Beobachtung und die sogenannte „dokumentarische Methode der Interpretation," ...

36

mit der beim befragten Gesellschaftsmitglied die Erzeugung einer Erzählung, d. h. Geschichtsdarstellung seiner Ich-Identität ... hervorgerufen werden kann. (Ethnotheorie und Ethnographie des Sprechens: 480 f.)

Eine Studie in dieser Art ist meine Arbeit über einen nubischen professionellen Musiker (Simon 1975). Andere Arbeiten, die in die autochtonen Konzeptionen oder emische Sicht hineinführen oder diese stark berücksichtigen sind unter anderem die von Nketia (1962), Simon (1978) und Zemp (1971).

Nketia berichtet zum Beispiel über seine Erfahrungen bei der Arbeit mit Akan-Musikern (Ghana):

> It was obvious that the musical tradition did not consist only of repertoire but also of a body of knowledge in terms of which music took place or was interpreted. This required to be sorted out and systematised. It was necessary for example to check "meaning" in their terms and how it operated in actual situations, to check and cross check individual information or interpretations, and local variations. Moreover what was referred to as meaning was not in one direction. Sometimes it was the circumstances that led to the creation of a particular piece, dance style or instrument. Sometimes it was something structural, something embodied in what one instrument or two instruments in an ensemble did. Many such problems came up when I took lessons in drumming from master drummers or read over song texts to different individuals in widely separated localities.
>
> Another point which I observed was that quite often references to music emphasized it as an event, as a process in time. Although there was no musical notation in the Western sense, no awareness of scales, etc., there was a method of quoting rhythm patterns or imitating drum rhythms in conversation when one had to talk about them or when in the course of the narration of a folktale one had to imitate verbally what some drums were playing or as often happened in the past when one had to teach someone to take up the office of drummer at the chief's court or drummer in some particular organisation. (See Nketia 1954). So far Jones seems to be the only non-African who has exploited this African approach in his descriptive analyses of rhythm. (See Jones 1952, 1959.) (Nketia 1962: 2)

Eine ausführliche Darstellung idiokulturaler Begriffsbildung und Konzeptionalisierung bringt Zemp in seiner Arbeit über die Musik der Dan (Westafrika), vor allem in dem Kapitel „Conceptions et verbalisations" (Zemp 1971: 67 ff.). Ähnlich ist der Ansatz in meinen Untersuchungen über eine Berglandkultur in West-Neuguinea (Simon 1978). In einer anderen Studie von mir zur Oboen-Trommel-Musik in Ägypten (Simon 1977) ergab die Terminologie der Musiker zu den einzelnen Partien im Zusammenspiel wichtige Aufschlüsse zur musikalischen Rollenverteilung im Ensemble und damit auch zur Struktur der musikalischen Gestaltung:

> Das Zusammenspiel ist präzise und aufeinander nach bestimmten Spielregeln abgestimmt, die schon aus der Bezeichnung der drei Oboen-Partien hervorgehen. Danach heißt die erste Oboe (sibs oder šalabiya) el-auwal oder rais, das heißt der „Erste" oder „Leiter", also derjenige, der die Melodie führt. Die zweite Oboe (šalabiya oder qabak) heißt tabī'a oder taba'a, mit der Bedeutung von „folgend",

37

281

„untergeordnet", „derjenige, der einem anderen folgt". Das heißt in unserem Sinne derjenige, der die Melodieführung unterstützt und dem Spiel der ersten Oboe folgt. Die dritte Oboe wird als *qarar* und *mīzān* bezeichnet. Ebenso wie bei der zweiten Oboe wird damit die Funktion sehr klar bezeichnet. Das Wort *qarar* geht zurück auf das Verb *qarra* mit der Bedeutung „sich niederlassen", „ruhen" oder „verharren". *El-qarar* läßt sich daher mit „Seßhaftigkeit", „Ruhe", „Dauer", „Permanenz", „Boden" oder „Grund" übersetzen, womit die Bordun-Funktion hinreichend charakterisiert ist. *Mīzān* dagegen heißt soviel wie „Balance", „Gleichgewicht" der Melodie), einer, der das melodische Geschehen der anderen beiden Oboen im Gleichgewicht hält (mit dem Bordun). (Simon 1977: 156 f.)

Bereits 1937 hatte Marius Schneider in seiner Arbeit über afrikanische Chorformen auf die Bedeutung der einheimischen Terminologie für eine kulturspezifische musikalische Analyse hingewiesen:

> Der Wechselgesang wird bei den Suaheli als „einfädeln, aneinanderreihen" (wie Perlen an einer Schnur), in Togo hingegen einfach durch „tauschen" bezeichnet. Es liegt auf der Hand, daß hier eine andere Vorstellung, d. h. eine andere psychologische Basis einer äußerlich ähnlichen Form, vorliegt.
> Die Erfassung der einheimischen Begriffsbildung allein kann uns also tiefer in die Psychologie der einzelnen Chorformen einführen. Sie wird noch manches wesentlich voneinander trennen, was äußerlich (der rein formalen Analyse nach) ähnlich ist und ebenso äußerlich Verschiedenes zusammenrücken. (M. Schneider 1937: 88)

In seiner Arbeit „Perzeptorische und kognitive Grundlagen der Musikgestaltung in Schwarzafrika" faßt Gerhard Kubik (1977) 40 Jahre später den Stand der ethnotheoretischen Forschung auf dem Gebiet der afrikanischen Musik zusammen, wobei er den folgenden Fragenkatalog als Richtschnur für bisherige und zukünftige Arbeiten aufstellt:

1. In welcher Weise erfassen afrikanische Musiker auditive Stimuli als Patterns? Gibt es spezifische Kriterien für die Wahrnehmung als Gestalt in der afrikanischen Musik, die für ganz Schwarzafrika oder für bestimmte musikalische Stilgebiete gültig sind?

2. Welche akustischen Phänomene sind für Angehörige verschiedener afrikanischer Kulturen bedeutsam und wie organisieren sie diese in ihrer Auffassung von Musik?

3. Auf welche Weise reflektieren Musikterminologie und -taxonomie in afrikanischen Sprachen die intrakulturell bestimmte Wahrnehmung und Auffassung von Musik/Tanz-Patterns?

4. Welche intrakulturellen und welche interkulturellen Variationsbreiten bestehen in der Wahrnehmung, im Erkennen und Auffassen von Patterns in den Musikkulturen Schwarzafrikas? Bis zu welchem Ausmaß kann ein Musik/Tanz-Pattern in varianter Form auftreten und von den Angehörigen afrikanischer Musikkulturen als identisch aufgefaßt werden?

5. Wie lassen sich individuelle Modelle und Auffassungen innerhalb einer Musikkultur von kognitivem Gemeingut abgrenzen?

6. Was läßt sich aus den Aussagen und dem Verhalten der Angehörigen einer schwarzafrikanischen Musikkultur mit verschiedenem Grad von Spezialisierung

über Grundlagen und Prozesse der Gestaltwahrnehmung und -auffassung ab-
leiten? a) im Rahmen einer ethnisch abgrenzbaren Musikkultur, b) im Rahmen ethnisch indifferenter Musikkulturen, c) im Rahmen einer musikalischen
Subkultur, etwa einer musikalischen Altersgruppierung, d) innerhalb einer
Musiziereinheit (Ensemble, Band etc.), e) auf der Ebene eines einzelnen, spe-
zialisierten Individuums.

7. Wie lassen sich universale Grundlagen der Gestaltwahrnehmung in der Musik
   von enkulturierten Verhaltensweisen im Bereich schwarzafrikanischer Kulturen
   abgrenzen? (Kubik 1977: 35–36)

6. Die *ethnopsychologische Analyse*, untersucht in Ergänzung zur kognitiven Analyse (5.) die idiokulturalen emotionalen Faktoren wie die *Hörgewohnheiten, Hörerwartungen* und die *Wirkung* der Musik, also alles das, was von den jeweiligen
Kulturträgern in der Regel nicht verbalisiert wird. Ob wir ein Musikereignis „gut"
oder „schlecht" finden, werden auch wir nur in extremen Fällen rational begründen
können, etwa dann wenn die Musik durch gravierende Fehler in der Aufführung von
den gewohnten Normen der Hörerwartungen abweicht. In manchen Kulturen wird
ein Sänger nach seinem Einfallsreichtum in den melodischen oder textlichen Erfindun-
gen oder den Nuancierungen in der Stimmgebung beurteilt, so zum Beispiel in einigen
Formen der arabischen Musik. Bei den Eipo im Hochland von Neuguinea (vgl. Simon
1978) gilt ein Vorsänger dann als besonders gut, wenn er eine kräftige, tragende
Stimme besitzt, während auf melodischen und textlichen Einfallsreichtum kein Wert
gelegt wird. Stark schablonisierte Melodie und Textabläufe sind die Folge.

Eine ethnomusikologisch eminent wichtige Frage, die der ethnopsychologischen
Analyse bedarf, wäre zum Beispiel die nach der Relevanz von Musikereignissen, die
wir in der bloßen musikalischen Strukturanalyse als mehrstimmig interpretieren
würden. Was von uns als mehrstimmig angesehen wird, kann von den betreffenden
Kulturträgern als einstimmig oder als bloße Klangverstärkung betrachtet werden.
Umgekehrt kennen wir Musikereignisse aus der afrikanischen Musik, die von uns als
einstimmig, von dem Afrikaner jedoch als mehrstimmiges Spiel im zeitlichen Nach-
einander gehört und empfunden werden.

Die ethnopsychologische Analyse benötigt dringend musikpsychologische Testver-
fahren, gegen die man nicht den Vorwurf der Eurozentrik erheben muß. Sie sind mei-
nes Wissens bisher nicht überzeugend entwickelt worden. Die für die Erforschung der
jeweiligen *sonischen Ordnung* so bedeutenden *Hörgewohnheiten* und *Hörerwartungen*
können auch – zumindest teilweise – durch genaue Beobachtung und Befragung sowie
in Kombination mit den anderen hier dargestellten Methoden ermittelt werden. Zum
Stand der Forschung sei auf die Aufsätze von Harwood (1976) und Laske (1975)
hingewiesen.

Der Versuch, die psychischen und physischen *Wirkungsmechanismen* in bestimmten
Musikereignissen ethnomusikologisch zu untersuchen, liegt in meiner Analyse eines
Krankenheilungsritus der Digo aus Tanzania (Simon 1970) und religiöser Riten im
Sudan (Simon 1975) vor.

39

7. Die *Funktionsanalyse,* untersucht die Funktionen der Musik im metafunktionalen Sinne, wie es von mir an anderer Stelle ausführlich dargestellt worden ist (Simon 1977). Danach werden folgende Metafunktionen unterschieden: 1. die soziale, 2. die psychische, 3. die religiöse, 4. die ästhetische, 5. die magische und 6. die kommunikative Funktion.

Diese Funktionskategorien haben idealtypischen Charakter. Sie sind nicht streng isoliert zu sehen, sondern in ihren mehr oder weniger wechselseitigen Beziehungen untereinander. Es dürfte nur selten Fälle geben, in denen nur eine der Kategorien allein zu erkennen ist.

> Ein wesentliches Merkmal ist gerade die Komplexität verschiedener Funktionen in Form eines Funktionsbündels aus zwei, drei und mehr Funktionen, die zwar qualifizierbar, aber nur selten quantifizierbar sind. (Simon 1977)

Die Funktionsanalyse stellt sich die Frage nach der Rolle der Musik als Stimulans und Stabilisator für Individuum und Gemeinschaft. Merriam unterscheidet folgende Funktionen der Musik:

> The function of emotional expression, ... of aesthetic enjoyment, ... of entertainment, ... of communication, ... of symbolic representation, ... of physical response, ... of enforcing conformity to social norm, ... of validation of social institutions and religious rituals, ... of contribution to the continuity and stability of culture, ... of contribution to the integration of society. (Merriam 1964: 219–226)

Diese Aufstellung ist von mir in den oben genannten sechs Kategorien zum Teil zusammengefaßt, zum Teil erweitert worden. Danach haben musikalische Ereignisse, Aktivitäten oder Verhaltensweisen eine *soziale Funktion,* wenn sie dem sozialen Zusammenhalt der ethnischen Gruppe dienen, deren Ethnizität fördern und zum Bestand der Gemeinschaft beitragen. Ist die Musik emotionaler Ausdruck des Individuums oder trägt sie zu dessen psychischen Stabilisierung bei, so hat sie eine *psychische Funktion.* Entspricht die musikalische Verhaltensweise den religiösen Vorstellungen und unterstützt sie diese, zum Beispiel als Bestandteil einer vorgeschriebenen Kulthandlung, so liegt eine *religiöse Funktion* vor. Das gleiche gilt entsprechend für die *magische Funktion.* Beide können eng miteinander verbunden sein, wie zum Beispiel in der tibetanischen Kultmusik. Dient eine Musik der Unterhaltung oder Erbauung und unterliegt sie hierbei den kulturspezifischen ästhetischen Werturteilen, so besitzt sie eine *ästhetische Funktion.* Die *kommunikative Funktion* liegt in jenen Spezialfällen vor, in denen verbale Mitteilungen in musikalische Signale transformiert werden, wie zum Beispiel in der sogenannten Trommelsprache.

Beispiele zur Funktionsanalyse sind von mir schon mehrfach publiziert worden (v. a. Simon 1977 und 1978), so daß sich eine weitere Erörterung an dieser Stelle erübrigt. Die Funktionsanalyse gibt uns einen Wertmaßstab an die Hand, der uns den Weg zum transkulturellen Vergleich weit besser eröffnet, als die von Lomax multiregional postulierten Zusammenhänge von musikalischer und sozialer Struktur (Lomax 1962, 1968), was als gescheitert angesehen werden kann (vgl. u. a. Henry 1976 und Simon 1977). Die Zusammenhänge zwischen musikalischer Struktur und Funk-

40

tion sind jedoch so evident, daß im transkulturellen Vergleich unbedingt darauf geachtet werden muß, auf welcher funktionalen Ebene man sich befindet. Mit anderen Worten: in einer ethnischen Gemeinschaft finden sich in der Regel mehrere musikalische Strukturen mit unterschiedlichen funktionalen Bezügen, aber nur eine soziale Struktur.

8. *Die Textanalyse*, untersucht die musikalische Relevanz der Gesangstexte und deren semantischen Gehalt. Der Ethnomusikologe interessiert sich hierbei für die Frage, in welcher Weise die Sprache oder der Gesangstext die musikalische Gestaltung beeinflußt oder nicht beeinflußt, ob der Text der Musik untergeordnet ist oder umgekehrt. Die Frage, in welcher Weise sich die Sprache im Gesang von den alltäglichen Sprechgewohnheiten der Sprachgemeinschaft unterscheidet, gehört eigentlich in die Kompetenz des Linguisten. Sie läßt aber auch Rückschlüsse auf die Funktion des Gesangs und dessen Rolle innerhalb der Gemeinschaft zu. Die interdisziplinäre Zusammenarbeit von Ethnomusikologie und Linguistik läßt hier die besten Ergebnisse erwarten. Merriam (1964: 187–208) hat einige wichtige Aspekte der Textanalyse aufgezählt, so daß hierauf verwiesen werden kann. Die Textanalyse ist in erster Linie ein kulturspezifisches Problem, daß heißt in jeder Kultur hat ihre Relevanz für die musikologische Analyse eine andere Gewichtung.

9. Die *interdisziplinäre Analyse*, arbeitet problemorientiert in Zusammenarbeit mit anderen Disziplinen, wie vor allem der Kulturanthropologie, Sozialanthropologie, Ethnopsychologie, (Ethno)linguistik, Humanethologie, Ethnomedizin und der systematischen Musikwissenschaft. Methodische Einflüsse kamen in jüngerer Zeit vor allem von der Anthropologie (vgl. auch Blacking 1974) und Linguistik (vgl. Nettl 1958; Bright 1963), von Richtungen wie denen des Kulturrelativismus, des Strukturalismus und der Ethnotheorie (Ethnosience).

Unter problemorientierter Zusammenarbeit versteht man das Mitwirken verschiedener wissenschaftlicher Disziplinen an der Lösung der gleichen, vorgegebenen Problemstellung. So kann, zum Beispiel, ein Krankenheilungsritus von dem Anthropologen, Mediziner, Psychologen und Ethnomusikologen kooperativ untersucht werden. Ideal ist die Zusammenarbeit, wenn die Disziplinen hierbei die gleichen Methoden anwenden. Die Methode der „Ethnographie der Kommunikation" kann zum Beispiel vom Ethnomusikologen und Linguisten bei der Frage nach der Rolle von Gesängen innerhalb einer Gemeinschaft angewandt werden. Diese interdisziplinäre Analyse hat bereits bei der gemeinsamen Feldforschung zu beginnen. (Als Beispiel hierzu – die Publikation der Ergebnisse steht bevor – ist meine Zusammenarbeit mit dem Linguisten Volker Heeschen im Hochland von West-Irian zu nennen.)

10. *Naturwissenschaftliche und experimentelle Methoden*. Die in Wien bestehende Tradition der Vergleichenden Musikwissenschaft (vgl. Lach 1924; Graf 1974) hat sich, unter Bevorzugung naturwissenschaftlicher und systematisch-musikwissenschaftlicher Methoden, vor allem der Klangforschung gewidmet (vgl. Graf 1972). Für den Ethno-

41

musikologen bedeutend sind, von den grundlegenden Erkenntnissen abgesehen, die Ergebnisse vergleichender Studien über außereuropäische musikalische Phänomene, wie sie zum Beispiel in einer Arbeit von Födermayr (1971) vorgelegt wurden. So vermochten diese Arbeiten einen wesentlichen Beitrag zur Objektivierung von Untersuchungen, wie zum Beispiel der gesanglichen Stimmgebung zu leisten, die bislang fast immer nach dem Höreindruck beschrieben wurde.

Eine Erweiterung des hier angewandten analytischen Verfahrens besteht in der von Födermayr (1977 a, b) vorgestellten experimentellen Methode, bei der ein musikalisch akustisches Phänomen experimentell nachvollzogen wird und bestimmte Parameter kontrolliert verändert werden. Födermayr hat auf diese Weise bereits den sogenannten „Gesang zur sich drehenden Pfanne" aus Südosteuropa (1977 a) und das Prinzip der paarigen Stimmung im balinesischen Gender-Spiel (1977 b) untersucht.

> Eine Untersuchung solcher Musikformen bloß auf der Basis der herkömmlichen Parameter (musikalische Form, Melodie, Rhythmus, Zusammenklang) wird nicht den ganzen Tatbestand erfassen können; es bedarf vielmehr des Zugriffs der musikalischen Schallforschung (Graf bes. 1969, 1972), um diese Musikformen erschöpfend beschreiben und verstehen zu können. Hierbei kann man zwei Wege beschreiten, einen analytischen und einen experimentellen (Födermayr 1971, S. 63 f.; 1976). Der erste Weg besteht in der genauen Analyse der jeweiligen musikalischen Erscheinungsform unter Einbeziehung der Möglichkeiten musikalischer Schallforschung und ihrer Interpretation vor dem Hintergrund der Erkenntnisse der Disziplinen der musikalischen Grundlagenforschung (bes. Akustik, Gehörphysiologie und -psychologie, Musikpsychologie). In vielen Fällen können hierbei schon durch diese Vorgangsweise Hypothesen über die Natur solcher Musikformen gebildet werden, etwa auch im Falle des „tepsijanje", in welchem man auf Grund allgemeiner akustischer Kenntnisse auf einen Modulatoreffekt schließen wird, wie er ähnlich beim Vibraphon, der Orgel und elektronischen Musikinstrumenten (zu letzteren s. Douglas 1976, S. 83 ff.) verwendet wird. Um aber einerseits solche Hypothesen zu prüfen, anderseits das Spezifische der jeweiligen musikalischen Erscheinungsform zu erfassen, wird es notwendig sein, den analytischen Ansatz durch den experimentellen fortzuführen, in dem die aus der Analyse bzw. der jeweiligen Aufführungssituation gezogenen Parameter planmäßig abgewandelt werden (experimentelle Musikwissenschaft). Daß hierbei eine Vereinfachung und Reduzierung der vollen Wirklichkeit erfolgt, liegt im Wesen des Experiments und begünstigt die Erkennung der im gegenständlichen Fall wirksamen Grundtatsachen. (Födermayr 1977 a: 97 f.)

3.4. Legitimation, Nutzen und Aufgaben ethnomusikologischer Arbeit.

> I am speaking, of course, about the field worker's obligation to the people who are helping him. Is he to present himself as a buyer or as a student? Should he help people to preserve their music whether they wish to have this done or not? Should he share with them some of the fruits of his work? We do face ethical and moral issues, for we have incurred debts. To be sure, most of us in ethnomusicology do not make much money from the issuing of recordings or books about the music of folk, tribal, and Oriental cultures. Nevertheless, most of us are building careers that result from the willingness of our so-called informants to help us understand their music. Do we have the right to study the music of

42

a tribal group if this tribal group will soon itself produce ethnomusicologists who may do an altogether different but in some ways better job? Do we have the right to record music and information that the majority of a people in a culture do not want recorded, even though the musician who is working with us is quite willing, for a price, to divulge the material? Is our duty as preservers something that transcends our duty to the people with whom we are working? These questions have always been with us but they have only been recognized in recent years. (Nettl 1976: 24 f.)

Wir leben in einer Zeit schnellen technologischen Wandels mit zum Teil radikalen und rücksichtslosen Veränderungen. Eine sich bis in die letzten Winkel der Erde ausbreitende moderne Zivilisation, mit ihren oft grotesken und inhumanen Erscheinungen einer Ersatzkultur, zerstört nicht nur die kulturellen Werte der Betroffenen, sondern schreckt, in vielen belegten Fällen, auch nicht vor dem Ethnozid zurück. Noch bevor sich der als „Bewahrer" gegen den Strom der Entwicklung arbeitende Wissenschaftler die von Bruno Nettl oben stellvertretend für uns alle angeführten Fragen stellen kann, muß er oft genug erleben, zu spät gekommen zu sein und daß die traditionelle Kultur, die er studieren und dokumentieren wollte bereits auf unwiederbringliche Weise zerstört worden ist. Er wird dann versuchen, aus dem noch vorhandenen Torso, die ursprüngliche sonische Ordnung zu rekonstruieren und die Gesetzmäßigkeiten und Elemente des Kulturwandels zu ergründen. In einem grotesken Wettlauf mit der Zeit versucht er, schneller zu sein als jene Zivilisationsbringer, die als Techniker, Touristen, Soldaten, Verwaltungsbeamte und Händler eine technokratisch und bürokratisch gelenkte Welt repräsentieren. Das soll hier nun nicht ein Plädoyer für einen Kulturpurismus sein, der versucht, die Welt in ein lebendes Museum zu verwandeln und die Menschen in bestimmten Regionen unter Kulturschutz zu stellen. Es gehört jedoch zu den legitimen und vorrangigen Aufgaben zum Beispiel des Ethnologen und Ethnomusikologen, die noch existenten traditionellen Kulturen zu dokumentieren und die in jenen anzutreffenden menschlichen Verhaltensweisen zu analysieren. Er sollte hierin unbeirrt seinen Weg verfolgen, auch wenn ihm beim Anblick der in den Slums der Großstädte Asiens, Afrikas und Amerikas dahinvegetierenden und entwurzelten Menschen ernste Zweifel am Sinn seiner Arbeit kommen. Kommt hier der Wissenschaftler zu spät, um die Ergebnisse seiner Arbeit auch praktisch zur Anwendung zu bringen, so gibt es eine Vielzahl von Fällen, in denen er die Möglichkeit hat, zum Beispiel auf den Prozeß des Kulturwandels oder den Aufbau eines organisierten Schulunterrichts mit seinen Erkenntnissen direkt Einfluß zu nehmen und dazu beizutragen, daß nicht aus Ignoranz und Gedankenlosigkeit den Menschen alle ihre Kulturgüter und damit in letzter Konsequenz ihre menschliche Würde genommen werden.

Spätestens hier stellt sich die Frage nach dem Sinn, Zweck und Nutzen ethnomusikologischer Arbeit. Hierbei haben wir einmal darin zu unterscheiden, welchen Nutzen unsere Arbeit für die Gesellschaft hat, in der wir selber leben und zum anderen, welchen Nutzen sie für jene Menschen erbringt, deren Kultur wir studieren. Selbstverständlich stellt sich die gleiche Frage dem einheimischen Forscher in umgekehrter Relevanz.

Grundsätzlich, im übergeordneten Sinne, ist die Ethnomusikologie genauso legitimiert wie jede Humanwissenschaft, wie zum Beispiel die Geschichtswissenschaft, Ar-

43

chäologie, Philosophie und andere. Die Ethnomusikologie beschäftigt sich mit einer elementaren und universalen menschlichen Verhaltensweise, deren Erforschung schon deshalb von großer Bedeutung ist, weil sie tief im sozialen und psychischen Bereich verwurzelt ist. In diesem Zusammenhang interessiert uns die Frage nach den biologischen Konstanten und kulturspezifischen Varianten.

Die Ethnomusikologie ist ein Kind abendländischer Wissenschaftlichkeit und Fragestellung. Sie arbeitet in der Regel in Kulturen, in denen diese Fragestellung und Methoden unbekannt oder zumindest ungewöhnlich sind, das heißt, daß die Menschen bei denen der Forscher arbeitet, im allgemeinen nur ein geringes Verständnis für dessen Arbeit aufbringen. Ethnotheorie und Ethnopsychologie versuchen, diese Barrieren abzutragen. In jedem Fall wird von dem jeweiligen Forscher ein hohes Maß an Einfühlungsvermögen verlangt, damit es nicht nur zu einem einseitigen „Nehmen" sondern auch zum „Geben" kommt, zu einem Austausch von Erkenntnissen.

In den Industriegesellschaften besteht der praktische Nutzen der Ethnomusikologie darin, Vorurteile, Ignoranz, Arroganz gegenüber den Kulturen der Menschheit abbauen zu helfen und den geistigen Erkenntnishorizont zu erweitern. Daraus ergibt sich die Forderung an den Ethnomusikologen, seine wissenschaftlichen Ergebnisse auch in allgemeinverständlicher Form der Öffentlichkeit zu unterbreiten, wo immer dazu eine Möglichkeit besteht. Eines der wichtigsten Medien ist hierbei der Rundfunk. Auch die praktische Anwendung wissenschaftlicher Ergebnisse in der Musikpädagogik ist hier zu nennen.

Es sollte heute selbstverständlich sein, daß die ethnomusikologischen Erkenntnisse auch jenen Kulturen zugute kommen, aus denen sie stammen. Es gibt bereits genug Beispiele dafür, daß allein die intensive Untersuchung einer Musikkultur durch westliche Wissenschaftler in einer Art Rückkopplungseffekt eine Wiederbelebung oder Unterstützung der musikalischen Aktivitäten in den betreffenden Kulturen bewirkte. Die Anwesenheit kulturexterner Beobachter trägt nicht selten zur Aufwertung jener Aktivitäten bei, die untersucht werden. Oft genug jedoch verläßt der westliche Wissenschaftler die Kultur, in der er gearbeitet hat, ohne jemals wiederzukommen. Seine Ergebnisse werden in Publikationen oder auf Schallplatten veröffentlicht, die nur in den Industrieländern Verbreitung finden. Man fragt sich in diesem Fall zu Recht, welchen Nutzen diese Arbeit für jene Leute hatte, die die Ergebnisse nie erfahren werden. Daraus ergibt sich die Forderung, die wissenschaftlichen Ergebnisse und Kopien der Dokumentation auch jenen Ländern zur Verfügung zu stellen, aus denen diese Materialien stammen. Hiermit verbunden ist ebenso die Forderung nach einer Mithilfe beim Aufbau entsprechender Dokumentationszentren in diesen Ländern. Darüber hinaus kann der Nutzen ethnomusikologischer Arbeit vielfacher Art sein. Die Erkenntnisse können in den Schulunterricht einfließen oder den offiziellen Stellen Direktiven in die Hand geben, welche Aktivitäten in welcher Weise gefördert werden können. Das ist politisch relevant, wenn Staaten ihre kulturelle Identitätskrise zu überwinden versuchen, wie zum Beispiel in einigen Regionen Afrikas. Nicht selten mangelt es bei der Abfassung von Liederbüchern oder Rundfunkprogrammen an gutem Quellenmaterial oder gar wissenschaftlich gesicherten Kenntnissen. Hier Abhilfe zu schaffen gehört heute zu den vorrangigen Aufgaben einer angewandten Ethnomusikologie.

44

Eine andere Frage ist die nach der Rolle des einheimischen Forschers. Es gibt eine radikale Auffassung, daß nur derjenige in der Lage sei, die Musik einer Kultur richtig zu studieren, der selber Angehöriger dieser Kultur ist. Es mag unbestritten sein, daß diese Konstellation zu hervorragenden Ergebnissen führt. Die Praxis hat jedoch gezeigt, daß der externe Forscher gegenüber seinem einheimischen Kollegen in bestimmten Punkten im Vorteil sein kann. Er kann als neutraler Beobachter mit dem nötigen Abstand seine Untersuchungen beginnen, während der Einheimische als Teil der Gesellschaft, an deren Restriktionen, Vorschriften und Gebräuchen gebunden ist. Er hat zwar den Vorteil der uneingeschränkten sprachlichen Kommunikationsmöglichkeit, die jedoch schon einige Kilometer weiter nicht mehr vorhanden sein kann, das heißt die Vorteile des internen Forschers sind im allgemeinen auf ein relativ kleines Gebiet beschränkt. Das spricht nicht gegen die Forderung, soviel interne Forscher wie möglich auszubilden, damit diese in ihren Ländern arbeiten können. Die ideale und optimale Konstellation besteht jedoch in der Kooperation von externem und internem Forscher.

Es ist hier versucht worden, die aktuellen Probleme und Aufgaben der Ethnomusikologie zu umreißen. Manche der hier gestellten Forderungen werden bereits verwirklicht, andere warten auf ihre Realisierung, die oft daran scheitert, daß es zu wenig Ethnomusikologen gibt, die die im Vergleich zu den anderen musikwissenschaftlichen Disziplinen vorhandenen Mehrbelastungen auf sich nehmen wollen. Das Problem mangelnder Anerkennung besteht hierbei für den europäischen Forscher genauso, wie für dessen Kollegen in anderen Ländern.

> Der afrikanische Musikforscher, den ich erwähnte, hat kaum Unterstützung von offizieller Seite, um seine Aufgaben durchzuführen, und er sucht vergeblich nach begabten jungen Musikern, die bereit wären, einige Jahre ihres Lebens in Afrika die musikalische „Feldarbeit" zu leisten, die notwendig wäre, um möglichst viel Musik, Tänze, Dramen, Legenden aufzuzeichnen. Solche Mitarbeiter müßten mehrere Sprachen – auch afrikanische Dialekte – lernen, sehr geschickt in Aufnahmetechnik sein, ein ausgezeichnetes Ohr haben, eine ungewöhnlich gute körperliche Konstitution, um diese harte und wenig ruhmreiche Arbeit zu leisten.
> (Stockhausen 1975: 16/17)

LITERATURVERZEICHNIS

Abraham, Otto und Erich Moritz von Hornbostel: Vorschläge für die Transkription exotischer Melodien.
In: Sammelbände der Internationalen Musikgesellschaft 9 (1), 1909/'10, S. 1–25.
Adler, Guido: Umfang, Methode und Ziel der Musikwissenschaft.
In: Vierteljahrsschrift für Musikwissenschaft 1, 1885, S. 5–20.
Ames, David W.: A sociocultural view of Hausa musical activity.
In: d'Azevedo (ed.): The traditional artist in African societies, Bloomington 1973.

45

Apel, Willi: Comparative musicology. Exotic music.
  In: Harvard Dictionary of Music, Cambridge 1946.

Baumann, Max Peter: Musikfolklore und Musikfolklorismus. Winterthur 1976.

Bielawski, Ludwik: Formale Aspekte der Ordnungsmethoden bei Volksliedweisen.
  In: D. Stockmann/J. Steszewski (Hrsg.): Analyse und Klassifikation von Volksmelodien, Krakow 1973, S. 31–40.

Bingham, W. V.: Five years of progress in comparative musical science.
  In: Psychological Bulletin 11, 1914, S. 421–433.

Blacking, John: How musical is man? Seattle 1973.

Blacking, John: Ethnomusicology as a key subject in the social sciences.
  In: In memoriam Antonio Jorge Dias, III, Lisbon 1974, S. 71–93.

Blacking, John: The Ethnography of musical performance. (Background paper for the 12th IMS Conference, Berkeley 1977),
  (im Druck im Kongreßbericht über den 12. Kongreß der Internationalen Gesellschaft für Musikwissenschaft).

Bose, Fritz: Vergleichende Musikwissenschaft heute.
  In: Musica 3, 1949, S. 255–259.

Bose, Fritz: Musikalische Völkerkunde, Freiburg 1953.

Bose, Fritz: Tonale Strukturen in primitiver Musik.
  In: Jahrbuch für musikalische Volks- und Völkerkunde 7, 1973.

Brandl, Rudolf: Der Einfluß der Feldforschungstechniken auf die Auswertbarkeit musikethnologischer Quellen.
  In: Bulletin of the International Committee on Urgent Anthropological and Ethnological Research 15, 1973, S. 73–88.

Brandl, Rudolf: Karpathos – eine griechische Inselkultur im Umbruch.
  In: International Committee on Urgent Anthropological and Ethnological Research. Bulletin 17, 1975, S. 35–64.

Brandl, Rudolf: Musiksoziologische Aspekte der Volksmusikinstrumente auf Karpathos.
  In: Studia instrumentorum musicae popularis V, Stockholm 1977.

Brandl, Daniela u. Rudolf: Zur Kritik eurozentristischer Hörmodelle aus erkenntnisanthropologischer Sicht.
  In: Steszewski/Stockmann (Hrsg.): Modelle und Modellbildung in der ethnomusikologischen Forschung. Poznan (im Druck 1977).

Bright, William: Language and music: areas for cooperation.
  In: Ethnomusicology 7 (1), 1963.

Bukofzer, Manfred: Observations on the study of non-western music.
  In: P. Collaer (ed.): Les Colloques de Wégimont I, Bruxelles 1956.

Chase, Gilbert: A dialectical approach to music history.
  In: Ethnomusicology 2, 1958, S. 1–9.

Chase, Gilbert: American musicology and social sciences.
  In: B. S. Brook, Downes, van Solkema (Eds.): Perspectives in Musicology, New York 1972, S. 202–226.

Dauer, Alfons M.: Afrikanische Musik und völkerkundlicher Tonfilm. – Ein Beitrag zur Methodik der Transkription.
  In: Research Film Vol. 5 (5), 1966, S. 439–456.

Despres (Ed.), Leo A.: Ethnicity and resource competition in plural societies. The Hague/Paris 1975.

46

Dundes, Alan: Introduction to the study of folklore.
In: A. Dundes (ed.): The study of folklore. Englewood Cliffs, N. J. 1965.

Elbourne, R. P.: The question of definition.
In: Yearbook of the International Folk Music Council 7, 1975, S. 9–29.

Elscheková, Alica: Methods of classification of folktunes.
In: Journal of the International Folk Music Council 18, 1966, S. 56–76.
—: Ethnotheorie und Ethnographie des Sprechens. (Hrsg. Arbeitsgruppe Bielefelder Sozio-logen).
In: Alltagswissen, Interaktion und gesellschaftliche Wirklichkeit. Reinbek 1973.

Födermayr, Franz: Zur gesanglichen Stimmgebung in der außereuropäischen Musik.
Ein Beitrag zur Methodik der vergleichenden Musikwissenschaft, Wien 1971.

Födermayr, Franz und Werner A. Deutsch: Zur Akustik des „tepsijanje".
In: Neue ethnomusikologische Forschungen (Fs. Hoerburger). Laaber 1977 (a).

Födermayr, Franz: Zur Frage einer experimentellen Musikwissenschaft.
In: J. Steszewski/E. Stockmann (Hrsg.): Modelle und Modellbildung in der ethnomusiko-logischen Forschung, Poznan (1977 im Druck), (b).

Gilman, Benjamin: The science of exotic music.
In: Science 30, 1909, S. 532–535.

Glazer, Nathan/Moynihan, Daniel P. (Hrsg.): Ethnicity. Theory and experience. Cambridge 1975.

Graf, Walter: Das biologische Moment im Konzept der vergleichenden Musikwissenschaft.
In: Studia Musicologica Acad. Scient. Hungaricae 10 (1–2), 1968, S. 91–113.

Graf, Walter: Die musikalische Klangforschung. Karlsruhe 1969.

Graf, Walter: Musikalische Klangforschung.
In: Acta Musicologica 44 (1), 1972, S. 31–78.

Graf, Walter: Die vergleichende Musikwissenschaft in Österreich seit 1896.
In: Yearbook of the International Folk Music Council 6, 1974, S. 15–43.

Harrison, Frank: American musicology and the European tradition.
In: F. Harrison, M. Hood, C. Palisca (Eds.): Musicology. Englewood Cliffs, N. J., 1963.

Harwood, Dane L.: Universals in music: a perspective from Cognitive Psychology.
In: Ethnomusicology 20 (3), 1976, S. 521–533.

Haydon, Glen: Introduction to musicology. NewYork 1941.

Heinitz, Wilhelm: Strukturprobleme in primitiver Musik. Hamburg 1931.

Henry, Edward O.: The variety of music in a North Indian village: reassessing cantometrics.
In: Ethnomusicology 20 (1), 1976, S. 49–66.

Herskovits, Melville J.: Patterns of Negro music.
In: Transactions, Illinois State Academy of Sciences 34, 1941, S. 19–23.

Herskovits, Melville J.: Cultural relativism and cultural values. (1955).
In: Cultural relativism, hrsg. von Frances Herskovits, New York 1973.

Herzog, George: On primitive music.
In: American Anthropologist 34, 1932, S. 546 ff.

Herzog, George: Comparative musicology.
In: The Music Journal 4, 1946.

Hood, Mantle: Training and research methods in ethnomusicology.
In: Ethnomusicology Newsletter 11, 1957, S. 2–8.

47

Hood, Mantle: The challenge of "bi-musicality".
  In: Ethnomusicology 4 (2), 1960, S. 55–59.

Hood, Mantle: Music the unknown.
  In: Frank L. Harrison, Mantle Hood and Claude V. Palisca: Musicology. Englewood Cliffs 1963, S. 215–326.

Hood, Mantle: Ethnomusicology.
  In: W. Apel (ed.): Harvard dictionary of music. Cambridge ²/1969, S. 298–300.

Hood, Mantle: The Ethnomusicologist. New York 1971.

Hornbostel, Erich Moritz von: Die Probleme der Vergleichenden Musikwissenschaft.
  In: Zeitschrift der Internationalen Musikgesellschaft 7 (3), 1905, S. 85–97.

Hornbostel, E. M. von, und Carl Stumpf: Über die Bedeutung ethnologischer Untersuchungen für die Psychologie und Ästhetik der Tonkunst.
  In: Bericht über den 4. Kongreß für experimentelle Psychologie (IV), Innsbruck 1910, S. 256 ff.

Hornbostel, E. M. von, und Robert Lachmann: Asiatische Parallelen zur Berbermusik.
  In: Zeitschrift für Vergleichende Musikwissenschaft 1, 1933, S. 4 ff.

Howes, Frank: Anthropology and music.
  In: Man 45 (83), 1945, S. 107.

Howes, Frank: Man, mind and music. Studies in the philosophy of music and in the relations of the art to anthropology, psychology and sociology. London 1948.

Hymes, Dell: Toward ethnographies of communication.
  In: American Anthropologist, Special Publication, Vol. 66, 6 (2), 1964.

Jones, Arthur M.: Studies in African music. London 1959.

Kaden, Christian: Methoden der graphischen Modellierung sozialhistorischer Prozesse als Hilfsmittel bei der Erforschung instrumentaler Volksmusik.
  In: Studia instrumentorum musicae popularis IV, Stockholm 1976, S. 39–45.

Kaden, Christian: Elementare Methoden der mathematischen Modellierung musikalischer Kommunikationsprozesse in der Musikethnologie.
  In: Steszewski/Stockmann: Modelle und Modellbildung in der ethnomusikologischen Forschung. Poznan (im Druck 1977).

Kubik, Gerhard: Transcription of Mangwilo xylophone music from film strips.
  In: African Music 3 (4), 1965, S. 35–51.

Kubik, Gerhard: Transmission et transcription des éléments de musique instrumentale africaine.
  In: Bulletin of the International Committee on Urgent Anthropological and Ethnological Research 11, 1969, S. 47–61.

Kubik, Gerhard: Aufbau und Struktur der Amadinda-Musik von Buganda.
  In: Musik als Gestalt und Erlebnis (Festschrift Walter Graf), Wien 1970.

Kubik, Gerhard: Perzeption und kognitive Grundlagen der Musikgestaltung in Schwarzafrika.
  In: Musicologica Austriaca I, 1977, S. 35–90.

Kuckertz, Josef: Zur Niederschrift der Musik außereuropäischer Kulturen.
  In: Bericht über den Kongreß der Gesellschaft für Musikforschung München 1977. Tutzing (im Druck).

Kunst, Jaap: Musicologica. Amsterdam 1950.

Kunst, Jaap: Ethnomusicology. The Hague 1959.

48

Laade, Wolfgang: Anthropologie der Musik.
  In: Musica 28 (6), 1974, S. 529–530.

Laade, Wolfgang: Musikwissenschaft zwischen gestern und morgen. Berlin 1976.

Lach, Robert: Die vergleichende Musikwissenschaft, ihre Methoden und Probleme. Wien/ Leipzig 1924.

Lach, Robert: Die Musik der Natur- und orientalischen Kulturvölker.
  In: Guido Adler: Handbuch der Musikgeschichte, Kap. I, Frankfurt 1924.

Lachmann, Robert: Die Musik der außereuropäischen Natur- und Kulturvölker.
  In: Handbuch der Musikwissenschaft, hrsg. von E. Bücken, Wildpark-Potsdam 1929.

Lachmann, Robert: Musiksysteme und Musikauffassung.
  In: Zeitschrift für Vergleichende Musikwissenschaft 3, 1935, S. 1–23.

Laske, Otto: On psychomusicology.
  In: International review of the aesthetics and sociology of music (Zagreb) 6 (2), 1975, S. 269–281.

Lenoir, Raymond: La musique comme institution sociale.
  In: L'Anthropologie 43, 1933, S. 47 ff.

Lévi-Strauss, Claude: Strukturale Anthropologie (deutsch). Frankfurt a. M. 1967.

List, George: Ethnomusicology in higher education.
  In: Music Journal 20, 1962.

List, George: Ethnomusicology and the phonograph.
  In: Reinhard/List (Eds.): The demonstration collection of E. M. von Hornbostel and the Berlin Phonogramm-Archiv. New York 1963. (Beiheft zur Schallplatte Ethnic Folkways FE 4175.)

List, George: Discussion of K. P. Wachsmann's paper.
  In: Journal of the Folklore Institute 6, 1969, S. 192–199.

Lomax, Alan: Song Structure and Social Structure.
  In: Ethnology 1, 1962, S. 425–451.

Lomax, Alan: Folk Song Style and Culture. Washington 1968.

McLeod, Norma: Ethnomusicological research and anthropology.
  In: Annual Review of Anthropology 3, 1974, S. 99–115.

Merriam, Alan P.: Ethnomusicology: discussion and definition of the field.
  In: Ethnomusicology 4 (3), 1960, S. 107–114.

Merriam, Alan P.: The purposes of ethnomusicology, an anthropological view.
  In: Ethnomusicology 7 (3), 1963, S. 206–213.

Merriam, Alan P.: The Anthropology of music. Evanston 1964.

Merriam, Alan P.: Ethnomusicology revisited.
  In: Ethnomusicology 13, 1969, S. 213–229.

Merriam, Alan P.: Ethnomusicology today.
  In: Current Musicology 20, 1975, S. 50–66.

Merriam, Alan P.: Definitions of „Comparative Musicology" and „Ethnomusicology": an historical-theoretical perspective.
  In: Ethnomusicology 21 (2), 1977, S. 189–204.

Meyer, Leonhard B.: Universalism and relativism in the study of ethnic music.
  In: Ethnomusicology 4 (2), 1960, S. 49–54.

Mühlmann, Wilhelm E.: Rassen, Ethnien, Kulturen. Neuwied 1964.

Mühlmann, Wilhelm E.: Geschichte der Anthropologie. Frankfurt a. M. 1968.

49

Myers, Ch. S.: The ethnological study of music.
In: Anthropological essays presented to Edward Tylor, Oxford 1907.

Nettl, Bruno: Music in primitive culture. Cambridge 1956.

Nettl, Bruno: Historical aspects of ethnomusicology.
In: American Anthropologist 60, 1958, S. 518–532.

Nettl, Bruno: Some linguistic approaches to musical analysis.
In: Journal of the International Folk Music Council 10, 1958, S. 37–41.

Nettl, Bruno: An introduction to folk music in the United States. Detroit 1960.

Nettl, Bruno: Reference materials in ethnomusicology.
In: Detroit Studies in Music Bibliography 1, Detroit 1961.

Nettl, Bruno: Folk and traditional music of the western continents. Englewood Cliffs 1965.

Nettl, Bruno: Ethnomusicology today.
In: The World of Music 17 (4), 1975, S. 11–15.

Nettl, Bruno: The state of research in ethnomusicology and recent developments.
In: Current Musicology 20, 1975 (a), S. 67–78.

Nettl, Bruno: On method in the study of indigenous musics.
In: Musica indigena. Rom 1976.

Nketia, J. H. Kwabena: The role of the drummer in Akan society.
In: African music 1 (1), 1954, S. 34–43.

Nketia, J. H. Kwabena: African Music.
In: E. P. Skinner (ed.): Peoples and Cultures of Africa. New York 1973 (zuerst in AMSAC Newsletter 3, 1961).

Nketia, J. H. Kwabena: The problem of meaning in African music.
In: Ethnomusicology 6 (1), 1962, S. 1–7.

Oesch, Hans: Musik in nicht-integrierten Gesellschaften.
In: Schweizer Beiträge zur Musikwissenschaft 1, 1972, S. 9–22.

Pike, K. L.: Emic and etic standpoints for the description of behaviour.
In: Pike: Language in relation to a unified theory of the structure of human behaviour. (^{1}/1954 Glendale), The Hague ^{2}/1966.

Redfield, Robert: The folk society.
In: American Journal of Sociology 52 (4), 1947, und
in: Redfield: Human nature and the study of society. The papers of Robert Redfield 1. Chicago 1962.

Redfield, Robert: Peasant society and culture. (Chicago 1938).
In: Redfield: The little community and peasant society and culture. Chicago ^{8}/1969.

Reinecke, Hans-Peter: Zum Problem der Strukturanalyse akustisch fixierter Musikbeispiele.
In: Musik als Gestalt und Erlebnis (Fs. Walter Graf), Wien 1970, S. 153–157.

Reinhard, Kurt: Bedeutung, Wesen und Erforschungsmöglichkeiten primitiver Musik.
In: Sociologus N. F. 1951, S. 81–96.

Reinhard, Kurt: Einführung in die Musikethnologie. Wolfenbüttel 1968.

Reinhard, Kurt: Über Erfahrungen mit einem Tonhöhenschreiber.
In: Mitteilungen der Deutschen Gesellschaft für Musik des Orients 13, Berlin 1975, S. 56 bis 68.

Rhodes, Willard: Toward a definition of ethnomusicology.
In: American Anthropologist 58, 1956, S. 457–63.

Roberts, Helen H.: Form in primitive music. New York 1933.

50

Roberts, Helen H.: The viewpoint of comparative musicology.
In: Proceedings of the Music Teachers National Association for 1936; 1937, S. 233–238.

Rouget, Gilbert: Transcrire ou décrire? Chant soudanais et chant fuégien.
In: Echanges et communications (Mélanges offerts à Claude Lévi-Strauss ... réunis par J. Pouillon et P. Marando), Tome 1, The Hague/Paris 1970.

Sachs, Curt: The rise of music in the ancient world east and west. New York 1943.

Sachs, Curt: Vergleichende Musikwissenschaft. Heidelberg 1959.

Sachs, Curt: The wellsprings of music. The Hague 1962.

Schaeffner, André: Ethnologie musicale ou musicologie comparée?
In: Les Colloques de Wégimont I. Bruxelles 1956.

Schneider, Albrecht: Musikwissenschaft und Kulturkreislehre. Bonn-Bad Godesberg 1976.

Schneider, Marius: Ethnologische Musikforschung. In: Preuss: Lehrbuch der Völkerkunde. Stuttgart 1937, S. 125 ff.

Schneider, Marius: Über die Verbreitung afrikanischer Chorformen.
In: Zeitschrift für Ethnologie 69, 1937, S. 78–88.

Schneider, Marius: Das Phonogramm-Archiv des Museums für Völkerkunde.
In: Archiv für Vergleichende Phonetik 1, 1938, S. 41–47.

Schneider, Marius: Die musikalischen Beziehungen zwischen Urkulturen, Altpflanzern und Hirtenvölkern.
In: Zeitschrift für Ethnologie 70 (3–5), 1938, S. 287–306.

Schneider, Marius: Primitive music.
In: E. Wellesz (ed.): Ancient and Oriental Music. London 1957, S. 1–82.

Schneider, Marius: Die Musik der Naturvölker.
In: Adam und Trimborn (Hrsg.): Lehrbuch der Völkerkunde. Stuttgart 1958.

Schneider, Marius: Die Gattung in der Musik der Naturvölker.
In: Arlt (u. a. Hrsg.): Gattungen der Musik in Einzeldarstellungen. Bern/München 1975.

Schünemann, Georg: Über die Beziehungen der Vergleichenden Musikwissenschaft zur Musikgeschichte.
In: Archiv für Musikwissenschaft 2, 1919/1920, S. 175–194.

Seeger, Charles: Toward a unitary field theory for musicology.
In: Selected Reports in Ethnomusicology, 1970, S. 172–210.

Simmel, Georg: Psychologische und ethnologische Studien über Musik. Berlin 1882.

Simon, Artur: Ein Krankenheilungsritus der Digo aus musikethnologischer Sicht.
In: Probleme interdisziplinärer Afrikanistik (Hrsg. von der Vereinigung von Afrikanisten in Deutschland). Hamburg 1970, S. 107–125.

Simon, Artur: Studien zur ägyptischen Volksmusik (Teil I, II). Hamburg 1972.

Simon, Artur: Dahab – ein blinder Sänger Nubiens. Musik und Gesellschaft im Nordsudan.
In: Baessler-Archiv N. F. 23, 1975, (Festschrift f. Kurt Reinhard), S. 159–194.

Simon, Artur: Islamische und afrikanische Elemente in der Musik des Nordsudan am Beispiel des Dikr.
In: Hamburger Jahrbuch für Musikwissenschaft 1, Hamburg 1975, S. 249–278.

Simon, Artur: Zur Oboen-Trommelmusik in Ägypten.
In: Baumann/Brandl (Hrsg.): Neue ethnomusikologische Forschungen (Fs. Felix Hoerburger), Laaber 1977, S. 153–166.

Simon, Artur: Über einige ethnomusikologische Zusammenhänge von Typus, Funktion und Struktur.

51

In: Steszewski/Stockmann: Modelle und Modellbildung in der ethnomusikologischen Forschung. Poznan (1977, im Druck).

Simon, Artur: Types and functions of music in the eastern highlands of West-Irian (New Guinea).
In: Ethnomusicology (1978 im Druck).

Smith, Michael G.: The social functions and meaning of Hausa praise singing.
In: Africa 27, 1957, S. 26–44.

Stockhausen, Karlheinz: Weltmusik.
In: Eduard Pütz/H. W. Schmidt (Hrsg.): Musik international. Köln 1975, S. 13–22.

Stockmann, Doris: Das Problem der Transkription in der musikethnologischen Forschung.
In: Deutsches Jahrbuch für Volkskunde 12, 1966.

Stumpf, Carl: Anfänge der Musik. Leipzig 1911.

Sturtevant, W. C.: Studies in ethnoscience.
In: J. W. Berry/P. R. Dasen (Eds.): Culture and cognition. Readings in cross-cultural psychology. London 1974. (Zuerst in American Anthropologist Special Publication Vol. 66, 3 [2], 1964.)

—: Symposium on Transcription and Analysis: A Hukwe Song with Musical Bow. (Mit Beiträgen von N. M. England, R. Garfias, M. Kolinski, G. List, W. Rhodes und Ch. Seeger).
In: Ethnomusicology 8 (3), 1964, S. 223–277.

Tiersot, Julien: Notes d'ethnographie musicale. (La musique chez les peuples indigènes de l'Amérique du Nord).
In: Sammelbände d. Intern. Musikgesellschaft 11, 1909/'10, S. 141 ff.

Wallaschek, Richard: Primitive Music. London 1893.

Wallaschek, Richard: Musikalische Ergebnisse des Studiums der Ethnologie.
In: Globus 1895.

Wiora, Walter: Ergebnisse und Aufgaben vergleichender Musikforschung. Darmstadt 1975.

Zemp, Hugo: Musique Dan. La musique dans la pensée et la vie sociale d'une société africaine. Paris 1971.

52

Ethnic Music, the Urban Area, and Ethnomusicology

By Adelaida Reyes Schramm

" Ethnic" and "urban" are terms which, of late, have been claiming an increasing share of our attention. The first has long been ensconced in the language of ethnomusicology; the second until recently has been no more than a peripheral concern, and the two were hardly ever associated with each other. Now, the accretions that are altering the semantic load of "ethnic", the rising interest in the urban area and the increasing awareness, particularly in the social sciences, of the relations between urban and ethnic phenomena are strongly suggesting a re-examination of our perspectives with respect to these developments, both for methodological reasons and for the sake of communicating better among ourselves and across disciplinary lines.

"Ethnic" — Then and Now

In early ethnomusicological discourse, "ethnic" derived directly from the Greek *ethnos* (in the sense of cultural group), and it served to delineate a major focus of our discipline: the music of ethnic groups in its cultural setting (Rhodes 1956: 459). By this was evidently meant the music of all culture groups, an ideal study-object undercut by a more circumscribed view which championed instead folk and non-Western music (Kunst 1969) or the music of foreign cultures (Sachs 1959). This view deprived "ethnic" of its prior omnibus connotations. To the extent that ethnomusicology's subject matter had come to be seen as music of some specific culture groups rather than as that of all culture groups, the meaning of ethnic as it applied to these corpora was correspondingly delimited.

Anmerkung des Herausgebers: Die Verfasser der Aufsätze, der Buchbesprechungen und sonstigen Mitteilungen tragen allein die Verantwortung für die von ihnen vorgebrachten Auffassungen.

Editor's note: The responsibility for opinions expressed in the articles, book reviews, and other communications published herein rests entirely with the authors.

As long as this constraint was understood and accepted, terminological problems could, in theory if not in actuality, be contained. But with the old boundaries now giving way and with the varied and evolving connotations of "ethnic" now commingling quite arbitrarily in ethnomusicological literature, the term has become ambiguous almost to the point of vacuity. It has become necessary to ask: do we know what we mean when we use the term "ethnic"? Do we have a common frame of reference, a common point of departure, a common base that is essential to fruitful discussion? What are the methodological implications embedded in these issues? These are the broad questions that this paper intends to address.

The Urban Area — Some Historical Observations

One of the principal deterrents to the study of music in urban areas has been the long-held view of ethnomusicology's subject matter: "all tribal and folk music and every kind of non-Western art music" (Kunst 1969: 1). The stipulation, "non-Western", coupled with a strong concern for "the authentic", by which was meant "the old, the unchanging ... untouched by the modern world" (Nettl 1975: 18) has had a specially powerful effect, blocking out major portions of musics in contemporary urban environments. Methods, as they reflect the way the subject for study is perceived, have therefore been geared toward closed systems, relatively self-contained and culturally homogeneous units. Cultural relativism pervaded ethnomusicological work, and the end product of many studies were trait lists — sets of static features which served to characterize musical corpora from particular culture or music areas. Like anthropology until the middle of the 20th century, ethnomusicology treated the world "as if it consisted of some 2000 Tikopias" (van den Berghe 1973: 962).

From this vantage point, the urban area was virtually a non-entity; and when its existence was at all acknowledged, it was either as an alien environment, outside the pale of ethnomusicological work, or as an environment hostile and threatening to that body of music — folk and traditional — which had the primary claim on our attention and our devotion.

It seems paradoxical, therefore, to note that it was folk music (as it has been conventionally understood) which began to draw ethnomusicologists to urban ground. The presence of immigrant groups — in the minds of many, folk music bearers (Klymasz 1972; Nettl / Myers 1975 among others) — brought scholars in pursuit of folk music to cities. This development, however, amounted to little more than a change of locale.

The urban area, though new to ethnomusicologists and essentially different from their accustomed milieux, was nevertheless treated merely as an extension of the old closed systems.

It was not until the hegemony of folk and traditional music was effectively challenged, not until popular and Western musics of all kinds were actually admitted into the domain of proper ethnomusicological study that music in urban areas began to escape treatment as simply an unusual kind of rural music (Nettl 1975: 18). Popular music in particular, because it has been assumed, rightly or wrongly, to be an urban product[1], has drawn attention to the urban area as its socio-cultural context. Now, with immigrant groups being equated — again rightly or wrongly — with ethnic groups, "ethnic music" is also beginning to be sought after in cities, invariably the immigrants' first stop and frequently also their permanent home in the new environment. Before long, it is hoped, the urban area as locus of musical activity, shall itself be taken as a unit of ethnomusicological study in its own right.

The Urban Area and Ethnic Phenomena

The association of urban area with ethnic phenomena is readily understood. Through the various discussions and definitions of the urban area[2], through the many accompanying arguments and points of contention, one feature emerges as incontrovertible: contemporary urban populations are by nature culturally heterogeneous[3]. And because in modern times this heterogeneity is largely the consequence of migration[4], the single most important factor in urban growth, the linkage of ethnic populations to urban centers appears to be inevitable[5]. As more and more people migrate from more and more diverse places to join and interact with larger agglomerations of groups in increasingly complex urban structures, cultural diversity and the ethnic components of the population to which it is frequently attributed have gained saliency as urban concerns. The questions: what is an ethnic

---

[1] *Ridgeway* and *Roberts* (1976), for example, identify popular music as an "urban genre".

[2] Among the most notable are: *Gulick* 1973, *Park* 1925, *Southall* 1973 and *Wirth* 1938.

[3] *Southall* (1973 b: 83), who at first glance appears to dissent, actually objects not to heterogeneity per se but to a lack of specificity in its usage.

[4] Following the practice in much social science literature, migration will here subsume immigration.

[5] As early as 1938, *Wirth* reported that "the foreign-born and their children constitute nearly two-thirds of all the inhabitants of cities of one million and over. ... in the rural areas, they comprise only one-sixth of the total population" (1974: 41). The relationship of ethnic population and "the foreign-born and their children" will be dealt with presently.

1*

group?, what constitutes ethnicity? engage the minds of a growing number of scholars in the urban field. They are questions which the ethnomusicologist must confront when he touches upon what he calls ethnic music.

But as social scientists grapple with these issues, ethnomusicologists barely begin even to ask, much less investigate these fundamental questions. Is our apparent indifference justified? Can we continue to use the term "ethnic music" without reference to the human groups which vest that term with much if not all of its meaning?

This paper intends to explore these questions and their ramifications, first by reviewing the more recent work on ethnicity and ethnic groups, and second, by examining their relevance to ethnomusicological work. The paper's premise is an elementary one, needing no re-statement were it not for the fact that it seems to have been lost sight of in our involvement with "ethnic music": ethnomusicologically, the musical product is not truly isolable from its makers and users; no treatment of "ethnic music" can be ethnomusicologically sound if it ignores the human component.

The Ethnic Group

The ethnic group has been variously defined. R. A. Schermerhorn's definition provides a springboard for discussion. An ethnic group is

> "a collectivity within a larger society having real or putative common ancestry, memories of a shared historical past, and a cultural focus on one or more symbolic elements of their peoplehood. Examples of such symbolic elements are: kinship patterns, physical continuity ... religious affiliation, language ... or any combination of these. A necessary accompaniment is some consciousness of kind among members of the group". (1970: 12)

Two interrelated elements implicit in the above definition have stimulated some of the most provocative and productive discussions on ethnicity. These elements are: 1. diacritica: by what are ethnic groups marked, by what are they identified?; and 2. ascription: who identifies the ethnic group — its members, the outsiders, or both?

Diacritica. Schermerhorn's definition lists some of those kinds of markers by which ethnic groups might be recognized. The implications of the phrase, "cultural focus on one or more symbolic elements of their peoplehood", have, however, only recently been coming to light. Up until the first half of the 20th century, the overriding tendency has been toward culture traits (in the cultural relativistic sense) as ethnic group markers. This is perhaps a consequence of identifying ethnic groups minimally as "immigrants and their children"[6], bearers of a culture alien to that of the host society[7]. Hence, the prevalence in early studies, of ethnic group characterization in terms of pre-migration culture patterns.

Recent work on ethnic groups, however, has revealed two serious flaws in this approach. First, it fails to account for the persistence of ethnic groups despite changes in the cultural content or in culture forms and institutions — transformations which, on occasion, have made their objects hardly distinguishable from the forms and institutions of the host society (Glazer and Moynihan 1975; Barth 1969). Second, the static nature of trait lists ignores the dynamism of the home culture and thus minimizes the lists' diagnostic value. Du Toit's insights on the nature of the "sending community", i. e., the migrant's place of origin, and of the migrant himself have a special relevance:

> "Migration in any intensity is unlikely to occur in a small isolated community. The larger the community and the more varied its external contacts, the greater the diversity of choices. As choice increases so does cultural diversity and the likelihood of cultural marginality. ... persons who are marginal due to exposure, experiences and knowledge, or who are dissatisfied and frustrated with their condition will tend to migrate." (1975: 3)

Lists of pre-migration traits further ignore both the societal and ecological conditions in the new environment, as well as the dynamic processes generated therein by the ethnic group-host society interaction (Charsley 1974; Cohen 1974; Knutsson 1969). Thinking on ethnic groups has therefore changed substantially in the past decade:

1. Cultural forms and pre-migration cultural content in general are no longer deemed a strict necessity for the identification of ethnic groups (Barth 1969; Charsley 1974; Glazer and Moynihan 1975; Schildkrout 1974). Ethnicity is not a matter of "cultural differences on the level of form" (Blom 1969) but a matter of boundaries set up through the articulation of differences and the use of symbols *perceived to be cultural or assigned a cultural meaning* by members of the group and by outsiders.

This argument gains in potency with Horowitz's finding that when ethnic group boundaries change through amalgamation, i. e., through the union of two or more groups to form a larger unit which differs from any of the component parts, the new ·identity will tend to be

---

[6] This is the sole criterion used by the U. S. Census Bureau, for example.
[7] The importance of pre-migration culture to the formation and understanding of ethnic identity has been discussed in more recent literature by *Charsley* (1974), *Dahya* (1974), *du Toit* (1975), and *Greeley* and *McCready* (1975).

"a 'least common denominator' culture of the amalgam". The cultural identity markers will thus be a *consequence* rather than a pre-condition of ethnic group identification (1975: 124 - 125; see also Charsley 1974: 359 - 360).

2. Nor are forms, institutions and practices which appear to be carry-overs from pre-migration culture to be regarded merely as survivals or extensions of previous practice, for all too frequently, their functions change dramatically in the new environment[8]. An undue emphasis on the pre-migration cultural content of ethnicity therefore inhibits our understanding of ethnicity as process and of the important role that it plays in socio-cultural change (Cohen 1974: ix ff.).

The question thus arises: if overt cultural forms are not essential to ethnic identity, why the insistence on *cultural* diacritica, on the assignment of *cultural* meanings to symbols? Indeed some scholars have suggested a shift of emphasis from ethnic groups as culturally defined groups to ethnic groups as interest groups (Cohen 1974), as political groups (Parkin 1974) or even as sub-nations (Patterson 1975). But their arguments have been outweighed, for the present at least, by the fact of large-scale migrations in the modern world and by the cultural diacritica which these force upon our attention. More importantly, the interaction of groups identified according to these differences, absolute or ascribed — an interaction inevitable and highly observable in urban centers where most migrants congregate — has induced a view of the ethnic group no longer as an isolate, a more or less self-contained unit, but as a *social category* within a larger social system. As such, it has assumed a structural role with a potentially long-lasting impact on urban social organization.

The culture-based dichotomization that ethnic groups bring to bear upon society spotlights "the strategic efficacy of ethnicity as organizing principle" (Glazer and Moynihan 1975: 15 - 18), for the ethnic group as "culturally defined communal group" (Bell 1975), besides being "too pervasive to escape", possesses a potent combination of instrumental

---

[8] Data supporting this view have been reported for China by *Pye* (1975), for Indonesia by *Bruner* (1974), for Guyana and Jamaica by *Patterson* (1975), for Uganda by *Charsley* (1974) and for the Upper Volta and Ghana by *Schildkrout* (1974). *Charsley* notes, in a passage that could apply for the other case studies, that in the new environment, pre-migration institutions may become alternatives and options rather than mandatory.

... [these] alternatives and options provide the basis on which ethnic sub-systems develop, each subsystem contributing an element of 'plurality' to the form in which the total society emerges from large-scale immigration. ... [These subsystems are] not simply the prolongation of pre-migration customs and patterns but are the result of an interaction between these and the values and requirements of the receiving society (1974: 354 - 355).

and affective ties with a cohesive force unmatched even by that which binds the best organized units dependent upon either instrumental or affective ties alone (ibid.: 175). The potency of this combination manifests itself in the ethnic group's power to mobilize collective action.

The cultural aspect of ethnicity thus remains, but it is no longer embedded solely in static pre-migration traits. Rather, it resides equally and perhaps even more significantly in the ascriptive aspect of ethnic identification.

Ascription. Fredrik Barth, the most persuasive exponent of ascription as the primary diagnostic tool for ethnic identification, defines ethnic groups as "categories of ascription" (1969: 10) by which members distinguish themselves from and are recognized by non-members. He does not deny that cultural features may signal the boundaries of ethnic units, but by concentrating on ascription, he allows for the continuity of ethnic groups despite the transformation of these features and despite changes in cultural content. The critical factor, therefore, is the boundary as created by the dichotomization inherent in self- and other-definitions.

Barth, however, does not adress the problem of discrepancies that may arise between these sets of definitions[9]. This issue — and its complexity — is brought to our attention by discussions such as Mitchell's (1974) which focus on the confusion arising from the many levels of abstraction and categorization subsumed by ethnicity. (He also demonstrates how these levels and categories may be turned to methodological advantage.) But the problem of disjunct ascriptions are attacked more directly by Horowitz (1975).

"Ascriptive identity", he writes, "is heavily contextual. It embraces multiple levels or tiers and it changes with environment. ... Ascriptive identities are not equally significant if only because all contexts do not remain so" (1975: 118)[10]. But context alone will not determine which, out of one's repertory of identities, will become the "'center of gravity'" of one's identity. The problem becomes more acute when ethnic boundaries shift, when groups fuse or divide, for "self- and other-definitions do not necessarily adjust at the same rate. ... What often happens

---

[9] In the United States, for example membership in the Hispano ethnic group is assigned by the larger society to immigrants (and their children) from Latin American countries and from Iberia. Some segments of this population accept the Hispano designation; others reject it in favor of the more specific "Puerto Rican", "Cuban", etc.; still others, when racial features make it feasible, adopt the identification "Black". This is only one of innumerable examples where self- and other-definitions do not coincide.

[10] *Patterson's* comparative study of Chinese in Jamaica and in Guyana (1975) is particularly illustrative of this point.

therefore is that there is a lag in identifications" (Ibid.: 131) and hence, a disjunction in the sets of identifications.

The key to understanding this disjunction, or put in positive terms, the interplay of self- and other-definitions, lies in recognizing ethnicity as a set of dynamic processes generated by interactions: a) within the group, b) between groups of the same order, and c) between these groups and the larger society. It therefore becomes crucial to ask: "What are the *criteria* for likeness and unlikeness[11]? . . . What kinds of collective experience are likely to have an impact on judgments of identity in a new milieu?" (Horowitz 1975: 123). What, ultimately, shapes and alters group boundaries?

Horowitz refers us to social judgment theory and illustrates how focusing attention on "who the others are" (1975: 124), on the ways by which groups "sort out affinities and disparities" (p. 121), on perceptual judgments and their relation to behavior, can clarify the ascriptive aspect of ethnicity and the role it plays in establishing ethnic identity.

Ethnicity, Ethnic Groups and "Ethnic Music"

The foregoing abbreviated review of concepts now dominant in studies of ethnicity and ethnic groups underscores a number of points the significance of which we are either missing or dismissing in our work on "ethnic music":

1. While on the grossest level, cultural difference marks an ethnic group, not every group so marked is automatically ethnic. "Cultural differences between isolated societies, autonomous regions or independent stocks of population . . . are . . . not ethnic differences" (Cohen 1974: xi). The critical ingredient is interaction between culturally defined groups and a host society. Southall (1973, 1975) reinforces this point when he proposes the host-migrant relationship as the most useful framework for studying ethnicity. By making no specific reference to migrant groups (thus accomodating scholars like Glazer and Moynihan [1970] who maintain that foreign origin is not the only determinant of culture difference), Cohen potentially broadens the ethnic group category while supporting interaction between dominant and subordinate

---

[11] *Horowitz* emphasizes the importance of distinguishing between criteria and indicia. The former are bases for judgments of *collective* likeness and unlikeness which define identity. Indicia are surrogates of criteria which give evidence of *individuals'* identity. They are "probabilistic and subject to contradiction" (1975: 120). Though indicia and criteria may merge at some point, the logical sequence, theoretically, is that indicia follow criteria. Criteria, in turn, derive from group boundaries, the formation of which is the core of *Horowitz's* essay.

groups as a necessary condition for its identification: problems of ethnicity are problems of the interdependence of social units and of the "processes of socio-cultural change involved in this development" (1974: ix).

2. Pre-migration culture does not encapsulate the criteria for identifying an ethnic group; it is nothing more than a body of data. It may provide a point of reference or a base for comparison, but it does not constitute the characterization of an ethnic group nor does it, by itself, constitute an explanation. An exclusive dependence on pre-migration culture as matrix of ethnic group markers negates the importance of ascriptive processes in ethnic identification.

3. It follows from the above that migrants, while potential ethnic group members are not automatically so; that ethnic group boundaries are not immutable but shift — with or without change of personnel — in response to internal and external pressures; that ethnicity must therefore be seen as dynamic process.

The usefulness of the above points to the study of "ethnic music" may be assessed initially by looking at the consequences of ignoring them and subsequently by examining the results of applying them to the interpretation of field data.

Assessment I: Consequences of a disregard for social science data. Some of the consequences are evident in the terminological confusion which lumps together under the label "ethnic music" such disparate items as musics from an alien culture in its native environment (most often seen in record catalogs) and musics transplanted to and/or transformed in an alien environment. They are evident in the ambiguity that arises from the undifferentiated use of ethnic and folk music. The potential usefulness of ethnic music as a category is undermined not only by the failure to differentiate but more importantly by the failure to explore and specify bases for differentiation. The almost exclusive use of pre-migration culture as framework for ethnic group and ethnic music identification leads to assumptions of homogeneity and ignores the probability of group segmentation and segmental response. Native perceptions tend to be discounted through unilateral, i. e., the researcher's, ascription. But the consequence that is perhaps the most crippling methodologically and the most misleading is the perpetuation — explicitly or implicitly through the methods employed — of the notion that the enclave is the principal habitat of ethnic music[12]. Because this exemplifies most of the above weaknesses in our treatment of ethnic groups and their music, it will be discussed at some length.

[12] See, for example, *Nettl / Myers* 1976, particularly pp. 135 - 136.

The Enclave. The assumptions persist that: 1) the music of ethnic groups is conserved in territorially bounded units discontiguous to its native state but culturally part of it[13]; and 2) the music of ethnic groups includes only that music which has been transplanted from pre-migration culture, a music whose identity depends upon the faithfulness with which it reflects that of its culture of origin at a given point in time.

These assumptions promote a static view both of the ethnic group and of its music. Methodologically, it strongly suggests the closed system of the functionalists, the holistic approach effective for the study of self-contained units but dysfunctional for the study of complex societies. By ignoring the host environment as a necessary variable, by negating the fact that pressures generated by this environment can not only suppress but also revitalize and strengthen ethnic identity, the enclave notion also suggests that there is no essential difference in the methods needed for the study of a music in its native and in an alien context. What stands to be gained from this is self-evident. What stands to be lost depends on the fit — or lack of fit — between data and method.

There is abundant evidence that the notion of enclave is obsolescent for the study of ethnic groups particularly in urban centers where they proliferate. Mobility characterizes much of urban life. Places of residence, of work and of musical activity coincide less and less in cities. Population distribution is determined by a highly complex interplay of economic, social and governmental pressures.

Klymasz (1972) and Qureshi (1972) have noted the mobility and dispersal of ethnic populations in Canadian cities. Bruner (1974) observes the same phenomena among the Batak ethnic group in Bandung, Gallin and Gallin (1974) among one group of migrants in Taiwan. Gonzalez (1974) and Kemper (1974) detail the rigors imposed by these circumstances on field work: in a one-year period, Gonzalez managed to track down and study a total of 98 migrants from Trinidad in Santiago de los Caballeros (Dominican Republic), a small city of 125 000; Kemper traveled 9000 miles in sixteen months to study Tzintzuntzeños spread out in more than forty neighborhoods within Mexico City.

New York offers a striking example particularly through the work of Kantrowitz (1973) whose central thesis is precisely that residential segregation persists and declines only minimally in that city. This, he

[13] This derives from *Melamid's* definition of enclaves: "discontiguous territories of states which are located within the territory of other states. Seen from the state within which the outlier is located, it is an enclave; seen from the state to which the outlier belongs, it is an exclave" (1968: 60).

has been able to substantiate only by defining the metropolis "in terms of the modern city's separation of workplace and residence" (p. 53) and by selecting data that are directly quantifiable. Ethnic population is defined according to the U. S. Census Bureau's criterion (the foreign-born and their children); by residence is meant owner-occupied dwellings which in New York constitute only 23,93 % of all housing (Goodman 1974: 86). Thus, he has had to concede that "any one part of the metropolis contains only a segment of whatever population is being investigated" (p. 78), and that characteristic of New York is its complex "population mix" (p. 61).

This mix owes not only to "natural forces" (Kaiser 1976)[14] but to legislation which discourages residential segregation (e. g., the Civil Rights Act of 1968) or moves people forcibly for reasons such as urban renewal. Thus, there is the mix of naturally integrated communities such as Greenwich Village, Upper West Side in Manhattan; Brooklyn Heights, Park Slope, Cobble Hill and Boerum Hill in Brooklyn (Ibid.: 8)[15]; the mix of communities like East Harlem in Manhattan and Sunset Park in Brooklyn where upwardly mobile ethnic groups have been replaced by newcomers who then share the community with the old-timers who were either left or chose to stay behind; and the enforced mix of government-subsidized housing such as the projects.

If the mix is complex residentially, it is even more so in the domain of musical activity. Musics of particular ethnic groups may be concentrated in certain localities — Chinese music in Chinatown, Arabic music in the Atlantic Avenue section of Brooklyn — but these do not hold the totality of those particular musics in New York. Radio stations air programs of music from different ethnic groups. Broadway, which runs through the entire length of Manhattan, is virtually a catalog of musical types. Churches, from Buddhist to Roman Catholic adapt musical repertories not only to the ethnic identity of their congregation (if it has one) but to the varying musical needs of segments of ethnic groups. The Fountain area of Central Park is a meeting ground for multi-ethnic music-making groups and the people who dance and listen to their music are marked more by age than by ethnic group affiliation.

Clearly then, population concentration as a primary methodological consideration in the study of ethnic groups and their music in cities is

---

[14] I. e., those not generated by government intervention.
[15] The Chinese population, believed concentrated wholly in New York's Chinatown, have been responding to market and population pressures. Fifty-thousand Chinese-Americans, a number equal to Chinatown's population, now reside in Little Italy, SoHo and other boroughs, particularly Queens (*Ellis 1976: 1, 6*).

being effectively challenged by population dispersal and distribution. The enclave notion has become an untenable presupposition not only for New York but for urban centers in general, first, because too large a body of data challenges its validity, and second, because at best, it holds no promise for methodological advancement.

In the increasingly real situation where ethnic groups and their musical activity are neither spatially nor socially confined, the impact of population distribution is immediately felt in the logistics for field work and in problem formulation (Kemper 1974). Where the ethnic group is geographically dispersed, what shall determine the unit of study and how far into the total population of the ethnic group might generalizations apply? Context becomes an ever more important variable: at work, in the larger society or in what Eidheim (1969) calls the public sphere, ethnic markers may disappear, be subdued or become exaggerated. In the closed sphere, i. e., among members of the same ethnic group, at home or in the neighborhood, they may be reactivated or normalized (Hannerz 1974: 68; Suttles 1968: 105). The resultant musical products may depart partially or wholly from their original cultural forms; they are not less ethnic for that reason. In fact, the departures may signal that the processes of ethnicity are at work.

Assessment II: Field data and the use of social science concepts in their interpretation. Data for the following illustrations were drawn from field studies done in New York[16].

A. East Harlem is a section of New York City about a square mile in size with a population of approximately 136 000 the majority of which is Hispano[17] and Black American. Government regulations governing the allocation of public housing reflect population distribution in the community: roughly 50 % Hispano, 35 % Black American and 15 % "Other". The first two figures represent a fraction of the total Hispano and Black American population of New York which are approximately 1000 000 and 3300 000 respectively.

---

[16] Data for the first illustration (A) come from *Reyes Schramm* 1975; those for the second illustration (B) come from *Fujie* 1976.

[17] The Bureau of Census uses the term Puerto Rican, and to the extent that the residents respond to census questionnaires, this term is also self-ascriptive. The more broadly inclusive term, Hispano, is used here, however, because many non-Puerto Rican residents of East Harlem identify themselves as Puerto Rican when this will give them certain advantages of U. S. citizenship. Furthermore, many upwardly mobile Puerto Ricans prefer the label Hispano which is believed to be more prestigious (*Wakefield* 1959: 37; *Alers-Montalvo* 1951: 87, 89).

Both Hispanos and Black Americans are recognized as ethnic groups by the larger society and each, particularly with reference to the other in East Harlem, ascribe to themselves (collectively) either a Hispano or Black American identity.

In East Harlem, the Hispanos and Black Americans are dispersed residentially throughout the community so that in some neighborhoods the former predominate; in others, the latter do. No neighborhood is exclusively one or the other.

East Harlem has no music distinctively its own. Over the media, on streets, in churches, in public institutions and private homes, a wide range of musical types can be heard — from popular music to the music of spiritualist rituals — and the residents, particularly the younger ones, being free to move in and out of the community, have access to virtually every kind of music that New York has to offer.

One of the most observable musical phenomena in East Harlem is the conga drumming which becomes ubiquitous from the onset of warmer weather in the late spring to late fall. It is generally recognized as a Hispano activity by the community's population, and its distinguishing features, according to its Hispano practitioners, are the following: 1. the core of the activity, which can mushroom into a complex that includes singing, dancing, handclapping and the playing of other percussion instruments, is the interplay of a pair of drums, one providing a basic rhythmic pattern (*tumbao*) repeated an indeterminate number of times, and the other improvising around this pattern; 2. the meter is unequivocally and markedly duple; and 3. the two-drum minimal ensemble and the form it generates is complete unto itself, the constellation of accompanying activities being complementary but nonessential.

These norms are traceable to Afro-Latin American roots (see for example, Ayestarán 1967: 23 - 31; List 1967: 118; López-Cruz 1967: 48 - 51; Manzanares 1967: 128; Muñoz 1966: 86 - 88; Ortíz 1965: 276, 435), a fact which validates and reinforces the Hispano identification of the East Harlem congueros' practice despite deviations from what is considered traditional in their pre-migration culture[18]. Through these norms, the Hispanos differentiate their practice from that of the Black Americans in the community who, the Hispanos acknowledge, also play congas.

In the context of the larger society, however, well-known Hispano congueros such as Armando Peraza and Ray Barretto violate these norms. They play their drums as part of popular music ensembles thus denying the autonomy of the conga ensemble. They have no compunction about using triple meter, particularly when they must adapt to

---

[18] Some of the drums, for example, are now made of plexiglass instead of wood, their drumheads secured by metal lugs instead of wooden pegs. The prior ritual context of conga drumming has very much receded into the background.

the repertory of the large ensemble of which they may now be but a part. The two or three congas traditionally played by as many drummers are played by one. Only the tumbao-improvisation relationship remains and even this, on occasion, gives way when the improvisation is replaced by fixed arrangements. Yet East Harlem congueros not only ascribe to these well-known Hispano congueros and their product a Hispano identity but set them up as objects of pride and as models to be emulated.

Why the apparent change in ascriptive criteria? Why the persistence of the identification despite radical changes in overt cultural form? Neither question can be answered without reference to context.

Among the Hispanos of East Harlem and among the Hispano adherents of conga drumming in particular, conformity to the norms designated as markers of Hispano identity — norms which derive from pre-migration culture — asserts and reinforces Hispano identity. Because the identity of actors and musical products, both drawing from common roots, coincide, the strength and validity of their claim is accepted without question by the ethnic other of the community. The dichotomization thus set up is important in the context of East Harlem where the need for Hispano self-identification is proportionate to the Hispanos' desire to be distinguished from the Black Americans with whom they share the community (see, for example, Chenault 1938: 150 - 151; Rand 1958: 130).

In the context of the larger society, however, the need for this dichotomization is attenuated. Adaptation to the larger society and upward mobility within it is a goal professed by many Hispano congueros in East Harlem. It is a goal that supersedes the community-specific one: differentiation from the Black American segment of the population. If other Hispano congueros have achieved larger-society-directed goals by adapting the form of their musical product to other norms, then these changes are justified. The musical product is therefore assigned an instrumental function in the service of which its form becomes "negotiable"; but the ascription remains to reinforce the cultural affective ties which ensure ethnic group membership.

B. Linda Fujie's study of a group of Japanese Americans focuses on a Buddhist church in New York. Its congregation, though predominantly Japanese American, includes a small number of Japanese nationals and non-Japanese — white and black Americans, and Hispanos. Residentially, the members are dispersed throughout New York's five boroughs, New Jersey and Connecticut; the church in New York serves as a center for social and religious interaction.

One of the study's primary sources of data was the music and ritual of the religious services of which two are held regularly on Sundays and other holidays. One is a Japanese service (for the native Japanese and for the Issei, first generation Japanese Americans who came to the United States around the first quarter of this century), and the other is an English service (for the Nisei and Sansei — second and third generation Japanese Americans — and for the non-Japanese members of the congregation).

Both services differ considerably from Buddhist services in Japan[19] but predictably, the ritual and music of the Japanese service adhere more closely to Japanese practice; that of the English service shows the strong influence of Western Christianity. These facts, however, become noteworthy in view of a development currently taking place in the congregation. There is growing pressure from the Sansei, the most Americanized segment of the Japanese-American group, and the non-Japanese members to "eliminate all Christian influences from the English service ... and to reinstate Buddhist ritual to a form in which it is practised in Japan" (Fujie 1976: 44). This development represents shifts in the dichotomization process accompanied by changes in personnel and in overt cultural forms. It does not, however, entail alteration of group identity.

Within the framework of this congregation, the original Japanese Buddhist group were the Issei. Before the influx of the non-Japanese[20], the segment from which they were differentiated within the congregation were the Nisei and the Sansei, Japanese Americans whose cultural ties had become dual and who, linguistically, had become perhaps more comfortable with English than with Japanese. Hence, the differentiated services (the Japanese and the English) and the heterogeneous musical repertoire (with Buddhist and Christian elements) functioned to unite a generationally segmented group under the identity label Japanese Buddhist.

The addition of non-Japanese members to the congregation has served to highlight other factors in the dichotomization process. This segment of the congregation has come from a background of Western

---

[19] For instance, regular Sunday services are not held in Japanese Buddhist temples; those held are not as structured as their American counterpart; sermons are not part of the Japanese service.

[20] Five years ago, according to Professor Paula *Rubel* of Barnard's Department of Anthropology, one of her students who studied the same institution reported that there were no non-Japanese among the congregation (personal communication). At the time of Fujie's study, the American and Hispano membership added to the Nisei and the Sansei had grown to the point where they were beginning to exert considerable influence upon church matters.

religions, largely Christian. For them, a call for closer adherence to Japanese Buddhist practice represents not only a definition of self as Buddhist but a definition of the other as Christian. For the third-generation Japanese Americans, strong advocacy of the same movement reflects the "'principle of third generation interest' ... according to [which] the more assimilated third generation, sufficiently confident of their identity as Americans, gain an interest in their ancestors' non-American cultural background" (Fujie 1976: 49 - 50).

The movement toward de-Christianization and toward a renewed emphasis on Japanese Buddhist practice signals a shift toward a less heterogeneous repertory for the congregation. It is, however, evident that this lessened heterogeneity will serve needs no less diverse and a congregation no less segmentary than it has been to the present time. Seen from the perspective of ethnicity as process, both repertories — that which contains Buddhist and Christian elements, and that which shall be deliberately Japanese Buddhist — are amenable to analysis as one corpus, identifiable despite changes in form, function and users as Japanese Buddhist.

Neither of the above two studies had set out to deal with ethnicity or with "ethnic music". Both were intended to be ethnomusicological studies of musical activity in an urban environment. But the ethnic identity of the actors involved, an identity ascribed to them by themselves as well as by others, emerged as a significant datum. It was a clue to understanding the way ethnic group members identified music as theirs or not-theirs, in turn a clue to understanding their intra- and extra-group relations. Musical identities, disjunct on the level of form, became unifiable ascriptively through the response of in-group and out-group members to context. The heterogeneity of musical corpora became systemic and functional rather than aberrant. Ascription, dichotomization, cultural diacritica assumed important and complementary positions in analysis and explanation, providing insights into ethnicity as process and reaffirming at the same time the validity of the ethnomusicological premise that music, actors and their environment are truly intrinsically related.

Coda

In the humanities and the social sciences, the term that means the same thing to all users is a rarity. This truism is cited merely to evoke the conditions under which researchers must nevertheless define. "Ethnic", commonplace in the vernacular as well as in scholarly literature, has come to have a range of meanings that confounds more than it simplifies. We are therefore confronted with the possibility either of a multitude of definitions so disparate as to be mutually nullifying or of replacing the term with another that has relatively little or no prior semantic luggage.

This paper has proceeded on the assumption that the disadvantages of having to unburden "ethnic" of its previous connotations in order to bring it into line with current usage are offset by the advantages of retaining a term used by other disciplines with which we must communicate. Groups labeled ethnic are a social reality and, on the basis of data from the United States at least, they have come to constitute a structural category in urban social organization. It appears, therefore, that we may have to live with the term a while longer.

The major thrust of this discussion has thus been directed not toward another definition of "ethnic" but toward establishing a need for and proposing components of a common base for discussion, for description and explanation. These precede and in fact lead to effective definition.

But by whatever name they come to be called, groups that distinguish themselves from others within a larger society through the use of markers perceived to be cultural will persist. The urban area in particular, where the impact of large population movements are most immediately felt, where demography most clearly bears the imprint of cultural heterogeneity, will see to their perpetration. And the dynamics generated by the interaction of these groups, the processes by which they select, adopt, adapt and transform their music will be the most challenging and the most revealing of the ways in which music changes. It is this — the understanding of change as it results from specific types of human interaction within certain environments — that studies of ethnicity shall ultimately serve.

References Cited

Alers-Montalvo (1951): The Puerto Rican migrants of New York City, a study of anomie. Unpublished master's thesis (Sociology), Columbia University.

Ayestarán, Lauro (1967): El tamboril Afro-Uruguayo. In: G. List and J. Orrego-Salas, eds., Music in the Americas. The Hague: Mouton. pp. 23 - 37.

Barth, Fredrik (1969): Introduction. In: F. Barth, ed., Ethnic groups and boundaries. The social organization of culture difference. Boston: Little, Brown. pp. 9 - 38.

Bell, Daniel (1975): Ethnicity and social change. In: N. Glazer and D. Moynihan, eds., Ethnicity. Theory and Experience. Cambridge, Mass.: Harvard University Press. pp. 141 - 174.

Blom, Jan-Petter (1969): Ethnic and cultural differentiation. In: F. Barth, ed., Ethnic groups and boundaries. The social organization of cultural difference. Boston: Little, Brown. pp. 74 - 85.

Bruner, Edward M. (1974): The expression of ethnicity in Indonesia. In: Abner Cohen, ed., Urban Ethnicity. London and New York: Tavistock Publications. pp. 251 - 280.

Charsley, Simon Robert (1974): The formation of ethnic groups. In: Abner Cohen, ed., Urban ethnicity. London and New York: Tavistock Publications. pp. 337 - 368.

Chenault, Lawrence (1938): The Puerto Rican migrant in New York City. New York: Columbia University Press.

Cohen, Abner (1974): Introduction. In: A. Cohen, ed., Urban Ethnicity. London and New York: Tavistock Publications. pp. ix - xxiv.

Dahya, Badr (1974): The nature of Pakistani ethnicity in industrial cities in Britain. In: A. Cohen, ed., Urban Ethnicity. London and New York: Tavistock Publications. pp. 77 - 118.

Du Toit, Brian M. (1975): Introduction: migration and population mobility. In: B. du Toit and H. Safa, eds., Migration and urbanization. Models and adaptive strategies. The Hague and Paris: Mouton. pp. 1 - 15.

Eidheim, Harald (1969): When ethnic identity is a social stigma. In: F. Barth, ed., Ethnic groups and boundaries. The social organization of culture difference. Boston: Little, Brown. pp. 39 - 57.

Ellis, Junius (1976): Chinatown breaking out of the shell. In: The New York Times, section 8 (July 18). pp. 1 - 6.

Fujie, Linda (1976): Japanese Americans in New York. A case study. Unpublished master's thesis (Music). New York: Columbia University.

Gallin, Bernard and Rita *Schlesinger Gallin* (1974): The rural-to-urban migration of an anthropologist in Taiwan. In: G. Foster and R. V. Kemper, eds., Anthropologists in Cities. Boston: Little, Brown. pp. 223 - 248.

Glazer, Nathan and Daniel P. *Moynihan* (1970): Beyond the melting pot. The Negroes, Puerto Ricans, Jews, Italians and Irish of New York City, 2nd ed. Cambridge, Mass. and London: MIT Press.

Glazer, Nathan and Daniel P. *Moynihan*, eds. (1975): Ethnicity. Theory and experience. Cambridge, Mass.: Harvard University Press. pp. 1 - 26.

Gonzalez, Nancie (1974): The city of gentlemen: Santiago de los Caballeros. In: G. M. Foster and R. V. Kemper, eds., Anthropologists in cities. Boston: Little, Brown. pp. 19 - 40.

Goodman, Roy (1974): New York: Problems of the metropolis. In: Rosemary Righter, ed., The exploding cities. The Sunday Times (London) and the United Nations Population Conference held in Oxford, England, April 1 - 6, 1974. Transcript. pp. 71 - 88.

Gordon, Milton (1964): Assimilation in American life: the role of race, religion and national origins. New York: Oxford University Press.

Greeley, Andrew M. and William C. *McCready* (1975): The transmission of cultural heritages: the case of the Irish and Italians. In: Glazer and Moynihan, eds., Ethnicity. Theory and experience. Cambridge, Mass.: Harvard University Press. pp. 209 - 235.

Gulick, John (1973): Urban anthropology. In: John J. Honigmann, ed., Handbook of Social and Cultural anthropology. Chicago: Rand McNally. pp. 979 - 1029.

Hannerz, Ulf (1974): Ethnicity and opportunity in urban America. In: A. Cohen, ed., Urban ethnicity. London and New York: Tavistock Publications. pp. 37 - 76.

Horowitz, Donald (1975): Ethnic identity. In: Glazer and Moynihan, eds., Ethnicity. Theory and experience. Cambridge, Mass.: Harvard University Press. pp. 111 - 140.

Kaiser, Charles (1976): "Resegregation": the urban challenge. In: The New York Times, section 8 (April 25). pp. 1, 8.

Kantrowitz, Nathan (1973): Ethnic and racial segregation in the New York metropolis. Residential patterns among white ethnic groups, Blacks and Puerto Ricans. New York, Washington and London: Praeger.

Kemper, Robert V. (1974): Tzintzuntzeños in Mexico City: the anthropologist among peasant migrants. In: G. M. Foster and R. V. Kemper, eds., Anthropologists in cities. Boston: Little, Brown. pp. 63 - 91.

Klymasz, Robert B. (1972): "Sounds you never before heard": Ukrainian country music in Western Canada. Ethnomusicology 16 (3): 372 - 380.

Knutsson, Karl Eric (1969): Dichotomization and integration. In: F. Barth, ed., Ethnic groups and boundaries. The social organization of cultural difference. Boston: Little, Brown. pp. 86 - 100.

Kunst, Jaap (1969): Ethnomusicology, 3rd ed. The Hague: Martinus Nijhoff.

List, George (1967): The folk music of the Atlantic littoral of Colombia, an introduction. In: G. List and J. Orrego-Salas, eds., Music in the Americas. The Hague: Mouton. pp. 115 - 122.

López-Cruz, Francisco (1967): La música folklórica de Puerto Rico. Sharon, Conn.: Troutman Press.

Mitchell, J. Clyde (1974): Perceptions of ethnicity and ethnic behavior: an empirical exploration. In: A. Cohen, ed., Urban ethnicity. London and New York: Tavistock Publications. pp. 1 - 35.

Manzanares, Rafael (1967): Instrumentos musicales tradicionales de Honduras. In: G. List and J. Orrego-Salas, eds., Music in the Americas. The Hague: Mouton. pp. 123 - 128.

Melamid, Alexander (1968): Enclaves and exclaves. In: Encyclopedia of the Social Sciences, vol. V. New York: The Macmillan Co., and The Free Press. pp. 60 - 62.

Muñoz, María Luísa (1966): La música en Puerto Rico. Panorama histórico-cultural. Sharon, Conn.: Troutman Press.

Nettl, Bruno (1975): The state of research in orally transmitted music. Working papers of the XXIIIrd Conference of the International Folk Music council (No. 1). Regensburg: IFMC.

Nettl, Bruno and Helen *Myers* (1976): Folk music in the United States, 3rd rev. ed. Detroit: Wayne State University Press.

Ortíz, Fernando (1965): La africanía de la música folklórica de Cuba. La Habana, Cuba: Editoria Universitaria.

Park, Robert E. (1925): The city. Suggestions for the investigation of human behavior in the urban environment. In: R. E. Park, W. Burgess and R. McKenzie, eds., The City. Chicago and London: University of Chicago Press. pp. 1 - 46.

2*

Parkin, David (1974): Congregational and interpersonal ideologies in political ethnicity. In: A. Cohen, ed., Urban ethnicity. London and New York: Tavistock Publications. pp. 119 - 157.

Patterson, Orlando (1975): On the subnations of Western Europe. In: Glazer and Moynihan, eds., Ethnicity. Theory and experience. Cambridge, Mass.: Harvard University Press. pp. 177 - 208.

Pye, Lucian W. (1975): China: ethnic minorities and national security. In: Glazer and Moynihan, eds., Ethnicity. Theory and experience. Cambrige, Mass.: Harvard University Press. pp. 489 - 512.

Qureshi, Regula (1972): Ethnomusicological research among Canadian communities of Arab and East Indian origin. Ethnomusicology 16 (3): 381 - 396.

Rand, Christopher (1958): The Puerto Ricans. New York: Oxford University Press.

Reyes Schramm, Adelaida (1975): The role of music in the interaction of Black Americans and Hispanos in New York City's East Harlem. Unpublished Ph. D. dissertation (Music), Columbia University.

Rhodes, Willard (1956): Toward a definition of ethnomusicology. American Anthropologist 58 (3): 457 - 463.

Ridgeway, Cecilia L. and John M. *Roberts* (1976): Urban popular music and interaction: a semantic relationship. Ethnomusicology 20 (2): 233 - 251.

Sachs, Curt (1959): Vergleichende Musikwissenschaft. Musik der Fremdkulturen, 2nd. ed. Heidelberg: Quelle und Meyer.

Schermerhorn, R. A. (1970): Comparative ethnic relations. A framework for theory and research. New York: Random House.

Schildkrout, Enid (1974): Ethnicity and generational differences among urban immigrants in Ghana. In: A. Cohen, ed., Urban ethnicity. London and New York: Tavistock Publications. pp. 187 - 222.

Southall, Aidan (1973 a): Introduction. In: A. Southall, ed., Urban anthropology. Cross-cultural studies of urbanization. New York, London and Toronto: Oxford University Press. pp. 3 - 14.

— (1973 b): The density of role-relationships as a universal index of urbanization. In: A. Southall, ed., Urban anthropology. Cross-cultural studies of urbanization. New York, London and Toronto: Oxford University Press. pp. 71 - 106.

— (1975): Forms of ethnic linkage between town and country. In: du Toit and Safa, eds., Migration and urbanization. The Hague and Paris: Mouton. pp. 273 - 283.

Suttles, Gerald (1968): The social order of the slum. Ethnicity and territoriality in the inner city. Chicago and London: University of Chicago Press.

van den Berghe, Pierre L. (1973): Pluralism. In: John J. Honigmann, ed., Handbook of social and cultural anthropology. Chicago: Rand McNally. pp. 959 - 977.

Wakefield, Dan (1959): Island in the city: Puerto Ricans in New York. Boston: Houghton-Mifflin Co.

Wirth, Louis (1938): Urbanism as a way of life. Reprinted from American Journal of Sociology, vol. 44: 1 - 24. In: J. Friedl and N. Chrisman, eds., City Ways. A selective reader in urban anthropology (1974). New York: Thomas Y. Crowell. pp. 26 - 45.

Synopsis

Die Musik ethnischer Minoritäten im urbanen Milieu als Gegenstand musikethnologischer Forschung

Im Bezugsfeld der Begriffe „ethnisch" und „urban" liegen Problembereiche, welche — im Rahmen angemessener historischer und interdisziplinärer Perspektiven — der Musikethnologie wichtige Impulse zu systematischer Sichtung und zu Neuerungen auf methodischem Gebiet geben können. In diesem Sinne ist die Untersuchung durchgeführt, wobei drei grundlegende Thesen erörtert werden: (1) die ethnische Gruppe ist ein geeigneter Ausgangspunkt für die Untersuchung von „ethnischer Musik"; (2) die Identifikation ethnischer Gruppen erfolgt durch ihnen zuerkannte, bewußt abgrenzende Merkmale; (3) die musikethnologische Untersuchungseinheit ist dasjenige Repertoire, das von den Angehörigen einer betr. ethnischen Gruppe selbst als das ihre angesehen wird. Die Gültigkeit dieser Thesen wird durch eine Überprüfung des „Enklave"-Begriffs, vor allem gegen den Hintergrund von Daten aus New York, auf der Basis von zwei Fallstudien illustriert. Es wird gefolgert, daß mit Hilfe der in der vorliegenden Diskussion implizierten Methoden der Übergang zu Studien des sozialen Wandels überhaupt — als einem über ethnische Unterschiede hinausgehenden Thema — möglich ist.

ETHNOMUSICOLOGY: A DISCIPLINE DEFINED

George List

A quarter of a century ago Jaap Kunst, dissatisfied with the term "comparative musicology," invented the new term "ethno-musicology." In so doing he placed the prefix or combining term "ethno" in front of the word "musicology" to indicate that the study was of the music of the races of man (1950:7). However, his definition was restrictive in that the study of Western art and popular music was excluded. In a later redefinition of the term, he indicated that the study also included the sociological aspects of music (1959:1).

Since that time that field of study known as ethnomusicology has expanded so rapidly that it now encompasses almost any type of human activity that conceivably can be related in some manner to what may be termed music. The data and methods used are derived from many disciplines found in the arts, the humanities, the social sciences, and the physical sciences. The variety of philosophies, approaches, and methods utilized is enormous. It is impossible to encompass them all within one definition. In my opinion, ethnomusicology cannot be adequately defined as an inter-disciplinary activity. It is too diffuse, too amorphous. Ethnomusicology can only be defined when we consider what the ethnomusicologist is better equipped to accomplish than the anthropologist, the folklorist, the historian, the linguist, the so-called historical musicologist, the psychologist, or the sociologist. If we focus upon this, that activity which is uniquely ethnomusi-cological, we are then in a position to define ethnomusicology. However, in this process ethnomusicology becomes a discipline in its own right and, like other disciplines, has not only its own focus, its own subject matter or particular type of activity, but shows some limitations in its fields of interest.

How then would one define ethnomusic^logy as a discipline, a *Wissenschaft*, a *scientia* in its own right? It is the study of humanly produced patterns of sound, sound patterns that the members of the culture who produce them or the scholar who studies them conceive to be music. Since the definition includes the words "humanly produced," bird song lies without the province of ethnomusicology. Since the definition includes the term "patterns of sound" the written or printed score that forms the guide to a performance is not the focus of our discipline. In this we differ from the

)014-1836/79/2301-0001$0.12

1

so-called historical musicologist. He focuses upon the written or printed score, we focus upon the performance of music whether or not a written prescription for its performance exists.

All humanly produced music shares to some extent a particular characteristic: two performances of what is considered to be the same item always differ in some manner. This is as true of a performance of a Mozart symphony as it is of a song sung by the Vedda. Not only do we deal with diverse cultures located in differing geographic areas but we also study a human product that is always in flux: this leads us to the social sciences as well as the humanities for the tools of our research.

The study of concomitant activities is necessary to our full understanding of the style and structure of music. Thus we study the texts of the songs sung, the making and playing of musical instruments, the kinetic activities that occur simultaneously with the music. Of particular interest are the concepts held by the members of the culture concerning the music they produce. These non-musical activities are of course of interest in themselves but the ethnomusicologist studies them in order to gain a greater understanding of various aspects of music. For example, a knowledge of what aspects of music are important to those who make it assists us in transcribing this music. The musical concepts held by the informants, however, are not always consonant with those of the ethnomusicologist. An informant, for example, may believe that he performs two items at the same tempo. When the recordings of both performances are checked with a metronome or a watch it may be seen that considerable change in tempo has occurred. Custom and psychological factors are operative here. A study based entirely upon the concepts held by the members of the culture, the results of which are not compared with the more objective conclusions within the capability of the ethnomusicologist is not, according to the definition offered, ethnomusicology. It lies within the scope of another discipline—psychology or perhaps one of those omnivorous disciplines, anthropology or sociology, which profess that they encompass all studies dealing with man and his works. For a study to be ethnomusicological the scholar must transcribe the music by one means or another, analyze its style and its structure, and compare his results with the concepts concerning the music held by the members of the culture in question if such concepts are available.

Music can obviously be studied as a means of solving a nonmusical problem. For example, Clark Wissler in his book concerning the American Indian (1922:155) suggested that music is a very stable cultural trait and therefore provides a useful means for determining the diffusion of other cultural traits. Such studies are of course feasible but they lie outside ethnomusicology as a discipline. For the study to be ethnomusicological the reverse purpose would have to be served. Other cultural traits would be studied in order to arrive at conclusions concerning the diffusion of music. It is a matter of focus. Thus Alan P. Merriam's *The Anthropology of Music* (1964), as its name indicates, is an anthropological rather than an ethnomusicological work. It is concerned primarily with human behavior in making and reacting to music rather than in the musical product itself. Were the work ethnomusicological in character a reversed title would be required, *The Musicology of Anthropos,* the study of the music of man.

A detailed example may clarify this problem of focus. A number of years ago I published in *Ethnomusicology* an article concerning song melody and speech melody in central Thailand (1960). The article was recently republished in a collection of essays entitled *Intonation,* edited by a linguist (Bolinger 1972). Five tones are utilized in the dialect of central Thailand. The purpose of my study was to determine how the tones of the language affect the melody of song. In other words, I was utilizing linguistic data in order to arrive at a better understanding of the melodies of the songs. The editor of *Intonation* apparently believed that the linguist could derive from my study information concerning the modification tones undergo when sung rather than spoken. In other words, musical data would be used to arrive at a better understanding of linguistic phenomena. Possibly the article is useful for this purpose. However, what I would consider basic linguistic data is missing. I do not offer the texts of the songs in either Thai characters or in phonetic or phonemic symbols. I secured from my informants merely the tones they would have utilized if they had spoken the text of the song. However, without listening to the text of the song the informants could not have distinguished the tones as such. Thus, in my opinion, my study better serves an ethnomusicological than a linguistic purpose.

I am not arguing against interdisciplinary studies. Such studies have been carried on, are being carried on, and should be carried on. Insofar as they focus on the study of humanly produced sound patterns they can be described as partially ethnomusicological in character. No work can be said to be fully ethnomusicological, however, unless its primary focus is on such study.

This leads us to methods or lines of inquiry. Ethnomusicology shares with other disciplines certain underlying points of view or methods. These are the securing of an adequate sample of the material to be studied, care and accuracy in all operations and procedures performed, and objectivity. The latter, objectivity, requires that one approach the problem—whether it be fieldwork, transcription, analysis, or comparison—with an open mind. The scholar should not be limited by one methodology or by one theoretical framework. Rather, he should apply the approach that seems most efficacious in solving the particular problem. Should no useful procedures be available he must invent those needed. One method in common use is for the scholar himself to learn to perform the music of the culture being studied. This method was suggested by von Hornbostel in the early part of this century (Abraham and von Hornbostel 1909-10:15). It is a useful method as long as the performance itself does not become the goal. Then the activity becomes applied music rather than forming an aspect of ethnomusicological research.

Our field methods are those of the anthropologist, the folklorist, and the sociologist modified to meet our particular needs. New developments derived from physics—acoustics, electronics, optics—are probably more useful to us than to most other field workers. We take advantage of every new tool of this type.

Any approach, theoretical framework, or method can be utilized if it proves efficacious: models, paradigms, ethnoscience, cognitive process, semiotics. A knowledge of these is certainly useful in securing grants. All should be viewed with a critical eye, however, before any are applied to a particular problem. Does the emphasis lie so strongly upon process that the process is rarely completed? Are the results produced by such a lengthy process such that one could arrive at equally valid conclusions through the use of a traditional procedure in much less time? Does the model bring together two events that do occur simultaneously in time but that in reality have no significant relationship one to the other? One of course wishes to be *au courant* but one should be cautious in dealing with fashions that change from time to time. Nevertheless, any method or data derived from any discipline or source can be used if it is helpful in developing a better understanding of humanly produced sound patterns. This is the interdisciplinary character of ethnomusicology as a discipline.[1]

NOTES

1. This article is a revised version of a statement made at a colloquium, "Future Directions in Ethnomusicology," at Indiana University, November 28, 1977.

REFERENCES CITED

Abraham, Otto and Erich M. von Hornbostel
    1909- "Vorschläge für die Transkription exotischer Melodien," *Sammelbände der*
    1910   *Internationalen Musikgesellschaft* 11:1-25.

Bolinger, Dwight, ed.
    1972   *Intonation.* New York: Penguin.

Kunst, Jaap
    1950   *Musicologica.* Amsterdam: Uitgave van het Indisch Institut.
    1959   *Ethnomusicology.* The Hague: Nijhoff.

List, George
    1960   "Speech Melody and Song Melody in Central Thailand," *Ethnomusicology*
           5:16-32.

Merriam, Alan P.
    1964   *The Anthropology of Music.* Evanston: Northwestern Univ. Press.

Wissler, Clark
    1922   *The American Indian.* 2nd ed. New York: Oxford Univ. Press.

Mervyn McLean

PRESERVING WORLD MUSICS:
PERSPECTIVES FROM NEW ZEALAND AND OCEANIA

No one who has had much to do with ethnomusicology can fail to be impressed with the remarkable variety of the world's musics and the immense richness of the musical principles exemplified by them. From Virginia mountain 'blue grass' to Balinese 'ketchak'; from Alpine yodelling to the disjunct rhythmic organization of the Kwakiutl; from the extraordinary range of timbres of the Australian didjeridu to the polyphony of the Manus; from Africa to Asia and from Europe and the Americas to Oceania the list is endless. Such styles, however, are a dwindling resource, vulnerable to the impact of an ever-encroaching Western way of life. Concern is mounting that they may soon be extinguished altogether. Increasingly the view is being expressed that they are part of the common heritage of all mankind which it is the duty of everyone who cares about music to preserve. Perhaps the most outspoken advocate of this view is Alan Lomax. He represents our age as one of 'ruthless destruction of cultures' with 'thousands of . . . cultures on the fringe, dying of neglect, that need recognition'.[1] Beyond this he sees Western influence upon other music systems as not only destructive but homogenizing. He speaks despairingly of 'the cultural greyout'. 'Soon', he says, 'there will be nowhere to go and nothing worth staying home for'.[2] Lomax is a crusader and it could be that in some of his remarks he goes too far. In its essentials, however, I believe his judgement is sound.

   That profound changes are taking place in the world's musics is undoubted. The debate is whether such changes are cause for concern and whether anything can or should be done about them. Against Lomax's view it has been argued that there has always been change, that the products of change have had an unjustifiably bad press, and that there is in any case no merit in opposing them. As always there is some truth on both sides. In the present paper I shall be examining some of these issues and looking also at the issue of collective and individual responsibility.

* This paper was read at the 53rd ANZAAS Congress (Section 36: Musicology), the University of Western Australia, May 16–20, 1983.

23

Should Traditional Oceanic Musics be Preserved?

Let us agree to begin with that some musical styles are more vulnerable than others and that we are speaking of styles that are in some danger of extinction. Setting aside for the moment the question of whether preserving a music style is possible in any true or complete sense, let us look at reasons which are commonly advanced to justify the attempt. It would seem useful to distinguish 'outsider' and 'insider' points of view. The great diversity of world musics has obvious interest and utility for Western composers and educationists as well as for ethnomusicologists. The intimate role played by folksong in the European art music tradition is well known; present-day composers are beginning to turn to less familiar forms of ethnic music in a search for 'new modes of aesthetic perception'[3] and 'world music' is playing an increasingly important role in elementary and advanced education. I venture to think, however, that such uses of world music may be amongst the least important. There is more to ethnic music than exotic sounds for composers or a new and rich source of materials for music appreciation. Nor is this necessarily to elevate the role of the ethnomusicologist. In the professional sense he too is motivated by self-interest. But he does tend often to be drawn to the more vulnerable musics and some of these, including most of those of Oceania, turn out to be completely unstudied. My own advocacy for more work on the musics of Oceania has been strong. For more than a decade I have been urging Unesco and anyone who would listen to begin urgent and immediate study programmes to salvage the vanishing musics of the Pacific Basin. In a recent paper addressed to Unesco,[4] I documented the vast gaps that exist in our present knowledge of Oceanic musics, advocated 'in depth' research of selected areas of Oceania that would attempt to recover *all* data about music-making and, as a necessary first step, argued the merits of a 'territorial survey' to meet the most pressing needs for information-gathering and to pinpoint areas within which future research could best be concentrated.

The few professional studies to date in Oceania have concentrated largely upon traditional non-acculturated forms, drawing some criticism[5] that such an emphasis has 'distorted our image of the character of Oceanic music cultures' and that in pursuing historical survivals and ignoring lack of distinction by native musicians between traditional and acculturated forms, ethnomusicologists could be seen 'to be promoting a division and value judgement of their own making'. As one of the apparent offenders, let me use this as a springboard for reintroducing the topic of acculturative change and whether it is as villainous a process as it is sometimes represented to be. Change as such is not, of course, the enemy. Indeed, studying the process of change is one of the interests of ethnomusicologists. But it is untrue to state that because change is inevitable it is not a matter for concern. Elsewhere[6] I have pointed out that a distinction needs to be made between change from within (which, while often slow, is generally benign and is indeed inevitable) and acculturative change or change from without (which is avoidable in principle and, as Lomax rightly emphasizes, can be overwhelming). But, this aside, is it justifiable to heap calumny on the acculturated forms? First, let it be stated at once that acculturated forms are indeed worthy of study in their own right and that this is not

24

something which, to my knowledge, any Pacific ethnomusicologist has denied. Second, contrary to the statement earlier quoted, I think it needs to be said that many Pacific islanders are well aware of the distinction between acculturated and non-acculturated forms and may even be articulate about their reasons for preferring one to the other. Vanuatuans, for example, distinguish 'custom music' from non-indigenous styles. Maoris distinguish *waiata kori* or action-songs from non-acculturated traditional forms, and at the South Pacific Festival of the Arts in Rotorua in 1976 the Niuean people distinguished 'old' or traditional and 'new' or acculturated songs in separate programmes. Finally, it ought to be obvious that acculturated forms cannot effectively be studied without a knowledge of their antecedents. To find out what a music has become, and how it has become so, one must know what it was. For this reason, if no other, ethnomusicologists have been right to give priority to the study of the most vulnerable forms whether or not they are guilty of 'bias', 'ethnocentric idealism' or an offended 'image of what a music should be'.'

What then of the insider view? Not surprisingly there is no unanimity here either. Many Pacific islanders are convinced that 'custom' music should be forgotten as speedily as possible because it is 'heathen'. Students at the University of the South Pacific argued seriously with me ten years ago that their own indigenous music is inferior to Western and for this reason is not worthy of preservation. There is feeling also that there is no justification in preserving items from the past as 'museum pieces' cut off from a no longer relevant cultural context which has long been overtaken by adjustive responses to the modern world. Finally there is some sentiment on the part of Pacific island intellectuals that the only value of traditional materials is as a starting point for contemporary efforts at 'development' in the creative arts and as a basis for something new and better. The latter is a thoroughly Western view which is not shared by Oceanic peoples at large who have traditionally practised and perpetuated their own musics unencumbered by Western notions of art and aesthetics. To understand the nature of this music one must realize that it is tribal in origin and is communicated almost exclusively by oral means, without benefit of notation systems. It follows that once the continuity of the oral tradition has been broken, the music becomes irretrievably lost. Moreover, as traditionally practised, and in common with other tribal cultures, worldwide, this music was and, up to a point, still is woven into the very fabric of life in ways that are no longer or may never have been true of the Western world. Songs were and are named and conceptualized in use categories such as funeral songs, game songs, lullabies, love songs, magical songs, taunting songs, war songs, work songs and a host of others. Such songs were not some kind of overlay or extra, above and beyond daily living, but were 'part and parcel of controlling one's environment, getting work done, making love, or performing some basic duty like demonstrating respect for the dead'.' As such they have become imbued with a powerful symbolic significance which is often retained long after the institutions which gave them birth have changed. In a word they have become an agent of national or cultural 'identity'. The literature upon music and identity is large and the concept is of key importance in understanding Third and Fourth World attitudes to traditional musics. Amongst the New Zealand Maori, to quote only one example, music is explicitly recognized as a

25

component of *Maoritanga* (or Maoriness). The late Sir Apirana Ngata listed traditional chant songs and posture dances as secondary in importance only to the Maori language itself and the sayings of the ancestors. This said, it must also be stated that authenticity is not a requirement for purposes of identity. In Maoridom if a traditional *waiata* is unavailable to serve as a 'relish' to speech-making, acculturated action-songs are now an acceptable substitute. And at the last but one South Pacific Festival of the Arts in Rotorua, in 1976, representatives of the small island of Guam saw no incongruity in presenting a Chamorro version of 'How Much Is That Doggy in the Window?', complete with enthusiastic 'woof woofs'.

In looking at the indigenous forms, let us turn attention, then, to the music itself. Does it have any intrinsic merit or worth that would justify its retention? Judging it as a sound product, should it be preserved for artistic reasons? Not so very many years ago a favourable response to this question would have been hard to find. The missionary, travel and even professional literature on Oceania is full of ethnocentric judgements. The most frequent epithet, no matter what the place or culture, is 'monotonous', with 'dull', 'dismal' or 'doleful' coming a close second and 'strange', 'weird', or 'peculiar' perhaps third. On the other hand, native responses to European music were often at first just as unfavourable. Some individuals were frightened by it, others puzzled or astonished; some were indifferent to it, bored by it, or found it funny or amusing. I will not dwell upon the reasons for this. For those who are 'in the know' it is by now a truism that music is not an international language and it is well understood that the aesthetic norms of one form of music are not necessarily applicable to another. I do not propose to develop this point at any length. Aesthetics is a notoriously difficult subject and its literature is both huge and inconclusive. As in religion, economics and politics, its nature is such that verifiable conclusions seem largely impossible. For every theory there is a counter-theory and—somewhere in the literature—for every argument a counter-argument. In the face of such mammoth difficulties and confusion, the most prudent response is simply to run for cover. Nevertheless my topic does require some attention to the vexed problem of the nature of aesthetic response as it applies to tribal musics such as those of Oceania. Almost twenty years ago, Alan P. Merriam[9] suggested that the 'idea of the aesthetic' is almost uniquely a Western concept, inappropriate in dealing with musics outside the narrow ambit of Western art musics. This view has since been challenged and it has, indeed, become fashionable to talk about the 'aesthetics' of various folk and tribal musics, sometimes after first redefining the term to make it fit the case. In his recent book on Kaluli society, for example, Steven Feld[10] applies Robert Plant Armstrong's concept of the 'affecting presence' thus avoiding the use of words like 'art' and 'beauty' which Armstrong[11] claims to be themselves ethnocentric. Adrienne Kaeppler,[12] in a paper on the aesthetics of Tongan dance, likewise avoids the problem by redefinition, defining 'art' as cultural forms that result from creative processes and 'aesthetics' as ways of thinking about such forms. If this definition is accepted, *any* style of music or dance becomes 'art' (so long as it is creative) and *any* cognitive activity concerning it becomes 'aesthetics'. Most of the evidence which has been mustered in support of a 'folk aesthetic' concerns the undoubted presence of performing

26

standards and in some cases highly developed associated terminologies. In the West, however, we are accustomed to making a distinction between performing standards (which by definition apply to performance alone) and aesthetic standards over and beyond these (which are meant to be applied to the musical work itself). I believe this to be a useful distinction and one worth retaining. It is not inconsistent to admire, let us say, the Brahms G minor Piano Quartet as a sublime work of art while simultaneously deploring a particular performance of it. The value of the work itself shines through. Conversely, a virtuoso performance of an inferior work can arouse intense feelings of admiration which could well be the analogue of the *mafana* response (inward warmth or exhilaration) which Kaeppler[13] says is aimed at in performances of Tongan dance. In another of his publications, Merriam[14] observes that one of the special characteristics of music is that it 'seems to be carried subliminally; that is, the patterns of musical style are held in the mind and are not usually objectified in a technical vocabulary'. If this is true, standards of judgement concerning such patterns must also be carried subliminally and an aesthetic as such cannot emerge without a matching technical vocabulary. In the absence of such a vocabulary, if an aesthetic is to be found at all in tribal music, it must reside largely in the domain of the implicit or, in Roy Sieber's words,[15] an 'unvoiced aesthetic'. Attractive as this idea may be, however, I believe it takes us only part way towards an answer. In the last analysis, the concept of 'the aesthetic' as it applies to tribal music may simply be irrelevant. A few years ago I was asked to select a piece of Maori music for a cross-cultural register of 'master works'. I responded by nominating a classic *oriori* or lullaby of the Maori people called 'Pine pine te kura'. But it was a response I had some difficulty in justifying. I was by no means sure that one could think of individual pieces in the Maori repertoire as 'master works'. I never heard what became of the register but I have no doubt that other respondees had similar problems to my own. The concept of the 'master work' is taken virtually for granted in Western aesthetics but, by and large, has no place in tribal musics. I have already emphasized that tribal music—like folk music—is a product of oral tradition. It has undergone the transforming process of the transfer from mind to mind and in doing so has passed the test of community selection. In light of this, I think I can offer an advance on Merriam which is supportive of his stance while offering some comfort to his critics. Most persons who have considered the so-called problem of the tribal aesthetic have done so without regard for the special character of music in oral tradition. The nature of the oral transmission is such that a far greater proportion of the community participates in the artistic process and the *whole* of the end-product may be regarded as exemplifying the artistic standards of the community. Over the generations, such music has been shaped collectively. Our own art music is practised less by communities than by individuals, and the product of these individuals is not dependent upon the approval of the whole community for its survival. As a result, different standards may co-exist, in contrast with the tribal community which typically operates by consensus. In such circumstances it becomes simply inappropriate to talk of individual art works, and the critical apparatus of the Western aesthetic (which depends upon the comparison of individual art works) becomes superfluous. It may be suggested,

27

then, that in the case of most tribal musics it is the style which is the art work and *every* piece within the tradition is exemplary of it. In such circumstances distinctions cannot usefully be made. Every work has the same artistic worth because if it did not it would not and could not be in the repertoire. Thus the worth of the work can be assumed and individual distinctions—which are at the very heart of Western aesthetics—are of small consequence. If this conclusion is correct, it is unnecessary to feel defensive about the absence in most tribal cultures of a highly verbalized, elaborated 'art for art's sake' aesthetic. The aesthetic may be 'unvoiced' but the music is art none the less.

PROBLEMS OF PRESERVATION IN OCEANIA

In Oceania at large, especially in Melanesia, there are numerous societies which could reasonably be regarded as 'multicultural'. One need look no further, indeed, than Australia's closest neighbour, Papua New Guinea. Of the two large language families present there, the non-Austronesian languages alone are said to number 700–800[16] and are so distantly related that only recently has it been possible to classify them. Not every language represents a distinct culture and there are, indeed, cultural institutions such as the 'big man' complex, pig festivals, men's clubs and initiations which are both important musically and widespread in Papua New Guinea and adjacent areas of island Melanesia. But there is more than enough cultural diversity to justify the label of 'multicultural'. The main distinguishing feature of Papua New Guinea compared with most other multicultural societies in Oceania is that its numerous ethnic groups are nearly all indigenous to the country. A contrasting case is Fiji with European and Chinese minorities and a still large indigenous Fijian population now somewhat outnumbered by Indians who first came to Fiji as indentured labourers in 1879.[17] Closer to the popular idea of a 'multicultural' country is America's fiftieth state, Hawaii, with a strong Japanese and Filipino presence together with some 40% of people of Caucasian origin and a dwindling minority of indigenous Hawaiians now numbering less than 10%. Yet another type of multicultural society is that of New Zealand with its outright majority of Europeans, 12% Maoris, 3% Pacific islanders and only tiny minorities from other ethnic groups. In view of the great differences between multicultural societies in Oceania, I shall not attempt detailed comparison. Some common elements may, however, be isolated. The first is the immense impact upon music and dance of European culture as introduced by the early missionaries. Almost everywhere in Oceania native singing was condemned and discouraged as 'heathen' or 'objectionable' and dancing was forbidden as 'sinful'. In many cases the missionary attitude was understandable if mistaken or over-zealous by contemporary standards. One could go further and concede that by their own lights missionary actions were even justified and their perceptions of the dangers of music and dance accurate. In Polynesia, for example, singing and dancing was part and parcel of the religious practices which the missionaries had dedicated themselves to stamp out. Destruction of the one was a logical if ruthless step towards the destruction of the other in the interests of bringing the heathen to Christ. Ribaldry is a culturally accepted and well-established component of much Oceanic humour and inevitably

28

found its way into song and dance, explaining missionary accusations of 'indecency', 'licentiousness' and 'obscenity'. In some cultures singing and dancing indeed led to culturally sanctioned relaxation of normal moral restraints, as in Samoa where an integral part of the *poula*, or 'night dance', was naked dancing which terminated the evening's entertainment and is reported usually to have resulted in a general orgy.[18] Finally, explicit sexuality and intentional eroticism was characteristic of some genres of song and dance in much of Micronesia and eastern Polynesia. An example from the Marquesas Islands is the class of erotic funeral songs called *uta* whose purpose it was to arouse the sexual energy of the ancestors who were believed to be mediums of fertility for the people and their food.[19] Another is the *hamath* dance of Ulithi which is a device for social criticism, performed publicly as a means of humiliating the person named in the accompanying song. If a woman is being attacked 'she may be accused of having an odd-sized sex organ or a large rectum'. Sexual indignities claimed to have been performed on her are described and she may be accused of masturbation or fellatio.[20] It is easy to see why a missionary might be upset by such a performance and might fail to be swayed in his attitude by its social significance.

Perhaps the most far-reaching effect upon music of missionary activities in Oceania has been the introduction of European hymn-singing. In places such as Tonga, which are known to have had a pre-European polyphonic tradition, the European idiom was readily incorporated into the native system. By contrast, in New Zealand and Hawaii, where harmony was unknown, native singers at first had difficulty with hymn-singing and missionaries despaired of ever teaching them.[21, 22] Maoris and Hawaiians soon, however, became bimusical, and for a while there was an interregnum during which the two music systems were practised equally side by side. But inevitably the European system came to dominate and eventually to displace the native forms. As late as 1938 when missionaries first came to the Polynesian outliers Bellona and Rennell[23] and more recently still in places like Papua New Guinea, missionaries and their converts have continued to ban traditional singing and dancing and have sought successfully to replace them with European hymn-singing.

Hardly less influential than the missionaries was the impact of colonialism. By the end of the nineteenth century almost every island group was in the possession of a colonial power and most had a long history of contact preceding formal annexation. In the main, those which have been in contact with Europeans the longest have fared the worst in their retention of song and dance tradition. In Papua New Guinea, unacculturated styles can still be found in areas which did not see a white man until the late 1930s. Part of Micronesia, on the other hand, was discovered by the Spanish as long ago as 1521. As a result, on the Micronesian island of Guam, where Spanish Jesuit missionaries set the scene for the rest of Oceania by suppressing most of the indigenous ceremonies, the only folksong style surviving today, the *chamorita*, is Spanish rather than Micronesian. Fortunately for Pacific music, few areas are as badly off as Guam. One reason for this is that many of the local languages are still alive and flourishing and, in places such as the Cook Islands, remain the language of instruction in primary schools. Language competence obviously has a vital role to play in the survival of a vocal music if it is

29

to remain a living tradition. Survival of the language, in turn, bears a direct relationship to the proportion of speakers in the population at large and to the status of the language as an everyday medium of communication. Ultimately the simplest measure of language decline, and with it music decline, may be the ratio of the minority population to the dominant one be it colonial or any other. The situation in New Zealand is an excellent case in point. New Zealand's population is predominantly European and mainly of British stock. Large-scale settlement was begun by the New Zealand Company which aimed to create in New Zealand a microcosm of British society. The first New Zealand Company settlers came mostly from the southern counties of England. Otago, in the South Island of New Zealand, was settled by Scots and remained largely Scottish until the goldrush days from 1861 onwards brought an influx of other nationalities. The Scottish presence in New Zealand is attested by numerous pipe bands and by Caledonian societies which periodically hold Highland games and sports.[24] Subsequent New Zealand settlers were carefully chosen for cultural compatibility and most soon became integrated. The largest increment to the nineteenth century population was provided by Germans and Scandinavians. By 1878 more than four-and-a-half thousand of each had settled in New Zealand but are described as now 'submerged and assimilated' or 'absorbed into the British stock'.[25] A musical survival exists at the small settlement of Puhoi north of Auckland where a German-speaking Bohemian group settled in the 1860s. Today, at the local old-time dances, music may be heard from 'folk' instruments such as accordion and dudelsack playing waltzes and other dance music popular in Bohemia more than 120 years ago. Some cultural survivals also occur amongst New Zealand's Yugoslavs, many of whom arrived from Dalmatia in the 1880s.[26] Large numbers found work in the gumfields of North Auckland where some intermarried into Maori families and where 'Bullocky' songs with texts that are a mixture of Maori and Dalmatian are still remembered. Today there are said to be 40,000 people of Yugoslav descent in New Zealand. Nearly half live in Auckland where each year in January, at a giant picnic held at Long Bay, cultural ties are renewed and Yugoslav music and dancing are traditionally performed.[27] In post-Second World War years the largest group of European nationals to migrate to New Zealand has been the Dutch. Now numbering about 45,000, of whom 30,000 live in Auckland, the Dutch have a reputation of being amongst the most completely integrated of New Zealand's immigrants.[28] Polynesians and Maoris excepted, extra-European people are few indeed in New Zealand. The most numerous are New Zealand Chinese, of whom there are 15,000, and Indians who number 10,000.[29] A striking proportion of all ethnic minorities, including Maoris and Polynesians, live in the largest urban centres. Auckland, Hamilton and Wellington claim the most Maoris; the inland timber town of Tokoroa and especially Auckland have large concentrations of Cook Islanders; Wellington has the greatest number of Tokelauans. The most cosmopolitan city, however, is Auckland. Although some 35% of all New Zealanders now live in greater Auckland, this proportion is exceeded for a number of ethnic minorities. Auckland is the home of about 40% of New Zealand's Yugoslavs, 46% of its Hungarians, 60% of the Chinese, 67% of the Dutch and no less than 80% of the Indians.[30] As a result of the last concentra-

30

tion, a visiting sitar player to Auckland can draw an Indian audience of 200–300. Amongst clubs and societies representing such minority groups are an Indian Association, a Welsh Society, a Yugoslav Society, a Chinese Community Centre, a Scandinavian Club and numerous others. The greatest contribution by far to Auckland's multiracial image, however, is provided by its Maoris and Polynesians. A frequently heard but never contradicted claim is that Auckland is 'the largest Polynesian city in the world'. In South Auckland and in the Western suburb of Te Atatu flourishing urban *maraes* have been established to service the large Maori population, while the inner suburb of Ponsonby is the home of most of Auckland's Polynesians, despite a recent upward trend in urban renewal which has displaced many of them. Niueans, Samoans, Tongans, and Tokelauans as well as Cook Islanders from Raro-tonga, Aitutaki, Pukapuka and elsewhere all have their own community organizations and an active social calendar of events in which music and dance play a prominent role. Pukapukans in Auckland, for example, number about 900. Combined churches hymn-singing competitions are held on Christmas Eve; dancing and singing takes place at annual church conferences; singing occurs at funerals and at memorial services for those who have died on the home island of Pukapuka; and during Christmas and New Year, sports tournaments and annual festivals of music and dance are organized at which singers are seated in a triangular spatial orientation representing the three villages of Ngake, Loto and Yato on the home island of Pukapuka.[11] The music at these events is newly composed following the stylistic models of older songs still remembered from Pukapuka. By contrast, the *waiata* singing which traditionally takes place at Maori tribal meetings, whether in rural settings or urban *maraes*, is a moribund tradition. New songs are seldom composed and those remaining are regarded as *taonga* or treasures from the past like heirlooms to be preserved and passed on scrupulously from one generation to the next. The repertoire is static and diminishing and there are supernatural restraints upon change. In this respect Maori music differs dramatically from Cook Island singing traditions which are still in full flower with an expanding repertoire and a non-conservative attitude towards change on the part of the performers.

The key to reconciling the foregoing is that every minority culture in New Zealand has the common problem of how to preserve its integrity in the face of the fully integrated European majority. There has been little interaction of immigrant groups each with the other. In their music all alike are dominated by the majority culture and by the majority's preference in music. From nursery songs through singing commercials, the 'top twenty' and Muzak, the New Zealand music-scape is uncompromisingly Western and overwhelmingly 'pop' orientated. It is already impossible to drink in a bar, eat in a restaurant, put petrol in one's car, fly in an aeroplane, have a tooth extracted or to visit a supermarket or department store without being assailed by someone else's choice of music: the blight has even spread to bookshops. In this respect New Zealand is the same as most other countries in the Western world. In practical terms, then, for each and every one of the minority cultures, including Maori, it is more accurate to think in terms of the bicultural than the multicultural. The differences between Maori and Pukapukan adjustive responses are readily

31

explainable. From 1840 onwards Maori culture has been under threat as a result of successive Government policies first of 'assimilation' and from 1961 onwards of 'integration'. Only recently have these policies been relaxed to permit the teaching of Maori in schools and the setting up of community programmes aimed at reinforcing Maori cultural values. Late last century the Maori was even thought to be a 'dying race'. Pukapukans by contrast are recent arrivals whose culture until now has been nurtured in a relatively isolated atoll environment 1150 kilometres distant even from the Cook Islands administrative centre of Rarotonga. English is no more than a second language and cultural and community bonds are tight. Nevertheless the need to preserve traditional cultural forms is recognized and 'has become a conscious issue in the minds of many [Auckland] Pukapukans'.[32] It can be confidently predicted that they too will eventually succumb to the same cultural pressures which for so long have beset the Maoris.

CAN TRADITIONAL OCEANIC MUSICS BE PRESERVED?

In a previous paper[33] I have discussed such means of conservation as workshops and song and dance schools; the provision of aids such as recordings, edited song texts and music transcriptions to supplement traditional methods of instruction; and the encouragement of performance by means of cultural competitions and festivals or by the establishment of professional song and dance companies. I have pointed out that although all of these methods have been tried in Oceania, all have their drawbacks. Competitions, festivals and—especially—professional companies are agents of rapid change both because of the need to achieve popular appeal and because of the interchange of traits that inevitably takes place when disparate groups get together. Workshops and special 'schools' are unable to achieve their aims unless the participants are already largely familiar with the styles they are trying to learn. Elsewhere[34] [35] I have documented and explained the unwitting transformations which occur in Maori songs when attempts are made to learn them without the checks and balances of the traditional learning context. Earlier in the present paper I explained that in most Oceanic cultures music genres occur in named use categories and as such are occasion bound. When there is no longer a reason for singing a song or when the social institution served by the song changes or is no longer extant, the song will eventually be lost unless some other reason is found to sing it. Loss of function is probably the most important continuing single reason for the disappearance of Maori songs[36] and there is no reason to suppose that the situation is any different for the rest of Oceania. It follows that 'Performing arts which are in danger of being lost can be successfully stimulated only by restoring to them their former function . . . or by providing them with a new function'.[37] But turning the clock back may be impossible or undesirable. The most ardent advocate would not wish to see the Maori *pioi* or 'head-brandishing song' restored to its former context. And, as I have stated, substitutes such as festivals and competitions are of doubtful worth and may even stimulate changes of the very kind they are seeking to prevent. Does this, then, invalidate efforts, few as they are, to perpetuate the traditional musics of

32

Oceania? Is near enough good enough? Is it worth trying at all? I shall try to answer these questions by turning once again to New Zealand.

Last year, when I first began thinking about this paper, I realized I would be delivering it on the 25th anniversary of the very month I began field work amongst the Maori people of New Zealand. Between May and July 1958 I recorded my first eighty-seven songs from singers of Tuuhoe, Ngaati Manawa, Tuuwharetoa, Te Arawa, Ngaaiterangi and other tribes living within a range of 90 km of Rotorua in the Bay of Plenty area. Some of the singers were as young as their early fifties, others were in their seventies, eighties or even nineties. They recorded for me despite a widespread belief that singers would die if they sang their songs to anyone other than members of their own tribe. Some individuals may well have feared, then, that by recording they were literally risking their lives. Why did they do so? Why indeed should they have taken any risk at all? In these days of rapid technical advancement, when any Western teenager or any Third World village is likely to possess a cassette recorder, and when a similar video revolution is almost upon us, it is easy to forget how recent such recording technology is. A landmark event, in 1936, was the first tape recording of a symphony orchestra. More than a decade went by before the widespread adoption of tape recording by the recording and broadcasting industry. And the tape recorder did not become domestically available until the early 1950s.[11] In 1958 there were still many Maoris, particularly of the older generation, who had neither seen nor heard of a tape recorder. They were quick, however, to see its immense potential for the future. I remember one old man in his nineties who sat in thought after recording in 1958 and then, albeit with no real assurance, said 'I think you might be a Maori prophet'. No one else put me in such a role, but in other respects this old man was representative. The old people who recorded for me had no great interest in advancing the cause of scholarly research. Their motives were simple, personal and direct. They saw themselves as the repositories of a sung tradition which was precious and already rare. The migration of young and middle-aged Maori people to the cities by this time was already well under way and the traditional means of learning songs had already broken down. My recording machine was an opportunity to rescue a valued tradition and against all expectations to communicate it after all to the next generation of singers. Although I had began work with no thought beyond studying the songs and penetrating the music system, I quickly became caught up also in the concerns of the singers and for the past dozen or more years I have been actively assisting the revival of Maori chant in Maori communities. The principal means of doing this has been through a free dubbing service offered by the Archive of Maori and Pacific Music which the University of Auckland agreed to establish in 1970. Some sixty individuals and groups a year receive dubbings and in several tribal areas there have been *waiata* schools which have used recorded materials supplied by the Archive. In the Waikato area, where it is said that only two songs were commonly sung in the 1960s, the tribal singing tradition is again strong and it is becoming commonplace once again for numerous songs to be performed at meetings. The effort, of course, has been successful only up to a point. I have already mentioned that unwitting transformations have occurred in the end-product. The easiest songs for neophytes to learn are tran-

33

sitional songs which are already to some degree Europeanized. The scales tend to be diatonic and metre is generally present. Non-metrical non-diatonic songs on the other hand, are generally modified during the learning process. The scale changes to major or minor; melodic ornament and melisma are glossed over, deleted or stereotyped; additive rhythms are regularized and made to conform to the Western metric system; and the manner of singing becomes markedly different, losing its distinctive 'edge' with the introduction of vibrato and portamento both of which are absent in the indigenous system. If 'authenticity' is the aim, then, the effort to revive the *waiata*-singing tradition must be said to have failed. I would suggest, however, that in cultural terms this 'failure' is of little significance. For its practitioners, *waiata* continues to be important because of its social relevance particularly as an ingredient of the 'rituals of encounter'³⁹ which are played out at every Maori meeting. And in this I believe there is a lesson. Efforts to 'revive' a singing tradition will be misplaced if the tradition in question is no longer of relevance for the people most directly concerned. Attempts in New Zealand to aid the revival of *waiata* singing have had some success only because they are a response to an expressed need. It is this need which has fuelled the current renaissance. The product may not be fully 'authentic' but it is here, paradoxically, that the real hope lies. In Western culture music may be thought of as stratified into categories such as 'classical', 'middle-brow' and 'popular'. Tribal musics are largely non-stratified, accessible to all and practised by most members of the community. Now that Western-derived island 'pop' has begun to displace the older music in the affections of the younger generations of Pacific peoples, the indigenous styles seem to have taken on some of the connotations of 'classical' music in the West. Just as few persons in the West now compose in the style of Beethoven or Brahms, so too Maori songs in non-acculturated style are static, non-living or, in a word, 'classical' survivals from the past. The barrier to composing in this style is that the rules—unlike those of the Western popular idiom—are no longer internalized and the best that can be hoped for is a more or less imperfect rote learning. Once *waiata* style has come fully to terms with the intrusive Western system, however, it is possible that a syncretic blend of old and new will emerge, composition will again become commonplace, and the long process of attrition which has so diminished the traditional Maori repertoire will at last be at an end.

WHOSE RESPONSIBILITY?

I hope I have demonstrated that salvaging minority musics is both desirable and, within limits, practicable. Who then should be trying to remedy the problem? Is there a role, to begin with, for music educationists and the general public? Alan Lomax is in no doubt. Having placed the blame for destroying human cultural and musical variety squarely in the court of the entertainment industry, he argues passionately that the agents of dissemination should now go into reverse thrust. Non-European music systems, he says,⁴⁰ must be 'taught, propagated and defended: . . . the media and the educational system must open their channels to the whole band-width of human music and human achievement'.⁴¹ It is a grand vision and one worthy of success. But there are obvious problems. We have seen that for music systems to be 'preserved' they must be maintained in living tradition. If it is difficult or, in some cases impossible, for the practitioners themselves to revive a tradition once continuity has been broken, how much more so for persons not familiar with the culture. Lomax himself recognizes this. It is no easier, he says,[42] for a bimusical performer to become a 'master' of a style not his own then it is to master (say) English as a second language. But unless this kind of competence is aimed at, the best that can be hoped for from music education is to raise the level of appreciation of world musics, leaving the problems of 'preservation' still unsolved. The ethnomusicologist is better equipped to help and I believe could and should do so. Firstly, rather than choose an area of study which has already been thoroughly explored by others, he could opt for one of the more vulnerable traditions such as most of those of Oceania. Secondly, having entered the field, he could collect more than is required for his own immediate purposes. Collecting music for no better reason than to record it before it is lost has never been an object of ethnomusicology as a discipline and there is no agreement on how large a sample is adequate for study purposes. But there can be no doubt that if the object were preservation, rather than recording the minimum amount necessary for stylistic analysis, the sample would need to be much greater. In such circumstances, indeed, the ultimate object might well be to recover every extant song or piece of music. Finally, having left the field, the ethnomusicologist should make sure first that his collection is properly archived in a safe repository and second that cassette copies of the tapes together with typed copies of song texts and other relevant documentation are repatriated to the host community. 'Rescue ethnography' of this kind would undoubtedly be helpful, would identify the ethnomusicologist more closely with the needs and concerns of the host community and would be seen by them as an appropriate *quid pro quo* for services rendered to the ethnomusicologist. What happens next will depend wholly upon the community concerned. I have stressed in this paper that it is impossible to 'preserve' a music tradition by descriptive accounts alone or by storing recordings unused in an archive. To be effective a preservation programme must be active and it must be aimed at the maintenance of a living tradition. Music can be collected, archived and even disseminated but will not be 'preserved' in any real sense unless it is used to revitalize the tradition from whence it came. I do not suggest that this can be done without effort and I have outlined some of the difficulties and problems. Others could be mentioned. Even when recordings get back to their home communities, factionalism can stand in the way. For everyone who would like a tape recording distributed to all and sundry, or even issued on a commercial gramophone record, there is someone else who would like to lock it up in a bank vault. But, in the final analysis, 'preservation' is up to the people themselves. No one can 'save' a music if the practitioners themselves do not want it to be saved. Our role as I see it, then, should be one of support. The Archive of Maori and Pacific Music experiment has worked in New Zealand and, as a model, might well prove useful elsewhere.

35

[1] Alan Lomax, 'Cantometrics: An Approach to the Anthropology of Music', *Life-long Learning* 46(57) (1977), p. 2.

[2] Lomax, *Folk Song Style and Culture*, Washington: American Association for the Advancement of Science, 1968, p. 4.

[3] Gregg W. Howard, 'Conservation and Composition: Some Thoughts on the Meaning of Ethnomusicology', in Goro Kalinoki (ed.), *International Symposium on the Conservation and Restoration of Cultural Property*. Tokyo: National Research Institute of Cultural Properties, 1981, p. 138.

[4] Mervyn McLean, 'UNESCO World History of Music Proposal: The Case for Field Research in Oceania', *Bulletin of the International Committee on Urgent Anthropological and Ethnological Research* (Vienna) 21 (1979), pp. 99–113.

[5] Alan Thomas, 'The Study of Acculturated Music in Oceania: "Cheap and Tawdry Borrowed Tunes"?', *Journal of the Polynesian Society 90(2) (1981), p. 184.*

[6] McLean, 'Innovations in *Waiata* Style', *Yearbook of the International Folk Music Council* 9 (1977), p. 33.

[7] Thomas, *op. cit.* p. 183.

[8] McLean, 'Sound Archiving as an Aid to Music Conservation in the Pacific', *Continuo* (Wellington) 4(1) (1974), p. 8.

[9] Alan P. Merriam, *The Anthropology of Music,* Evanston, Illinois: North-Western University Press, 1964, p. 99.

[10] Steven Feld, *Sound and Sentiment: Birds, Weeping, Poetics and Song in Kaluli Expression,* Philadelphia: University of Pennsylvania Press, 1982, p. 233.

[11] Robert Armstrong, *The Affecting Presence: An Essay in Humanistic Anthropology,* Urbana: University of Illinois Press, 1971, p. 10.

[12] Adrienne Kaeppler, 'Aesthetics of Tongan Dance', *Ethnomusicology* 15(2), p. 175.

[13] Kaeppler, *op. cit.,* p. 177.

[14] Alan P. Merriam, *A Prologue to the Study of African Arts,* Antioch College Founders Day Lectures No. 7, Yellow Springs, Ohio: Antioch Press, 1961, p. 25.

[15] Roy Sieber, 'The Esthetic of Traditional African Art', in Froelich Rainey (ed.) *7 Metals of Africa*, Philadelphia: The University Museum; cited in Merriam, *The Anthropology of Music*, p. 271.

[16] Peter Bellwood, *Man's Conquest of the Pacific: The Prehistory of Southeast Asia and Oceania*, Auckland: Collins, 1978, p. 119.

[17] Stuart Inder, *Pacific Islands Yearbook*, 12th edition, Sydney: Pacific Publications, 1977, p. 59.

[18] Richard Moyle, 'Samoan Traditional Music', doctoral dissertation, University of Auckland, 1971, p. 799.

[19] E. S. Craighill Handy and Jane L. Winne, *Music in the Marquesas Islands*, Honolulu: B. P. Bishop Museum Bulletin 17, 1925, pp. 18–19.

[20] William A. Lessa, *Ulithi: A Micronesian Design for Living,* New York: Holt, Rinehart and Winston, 1966, p. 82.

[21] McLean, 'An Analysis of 651 Maori Scales', *Yearbook of the International Folk Music Council*, 1 (1969), pp. 155–6.

[22] Dorothy M. Kahananui, 'Influences on Hawaiian Music', in *Kamehameha Schools 75th Anniversary Lectures*, pp. 118–19.

[23] Jane Mink Rossen, 'Some Bellonese Musical Concepts and Points of Conflict with the Church', *Antropologiska Studier* (Stockholm), 25–26 (1978), p. 26.

[24] James Oakley Wilson, 'National Groups', in A. H. McLintock (ed.), *An Encyclopaedia of New Zealand*, Wellington: Government Printer, Vol. 2, pp. 623–5.

[25] *Ibid.*, pp. 626–7.

[26] *Ibid.*, p. 628.

[27] Iain MacDonald, 'A Placid Ethnic Melting Pot', *NZ Herald* July 17, 1982.

[28] *Ibid.*

[29] *Ibid.*

[30] *Ibid.*

[31] Kevin Salisbury, 'Pukapukan People and their Music', Master's dissertation, University of Auckland, 1983.

[32] *Ibid.*

36

[33] McLean, 'Sound Archiving as an Aid to Music Conservation in the Pacific'.

[34] McLean, 'Innovations in *Waiata* Style'.

[35] McLean, Review of *Nga Moteata: Traditional Song-Poetry of the Maori Sung by Rangi Te Kura Dewes, Journal of the Polynesian Society* 86(1) (1977), pp. 142–3.

[36] McLean, 'Song Loss and Social Context Amongst the New Zealand Maori', *Ethnomusicology* 9(3) (1965), p. 303.

[37] McLean, 'Sound Archiving as an Aid to Music Conservation in the Pacific', p. 9.

[38] Jerry McWilliams, *The Preservation and Restoration of Sound Recordings*, Nashville: American Association for State and Local History, 1979, p. 16.

[39] Anne Salmond, *Hui: A Study of Maori Ceremonial Gatherings*, Wellington: Reed, 1975, p. 115.

[40] Lomax, 'Cantometrics: An Approach to the Anthropology of Music', p. 2.

[41] Lomax, *Cantometrics: An Approach to the Anthropology of Music*, Berkeley: University of California Press, 1976, p. 9.

[42] *Ibid.*, p. 63.

ACKNOWLEDGMENTS

Benjamin I. Gilman, "The Science of Exotic Music," *Science* 30 (1909): 532–535. Reproduced by permission of the American Association for the Advancement of Science. Courtesy of the Library of Congress.

Frances Densmore, "The Study of Indian Music in the Nineteenth Century," *American Anthropologist* 29 (1927): 77–86. Reproduced by permission of the American Anthropological Association. Courtesy of Yale University.

George Herzog, "Study of Native Music in America" *Proceedings of the Eighth American Scientific Congress* 2 (1942): 203–209. Courtesy of New York Public Library

Charles Seeger, "Systematic Musicology: Viewpoints, Orientations, and Methods," *Journal of the American Musicological Society* 4 (1951): 240–248. Reproduced by permission of the American Musicological Society. Courtesy of Yale University Music Library.

Willard Rhodes, "Toward a Definition of Ethnomusicology," *American Anthropologist* 58 (1956): 457–463. Reproduced by permission of the American Anthropological Association. Courtesy of Yale University.

Bruno Nettl, "Historical Aspects of Ethnomusicology," *American Anthropologist* 60 (1958): 518–532. Reproduced by permission of the American Anthropological Association. Courtesy of Yale University.

Anonymous, "Whither Ethnomusicology?" "The Scope and Aims of Ethnomusicology," (two panel discussions held in 1958) *Ethnomusicology* 3:2 (1959): 99–105. Reproduced by permission of *Ethnomusicology*. Courtesy of Yale University Music Library.

Alan P. Merriam, "Ethnomusicology, Discussion and Definition of the Field," *Ethnomusicology* 4:3 (1960): 107–114. Reproduced by permission of *Ethnomusicology*. Courtesy of Yale University Music Library.

Gertrude P. Kurath, "Panorama of Dance Ethnology," *Current Anthropology* 1:3 (1960): 233–254. Reproduced by permission of the University of Chicago Press. Courtesy of Yale University.

André Schaeffner, "Contribution de l'ethnomusicologie à l'histoire de la musique," *International Musicological Society Report of the 8th Congress* (1961), Jan La Rue, ed. (Basel: Bärenreiter Kassel, 1961), Vol. 1, 376–379. Reproduced by permission of the International Musicological Society.

David P. McAllester, "Ethnomusicology, the Field, and the Society," *Ethnomusicology* 7:3 (1963): 182–186. Reproduced by permission of *Ethnomusicology*. Courtesy of Yale University Music Library.

Charles Seeger, "Preface to the Critique of Music," *Inter-American Music Bulletin* 49 (1965): 2–24. Reproduced by permission of the Organization of American States.

Walter Wiora, "Ethnomusicology and the History of Music," *Studia Musicologica* 7 (1965): 187–193. Reproduced by permission of Akademiai Kiado. Courtesy of Yale University Music Library.

Mantle Hood, "Ethnomusicology," in *Harvard Dictionary of Music* (2nd rev. ed.) Willi Apel ed. (Cambridge: Harvard University Press, 1969): 298–200. Reproduced by permission of Belknap Press. Courtesy of Yale University Music Library.

Christopher Marshall, "Two Paradigms for Music: A Short History of Ideas in Ethnomusicology," *Cornell Journal of Social Relations* 7 (1972): 75–83. Reproduced by permission of the *Sociological Forum*. Courtesy of *Sociological Forum*.

Norma McLeod, "Ethnomusicological Research and Anthropology," *Annual Review of Anthropology* 3 (1974): 99–115. Reproduced by permission of the *Annual Review of Anthropology*.

Alan P. Merriam, "Ethnomusicology Today," *Current Musicology* 20 (1975): 50–66. Reproduced by permission of the American Musicological Society.

Bruno Nettl, "The State of Research in Ethnomusicology, and Recent Developments," *Current Musicology* 20 (1975): 67–78. Reproduced by permission of the American Musicological Society.

Steven Feld, "Ethnomusicology and Visual Communication," *Ethnomusicology* 20:2 (1976): 293–325. Reproduced by permission of *Ethnomusicology*. Courtesy of Yale University Music Library.

Fredric Lieberman, "Should Ethnomusicology Be Abolished?" and responses by E. Eugene Helm and Claude Palisca. *Journal of the College Music Society* 17:2 (1977): 198–206. Reproduced by permission of the College Music Society. Courtesy of Yale University Music Library.

Alan P. Merriam, "Definitions of 'Comparative Musicology' and 'Ethnomusicology': An Historical-Theoretical Perspective," *Ethnomusicology* 21:2 (1977): 189–204. Reproduced by permission of *Ethnomusicology*. Courtesy of Yale University Music Library.

Artur Simon, "Probleme, Methoden und Ziele der Ethnomusikologie," *Jahrbuch für Musikalische Volks- und Völkerkunde* 9 (1978): 8–52. Reproduced by permission of *Jahrbuch für Musikalische Volks- und Völkerkunde*. Courtesy of Yale University Music Library.

Adelaida Reyes Schramm, "Ethnic Music, the Urban Area, and Ethnomusicology," *Sociologus* 29 (1979): 1–21. Reproduced by permission of Duncker & Humblot. Courtesy of Yale University.

George List, "Ethnomusicology: A Discipline Defined," *Ethnomusicology* 23:1 (1979): 1–4. Reproduced by permission of *Ethnomusicology*. Courtesy of Yale University Music Library.

Mervyn McLean, "Preserving World Musics: Perspectives from New Zealand and Oceania," *Studies in Music* 17 (1983): 23–37. Reproduced by permission of *Studies in Music*.